# Oracle Identity Management

# OTHER INFORMATION SECURITY BOOKS FROM AUERBACH

**802.1X Port-Based Authentication**
Edwin Lyle Brown
ISBN: 1-4200-4464-8

**Audit and Trace Log Management: Consolidation and Analysis**
Phillip Q. Maier
ISBN: 0-8493-2725-3

**The CISO Handbook: A Practical Guide to Securing Your Company**
Michael Gentile, Ron Collette and Thomas D. August
ISBN: 0-8493-1952-8

**Complete Guide to Security and Privacy Metrics: Measuring Regulatory Compliance, Operational Resilience, and ROI**
Debra S. Herrmann
ISBN: 0-8493-5402-1

**Crisis Management Planning and Execution**
Edward S. Devlin
ISBN: 0-8493-2244-8

**Computer Forensics: Evidence Collection and Management**
Robert C. Newman
ISBN: 0-8493-0561-6

**Curing the Patch Management Headache**
Felicia M Nicastro
ISBN: 0-8493-2854-3

**Cyber Crime Investigator's Field Guide, Second Edition**
Bruce Middleton
ISBN: 0-8493-2768-7

**Database and Applications Security: Integrating Information Security and Data Management**
Bhavani Thuraisingham
ISBN: 0-8493-2224-3

**Guide to Optimal Operational Risk and BASEL II**
Ioannis S. Akkizidis and Vivianne Bouchereau
ISBN: 0-8493-3813-1

**How to Achieve 27001 Certification: An Example of Applied Compliance Management**
Sigurjon Thor Arnason and Keith D. Willett
ISBN: 0-8493-3648-1

**Information Security: Design, Implementation, Measurement, and Compliance**
Timothy P. Layton
ISBN: 0-8493-7087-6

**Information Security Architecture: An Integrated Approach to Security in the Organization, Second Edition**
Jan Killmeyer
ISBN: 0-8493-1549-2

**Information Security Cost Management**
Ioana V. Bazavan and Ian Lim
ISBN: 0-8493-9275-6

**Information Security Fundamentals**
Thomas R. Peltier, Justin Peltier, and John A. Blackley
ISBN: 0-8493-1957-9

**Information Security Management Handbook, Sixth Edition**
Harold F. Tipton and Micki Krause
ISBN: 0-8493-7495-2

**Information Security Risk Analysis, Second Edition**
Thomas R. Peltier
ISBN: 0-8493-3346-6

**Investigations in the Workplace**
Eugene F. Ferraro
ISBN: 0-8493-1648-0

**IT Security Governance Guidebook with Security Program Metrics on CD-ROM**
Fred Cohen
ISBN: 0-8493-8435-4

**Managing an Information Security and Privacy Awareness and Training Program**
Rebecca Herold
ISBN: 0-8493-2963-9

**Mechanics of User Identification and Authentication: Fundamentals of Identity Management**
Dobromir Todorov
ISBN: 1-4200-5219-5

**Practical Hacking Techniques and Countermeasures**
Mark D. Spivey
ISBN: 0-8493-7057-4

**Securing Converged IP Networks**
Tyson Macaulay
ISBN: 0-8493-7580-0

**The Security Risk Assessment Handbook: A Complete Guide for Performing Security Risk Assessments**
Douglas J. Landoll
ISBN: 0-8493-2998-1

**Testing Code Security**
Maura A. van der Linden
ISBN: 0-8493-9251-9

**Wireless Crime and Forensic Investigation**
Gregory Kipper
ISBN: 0-8493-3188-9

## AUERBACH PUBLICATIONS

www.auerbach-publications.com
To Order Call: 1-800-272-7737 • Fax: 1-800-374-3401
E-mail: orders@crcpress.com

# Oracle Identity Management

Governance, Risk, and Compliance Architecture

Third Edition

Marlin B. Pohlman

**CRC Press**
Taylor & Francis Group
Boca Raton  London  New York

CRC Press is an imprint of the
Taylor & Francis Group, an **informa** business

AN AUERBACH BOOK

CRC Press
Taylor & Francis Group
6000 Broken Sound Parkway NW, Suite 300
Boca Raton, FL 33487-2742

© 2008 by Taylor & Francis Group, LLC
CRC Press is an imprint of Taylor & Francis Group, an Informa business

No claim to original U.S. Government works

ISBN 13: 978-1-138-44044-9 (hbk)
ISBN 13: 978-1-4200-7247-1 (pbk)

---

**Library of Congress Cataloging-in-Publication Data**

---

Pohlman, Marlin B.
   Oracle identity management : governance, risk, and compliance architecture / Marlin B. Pohlman.
-- 3rd ed.
      p. cm.
   Includes bibliographical references and index.
   ISBN 978-1-4200-7247-1 (hardback : alk. paper) 1. Oracle (Computer file) 2. Computers--Access control. 3. Computer security. I. Title.

QA76.9.A25P645 2008
005.8--dc22                                                                    2008002930

---

**Visit the Taylor & Francis Web site at
http://www.taylorandfrancis.com**

**and the Auerbach Web site at
http://www.auerbach-publications.com**

# Contents

## PART III: GOVERNANCE LANDSCAPE

# Preface

An identity management system is defined as the management of the identity life cycle of entities (subjects or objects) during which the identity is established, described, and destroyed. What this definition fails to cover is the social, personal, and financial impact of the identity life cycle.

Before I joined Oracle as director of GRC Product Strategy with the goal of creating a product that would address corporate governance, shareholder risk, and regulatory compliance, I had been a specialist in identity management for 14 years. Having worked at Netscape with Tim Howes and Frank Chen, and having participated in IETF working groups, I was no stranger to the social impact of technologies.

After Netscape was aquired by AOL and then Time Warner, I learned that the corporate officers had acted unethically, issuing three times the stock options for which they had shares. I was crushed, because I not only believed in my former employer but I believed in the value of the stock options. During that time in my life, I had been diagnosed with a rare form of Hodgkin's lymphoma and was in need of a stem cell transplant. The insurance handled most of the medical bills, but the co-payments were costly. Without the ability to exercise my stock options, I lacked the funds for the insurance co-payments.

Fortunately, I still had professional worth despite my partial inability to work, and an excellent manager from Oracle hired me. I found Oracle to be an ethical company for giving me health benefits while I was ill, and due to my employment with them, I was able to receive treatment through two years of stem cell transplant and chemotherapy while working remotely. It was at this juncture that I realized my career was more than a way to increase the wealth and efficiency of the corporation for which I worked; it was a way for me to take this life lesson and become an instrument of change.

# Introduction

Corporations are often seen as inherently amoral and driven to secure profits for their shareholders. This is because those empowered to insure accountability often have no visibility into the inner workings of the business. Legislation is the tool society uses to hold those in power responsible to the community in which they interact, but without a strong regulatory "immune system," cancers of injustice and fraud can spread through the corporate entity in the same way cancer cells injured a body.

Identity management is the first line of defense in the corporate internal ecosystem; it enables the corporate structure to know who is doing what, where. From this base knowledge of identity patterns, behavior and governance can then be established to ensure the corporate entity behaves in a healthy, symbiotic manner with its partners, shareholders, employees, and society. In this work we strive to create a governance ecosystem that enables a business to act in a profitable manner, employing enlightened self-interest to create a better world. This is the best I can do with the second chance I have been given.

The goal of this work is to enable you to leverage the Oracle Identity Management Suite in conjunction with Oracle's other governance, risk, and compliance products to facilitate regulatory compliance and good corporate governance. In the first four chapters we cover the nature of what has come to be called governance, risk, and compliance or GRC for short. We outline a common taxonomy for the GRC space, cite standards that are used, and illustrate compliance frameworks that information systems auditors and corporate performance experts use to measure good corporate governance and security. We then present a meta-framework that we at Oracle use to abstract the control criteria defined by legislation and the compliance frameworks themselves, which often have overlapping interpretations and measures.

Using this metamodel, we present you with a detailed method to implement and configure our identity management product suite to obtain the control objectives we have identified through analysis of auditor reports, compliance frameworks, and the legislation itself. Finally, we provide a taxonomy of the legislation we have encountered throughout the world, and in Appendix A, illustrate how our applications and technology, including our Identity Management product suite, enables a corporation to meet the legal mandates within multiple legal jurisdictions with a single unified solution.

A secondary goal of this book is to empower those charged with stewardship of the corporation, be they corporate board members, legal expert witnesses, or auditors, with a tool they can use to measure their own efforts in meeting the compliance duties entrusted to them. Board members and executive management need technical guidance when reviewing the solutions presented. Consultants and vendors alike often pitch product and service without mapping the solution back to the legislative driver that spawned its adoption. This soloed approach leads to redundancy of effort and excessive expense, directly counter to the board members' duties to shareholders. Using this text, a corporate steward can map those solutions directly to region and legislation, and can hold service providers accountable for the proper deployment and configuration of those service.

# About the Author

In addition to serving on the board of directors for three publically traded multinational corporations, Dr. Marlin Pohlman is director of governance, risk, and compliance (GRC) product strategy at Oracle Corporation. Dr. Pohlman has lectured in the university systems of New Mexico, Arizona, and Minnesota, as well as speaking at Burton Group, Gartner, AMR, BC Government Identity Management Symposium, and the Veritas Nobel Laureate invitational. Dr. Pohlman is recognized as one of the primary educators worldwide on identity management, regulatory compliance, and corporate governance. His affiliations in this field include the Information Systems Audit and Control Association (ISACA), The Burton Group, the Institute of Internal Auditors, RSA Security Confrence, DefCon, AMR research, and Gartner. With over 18 years experience in x.500 and LDAP based directory structures, he has led directory server implementation for companies such as Ford Motor Company, the Automotive Industry Action Group, Home Depot, Citigroup, AXA Insurance, Bank of New York, Alliance Capital, GE Equity, Federal Express, and the U.S. Department of Defense credit card issuance system. An original contributor to the IETF ASID and DIX working group, Dr. Pohlman implemented the world's second implementation of RFC 1777 for Sanlam Insurance in Cape Town, South Africa. The directory structure implemented in Sydney, Australia, for the 2000 Olympics held the record for the largest non-x.500 meta-directory implementation in a client–server environment. Dr. Pohlman received his Ph.D. in computer science from Trinity College and University, SD, with a thesis "Scaling Factors in Very Large, High Availability Directory Architectures." He has authored three texts on identity management, two texts on GRC, and is a Licensed Professional Engineer, Certified Information Systems Auditor, Certified Information Security Manager, and Certified Information Systems Security Professional. While at Oracle, Dr. Pohlman has worked on wide-ranging security programs for various customers including governmental agencies, educational intuitions, financial services companies, and healthcare organizations. He is coauthor of the Oracle Unified Method, an iterative and incremental development process framework developed by Oracle. In the area of identity management and GRC he created a roadmap for achieving successful implementation of all Oracle products, including applications and middleware. In this comprehensive work, Dr. Pohlman leverages his experience as both a corporate board member and corporate governance solution implementer to provide a mechanism for promoting corporate accountability and stewardship of personally identifiable information within daily business operations.

Also By Marlin Pohlman:

*Oracle Identity Management: Governance, Risk and Compliance,* ISBN: 0-07-148926-6 Oracle Press Osborne
   Publishing, a McGraw Hill Company.
*LDAP Metadirectory Provisioning Methodology: A Step-by-Step Method to Implementing LDAP Based Metadi-*
   *rectory Provisioning & Identity Management Systems* ISBN:0-595-26726-2 **HC** ISBN: 0-595-65619-6,
   Writers Showcase Publishing.
*LDAP and Metadirectory Architecture* ISBN: 1-590-59090-2, Apress.

# Implement Multinational Regulatory Compliance Solutions

This comprehensive new resource from Oracle details the legal and technological aspects of Oracle Identity Management, the integrated suite of database security tools. You will get installation and configuration instruction as well as in-depth coverage of multinational regulations and guidelines to ensure compliance at minimal effort. This work covers over 220 legislative mandates in over 60 countries and provides metrics against such frameworks as ITIL, COBIT, ISO, BSI IT-Grundschutz, GAIT, and FISMA.

# Summary

The Oracle Identity Management Suite, when properly configured, deployed, and used, provides all the technical controls necessary to meet the legal challenges imposed by a global marketplace. It is important to remember that no software product, no matter how sophisticated and complex, will manage regulatory compliance for a company. Regulatory compliance and good corporate governance happen as a result of policy, process, and procedure implemented by the employees, managers, and executives of a corporation. It is the individual's responsibility to act from a perspective of enlightened self-interest to further the symbiosis of the corporate structure and the environment in which that corporate structure functions. The environment must be expanded from the traditional market perspective to encompass all those aspects that make up the marketplace. This holistic approach must include social responsibility and environmental stewardship and must result in the corporation assuming a position of moral and ethical leadership if the era of the corporation is to survive.

# FUNDAMENTAL CONCEPTS

# Chapter 1

# Enterprise Risk

Identity and its governance has become the principal concern of chief information security officers and those charged with the management and compilation of personally identifiable information. This chapter provides a primer for the information professional. This chapter details elements of risk management, risk analysis, and the measures to which the efforts of those charged with the custodianship of personally identifiable information are held in multiple jurisdictions and regions.

## What Is Risk Management?

Risk management planning is about making informed business decisions. Mitigating risk means to reduce the risk until it reaches a level that is acceptable to an organization. This involves achieving the appropriate balance between realizing opportunities for gains while minimizing losses. As such, risk management can be defined as the identification, analysis, control, and minimization of loss associated with events that affect the enterprise. As such, risk management is an integral part of good management practice and an essential element of good corporate governance. It is an iterative process consisting of steps that, when undertaken in sequence, enable continuous improvement in decision making and in performance. It is important to remember that totally eliminating risk in an enterprise cannot be achieved without ceasing operations.

## *Risk Mitigation*

Risk mitigation means finding out what level of risk the enterprise can safely tolerate and still continue to function effectively. To enable this process, some properties of the various elements will need to be determined, such as the value of assets, threats, and vulnerabilities, and the likelihood of events. There are many practical benefits to performing a risk analysis. Performing a risk analysis creates a clear cost-to-value ratio for security protections and influences the decision-making process dealing with hardware and software systems design. However, more importantly, risk analysis helps a company to focus its resources where they are needed most, influencing planning and growth. Organizations that manage risk effectively and efficiently are more likely to achieve their objectives and do so at lower overall cost.

# What Is Risk Analysis?

The first major element of risk analysis is to access the value of the information itself. Information asset value is the heart of the risk assessment process. Any security analysis must include a detailed inventory and empirical assessment of the value of the information resources. Although it is possible to make a detailed assessment of security functionality of specific IT components without considering the value of the data they transmit, store, and process, it is impossible to define security requirements for a system without the value of the data in question. The consequences of damage by a risk incident might not just be quantifiable initially in monetary terms, such as in the loss of valuable assets or by destructive levels of litigation, but by criminal penalties levied against a company's officers and board members. Risk management planning is about making informed business decisions.

Risk has two primary components for a given event:

■ The probability (likelihood) of occurrence of that event
■ Impact of the event occurring (amount at stake)

The first step in risk management is to identify all potential risk issues. The second step is to quantify and document the threats, assets, vulnerabilities, exposure factors, and safeguards.

## *Definitions Used in the Risk Analysis Process*

Definitions are important to establish a common lexicon for discussion to provide background and a general understanding of the governance initiative within the software industry. The term *risk analysis* means many things to different people. All of these definitions have merit; thus, it is important to establish the context for the definition in use at the moment.

For our purposes, we will use the following general definition:

> **Asset**: An asset is a resource, product, process, or digital infrastructure element that an organization has determined must be protected.

The identification of risk to an organization entails defining the following four basic elements:

■ The actual threat
■ The possible consequences of the realized threat
■ The probable frequency of the occurrence of a threat
■ The confidence level that a threat will happen

In that light, the following definitions are vital to the process of risk management:

> **Threat**: The presence of any potential event that causes a detrimental impact on the organization.
> **Vulnerability**: The absence or weakness of a safeguard counter to a threat.
> **Safeguard**: A control or countermeasure employed to reduce the risk associated with a specific threat or group of threats.

**Exposure factor (EF):** The percentage of loss a realized threat event would have on a specific asset.

**Single loss expectancy (SLE):** A financial amount assigned to a single realized threat event representing a loss to the organization.

$$Asset\ Value \times Exposure\ Factor\ (EF) = SLE$$

**Annualized rate of occurrence (ARO):** A number that represents the estimated frequency of an expected threat.

**Annualized loss expectancy (ALE):** A financial figure that represents the annual expected loss from threats. It is derived from the following formula:

$$SLE \times ARO = ALE$$

**Preliminary security examination (PSE):** A PSE is often conducted before the actual quantitative risk analysis (RA). The PSE helps to gather together the elements that will be needed when the actual RA takes place. It also helps to focus risk analysis.

The difference between quantitative and qualitative RA is fairly simple: Quantitative RA attempts to assign independently objective numeric values. Risk analysis begins with a detailed study of the risk issues that have been identified and approved by decision makers for further evaluation. The objective is to gather enough information about the risk issues to judge the likelihood of occurrence and cost, schedule, and technical consequences if the risk occurs.

There are a number of approaches to risk:

■ Accept the risk.
■ Avoid the risk.
■ Reduce the risk.
■ Contain the risk.
■ Transfer the risk.

However, before we determine how to deal with risk, we must first identify the risk in a concrete, auditable format. The following are common risk identification methods:

■ **Objective-based risk identification:** Organizations set objectives. Any event that may endanger achieving an objective is identified as risk. Objective-based risk identification is at the basis of COSOs (Committee of Sponsoring Organizaitons of the Treadway commission).
■ **Scenario-based risk identification:** In scenario analysis different scenarios are created. The scenarios may be the alternative ways of achieving an objective or an analysis of the interaction of forces. Any event that triggers an undesired scenario alternative is identified as risk.
■ **Taxonomy-based risk identification:** A breakdown of possible risk sources. Based on the knowledge of best practices, this methodology is questionnaire oriented.
■ **Common-risk checking:** In industries with known risks. Each risk in the list can be checked for application to a particular situation.

## Risk Analysis Standards

Once identity information professionals get a firm grasp of the elements of risk, they must become familiar with the standards against which their efforts and activities will be measured. Many formulas and processes are designed to help provide some certainty when answering these questions. However, not every possibility can be considered, because life and nature are constantly evolving and changing. Risk analysis tries as much as possible to anticipate the future and to lower the possibility of a threat's impact on companies.

Risk is a measure of the frequency or probability of a negative event and the associated consequences. You do not have to plan for events with zero probability or events that have no consequences. The probability of a threat is a measure of the capabilities, impact, intentions, and past activities of potential miscreants. The capability of perpetrating a terrorist act depends the ability to manufacture or acquire a weapon and to carry out the terrorist act. The impact is the consequence of the act, including casualties, property damage, and business interruption. Intentions are the motivations of a terrorist or terrorist organization to perpetrate acts of terror.

In the physical domain, a nuclear or radiological incident could involve the detonation of a thermonuclear device, explosion of a "dirty bomb" (radiological dispersion device), or the release of radioactive material from an attack on a facility that uses or stores radioactive materials (e.g., bomb, aircraft, or missile attack on a nuclear power plant). An attack with biological agents could include the intentional dispersal or distribution of biological agents such as anthrax, smallpox, botulism, and the plague. Anthrax can be sent through the mail system, and food can be contaminated with salmonella. Smallpox and plague are infectious diseases that could spread widely. A vulnerability assessment is the process of identifying weaknesses in perimeter security, buildings, utility systems, personnel protection systems, or computer systems that can be exploited. In this context, the role of information risk management is to optimize outcomes such as profit objectives, return on investment, and performance measures, which results in value creation.

## Common Vulnerabilities

**Domain name servers:** The domain name service architecture should be evaluated to avoid creating a single point of failure that could result in an extended loss of connectivity. Cyber attacks by definition strike computer systems that are connected via local and wide area networks to computer networks outside the building, including, and especially, the Internet.

**Software vulnerabilities:** These account for the majority of successful attacks, simply because attackers are opportunistic and take the easiest and most convenient route. Attackers exploit the best-known flaws with the most effective and widely available attack tools. They count on organizations not fixing the problems, and they often attack indiscriminately, scanning the Internet for vulnerable systems.

**Default installs of operating systems and applications:** Most software packages, including operating systems and applications, come with installation scripts or programs. The goal of these installation programs is to get the systems installed as quickly as possible, with the most useful functions enabled and the least amount of work by the system administrator. To accomplish this goal, the scripts typically install more components than most users need. This opens an avenue of attack to miscreants.

**Accounts with no password or a weak password:** Most systems are configured to use passwords as the first, and only, line of defense. User IDs are fairly easy to acquire, and most companies have dial-up access that bypasses the firewall. Therefore, if an attacker can determine an account name and password, he or she can log on to the network.

**Nonexistent or incomplete backups:** When an incident occurs, recovery from it requires up-to-date backups and proven methods of restoring the data. Some organizations make daily backups but never verify that the backups are actually working. Others construct backup policies and procedures but do not create restoration policies and procedures.

**Large number of open ports:** Both legitimate users and attackers connect to systems via open ports. The more ports that are open, the more possible ways that someone can connect to your system. Therefore, it is important to keep the least number of necessary ports open on a system. All other ports must be closed.

**Not filtering packets for correct incoming and outgoing addresses:** Spoofing IP addresses is a common method used by attackers to hide their tracks when they attack a victim. For example, the very popular smurf attack uses a feature of routers to send a stream of packets to thousands of machines. Each packet contains a spoofed source address of a victim. The computers to which the spoofed packets are sent flood the victim's computer.

**Nonexistent or incomplete logging:** You cannot detect an attack if you do not know what is occurring on your network. Logs provide the details of what is occurring, what systems are being attacked, and what systems have been compromised. Without logs you have little chance of discovering what the attackers did.

When applying risk management, the regional circumstances dictate the model that must be used to express the risk. Australia, New Zealand, Canada, the United Kingdom, Germany, South Africa, the United States, and the United Nations through the International Standards Organization have all devised risk analysis standards designed to assist in the risk mitigation process and protect shareholders within their populations.

## Australia/New Zealand Standard 4360:1795, 1799, and 1800

AS/NZS 4360 was developed in response to a perceived need for practical assistance in applying risk management in public sector and private sector organizations. The reason AS/NZS 4360 has been so widely accepted in Australia, New Zealand, and globally may lie in the way standards were developed and approved there. The process started in 1992 when a Standards Australia questionnaire was submitted on behalf of the Association of Risk and Insurance Managers of Australasia (ARIMA). This led to the distribution of a further questionnaire to a wide range of industry and professional organizations to determine both need and interest. Satisfied of the need and the availability of a representative range of potential members, Standards Australia and Standards New Zealand established a Joint Technical Committee composed of 27 members representing 22 industry, professional, and government (federal, state, and local) organizations. The committee first gathered all available information. All submissions and documents were copied and supplied to the members. After several drafts, the committee produced one for public comment. To ensure maximum exposure, the representative organizations were asked to encourage responses from their membership, advertisements were placed in the daily press seeking input from the general public, and copies were supplied to all member organizations of the International Federation of

Risk and Insurance Management Associations (IFRIMA). The committee received 326 specific comments from 55 individuals or organizations. Each comment was addressed, resulting in many changes to the draft. The final document received unanimous approval and was published in November 1995.

AS/NZS 4360 was prepared by the Joint Standards Australia/ Standards New Zealand Committee OB-007, Risk Management, as a revision of AS/NZS 4360:1999, Risk Management. AS/NZS 4360 provides a generic framework for establishing the context and identifying, analyzing, evaluating, treating, monitoring, and communicating risk. This handbook states in clause 4.2 that "risk is the chance of something happening that will have an impact on objectives." The stated objective of this standard is to provide guidance to enable public, private, or community enterprises, groups, and individuals to achieve the following:

- A more confident and rigorous basis for decision making and planning
- Better identification of opportunities and threats
- Gaining value from uncertainty and variability
- Proactive rather than reactive management
- More effective allocation and use of resources
- Improved incident management and reduction in loss and the cost of risk, including commercial insurance premiums
- Improved stakeholder confidence and trust
- Improved compliance with relevant legislation
- Better corporate governance

The model of the risk management process AS/NZS 4360 consists of three major elements: the risk management workflow, monitor and review, and, finally, communication and consult. The latter two continuously interact with the steps of risk management workflow. AS/NZS 4360 defines risk management as "the culture, processes and structures that are directed towards the effective management of potential opportunities and adverse effects." AS/NZS 4360 defines risk as "the chance of something happening that will have an impact upon objectives. It is measured in terms of likelihood and consequences."

Figure 1.1 illustrates the bidirectional flow from context and risk to communication and consultation in parallel with monitoring and reviewing activities. These serve as a logical check on the risk analysis process, where risk is evaluated, mitigated, or accepted in sequential steps as follows:

- **Establish the context**: It is necessary to fully understand the external and internal aspects of the organization or organizational part, which is subject to risk management.
- **Identify risks**: This step uncovers risks, their location, time frame, root causes, and scenarios.
- **Analyze risks**: The output of risk analysis is the likelihood of a risk and the consequences of risk occurrence.
- **Evaluate risks**: Risk analysis provides an outcome, which is the basis for deciding which risks need treatment and in what priority.
- **Treat risks**: Treatments are responses to risks. Alternative treatments need to be identified, assessed, selected, planned, and implemented.
- **Monitor and review**: The purpose of this step is to ensure that the risk management plan remains relevant and all input data, including likelihood and consequence, are up to date.

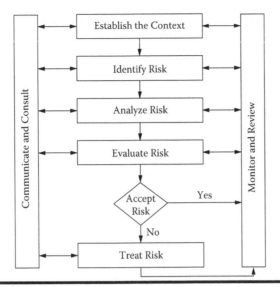

**Figure 1.1    The AS/NZS 4360 risk analysis process.**

Monitor and review relates to all of the five elements of risk management workflow mentioned previously.

■ **Communication and consult**: Successful risk management relies on communication with all stakeholders. Communication will improve the level of understanding and treating risks. Communication is important throughout the entire risk management cycle.

The risk management process flow consists of the following elements:

■ **The organization's strategic objectives**: Ensure that risk management activities meet the strategy of the organization.
■ **Risk identification**: Uncover and list risks.
■ **Risk description**: Display the identified risks in a structured format.
■ **Risk estimation**: Provide values for probability of a risk and consequence in case of risk occurrence.
■ **Risk evaluation**: Compare against risk criteria to analyze whether the risk is accepted or requires any treatment.
■ **Risk reporting**: Report the risks identified. There are different requirements on reporting depending on the level inside (internal reporting) or outside (external reporting) the organization.
■ **Decision**: Make a decision about whether and how to respond to a risk.
■ **Risk treatment**: Select and implement treatments against risks.
■ **Residual risk reporting**: Report the progress made by mitigating the risk.
■ **Monitoring**: Check results. The monitoring step loops back to the previous steps of improvement and update.

### *British Standard BS 6079 3:1800 and PD-6668:2000*

Lord Berkeley stated the course of empire was westward. The course of risk management standards, however, appears to be in reverse. The first national standard was created in Oceania by the Kiwis and Aussies in 1995 (ANZ Standard 4360:1995 and 1999). The Canadians followed in 1997 (CSA-Q850-97) with their version. Eastward, the British published BS 6079-3:2000 after a revision of ISO/IEC 17799 led to a modification in the controls, which triggered a change to Annex A of BS 7799 Part 2 to keep it in line with the new Part 1. This resulted in the creation of BS 6079 as a method to quantify risk in the security audit process. In the British standard, BS 6079, risk is defined as "uncertainty inherent in plans and the possibility of something happening that can affect the prospects of achieving business or project goals." Uncertainty may be positive or negative. Risk is therefore a possible hazard or opportunity that if it occurred or was captured would threaten or benefit business outcomes.

PD 6668:2000 provides guidance on how organizations can establish and manage their strategic and operational risks. Some risks must be taken to be successful and survive. Other risks, if realized, can put an organization in jeopardy, and these risks should be mitigated. BS 6079-3:2000 provides specific guidance on the management of business-related project risk. The standard describes a process for identifying, assessing, and controlling risk within a broad framework.

Risk management then is the systematic application of policies, procedures, methods, and practices to the tasks of identifying, analyzing, evaluating, treating, and monitoring risk. BS 6079 confirms that risk involves three key issues: the frequency, the consequences, and the perception of loss. BS 6079 focuses on how risk affects all stakeholders. It emphasizes the importance of communications among stakeholders in the process of seeking responses. It identifies a "risk cycle" of estimation, evaluation, and control in which methods of financing are implicitly included. It recommends the creation of a "risk management team," a multidisciplinary group of internal and external experts, as well as perhaps some stakeholder representatives, to address the major risk issues facing an organization. It suggests creating a "risk information library" that includes documentation of issues, scope of decisions, identification of roles and responsibilities, identification of decision makers, details of analyses, stakeholder responses, and support documentation for decisions.

$$Risk = Hazard \times Consequence$$

Risk can be rated for a specific resource or value (specific risk), or it can be determined for all resources and values (total risk).

The framework comprises an iterative process embracing the following:

- **Understanding context**: Project objectives and business objectives—project in the business context and business in the project context
- **Identifying risk**: The sources of risk, and understanding how risks arise
- **Analyzing risk**: Characterization
- **Evaluating risk**: Identifying priorities
- **Treating risk**: Taking action

## Maintaining the Knowledge Pool, Plans, and the Management Process

The risk management culture is exemplified by encouraging everyone, especially managers, to continuously consider and monitor risk, including that arising from their own decision making and actions. Training and simulations can heighten awareness and responsibilities of decision makers (BS 6079-3:2000 cls 4.4), and help them adopt a priority of actions for treating risk (BS 6079-3:2000 cls 4.3.4). The phases outlined by BS 6079 are as follows:

1. Eliminate risk.
2. Avoid risk.
3. Share risk.
4. Reduce the probability of occurrence of risk.
5. Reduce the consequences of risk.

## Canadian Standard 1797 (CSA-Q85-97)

Canada followed Australia and New Zealand in creating a "guideline" on risk management. The Australasian "Standard" #4360:1995 broke the ice and received global applause. In response, the Canadian Standards Association published CAN/CSA-Q850-97 in October 1997, "Risk Management: Guideline for Decision Makers, a National Standard for Canada." It is more a public policy risk document than a financial or operational risk management guide. CSA-Q850-97 confirms that risk involves three key issues: the frequency, the consequences, and the perception of loss. The Canadian guideline also focuses on how risk affects all stakeholders. It emphasizes the importance of communication among stakeholders in the process of seeking responses. It identifies a "risk cycle" of estimation, evaluation, and control, in which methods of financing are implicitly included. It recommends the creation of a "risk management team," a multidisciplinary group of internal and external experts, as well as stakeholder representatives, to address the major risk issues facing an organization.

The decision-making process described in the CSA Risk Management Guideline (CAN/CSA-Q850-97) consists of six steps, which follow a standardized management or systems analysis approach. The process is iterative and allows for the return to previous steps at any time throughout the process. The features of the Q850 approach are as follows:

■ It incorporates stakeholder perceptions of the acceptability of the risk into the decision process, providing for more informed decision making and ensuring that the legitimate interests of all affected stakeholders are considered.
■ It incorporates a risk communication framework into the decision process, ensuring reasonable and effective communication among stakeholders.
■ It provides a standardized terminology used to describe risk issues, thus contributing to better communication about risk issues.
■ It provides for an explicit treatment of uncertainty.

The CSA risk management process is illustrated in Figure 1.2.

Walking through the CSA risk management process, one begins with the initiation phase. Risk Assessment and Analysis begins in the Preliminary Analysis phase, coming to completion in Risk Estimation. Risk Assessment ends in Risk Evaluation. Risk Control and Action Monitoring complete the risk management process.

The definition of risk for the CSA risk management process involves three key issues: the frequency, consequences, and perception of loss. The process focuses on how risk affects all stakeholders. It emphasizes the importance of communication among stakeholders in the process of seeking responses. It identifies a "risk cycle" of estimation, evaluation, and control, in which methods of financing are implicitly included. The CSA process recommends the creation of a "risk

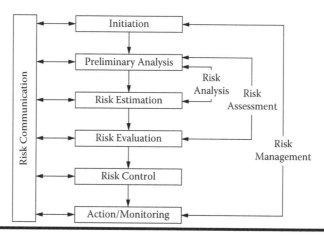

**Figure 1.2   The risk analysis, assessment, and management process.**

management team," a multidisciplinary group of internal and external experts, as well as perhaps some stakeholder representatives, to address the major risk issues facing an organization. The process suggests creating a "risk information library" that includes documentation of issues, scope of decisions, identification of roles and responsibilities, identification of decision makers, details of analyses, stakeholder responses, and support documentation for decisions.

## *Germany IT-Grundschutz 100-3*

German-headquartered global businesses follow ISO 17799 as their horizontal best standard practice of corporate security. If more than 50 percent of their business remains in Germany, corporations will generally opt for the BSI-issued IT Grundschutz. IT Grundschutz is a more detailed version of ISO 17799, and Germans argue over which came first, Grundschutz or the British BS 7799. They see theirs as the more stringent, realistic approach to a baseline. Under the IT-Grundschutz risk analysis approach, the threats are identified and assigned a likelihood of occurrence. The results of this analysis are then used to select the appropriate IT security measures, following which the residual risk can be assessed. Figure 1.3 outlines how threats are managed.

The procedure illustrated in Figure 1.3 can be used to reveal the most important areas in which there is still a need for action after application of the IT Baseline Protection Manual with the least possible effort and expense. Threats listed in the IT Baseline Protection Manual that are relevant to the IT asset under review are used as the starting point for risk analysis.

> *Preparing the threat summary*—When determining relevant threats, the protection requirement for the target object under review must be considered in terms of the three basic parameters for IT security: confidentiality, integrity, and availability.
>
> *Determination of additional threats*—Regardless of the protection requirements of the target object under review, it is important to determine additional relevant threats when there exists a special need for analysis. This is the case, for example, if there is no appropriate module in the IT Baseline Protection Manual.
>
> *Threat assessment*—The threat summary is worked through systematically. It is checked to see if the IT security safeguards are already implemented or at least planned in the IT security concept and do provide adequate protection for each target object and threat. These are usually standard security safeguards from the IT Baseline Protection Manual.

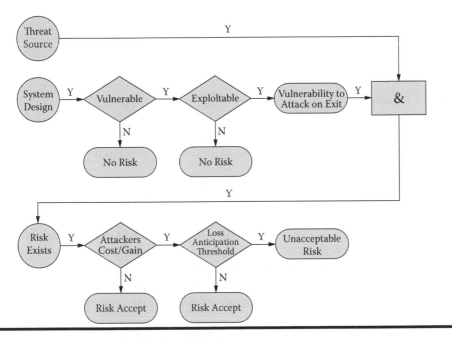

**Figure 1.3   Threat assessment process flow.**

From this point three options exist: risk reduction, risk transference, and risk acceptance. Risk reduction is accomplished through further security safeguards, where the threat remaining is removed by preparing and implementing additional security measures that counteract the threat adequately; risk transference through restructuring, where the remaining threat is removed by restructuring the business asset; or risk acceptance, where the remaining threat and the risk arising from it are accepted.

## South Africa: IRMSA and King II Report Section 2

In 1994 the King Committee on Corporate Governance, headed by former High Court judge Mervyn King S.C. King I, published the King Report on Corporate Governance (King I), incorporating a code of corporate practices and conduct. It was the first of its kind in the country and was aimed at promoting the highest standards of corporate governance in South Africa.

Over and above the financial and regulatory aspects of corporate governance, King I advocated an integrated approach to good governance in the interests of a wide range of stakeholders. Although groundbreaking at the time, the evolving global economic environment, together with recent legislative developments, has necessitated that King I be updated. To this end, the King Committee on Corporate Governance developed the King Report on Corporate Governance for South Africa, 2002 (King II). King II acknowledges that there is a move away from the single bottom line (that is, profit for shareholders) to a triple bottom line, which embraces the economic, environmental, and social aspects of a company's activities. The South African corporate governance report provides a unique definition of risk in the context of regulations designed to promote operational transparency and stakeholder accountability, and to that end we will break down the report into its core areas of focus to differentiate it from the purely operational or purely risk-oriented taxonomies, which occupy a common subject area. Although focused on South Africa, the rigor of the King reports has earned international recognition and acclaim. King II requires the majority of members of the audit committee to be financially literate and, in four chapters, defines risk for the purpose of legislative accountability. The following paragraphs present an overview of the report broken down by chapter:

*Chapter 1: Introduction and definition*—Risk management is defined as the identification and evaluation of actual and potential areas of risk as they pertain to a company, followed by a procedure of termination, transfer, acceptance (tolerance), or mitigation of each risk. Risk management is therefore a process that utilizes internal controls as a measure to mitigate and control risk.

*Chapter 2: Responsibility for risk management*—The board is responsible for setting risk tolerance and related strategies and policies. It is also the board's responsibility to review the effectiveness of these policies on a regular basis and in a manner in which its objectives are clearly defined for the benefit of management to guide them in carrying out their responsibilities. The board is responsible for ensuring that the company has implemented an effective ongoing process to identify risk, measure its potential impact against a set of assumptions, and then activate what it believes is necessary to proactively manage these risks. The board must then decide on what risk that company is prepared to take and what risks it will not take in pursuance of its goals and objectives.

*Chapter 3: Assimilating risk to the control environment*—The board is required to implement a comprehensive system of controls to ensure that risks are mitigated and that the company's objectives are attained. The control environment must then set the tone of the company and cover ethical values, management's philosophy, and the competence of employees. Any vulnerability in the achievement of the company's objectives, whether caused by internal or external risk factors, should be detected and reported by the systems of control in place and met with appropriate intervention. This is intended to improve the company's risk profile, enhancing the company's investment attraction, and increase the positive influences of risk on the business.

Five essential aspects of control are identified in the standard:

Corporate control environment
Risk assessment
Control activities
Information and communications
Monitoring

*Chapter 4: Application of risk management*—The risk management review processes must identify areas of opportunity, in which, for example, effective risk management can be turned into a competitive advantage for the company. Risk management in this context goes beyond the control of financial risks. Reputation and a company's future survival are also taken into consideration. Companies under King II must ensure that the governance surrounding risk management is transparent and disclosed to its stakeholders. In King II, risk management is viewed as a continuous process of identifying, evaluating, and managing risk.

Risk assessment in this context addresses the company's exposure:

■ Physical and operational risks
■ Human resource risks

- Technical risks
- Business continuity and disaster recovery
- Credit and market risks
- Compliance risks

Here are a few sections of the act, which preserve the integrity of the risk management process:

> *Section 275A*: Prohibits the provision of nonaudit services; requires the auditor to subject the nonaudit service to his or her own external audit procedures.
>
> *Section 275A(3)(b)*: Prohibits an auditor having financial interest in a company.
>
> *Section 287*: States that directors will be guilty of an offense when incomplete or noncompliant financial reports are issued. Directors are guilty of an offence in cases where the auditor expressed either a qualified opinion or an adverse opinion.
>
> *Section 287 and section 440FF*: State that it will be an offense for any director to issue incomplete or noncompliant financial reports.
>
> *Section 287A*: False or misleading statements—directors of a company are accountable to their stakeholders, and the major exposure to liability should rest with the directors or executives responsible for making the decisions or preparing the financial statements that mislead stakeholders.

Figure 1.4 illustrates how vulnerabilities and hazards are managed in the King Report.

Finally, the risk analysis process must maintain independence. As cited from the Executive Summary of the King Report, 2002, ISBN 0-620-28852-3, March 2002:

> Independence of mind—The state of minds that permits the provision of an opinion without being affected by influences that comprise professional judgment, allowing an individual to act with integrity, and exercise objectivity and professional skepticism.
>
> Independence in appearance—The avoidance of facts and circumstances that are so significant that a reasonable and informed third party, having knowledge of all relevant information, including safeguards applied, would reasonably conclude a firm's, or a member of the assurance team's, integrity, objectivity, or professional skepticism had been compromised.

## United States NIST SP 800-30

NIST SP 800-30 consists of three sections: risk assessment, risk mitigation, and control evaluation. It is a questionnaire, interview-, and tool-based risk methodology. Risk management encompasses three processes: risk assessment, risk mitigation, and evaluation and assessment. Section 1 describes the risk assessment process, which includes identification, evaluation of risks and risk impacts, and recommendation of risk-reducing measures. Section 2 describes risk mitigation, which refers to prioritizing, implementing, and maintaining the appropriate risk-reducing measures recommended from the risk assessment process. Section 3 provides an evaluation and assessment of the processes.

**Figure 1.4   Risk analysis and assessment process flow.**

Nine steps of risk assessment:

**Step 1:** *System characterization*—The first step is to define the scope of the effort. In this step, the boundaries of the IT system are identified, along with the resources and the information that constitute the system. Characterizing an IT system establishes the scope of the risk assessment effort, delineates the accreditation boundaries, and provides information essential to defining the risk.

**Step 2:** *Threat identification*—The goal of this step is to identify the potential threat sources and compile a threat statement listing potential threats and threat sources that are applicable to the system being evaluated.

**Step 3:** *Vulnerability identification*—The goal of this step is to develop a list of system vulnerabilities, flaws, or weaknesses that could be exploited by the potential threat sources. Methods for identifying system vulnerabilities are the identification of vulnerability sources, the performance of system security testing, and the development of a security requirements checklist.

**Step 4:** *Control analysis and methods*—The goal of this step is to analyze the controls implemented, or planned for implementation, by the organization to minimize or eliminate the likelihood or probability of a threat's exercising system vulnerability.

**Step 5:** *Likelihood determination*—The likelihood rating indicates the probability that a potential vulnerability may be exercised within a threat environment. The factors that must be considered are threat source, motivation, capability, the nature of the vulnerability, existence, and effectiveness of current controls. The likelihood that a potential vulnerability could be exercised by a given threat source is then rated as high, medium, or low.

**Step 6:** *Impact analysis*—The next step in measuring the level of risk is to determine the impact resulting from a successful threat exercise of vulnerability.

**Step 7:** *Risk determination*—The purpose of this step is to assess the level of risk to the IT system. The determination of risk for a particular threat and vulnerability pair can be expressed as a function of the likelihood of a given threat source attempting to exercise a given vulnerability, the magnitude of the impact should a threat source successfully exercise the vulnerability, and the adequacy of planned or existing security controls for reducing or eliminating the risk.

**Step 8: *Control recommendations*—**During this step of the process, controls that could mitigate or eliminate the identified risks, as appropriate to the organization's operations, are provided. The goal of the recommended controls is to reduce the level of risk to the IT system and its data to an acceptable level. The factors that should be considered in recommending controls and alternative solutions to minimize or eliminate identified risks are effectiveness of recommended options, legislation and regulation, organizational policy operational impact, and safety and reliability.

**Step 9: *Results documentation*—**Once the risk assessment has been completed, threat sources and vulnerabilities identified, risks numerically assessed, and recommended controls provided, the results should be documented in an official report or briefing. A risk assessment report is a management document that helps senior management—the mission owners—make decisions on changes needed—in policy, procedures, budgets, and operation and management of the system.

Risk mitigation is the second process of risk management. It involves prioritizing, evaluating, and implementing the appropriate risk-reducing controls recommended from the risk assessment. Because elimination of all risk is usually impractical or close to impossible, it is the responsibility of senior functional and business managers to use the least-cost approach and implement the most appropriate controls to decrease mission risk to an acceptable level.

*Phase 1. Options*—The goals and mission of an organization should be considered in selecting any of these risk mitigation options. It is not practical to address all identified risks, so priority should be given to the threat and vulnerability pairs that have the highest potential to cause significant impact or harm. NIST SP800-30 defines the following options when addressing risk:

■ Risk assumption: Accept the potential risk and continue operating.
■ Risk avoidance: Avoid the risk by eliminating the risk cause or consequence or both.
■ Risk limitation: Limit the risk by implementing controls that minimize the adverse impact of a threat's exercising a vulnerability.
■ Risk planning: Manage risk by developing a risk mitigation plan that prioritizes, implements, and maintains controls.
■ Research and acknowledgment of risk: Lower the risk of loss by acknowledging the vulnerability or flaw and researching controls to correct it.
■ Risk transference: Transfer the risk by using other options to compensate for the loss.

*Phase 2. Risk mitigation strategy*—Figure 1.5 outlines the risk mitigation strategy set out in NIST SP800-30.

■ When a vulnerability or flaw exists, implement assurance techniques to reduce the likelihood of a vulnerability exploit.
■ When a vulnerability can be exercised, apply layered protections and administrative controls to minimize the risk of an exploit or prevent it.
■ When the attacker's cost is less than the potential gain, apply protection to decrease an attacker's motivation by increasing the attacker's effort.
■ When loss is too great, apply technical and nontechnical protections to limit the potential for loss.

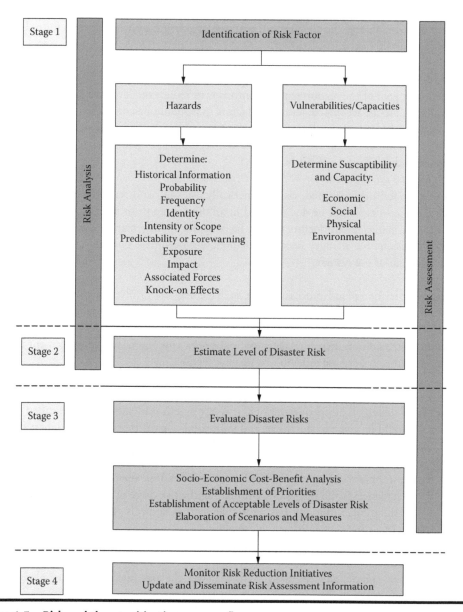

**Figure 1.5   Risk and threat mitigation process flow.**

*Phase 3. Control implementation*—When control actions must be taken, address the greatest risks and strive for sufficient risk mitigation at the lowest cost with minimum impact on other mission capabilities by the following:

- Prioritizing actions
- Evaluating recommended control options
- Conducting cost–benefit analysis
- Selecting control based on the results of the cost–benefit analysis

- Assigning responsibility to appropriate persons who have the expertise and skill sets to implement the selected controls
- Developing a safeguard implementation plan

*Phase 4. Control categories:*

- Technical security controls: These controls may range from simple to complex measures and usually involve system architectures, engineering disciplines, and security packages with a mix of hardware, software, and firmware.
- Management security controls: Management controls focus on the stipulation of information protection policy, guidelines, and standards, which are carried out through operational procedures to fulfill the organization's goals and missions.
- Operational security controls: Operational controls, implemented in accordance with a base set of requirements, technical controls, and good industry practices, are used to correct operational deficiencies that could be exercised by potential threat sources.

*Phase 5. Cost–benefit analysis*: The cost-benefit analysis can be qualitative or quantitative. Its purpose is to demonstrate that the costs of implementing the controls can be justified by the reduction in the level of risk.

## International Standards Organization/UN: ISO/IEC 13335-2

ISO/IEC 13335-3 identifies three sources for establishing the organization's information security requirements: the risks that the organization faces, risks arising from compliance, and contractual requirements.

The first step is to determine the assets within the scope. The next step is to identify the threats or potential events that can "assault" the identified assets. Threat modeling comprises three high-level steps: understanding the adversary's view, characterizing the security of the system, and determining threats. External threats originate from outside sources, either targeted at the company or randomly spread to the network through users or the Internet. External threats can range from Web site defacement and attacks targeting a business to nasty viruses and worms that tunnel their way into any network and destroy or alter data and applications or monopolize system resources (denial of services) by duplicating and spreading themselves. Internal threats are varied and range from unprivileged local access to administrative abuse of privileges. The developers of kernel-level rootkits are orchestrating very complicated and effective schemes for compromising a system and remaining undetected. Malicious software worms spread faster than systems can be patched; however, they can be detected because most leave some type of imprint. The next step is to determine the vulnerabilities. These are events that leave a system open to attack by a threat or allow an attack to have some success or greater impact.

The next step in the process is to determine the impacts. These are the successful exploitation of a vulnerability by a threat, thereby impacting the asset's availability, confidentiality, or integrity. The impacts are then identified and assigned a monetary value. This effort constitutes risk assessment in which risks are assessed in light of the true harm they pose. From this point, an assessment of the likelihood of the system failure ensues. In remediation, the controls in place against the risks are activated. Controls are the countermeasures for vulnerabilities. Apart from knowingly accepting risks that fall within the criteria of acceptability or transferring the risk (through contract or insurance) to others, there are four types of risk mitigation controls:

- Deterrent controls reduce the likelihood of a deliberate attack.
- Preventative controls protect vulnerabilities and make an attack unsuccessful or reduce its impact.
- Corrective controls reduce the effect of an attack.
- Detective controls discover attacks and trigger preventative or corrective controls.

Countermeasures or controls must be cost effective. In the best interest of the business, the cost of implementing and maintaining a control must be less than the cost of the impact. Total security is not possible, but it is possible to provide effective security against known risks provided periodic reevaluation practices are in place.

The process for assessing risk builds on the scoping document, is focused on critical systems and information assets, and can be broken down into clearly defined steps:

- Identify the boundaries of what is to be protected.
- Identify systems necessary for the reception, storage, manipulation, and transmission of information within those boundaries and the information assets within those systems.
- Identify relationships between these systems, the information assets, and the organizational objectives and tasks.
- Identify systems and information assets that are critical to the organizational objectives and rank them in order of priority.
- Identify the potential threats to those critical systems and assets.
- Identify the potential vulnerabilities of those critical systems and assets.

With the key objectives clearly identified, the systems that are most important to their delivery are identified. It is possible that some objectives will have more than one system, and these interdependencies should also all be noted. The resulting report is a schedule that shows prioritized critical systems as dependencies of key organizational objectives, which is then reviewed and agreed upon by the senior management. The final step in this exercise is to transfer the risk-level assessment for each impact to the asset and risk log.

## Academia: Octave® Method from Carnegie Mellon

For an organization looking to understand its information security needs, OCTAVE is a risk-based strategic assessment and planning technique for security. OCTAVE is self-directed, meaning that people from an organization assume responsibility for setting the organization's security strategy. The technique leverages people's knowledge of their organization's security-related practices and processes to capture the current state of security practice within the organization. Risks to the most critical assets are used to prioritize areas of improvement and set the security strategy for the organization. The Operationally Critical Threat, Asset, and Vulnerability Evaluation (OCTAVE) defines the essential components of a comprehensive, systematic, context-driven information security risk evaluation. OCTAVE is a risk-based strategic assessment and planning technique for security. Octave leverages people's knowledge of their organization's security-related practices and processes to capture the current state of security practice within the organization. Risks to the most critical assets are used to prioritize areas of improvement and set the security strategy for the organization. OCTAVE is self-directed, meaning that people from an organization assume responsibility for setting the organization's security strategy. The OCTAVE approach is driven by

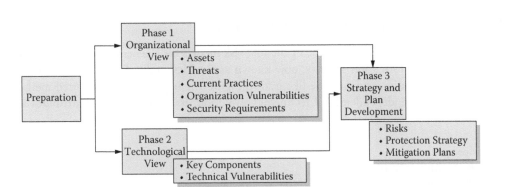

**Figure 1.6   Phase 1, 2, and 3 of OCTAVE risk management.**

two of the aspects: operational risk and security practices. Technology is examined only in relation to security practices, enabling an organization to refine the view of its current security practices. OCTAVE distinguishes itself in organization evaluation, security practices, strategic issues, and self-direction. OCTAVE phases of technical, organizational strategy are illustrated in Figure 1.6.

Founding philosophy of OCTAVE:

■ One cannot mitigate all information security risks.
■ The enterprise budget is limited. So are other resources.
■ One cannot prevent all determined, skilled incursions.
■ The enterprise needs to recognize, resist, and recover from incidents.

The enterprise needs to determine the best use of limited resources to ensure the survivability of its view and focus on critical issues.

Analysis teams must do the following:

■ Identify information-related assets that are important.
■ Focus risk analysis activities on those assets judged to be most critical to the organization.
■ Consider the relationships among critical assets, the threats to those assets, and vulnerabilities that can expose assets to threats.
■ Evaluate risks in an operational context—how they are used to conduct an organization's business and how those assets are at risk on account of security threats.
■ Create a practice-based protection strategy for organizational improvement as well as create risk mitigation plans to reduce the risk to the organization's critical assets.

OCTAVE drivers:

■ Risk-based—to prioritize effective use of minimum resources
■ Practice-based—serves as a platform for improving security

OCTAVE is part of a continuum:

■ Identify the organization's information security risks.
■ Analyze the risks to determine priorities.
■ Plan for improvement by developing a protection strategy for organizational improvement.

## *Academia: McCumber Cube Methodology*

In 1991, John McCumber created one of the first risk models for a general architectural description of computer information security, now known as the McCumber Cube. This risk model is depicted as a three-dimensional cube-like grid in Figure 1.7. It provides a structured methodology that functions independently of technology evolution. Its dimensions and attributes are as follows:

Desired goals
- Confidentiality
- Integrity
- Availability

Information states
- Storage: in memory
- Transmission: over network
- Processing: in execution

Reaction states
- Policy: directives from management or IT department
- Education: of users in process and procedure
- Technology: software and hardware enablers

The 27 individual cubes created by the model can be extracted and examined individually. This key aspect can be useful in categorizing and analyzing countermeasures. It is also a tool for defining

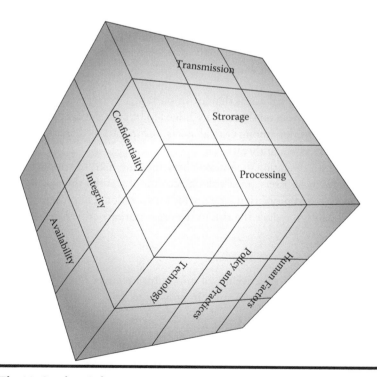

**Figure 1.7 The McCumber Cube.**

organizational responsibility for information security. By considering all 27 cubes, the analyst is assured of a complete perspective of all available security measures. Unlike other computer security standards and criteria, this model connotes a true systems viewpoint. The McCumber cube was originally published as "Information Systems Security: A Comprehensive Model," in October 1991. The model is the baseline used by the National Security Telecommunications and Information Systems Security Committee (NSTISSC) and was published in National Security Telecommunications and Information Systems Security Instruction's (NSTISSI) National Information Systems Security (INFOSEC) Glossary.

## Basel II

International Convergence of Capital Measurement and Capital Standards—A Revised Framework is the second Basel Accord and represents recommendations by bank supervisors and central bankers from the 13 countries making up the Basel Committee on Banking Supervision (BCBS) to revise the international standards for measuring the adequacy of a bank's capital. It was created to promote greater consistency in the way banks and banking regulators approach risk management across national borders. Basel II uses a "three pillars" concept—(1) minimum capital requirements, (2) supervisory review, and (3) market discipline—to promote greater stability in the financial system:

The first pillar: The first pillar provides improved risk sensitivity in the way that capital requirements are calculated for three major components of risk that a bank faces: credit risk, operational risk, and market risk. In turn, each of these components can be calculated in three ways of varying sophistication. Terms defining market risk include VaR (value at risk) and EL (expected loss, more commonly known as loss function) whose components are PD (probability of default), LGD (loss given default), and EAD (exposure at default). Calculation of these components requires advanced data collection and sophisticated risk management techniques.

The second pillar: The second pillar deals with the regulatory response to the first pillar, giving regulators improved measures to help them implement the accord. It also provides a framework for dealing with financial risk, including name risk, liquidity risk, and legal risk, which the accord combines under the title of residual risk.

The third pillar: The third pillar greatly increases the disclosures that the bank must make. This is designed to allow the market to have a better picture of the overall risk position of the bank and to allow the counterparties of the bank to price and deal appropriately.

## Summary

We are at the precipice of a new risk management frontier with operational risks, and clearly, there is still much further to go. Because operational losses today are more intensely scrutinized, and therefore visible, operational performance demands are greater than ever.

In addition to modeling operational risk, there is much to be said for simply improving on the availability of information about operational risk information for management decision making. Technology will be the essential mortar needed to aggregate, cement, and simplify all the pieces in place, thereby linking all of the functional areas, initiatives, and data sets, both hard and soft, firmwide. Aggregated operational risk reporting will become commonplace, much as portfolio market and credit risk reports have. Because of the softer issues involved, such as the vagaries of human behavior (i.e., people risk), a mix of tools will be needed to represent operational risk fully. The risk complexities also require more effective risk management programs to link initiatives and variables together, not just periodically but continuously.

# Chapter 2

# Compliance Frameworks

Compliance frameworks are the connection between regulatory mandates and software practices. In the following chapter, we explore the nature of compliance frameworks and best practices in an attempt to direct the identity professional toward standards that enable auditable stewardship and governance of identity-related information.

Management should perceive the self-assessment phase provided by the use of these tools as an opportunity for business process reengineering. For the manager, a regular self-assessment of control operations should also reveal potential improvements in process. The exceptions found in detective, back-end controls can recommend more appropriate front-end controls to reduce error correction and rework. Often, these exceptions can point to refinements for system input screens that shift the control function from detective or manual to preventative or automated and result in a net increase in value for the company.

## Compliance Framework Taxonomy

Identity management has the greatest impact on a company's ability to achieve regulatory compliance. Operational transparency and financial accountability derive from the enterprise's ability to assign access and authority to the right people. Accountability also derives from the ability to track users' identity as expressed in the role and responsibility assigned by the company. As a result, companies are discovering that their ability to win and perform on contracts is as subject to investigation of their identity management processes as it is of their company's balance sheets or stock value.

Accompanying a flock of identity-related compliance mandates are multiple frameworks and methodologies for managing operational risk in a way that can be verified. This can be good or bad depending on perspective. Either way, these frameworks should not be unfamiliar to the identity management professional. The number of frameworks against which companies' processes are evaluated continues to increase; however, it is evident that companies may need to consider a daunting number of frameworks. The field truly is a quagmire in which compliance efforts can stall if an organization is not careful. The first step toward making sense of the regulatory quagmire is to categorize the frameworks by purpose and focus. In general, these frameworks define characteristics of good processes, but do not prescribe how they should be enacted.

## Joint EU Framework

ISO/IEC 27001:2005, ITIL, and CobiT are the three most important best-practice IT-related frameworks. ISO/IEC 27001 is the international Code of Best Practice for Information Security from the International Standards Organization in Geneva. ITIL is the IT Infrastructure Library, created by the United Kingdom's Office of Government Commerce, and CobiT is Control Objectives for Information and Related Technology, from the IT Governance Institute, in the United States. ISO 17799, ITIL, and COBIT are all best-practice IT approaches to regulatory and corporate governance compliance. The challenge is to craft an integrated framework that encompasses all three standards. The Joint Framework established by the IT Governance Institute and the British Office of Government Commerce forms one of the two most comprehensive frameworks.

*Aligning COBIT, ITIL and ISO 17799 for Business Benefit* was published in 2005 and serves to formalize the relationship between these three best-practice frameworks. The recommendation is that COBIT should be used to provide "an overall control framework based on the (generic) IT-process model" at the governance level.

- ITIL describes how service management aspects should be handled.
- ITIL and ISO 27001 are mapped to high-level COBIT process and control objectives.
- ISO 27001 defines what must be done in terms of information security controls.
- Appendix I maps CobiT controls to ITIL processes and ISO 27001 controls.
- Appendix II maps ITIL processes to COBIT control objectives.
- ITIL, COBIT, and ISO 27001(17799) projects are enabled to be cross-linked/integrated.

Organizations that use the Joint Framework will have a single, integrated, compliance approach that delivers corporate governance general control objectives, meets the regulatory requirements of data- and privacy-related regulation, and enables the organization to prepare for external certification to ISO 27001 and ISO 20000, both of which demonstrate compliance. The Joint Framework prepares the enterprise for emerging regulatory requirements, enabling compliance with multiple regulations and meeting complex compliance requirements.

The Joint Framework helps organizations improve business performance; it focuses on business processes, as opposed to controls, and builds controls into the business processes. The Joint Framework enables a broad-based shift from reactive to proactive compliance operations.

A benefit of increased standardization in compliance efforts is reduced costs, improved efficiency, and increased quality. Because the framework applies across the enterprise, it reduces vertical silos of expertise and practice, improving communication and business effectiveness. In observation, the framework can be deployed quickly and can reduce an organization's dependence on multitudes of experts and methodologies. Choosing the implementation of the Joint Framework not only leads an enterprise toward effective regulatory compliance but also helps improve the organization's competitiveness.

## Control Mapping—Joint EU Framework

ISO/IEC 27001:2005, ITIL, and CobiT make up the Joint EU Framework, addressing the domain control requirements of

- Trusted access
- Change management
- Business continuity and availability
- Operational monitoring
- Records management
- Audit and risk management
- Operational controls

The standard concedes as out of its scope the control areas of

- Operational transparency
- Segregation of duties

## *COBIT*

The Control Objectives for Information and Related Technologies (CobiT), in its fourth edition, is widely adopted in North America and is increasingly being accepted in Europe. It is a broad principles-based framework that looks at the management of the IT organization and is aimed at board members, managers, and auditors. CobiT identifies 34 key information technology processes and a further 318 control objectives, each of which has an audit guideline. It maps to the specific requirements of the recommended internal control framework for Sarbanes–Oxley compliance and underpins the recommendations of the Turnbull Guidance.

This framework has four major domains, which follow the general systems development life cycle:

- Planning and organization (PO, plan and organize): The planning and organization domain has 11 high-level control objectives that cover everything from strategic IT planning and the creation of a corporate information architecture to the management of specific projects.
- Acquisition and implementation (AI, acquire and implement): Companies need to acquire and implement information systems. This domain has six high-level control objectives.
- Delivery and support (DS, deliver and support): Most of the IT project life cycle takes place after implementation. The CobiT framework has 13 high-level control objectives for delivery and support.
- Monitoring (M, monitor and evaluate): Firms must monitor processes, assess the adequacy of internal controls, obtain independent assurance, and provide for independent auditing.

Each process is described by using the following information:

- High-level control objectives
- Detailed control objectives
- Information criteria affected by the process
- IT resources used by the process
- Typical characteristics depending on the maturity level
- Critical success factors
- Key performance indicators
- Key goal indicators

## Information Criteria

Information delivered to the core business processes has to fulfill certain criteria, categorized as follows:

*Quality requirements*
- *Effectiveness:* The relevance and pertinence of information to the business process as well as the timely, correct, consistent, and usable delivery.
- *Efficiency:* The provision of information through the optimum (most productive and economical) use of resources.

*Security requirements*
- *Confidentiality:* The protection of sensitive information from unauthorized disclosure.
- *Integrity:* The accuracy and completeness of information, as well as its validity, in accordance with business values and expectations.
- *Availability:* Information being available when required by the business process now and in the future. It also concerns the safeguarding of necessary resources and associated capabilities.

*Fiduciary requirements*
- *Compliance:* Deals with following those laws, regulations, and contractual arrangements to which the business process is subject (i.e., externally imposed business criteria).
- *Reliability:* Relates to the provision of appropriate information for management to operate the entity and for management to exercise its financial and compliance-reporting responsibilities.

## Control Mapping—COBIT

COBIT addresses the domain control requirements of

- Trusted access
- Business continuity and availability
- Operational monitoring
- Records management
- Operational controls

The standard concedes as out of its scope the control areas of

- Change management
- Audit and risk management
- Operational transparency
- Segregation of duties

# ISO 27001

This international standard promotes the adoption of a process approach for establishing, implementing, operating, monitoring, reviewing, maintaining, and improving an organization's information security management system (ISMS). An organization needs to identify and manage many activities to function effectively. Any activity using resources and managed so as to enable the transformation of inputs into outputs can be considered to be a process. Often, the output from one process directly forms the input of the following process.

ISO (International Organization for Standardization) and IEC (International Electrotechnical Commission) form the specialized system for worldwide standardization. National bodies that are members of ISO or IEC participate in the development of international standards through technical committees established by the respective organization to deal with particular fields of technical activity. ISO and IEC technical committees collaborate in fields of mutual interest. Other international organizations, governmental and nongovernmental, in liaison with ISO and IEC, also take part in the work. In the field of information technology, ISO and IEC have established a joint technical committee, ISO/IEC. This international standard adopts the "Plan-Do-Check-Act" (PDCA) process model, which is applied to structure all ISMS processes. This international standard is aligned with ISO 9001:2000 and ISO 14001:2004 to support consistent and integrated implementation and operation with related management standards.

The focus of ISO/IEC 17799:2005, the precursor to ISO 27001, is the assurance of the availability, confidentiality, and integrity of an organization's information. These principles are at the heart of all of today's information-related regulations. The standard's key controls all mapping to specific requirements of existing data protection legislation and, through ISO/IEC 27001:2005 (the ISMS specification standard), it is recognized as a means of complying with EU regulations on data protection and privacy.

## Control Mapping—ISO 27001

ISO/IEC 27001:2005 addresses the domain control requirements of

- Trusted access
- Business continuity and availability
- Operational monitoring
- Records management
- Audit and risk management
- Operational controls

The standard concedes as out of its scope the control areas of

- Change management
- Operational transparency
- Segregation of duties

## ITIL

The Information Technology Infrastructure Library (ITIL) is growing in popularity among financial institutions seeking to improve service quality and to align IT with larger business objectives. It is an IT management approach that bridges tools and standards with business processes. As one of the three compliance structures of the Joint EU Framework, ITIL will only increase in importance. It was developed in England in the 1980s for the Central Computer and Telecommunications Agency (CCTA), and is a set of documents focused on best-practice processes for IT service management. ITIL is technology neutral and focuses on processes. Unlike ISO 17799, ITIL security management describes "how" security measures can be implemented.

The ITIL book has five chapters along with annexes at the end of the book. The first two chapters consist of an introduction, a section on the fundamentals of information security, and a section on the links between information security and IT processes. The first two chapters primarily deal with basic security management information, including the importance of upper management commitment and the view of information security being a business enabler instead of a cost. These are important concepts worthy of being reviewed and discussed to help identity stewards look at information security from a business perspective as opposed to a technical product perspective.

The next three chapters discuss security management for a number of key security processes. In the third chapter, there is a discussion about determining the security-related service-level requirements for various business processes. The service-level requirements help determine key operational areas that must be in place before effective security management can take place. The operational areas include

- ◼ Configuration and asset management
- ◼ Incident control and help desk
- ◼ Problem management
- ◼ Change management
- ◼ Release management

The final two chapters provide best-practice processes for some key information security areas, including

- ◼ Asset classification
- ◼ Personnel security
- ◼ Communications and operations management
- ◼ Access control
- ◼ Auditing and evaluation

## ITIL Process Description

- ◼ *Configuration management:* Creation and maintenance of a database of all IT configuration items, their relationship with other items, and their proper state.
- ◼ *Incident management:* Receiving, recording, and classifying user reports of malfunctions, primarily received through the help desk.
- ◼ *Problem management:* Analysis of incidents to uncover patterns of repetition that might indicate a common root cause. Positive conclusion results in a request for change (RFC), and the cycle repeats.
- ◼ *Change management:* Response to and action on requests for change. The process includes solution evaluation and design, risk analysis, prioritization, approvals, and feasibility testing.
- ◼ *Release management:* Sequence of events for rolling out a change to the user environment in order to minimize disruption, prevent errors and loss of data, and maintain proper documentation.

## Terms and Definitions Associated with ITIL

- *SLM (service-level management)*—The monitoring of required service levels.
- *SLA (service-level agreement)*—Specific targets identified by SLM for each unit within the IT organization.
- *SLC (service-level contract)*—Specific targets identified by SLM for each unit within an external IT supplier.
- *OLA (operation-level agreement)*—Specific targets for the service being supplied by internal service providers (network services, LAN services, and so on).
- *UC (underpinning contract)*—Specific targets for the service being supplied by an external service provider (such as GE Capital, Decision One).
- *Service catalogue*—A collection of all the services being provided and the customers of each.
- *SLR (service-level requirements)*—SLM will ask each IT customer what his or her requirements are. This will be embedded into the SLA.
- *SIP (service improvement program)*—After the review of an SLA, service improvements may be necessary. A service improvement plan will be designed and acted on.
- *CI (configuration item)*—Anything within IT that is decided to be within scope and can be changed should be considered a CI. This could be hardware, software, an SLM, a job description, and so on.
- *CMDB (configuration management database)*—The CMDB holds all details, and relationship information of all CIs, associated with the IT infrastructure.
- *SCOPE (scope)*—The activities of configuration management include identification, control, status accounting, and auditing.

## Control Mapping—ITIL

ITIL addresses the domain control requirements of

- Change management
- Business continuity and availability
- Operational monitoring
- Records management
- Operational controls

The standard concedes as out of its scope the control areas of

- Trusted access
- Audit and risk management
- Operational transparency
- Segregation of duties

# BSI IT-Grundschutz Methodology

The IT-Grundschutz methodology is a procedure for IT security management that can be adapted to the situation of a specific institution. It is described in BSI Standard 100-1 MSIS. This document describes the steps required by the IT-Grundschutz methodology. It represents a standard for establishing and maintaining the appropriate level of IT security in an institution. The method, which was introduced by BSI in 1994, has been developed to provide a methodology for setting up an information security management system for establishing a comprehensive basis for assessing risk, monitoring the existing IT security level, and implementing appropriate IT security.

One of the most important objectives of IT-Grundschutz is to reduce the expense of the IT security process by providing established procedures to improve information security. The methodology describes an efficient management system for information security and how the IT-Grundschutz catalogues can be used for this task. Each of the documents focuses on a differing area:

- The BSI Standard 100-1 MSIS describes the general methods for the initiation and management of information security in an institution.
- The BSI Standard 100-2 provides a summary of the important steps in introducing an ISMS and the approach to producing an IT security concept.
- The BSI Standard 100-3 describes how the fundamental phase in initiating the IT security process could look, and which organizational structures are appropriate for it. In addition, a systematic path is shown for setting up functional IT security management and for developing it further in ongoing operations.
- The BSI Standard 100-4 describes the IT-Grundschutz methodology for producing an IT security concept. This first lists how the basic information on IT assets can be collected and simplified by forming groups.

The IT-Grundschutz catalogues describe how to produce and monitor IT security concepts on the basis of standard security measures. Modules of standard security measures are available for common IT processes, applications, and components. The modules are classified into five layers according to their focus:

- Layer 1 covers all the generic IT security issues.
- Layer 2 covers all the physical, technical issues.
- Layer 3 relates to individual IT systems.
- Layer 4 concerns the issues relating to networking IT systems.
- Layer 5 handles the actual IT applications.

## Control Mapping—BSI IT-Grundschutz Methodology

The BSI IT-Grundschutz methodology addresses the domain control requirements of

- Trusted access
- Change management
- Business continuity and availability
- Operational monitoring
- Records management
- Audit and risk management
- Operational transparency
- Operational controls

The methodology only concedes as out of its scope the control areas of

- Segregation of duties

## CMMI-SEI

Capability Maturity Model Integration (CMMI) is a process improvement approach that provides organizations with the essential elements of effective processes. It is used to guide process improvement across projects, divisions, and entire organizations. CMMI helps integrate traditionally separate organizational functions, set process improvement goals and priorities, provide guidance for quality processes, and afford a point of reference for appraising current processes. Although it is not a specific compliance methodology, its use in conjunction with other compliance methodologies in remediation efforts may serve as proof of intent to comply.

The Carnegie Mellon Software Engineering Institute (SEI) is a federally funded research and development center in the United States. Its core purpose is to help organizations improve their software engineering capabilities.

### Control Mapping—CMMI-SEI

The CMMI methodology addresses the domain control requirements of

- Trusted access
- Change management
- Business continuity and availability
- Operational monitoring
- Records management

The methodology only concedes as out of scope of the standard the control areas of

- Audit and risk management
- Operational transparency
- Segregation of duties
- Operational controls

## SoGP

In 1998, the Information Security Forum (ISF) developed a comprehensive list of best practices for information security, the Standard of Good Practice (SoGP). The foundation offers an assessment to identify benchmark environments and measure compliance with the SoGP. The SoGP provides a biannual review cycle during which existing sections are revised and new sections are added according to ISF member information and best-practices research.

The standard is developed from research based on practices of and incidents in major corporations. The standard is used as the default governing document for information security behavior by many major organizations, by itself or in conjunction with other standards such as ISO 17799 or COBIT.

The standard is divided into five aspects:

■ *Security management (SM):* Aligns business risks associated with information with senior management.
■ *Systems development (SD):* Builds security into every component from inception at each stage of the cycle. This approach proves more cost effective and efficient than grafting it on after development. SD encourages a coherent approach to systems development and sound discipline throughout the development cycle, ensuring that information security is addressed.
■ *Critical business applications (CB):* By understanding the business impact surrounding a loss of confidentiality, integrity, or availability of information, it is possible to establish the level of criticality of an application. This provides a sound basis for identifying business risks and determining the level of protection required to keep risks within acceptable limits.
■ *Computer installations (CI):* This aspect provides a common standard of good practice for information security that should be applied irrespective of where, or on what scale or type of computer, information is processed.
■ *Networks (NW):* Secure network design is essential to network services. This aspect enforces sound discipline in running networks and managing security. This discipline applies equally to local and wide area networks, and to data and voice communications.

## Control Mapping—ISF Standard of Good Practice (SoGP)

The ISF Standard of Good Practice (SoGP) addresses the control requirements of the domains of

■ Trusted access
■ Change management
■ Business continuity and availability
■ Operational monitoring
■ Audit and risk management

The standard concedes as out of its scope the control areas of

■ Records management
■ Operational transparency
■ Segregation of duties
■ Operational controls

## GAIT and GAISP

GAIT stands for Guide to the Assessment of IT General Controls Scope Based on Risk. GAIT provides guidance in support of the internal control objectives of the IT-related Committee of Sponsoring Organizations of the Treadway Commission (COSO), including operational and financial reporting. Although not a control framework, GAIT provides information to appropriately identify and link COSO constructs of internal control assertions, risks, controls, and objectives. These principles define the relationship between IT and business objectives, how IT differs from company to company, and how to make assertions on IT processes, for example, how to reach an educated decision on which controls to include and exclude. GAIT also addresses the balance of manual and automated controls, entity and process- or activity-level controls, and percentage of business automation supported or enabled by IT.

Related to GAIT is GAISP, the successor project to the Generally Accepted System Security Principles (GASSP). GAISP is organized in a three-level hierarchy, comprising

- *Pervasive principles*—Fundamental in nature, and rarely changing (target: governance)
- *Broad functional principles*—Subordinate to one or more of the pervasive principles; change only when reflecting major developments in technology or other affecting issues (target: operational management)
- *Detailed principles*—Subordinate to one or more of the broad functional principles; change frequently as technology and other affecting issues evolve (target: the information security practitioner)

## Control Mapping—GAIT and GAISP

GAIT and GAISP address the domain control requirements of

- Trusted access
- Records management
- Audit and risk management
- Operational controls

Functionally, the standard concedes as out of its scope the control areas of

- Change management
- Business continuity and availability
- Operational monitoring
- Records management
- Operational transparency
- Segregation of duties

## NIST 800 Series

NIST special publication 800-12 provides a broad overview of computer security and control areas. The standard highlights the importance of the security controls and details ways to implement them.

The first section establishes the basic elements of computer security, defines the associated roles and responsibilities, and exposes common threats. The second section on management controls defines the computer security policy and how to implement this in the computer security program management, computer security risk management, security and planning in the computer security life cycle, and the required assurance measures. The third section outlines the operational controls. These include personnel and user issues, how to prepare for disasters, computer security, incident handling, training and education, security considerations in computer support and operations, and physical and environmental security. The fourth section outlines the technical controls, defining identification and authentication controls, logical access controls, the necessary audit trails, and cryptography techniques.

The Management Controls section addresses security topics that can be characterized as managerial. They focus on the management of the computer security program and the management of risk within the organization. The Operational Controls section addresses security controls that focus on controls that are implemented and executed by people. These controls are put in place to improve the security of a particular system (or group of systems). The Technical Controls section addresses security controls that the computer system executes. These controls are dependent on the proper functioning of the system for their effectiveness.

NIST special publication 800-14 describes common security principles. The standard provides a high-level description of what should be incorporated within an information security policy. Eight principles and fourteen practices are described within this document.

The eight principles are

1. Computer security supports the mission of the organization.
2. Computer security is an integral element of sound management.
3. Computer security should be cost effective.
4. Systems owners have security responsibilities outside their own organizations.
5. Computer security responsibilities and accountability should be made explicit.
6. Computer security requires a comprehensive and integrated approach.
7. Computer security should be periodically reassessed.
8. Computer security is constrained by societal factors.

NIST special publication 800-26 provides guidance on managing IT security. The standard emphasizes the importance of self-assessments as well as risk assessments.

The MIST self-assessment questionnaire defines specific control objectives and suggested techniques against which the security of a system. The questionnaire can be based primarily on an examination of relevant documentation and a rigorous examination and test of the controls.

Most controls cross the boundaries between management, operational, and technical. Each chapter in the three sections provides a basic explanation of the control; approaches to implementing the control; some cost considerations in selecting, implementing, and using the control; and selected interdependencies that may exist with other controls.

## Control Mapping—NIST 800 Series

NIST addresses the domain control requirements of

- Records management
- Operational monitoring
- Records management
- Operational transparency
- Segregation of duties

The standard functionally, concedes as out of its scope the control areas of

- Trusted access
- Change management

- Business continuity and availability
- Audit and risk management
- Operational controls
- Operational transparency

## COSO and Turnbull Guidance

The COSO framework is a document called Internal Control, Internal Framework (COSO, 1994). The acronym COSO comes from the organization that created the document, the Committee of Sponsoring Organizations of the Treadway Commission (http://www.coso.org).

In the COSO framework, there are three objectives:

- *Operations*—The firm wishes to operate effectively and efficiently. It is necessary for the firm to control its general internal operations to do this.
- *Financial reporting*—The firm must create accurate financial reports.
- *Compliance*—The firm wishes to be in compliance with external regulations.

### Control Environment

The component at the base of the COSO framework is the corporation's control environment. This is the company's overall control culture. It includes the "tone at the top" set by top management, the company's commitment to training employees in the importance of control, the punishment of employees (including senior managers) who violate control rules, attention by the board of directors, and other broad matters. If the broad control environment is weak, other control elements are not likely to be effective.

### Risk Assessment

A company needs to assess the risks that it faces. Without systematic risk analysis, it is impossible to understand what level of controls to apply to individual assets. Risk assessment must be an ongoing preoccupation for the firm because the risk environment constantly changes.

### Control Activities

An organization will spend most of its control effort on control activities that actually implement and maintain controls. This includes approvals and authorization, IT security, the separation of duties, and many other matters. Controls usually have two elements: One is a general policy, which says what must be done. The other is a set of procedures, which explain how to do it.

### Monitoring

Having controls in place means nothing if organizations do not monitor and enforce them. Monitoring includes both human vigilance and audit trails in information technology. It is essential to have an independent monitoring function that is free to report on problems even if these problems deal with senior management.

## Information and Communication

For the control environment, risk assessment, control activities, and monitoring to work well, the company needs to ensure that it has the required information and communication across all levels of the corporation.

Page 49 of the COSO framework notes the existence of manual controls, computer controls, and management controls. On page 50, it provides the following process:

*Top-level review:* Comparing budgets with actual performance, tightly monitoring major initiatives.

*Direct functional or activity management:* Examining the appropriate reports for their level in the role of managers who run individual operations.

*Information processing:* Including the enforcement of manual procedures. Information processing must focus on business processes, not merely on IT processes.

*Physical controls:* Taking inventory of cash stores and archival media.

*Performance indicators:* Relating different sets of data to each other for checking inconsistencies, noting deviations from normal performance (in either direction), unusual trends, and so forth.

*Segregation of duties:* Requiring sensitive processes to be completed by two or more people so that no single person can engage in improper activities without this becoming apparent.

## Controls for Information Systems

On pages 52–55, Internal Control Internal Framework specifically lists some controls over information systems. At a most basic level, the framework discusses the differences between application controls and general controls:

■ *Application controls:* Involve individual applications (accounting applications, spreadsheets, and so forth), including manual operations in using them.
■ *General controls:* Cover levels beneath the application, together with manual operations in using them.

## Control Mapping—COSO and Turnbull Guidance

COSO and Turnbull Guidance address the domain control requirements of

■ Trusted access
■ Records management
■ Operational monitoring
■ Operational transparency
■ Segregation of duties
■ Audit and risk management
■ Operational controls

Functionally, the standard concedes as out of its scope the control areas of

- Change management
- Business continuity and availability

## *SAS 70*

SAS 70 is an international auditing standard developed by the American Institute of Certified Public Accountants (AICPA). More precisely, this standard is defined in the Statement on Auditing Standards (SAS) No. 70 (Service Organizations); hence, SAS 70. The results of an SAS 70 audit are displayed in an SAR (service auditing report or service auditor's report). There are two versions of an SAR, known as Type I and Type II reports. A Type I report provides a description of a service organization's controls as of a point in time. A Type II report provides assurance over the operating effectiveness over controls for a period of time. Type II testing procedures are required to be performed for a period not less than six months. Type II SAS 70 reports cover a 6-month or 1-year period of time.

The report includes the following information:

- Independent service auditor's opinion
- Service organization's description of controls
- Information provided by the independent service auditor, including description of the service auditor's tests of operating effectiveness and the results of those tests (Type II only)
- Glossary

The report assesses four main indicators:

- Description of controls is presented fairly.
- Controls are designed effectively.
- Controls are placed in operation as of a specified date.
- Controls are operating effectively over a specified period of time (for Type II reports).

### *Control Mapping—SAS 70*

SAS 70 addresses the domain control requirements of

- Change management
- Business continuity and availability
- Operational monitoring
- Operational transparency
- Segregation of duties
- Operational controls

Functionally, the standard concedes as out of its scope the control areas of

- Trusted access
- Records management
- Audit and risk management

## Summary

Table 2.1 illustrates the strength and scope of each framework cited.

It is hoped this will assist in the framework selection process for the client's operational structure and audit requirements.

**Table 2.1    Framework to Control Domain Mapping**

| | Trusted Access | Change Management | Business Continuity and Availability | Operational Monitoring and Report | Records Management | Audit and Risk Management | Operational Transparency | Segregation of Duties | Operational Control |
|---|---|---|---|---|---|---|---|---|---|
| Joint EU Framework (ISO/IEC 27001:2005, ITIL and CobiT ) | X | X | X | X | X | X | X | * | * |
| COBIT | X | X | X | X | X | X | * | X | * |
| ISO/IEC 27001:2005 | X | * | X | X | X | X | X | X | * |
| ITIL | * | X | X | X | X | X | * | * | * |
| BSI IT-Grundschutz Methodology | X | X | X | X | X | X | X | * | X |
| Capability Maturity Model Integration (CMMI) | X | X | X | X | X | * | * | * | * |
| ISF Standard of Good Practice (SoGP) | X | X | X | X | * | * | X | * | * |
| GAIT and GAISP | X | * | * | * | * | X | X | * | * |
| NIST | * | * | * | * | X | X | * | X | * |
| COSO and Turnbull Guidance | X | * | * | X | X | X | X | X | X |
| SAS 70 | * | X | X | X | * | X | * | X | X |

*Notes:*  X Denotes the framework may be used to measure the control requirement.

* Denotes the framework does not express a metric used to measure the control requirement.

# Chapter 3

# Oracle Governance, Risk, and Compliance Management Architecture

Most Fortune 50 companies are using compliance architectures to aid their compliance efforts. *Compliance architecture* aligns regulatory drivers, covered in Chapter 4, with compliance frameworks, covered in Chapter 1, and enables the enterprise to implement automated controls to address regulatory mandates interpreted through the chosen compliance framework. In an Oracle context, automated controls take the form of applications, middleware, or embedded database control mechanisms designed to enforce confidentiality, integrity, availability, and operational transparency and report on their effectiveness.

Until now, many companies have responded to new compliance mandates as a series of individual efforts centered on one of the regulatory mandates searching for products that will help satisfy government regulations rather than engage in a proactive, comprehensive compliance program. Complexity can be very costly from a compliance standpoint. A simplified infrastructure allows for less expensive compliance sustainability through standardization and automation. This concept is at the heart of Oracle's compliance architecture. According to Gartner, "Companies that choose one-off solutions to each regulatory challenge they face will spend 10 times more on compliance projects than their counterparts that take a proactive approach."

Containing costs is possible only if you approach compliance as a broad business requirement, implementing systems and processes that will develop with evolving regulatory mandates and satisfy multijurisdictional business controls. As a consequence, companies need a systemic way to manage evolving compliance requirements across the organization and across jurisdictions. Only Oracle delivers a complete compliance architecture and product set that combines data and identity management, enterprise content management, business processes and controls, risk management, learning management, and performance management and reporting. Oracle's approach to compliance delivers auditable control visibility with the inherent process efficiency needed to support any compliance or governance mandate. A compliance architecture is more sustainable, cost effective, and adaptable than ad hoc approaches to governance and compliance. The breadth of governance, risk, and compliance architecture allows for multiple ways to implement automated controls against compliance frameworks such as BSI, COBIT, ISO 27001, ITIL, and others. This can allow companies to attain compliance with many multinational regulations, which could greatly reduce their cost to attain compliance.

Oracle's governance, risk, and compliance framework allows for companies to simplify their infrastructure, reduce their cost, and attain compliance. According to Hackett, "The first look at *Hackett's 2005 Book of Numbers* analysis found that typical companies now spend $940,000 per billion dollars of revenue on compliance management, while world-class companies spend 36 percent less." According to Hackett, "World-class CFOs rely on standardization and reduced complexity to more effectively manage compliance costs. World-class finance organizations ... make better use of technology they have by simplifying and optimizing their infrastructure."

## Governance, Risk, and Compliance Control Domain Approach

The sheer number of regulations facing companies is daunting, but the real challenge is that companies have tended to respond to each new compliance mandate as an individual project rather than as part of a proactive compliance program based on sustainable processes. The human and financial costs of responding to each regulatory challenge with one-off solutions are simply not sustainable.

The first step should be the execution of a comprehensive analysis of the regulatory environment in which the company conducts business and how compliance is assessed by regulators. The starting point should be to address the corporate responsibility the company assumes while doing business (Figure 3.1). From this analysis, the business process definition becomes critical in determining how those responsibilities are met. This process is governed by the directives that are an aggregate of the business rules and business policy under which the company operates. The objectives and assessment criteria form the basis of the goals for the compliance effort.

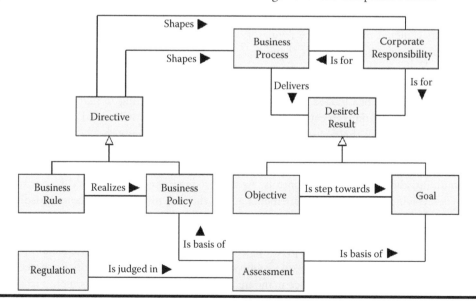

**Figure 3.1   The oracle corporate analysis process flow.**

As a result of all the frameworks and laws, the most efficient way to address the myriad of issues is to break the issue of compliance into nine control domains against which all existing compliance regulations and frameworks may be mapped:

- Trusted access
- Change management
- Business continuity and availability
- Operational awareness
- Records management
- Audit and risk management
- Operational accountability and transparency
- Segregation of duties
- Operational controls

Each of these nine may then be mapped to products and the compliance frameworks against which the regulations and legal mandates are measured. In the following chapters, each of the regulatory mandates are measured against the nine axioms. Each of the governance, risk, and compliance software components is presented as a preventative, detective, or corrective control against one or more of the nine axioms. Figure 3.2 diagrams the GRC mapping process.

Figure 3.3 illustrates an example of the control domain relationship. In this illustration, Health Insurance Portability and Accountability Act (HIPAA) and Sarbanes–Oxley (SOX) have been chosen as two examples of how the control domains intermediate the relationship between the control activities, which comprise the control and the frameworks, that may be used to measure the control's effectiveness. For the sake of brevity, the example has been limited to three of the nine control domains.

It is beyond the scope of this work to detail all the control activities for all the products one may encounter. However, this work endeavors to detail the control activities that must be

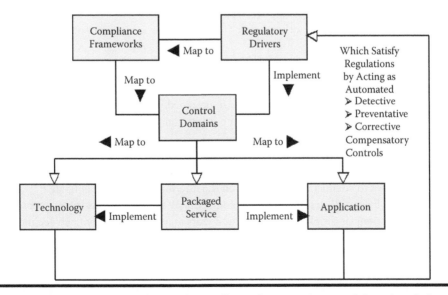

**Figure 3.2   The regulatory mandate and compliance framework control domain relationship.**

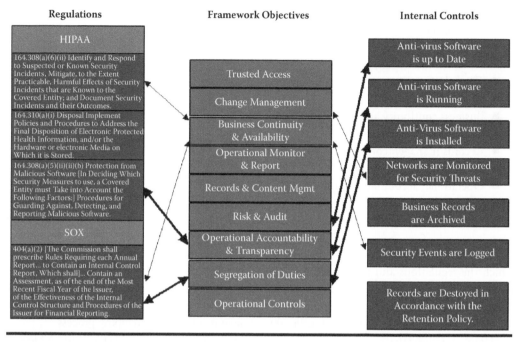

**Figure 3.3 An example of how the nine control domains (limited to three in this case) inter-mediate between overlapping frameworks, legal mandates, and control activities.**

accommodated within an identity management platform to achieve regulatory compliance within a given jurisdiction and line of business.

Each of these functional areas has multiple applications that may serve as internal controls. Internal controls can be detective, corrective, or preventive by nature.

1. Detective controls are designed to detect errors or irregularities that may have occurred.
2. Corrective controls are designed to correct errors or irregularities that have been detected.
3. Preventive controls, on the other hand, are designed to keep errors or irregularities from occurring in the first place.

Following this process one may move from regulatory drivers to product, process, and procedure implemented as controls in response to regulatory frameworks.

No matter how well the internal controls are designed, they can only provide a reasonable assurance that objectives will be achieved. Some limitations are inherent in all internal control systems. These limitations include the following:

- *Judgment*: The effectiveness of controls will be limited by decisions made with human judgment under pressures to conduct business based on the information available at hand.
- *Breakdowns*: Even well-designed internal controls may fail. Employees sometimes misunderstand instructions or simply make mistakes. Errors may also result from new technology and the complexity of computerized information systems.
- *Management override*: High-level personnel may be able to override prescribed policies or procedures for personal gains or advantages. This should not be confused with management intervention, which represents management actions to depart from prescribed policies and procedures for legitimate purposes.

- *Collusion*: Control systems can be circumvented by employee collusion. Individuals acting collectively can alter financial data or other management information in a manner that cannot be identified by control systems.

The objective of internal control systems is to ensure the following:

- *Authorization*: Responsible personnel, in accordance with their specific or general authority, approve all transactions.
- *Completeness*: No valid transactions have been omitted from the accounting records.
- *Accuracy*: All valid transactions are accurate, consistent with the originating transaction data, and information is recorded in a timely manner.
- *Validity:* All recorded transactions fairly represent the economic events that actually occurred, are lawful in nature, and have been executed in accordance with management's general authorization.
- *Physical safeguards and security*: Access to physical assets and information systems is controlled and properly restricted to authorized personnel.
- *Error handling*: Errors detected at any stage of processing receive prompt corrective action and are reported to the appropriate level of management.
- *Segregation of data*: Proper data governance and information assurance are in place. In many jurisdictions, logical separation of data is not considered an adequate control with regard to security and governance.
- *Segregation of duties*: Duties are assigned to individuals in a manner that ensures that no one individual can control both the recording function and the procedures relative to processing a transaction. This requirement is unique in that many regulations such as SOX, J-SOX, and EU 8th Company Law Directive mandate a role-based approach cited in Figure 3.4.
- *Approved use of data*: Data is used in the manner in which its collectors intended and is not diverted for an incidental function or aggregate operation.

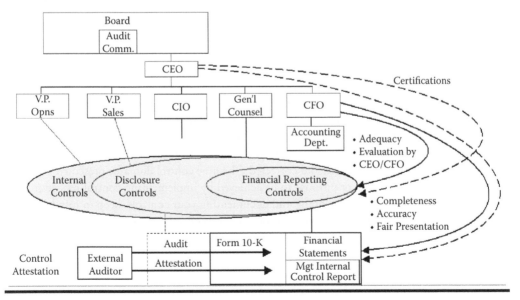

**Figure 3.4   Segregation of duties attestation by corporate role and responsibility.**

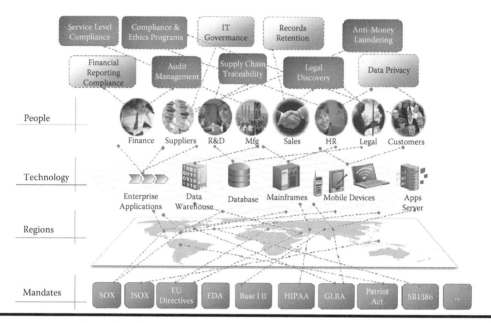

**Figure 3.5  People, technology, region, and legal mandate.**

The final step in this process is to step back from the analysis with the information gathered and review the corporate position in the context of people, technology, region, and legal mandate. This approach is illustrated in Figure 3.5, and the process is outlined in Appendix A.

## Conclusion

It is important to remember that no product can make an enterprise compliant. Only proper process and procedure in conjunction with automated solutions may effect compliance. Select the business process, policy, or procedure you wish to review for compliance. The "self-assessment checklist" is the first compliance method in any compliance plan. The nine control domains discussed offer an umbrella approach that can be used with any of the aforementioned frameworks to perform a self-assessment prior to a certification audit with legal mandates for specific frameworks (e.g., EU 97 Data Compliance tested versus the Joint EU Framework or BSI or IT-Grundschutz). A control checklist provides a form of feedback about a business process, policy, or procedure. According to quality definitions, the word *checklist* means a data-gathering tool. Entity-level controls gathered in this exercise consist of the policies, procedures, practices, and organizational structures intended to assure that the use of IT will enable the accomplishment of business objectives and that planned events will be prevented, or detected and corrected. The nine control domains presented provide a statement of the desired result or purpose to be achieved by implementing control procedures for a particular IT activity. When developing and documenting your controls, keep in mind the nine control objectives' characteristics so your controls will be as effective as possible.

# IDENTITY
# MANAGEMENT SUITE

# Chapter 4

# Oracle Identity and Access Management Suite

The advent of directory services gave rise to the broad spectrum of technologies that are collectively referred to as *Identity Management* (IdM). As it has matured, the identity market has gone through waves of stratification as innovative new solutions have been conceptualized, and progressed through the technology maturation life cycle. As a result of this natural evolution, many of the more mature technology components have been consolidated into IdM "suites." Such suites typically comprised of those services and elements that are broadly applicable to the vast majority of applications and network services. These identity services range from authentication, enterprise Single Sign-On (eSSO), and physical access control to life-cycle provisioning and auditing. However, the majority of commercial technology solutions are not considered holistically with IdM from the perspectives of design, implementation, and ongoing operational management. Although many vendors have invested in making their individual products well integrated, attention has not yet been paid to the interoperability and "interdeployability" of those suites with the types of adjacent technologies. This results in fragmentation of the solution model for enterprises that aim to benefit from the aggregate deployment of "classic" IdM services in conjunction with other security technologies.

The value proposition for the Oracle Identity and Access Management suite has been built around three key areas: improved compliance, reduced costs, and enhanced security. Expanding the scope of management for the IdM platform to include the other components of the ecosystem can enhance these benefits. In addition, the ecosystem approach to identity management delivers added benefits by reducing the overall integration risk of codeploying the various components as well as providing a near seamless user experience.

## Overview

The Oracle Identity and Access Management Suite allows enterprises to manage the end-to-end life cycle of user identities across all enterprise resources. Oracle Access Manager (OAM) delivers the functionalities of Web Single Sign-On (SSO), access policy creation and enforcement, user self-registration and self-service, delegated administration, password management, and reporting and auditing. It supports all leading directory servers, application servers, Web servers, and enterprise applications. When implemented as a suite, these products allow enterprises to manage the end-to-end life cycle of user identities across all enterprise resources both within and beyond the firewall. Implementers can deploy applications faster, apply the most granular protection to enterprise resources, and automatically eliminate latent access privileges to meet the unique needs of the business. The Oracle Identity and Access Management Suite is a member of both the Oracle Fusion Middleware family of products as well as the Oracle Governance, Risk, and Compliance family OS solutions.

Delving into the products themselves, we will explore the niche each of these software components occupy within the greater identity management ecosystem, and in later chapters we will explore how each product may be configured to comply with industry best practice.

## Oracle Identity Federation

This is a federation solution providing a self-contained and flexible multi-protocol federation server deployable with existing identity and access management systems. Federation enables organizations to create virtual communities for their employees as well as customers and partners with SSO capabilities. Federation delegates the management of users' information to their respective owners, preserving privacy and data ownership while enabling users to securely communicate and conduct business within their virtual communities. Oracle Identity Federation is Liberty Alliance certified for Liberty ID-FF and SAML 2.0.

## Oracle Enterprise Single Sign-On

This is a unified sign-on and authentication across enterprise resources, including desktops, client/server, and host-based mainframe applications. Oracle SSO is integrated into the ecosystem in two ways. From an administrative perspective, they are tied into user provisioning solutions via SPML interfaces such that, when a user is provisioned with a resource, those credentials are also immediately propagated to the Oracle enterprise Single Sign-On (eSSO) credential store via a secure channel. From a runtime perspective, when a user successfully authenticates to Oracle SSO, that authentication is also communicated to the Oracle Access Management component, resulting in a seamless experience for the user during transitions from thick client applications to Web-based applications.

## Oracle Internet Directory (OID)

These directory services are key building blocks for identity-enabled business applications. The central component of Oracle IdM, the Oracle Internet Directory (OID) is an LDAP v3 service that combines Oracle's database technology with the flexibility and compatibility of the LDAP v3. OID includes the Directory Integration Platform, a consolidated point of certification for such configurations, thereby simplifying the support and maintenance of such configuration with integrated synchronization against third-party directories, which enables customers to synchronize data between various directories and the OID. The Directory Integration Platform is a set of services and interfaces that enable synchronization with other enterprise repositories, including Microsoft Active Directory, SUN Java System Directory Server, Novell eDirectory, and Open-LDAP. It can also be used to provide OID interoperability with third-party metadirectory solutions. OID supports "multimaster" replication between the various directory server nodes.

## Oracle Virtual Directory (OVD)

This is a directory abstraction layer that allows system integrators to rapidly deploy secure directory-enabled applications by providing a real-time, virtual view of identity data from any data store, including directories, databases, and Web services, without synchronization. By leveraging an abstraction layer, architects can logically join identity attributes stored in multiple data stores and prioritize requests to back-end directories based on server, location, or connection, maximizing the native directory's processing potential.

## Oracle Security Developer Tools

These are the essential Java toolkit libraries that provide standards-based implementations of the key security elements needed for basic cryptographic tasks such as secure messaging to more complicated projects such as securely implementing a Service Oriented Architecture (SOA). These include standard symmetric and asymmetric algorithms, a NIST FIPS 140-2, an X.509 security engine, a Smartcard Cryptoki, Oasis WSS and SAML, an S/MIME toolkit, an implementation of the IETF Cryptographic Message Syntac, and Oracle Centuris PKI life-cycle management.

## Oracle Access Manager

This is a solution for centralized identity administration and access control. OAM delivers the functionalities of Web SSO, access policy creation and enforcement, user self-registration and self-service, delegated administration, password management, and reporting and auditing. OAM consists of the Access System and the Identity System. The Access System secures applications by providing centralized authentication, authorization, and auditing to enable SSO and secure access control across enterprise resources. The Identity System manages information about individuals, groups, and organizations. It enables delegated administration of users, as well as self-registration interfaces with approval workflows. These systems integrate seamlessly and may be deployed together or individually. Together they support all leading directory servers, application servers, Web servers, and enterprise applications.

## Oracle Web Services Manager (OWSM)

This is a solution for adding policy-driven security and management capabilities to service-oriented architecture. OWSM provides the visibility and control required to deploy Web services into production. With OWSM, organizations can enjoy a common security infrastructure for all Web service applications. This allows best-practice security policies and monitoring to be deployed across existing or new services.

### Oracle Identity Manager (OIM)

This is a flexible and scalable enterprise IdM system that centrally controls user accounts and access privileges. Identity Manager provides identity and role administration, approval and request management, policy-based entitlement management, technology integration, and audit and compliance automation. OIM delivers flexibility and scalability with product features such as J2EE implementation, N-tier deployment architecture, browser-based user interfaces, and Oracle Grid compatibility.

### Oracle Identity Tracker

Recently acquired from Bharosa, Oracle Identity Tracker works behind the scenes to verify a host of factors used to confirm a user's identity, including the user's computer, location, and online behavior. Tracker scores risk through a unique and proprietary "gated" security method and responds to risk in real-time by increasing online security. It offers strong asset and transaction authentication security that can be implemented without requiring any change to the online experience.

### Oracle Identity Authenticator

Also acquired from Bharosa, Oracle Identity Authenticator protects sensitive password credentials data from phishing, trojans, and proxy-based fraud. The results of these tools offer the industry a business-friendly suite of solutions to securely manage user identities and protect against the growing threat of online fraud. The combined offering of solutions helps businesses satisfy increased compliance requirements with information security and industry regulations, such as the Payment Card Industry (PCI) data security standards, Financial Institutions Examination Council (FFIEC) guidance, Health Insurance Portability and Accounting Act (HIPAA), and Sarbanes–Oxley (SOX) requirements.

## Oracle's Extended Identity Management Ecosystem and Control Effectiveness

Oracle's Extended IdM Ecosystem Approach and its Identity and Regulatory Governance Architecture enables implementers to seamlessly connect existing security systems with Oracle's standards-based IdM framework to help enhance overall security and system management, lower costs, and realize further convergence between their physical and logical security initiatives. The ecosystem identity approach enables identity service to span a wide range of technologies.

In the deployment of the IdM Suite, it is important to first ensure adequate documentation of significant controls. The documentation of a control is an important design element of the internal control system. For example, it is difficult for control procedures to be reliable consistently if there is no formal means for communicating the requirements of the procedure. For this reason, management should review the entity's documentation of significant controls to ensure that it is adequate.

Once the documentation of the controls within each IdM component is complete, the platform must be deployed as an automated control with the proper configuration and settings to ensure effective operation. These steps are outlined in Chapters 5 through 14. Once deployed, it is equally important to evaluate the design effectiveness of significant controls. To evaluate the design of controls requires that procedures be performed to determine whether the control is suitable to prevent or detect material misstatements. The nature of the procedures performed will vary according to the circumstances.

Before beginning any implementation of automated activity-level controls, the IdM compliance professional should have a thorough understanding of

- The company's overall business objectives
- The significant classes of identity transactions that the company routinely enters into to achieve those objectives
- The financial reporting risks associated with those transactions
- The control objectives related to those risks

Understanding these items will allow you to focus your efforts on implementing and documenting only the controls that matter. Upon deployment, the documentation of controls should be sufficiently detailed and clear to allow those affected by the procedure to understand it and either perform the procedure or monitor its performance. To do this, the Identity Management project team must

1. Assess design effectiveness
2. Design tests of operating effectiveness

Designing a documentation architecture around your IdM deployment that meets these two objectives will allow you to meet your compliance obligations.

Documentation of the use and governance of personally identifiable information (PII) is an integral part of the internal control structure. High-quality documentation enables the effective communication of prescribed PII control procedures across the organization and over time. Documentation allows for consistent performance and monitoring of controls, which enables internal controls to be institutionalized and become part of a system, less reliant on the competency and diligence of individual employees. As you design your control documentation, consider whether it is capable of achieving these broader objectives.

This work recommends three basic documentation techniques around the flow and governance of PII:

- Flowcharts illustrating chain of custody and data stewardship
- Narratives and use cases denoting intended use and segregation of duties
- Matrices outlining role responsibility overlap

When properly implemented, the Oracle IdM Suite serves the following functions:

- *Warehouse of internal control documentation around data access*: When properly used, the IdM suite provides a repository for all of the entity's documentation relating to the design of internal identity control and data access. In those instances in which the documentation of the access control or the control itself either does not exist or is deficient, the software allows the company to either efficiently document existing access policies or design and document new ones.
- *Tool to automate business processes*: OIM and Oracle Web Services are designed to automate business processes.

Within the context of compliance, this automation can occur on two different levels:

■ *Testing and evaluation of internal access controls*: To support its assessment of internal controls, management must test both its design and operating effectiveness. The Oracle IdM Suite can help manage this process, for example, by tracking the progress of provisioning requests or accumulating the conclusions reached about the achievement of segregation of duties.

■ *Implementation of internal access control policies and procedures*: Oracle IdM serves to automate or make systematic the performance of a wide variety of business tasks, including the performance of access control procedures. For example, the provisioning components automatically may send an e-mail to an employee to remind him or her to enter a new password. The Access Manager software may then facilitate the actual performance of this control procedure, including its subsequent review by a supervisor. Within this context, the software can help monitor the performance of access control procedures, for example, by providing summaries for supervisors on which control tasks have been completed.

In this process, once all control objectives have been considered, control policies and procedures must be documented for each and every control objective.

There must be sufficient documentation to allow management and the independent auditor to

■ Evaluate the effectiveness of design
■ Design and perform procedures to test the operating effectiveness of the controls

The documentation of individual control policies and procedures should contain

■ A link between the control objective and the control policy or procedure
■ A description of the control policy or procedure that achieves the control objective

The documentation should contain information about

■ How transactions are initiated, recorded, processed, and reported
■ The flow of transactions to identify where material misstatements due to error or fraud could occur

The documentation should contain a description of

■ How the control procedure is to be applied
■ Who is responsible for performing the procedure
■ How frequently the procedure is performed

Formal documentation of policies and control procedures will enhance the reliability of internal controls. Entities that use software tools, such as the Oracle IdM Suite, to automate business processes need to make decisions about how the tool should be configured and deployed. To make these decisions, management must consider carefully the processes they put in place, the information resources people need to perform their assigned task, and how controls are monitored and exceptions handled. All of these considerations will add further definition to the entity's internal control and improve its effectiveness.

## Regulatory Governance Mapping

Together, the Oracle Identity and Access Management Suite addresses all nine control domains outlined in Chapter 3. Within those domains only the financial operational control remains outside the reach of the aggregate capability of the eight components, their frameworks, and supporting applications. In the following chapters, each of the IdM applications within the ecosystem will be mapped in capability and deployment into the nine control domains, against which all known compliance regulations and frameworks that Oracle has encountered in the field and documented may be mapped. The regulations and frameworks are documented in Appendix A. These control domains identified include

- Trusted access
- Change management
- Business continuity and availability
- Operational awareness
- Records management
- Audit and risk management
- Operational accountability and transparency
- Segregation of duties
- Operational controls

Each of these nine will then be mapped to deployment configurations chosen to optimize the ability of an IT audit and control specialist to generate the attestation reports formatted to the compliance frameworks such as BSI, COBIT, ISO 27001, and ITIL against which the regulations and legal mandates are measured. It is the hope of the author and Oracle Corporation that proper configuration and management of Oracle's software solutions in the form of an automated control will assist and facilitate your governance risk and compliance goals.

## Summary

Chapters 1 through 4 of this book describe a risk-based, top-down overall approach to designing and implementing software products in the context of automated controls.

In the review of the legislation contained in Chapters 16 through 19, this work endeavors to identify significant controls common to all legislative risk models. It is understood that management's assessment is based on the effectiveness of internal controls taken as a whole, not on the effectiveness of individual components of controls or individual controls. The holistic approach to assessing effectiveness recognizes the interdependence of the control components. Implicit in this approach is the notion that some individual controls are more significant to the overall operating effectiveness of internal controls than others. For example, the effectiveness of an entity's control environment or computer general controls is a prerequisite for the effective operation of an individual control procedure for a specific transaction.

For these reasons, the first step in evaluating the effectiveness of internal controls taken as a whole is to identify significant individual controls, both at the entity level and, next, at the business process level, and assign nine objectives against which the nine control domains may be measured.

# Chapter 5

---

# Oracle Identity Federation

---

Oracle Identity Management is a comprehensive suite of solutions intended to address all the aspects of implementing the necessary mechanisms and controls for managing the data related to people's identities in a secure, reliable, compliant, and highly available environment, while providing a positive end-user experience when accessing the services provided by an infrastructure based on Oracle's Identity Management (IdM) Product Suite.

The need for business-to-business transactions has grown tremendously in the past decade, and companies face the difficult situation of exposing their internal applications to external parties while maintaining the security of those applications and avoiding antitrust issues, which expose the company to regulatory risk. The challenge is that it is not cost effective for the enterprise to devote resources to manage the external identities of users accessing applications from outside the corporation. However, to treat those outside the corporation as "virtual" employees brings serious legal peril.

This chapter will describe in detail the role of the Oracle Identity Federation (OIF) product as a member of the Oracle IdM Product Suite, which provides services that allow companies to provide access to their internal applications without compromising security and without having to maintain the identity information of the external users accessing the applications.

## Overview

OIF enables cross-domain single sign-on (SSO) and multicorporate role-based access control, leveraging a multitier distributed architecture comprising four components and integration points:

- Source domain federation components
- Destination domain federation components
- Service providers
- Integration points

*Source domain federation components*: These components are responsible for the generation and exchange of user identity assertions, which are used to communicate a user's identity to the destination party. The destination site will determine if the user identified by the assertion is in fact authorized to access the internal application being requested. This component provides the level of distance required to satisfy antitrust allegations on a technical level.

*Destination domain federation components*: These components provide mechanisms to receive, evaluate, and process user assertions coming from external parties requesting access to internal applications published by the destination party through the federation channel.

*Service providers*: These components implement the interfaces to authenticate users locally on each side of the federation, facilitate the exchange of user identity assertions, and perform the actual processing of the assertion's content.

*Integration points*: These components provide the necessary mechanisms to integrate with an IdM platform such as Oracle Access Manager (OAM).

OIF can be deployed in multiple configurations, depending on the business requirements; the multitier architecture allows the deployment of components of different categories without compromising functionality, security, or purpose.

Table 5.1 describes some of the components and their functionality as part of a typical deployment.

## Typical Deployment Architecture

### *Preliminary Concepts*

Federated IdM is a relatively new trend, which is based on the following concepts:

- Assertion sources
- Assertion consumers
- Assertion exchange profiles—POST and Artifact

### *Assertion Sources*

In OIF, these are known as source domains or spokes. Source domains generate assertions and exchange those assertions with other parties that expose access to internal applications through the federation channel. The assertions establish the user's identity to the destination, but the ultimate decision on whether access is granted or not is up to the destination policies. This enables policy enforcement and corporate governance at a level above the implementation.

### *Assertion Consumers*

To establish the identity of an external user trying to get access to an application exposed through the federation channel, the destination domain or HUB (as known in OIF) has to consume assertions from the source domain.

**Table 5.1  The Components and Their Functionality as Part of a Typical Deployment**

| Component | Category | Description |
|---|---|---|
| Transfer service | Source domain federation and Service Providers | This component verifies the identity of the user and generates an assertion about that user. For assertion exchange profiles, it also generates a reference to itself, called the Artifact, which will be used by the destination's federation engine to request the actual Security Assertion Markup Language (SAML) assertion from the source. The assertion exchange profiles will be discussed in more detail in sections to come |
| Receiver service | Destination domain federation components and Service Provider | This component, as its name implies, receives assertions, artifacts from the source, or both |
| Requestor service | Service Provider and destination domain federation components | The Requestor is only used in the Artifact profile. It uses the Artifact to determine the origin of the SAML assertion; then, the Requestor retrieves the assertion from the source |
| Responder service | Service Provider and source domain federation components | The Responder is only used in the Artifact profile. The source includes a reference to this component in the Artifact, so the destination site knows where the assertion is coming from, and can request it |
| IdM bridges | Integration points | User account information may come from many sources: directory servers, databases, or third-party IdM applications. IdM Bridges are used to connect to these repositories and extract the information to be included in SAML assertions |

## Assertion Exchange Profiles—POST and Artifact

The exchange of Security Assertion Markup Language (SAML) assertions can be accomplished in two different ways. The POST and Artifact profiles describe two different mechanisms used to exchange SAML assertions with the destination site. The POST profile is also known as the PUSH method because the Source generates the assertion and sends it immediately to the destination. The Artifact profile, on the other hand, is known as the POLL profile because the Source generates a token known as the "Artifact," which is then used by the destination to retrieve the assertion from the source. Both profiles serve the same purpose, but the decision on what is the best mechanism to use is up to the requirements of each implementation. Some trends of thought promote the concept of the Artifact profile being more secure than the POST, although POST is a little faster and, as the POST profile is stateless by nature, load balancing and failover are easier to implement.

## Assertion Profiles

Usually, OIF is deployed to control access to applications outside the corporation. The destination site keeps complete control of the policies dictating who is authorized to access their internal resources. The federation per se is not responsible for authorizing access, although the source may participate in the authorization process by request from the destination. SAML 2.0 allows this because the SAML protocol includes authorization assertion elements as extensions to the typical authentication elements.

### Source Domain Deployment

Install OIF on an internal host hosting the Transfer Service, Receiver Service, and, in the case of Artifact profile, the Responder Service.

If OAM is available, then SSO is possible between internal applications and federated resources (external applications accessible through the Federation Channel). The integration is accomplished via the OAM IdM Bridge.

(*Note:* Other IdM and SSO engines are supported by OIF out of the box to leverage infrastructures such as Netegrity Site-Minder via the Site Minder IdM Bridge.)

### Destination Domain Deployment

For OIF, it is a requirement that OAM is installed, because the only IdM Bridge supported by OIF in destination mode is the OAM IdM Bridge.

Install OIF on an internal host hosting the Receiver Service and, in the case of Artifact profile, the Requestor Service.

## Deployment Scenarios

OIF is based on standards, which leads to interoperability. OIF can be used as an assertion producer whose assertions may be consumed by other SAML-compliant assertion consumers, may be deployed as an assertion consumer from another OIF domain acting as a source, or may be set up as a consumer for assertions generated by non-Oracle federation engines. The possibilities are very diverse. OIF can participate or be the foundation of an intricate federated network in which the roles of source and destination can be performed by the same site, being the source for access to external applications or exposing secure access to internal assets. The following sections explain some of these scenarios and describe the deployment architecture typically used for each kind of scenario.

### Scenario One

The first scenario to be discussed involves OIF as a destination domain site consuming assertions from another OIF domain acting as an assertion source. One important aspect to notice in this scenario is that the source site interacts with OAM as the identity data source via SSO based on the ObSSOCookie. Users establish their identity internally to a portal or an application exposing the federation channel via a special link to a service provider serving as an entry point to the federated access mechanisms. Once the identity of the user has been established, it can be leveraged to obtain the information contained in the assertion.

In this particular case, the source domain interfaces with OAM via the Access Server SDK APIs available. These API calls request special policies generated automatically when the OAM IdM Bridge is configured in the source domain. These policies extract the values of user profile attributes, which will be included as the contents of the assertion. Details such as user roles, e-mail address, special identifiers, etc., are some examples of possible attributes to be included in SAML assertions as a proof of identity for the users. It is also very important to mention that the information included in the assertions is meaningless unless there is an agreement between the two parties involved in the federated access to applications at the destination site. This agreement defines the mapping of the contents of the assertion to a local user at the destination site, who in turn has access to the requested application. This is the reason why the destination does not have to maintain information about the users at the source site, which is one of the main benefits of a federation.

The destination will extract the contents of the assertion and try to find a local user through mapping the contents of the assertion to a local user account. In this case, the mapping is also achieved by leveraging OAM. In fact, OIF as a destination requires OAM to be the identity data source. The mapping is performed via special access policies automatically generated by the configuration process for the OAM IdM Bridge at the destination site. The authorization policies are applied to the local user resulting from the assertion content mapping, and access is granted or denied accordingly. Figure 5.1 outlines a typical federation deployment scenario.

Figure 5.1 demonstrates, at a high conceptual level, the architecture of the deployment for this scenario; the actual assertion exchange process represented in the diagram as the "Send Assertion" step varies depending on the profile being used to exchange assertions from the source to the destination. These processes will be described in detail later.

## Scenario Two

An OIF destination domain site consuming assertions from a non-OIF source domain comprises the next scenario. Figure 5.2 shows the components in this scenario and the corresponding deployment architecture.

The main concept illustrated here is the interoperability of OIF with other SAML-compliant solutions in the market. Users establish their identity using the mechanisms available in their internal infrastructure, and the federation engine generates and populates the contents of the assertion based on the user's identity. In this particular case, the source domain may interface with an (LDAP) directory or have a complete SSO solution deployed, similar to the one provided by OAM in scenario one for the source domain. The federation components of the third-party federation engine extract the user's data as part of the authentication process and include it in the assertion. Based on the agreement between source and destination, the mapping of the contents of the assertion to a local user at the destination site happens just as described in scenario one.

The destination will extract the contents of the assertion and try to find a local user through mapping the contents of the assertion to a local user account. In this case, the mapping is also achieved as described in the previous scenario. The authorization policies are applied to the local user resulting from the assertion content mapping, and access is granted or denied accordingly, just as in the previous scenario.

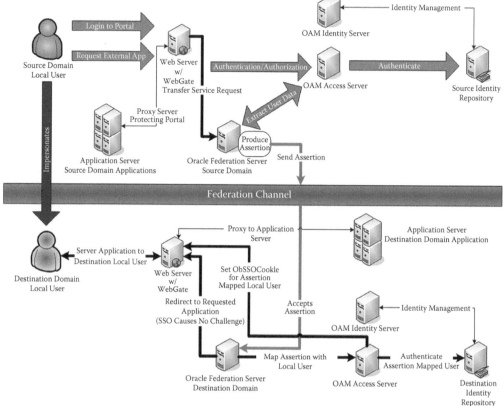

**Figure 5.1   Deployment architecture for scenario one—Oracle Identity.**

## Scenario Three

The next scenario involves an OIF source domain site interoperating with a non-OIF destination domain site. Figure 5.3 shows this scenario's architecture.

To reinforce the concept illustrated in scenario two about the interoperability of OIF with other SAML-compliant solutions in the market, users establish their identity using the mechanisms available in OAM just as in scenario one.

The destination will extract the contents of the assertion and will try to find a local user through mapping the contents of the assertion to a local user account. In this case, the mapping is also achieved using the mechanisms available in the third-party federation solution, which are specific to that solution. As long as the mapping to a local user is achieved and the local user has access to the resource, the source domain user should be able to access the requested external application. This is very critical because it serves the very purpose of the federation—controlling access to protected resources by external entities without having to maintain the identity profile of the external users at the destination site. If the third-party federation solution requires the user to be physically present on the destination domain identity repository for any reason other than for auditing purposes, then it totally defeats the purpose of the federation.

It is time to look at the actual process to generate the assertion and exchange it according to the two profiles serving as a model for such purposes.

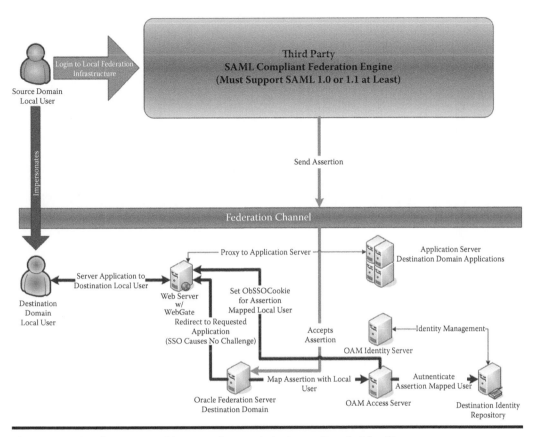

**Figure 5.2    Deployment architecture for scenario two—Oracle Identity.**

## POST Profile Revisited: OIF Implementation

The POST profile—as its name implies—generates an assertion, which will be immediately POSTed to the destination domain. The implementation of this mechanism provided by OIF is illustrated in Figure 5.4.

The figure describes the steps taken by a user at the source domain to access an external application hosted at the destination domain without having to be reauthenticated and, more important, without the need for the user account to be stored in the destination's identity repositories.

A source domain user establishes his or her user identity to the local system, which is supposed to recognize the account because it is local to the identity repositories at the source domain. Part of this identity data will be conveyed to the destination domain via the assertion. Once the user can access the local infrastructure, it will be possible to request access to an external resource through the federation channel. To start the generation of the assertion, the user must request the application via the Transfer Service of OIF. This is done via a special http URL that points to the Transfer Service (this is a servlet running on an instance of Tomcat bundled with OIF). One of the arguments of this URL is the URL of the actual application being requested.

The URL for the Transfer Service is protected by OAM's Access System, which is required to prevent the user from being challenged for authentication by leveraging SSO. OAM enforces the Access Policy upon the Transfer Service URL and extracts the values for the assertion from the authenticated user's profile. Once the assertion is built, it is transferred to the destination.

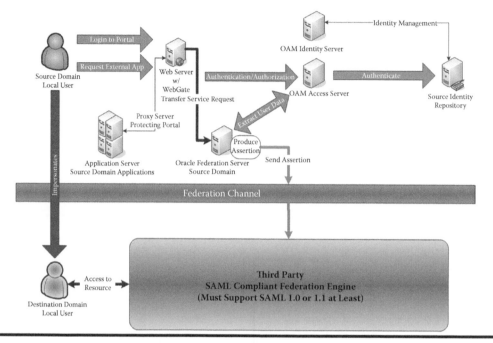

**Figure 5.3** **Deployment Architecture for scenario three—Oracle Identity.**

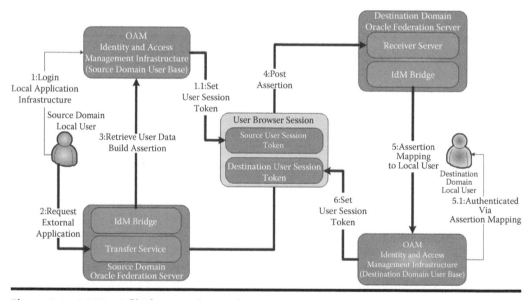

**Figure 5.4** **POST profile for assertion exchange—OIF detailed implementation.**

The Receiver Service (whose URL is configured on the source domain configuration when configuring a destination domain) intercepts the assertion and processes it by extracting the attributes from the assertion and requests a special authentication scheme that accepts the data from the assertion. This authentication scheme is automatically generated by OIF at the destination site when an assertion mapping policy is created. The authentication scheme performs a search based on the values provided in the assertion against the LDAP server and, if a match is found (must be a single match—multiple users are not allowed), then an authenticated user session token for the matching user is created and set up on the user's browser as a cookie. Then, a redirection to the requested resource is performed, which is also protected by OAM; if the policy states that the authenticated user is authorized to access the resource, then the browser will display the requested application without challenging the user for authentication. The scope of authority for the source domain's user is that of the destination domain's user who was mapped via the assertion.

## Artifact Profile Revisited: OIF Implementation

The Artifact profile, as its name implies, generates an assertion and a reference to the assertion's source called the Artifact, which will be immediately sent to the destination domain instead of the assertion as viewed in Figure 5.5. The implementation of this mechanism provided by OIF is depicted in the figure.

The figure describes the steps taken by a user at the source domain to access an external application hosted at the destination domain, but this time the mechanism implemented to exchange assertions with the destination has changed a little.

A source domain user still establishes his or her user identity to the local system, and part of this identity data will be conveyed to the destination domain via the assertion. Everything up to the point the user requests access to the external application is the same in both cases; then arises the difference. Whereas in the previous case, the assertion was submitted to the destination right after its being generated, in this profile that does not happen immediately. In fact, it only happens

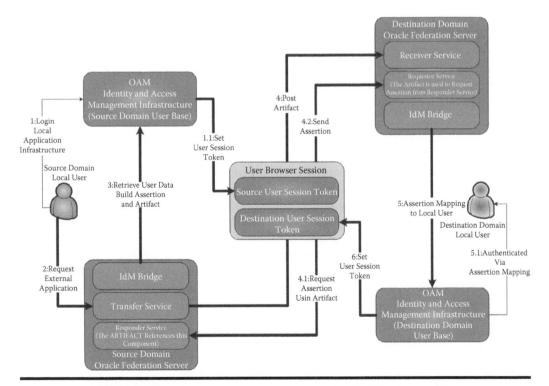

**Figure 5.5  Artifact Profile for assertion exchange—OIF detailed implementation.**

when the destination itself requests for the assertion using a reference to the source domain; this is known as the artifact. Two additional components are introduced in the Artifact profile's implementation of OIF: the Requestor Service and the Responder Service.

The Requestor Service receives the Artifact received initially by the Receiver Service and uses it to reach the Responder component at the source domain side and request for the assertion. After the assertion has been submitted, the steps continue as for the POST profile.

## Installation and Configuration Overview

This section does not intend to replace the documentation for installation and configuration of OIF; it provides useful information about the parameters available in the configuration of every component and complements the installation process described in OIF's documentation.

The installation procedure for a source domain is not different from that for the destination domain; the differences arise at the time of configuration. In fact, the installation is merely the execution of the installer program on the target server, which is described in the OIF documentation. The following section will focus on the configuration steps for the IdM Bridge and the elements related to each domain type.

## *OIF Source Domain*

Before beginning the installation of OIF as a source domain, it is important to collect the following information (as described in the prerequisites for installing OIF as a source domain presented in the OIF installation guide):

- Be sure you have the fully qualified DNS name of the machines on which you are installing OIF or the OIF Proxy Server. You must provide the fully qualified DNS name to ensure that your federation services, URLs, default keys, and certificates are configured correctly.
- When installing OIF, be sure to record the name of the host machine on which it is installed, and the OIF listener ports. You will need to provide this information to all external domains that your domain communicates with. Note that the information you exchange with other domains in your partner network will be affected by whether you also install an OIF proxy to be used with OIF.
- Ensure that the source and destination machine times are synchronized. Your site and your partners' sites may want to use a product to synchronize each host machine to an atomic clock, or you can increase the assertion validity period for an assertion after installing OIF.

There are three elements that must be configured for the source domains in OIF: IdM Bridge, assertion profiles, and one or more destination domains.

IdM Bridge Configuration—Depending upon the implementation of the repositories hosting user data, an IdM Bridge must be configured to extract the information to build an assertion about a user. The choices for an IdM Bridge at a source domain are

- LDAP
- OAM
- Netegrity Site Minder (owned now by Computer Associates)
- Oracle Database

There are advantages and disadvantages to each approach. For instance, LDAP IdM Bridge simply connects to an LDAP server to extract the information required for the assertion. OIF provides an authentication mechanism that communicates with LDAP via the IdM Bridge, validates the user identity (authentication), and then extracts the data after a successful authentication. The advantage of this mechanism is that it is very simple to configure. The disadvantage is that it is not very flexible and only provides one challenge mechanism to allow for user authentication.

If OAM is also installed on the source domain, an IdM Bridge configured to leverage OAM's infrastructure allows for a more flexible mechanism to generate assertions because features such as SSO are also available for OIF to take advantage of. Another advantage is that OIF is not responsible for the local authentication mechanisms; OAM is. So, all the challenge methods supported by OAM can potentially be used to authenticate the users at the source site. OIF supports integration with Netegrity Site Minder, which should provide functionality similar to the one offered by OAM.

The following discussion will focus on integration with OAM via the OAM IdM Bridge.

## OAM IdM Bridge Configuration

As previously stated, using OAM as the authentication and SSO services infrastructure adds a lot of flexibility to the OIF implementation when generating user assertions. This section focuses on the procedure to configure OIF integration with OAM via the IdM Bridge for OAM.

### Access Server SDK: Access Management API

As the interaction using OAM is with the Access System, the Access Server SDK is the API used by OIF to communicate with the Access System to extract the information to be included in the user assertions. OIF does this by applying predefined policies generated by it via the Access Manager API (part of the Access Server SDK), which allows the creation of such policies and configuration elements necessary for OIF to work in conjunction with OAM. On the source domain, whenever an assertion profile is created, some modifications are performed on some predefined policies used to extract user profile values by means of policy return actions (return actions are discussed in Chapter 10). It is important to mention that the Access Server SDK must be installed in the following directory:

**`<Oracle's Home Directory>/fed/shareid/AccessServerSDK`**

Version 10.1.4 of OIF is installed on an OC4J instance part of the Oracle Application Server 10g. The OAM data store expects the Access Server SDK to be installed in that directory; otherwise, the creation of access policies and Access System elements (authentication schemes) used and managed by OIF will not work. Also, the following host identifiers set must be created in OAM Access System Console:

**`Name: Fed HostID`**
**`Hosts: <your host>:<port>`**

(The host is the one in which OIF is installed, and the port is 7777 if the default was used).

Make sure to include all possible variations of host names and IP addresses to avoid security holes. Finally, the environment variable LD_ASSUME_KERNEL must be set to 2.4.19 for the

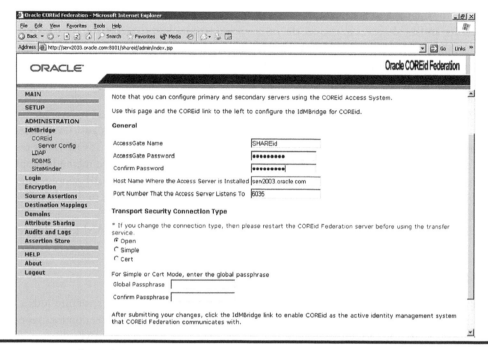

**Figure 5.6  Configuration parameters for Oracle Identity Federation integration with Oracle Access Manager.**

OC4J instance hosting OIF (OC4J_FED). Log into Enterprise Manager's Web console for OIF and select the OC4J_FED instance; navigate to Administration | Server properties and scroll to the bottom of the screen; add a new environment variable called LD_ASSUME_KERNEL and assign the value 2.4.19 to it. The AS 10g console will prompt you to restart the server after this; click Yes. If the Enterprise Manager console is not started, go to the Oracle Home directory and then go to the bin directory and issue the following command:

```
./emctl start iasconsole
```

To configure the OAM IdM Bridge, it is necessary to add an Access Gate in the Access System Console of OAM (see the proper documentation on how to create an Access Gate in OAM Access System Console). This information is required by OIF configuration screens to enable the integration with OAM Access System and create the proper policies automatically. In OIF's console, navigate to IdM Data Stores | User Data Store and select the OAM radio button if not already selected. The parameters shown in Figure 5.6 are presented:

## Repository Parameters

Connection URLs: This parameter has an LDAP-like URL to connect to the directory server where the configuration information of OAM resides. This assumes that version 10.1.4 of OAM is connected to the specified LDAP server the URL refers to.

BindDN: The DN of the account used by OAM to bind to the directory server specified by the previously mentioned URL.

Password: The password for the Binding Account specified in the previous field.

User ID attributes: The attribute associated with the log-in semantic type in OAM.

User description attribute: The attribute associated with the DN prefix and full name—this is usually the class attribute configured for the person object class in OAM.

Person object class: The LDAP object class configured as the person object class in OAM.

Base DN: This is the base user search base as specified in the configuration of OAM.

## OAM Configuration Parameters

Master Admin log-in ID: Username and password of the Master Administrator account for OAM. This is required to ensure proper privileges to create policies and authentication schemes in the OAM Access System.

Master Admin password: The password of the Master Administrator account for OAM.

Authorization result for unprotected resources: This is a flag used to allow/deny access to resources having no policy protecting them at the destination site. If the destination site is not an OAM-protected Web site, this should be set to Allow. If the destination site is an OIF domain, OAM must be installed, so this may be set to Allow or Deny depending on the agreement reached by the parties involved.

OAM cookie domain: This is a new parameter for OIF. The OAM IdM Data Store is the OAM cookie domain for the purposes of SSO. This must be set to the cookie domain, which, as of 10.1.4, is a required parameter for WebGates configured in an OAM 10*g* installation.

Basic authentication scheme name: This must be set with the name as it appears in OAM for the Basic Over LDAP authentication scheme. If this was created during OAM setup, the name should be "Oracle Access and Identity Basic Over LDAP." Verify that the case and spelling of this is correct; otherwise, OIF integration with OAM will not work as expected.

After the configuration data for this access gate has been provided to OIF, restart the OC4J container using the Enterprise Manager Web console or via opmnctl stopall | startall command. This will attempt to configure the access gate and connect with the corresponding access server associated with the access gate. At this time, the corresponding access system configuration elements will also be created automatically. Once this is complete, the IdM Bridge for OAM can be set as the IdM Data Store used by OIF by selecting the OAM radio button.

## Assertion Profiles

Assertion profiles determine the contents of the assertions exchanged with a destination domain. Assertion profiles are associated with domains in a one-to-one relationship. This association is configured when a domain is created. Domains represent external entities. MyDomain represents the local domain's configuration settings.

To create an assertion profile, log into the source domain administration console as the Admin account and select the SAM/WS-Federation tab, and select the assertion profiles link and then click the Add button. Figure 5.7 shows the Add assertion creation screens that the user will use to add profiles.

Provide a descriptive name and a description. Then proceed to configure the following parameters:

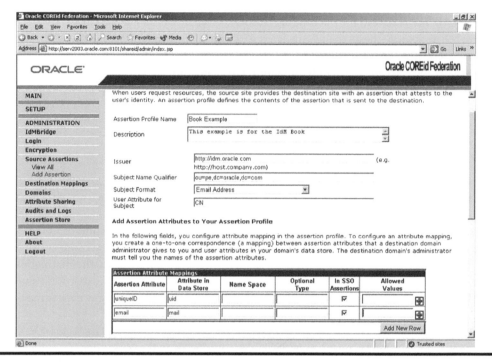

**Figure 5.7    Assertion profile configuration—upper section.**

- Issuer: The host name where OIF is installed within the source domain.
- Subject name qualifier: Usually the Directory Tree base location for the user accounts. This is used to create the ObMappingBase parameter for the Credential_Mapping plug-in of the authentication scheme used to authenticate users trying to access the Transfer Servlet of OIF. Any user trying to gain access to a federated resource must go through the Transfer Service URL (aka the Transfer Servlet).
- Subject format: The subject of an assertion is a label representing the individual identified by the assertion. The format of the subject can be one of the following:
  - E-mail address: The subject is formatted as <The value of User Attribute for Subject>@<issuer>. For instances, Joe_Smith@idm.oracle.com.
  - X.509 subject name: The subject is formatted as expressed in an X.509 certificate.
  - Windows Domain: The subject is formatted similar to a Windows Domain: \\ORACLE\ Joe_Smith
  - Unspecified: The default is used (e-mail).
  - None: The value of the user attribute for subject is simply used as the subject.
  - Other: This is not documented.
- User attribute for subject: An LDAP attribute whose value will be used in the assertion's subject label.
- Assertion attributes: The attributes and the source of their values to be included in the assertion. The configuration items for an assertion attribute are
- Attribute name: The name of the attribute in the assertion. It does not necessarily need to be the same as the attribute name in LDAP.
- Attribute in data store: The name of the LDAP attribute.

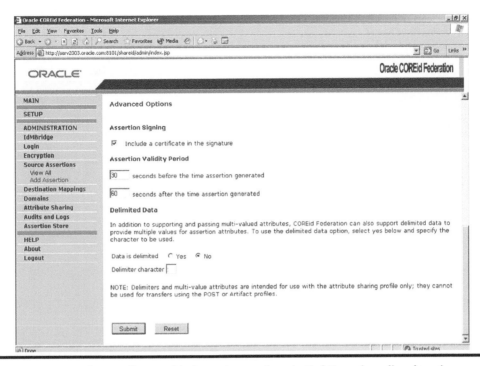

**Figure 5.8    Assertion attributes added as return actions in Fed Domain policy domain.**

- Name space: This is rarely used, but it contains an XML namespace in the SAML assertion and prefixes the assertion attribute tag with that name space. For example, an Oracle namespace would be created as follows:
- xmlns:oracle="http://idm.oracle.com/" xmlns=http://idm.oracle.com/
- Optional type: A data type: int, string, float, double, binary, etc. This will be represented as a SOAP data type for the attribute.
- In SSO assertions: This flag indicates that the value would be extracted from an SSO token, similar to the ObSSOCookie for OAM or the SSO token for Site Minder.
- Allowed values: The values can be restricted to enhance security of the assertions and prevent randomly generated assertions from being accepted.

It is not recommended that the advanced options be changed unless special networking conditions prevail and require adjusting the values of these parameters. They are self-explanatory and, as such, warrant no further discussion. After creating the assertion profile, OIF tries to modify the user attributes authorization rule in the "Fed Domain" policy domain in OAM, so as to add the subject attribute and the assertion attributes specified in the assertion profile as return actions for the authorization rule. The screen in Figure 5.8 shows OAM Fed Domain policy domain modified after creating the previously described assertion profile.

## *Domains*

Domains represent either side of the equation. For source domains, you create other domains to represent the destination sites. The MyDomain represents the local domain and may be configured as a source or as a destination domain. The configuration of MyDomain is shown in Figure 5.9.

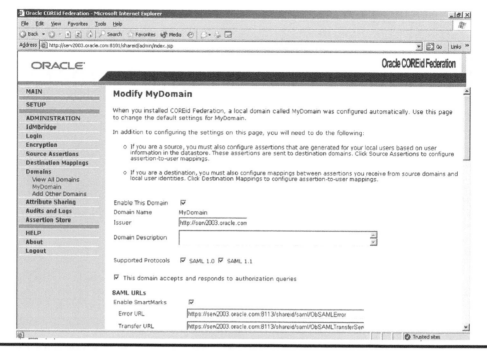

**Figure 5.9   MyDomain configuration—general settings.**

The figure describes the configuration for the domain itself and the SmartMarks enablement configuration data. The SmartMarks feature allows users to be authenticated at the source site when trying to access a protected resource through the federation channel and their user session has expired, or they are doing it through a bookmark and can potentially hit the URL before authenticating locally. The SmartMarks is configured only at destination domains, which require OIF using the OAM IdM Bridge. SmartMarks uses a special authentication scheme (for more information about authentication schemes see Chapter 10), which authenticates users from the source domain by redirecting them to a log-in form located at their local domain, so they can authenticate and regenerate an assertion. Destination users with expired sessions will be authenticated again by this scheme and redirected to their local domain, which is the destination domain; thus destination domain users do not notice any difference when the resource is protected with the SmartMarks Authentication Scheme, as the authentication is carried out as usual. The SmartMarks scenarios are discussed in the configuration of MyDomain as a destination. Other parameters to highlight here are the profiles supported by this domain, which should be already familiar: POST and Artifact profiles. A source domain can implement either one or both profiles depending on the requirements of the destination domain. Optionally, the domain can respond to authorization queries. The supported protocols are SAML 1.0 and SAML 1.1—in the near future SAML 2.0 will also be supported. The diagram in Figure 5.10 illustrates the configuration settings for a common domain.

SAML assertions are most commonly exchanged via SSL-encrypted transport channels due to the nature of the information being exchanged, so, for security reasons, SSL is a critical component in any federation solution. For the POST profile, it is required that the source domain identifies itself to the destination so the destination domain can verify that the assertion comes from a known and trusted source. For the Artifact profile, an Id is associated to the source, and this is

**Figure 5.10   MyDomain configuration—general settings ... (continued).**

communicated to the destination. Notice that there is a URL specified, pointing to the Responder Service. This service will receive the artifact from the destination and will respond with the assertion previously generated.

For the destination domain, MyDomain has the option of configuring SmartMarks. As already mentioned, SmartMarks provides an authentication mechanism for situations when a user needs to be authenticated either because the user session is expired or because the user is accessing a protected resource through the federation channel before authenticating locally. This section presents a detailed description of the most common scenarios where SmartMarks comes into action.

As previously described in this chapter, the SAML assertion is mapped to a local user on the destination site. A user session is established for the user, resulting from the mapping of the SAML assertion content against the local identity data repository. But what happens when this session expires and the user tries to access a federated application? The process is described in the following sections.

## Scenario One: Source User's Session Expired

This scenario assumes that a user on the source domain has been authenticated for the federation channel but the person's session has expired at the destination domain.

■ When this user clicks on a link within the external application (federated resource), the request goes through a WebGate on the destination side, which in turn communicates to the access server also on the destination domain.

■ The aforementioned access server determines that the user session has expired, because the ObSSOCookie is no longer valid, and challenges the user via WebGate with an authentication scheme, which happens to be the SmartMarks authentication scheme. The Challenge

Redirect parameter of the SmartMarks Authentication Scheme points to the OIF Smart-Marks log-in service (SmartMarks Login Facility as referred to in the documentation).

■ The SmartMarks Login Facility verifies the presence of the ObSAMLDomain cookie; this determines whether the user belongs to the source domain or the destination domain (local domain).

■ Assuming that the ObSAMLCookie is present (this cookie is refreshed every time an assertion transfer is completed and has a default expiration time of one year), the user is then redirected to the source domain's authentication mechanism (whatever that is). If OIF with an OAM IdM Bridge is present at the source, the users are redirected to the Transfer Servlet at the source domain.

■ The URL of the Transfer Servlet is protected by OAM and causes the user to be challenged by a log-in form.

■ The user logs in again as usual and an assertion exchange process starts, which eventually will generate a new ObSSOCookie at the destination site and will refresh the ObSAML-Domain cookie.

## Scenario Two: User at Source Domain Requests the Federated Resource via a Bookmark

This scenario assumes that a user on the source domain has not been authenticated for the local infrastructure or the federation channel, but tries, as a first act, to access the resource at the destination domain.

■ The user requests the federated resource, which means that the individual requests either the Transfer Servlet for the first time or an application bookmark.

■ If the Transfer Servlet is requested, the Source Domain challenges the user for authentication because the Transfer Servlet URL is protected by OAM (assuming the IdM Bridge for OAM is being used). The assertion process is started and will eventually generate an ObSSOCookie at the destination side for the user session.

■ If an application bookmark was requested, the WebGate at the destination domain receives the request directly. The process described in scenario one kicks off.

## Assertion Mappings

Assertion mappings are defined at the destination domain as part of the agreement between the source and the destination to map the values in the assertion to a local user at the destination domain. OIF configured as a destination domain extracts the attributes of the assertion and replaces the extracted values into the parameters for the authentication scheme created for user mapping. OIF Installer creates this authentication scheme when an assertion mapping template is created. The assertion mappings definition screen is shown in Figure 5.11.

The picture describes how to create destination mappings in OIF. Select Destination Mappings from the left-hand menu bar and then select the Add Mappings link. As Assertion Mappings will be responsible for authenticating the local user at the destination side once a mapping has been found for the data in the assertion, OIF creates a special authentication scheme. The authentication scheme requires a level, a search base (this is the ObMappingBase parameter of the authentication scheme), and the object class representing user entries in LDAP.

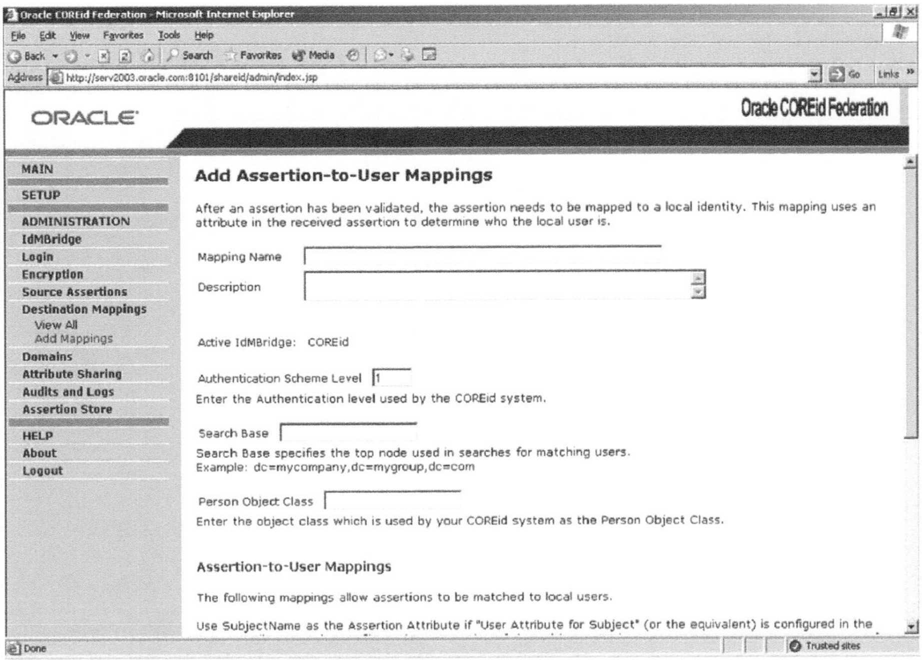

**Figure 5.11    Assertion to user mappings—upper section.**

**Figure 5.12    New authentication scheme generated from assertion mapping in OIF.**

Given the information mentioned previously, the authentication scheme as in Figure 5.12 through 5.14 is created in OAM.

As shown in Figure 5.13, the level of authentication is taken from the Assertion Mapping definition.

Finally, the Person Object Class and the assertion attributes are used to create the Credential_Mapping plug-in entry in OAM's authentication scheme as shown in Figure 5.14.

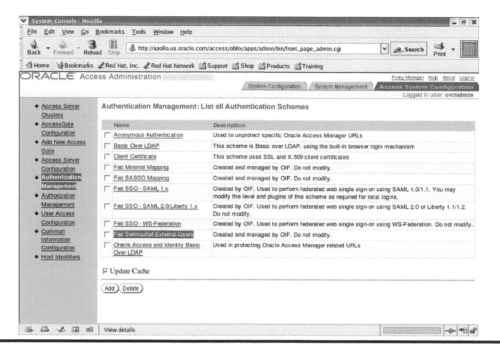

**Figure 5.13    General details of authentication scheme generated from assertion mapping.**

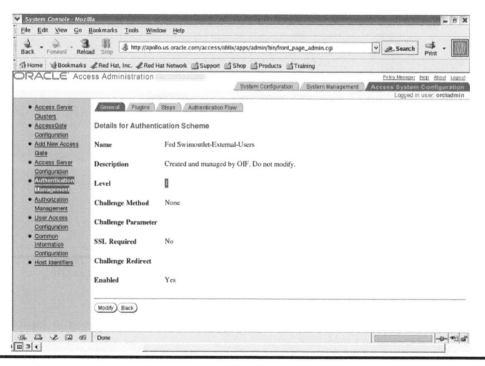

**Figure 5.14    Credential mapping entry in OAM authentication scheme, generated from assertion mapping.**

# Summary

OIF allows for a secure interaction of two or more parties while accessing each other's applications protected by internal policies within each organization and not having to maintain others' identities or exposing others' identity repositories.

OIF supports SAML 1.0, 1.1, and 2.0; other federation standards such as WS-Federation are also supported, making OIF the most comprehensive solution in the market for federated access to corporate resources.

OIF may perform in two different roles—as an identity provider or an identity consumer. In OIF terminology, it can act as a source domain or a destination domain.

OIF can create assertions from direct LDAP access or by integrating with an access management system such as OAM and Netegrity.

The assertion content is determined by an assertion profile created in OIF's administration console.

Assertions are consumed and mapped to local users at the destination site via assertion-to-user mappings defined in OIF's administration console.

Session expiration causing reauthentication is managed by SmartMarks. This feature of OIF allows users to be reauthenticated by their source and generates a new assertion that will refresh the tokens representing the authenticated session at the destination site.

# Oracle Identity Governance Framework

Oracle's Identity Services Framework, an instance of the Identity Governance Framework (IGF) standard, is a framework that will enable enterprises to integrate identity services into their application development and application runtime environments. Applications written to the ISF (Identity Service Framework) can embed IAM (Identity Access Manager) functionality as part of their inherent business processes without having to code it themselves. This identity governance approach conforms to the SOA approach to enterprise development, promoting loose coupling to ensure long-term viability and heterogeneity of business solutions.

## *ISF Feature Function*

Authentication:
- Multi-token authentication support via WS-Trust
- Security Token exchange Service (STS)
- Graded authentication support
- Assurance levels
- Strong authentication
- Authentication w/context

Federation:
- Multi-protocol federated support for IdP (Identity Provider) and SP (Service Provider)
- Seamless integration with WAM (Web Access Manager) systems (SP side)
- Support for browser- and SOA-based federation
- Federated provisioning

Authorization:
- Multi-protocol federated support for IdP and SP
- Seamless integration with WAM systems (SP side)
- Support for browser- and SOA-based federation
- Federated provisioning

Identity provisioning:
- Virtualize multiple identity data sources into single view:
  - End users
  - Business partners
  - Departmental systems
  - Applications (HR, CRM)
- Support both definitive (date of birth) and derived (over 21) identity data retrieval
- Declarative model for consumption of attributes by applications
- Declarative security model for authorities that provide attributes
- Full support for delegated permission model

Role provisioning:
- Enable RBAC adoption
- Support enterprise roles as well as application roles
- Support context-sensitive, relationship-based role structures
- Support session-based role determinations
- Graded authentication
- Dynamic SoD

Administration:
- Allows applications to register as authoritative for identities and attributes
- Support management of the identity information
- Support role and relationship management
- Provide necessary security and business controls: workflow, rules, audit, SoD

Internal provisioning:
- New concept: internal provisioning
- Applications delegate their own account creation and management responsibilities to IdM service
- Allows for better enforcement of policies: workflow, business rules, SoD, audit

Audit:
- Provide centralized identity-related audit service
- Support audit data retrieval by authorized applications

Compliance:
- Provide centralized SoD policy enforcement engine
- Detective controls
- Preventive controls
- Proactive detection
- Support comprehensive attestation, exception management, and security controls

Identity services interface:
- Abstraction layer that provides interface into the identity services
- Includes APIs, protocols, and policies
- Standards-based

- Current: SAML, SPML, XACML, WS-*, CARML, AAPML, JAAS, DSML, LDAP
- Integration with IDEs
- Contains provider framework for adapters, plug-ins, and connectors

These features are made possible by the contextual rich application of the Identity Governance Framework (IGF) standard applied to Oracle applications.

IGF is an open initiative to address governance of identity-related information across enterprise IT systems. It provides specifications establishing a common framework for defining usage policies, attribute requirements, and developer APIs pertaining to the use of identity-related information. This enables businesses to ensure full documentation, control, and auditing regarding the use, storage, and propagation of identity-related data across systems and applications.

The major components of IGF include

- Client Attribute Requirement Markup Language (CARML)—a declarative contract document defined by application developers that informs deployment managers and service providers of the attribute usage requirements of an application.
- Attribute Authority Policy Markup Language (AAPML)—a set of policy rules regarding the use of identity-related information from an identity source. AAPML allows identity sources to specify constraints on use of data provided by the source.
- CARML API—an API that makes it easy for developers to write applications that consume and use identity-related data in a way that conforms to policy set around the use of such information.
- Identity Attribute Service—a policy-enforced service for accessing identity-related data from multiple identity sources.

The IGF is a layered approach to the enforcement of operational control within a service-oriented architecture. Figure 5.15 illustrates IGF as a TCP/IP-like stack. The idea is that vendors are free to build products as they wish. This stack could be self contained within a single application or built in a client/server approach or as an identity gateway or brokerage service. The standards proposed allow for all types of implementations. Figure 5.15 outlines the governance framework and how it relates to a service-oriented architecture.

The two core expression languages of the service framework are CARML and AAPML.

CARML describes requirements and intended use of data based on SAML attribute definition. These include

- Group attributes into named sets (interactions)
- Keys, attributes, properties (entitlements)
- Legal use and data quality documentation
- Caching and propagation requirements
- Metadata about attributes
- Cardinality
- Schema
- Optionality
- Modifiability

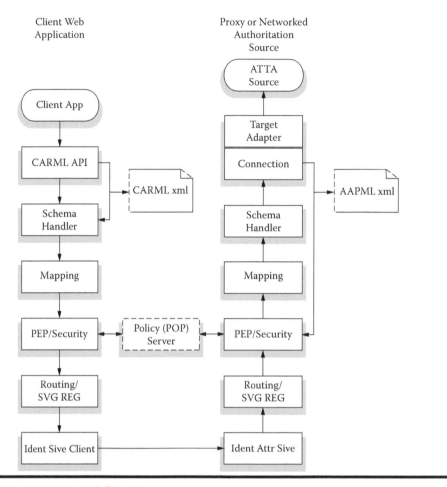

**Figure 5.15 IGF SOA stack flow diagram.**

Application developers list their identity requirements in the CARML file. This can include

- Last four digits of user social security number
- User employment level
- Office location in which user is employed

Administrators then review the CARML file and connect to appropriate back-end resources. In this example, the CARML spec indicates that the client wishes to propagate this information to servers under *.oracle.com domain. URLs are provided for the legal and data quality SLA agreements between the provider and the application as consumer. The client also indicates a desire to cache information for up to 12 hr.

```
<IRData>
  <NamedInteraction Name="UserProfileUS">
  <PropagateTo><Partner>*.oracle.com</Partner> </PropagateTo>

  <LegalUseRef>http://www.myorg.com/PartnerIdentityUseAgreement.htm</
LegalUseRef>
```

```
<DataQualityRef>http://www.myorg.com/PartnerIdentityQualityAgreement.
htm</DataQualityRef>
  <CacheTTL>12:00:00.00</CacheTTL>
  <SubjectIndexes>
  <IndexNameIdentifier>
    urn:oasis:names:tc:SAML:1.1:nameid-format:emailAddress
 </IndexNameIdentifier>
  </SubjectIndexes>
</NamedInteraction>
  </IRData>
```

AAPML is an XML document format designed to allow owners of identity-related data (I-R data) to specify the conditions under which information may be used by other applications. AAPML expresses the constraints under which identity data is released. Rules may include

- Subject—characteristics of application, user, strength of authentication
- Resources—attribute names
- Actions—read or write
- Environment—Internet, intranet, VPN, or others

Rules may also stipulate obligations such as

- Consent—availability of specific consent records
- Relationship between subject and requested identity information
- Whether data can be cached or propagated further

In this example, access to attributes, in this case e-mail, is conditionally specified with the restriction that the address is not cached.

```
<?xml version="1.0" encoding="UTF-8"?>
<Policy xmlns="urn:oasis:names:tc:xacml:2.0:policy:schema:os"
xmlns:xsi="http://www.w3.org/2001/XMLSchema-instance"
xsi:schemaLocation="urn:oasis:names:tc:xacml:2.0:policy:schema:os
http://docs.oasis-open.org/xacml/access_control-xacml-2.0-policy-
schema-os.xsd"
  PolicyId="urn:oasis:names:tc:example:deny-attrs-2"
  RuleCombiningAlgId="identifier:rule-combining-algorithm:deny-
overrides">
  <Description>
  AAPML Policy to allow marketing apps to access attributes provided
  consent is available.
  </Description>
  <Target>
  <Subjects>
  <Subject>
  <SubjectMatch
  MatchId="urn:oasis:names:tc:xacml:1.0:function:anyURI-regexp-match">
  <SubjectAttributeDesignator
  AttributeId="urn:aapml:1.0:names:subject:service-name"
  DataType="http://www.w3.org/2001/XMLSchema#string"/>
<AttributeValue DataType="http://www.w3.org/2001/XMLSchema#string">
```

```
http://www.example.com/marketing/*
</AttributeValue>
</SubjectMatch>
</Subject>
  </Subjects>
  <!-- This policy permits access to any/all of the following resources -->
  <Resources>
  <!-- EmailAddress -->
  <Resource>
  <ResourceMatch
  MatchId="urn:oasis:names:tc:xacml:1.0:function:string-equal">
  <ResourceAttributeDesignator
  AttributeId="urn:aapml:1.0:names:resource:generic"
  DataType="http://www.w3.org/2001/XMLSchema#string"/>
  <AttributeValue
  DataType="http://www.w3.org/2001/XMLSchema#string"
  >EmailAddress</AttributeValue>
  <Obligations>
  <!-- This is an example obligation that refers to a legal restriction -->
  <!-- document, referencible at the state government site, which the -->
  <!-- PEP must notify the requestor is condition for use of the -->
  <!-- returned data. -->
  <Obligation
  ObligationId="urn:aapml:1.0:names:obligation:consent"
  FulfillOn="Permit">
  <AttributeAssignment
  AttributeId=
  "urn:aapml:1.0:names:obligation:consent:agreement-identifier"
  DataType="http://www.w3.org/2001/XMLSchema#anyURI"
  >http://www.state.gov/userdata#PublicGenLaw2005</AttributeAssignment>
  </Obligation>
  <!-- This obligation says that any data returned from this request -->
  <!-- must not be cached, which the PDP must notify the requestor -->
  <Obligation
  ObligationId="urn:aapml:1.0:names:obligation:do-not-cache"
```

These SAML statements will be enforced through an attribute service and will express themselves to the attribute authorities via a common governance API, as shown in Figure 5.16.

In summary, IGF helps enterprises determine and enforce how identity-related information (including personally identifiable information [PII], entitlements, attributes, etc.) is used, stored, and propagated between their systems. It enables organizations to define enterprise-level policies to securely and confidently share sensitive personal information between applications that need it, without having to compromise on business agility or efficiency. The IGF assists in satisfying transparency and demonstrable compliance with respect to policies for identity-related data. As such, it acts as a fine-grain operational control, enforcing conditions in which user social security numbers may be accessed by applications or by answering which applications had access to customer account numbers, say, at 3:45 AM on March 12, 2015.

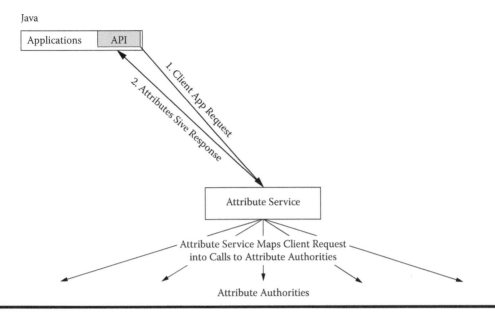

**Figure 5.16    IGF SAML attribute authority flow.**

## *Regulatory Governance Mapping*

As we have seen in the implementation, OIF adds a level of abstraction into the access control process. By dividing the responsibility and enacting grassroots policy enforcement, OIF serves as an automated technical control that helps mitigate both the risk of insecure systems and the legal risk of treating business partners as an extension of operation violating antitrust legislation. When viewed abstractly, of the nine control domains against which the existing body of compliance regulations and frameworks may be mapped, OIF best satisfies

- Trusted access
- Audit and risk management
- Segregation of duties
- Operational controls

OIF serves to implement domain-centric access control structures into a functional extranet, using the configuration cited in Figure 5.8. The control domain of Audit and Risk Management is an effective control domain as opposed to Operational Accountability and Transparency due to the external nature of those afforded access rights. Applied as outlined in Figure 5.9 through 5.11, the assertion structure may be used to enforce proper segregation of duties when dealing with external business units. Other domain assertions may be made more complex, affording a fine degree of operational control, thus acting as a mechanism for enforcement of that control domain.

# Chapter 6

# Oracle Enterprise Single Sign-On

Ensuring that the data is secure begins with authenticating the users, making certain they are who they claim to be. Once a user has been authenticated, it must be determined what data he or she may access. A Single Sign-On (SSO) framework is a mechanism that allows several different applications common to an enterprise to share a user authentication service. SSO, as it will henceforth be referred to, provides a secure way for users to be authenticated just once while enabling enterprisewide access to the data. It also simplifies the administration of tasks such as disabling a user account. In an SSO environment, the network administrator, whose time is surely tight, can disable just one account and be assured that there is no lingering access on a machine somewhere in the network. There are many methods available to enable an SSO in one form or another, and many are costly and difficult to implement. They can benefit us by creating a more efficient authentication process, but there are precautions to be taken to prevent hackers from exposing SSO weakness and killing many resources with one stone.

With Oracle's enterprisewide SSO, a user is required to log on, or authenticate them only once. That verification of identity is valid for the duration of the user session, and for every application participating in the SSO framework. The user session ends, across every application, when the user logs out. An SSO also enables a single point of administration. Usernames and passwords can be stored and maintained outside the application logic.

## Overview

SSO is a mechanism whereby a single action of user authentication and authorization can permit a user to access all computers and systems where that user has an access permission, without the need to enter multiple passwords. SSO is the holy grail of many organizations. Broadly, by achieving SSO, users will log in once to an SSO domain and then never be challenged again while accessing multiple secured resources. SSO provides a common, secure infrastructure that can be leveraged enterprisewide, carefully managed, and secured. An SSO scheme allows the user to log

**Figure 6.1  Five components of SSO.**

into (ideally) all relevant systems and applications, using only one set of authentication credentials (e.g., only one username and password pair).

There are three main motives for SSO:

Usability: The user no longer has to maintain a set of authentication credentials for each SP (service provider). Moreover, he or she does not have to do so securely.

User management: A supporting management system can enforce a global policy. Apart from unifying rules and trust relationships among a group of entities, such a system has the potential to reduce operational costs enormously. For instance, users could be added to, or removed from, the system by being granted or being revoked, respectively, by their (single) authentication credential.

Security: SSO has the potential to increase the overall level of security. First, from the user perspective, it is easier to securely maintain only one set of authentication credentials rather than many. Second, from the SP perspective, a globally enforceable policy is highly desirable because it significantly mitigates the threat of human error and abuse.

Figure 6.1 describes the five components of the enterprise Single Sign-On (eSSO) platform.

- Oracle Enterprise Single Sign-On Authentication Manager (eSSO AM)
- Oracle Enterprise Single Sign-On Provisioning Gateway (eSSO PG)
- Oracle Enterprise Single Sign-On Kiosk Manager (eSSO KM)
- Oracle Enterprise Sign-On Logon Manager (eSSO LM)
- Oracle Enterprise Single Sign-On Password Reset (eSSO PR)

Figure 6.2 describes the SSO architecture within the suite.

Oracle eSSO AM extends Logon Manager to leverage strong authentication option such as biometrics, smart cards, etc. Authentication manager supports multiple authenticators: smart card, biometric, or token. Adjust SSO authorizations based on grade of provided user authentication.

Oracle eSSO PG provides interface to Oracle Identity Manager (OIM) to accept credentials and settings from the provisioning system. User never knows or touches their application credentials.

Oracle eSSO KM monitors kiosk sessions and provides security controls for sessions left unattended, Safe application termination, and fast user switching.

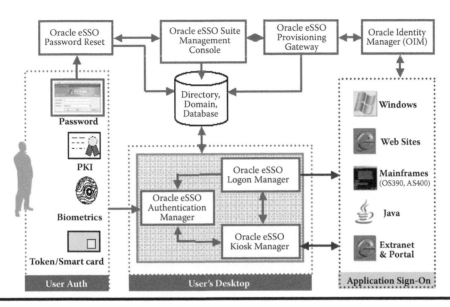

**Figure 6.2 Oracle SSO Architecture.**

Oracle eSSO LM is the desktop resident password manager for virtually any application, presenting users with an authentication request. eSSO LM extends Logon Manager to support kiosks/shared workstations with appropriate session and security controls.

Oracle eSSO PR is an enterprise level self-service password reset solution for Windows with both a Web interface and a windows desktop log-on interface. eSSO provides a flow-based reset for Windows password from GINA (Graphical Identification aNd Authentication) prompt. Confidence scoring allows errors instead of forcing call to helpdesk.

To understand how Oracle eSSO works within a Windows environment, one must understand GINA. GINA refers to the graphical identification and authentication library, Microsoft Windows XP operating systems that provide secure authentication, and interactive log-on services. GINA is a dynamically linked library that is loaded in the context of the Winlogon process when the machine is started. It is responsible for handling the secure attention sequence (SAS), typically Control-Alt-Delete, and interacting with the user when this sequence is received. GINA is also responsible for starting initial processes for a user (such as the Windows Shell) when he or she first logs on. MSGINA.DLL is provided by Microsoft as part of the XP operating system and provides

- Authentication against Windows domain servers with a supplied username and password combination.
- Legal notice to the user before presenting the log-on prompt.
- Automatic Logon, allowing for a username and password to be stored and used in place of an interactive log-on prompt.
- A restricted number of log-on attempts.

Windows log-on can be configured to use a different GINA, providing for nonstandard authentication methods such as smart card readers or identification based on biometrics. It is this feature that Oracle SSO employs to execute in Windows environments.

Within UNIX and LINUX variants, three authentication pathways are available to implementers.

## User Datafiles

With NIS (Network Information Systems), user data are kept in the same format as in /etc/passwd and /etc/group in a central database and are collected by remote machines via a remote procedure call (RPC). To use NIS, no changes have to be applied to existing applications; only the C library has to be changed.

## NSS

To be able to configure the source for the data in /etc/passwd and /etc/group, Unix vendors introduced the Name Service Switch (NSS). In terms of NSS, a name service refers to the data in one of the configuration files traditionally kept in /etc/ (such as /etc/passwd) and is named according to the file name where the data are traditionally kept in (such as passwd). With NSS, the source of a certain type of data such as passwd, but also including others such as hosts for data from /etc/hosts, is kept in a configuration file /etc/nsswitch.conf. This file is read by the C library, which decides for each name service where the data is gathered from (files, nis, etc). This method is very flexible, allowing for the implementation of arbitrary sources through dynamic libraries. For example, data can be gathered from an LDAP (Lightweight Directory Access Protocol) directory through the use of nss_ldap.

## PAM

All methods described in the preceding text have one common problem. The methods described rely on authentication information solely represented by the old crypt(3)-encrypted password. To gain flexibility Pluggable Authentication Modules (PAM) was invented. With this library, it is possible to have any number of authentication mechanisms such as smart cards, fingerprint scanners, etc. Authentication is no longer carried out by applications themselves but rather by the library which, depending on the actual configuration, can delegate the authentication step to various means. Unfortunately, using PAM makes it necessary to change all authenticating applications in order for them to use PAM instead of getpwent(3) and crypt(3) for authentication purposes.

To understand how authentication models preserve security while facilitating access, one must examine the issue of passwords and the fact that secure directories store the hashed value of the password. For this you need to understand the authentication process. When a user provides a log-on name (ID) and password, the password string is hashed, then compared to the stored password hash value in the directory. A good example of this process is the LDAP bind request that occurs when using an LDAP directory for credentials. If the hash from the log-on matches the hash stored in the directory, the bind is successful. Although some directories store both the original password and the hash value, a secure directory does not provide a means of accessing the original password; you can only access the hash.

The following is an example: A user password is set to the string "password" and gets stored in an Oracle Internet Directory as the hash value "[B@7a8ea817". If we try to synchronize this hash value in the Oracle directory in the user's personal document, what happens? The hash value our access server generates when we log in (bind) with a password of string "password" is "355E98E7C7B59BD810ED845AD0FD2FC4". Because this is not equal to the hash value we synchronized in from the Oracle directory of "[B@7a8ea817", authentication using the Application directory will fail.

Oracle eSSO Sign-On Manager allows for a variety of Primary/Front End Authentication methods as it ships with authenticators for Windows Logon, Windows Active Directory or Domain Logon, LDAP, public key infrastructure (PKI) Systems, smart card, and biometrics. Additionally, Oracle can enable the support for virtually any specific authentication device that you require using our Authenticator application programming interface (API). The Oracle eSSO Sign-On Manager Authenticator API is a set of plug-in interfaces used to integrate the authentication user interface with the main Oracle eSSO Sign-On Manager client. It serves as a conduit between the authentication service and Oracle eSSO Sign-On Manager. Third-party authentication services can integrate with Oracle eSSO Sign-On Manager by utilizing the Authenticator API. For more information on the Authenticator API, contact Oracle. Using the authenticator, an eSSO Sign-On Manager supports access to credentials anywhere, in any mode: connected, disconnected, roaming, shared workstations, kiosk workstations, etc. The authenticator allows users to prove their identity, whether through a Windows Domain Password, biometric, or smart card. The authenticator takes the user's proof and passes it to the authentication service. The authentication service validates the credentials provided by the authenticator against either its own store or a system authentication Service such as a Windows domain or a PKI. If validated, it passes the validation to the Authenticator API. An authentication service can support "disconnected" mode if it meets the requirements of the Oracle eSSO Sign-On Manager Authenticator API. This allows users to access their credentials even when the system authentication services are not available.

## *Administrative Console*

Administration of Oracle eSSO Sign-On Manager is done either via Microsoft Management Console (MMC) snap-in or via the Oracle eSSO Sign-On Manager Administrative Console, a .Net-based application that resides on the eSSO Sign-On Manager Administrator's desktop. This console has the wizards needed to gather the data required to configure application templates (required for Oracle eSSO Sign-On Manager to uniquely recognize and respond to enterprise applications), configure eSSO Sign-On Manager client settings, and define the user enrollment process (if necessary). The intuitive eSSO Sign-On Manager Administrative Console then "pushes" the administrative data to a central repository (typically a directory), where it is inherited by the appropriate Oracle eSSO Sign-On Manager end users. The Oracle eSSO Sign-On Manager Administrative Console uses the existing access right of the directory for object creation, modification, and deletion. Additionally, the administrative function of Oracle eSSO Sign-On Manager can be either centrally managed or delegated out to groups based on the configuration of your LDAP/directory service.

Oracle eSSO Sign-On Manager, when deployed with Oracle eSSO PG, will fully interface with OIM to enable the Sign-On Manager to fully participate in OIM's provisioning and workflow. Oracle eSSO Sign-On Manager is designed so that your technical team does not need to engage in the time-consuming and costly process of creating, implementing, and administering proprietary connectors, scripts, or agents. This ensures that the enterprise deployment of SSO can be managed in house.

Oracle provides you with the Oracle eSSO Sign-On Manager Administrative Console, which is a graphical user interface (GUI)-based wizard-driven configuration console for Oracle eSSO Sign-On Manager. It allows delegated parties to

■ Configure all of the Oracle eSSO Sign-On Manager agent settings
■ Configure all application specific settings for SSO

- Extend the schema for your directory
- Manage, add, and update Oracle eSSO Sign-On Manager-specific configuration settings across your enterprise via your existing LDAP or Active Directory (AD)
- Manage, add, and update Oracle ESSO Sign-On Manager application configurations across your enterprise via your existing LDAP directory

# Example of an Administrator Adding a New Application

First, run the Oracle eSSO Sign-On Manager Administrative Console Logon Form Wizard against the application that you wish to have the Oracle eSSO Sign-On Manager clients recognize, and the Administrative Console will create a configuration/signature for the targeted application. Then, using the Console, you simply publish that new application configuration to their Directory or Network File server, and all of their Oracle eSSO Sign-On Manager clients will be updated with the configuration for the new application.

## *Encryption*

Once the user has authenticated successfully to Oracle eSSO Sign-On Manager, via one of the configured authenticators, their Credential Repository (password purse) is unlocked. However, the credentials remain encrypted at all times while stored locally, in memory, in transit to the central repository (directory or database), and while stored on the central repository. In fact, the only time the Oracle eSSO Sign-On Manager exposes the user's credentials is during the brief moment it has been requested by an application for a log-on when it is unencrypted to be used, followed by an immediate housekeeping task that cleans the memory space used for that credential. Oracle eSSO Sign-on Manager protects each user's credential store using one of several selectable encryption algorithms. By default, Oracle eSSO Sign-On Manager uses the Microsoft CAPI (C Application Program Interface)–supplied Triple DES (Data Encryption Standard) (3DES) symmetric-key encryption algorithm to secure all user credentials locally on the desktop and to remote directories or network drives. MS CAPI 3DES is certified to meet FIPS 140-2 requirements. Oracle eSSO Sign-On Manager also includes MS-CAPI AES 256 bit (FIPS 140-1), RC4, Blowfish 448, and Cobra 128 as administratively selectable algorithms. The Oracle eSSO Sign-On Manager Encryption API enables the substitution of practically any other symmetric encryption algorithm beyond what is shipped with it. This enables companies to meet their security/audit requirements or comply with local government regulations. Oracle eSSO Sign-On Manager uses cryptography to confirm user authentication and to secure storage of the user credential data. Upon first-time use, it generates and maintains a cryptographically unique *primary authentication key* that is Authenticator independent and requires successful completion of the authentication process to be viably unlocked. Upon successful authentication, this key becomes available internally to the eSSO Sign-On Manager and is then used to unlock and access user credentials. Each credential is only decrypted on an as-needed basis and is never stored or cached in the clear.

For Random Number Generation (RNG), such as for generating the primary authentication key or for generating a new password for applications based on password policies, Oracle eSSO Sign-On Manager supports using Microsoft CAPI. In particular, the Intel Hardware RNG and RSA CSPs are utilized.

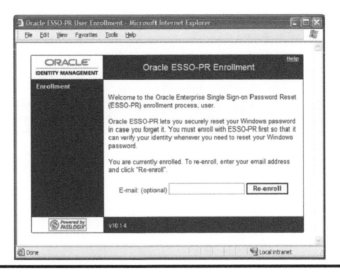

**Figure 6.3    eSSO Enrollment Screen.**

## Deployment Architecture

In the Figure 6.3, the eSSO enrollment screen is displayed. The challenge to provide SSO is working with independent security architectures, directories, etc., for each different existing application platform without compromising the integrity of those systems. To facilitate SSO, we need to provision all our applications to use a common security infrastructure for authentication that can be passed seamlessly between applications. This requires the use of a common entry point for distributing authentication information or credentials that all the applications can understand and accept.

Figure 6.3 describes the eSSO enrollment screen.

All SSO methods must address three issues:

1. Authenticating the identity of the user
2. Assigning the correct application access controls based on user identity
3. Rendering user credentials (identity) in a format recognized by other applications

The eSSO suite accomplishes this through the use of the eSSO, the Kiosk Manager, and the password reset architecture.

Figure 6.4 describes the eSSO PG.

Access administrators create the accounts and credentials for each application, system, or platform on behalf of each end user. This takes place manually, through the use of scripts, or via a provisioning solution. Once administrators create the accounts and the credentials, they provide them to the user by e-mail or even on a piece of paper. The end user logs in with these credentials and is immediately asked to change the password. Oracle eSSO PG simplifies this process by automating the sign-on and password-reset process. It receives instructions from OIM (or other provisioning systems) that contain credential data for provisioned targets. It normalizes these instructions into a format that the Oracle Logon Manager can understand and places them into the directory object for the appropriate user. When the Logon Manager syncs to the directory, it reads and processes the instructions and updates the entries as needed in its local credential cache.

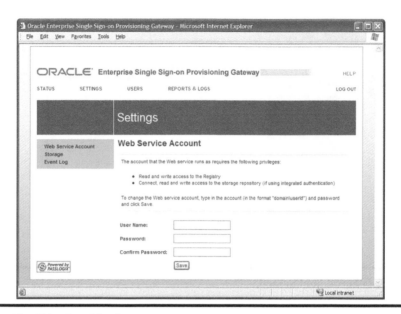

**Figure 6.4    The ESSO Provisioning gateway.**

Depending on the instructions it receives, the Logon Manager adds, modifies, or deletes credentials in the appropriate user's local credential cache. Finally, it syncs the credentials back to the directory object for that user. Password synchronization also alleviates help-desk overflow by letting users log on to different systems with a single password, reducing the chance that they will forget one of the passwords. However, unlike SSO, the user must enter an ID and password for each application. Synchronization products also do not necessitate the changes to existing IT infrastructure because the software usually resides on an existing server. Oracle eSSO ties the OIM to the Management console and the directory domain database, permitting eSSO to provision and deprovision username and password pairs to applications, managing the user identity life cycle. It automatically creates out-of-the-box provisioning and compliance workflows with preconfigured connectors to target applications and resources key derivation, hashing, RNG, symmetric algorithms (with salting and IV in CBC mode), and asymmetric support. Oracle provisioning also monitors for debug attachment and attempted early termination and re-encrypt keys in memory for user protection all DLLs signed and runtime validated bidirectionally. Components of the ESSO Provisioning Gateway include

■ The Oracle SSO client agent (resides on user's client workstation)
■ The Oracle Administrative Console (resides on the administrator's client workstation)
■ The Oracle SSO data repository—Oracle SSO leverages virtually any existing central repository as a store for user configuration and administration data. This data repository can be an enterprise directory server (e.g., AD, ADAM, Sun Directory Server, Oracle eDirectory, IBM Directory Server, etc.), databases (MS SQL, Oracle, and IBM DB2), or even a simple network file share.

To provide session-level security, eSSO KM enforces session integrity conditionally, prompting authentication in the screen shown in Figure 6.5.

The provisioning gateway receives instructions from OIM (or other provisioning systems) that contain the credential data for provisioned targets. It normalizes these instructions into a format

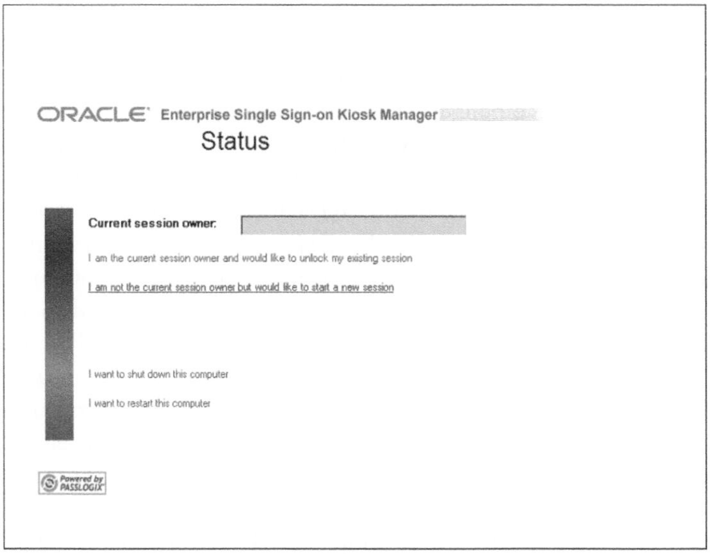

ORACLE Enterprise Single Sign-on Kiosk Manager
Status
Current session owner:
I am the current session owner and would like to unlock my existing session
I am not the current session owner but would like to start a new session
I want to shut down this computer
I want to restart this computer
Powered by PASSLOGIX

**Figure 6.5 eSSO Kiosk Manager Entry Session Screen.**

that the Oracle Logon Manager can understand and places them into the directory object for the appropriate user. When the Logon Manager syncs to the directory, it reads and processes the instructions and updates the entries as needed in its local credential cache. Depending on the instructions it receives, it adds, modifies, or deletes credentials in the appropriate user's local credential cache. Finally, it syncs the credentials back to the directory object for that user, as illustrated in Figure 6.6.

Oracle SSO Logon Manager detects and responds password-related events to automate password management task for the end user. These tasks include log-on, password selection, password

Oracle eSSO Suite Management Console
Directory, Domain, Database
Windows
Web Sites
Mainframes
(OS390, AS400)
Java
Extranet & Portal
Password
Oracle eSSO Logon Manager
User Auth
User's Desktop
Application Sign-On

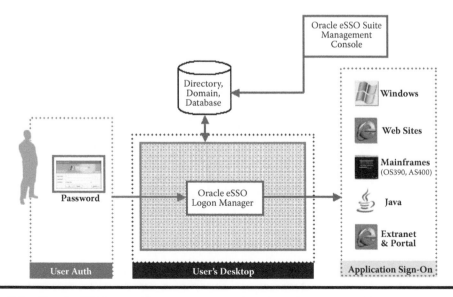

**Figure 6.6 Oracle SSO Logon Manager.**

change, and password reset. Oracle SSO keeps passwords and related data protected wherever they are located—in the directory, in transit from the directory to the client, in client local disk cache, and in client memory. It uses multiple cryptography libraries, including TripleDES and AES. Oracle SSO's FIPS 140-2 compliance helps financial institutions, government agencies, and healthcare and other organizations comply with privacy and security regulations that govern their operations. Oracle eSSO supports Microsoft Windows 2000, XP, and Windows 2003, as well as roaming profiles for user mobility, and Windows authenticator for certificate, smart card, biometric, or token. It includes an optional password change passphrase to protect against administrative breach as well as to integrate GINA for enhanced security. Oracle eSSO supports authentication from any LDAP directory such as Oracle Internet Directory or other third-party directory servers, the Certificate Authority Server, Oracle eDirectory, etc. It supports PKI authentication by employing PKI cryptographic services for key encryption and strong authentication. Oracle eSSO also supports MS CAPI CSP-based smart card as well as SAFLINK. It does this securely by relying on two independent factors that are disclosed at run-time and randomly encrypted during the session in memory. This enables the credentials to be cryptographically secured within the directory, in transit, on the client, and in memory. Individual credentials are decrypted on—as needed. In this manner eSSO supports FIPS 140-2–compliant MS CAPI support for 3DES, AES, and RC4 as well as for key generation and hashing, as illustrated in Figure 6.7.

Oracle eSSO Sign-On Manager fully supports roaming users, defined as users who move from workstation to workstation. This is done by either taking advantage of Windows Roaming profiles to supply users with their SSO configuration and SSO credentials, or preferably by utilizing the synchronization support for use an existing Directory Server or a Network File Server to provide users access to their unique credential repository from virtually any workstation with connectivity to the Server. Oracle SSO enables single sign-on by uniquely recognizing and responding to application log-in requests on behalf of the end user. Administrators easily create templates for virtually any application by using wizards contained in the Oracle SSO Administrative Console, a ".Net"-based application that is available as a either a stand-alone application (residing on the administrator's desktop) or as an MMC plug-in. The intuitive wizards within the Console enable administrators to create an application template by gathering the data required for Oracle SSO to

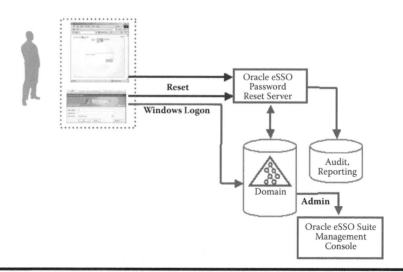

**Figure 6.7   Oracle eSSO Password reset architecture.**

uniquely recognize and respond to application sign-on requests, including URL, Window Title, Executable, Mainframe Session name, and field characteristics.

From within the Oracle SSO Administrative Console, Administrators configure

1. Password Policies—Oracle SSO responds to application password change requests and can generate a complex password on behalf of the end user (who no longer needs to remember application passwords). Whether selected by the end user or administrator, Oracle SSO generates the new password, and it must comply with the password policy for this application (or global password policy). These password policies are set from within the Oracle SSO Administrative Console.

2. Password Share Groups—Virtually every organization has applications that authenticate against a common database or system. Examples include Microsoft applications that authenticate against the domain or RACF (Resource Access Control Facility) application. If the password changes in one of these synchronized applications, it must change for all applications authenticating against that source. To accommodate this requirement, Oracle SSO can create password share groups—if the password changes in one of these applications, it is propagated to the others.

3. Enrollment process—On day one, Oracle SSO must learn the end user's existing usernames and passwords. As such, it can be deployed to either ask the end user for all known credentials during initial setup or simply add credentials as the user encounters new, password-protected applications.

4. Client settings—There is a myriad of client settings that can be configured by the administrators to customize Oracle SSO deployment. These settings include usability settings (e.g., which menus can the end user access), security settings (e.g., which cryptographic algorithm will Oracle SSO use for credential encryption), authentication settings (which form of authentication must the end user use), and many others.

Once the administrator has created all enterprise application templates and configured the client settings, all of this administrator data is exported to the central repository. Please note that users can, optionally, add additional applications as needed. Once users enroll in Oracle SSO, they will look to this repository and inherit all of this information. To change any settings or add/delete/modify any application templates, end users simply push new information to the central repository where they pull down the new data. This is the basic administrative process for Oracle SSO. Once deployed, end users transparently authenticate to the Oracle SSO client via the standard Windows network log-in, using either basic username/password combination, smart card, biometric, or token. Once authenticated, users benefit from SSO to all applications, including support for log-on and password-change requests. In addition, Oracle SSO can optionally store the encrypted end-user credential database on the client (enabling disconnected SSO) or in the directory (enabling support for shared workstations, kiosks, and roaming users). When deployed using Windows as the primary authentication means, if end users forgets their Windows log-in, they can perform a self-serve Windows password reset via Passlogix Oracle SSO. Oracle SSO provides a challenge–response mechanism that enables users to reset this password in-the-flow, meaning from the desktop they been locked out of. Oracle SSO also has an event logging capability that monitors specific end-user application access events, including which applications are accessed, the time accessed, the IP address from which applications were accessed, and much more. All of this event logging data can be pushed to the Windows Event Viewer or exported as an XML (eXtensible Markup Language) dump for auditing and compliance purposes. Figure 6.8 describes the authentication manager architecture.

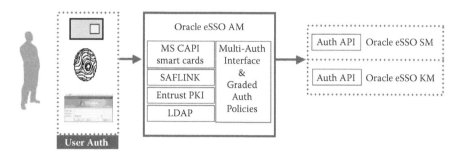

**Figure 6.8    Authentication manager architecture.**

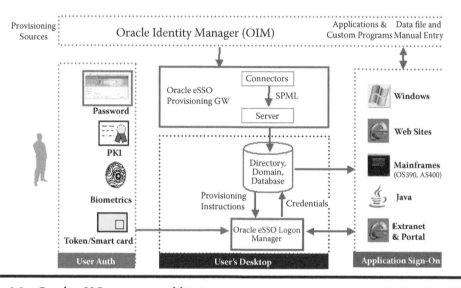

**Figure 6.9    Oracle eSSO gateway architecture.**

Oracle eSSO automates this process by serving as gateway for authentication. The information flow is graphically illustrated in Figure 6.9.

Within Oracle eSSO, the systems serve as facilitators linking users to applications and linking back to OIM through the Oracle eSSO provisioning engine. Figure 6.10 illustrates how the Oracle eSSO kiosk maintains session integrity, linking users to application and conditionally suspending the session on cessation of activities.

Oracle eSSO KM addresses the security threat posed by users inadvertently abandoning an open session by providing automated termination of inactive sessions and application shut-down. Inactive sessions end after a period of time predetermined by a systems administrator, and the kiosk returns to a ready state for the next user. KM-enabled kiosks know who is using the kiosk at any given time by prompting each user to log into an OID. Kiosk users who inadvertently walk away without logging off allow the next user to access systems in the prior user's session or may expose sensitive data to anyone using the kiosk.

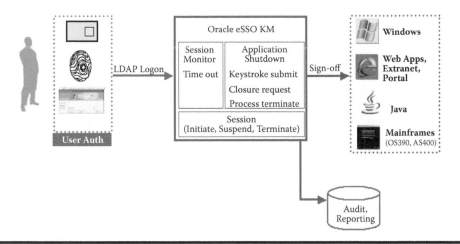

**Figure 6.10   Oracle eSSO Kiosk Manager.**

# Installation and Administration

## Unlocking Users

The following steps are the minimum permissions that are required for the Reset Service account to be able to unlock users.

Steps:

1. Run ADSIEdit and connect to AD.
2. Right-click the domain root (e.g., "dc=passlogix,dc=com") and select Properties.
3. Click on the Security tab and click the Advanced button.
4. Click Add...
5. Enter (or browse) the user to delegate to.
6. For "Apply onto", select "User objects"
7. Set the following permissions:
   a. Write All Properties
   b. Modify Permissions
   c. Reset Password

In the event the issue is password related, follow these steps to set the Default Domain Policy to work in conjunction with SSPR:

1. Open the MMC (Click Start > Run > and type MMC.)
2. Click File > Add/Remove Snap-in.
3. Click Add and select the Group Policy Object Editor snap-in (edit the "Default Domain Policy" object).
4. Expand Computer Configuration > Windows Settings > Security Settings > Account Policies > Password Policy and locate the "Minimum password age" entry.
5. Set the value to "0 days".
6. Run DOS Prompt, type in "gpupdate /force" (this will apply the policy changes).

One can also use AD to manage passwords. To do this

1. Open the MMC (Click Start > Run > and type MMC).
2. Click File > Add/Remove Snap-in.
3. Click Add and select the ADSIEdit snap-in.
4. Browse to the root of the tree, right-click, and select Properties.
5. In the Advanced Security tab, click the Advanced button and browse to bottom of the list. Two entries with the name "SELF" should be there. Highlight the first entry and click Edit.
6. In the Permission Entry dialog, select the Properties tab.h.
7. Browse to the bottom of the list and confirm that the "Create vGOUserData Objects" and "Delete vGOUserData Objects" exist and are set to "Allow".
8. Repeat these steps, except this time examine the properties of an individual user object in the tree to make sure the rights inherit all the way to the user object. Passlogix assumes that rights inheritance is not blocked between the root of the tree and the user object.

If an administrator renames an AD user container to a name that contains a comma (e.g., user container renamed to "First MI. L,ast"), the SSO container within the user container will also need to be renamed.

Follow these steps to rename an AD user container.

1. Open the AD Users and Computers dialog.
2. Rename the User Container (e.g., "First MI. L,ast").

The SSO will not be able to find the user, and an AD synch attempt will result in a First Time Use wizard appearing. Follow these steps to fix this:

1. Rename the SSO Container within the user container to the same name.
2. Replace any commas with a space.

For example, let us say your User Container is in the format "First MI. L,ast"; the SSO Container should now be named "First MI. L ast". A space is substituted for the comma.

The SSO Agent is now ready to reuse the correct credential set.

## Building Users in AD

You can also use the process of building users in an AD environment. It has been found to be helpful in recreating large user environments.

Follow these steps:

1. Change the OU where the user objects will be stored.
2. Change the user principal name information.
3. You may also want to change the amount of users you would like to create (currently 30,000).
4. Run it on your domain controller.

## Language Packs

To install the language packs, a "Modify" installation must be performed. To do this, install the English version of SM, then open the Control Panel, select Add or Remove Programs, and double-click Oracle SSO Session Manager (or you can re-execute the Oracle SSO SM installer). Click Next on the Welcome Panel, then select Modify and click Next. The Custom Setup panel appears. Click the + sign next to Language Packs and select the Language to be installed. Follow the prompts through the rest of the installation.

## Password Changing

Oracle eSSO Sign-On Manager can recognize a password expiration/password change request, and either prompt the user to compose a new password (forcing the user to comply with the password policy) or automatically (and transparently) generate a random password that complies with password policies set by an administrator on behalf of the end user. Customers frequently cite this feature as a competitive advantage of the eSSO Sign-On Manager. Additionally, it has the ability to monitor the age of a stored password and, at a preconfigured time interval (30 or 60 days, for example), initiate the password change process at the local application level.

## Password Generation Policies

Oracle eSSO Sign-On Manager allows the administrator to define a default global password policy, application-specific password policies, as well as subscribe several applications to one password policy.

The administrator can specify

- Maximum/minimum password lengths
- Maximum repetition of a character
- Number of times a character can be adjacent to itself
- Allow numeric characters
- Maximum/minimum occurrence of numeric characters
- Allow numeric to start password
- Allow numeric to end password
- Allow special characters (specify the characters to allow and exclude)
- Maximum/minimum occurrence of special characters
- Alpha usage (none, upper, lower, and upper and lower)

## Example: SSO in Operation

The following example shows how easy Oracle SSO is to use. Suppose you want to retrieve a stock portfolio and track preferred stocks using the Yahoo! Finance Web site. When you access the Yahoo! Finance Web site and select sign-in, Yahoo! requests a username and password. At this point, Oracle SSO automatically launches a dialog box, indicating it did not find log-in information for this Web site. This dialog box allows you to choose whether or not you want to create this information. When you select OK, the Oracle log-on wizard automatically launches. (See Figure 6.11.)

The Oracle SSO Logon Wizard enables users to easily configure Oracle SSO to automatically log in to resources, such as a Web site, that require a username and password. Next, Oracle SSO prompts you to identify this site. By default, Oracle SSO uses the title of the Web page (in this case: Welcome to Yahoo! Finance). It also lets you enter a description to help you identify the site

**Figure 6.11    The Oracle SSO Logon Wizard.**

**Figure 6.12    The Oracle SSO Logon Wizard stores and encrypts passwords.**

in your secret store. Next, it prompts you to enter a complete or partial URL. This URL helps Oracle SSO to identify the site the next time you access it. (Of course, an application does not require a URL.) The next dialog box that appears prompts you to enter a username. If you have an existing identity (username and password) for this Web site, you enter that information. If you have not logged in to this Web site before, you can use Oracle SSO to create an identity for this Web site. Next, the password dialog box appears. (See Figure 6.2.) You then enter the password for your existing identity, or the password for the new identity, as shown in Figure 6.12.

As Figure 6.12 shows, the password dialog box has a few interesting options. For example, if you select the Generate button, Oracle SSO generates a random password, which is a complex mixture of alphanumeric characters (such as 456y78IH8dO) that is difficult for a hacker to guess. Because Oracle SSO 2.0 will always provide the log-in credentials for this Web site, it can use a complex password, and the user does not have to worry about forgetting that password. All users need to remember their OID username and password—Oracle SSO completes the operation. The Properties button is also worth mentioning. You can use this option to view the password policy, which defines the password rules such as minimum and maximum password lengths, and uppercase and lowercase character supports. You can use the default password policy or configure your own in OID. After you enter this information, you never have to enter log-in credentials for this Web site again. Oracle SSO automatically supplies this information for you. If you use the disconnected feature, Oracle SSO can automatically log you in to this Web site even when you are not logged in to OID.

## *Integrating Oracle eSSO with OIM*

The Oracle eSSO PG provides the ability for an administrator to automatically provision eSSO LM with a user's ID and password by using the OIM. The OIM connector that is made available along with the eSSO PG enables an administrator to add, modify, and delete IDs and passwords for particular applications within the provisioning system and have the changes reflected in eSSO LM. From OIM, all usernames and passwords inside the eSSO can be deleted so that a user's access to all protected applications is eliminated.

eSSO PG is installed as an add-on component to the eSSO environment. eSSO LM must be installed before installing Provisioning Manager. In order for eSSO PG to install and function properly, your system must have the following applications installed:

- Internet Explorer 6.0 or higher with 128-bit encryption
- Microsoft° .NET Framework 1.1 (installed by Provisioning Manager installer)
- Microsoft Web Services Enhancements (WSE) 2.0 SP3 for Microsoft .NET (installed by Provisioning Manager installer)
- An X.509 Certificate for SSL must be obtained from a Certificate Authority.
- eSSO PG can use any the following as the repository:
- Oracle Internet Directory (OID)
- Microsoft AD or Active Directory Application Mode (ADAM). The AD server or ADAM instance (that is, AD running as a user service) can be on any server and in the same domain.
- Sun Java System Directory
- IBM LDAP Directory

## Installation and Configuration of eSSO-PG with OIM Connector

Following are the steps to set up eSSO PG with OIM.

### Step 1: Installation of the eSSO PG Server

1. On the desktop of the Windows 2003 Server.
2. Navigate to the C:\oracle eSSO Suite 10.1.4.0.1\ESSO-Provisioning Gateway 10.1.4.0.1 folder.
3. Double-click the ESSO-PG Server.exe file to begin the installation.
4. The Welcome Panel appears. Click Next.
5. The License Agreement panel appears. Read the license agreement carefully. Click the I accept the terms in the license agreement button and click Next to continue.
6. The Setup Type Panel appears. Select Complete or Custom. Complete installs all program files. Custom allows you to choose what program files are installed and the location. Custom installations are only recommended for advanced users. Click Next.
7. Provisioning Manager is ready to be installed. Click Install. Wait for the installation to complete. When it is done, click Finish.

### Step 2: Create or Identify a User Account for Anonymous Log-In

A dedicated Anonymous User account through which Provisioning Gateway users and administrators access Provisioning Gateway Web Services must be created or identified. This Anonymous User account should be a member of the Administrators group.

*Note:* Because the default Anonymous User account for a Web service, IUSR_<MACHINE_ NAME>, is not a member of the Administrator group, you must create or choose a domain user account that is an Administrator. To accomplish this, use the AD Users and Computers console (for an AD domain) or the Computer Management console (for non-AD domains).

For this, create an SSPGadmin (with a password of Password1) as a member of the Administrator and Domain Admins group, who will be specified as the Anonymous User. The SSPGadmin user needs access to

- Start, stop, and change services
- Read from/write to the directory
- Write to the local-machine registry (HKLM)

1. Go to Windows 2003 Server. Click Start, point to Program Files, point to Administrative Tools, and click Internet Information Services (IIS).
2. Locate the Provisioning Manager Console (v-GO PM Console) node in the tree, right-click on it, and click Properties.
3. Click the Directory Security tab and click the Edit button next to Anonymous Access. Check the Anonymous Access checkbox and type in the username (ssolab\SSPGadmin) and password (Password1) of the anonymous user.
4. Make sure the user SSPGadmin has the permission to write to the Windows 2003 Server's registry (HKLM), where the eSSO-PG Web service is running. This is done by adding SSOLAB\Domain Admins into the Administrators group.

## Step 3: Enable SSL for eSSO-PG Web Services

An X.509 Certificate for SSL must be obtained from a trusted Certificate Authority (CA). This trusted CA must be installed in the list of trusted Root CAs.

Our trusted root authority is the domain controller, SSOLABDC, and a certificate has already been added to the server for you.

The following steps are done on Windows 2003 Server:

1. To configure SSL for the eSSO-PG Web services, right-click v-GO PM Console on IIS and select Properties.
2. Select Directory Security, and under Secure Communications, click Edit.
3. Click Require secure channel (SSL) and Require 128-bit encryption, and click OK.
4. Select the ASP.NET tab (on the v-GO PM Console -> Properties dialog). Make sure the ASP.NET version is set to 2.0.x. (Please note that if it was not set to 2.0, click Apply after changing the setting). Click Edit Configuration.
5. Under Application Settings, select localhost.UP and click Edit.
   Enter the value as : https://localhost/v-GO%20PM%20Service/UP.asmx.
   In the Value field, changing the prefix of the URL to https; the console will now communicate over SSL with the Web service.
   Click OK.

## Step 4: Configuring the eSSO-PG Server Settings

Because we enabled SSL on the PG Site, we must access it via HTTPS.

1. Access the eSSO-PG admin Console by entering the following link on Windows 2003 Server:
   https://localhost/v-GO%20PM%20Console/webservice.aspx
   *Note:* when we go to https://localhost/v-GO%20PM%20Console/logon.aspx, it gives a security error—REVOCATION INFORMATION FOR THE SECURITY CERTIFICATE FOR THIS SITE IS NOT AVAILABLE DO YOU WANT TO PROCEED Click Yes. It gives another security alert; click Yes to that as well.
2. Enter ssolab\Administrator for the Username and Password1 for the Password, and click Log On.
3. When logged in properly, you should see a screen.
4. Click on Settings. You will see the Web Services Account screen. In the Username field, enter SSOLAB\SSPGadmin with a password of Password1 and click Save.
5. From the Settings page, click on Storage.
6. Select AD from the drop-down list and enter the settings to configure storage.
7. Click Save Changes, and this will return you to the log-in screen.
8. Log back into the eSSO-PG admin console.
   User Name: ssolab\Administrator
   Password: Password1
   Click on Users. If you have properly configured the storage settings, you should see a screen with all of the application templates when you click on Users.

## Step 5: Installing the eSSO-PG Client Program Files

Follow these steps to install and configure the eSSO-PG Support for Agent. This process is to be run on the CLIENT machine.

1. Close all programs.
2. Navigate to C:\oracle eSSO Suite 10.1.4.0.1\eSSO-Provisioning Gateway 10.1.4.0.1 folder.
3. Double-click the eSSO-PG Client.msi file to begin the installation.
4. The Welcome Panel appears. Click Next.
5. The License Agreement panel appears. Read the license agreement carefully. Click the I accept the terms in the license agreement button and click Next to continue.
7. Provisioning Manager is ready to be installed. Click Install.
8. Wait for the installation to complete. When it is done, click Finish.
9. Set CycleInterval Registry Key.

In order for eSSO PG to function properly, the agent must synchronize to retrieve the provisioning instructions from the directory.

When deploying, one of the decisions that must be made is the synchronization interval. The CycleInterval registry key is used to force synchronization to occur on a regular interval. If this is zero, synchronization only occurs on some user action, which is not the desired behavior with Provisioning Manager. It is recommended that this key be set to some value. If, for example,

CycleInterval is set to 5 min, the provisioning instructions will be pulled down from the directory within 5 min of when they are put there by the Provisioning Manager Server.

The CycleInterval registry key can be set through the eSSO-LM Console:

- Open the Administrative Console by clicking Start, point to Programs > Oracle > ESSO-LM > click on ESSO-LM Console.
- Expand Global Agent Settings, expand Live, and click Synchronization.
- Set the Interval for automatic resync setting to the desired value.
- Click Tools > Write Global Agent Settings to HKLM.

The Apply Settings dialog appears. Click Yes.

*Note:* Synchronization will only occur with agents that are running.

Processing the provisioning instructions requires that the user be authenticated. If the user is not authenticated (for example, the time-out expired), then an authentication UI is presented and the synchronization process is blocked until the user authenticates.

## Step 6 : Deploying the OIM Connector

*Note:* All the following steps are done on Windows 2003 Server.

Here are additional setup instructions that are required for the OIM connector that is deployed in E:\OIM\Server\xellerate\JavaTasks:

1. Unjar the C:\Oracle eSSO Suite 10.1.4.0.1\eSSO-Provisioning Gateway 10.1.4.0.1\Libraries\ OIM\bin\OIMConnector-6.0.jar.
   - Run this command at the command prompt on Windows 2003 Server to unjar OIM-Connector-6.0.jar. Make sure you are pointing to the right directories.
     - cd C:\Oracle eSSO Suite 10.1.4.0.1\eSSO-Provisioning Gateway 10.1.4.0.1\Libraries\ OIM\bin\
     - C:\j2sdk1.4.2_13\bin\jar -xvf OIMConnector-6.0.jar C:\TEMP
   - Navigate to unjared package com\passlogix\integration\provision\conf\PMClient-Configuration.properties and edit the values of these three attributes in the configuration file:
     - javaCLI.serviceurl= https://localhost/v-GO PM Service/UP.asmx
     - javaCLI.serviceuser = ssolab\\SSPGadmin
     - javaCLI.serviceuserpassword= Password1
   - After these changes are included, jar this file and deploy the OIMConnector-6.0.jar under the E:\OIM\Server\xellerate\JavaTasks. Run this command at the command prompt. Make sure you are pointing to the right directories:
     - cd C:\Oracle eSSO Suite 10.1.4.0.1\eSSO-Provisioning Gateway 10.1.4.0.1\Libraries\ OIM\bin\
     - C:\j2sdk1.4.2_13\bin\jar -cvf E:\OIM\Server\xellerate\JavaTasks\OIMConnector-6.0 .jar com META-INF
2. Copy all the jars (xalan.jar, xercesImpl.jar,jaxp-api.jar,dom.jar,sax.jar) from C:\Oracle eSSO Suite 10.1.4.0.1\eSSO-Provisioning Gateway 10.1.4.0.1\Libraries\PMSIM\SIMUpgrade\1.4\ endorsed to the appserver endorsed directory. If deploying in jBOSS, the location is jboss-4.0.2\lib\endorsed). The OIM connector requires the JDK 1.4 version.

## *Step 7: Additional Configurations for the OIM Connector*

1. In the final step, you will
   - Add the users who will be provisioned to the Employee HR Database
   - Add the application template "Employee HR Database" to the OIM repository
   - Add the administrators to the Provisioning Gateway

   Save these configuration updates:

   a) You need an Application template for the ROOT_RESOURCE_NAME assigned value (this is the repository where the user credentials for eSSO are stored). An application template called "Employee HR Database" has to be created on CLIENT, which has a username, password, and OK fields. (In the lab environment, we are using AD for this repository.)

   Here is how to create Employee HR Database application template on CLIENT.
      - Go to CLIENT.
      - Bring up eSSO LM Admin Console.
      - Click Applications -> New windows Application.
      - Enter Name of Application as Employee HR Database, and click Finish and select Logon.
      - Because this is a dummy template, select any on the list and click Next.
      - Click Next and Finish.
      - Select Fields Tab and click Add.
      - Add three fields Username/ID, Password, and OK (specify the control IDs for these fields).
      - Click OK to complete the application template creation at the eSSO LM admin console.

   b) Go to Applications -> select Employee HR Database (the application template created for the repository) -> click on the Provisioning tab on the right panel -> Add -> include the user/users who will be provisioned.

   Right-click on the entry and select Modify and Delete Login options for the Authenticated Users.

   c) Click on Repository on the console and Connect to Repository -> Configure SSO Support.

   Add the Employee HR Database template configuration into the Repository

   d) Navigate to Provisioning Gateway.

   Select Default Rights tab -> Add -> include the administrators who will need access ->Right-click on the user added -> enable Add, Modify, and Delete Logon.

   Select Delete SSO User Right -> Add -> include the administrators who will need delete access ->Right-click on the user added -> enable Delete SSO User.

   e) Save the changes into the local registry by going to Tools -> Write Global Agent Settings to HKLM.

## *Step 8: Testing the Provisioning to eSSO Using OIM Connector*

1. On Windows 2003 Server, log into the OIM Web page at http://gamma.ssolab.com:8080/ xlWebApp. Log in as administrator with username/password - xelsysadm/xelsysadm.
2. Click on Users-> Create.

3. Enter all the user attributes as follows, enter Password as 'Password1', then click Create User.
4. Provision this user to AD, which is the eSSO user credential repository. Select the AD server as 'Employee HR Database' and password as 'Password1'.
   *Note:* The application template in eSSO LM (Employee HR Database) was previously set up for the AD root resource.
5. If the OIM connector has provisioned the user successfully to eSSO, you will see the status of user provisioning in OIM as completed.
6. Go to the eSSO Provisioning Admin console at https://gamma.ssolab.com/v-GO%20 PM%20Console/overview.aspx. Log in as
   Username: ssolab\Administrator
   Password: Password1
   Click on Users.
7. Click on Find Users.
8. Scroll down to demo123 user that was provisioned through OIM connector. You will see that the "Employee HR Database" is under Pending Provisioning Instruction. The status for this application will change once the user has done the FTU (first time use) setup.
   This shows the behavior for the user who has been provisioned to the eSSO application templates directly through the OIM connector.
9. Log on to the CLIENT machine as the demo123 user you just provisioned and see if the logon credentials are populated in the log-on manager. If the credential appears in eSSO-LM, you have successfully provisioned an application for a user. Here is what you will find for the demo123 user before FTU setup.
10. Once you provision a user through the connector, if all has gone well, then you will see that a key called SSOProvisioning will be created for the user. After the user goes through FTU, two additional keys are created: SyncState and a 36-character alphanumeric key.

## Regulatory Governance Mapping

Oracle eSSO Sign-On Manager can log all SSO system events, including credential use, credential changes, global credential events, Oracle eSSO Sign-On Manager events, and Oracle eSSO Sign-On Manager feature use. Oracle eSSO Sign-On Manager can also log specified fields. Events can be logged locally or to any external destination through the Event Logging API. These destinations can include a directory, an SNMP (Simple Network Management Protocol) service, a Windows server (for viewing via the Windows Event log), or even a local XML log file for simplified parsing and reporting. Oracle eSSO Sign-On Manager can log all events, including credential use, credential changes, global credential events, Oracle eSSO Sign-On Manager events, and Oracle eSSO Sign-On Manager feature use. Oracle eSSO Sign-On Manager can log the fields that administrators specify. Specifically, Oracle eSSO Sign-On Manager can log

■ Credential use events: log-ons, manual password changes, and automatic password changes
■ Credential changes: add credentials, delete credentials, change credentials, copy credentials, etc.
■ Global credential events: backup, restore, synchronize, etc.
■ Oracle eSSO Sign-On Manager events: startup, shutdown, etc.

- Oracle eSSO Sign-On Manager feature use: Logon Manager, Settings, Help, About, etc.
- Administrator-specified fields: Domain, Windows username, Oracle eSSO Sign-On Manager username, Application name, Application username, Application third field, Date, Time, etc.

Events can be logged to any desired destination: Local XML storage, SNMP service, Windows Event log, directory server, Tivoli, etc. Customers can easily create their own audit reports from the event-logging data provided by Oracle eSSO Sign-On Manager. Oracle SSO also has an event-logging capability that monitors specific end-user application access events, including which applications are accessed, the time accessed, the IP address from which applications were accessed, and much more. All of this event-logging data can be pushed to the Windows Event Viewer or exported as an XML dump for auditing and compliance purposes. Properly implemented, SSO maintains the security of countless applications, tracks and logs access of PHI, and speeds access to critical information. SSO is a simple way to

1. Tie together proper user authentication and application access
2. Enable proper privacy controls

One ID and password authenticates the user for all required applications, such as prescription orders and patient records. Single sign-on eliminates the need for attorneys, health practitioners, and service workers to remember multiple passwords, while retaining a high level of security for each application. A doctor can access patient records and prescription information, an attorney gains access to proceeding minutes and court records, or a service worker gains access to information crucial to his or her role and responsibility, all using one-time authentication. Revisiting Chapter 3 and examining the benefits of eSSO, the mapping becomes directly mapped to the Trusted Access control domain. However, Operational Control and Segregation of Duties control domains are also areas in which an Access Control framework may be mapped:

- Trusted access
- Operational accountability and transparency
- Segregation of duties
- Operational controls

Of primary interest to those implementing Access Control to satisfy a regulatory requirement is the event-logging capability. From the Oracle eSSO Sign-On Manager Administrative Console, the administrator can initiate an eSSO Sign-On Manager Usage report against the data stored in the central repository to export a report containing the credential usage information by user so that you can easily and quickly see which users have credentials for which applications and identify their usage and last change. As a result, the Operational Accountability and Transparency control domain may also be satisfied by implementation of an Access Control system.

## Summary

In summary, the eSSO suite is composed of

- Oracle Enterprise Single Sign-On Authentication Manager (eSSO AM)
- Sign-On Provisioning Gateway (eSSO PG)

- Oracle Enterprise Single Sign-On Kiosk Manager (eSSO KM)
- Oracle Enterprise Sign-On Logon Manager (eSSO LM)
- Oracle Enterprise Single Sign-On Password Reset (eSSO PR)

Once deployed, Oracle SSO significantly reduces help-desk costs, simplifies the end-user experience, and enhances security by eliminating poor end-user password management, all without requiring any modification to target applications or significant modification to your enterprise infrastructure. Oracle SSO is easy to configure, deploy, and administer.

# Chapter 7

# Oracle Internet Directory and Related Services

A directory is a distributed database of named objects called *entries*. It employs a hierarchical naming scheme similar to the Domain Name System (DNS). The directory-naming scheme is more general than DNS in that its components are not restricted to domains. The naming components could be geographic and organizational entities, such as countries and corporations, or any arbitrary application entity. The directory applications have the freedom to extend the enterprise namespace as appropriate for their needs. Each directory entry is a collection of attributes. Directories are databases that are optimized for reads and contain key institutional and personal data for use by a wide variety of applications. They need ways to describe the sequence of fields in the database (a schema), the names of the fields (a namespace), and the contents of the fields (attribute values). They also need indices in the database (identifiers). The directory entries have a well-defined type or structure defined by their object class. The object class determines the legal set of attributes that can be present in an entry. The attributes, in turn, have type information, including the syntax of its values, and rules for how two related values can be matched or compared. The latter rules are called *matching rules*. Object classes, attributes, syntax, and matching rules are some of the most significant directory metadata elements. These elements constitute the directory schema. Typically, applications extend the directory schema to suit their information-modeling needs. The first step in developing a directory schema and namespace lies in understanding the nature of the schema and its constituent components. A schema is a set of rules determining what data can be stored in a directory service. The directory schema contains object names and object attributes used to define each object class. Each object class describes an entry, such as a person or asset. Directory entries (or object instances) are then structured and organized in a directory namespace. When a directory designer organizes this collection of object names and associated attributes hierarchically, these object names and attributes form a directory information tree (DIT). Within the DIT, each instance of an object class has a relatively distinguished name that, when combined with a top-level hierarchic name, forms a unique distinguished name (DN). Directory objects are hierarchically organized in a single-tree format known as the DIT. All objects are unique in this structure; even a copy of an object is considered a separate, unique object with the same values for all its properties as the original. To maintain object uniqueness, every object has a name. This name differentiates it from all other objects and is defined by its position in the tree. The Oracle Internet Directory (OID) provides this service.

## Overview

OID is an LDAP v3 implementation, providing you with a powerful combination found nowhere else—the mission-critical capabilities of the Oracle10*g* database, plus adherence to most of the LDAP v3 directory standards specifications. In addition, it plays a central role in the management and security infrastructure for the Oracle Application Server 10*g* and is certified by Oracle to provide centralized identity, naming, single sign-on, and other security services for the Oracle10*g* Database, Oracle10*g* Portal, Oracle E-Business Suite, and Oracle Collaboration Suite. As such, it is the LDAP directory of choice for several Oracle customers and serves as a central point of user provisioning for these Oracle installations.

In short, the OID's scalability, high availability, and security features make it the ideal customer choice for high-end carrier and online service provider implementations as well as a security and compliance centerpiece for large Oracle installations involving several different Oracle products.

### *Scalability*

OID is the only LDAP v3 directory built on the incredible Oracle10*g* database. This fact enables it to be deployed in immensely complex, huge enterprises and for Internet-scale applications requiring *millions* of distinct user identities. Like its database, the OID scales to support terabytes of real-world directory information on a single server. A multi-process and multi-threaded LDAP implementation, combined with database connection pooling, enable the OID to support tens of thousands of concurrent client requests, taking milliseconds to respond to normal directory requests.

OID also supports LDAP referral objects, which enable the physical partitioning of directories according to geographic or organizational boundaries. An administrator stores pointers in the OID; these pointers serve as the "glue" that connects the various partitions (known as *naming contexts* or *realms*) so that each is accessible to the other. Partitioned directories allow delegated administration of the physical directory segments, although maintaining a logically contiguous view of the directory as a whole. This is indispensable to service providers and enterprises hosting large directories because smaller, independent organizations or end-user communities typically overwhelm IT staff. Other OID capabilities such as server-side LDAP chaining make integration of external directories such as the SUN Java System Directory Server or Microsoft Active Directory transparent to directory clients. A call is issued to one directory and returned from that directory—regardless of which LDAP directory had to be consulted for the information requested.

As previously mentioned, OID provides data management tools for manipulating huge volumes of LDAP data. For example, with the OID bulk loader (based on SQL*Loader), administrators can populate a million-user-entry directory in just minutes. Bulk population of the directory is done by converting LDIF files into SQL*Loader files using a conversion utility called "bulkload.sh", with the OID server shut down, as follows:

```
$ORACLE_HOME/ldap/bin/bulkload.sh -connect LDAP1SID -generate
newcustomers.ldif
```

Additional flags to bulkload.sh support checking huge LDIF files for schema violations (-check) and then load in the results of a "generate" directly into OID's database files (-load). Over the years, several customers have reported finding schema violations with "bulkload.sh –check" in LDIF files generated by third-party LDAP servers!

## High Availability

OID was built for mission-critical deployments. The underlying Oracle10*g* database, running with massive data stores and heavy loads, can recover from system failure in a matter of seconds even when running stand-alone. However, typically, in a security-conscious world, OID is deployed using one or more of the supported highly available solutions and techniques, including hot back-ups, clustered "logical hosts," real application clusters, failover, and full multimaster replication. Thus, if one OID server in a clustered or replicated community is unavailable for any reason, clients see no service outage, and administrators can perform administrative tasks—such as directory user administration, schema extensions, and entry modifications—using one of the other (available) nodes.

OID also supports multimaster replication based on the LDAP protocol, providing the power to deploy highly available topologies in the presence of firewalls and limited port availability.

## Security

OID offers comprehensive and flexible support for directory access control for the information stored within it. This includes entry-level, attribute-level, and inheritable (or "prescriptive") access controls to provide varying levels of security as required by large enterprises and service providers. An administrator can grant or restrict access to a specific directory attribute, entry, group, or naming context—once—and naturally expect OID's built-in access control engine to ensure that all information within the directory store is properly protected.

OID supports anonymous binds (for things such as e-mail address lookups when addressing e-mail messages), password-based ldapbind and ldapcompare mechanisms (the norms when an application is using OID to determine whether a client should be permitted access to a resource), and certificate-based binding using Secure Sockets Layer (SSL) v3 (for strong, non-repudiatable authentication and access to highly sensitive or private data).

OID's built-in password policy capabilities enable virtually any corporate security policy to be reflected within the directory. Using a mixture of the password "state" (e.g., how long has it been since the password was last changed) and "value" policies (e.g., are both upper- and lower-case characters being used?), password policies can be created for an entire realm (directory subtree) or for individual entries in the directory.

Beyond these sophisticated password policy management capabilities, OID offers the ability to hash (or render unreadable) any password using a variety of open standards-based schemes. These mechanisms allow administrators to define consistent security policies across applications and comfortably share password "stand-in strings" with other systems.

Often, credentials such as passwords are stored in other places. In these situations, OID knows how to authenticate entries against credentials stored in mapped entries in external sources such as the Microsoft Active Directory, SUN Java System Directory Server, Novell eDirectory, and Open-LDAP. For this, OID provides a configurable "external authentication plug-in."

## Integration

The OID server is implemented as an application running on top of an Oracle10*g* database and effectively leverages the features of the Oracle platform to make it the compelling choice for mission-critical applications. For example, backing up most LDAP v3 directories involves the painstaking creation of standard LDIF flat files from potentially 100,000s of LDAP entries and storing the file on disk or tape. With OID, LDIF files are also an option, but so are fast database backups. Similarly, initial product data importation need not require LDIF files and one-at-a-time entry creation via protocol calls. Instead, OID administrators have the option of using SQL*Loader's fast-path direct-loading capabilities to bootstrap their OID instances.

Within the Oracle Application Server 10*g* environments, OID enables users to be created centrally and shared across components such as Oracle Application Server 10*g* Portal, Oracle Access Manager, Oracle Identity Manager, Oracle Collaboration Suite, Oracle E-Business Suite 11*i*, and others. When users log in, they are authenticated once by the Oracle Application Server 10*g* Single Sign-on Server or by the Oracle Access Manager, having compared the supplied credential with a stored credential found either within the OID or in a repository accessible to the OID. Beyond credentials—user passwords, X.509 v3 certificates, PINS, and other verifiers—OID can store enterprise user and role information for your Oracle9*i* and Oracle10*g* databases, thereby eliminating redundant user schemas and enabling better security management and more seamless access to multiple applications.

All OID installations are accompanied by Directory Integration Platforms, which enable customers to synchronize data between various directories and the OID (a necessary precondition for functions such as configuring an external authentication plug-in). The Directory Integration Platform is a set of services and interfaces that allow the OID to interoperate with third-party directory and metadirectory solutions. Oracle includes agents out-of-the-box for synchronizing OID with Oracle human resources, Oracle9*i* and Oracle10*g* databases, and nearly all other popular LDAP servers—SunONE/iPlanet Directory Server, Microsoft Active Directory, Novell eDirectory, and OpenLDAP.

Using the Directory Integration Platform, customers can use OID as their consolidation "hub" for all enterprise directories needed for global application data from such diverse sources as human resources applications, LDAP directories, and other data repositories. The Oracle Directory Integration Platform (OIDP) has both user and configuration data in the OID, so no additional directory infrastructure is required for this.

## Integration with, and Extensions for, Oracle Environments

OID provides LDAP directory services to a variety of Oracle products and options, such as Enterprise User Security, Oracle Label Security, Oracle Application Server 10*g*, and Oracle Collaboration Suite. So, other Oracle products, such as the Oracle E-Business Suite, that rely on the Oracle Application Server, use OID as well. It is also the preferred product for storing Oracle database service names and, in fact, has replaced Oracle Names for this purpose with version Oracle10*g*.

OID also includes a stand-alone Self-Service Console, a pure Web-based interface allowing end users and application administrators to configure, search for, and manage the data stored with it. A Delegated Administration Service console gives Oracle Application Server 10*g* application administrators a built-in way to deploy end-user self-service in the Oracle environment. Oracle Application Server 10*g* environments naturally know how to store data about users and groups in the OID, so that various kinds of user information stored in local application instances can be guaranteed to reflect a "single source of truth."

Even applications outside the Oracle Application Server 10*g* environment can keep track of changes in user and group data via the OID Integration Platform so that their private user repositories can be kept synchronized with the data in the central directory.

Oracle10*g* Database's Enterprise User Security uses OID and the Directory Integration Platform to enable you to establish Microsoft Active Directory as the source for enterprise user passwords, using a feature called the "Oracle Password Filter for Microsoft Active Directory." This feature synchronizes password changes in the Active Directory with OID enterprise user constructs.

Enterprise User Security can also use the aforementioned server-side-chaining feature as a means of communicating through OID with the Active Directory whenever the database's users are configured to use Kerberos tickets as credentials. This handy combination eliminates the use of passwords altogether, does not require the Directory Integration Platform to be configured, and eliminates the need for the "Oracle Password Filter for Microsoft Active Directory" as well.

## Manageability and Monitoring

OID ships with a Java-based graphical directory administration tool called Oracle Directory Manager, or ODM for short. ODM is used for administration of several operational aspects of OID, such as location of directory metadata, password policies, LDAP schema, and access control information.

Stand-alone deployments of OID and Directory Integration Platform can be monitored using the Identity Management Grid Control; it enables them to be seen in Enterprise Manager alongside all other managed IT components. Deploying the Identity Management Grid Control with Enterprise Manager improves security by simplifying and centralizing the administrative tasks required to monitor and maintain directory services, replication, and integrations in distributed environments. Essential features include a graphical topology viewer, performance monitoring tools, a centralized reporting framework, and process monitors and controls.

Of course, none of this would be possible if OID were not implemented with a comprehensive and efficient Server Manageability infrastructure that gathers the information necessary for monitoring and management of the OID. The information gathered by the Server Manageability infrastructure in OID can be exposed to various industry-standard-monitoring agents and presented to directory administrators through any compatible GUI interface of choice.

## LDAP-Aware Application Development

OID supports the development of custom applications that are natively LDAP-aware by providing C, Java, and PL/SQL APIs. Developers are free to use other toolkits available for popular languages such as PERL and PHP as long as they provide hooks for standard LDAP v2/v3 interoperability.

Within the context of an LDAP command to OID, Oracle provides a *server-side plug-in framework* for you when you want to customize the off-the-shelf LDAP functionality. Examples of this sort of thing include referential integrity of data ("delete group entries corresponding to deleted user entries"), special auditing and report functionality ("log every change to an organization's access-control policy"), customized password policies ("check that changed passwords do not match with any of a list of stop words"), etc. The plug-in framework uses PL/SQL or Java, so user-customized operations can be invoked by the directory server before, during, or after the normal LDAP processing has taken place.

By using the DSML (Directory Services Markup Language) v2 Web service provided by Oracle Virtual Directory (described in the next chapter), developers can access OID via SOAP/HTTP using eXtensible Markup Language (XML).

The rest of this chapter is devoted to several useful procedures in deploying security built around a centralized LDAP infrastructure with OID.

# Implementation Detail

Oracle Enterprise Manager (EM) is the tool of choice for managing the Oracle Application Server and Oracle Database installations. It provides a clean easy-to-use browser-based interface for most management functions. Using EM, the implementer can start, stop, restart, monitor, and configure Oracle server instances and components.

The EM controls run as different processes from the server instances that they control, and need to be started and stopped separately. In a Windows environment, they can be controlled from the Start menu or from the Windows Services panel.

There are three types of Oracle Enterprise Manager 10*g* tools:

Application Server Control Console (ASC) is used to manage the Oracle Application Server and the applications deployed on its framework.

Database Control Console is used to manage Oracle Database instances (and thus the Identity Management Metadata Repository).

Grid Control is an enterprise-management tool with a plug-in framework for managing enterprise applications.

Oracle Directory Manager is a Java-based tool specifically used for administering OID. It enables the implementer to connect to one or more OID instances and to configure and monitor their behavior and performance. Oracle Directory Manager cannot be used to start or stop OID; OID must be running for Oracle Directory Manager to connect to it.

*Note:* The implementer cannot use the Oracle Directory Manager to administer Lightweight Directory Access Protocol (LDAP) directories other than OID.

## *Oracle Identity Management Start Sequence*

Each tier of the Oracle Identity Management (IdM) infrastructure provides services that are relied upon by the tiers above it. For this reason, it is important to start up IdM components beginning from the lower tier; starting an upper tier before a lower tier will result in errors because supporting resources are unavailable. So, the proper start-up sequence is the following:

1. OracleAS metadata repository: Starting the metadata repository involves the start-up of three services—the database listener, the database service, and the EM database control. The implementer can start up the database control at any time, but it is recommended that the implementer start Net Listener before starting the database service.
2. Oracle Internet Directory: To start OID and Middle Tier, start the Oracle Process Manager and Notification Server (OPMN) and the EM Application Server Control Console. OPMN starts up OID by using the OID control (OIDCTL) and starting the OID Monitor (OIDMON). If OID and Middle-Tier applications are deployed on two different machines, start OID first.

## Start Summary

1. OracleAS Metadata Repository
   a. Oracle Database Net Listener
   b. Oracle Database Service: OracleServiceorcl
   c. Oracle Enterprise Manager Database Control
2. Oracle Internet Directory
   a. Oracle Process Manager and Notification Server (OPMN)
      a sub 1. Oracle Internet Directory Monitor (oidmon)
      a sub 2. Oracle Internet Directory Control (oidctl)
   b. Enterprise Manager Application Server Control Console (ASC)
3. Middle-Tier instances
   a. OPMN and ASC

## Stopping Oracle Internet Directory

Because of service dependencies, stop the IdM tiers from the top down, that is, stop OIM components in the following sequence:

1. Middle-Tier instances
   a. OPMN and ASC
2. Oracle Internet Directory
   a. Oracle Process Manager and Notification (OPMN) server
   b. Oracle Internet Directory Monitor (oidmon)
   c. Oracle Internet Directory Control (oidctl)
   d. Enterprise Manager Application Server Control Console
3. OracleAS Metadata Repository
   a. Oracle Database Service: OracleServiceorcl
   b. Oracle Database Net Listener
   c. Oracle Enterprise Manager Database Control

## Changing Password for OID Administrator

By default, the OID Administrator (cn=orcladmin) is assigned the ias_admin password specified during installation. To change the OID Administrator password, choose one of the following three approaches:

Oracle Directory Manager
> Select the root DSE node in the navigation tree, and then select the System Passwords tab.
> Edit the Super User Password field and click Apply.

Use ldapmodify to modify the root DSE by using an LDIF file containing:
> dn:
>> changetype:modify
>> replace:orclsupassword
>> orclsupassword:newpassword

> OID password utility
>> At a command prompt, enter oidpasswd [connect=connect_string] reset_su_password=-true

## Changing Password for Metadata Repository

OID connects to the Metadata Repository using the username ODS. By default, the password for the ODS user is set to the ias_admin password specified at installation. The OID password utility can also be used to change the password for the ODS user; oidpasswd will then prompt for the old and new passwords.

A server can run more than one instance of OID provided the instances run on different port numbers. To configure multiple OID instances, create configuration sets that contain the settings for the different server instances.

Configuration sets include settings for parameters such as the non-SSL and SSL port numbers, type of SSL authentication, maximum number of DB connections, and SASL parameters. These sets are stored according to the type of instances being configured (directory server, integration server, or replication server) under the cn=subConfigSubEntry node of the root DSE.

Governance requires the auditing of critical systems. The OID is designed to be able to log an incredible array of system events.

The primary tool for configuring OID logging is the OID Oracle Directory Manager; command-line tools are available to configure the same settings.

OID provides two logging parameters to provide flexibility in its logging configuration so that the implementer can capture only the desired events:

> Debug logging level—This specifies the level of detail and types of process traces provided in the log. The debug logging levels are binary bit masks represented as decimal values. For Trusted Access, set the debug logging level by adding the following values:
> 256—Connection management, related to network activities
> 8192—Access control list processing
> 8388608—Log of entries, operations, and results for each connection
> 67108864—Number and identity of clients connected to this server
> Operation debug dimensions—This chooses the LDAP operations that will be logged. Again, the dimension values are binary bit masks represented as decimals. So, add the values of the following:
> 511—All LDAP operations
> At a minimum for noncritical repositories

1—ldapbind
2—ldapunbind

Configure OID logging using command-line tools for trusted access compliance.

### Edit via Permanent Configuration

Use ldapmodify to change the orcldebugflag and orcldebugop attributes located in the root DSE node. The debug_level and operations_num parameters are decimal numbers representing the sum of the desired debug levels and operations for logging.

### Monitoring OID Servers for Business Continuity Compliance

OID uses the OID Server Manageability framework to collect performance statistics and to store them in the metadata repository using low-priority processes. Metrics can then be extracted for monitoring and reporting purposes. The implementer must use Application Server Control Console, ODM, or ldapmodify to enable collection of data and to configure parameters such as the frequency of data collection and level of critical events to capture. To view performance metrics, use Application Server Control Console and navigate to the LDAP instance page and the Metrics links there, or use the oiddiag tool to generate a report.

### Backing Up and the Restoring of Metadata Repository

For larger directories, it is generally better to use the backup and recovery tools designed for use with Oracle Database 10*g* to back up and restore the entire database. The Application Server Control Console, in particular, provides an easy-to-use interface for backing up both metadata repository and application server configuration files.

1. From the instance home page, select the Backup/Recovery tab.
2. On the Backup/Recovery page, there are links to configure the backup/recovery process and to perform the backup or recovery.
3. To configure the process, specify the directories for the configuration and the metadata repository backup files for the database.

## Data Integrity Protection

Relational database engines usually store very structured data and protect the integrity of data by verifying data manipulations against the database schema and table keys. In a similar manner, directories have mechanisms to protect the integrity of directory data. OID uses three mechanisms for this:

Attribute uniqueness constraints—These define the attributes that need to be unique (for example, an employee number) and the scope of the uniqueness in the directory.

Directory schemas—These define directory entries as data objects with mandatory and optional attributes that must conform to defined data types and formats.

Referential integrity—When one entry is moved or deleted, attributes of other entries that refer to the source entry are also updated or deleted.

Access control for OID has four special users:

Super-user: Administrator account for OID.
Anonymous user: User assigned to those who bind without specifying a username (if anonymous binds are allowed). Anonymous users have very few privileges.
Guest user: User who is not anonymous but does not have a specific user entry.
Proxy user: User account used for users connected through another authenticated identity (usually a middle-tier application).

## Managing Super-User, Guest User, and Proxy User

Usernames and passwords for these special users can be set using ODM by choosing the System Passwords tab for the OID node. In should be obvious that the super-user and anonymous user present security issues when addressing governance and compliance relating to personally identifiable information.

## Controlling Anonymous Binds

By default, anonymous binds are enabled. For trusted access systems, the implementer should disable anonymous binds in the ODM by navigating to the Allow Anonymous Binds parameter on the System Operational Attributes tab of the OID instance node and changing its value from 1 (enabled) to 0 (disabled). The implementer can also use ldapmodify to modify the orclanonymousbindsflag attribute of the root DSE node.

## Password Storage in OID

Password security is a critical part of any identity-management solution. OID stores a user's password in the userPassword attribute of the user's entry in the DIT.

OID protects passwords using one of the following one-way hashing algorithms:

MD4: 128-bit hash
MD5: Updated version of MD4
SHA-1 (default): 160-bit hash
SSHA: Salted Secure Hash algorithm
SMD5: Salted MD5 algorithm
UNIX Crypt: UNIX encryption algorithm
No encryption: Cleartext storage of password

OID protects user passwords that are stored in the directory by using a one-way hash algorithm (as opposed to a reversible encryption algorithm) to secure them. By default, it uses the SHA-1 algorithm, though the implementer can configure OID to use any of the algorithms to comply with the implementer organization's security requirements. To change the password-hashing algorithm, use ODM or ldapmodify. In ODM, modify the password encryption field on the System Operational Attributes tab of the OID instance node. Otherwise, using ldapmodify, change the orclcryptoscheme attribute of the root DSE node.

## Password Policies

Passwords are often compromised by poor password hygiene. Password policies help to mitigate the problem by requiring passwords that are harder to guess and that are regularly changed. OID supports the following types of password policies.

Password rotation policies:
> Maximum length of time a given password is valid
> Users to change their passwords periodically
> Minimum and maximum time betThe developeren password changes
> Grace period for log-ins after password expiration by time or by number of log-ins
> Users unable to reuse used passwords

Password complexity policies:
> Minimum number of characters a password must contain
> Minimum number of numeric characters required in a password
> Minimum number of alphabetic characters
> Minimum number of repeated characters
> Use of upper and lower case
> Minimum number of special (nonalphanumeric) characters

For additional flexibility, OID allows the implementer to specify different password policies for different DIT subtrees to mirror existing security policies for different parts of an organization.

To apply a password policy to the entries of a subtree (including a subtree consisting of only one entry), add a pwdPolicySubEntry attribute to the root entry of the subtree with a value for the DN of the password policy to be applied. pwdPolicySubEntry is an attribute supported by all structural entries because it is an optional attribute of the top object class.

## Managing Audit Log Entries

- Creating audit log entries: The implementer cannot create audit log entries in the DIT; audit log entries can be created only by the OID server. For example, the implementer cannot create audit log entries using ldapadd.
- Searching audit log entries: Audit log entries are not returned by general searches in the directory. To search for audit log entries, either use ODM and select the Audit Log Management node in the System Objects navigation tree under the OID instance (shown in the slide) or use ldapsearch to perform a search with a base DN of cn=auditlog.
- Purging audit log entries: To purge accumulated audit logs, use bulkdelete with a base DN of cn=auditlog.

## Access Control for DIP Server and Profiles

The Oracle Directory Integration server binds to the directory, both as itself and on behalf of the profile, as follows: When it binds as itself, it can cache the information in various integration profiles. This enables the directory integration server to schedule synchronization actions to be carried out by various connectors. When the directory integration server operates on behalf of a profile, it acts as proxy for the profile—that is, it uses the profile credentials to bind to the directory and perform various operations. The directory integration server can perform only those operations in the directory that are permitted in the profile.

# Directory Replication Groups

OID supports the following types of directory replication groups.

■ Single-master DRG: In this type of DRG, there is only one master replica, which supplies changes to one or more consumers. Clients can update only the master node, and can only read data on any of the consumers. This type of group typically uses LDAP. It is also possible to configure Advanced Replication as single-master DRG by switching all nodes in a group, except one, to the read-only mode.
■ Multimaster DRG: In this type of DRG, multiple OID servers are involved in managing the replication data. Each OID server involved acts as both supplier and consumer. Multimaster replication requires Advanced Replication as its transport mechanism. The full DIT is replicated on each node. Replication is always peer to peer.
■ Fan-out DRG: In this type of DRG, a supplier replicates data to consumers, which in turn supplies it to other consumers. It is also called a point-to-point replication group and has a supplier replicating directly to a consumer. That consumer can then replicate to one or more other consumers. Fan-out replication uses LDAP as its transport mechanism. The replication can be either full or partial. It can be either one-way or two-way.
■ Multimaster replication in conjunction with fan-out replication: This is a combination of both multimaster DRG and fan-out DRG.

## Single-Master DRG

In single-master DRG, there is only one master OID server. LDAP clients and LDAP-enabled applications write and read from the master OID server, and can only read directory data from servers A and B. In single-master DRG, there can be one or more consumers but only one supplier. The replication protocol between OID server is LDAP. This is also sometimes referred to as one-way replication—one node is configured as the supplier and the other as the consumer. The consumer is read-only.

Single-master DRG uses LDAP-based replication or Advanced Replication (by switching all masters in a multimaster configuration except the one to the read-only mode), and updates can be made on the master node (supplier) only, which will be replicated to all other read-only or consumer replicas.

## Multimaster DRG

In a multimaster DRG, all the OID servers that are involved in replication are both suppliers and consumers. An LDAP client or LDAP-enabled application can connect to any of the OID servers in the DRG to read and write directory data. Any change made to any of the OID servers is replicated to the other OID servers. The change is replicated to the other OID servers by using Oracle database replication. A multimaster DRG is also called peer-to-peer or n-way DRG.

## Fan-Out DRG

A fan-out replication group, also called a point-to-point replication group, has a supplier replicating directly to a consumer. That consumer can then supply the same data to one or more other consumers. The replication can be either full or partial and either one-way or two-way. Fan-out DRG uses LDAP-based replication. For one-way fan-out, updates can be made only on the supplier replica and will be replicated to the consumer replica. For two-way fan-out, updates can be made on either replica and will be replicated to the other replica.

## Multimaster and Fan-Out DRG

Multimaster and fan-out DRG is a combination of two replication methods—multimaster and fan-out. In this DRG, some OID servers replicate directory data by using multimaster replication and some by using fan-out replication. The changes from master OID servers are propagated to other OID servers in the multimaster DRG by using Oracle Database Replication. Subsequently, these changes are propagated to the OID servers that are part of fan-out DRGs by using LDAP. OID enables any node in a multimaster replication group to also participate in an LDAP-based replication agreement. The node it connects to using LDAP can, in turn, supply data to other nodes in a fan-out configuration. Within the multimaster replication agreement, data transfer between the nodes occurs by way of Oracle Database Advanced Replication. Within the fan-out replication agreement, data transfer from supplier to consumer occurs by way of LDAP. The LDAP replication agreements can be either one-way or two-way.

Replication configuration details of a replication are stored in the OID server. The objects that store replication configuration details are

- Replication configuration container
- Replica subentry
- Replication agreement

# Oracle Directory Integration Platform

The Oracle Directory Integration Platform (DIP) is a set of services and interfaces that make it possible to develop synchronization solutions with third-party metadirectories and other enterprise repositories, such as Microsoft Active Directory, Novell NDS, and PeopleSoft. With the Oracle DIP, it is possible to build a single directory with a global directory entry containing data

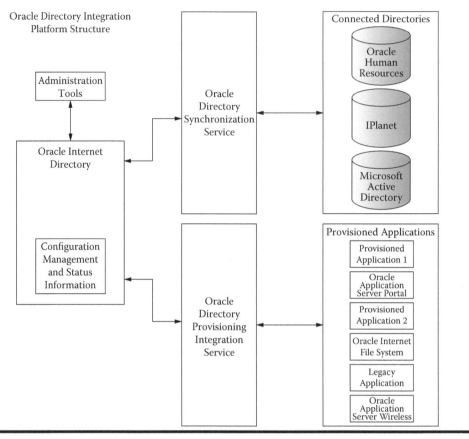

**Figure 7.1  Oracle directory integration platform.**

from such diverse sources as human resources applications, e-mail services, and NOS databases. DIP uses OID as the central store for both user and configuration data, as shown in Figure 7.1.

The following are the DIP components:

- DIP assistant (dipassistant): Migrates large amount of data between directories
- OID provisioning tool (oidprovtool): Used by applications to configure provisioning profiles
- External authentication plug-in:Used for authenticating Windows users when user passwords are available only in the active directory
- Self-Service Console (DAS-based)
- User and group management: Realm, user, and group search base management
- Oracle Directory Manager (ODM): Synchronization profile management
- Access policy management
- Integration and provisioning server: Executes a set of connectors for either synchronizing data or for provisioning user or group information

## Connectors

Supported interfaces include relational DB, LDAP, and tagged or LDIF flat file. Unsupported interfaces, however, require separate agents (e.g., Oracle HR agent), or that they be built separately. The configuration information managed in profile include the profile itself, direction of synchronization, type of interface, mapping rules and formats, and connection details of the connected directory.

Other information:

Directory synchronization service feature function
1. Scheduling: Processing a synchronization profile based on a predefined schedule
2. Mapping: Executing rules for converting data between connected directories and OID
3. Data propagation: Exchanging data with connected directories by using a connector
4. Error handling
5. Synchronization
   ▪ One-way: uses import connector (as seen from OID)
   ▪ Two-way: uses import and export connectors (as seen from OID)
6. Synchronization activities triggered by the OID change log

Directory synchronization service process flow
1. Monitors the change log.
2. Takes action whenever a change corresponds to one or more synchronization profiles.
3. Supplies the appropriate change to all other connected directories whose individual profiles correspond to the logged change.
4. Supplies these changes using the interface and format required by the connected directory.

## How Synchronization Works

Depending on where the changes are made, synchronization can occur as follows:

▪ From a connected directory to OID
▪ From OID to a connected directory

During synchronization, incremental changes made on one directory are propagated to the other. Once synchronization is complete, the information maintained on both directories is the same. Each time the Oracle Directory Synchronization Service processes a synchronization profile, it

1. Retrieves the latest change log number up to which all changes have been applied
2. Checks each change log entry more recent than that number
3. Selects changes to be synchronized with the connected directory by using the filtering rules in the profile
4. Applies the mapping rules to the entry and makes the corresponding changes in the connected directory

## Command Line Tool for Active Directory Synchronization

Dipassistant–gui

Input required: Active Directory host, port

Credentials: Name of the profile to be created

Function: Copies the existing profiles

Populates the required parameters: host, port, credentials, and domain name

Applies the ACIs to the various containers where the users/groups are to be created

Provides the right privileges to the profile for making changes in the directory.

Realm components

User search base (orclcommonusersearchbase)

- Pointer to the users containers in the DIT.
- Default is set to "users" under the default realm.
- Oracle applications look for users in this container.

Group Search Base (orclcommongroupsearchbase)

- Pointer to the groups containers in the DIT.
- Default is set to "groups" under the default realm.
- Oracle applications look for groups in this container.

User Create Base (orclcommonusercreatebase)

- Pointer to the container where DAS creates users.
- Default is set to "users" under the default realm.

Group Create Base (orclcommonusercreatebase)

- Pointer to the container where DAS creates groups.
- Default is set to "groups" under the default realm.

Nickname (orclcommonnicknameattribute)

- Used by single sign-on as the log-in ID.
- Default value is set to "uid".

  *Note:* Active Directory stores both users and groups under the "users" container only.

  Users and groups from Active Directory are usually synchronized under the "users" container in OID. This requires changing the Group Create and Search base attributes.

Supported domain mapping—deployment scenarios

- No mapping
- Both DITs are equivalent.

  One-to-One ( One AD domain–One OID domain )

  Cn=users,dc=oracle,dc=com => cn=users,dc=mycompany,dc=com
- Many-to-One ( Multiple AD domains–One OID domain )

  Ou=ou1, dc=oracle,dc=com => cn=users,dc=myc,dc=com

  Ou=ou2, dc=oracle,dc=com => cn=users,dc=myc,dc=com
- Attribute mappings

  Mapping rules supported: Concatenation   (string a + string b)

  Truncation: Case conversion (uppercase, lowercase)

  Binary and Base 64 conversion

Prebuilt mapping rules are available in

$ORACLE_HOME/ldap/odi/conf/*.map.master files

## Regulatory Compliance Key Feature

Using the DIP server logfile within the ldap log directory, the directory server may be employed as an automated detective control. The location of this is in

```
DIP Server logfile
$ORACLE_HOME/ldap/log/odisrvxxx.log
```

where xxx is the pid of the process that is running. Map it to the Control dashboard for attestation of data flow.

Using the process id and employing an aggregating tool such as Oracle GRC Manager in conjunction with Oracle Access Manager or Oracle Virtual Directory, the operational control and segregation of duties control the domain with regard to data access.

# Oracle Certificate Authority

Oracle Certificate Authority (CA) allows corporations to generate and publish X.509 v3 PKI certificates. The system integrates tightly with Oracle Single Sign-On and OID, and includes a Web-based interface for certificate management and administration. The CA is part of the Identity Management (IdM) solution of, and is designed to make it easy to deploy, public key certificates. Public key infrastructure (PKI) enables secure network transmission and supports secure e-mail, data integrity, and digital signatures. The CA creates and publishes X.509 V3 certificates to support PKI-based authentication methods. The authority is a trusted third party that authenticates the public key owner's identity and validates the connection between the public key and a person through the creation of a certificate. The digital certificates issued by the authority contain the public key and important information about the key owner and the certification authority.

## Process Flow

When an entity wishes to send an encrypted message to another entity, it first contacts the CA and obtains a certificate that authenticates the entity and binds it to its public/private key pair. The entity then sends its encrypted message to another entity along with the digital certificate from the CA. When the CA sends out a digital certificate, it signs it using its private key. Thus, anyone can use the published public key of the CA to verify the CA's signature and thus ascertain the veracity of a certificate. Once the recipient of a message validates the certificate in this way, it can use the certificate owner's public key to send encrypted messages.

## Features Summary of the Certificate

The CA supports open standards X.509 version 3 certificates, which helps in communicating with heterogeneous computing environments. It provides only a few default policy rules to restrict the certificate properties, which a site can easily configure to suit its own PKI requirements. These are restricted to the ITU X.500 certificate format, which supports hierarchical certificate authorities, enabling a subordinate CA installation to obtain certificates from any other standards-compliant

CA. Administrators can use the administrative Web interface of the CA to manage certificate requests and to generate certificate revocation lists (CRLs). Users can use the end-user Web interface to request new certificates, check on the status of their certificate requests, and save the CRL or install it in their browser. Using the Oracle database as the repository, CA automatically provides scalability and high availability benefits, and may be employed for business continuity and availability technical control.

An application authenticating to the single sign-on server can obtain certificates using one of the three methods. An application may use the enterprise Single Sign-On Server authentication to issue certificates to users who have been authenticated automatically by the ESSO Server. This may be employed to relieve an administrator from reviewing and issuing certificates. An application may implement certificate-based authentication through the automatic provisioning of certificates by the CA using ESSO and TLS. This is much less labor intensive than the manual operation of a CA.

## Oracle Certificate Authority Components

Oracle Internet Directory. The OID enables PKI-based single sign-on, and the CA uses the OID to store certificates. The OID enables the CA to simplify certificate provisioning by enabling it to easily publish the certificates it issues to entities contained within it. The OID enables the propagation of certificate information to all connected databases.

The CA consists of two main working components:

- The Registration Authority (RA)
- The Certificate Authority (CA)

The RA is an interface between the CA and the end user and performs tasks such as the verification and certification of entity identification. The RA receives requests to issue new certificates, renew expired certificates, and revoke existing certificates. The RA is responsible for the verification of the requestor's identification and the requestor's privileges to use the supplied identification and public key. Upon verification of the user's credentials and privileges, the RA approves the request (if everything is approved) and sends the request to the CA. The RA consists of the following modules:

- Authorization module: Enforces the privilege requirements for the various certification-related user requests
- Validation module: Validates the security certificates
- Policy module: Enforces the certificate policies created by the CA Administrator

## Using the Certificate Authority

Users request certificates from the CA once they are registered in the OID and authenticated through the single sign-on server. The CA will immediately issue the certificate automatically and provision it in the OID, which enables the SSO to identify the users and fill in the required information in the user's certificate request. This enables future use of the certificate for single sign-on authentication.

## Starting and Stopping the Oracle Certificate Authority

You use the command-line tool ocactl, found in the Oracle Home/bin directory, to start and stop the OracleAS Certificate Authority. First, verify that the following infrastructure components are running:

- Oracle HTTP server
- Oracle Internet directory

The following process uses the opmnctl command to verify that the necessary components are running:

```
$ opmnctl status
```

The OracleAS CA is started by using the ocactl utility. Once you start the Oracle CA, the administrator may access the home page via the following URL:

https://hostname.hostdomain:ssl_port/oca/admin

The port number for the OracleAS CA can be found in the portlist.ini file under the following:

- Oracle Certificate Authority SSL Server Authentication port
- Oracle Certificate Authority SSL Mutual Authentication port

## Certificate Management

The three tabs on the home page correspond to various Oracle CA administrative task areas. Certificate management uses these tabs to manage certificates, for certification requests, and certificate revocation lists. The following tasks can be performed in this screen:

- Viewing certificate details
- Approving and rejecting certification requests
- Searching and listing issued certificates and certificate requests
- Revoking certificates
- Managing the Certificate Revocation List (CRL)

The command line interface include the following:

Starting and stopping the Oracle CA

- Checking the Oracle CA status
- Turning the tracing on and off
- Clearing log information from the Oracle CA database repository

## Policy Enforcement—a Key to Compliance

Using conditional operators such as (==,!=,and), administrators can customize enforcement of policies to meet regulatory mandates. For example, certificate requests coming from the legal department may require different validity periods than certificates coming from the development organization. The predicates can be applied to the certificate policy using the Web administration interface. In addition, multiple predicates can be defined for the same policy rule.

### Predicates in Policy Rules

- Validity rule—Restricts the validity period on new certificates
- Unique certificate constraints—Restricts certificates from being issued to the same name for the same purpose
- RSA key constraints—Restricts the key length used for new certificates
- Trust-point DN custom rule—Prevents the use of trusted certificate chain's DNs in user certificate requests

# Oracle Wallet

An Oracle Wallet is a secure (i.e., encrypted) container for storing private keys and security credentials to safeguard the identity of the client or the server. You can use Oracle Wallet Manager to acquire, use, and store digital certificates. The X.509 version 3 standard is an international standard that defines and provides specifications for the certificates. In this function, Oracle Wallets are logical containers used to store security credentials such as certificates and public/private key pairs. Users store an Oracle Wallet in the OID itself or within the file system. The Oracle Wallet Manager is a GUI interface that users may use to manage the Oracle Wallets. Using the Oracle Wallet Manager, a system administrator may create Oracle Wallets, private keys, and certificate requests—you can download certificates into the Oracle Wallet, upload certificates to the OID directory, and perform other certificate-management tasks. Integrators may use the Oracle Wallet Manager to manage security credentials on the Oracle database and other clients.

Tasks performed using the Oracle Wallet Manager:

- Importing and exporting Oracle Wallets
- Creating new Oracle Wallets and deleting Oracle Wallets
- Generating public/private key pairs and creating certificate requests for submitting to the CA
- Installing certificates
- Configuring trusted certificates
- Opening and closing existing Oracle Wallets
- Uploading and downloading certificates to and from the OID and third-party LDAP directories

Wallets are stored in the $ORACLE_HOME/Apache/Apache/conf/ssl.wlt/default directory.

### Starting Oracle Wallet Manager

On a Windows platform, the administrator starts the Oracle Wallet Manager by going to Start => Programs => 10*g* Home => Integrated Management Tools => Wallet Manager. You start the Oracle Wallet Manager on a UNIX/Linux server using the following command:

```
$ owm
```

****DISPLAY environment variable not set!

Oracle Wallet Manager is a GUI tool, which requires that DISPLAY specify a location where GUI tools can display.

Set and export DISPLAY, then rerun.

```
$ owm
```

To open an existing wallet, select Wallet=> Open from the Menu bar. Once the wallet is opened, you will see it displayed in the directory tree where you opened it. You can save a wallet by using one of the three following options:

- Save in system default—Saves an open wallet to the default directory location and makes it the wallet used by TLS/SSL
- Save as—Saves the open wallet in a new directory location
- Save—Saves the wallet after you make changes to an open wallet

By default, each should return as follows: "Wallet saved successfully in: etc/ORACLE/WALLETS/ Oracle".

## *Uploading Wallets*

To upload a wallet to an LDAP directory, the target wallet must be open, and it must contain at least one user certificate. You can use the directory password to upload the wallet only if the wallet contains a TLS certificate, in which case you must use the TLS Select Wallet> Upload Into the Directory Service option. You must first save the wallet before you can upload it to the OID.

Select Yes to continue with the wallet upload process. At this point, the wallet certificates are checked to see if they are using a TLS key. If at least one certificate has TLS key usage, enter the LDAP directory server name and port information, and click OK. The Oracle Wallet Manager will then use TLS to connect to the LDAP directory server. If none of the certificates are using a TLS key, enter the user's DN, the LDAP server host name, and the port number, and click OK. The Oracle Wallet Manager will connect to the LDAP directory server using simple password authentication.

To download a wallet from the OID, choose Wallet > Download from the directory service. The Oracle Wallet Manager will connect to the OID using simple password authentication.

## Summary

Directories are the operational lynchpins of almost all middleware services. They can contain critical customization information for people, processes, resources, and groups. By placing such information in a common storage area, diverse applications from diverse locations can access a consistent and comprehensive source for current values of key data. A common theme across most Intranet/Extranet applications is the need for directory information about user, system, and organizational objects. The application's requirements can be described very simply: they need to find out who users are, what they are trying to do, whether they are allowed to do it, and how the company wants it done. In technical terms, these requirements are called authentication, certification, access control, profiling, policy representation, and policy or business rule enforcement. Most of the information to support such requirements should be stored in an enterprise directory.

# Chapter 8

# Oracle Virtual Directory

## Overview

Oracle Virtual Directory is a lightweight virtual directory service that accesses and audits identity information (who the user is, what roles they belong to, and what privileges they have) data directly from the sources in real-time rather than storing it in a separate repository. It provides a uniform way to access identity information that may be stored in multiple repositories without needing to synchronize information into a central store as required by a metadirectory. Oracle Virtual Directory allows applications to leverage identity data in place, without synchronizing or moving data from their native locations. As a result, applications can be configured much more quickly to handle dynamic operational scenarios and changing joint, coalition, and interagency user populations. The Oracle Virtual Directory provides a single, consolidated directory interface to identity data—regardless of the type of repository it exists in—without needing to synchronize the information into a central repository. A typical virtual directory deployment is highlighted here in Figure 8.1.

## Benefits

Based on analyst reports and the author's own personal experience, the average organization has identity information in over 100 different repositories. At the same time, most organizations are trying to deploy applications that can make use of this data effectively and efficiently while still meeting the various regulations that govern identity data.

Although this has been a known problem for many years, the original recommended solution, to synchronize all of the identity data into a single repository using a meta-directory, has basically failed. Metadirectories do exist, but they are not complete and can take years to deploy, not to mention the costs of designing, deploying, and maintaining synchronization-based systems.

OVD utilizes an architecture called Direct Data Access, which means the identity data is kept in its authoritative repository and is accessed only when needed. Because it leverages existing data

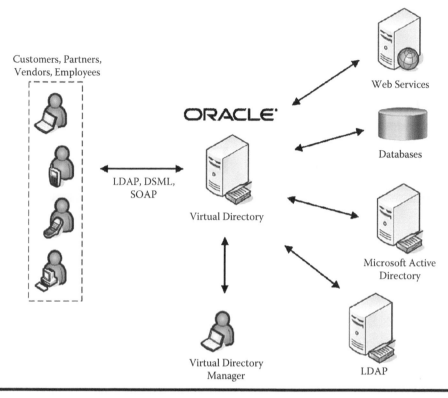

**Figure 8.1 Typical virtual directory deployment.**

and maps this data into required virtual identity structures, it can be deployed much more easily and rapidly. There are a number of OVD customers who have deployed OVD into production in less than 90 days—some have required as few as 30 days.

## Benefits of Deploying Oracle Virtual Directory

Here are a few of the benefits of deploying OVD:

- Decouple client applications for the identity data structure. Through virtualization, an organization has more flexibility in how it chooses to manage its identity information, including changing storage types, storage structure, or even tasks such as adding temporary test user data without affecting primary data stores.
- Virtually consolidate multiple heterogeneous directories into a single consistent view.
- Provide LDAP interface to relational and Web-service-based data stores without synchronization.
- Provide application-specific views of data, including independent schema and directory tree structures.
- Improve security by acting as a directory firewall/proxy.
- Simplify compliance requirements by avoiding synchronizing information and providing a complete real-time view of identity information.

## *Oracle Virtual Directory Scenarios*

Here are reasons why organizations have deployed the Oracle Virtual Directory:

■ LDAP-enabled applications such as portals or SSO products need a single LDAP server, but organization has multiple LDAP servers.

■ Organization wishes to deploy LDAP-enabled applications, but all of its user identity information is managed in relational databases.

■ Organization needs to aggregate data from multiple sources such as directories, databases, and Web services to satisfy application or audit requirements in real-time.

■ Provide application-specific views of data to satisfy application requirements or for better information security.

## *Benefits of Oracle Virtual Directory and Oracle Internet Directory*

Oracle is currently the only vendor that offers a complete integrated directory services stack. A complete directory services stack includes directory storage, directory synchronization, directory virtualization, and directory management.

One question that can come up when viewing Oracle Directory Services is the relationship between Oracle Internet Directory (OID) and Oracle Virtual Directory.

OID provides Internet-scale directory storage, which utilizes the Oracle database to facilitate data integrity, security, and reliability. OID is particularly useful when you need to deploy a directory that requires local storage for several hundred thousand users or more. This is because OID architecture limits the need to replicate data to scale. An example of this type of Internet-scale directory would be a business-to-consumer company (B2C) that needs to store usernames and passwords to provide personalized access to their Web site.

OID is also currently integrated and certified with more legacy Oracle products such as E-Business Suite, though OVD continues to add more certifications. However, most organizations cannot consolidate all of their data into a single directory structure—even one as scalable as OID. This is because the data does not lend itself to easy replacement (for example, if you run Windows, you cannot replace Active Directory), regulatory requirements (certain regulations prevent you from copying certain types of data into single source), or data politics (the fight that results from who "controls" the data when a copy is made). Also, it is almost impossible to come up with a single schema to meet all of an organization's attribute requirements while still maintaining data security and retaining flexibility for future application data requirements.

Because of OVD's architecture and capabilities, these issues can be avoided.

For example, the use of direct data access means that issues pertaining to maintaining multiple copies of identity data are avoided. The problems of determining a single schema and security requirements are avoided because OVD can provide application-specific views of the identity data, including completely different Directory Information Trees (DITs) for different applications from a single OVD service. Finally, because of these capabilities, OVD makes it quicker and easier to deploy, without requiring external consultants just to deploy the solution.

# Deployment Architecture

Now that you understand why you would want to use a virtual directory, this section will cover the Oracle Virtual Directory architecture.

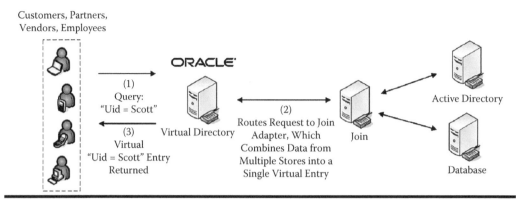

**Figure 8.2 Virtual directory data flow.**

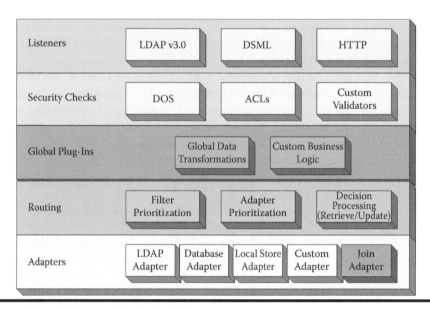

**Figure 8.3 Virtual directory logical architecture.**

Figure 8.2 shows an example of OVD data flow. In this example, an LDAP client application has issued an LDAP search to find the user entry with the uid value of "scott". In this hypothetical example, imagine that the data for "scott" is contained in two stores: Microsoft Active Directory contains his username, but the HR database contains the rest of the identity information.

Figure 8.3 provides a high-level, conceptual view of how OVD is deployed in an organization. Directory-enabled applications connect to OVD as if it was any other LDAP server, and then OVD translates those requests into requests to the authoritative data stores. It then consolidates, transforms, and normalizes the data before sending it to the client. Although this does sound like a lot of overhead, in reality it is not.

This is because OVD is most often deployed in the same data center as its authoritative sources, and these sources are already highly optimized systems with fast network connections and their own embedded caching systems. OVD in most cases only needs to make a single request to fetch the data, and OVD's own processing of the data is on average under 25 ms.

If necessary, OVD can be deployed with an in-memory cache, though it is most often unnecessary because the data sources themselves have their own optimized caches; so any additional cache actually causes more delay!

OVD gets the request, looks up the user in Active Directory, and once the scott user is found, it will then fetch the rest of the attributes from the HR database, combine them, and return them to the user.

The data is combined using a join adapter. A join adapter is similar in concept to a SQL join: it combines data from two or more data stores into a single virtual entry. By virtual entry we mean an entry that only exists on demand—the data is not synchronized into any other data store before sending it back to the client. OVD provides several out of the box rules—the one most often used is to combine entries based on a single shared attribute like uid, but it is also possible to write your own.

# Installation and Configuration

In this section, we will learn how to install and configure OVD. One of the real benefits of OVD is that it can most often be deployed without the need for outside consultants. All that is needed is a very basic understanding of LDAP concepts, the data stores to connect to, and of course, the credentials to connect to the data stores.

## *OVD Components*

Oracle Virtual Directory has two components: a server and a management client called Oracle Virtual Directory Manager. The OVD Server provides all of the functionality that has been discussed earlier in this chapter. It is a Java-based application and runs on the most popular operating systems including Microsoft Windows and Linux as well as Solaris, AIX, and HP-UX. The current management client is based on the Eclipse Rich Client Platform framework and runs on Microsoft Windows or a Linux Workstation that has Gnome or KDE installed on it.

You can download OVD from OTN. Follow the instructions on the OTN site on how to properly unpack the Unix/Linux distributions.

## *OVD Server*

Start the OVD Server installation for your platform. As of 10.1.4 OVD the installer was still based on its preacquisition installer, so the installation process is slightly different than other Oracle applications that use the Oracle Installer.

The first screen will ask you where to install OVD server in your server's file system. The next screen will ask you what port to run the OVD Administration service on. By default this port is 8888 and is set to be secured by SSL; you can optionally limit the admin service to a specific IP address. The OVD Administration service is a set of Web services used by the OVD Manager client.

The next screen will ask you what port to run the initial LDAP listener on. Its default choice is port 389 and set to non-SSL; you can also limit which IP address the LDAP listener is available for. You can add other LDAP listeners (for example, it is common to have one non-SSL and one-SSL enabled listener) post installation. If you want to run the initial listener as SSL, change the port number to 636.

The next screen asks if you want to run any of the default HTTP services such as DSML or the Web Gateway. DSML, which stands for Directory Services Markup Language, is a protocol for querying LDAP servers using XML. The Web Gateway is an XSLT-based Web application that can be used to provide an out of the box White pages service. By enabling the Web gateway, it will also enable the generic OVD HTTP listener, which would allow you to deploy your own custom Java servlet—for example, to deploy a customized Web service. You can leave them disabled by default.

The next screen will ask you to specify the default root RDN for your directory tree. This is used by OVD to set up initial ACLs. It is recommended that the default be changed from dc=MyCompany,dc=com to dc=com. Change dc=com to the proper ending element if your tree will not end in dc=com. Other examples could be dc=uk, o=Oracle, or c=US.

If you selected to SSL-enable the admin service port (the default setting), OVD will generate a self-signed certificate. To do this, it needs to collect some information. Leave the name "localhost" and click next. Then fill in the fields OVD asks for and click next.

The installer will then install OVD.

After the installer finishes, you can start OVD. On Windows, it will install itself as a service (default OViD_8888) and on Unix systems, you start OVD by typing `vde.sh start` on a command-line prompt while in the OVD home directory.

## Installing OVD Manager and Connecting to OVD Server

The OVD Manager is written using the Eclipse framework. Eclipse is more commonly known for being a popular Java integrated development environment (IDE); however, it was designed to facilitate the development of desktop-based applications as well. The original goal of the OVD Manager was to allow for easy system management of the virtual directory while also making it easy to extend OVD's functionality through the use of OVD's Java-API- and Python-based bidirectional mappings.

OVD Manager installation is rather simple; once you start the installer, it asks where you want to install the OVD Manager. The default on Windows is "C:\Program Files\Oracle\Ovid Manager". After you install OVD Manager, start the management client.

Before you can connect to an OVD server, you must create an OVD Server Project. This is because the Eclipse framework is project based (an artifact of its IDE origins). To do this, choose File->New->Directory Management Project. Call it "OVD 1".

Next, you create an OVD Server instance within this project by choosing File->New->Virtual Directory Server.

Ensure that the document folder is set to OVD 1, and give the server name as "OVD 1"v. The Manage Existing Server box should be checked—this is the default. Enter the hostname and admin port (8888 is default), the Admin DN (cn=Admin is default), and the admin password. Finally, check the Secure box, and this will bring up a screen for you to validate the SSL certificate that was generated during OVD installation.

Now click Finish; this will create the Virtual Server administrative instance within OVD Manager and connect the OVD Manager to the server.

In OVD 10.1.4 the server configuration files are maintained in a set of XML files. A copy always exists in the OVD Manager and the server. And the files can be restored to the server from the OVD Manager or vice versa.

You can also manage multiple OVD servers in OVD Manager, either in their own projects or within a single project. You can use drag and drop copy to copy configuration from one server to another server within the same project. This is most often used to rapidly deploy multiple servers in an OVD server cluster.

After starting OVD Manager again, you will need to connect to the OVD server before you can do any monitoring or server changes. To do this, right-click on the OVD server you wish to connect to. Then choose "Connect to Server," enter your OVD admin password, and click OK.

## OVD Manager

Figure 8.4 displays the virtual directory manager interface that DVD Manager provides to a comprehensive toolset to manage OVD and provide basic service monitoring.

OVD Manager follows the standard Eclipse pattern of having a navigation system in the left panel, and most of the tasks are performed in the right main panel. The left-side panel provides a tree-based navigation system called Server Navigator. The right side of the screen is primarily reserved for providing the configuration/administration tasks. However, the right-side panel also provides navigation tasks specific to a server, whereas the Server Navigator window lets you more easily move between servers.

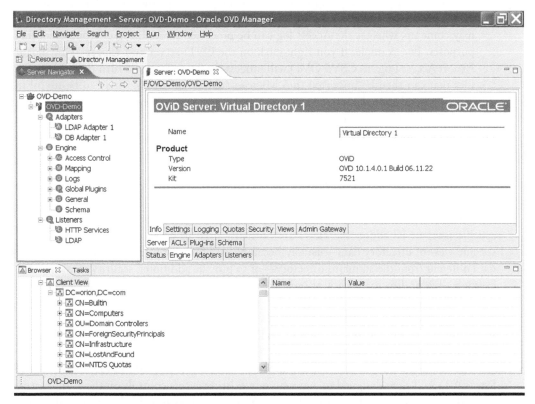

**Figure 8.4   Oracle virtual directory manager.**

Status tab: The Status tab provides a real-time view of activity on the OVD server. It shows the current number of connections coming from authenticated and anonymous clients, where the IP addresses connections are coming from, and activity on the active OVD adapters.

Engine tab: The Engine tab provides management tasks for the core service layer of the product.

Server tab: The Server subtab provides access to core server logic. This includes the following further subtabs.

Info tab: The primary purpose of this tab is to tell you the OVD version information, which can be useful for support if you need to file a service request. It has a License section, which is a legacy field because the OctetString version of the product used a license key—Oracle does not use license keys.

Settings tab: The Settings tab allow you to specify which OVD schema files you wish to enable. By default OVD's schema resembles the original University of Michigan standard LDAP schema. However, you could choose by default to appear as another directory server type; for example, you could choose to make the OVD schema appear as Microsoft Active Directory schema. This screen also lets you choose to enable or disable Access Controls. The Root DN field is only used in cases where you are using OVD as a LDAP proxy/firewall for a single directory service, which includes proxying the LDAP server's Root DSE object. Please note that Replication is currently not supported by OVD, so those fields can be ignored.

Logging: OVD currently uses the Apache Log4J logging system. This logging includes a service log (VDE General Log) and an access log that logs the client connections and basic operations. The general log is most often used to troubleshoot any problems that may come up, whereas the Access log can be processed for auditing or troubleshooting purposes. For example, if you right-click on the OVD server and choose "Download/ Export Access Logs to CSV," OVD will process the access logs and turn them into CSV files that can then be imported into Microsoft Excel for review. This can be useful in showing trend analysis or in identifying whether you have a client application that is not properly closing connections.

Quotas: The Quotas tab allows you to restrict the number of connections and operations a client may perform against OVD. This is often used to provide a directory firewall type of functionality.

Security: The primary use of the Security tab is to specify an LDAP URL to identify a group of users' accounts that can perform OVD administrative functions.

Views: Views are an OVD mechanism to allow you to restrict access to specific adapters to specific users or IP addresses. Views are normally used to either provide an application-specific view of directory data—usually because that application needs a view of directory data different from the standard directory—or to provide additional security measures. For example, if your directory contains sensitive information and you wish to limit access to it, you could create a view that in conjunction with the proper OVD ACLs and adapter configuration provides a multilayered firewall to access this data.

Admin gateway: This tab is to allow you to update any configuration information in regard to the Admin gateway HTTP interface.

ACLs: The ACLs subtab allows OVD Administrators to create and edit OVD access control lists. OVD ACLs are designed to augment any existing access controls on the authoritative data. They support all of the modern features of ACLs such as applying by branch, attribute, by IP address, account name, and group membership.

Plug-ins: This subtab lets you manage global plug-ins and mappings. These will be covered later in the chapter.

Schema: This subtab manages OVD schema attributes and object classes.

Adapters: This tab is used to manage individual adapters. OVD uses adapters to connect to the authoritative data stores. There are several types of adapters:

LDAP connects to practically any LDAP-v3-compliant directory service, including Microsoft Active Directory

Database connects to any database that provides a JDBC driver

NT adapter connects NT 4 domain controllers

Custom adapter—primarily used to expose in-house services such as Web services or EJBs as LDAP that cannot be accessed

Local store adapter—can be used to store relatively small (<100,000 entries) of data. Primarily used for development and testing environments. If an organization needs true directory-based storage, Oracle Internet Directory is the preferred option. Both OVD and OID are part of the Oracle Directory Services suite.

Join view adapter—combines two or more data stores virtually together using a Join rule such as a shared attribute value between each system. This is useful when, for example, part of a person's entry exists in one data store and part in another, but client applications wish to see a complete picture of the person's record.

Each adapter instance has three common tabs, which are described as follows.

Config: The Config subtab allows for general configuration of the data store. The name of the adapter is how it is referenced in the OVD Manager administrative interface, whereas the Root value specifies the directory namespace exposed to OVD clients. The Active checkbox allows OVD administrators to enable and disable individual adapters without having to actually remove the adapter from service. There will also be configuration settings specific to each adapter. LDAP and database adapter configuration will be discussed later in this chapter.

Routing: This subtab is standard regardless of the adapter.

It is divided into three sections: Selection, Attribute Flow, and General Settings.

Selection: The Priority option defines the order in which this adapter should be processed if multiple adapters are used. The Filters to Include allows managers to specify which type of LDAP filters should only be used for this adapter. Filters to Exclude lets managers specify which types of LDAP queries are not allowed. DN Matching helps specify which types of DNs are used for this adapter and Levels specify how many levels deep a search is allowed to proceed on this adapter.

Attribute flow: The Retrievable Attributes field can be used to restrict the attributes that can be retrieved from this attribute. If left empty, any attributes can be retrieved (whether they can be returned or not to the client is further controlled by OVD ACLs). This is useful, for example, if you have sensitive information in the data store mixed with public information. You could, for example, restrict access to just name attributes. Any attributes that are not listed are completely hidden from the client.

The Storable Attributes field can be used to limit the attributes that can be stored in the adapter (assuming all other access conditions are met). If it is empty, all attributes are allowed. If the assigned value is "None", no attributes at all can be updated.

The Unstoreable attributes field is used when the administrator wants all attributes but a specific few to be allowed to be updated.

General settings: The Visibility option is the most common value set in the Routing tab. If left at Yes, then when an LDAP client queries the Root DSE object, it will show this adapter's Root namespace as one of the namespaces available to clients. If set to No, then it is still available for clients to search, but not as a namespace. This is useful when you wish to have virtual DIT, because it allows you to make your adapters appear as branches of another adapter, even from different sources and, of course, without any synchronization. The internal visibility option means the adapter is only searchable by the Join adapter and plug-ins. This is primarily used by adapters that are intended to only be visible via Join View adapter instances.

The Views section lets you choose which views the adapter is visible to. By default it is available to the Default view.

Bind Support allows you to choose whether this adapter supports Binds or not.

Criticality allows you to define how you want errors to be handled. If left as default, then any operation that affects this adapter will affect its availability (for example, if the LDAP server is down for maintenance, then OVD will throw an error message). If set to false, operations will always succeed if another adapter can provide results. Finally, if set to partial, then data will be returned from other servers, but a "partial results set" error will be returned.

Include Binds From is used in cases when a user account exists in multiple adapters and you wish to allow a user authenticated in a different adapter to allow OVD to transparently use those credentials to connect to another adapter.

Exclude Binds From is used to tell the adapter to ignore bind requests that map to the namespaces for other adapters. This is most useful when one adapter namespace is under another and you want to prevent the parent adapter from intercepting the bind request, which would most likely cause an "incorrect bind failed" message.

Plug-ins: This is similar to the Global Plug-Ins covered earlier. Specific plug-ins and mapping behavior will be covered later in this chapter.

Listeners: Listeners are the connection points that clients communicate with. Currently, OVD supports HTTP(S) and LDAP(S) listeners. Common options for listeners are:

Lister Name—is the name for the listener in OVD Manager

Host Address—is used to restrict the socket to listen on a specific IP address/hostname on a multi-homed system. By default it will listen for any requests on all IP address/hostnames on the server.

Host Port—is the port used for the listener

Threads—the number of threads used to process incoming connections. Default is 10, which is fine for test and proof of concept, but 50 is more commonly used in production.

Secure—check box tells OVD whether this listener is SSL enabled or not.

Server Key Alias—lets you change the SSL certificates used for the SSL, which allows you to use one certificate for admin services and another for clients.

Server navigator: Most of the Server Navigator options are the same as described earlier, though there are a few additional options.

Server status: These include visual cues regarding the status of the server.

Once connected to the server, active adapters and listeners will have green arrows next to their names. If they are down or inactive, they will be red.

Export logs: OVD Manager allows you to download the OVD server log files to the OVD Manager workstation for easier viewing—in particular, if the administrator does not have command-line access to the server.

It can also process the Access logs into CSV format for easier importing into other applications for reporting purposes.

One-step configurations: OVD 10.1.4 added a new feature that had been in the design stage when Oracle acquired OctetString (which created the initial virtual directory product). This was the One-Step Configuration task wizards. These wizards simplify the setup of common OVD deployment tasks such as configuring OVD to be used as a Microsoft Active Directory firewall. It is planned that a future version will add additional one-step configuration tasks such as preparing OVD to be used with Oracle Access Manager.

## A Simple OVD Deployment

This section will discuss how to deploy a simple OVD. The assumption is that the example organization will have the following:

Microsoft Active Directory containing employees, which will be connected via LDAP adapter
Oracle Database containing customer records connected via Database adapter

The virtual directory topology will be as follows: the Active Directory will be considered to be the "root" of the Directory Information Tree (DIT), and the customer database will be deployed as a branch.

### Connecting to Active Directory via LDAP Adapter

Figure 8.5 illustrates the LDAP configuration screen and the steps to connect an LDAP server.

Here are the steps to connect an LDAP adapter (the steps are basically the same regardless of the type of LDAP server):

Start OVD server.
Start OVD Manager.
Connect to the OVD server.
Right-click on the OVD server instance, and choose New->LDAP Adapter.
Choose the template "Microsoft Active Directory." Templates can be used to deploy preconfigured options for different directories, though out of the box only the templates designed for Oracle Access Manager (they have an OAM prefix) currently take advantage of this.
Give it an Adapter Name of "AD". In production this can be the administrator's choice; it is used only to reference it in the OVD Manager, Join View Adapter, and custom plug-ins that need to operate on specific adapters.
DNS Host Discover option is used if an organization's DNS deployment maintains LDAP SRV records. OVD can leverage either the standard DNS or Microsoft's Dynamic DNS option. The default is No.

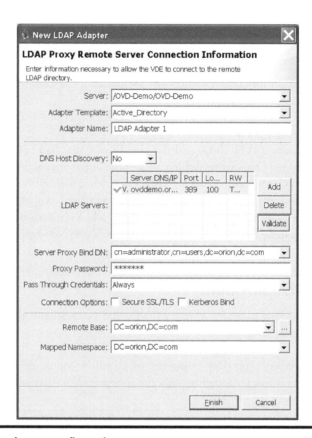

**Figure 8.5** **LDAP adapter configuration.**

Click the Add button to add a server. Enter the hostname or IP address and the port. The Load % field is used if there are multiple LDAP servers. OVD provides load balancing between multiple LDAP servers and will default to evenly splitting the load. An administrator can adjust the load by giving a higher percentage to one server and lower percentage to another. The RW field is a Boolean field that dictates if a server is Read/Write capable (True—which is the default) or only Read capable (R/W set to False). The latter is used if there are read-only replicas deployed in the organization.

Next are the Server Proxy credentials. These credentials are used by OVD for anonymous connections or when it cannot pass the client that is connected to OVD credentials to the back-end directory. This could happen if the client communicating with OVD is authenticated to another adapter (regardless of whether it is LDAP or database or custom) and does not have any credentials to connect to the server managed by this adapter.

The Pass Through Credentials option tells OVD when to attempt to pass through credentials to the servers connected through this adapter. The default is Always. BindOnly is used when the LDAP adapter is setup to use Kerberos authentication and Never is primarily used when clients are authenticating to OVD via digital certificates, because there is no way in the current PKI architectures to pass the client certificate directly to the back-end source to authenticate the end user.

The next field is the Remote Base field. This field specifies where in the LDAP server's tree to connect to; for this example, assume it is the AD base, such as "dc=orion,dc=com."

The Mapped Namespace field allows administrators to choose how this adapter will present its namespace to OVD clients. This can be different from the Remote Base; however, for this example, it will be the same.

Once the data is entered, click OK.

The adapter should now be in the OVD Manager Server Navigator. There should be an asterisk "*" next to the adapter's name. The asterisk means the OVD Manager configuration has something new to update to the OVD server.

Right-click on the OVD server instance, and choose "Save to Server."

## Connecting to Database

Figure 8.6 displays an example of the attribute database mapping when connecting virtual directory to a relational data store.

The OVD Database adapter supports connecting to practically any relational database that has a JDBC driver. For this example, the steps shown are for an Oracle 10g database using the standard Oracle OE example schema:

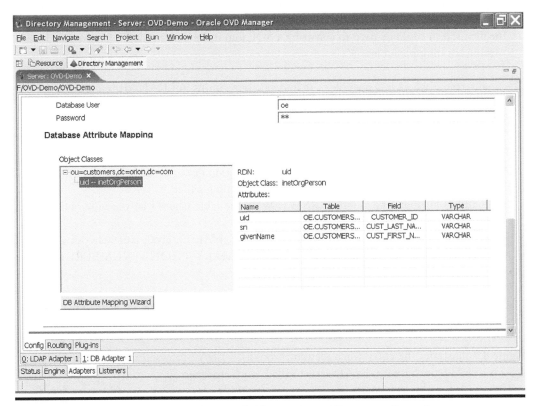

**Figure 8.6   Database adapter—database field to LDAP attributes configuration.**

The first step is to deploy the proper JDBC libraries. Oracle JDBC drivers can be found at http://www.oracle.com/technology/software/tech/java/sqlj_jdbc/index.html.

After connecting to the OVD Server instance, right-click on the server instance and choose Manage->Server Libraries.

Click on the Select New button.

Choose the proper JDBC JAR files.

Click Deploy.

Right-click on the server instance, and choose New->Database Adapter.

Leave the template as Default.

Give this a name of "OE."

Set the Adapter suffix to "ou=customers,dc=orion,dc=com." This will make this a virtual branch under the LDAP adapter configured in the previous section.

Select use Pre-Defined Database.

Select the type of database to connect to. For this example, it is Oracle Thin driver.

Enter a hostname and port.

Enter the Database name (e.g., Oracle Database SID value).

Enter a schema username and password. For this example, it is the default oe/oe values.

Then click validate. OVD server will validate that it can connect to the database.

Then click next.

The next screen shows the possible schema and table/views that can be used. Select the OE.CUSTOMERS_VIEW view.

The next screen could be used to construct a SQL join if the data needed to be exposed is contained in multiple tables.

The final screen is where it is possible to map database columns to LDAP attributes.

Select the namespace listed on the screen, and click the Add button.

For object class enter "InetOrgPerson."

For RDN value enter "uid" and click OK.

Next, select the new child of the "ou=customers,dc=orion,dc=com" namespace.

Click the Add button under the Field/Attributes mapping panel.

Select uid as attribute, CUSTOMERS_VIEW as the table (should be the only option), and column CUST_EMAIL.

Repeat the same process for sn (choose CUST_LAST_NAME), givenname (choosing CUST_FIRST_NAME), telephonenumbe (choosing PRIMARY_PHONE_NUMBER), and userpassword (choosing CUSTOMER_ID).

After completing the mapping, click OK.

Click on the OE adapter's Routing tab and go to the Visibility setting; set it to "No."

Right-click on the OVD server instance and save to server.

Figure 8.7 illustrates the entry when viewed through an LDAP browser; it now looks as though there is a child branch under the AD server called "ou=Customers."

By creating multiple adapters in this way, it effectively creates a union of identity data from multiple sources. In the next section it will be shown how it is possible to combine data from multiple sources into a single view using OVD Join Adapter.

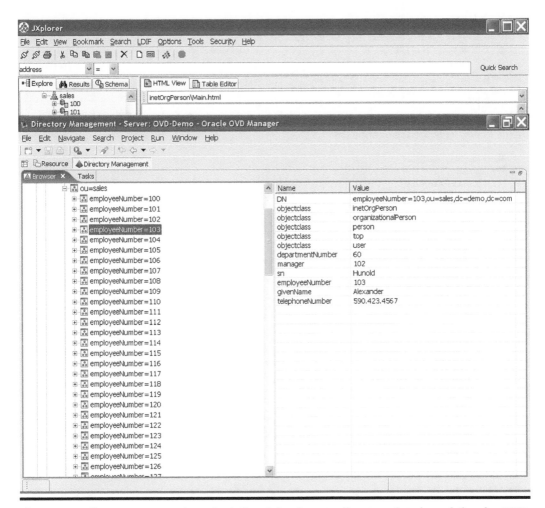

**Figure 8.7 Illustrates conversion of relational database to directory data in real-time by OVD.**

## Join Adapter

Imagine this scenario: part of the customer's record exists in the Active Directory server and another part exists in the customer database. However, the directory-enabled applications need all this data in a single record to make decisions.

The OVD Join View Adapter is designed for this kind of scenario.

With the Join View Adapter, it is possible to link entries from two or more sources into a single virtual entry. The joins are constructed using a Join Rule. There are built-in rules such as Simple Join Rule, and it is possible to construct custom rules.

The most common way to build a Join adapter is to link entries using the Simple Join Rule. This rule links entries together using a shared attribute value very similar to a simple SQL join. For example, the values of employeeid in one adapter and the empid in another adapter may be the same. Thus OVD could link them together on the fly.

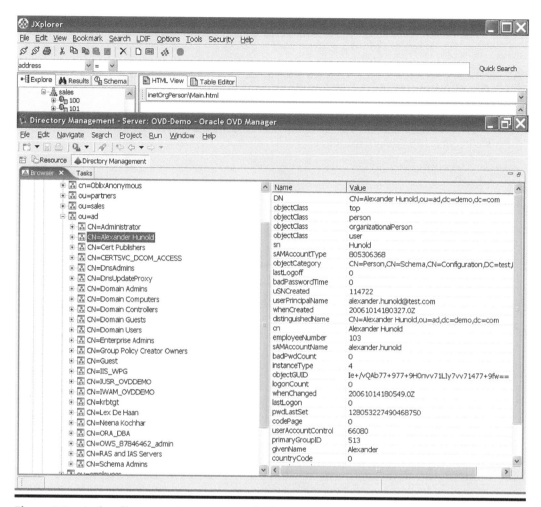

**Figure 8.8  Active directory view as source for join adapter.**

And the final figures (Figure 8.8 to 8.10) show the results of combining data from Active Directory and HR database. In this case, the givenname, sn, uid, and telephone attributes come from the HR database, whereas cn, givenname, sn, and uid come from AD. Microsoft proprietary attributes are removed from this shot to make it easier to read.

# OVD Bidirectional Mappings and Plug-Ins

OVD is a very versatile and flexible system not only because of its direct access technology but also because of its plug-in and bidirectional mapping frameworks.

Here is some of the functionality these frameworks can provide:

■ Rename attributes and object classes such as transforming Microsoft Active Directory entries into standard InetOrgPerson entries
■ Hide particular attributes from being returned based on business rules

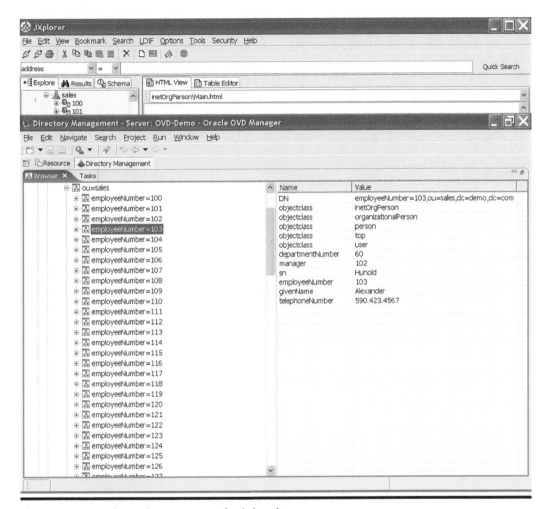

**Figure 8.9   Database view as source for join adapter.**

■ Guaranteeing that only one entry with a particular uid value is returned even if that user exists in multiple data stores
■ Caching search results

## Bidirectional Mapping

The bidirectional mapping framework allows simple transformations of attribute names and values. Most mapping deployments leverage one of the mappings provided out of the box either as is or by adjusting a configuration parameter. In the rare cases when a new mapping is needed, it should be pointed out that mappings use the Jython variant of the Python language as a simple scripting language. Mapping functionality is a subset of the plug-in functionality and most customers who edit the mappings have no previous Python experience. And there is no need to become a Python expert either, because the entire mapping grammar ultimately comprises less than 10 functions and most new mappings are derivatives of existing mappings, which further simplifies the work.

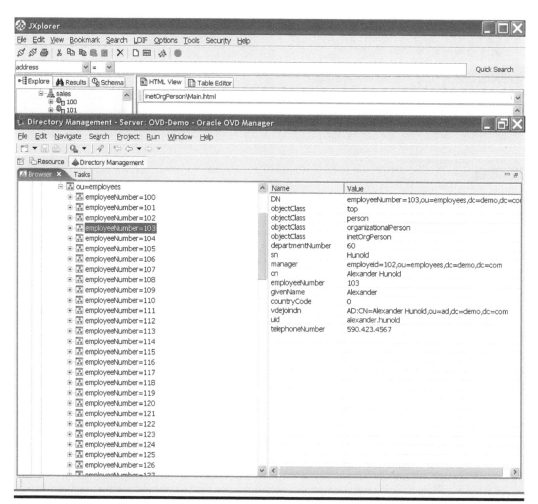

**Figure 8.10** **Completed join view—consolidated attributes from multiple sources without synchronization.**

## *Java Plug-In Framework*

The Java Plug-In Framework can do everything a mapping can, plus more—such as creating custom adapters to connect to Web services, rerouting requests to different adapters based on custom business logic, and synchronizing updates across multiple data stores during an LDAP update.

Although plug-ins are written in Java, do not get the impression that writing Java plug-ins is as complex as writing a J2EE application. Plug-ins are generally confined to a single class and often even limited to implementing a single method with a total code size of well under 100 lines of code. Even a novice Java developer can usually write an OVD plug-in very quickly. As with mappings, there are a number of inbuilt plug-ins available out of the box, and many implementations are able to go live without the need for any custom development.

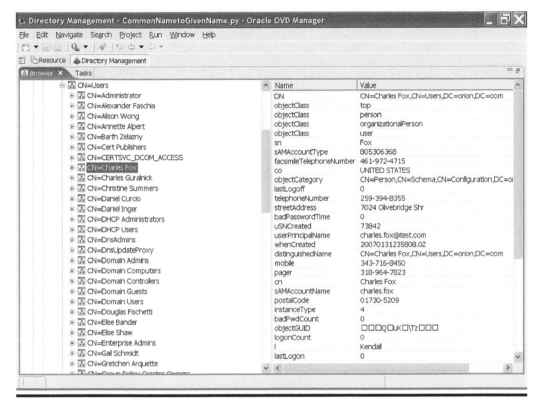

**Figure 8.11   Active directory view prior to transformation.**

## *Example: Data Transformation*

The next set of figures demonstrate data transformations using the example mappings included in OVD.

The first mapping in Figure 8.11 and Figure 8.12 shows an example of transforming Microsoft Active Directory from its proprietary *user* schema to the standard *inetorgperson* schema.

The next set of mappings (Figure 8.13 to Figure 8.15) show how to solve the use case of where a database may only have data to provide givenname (e.g., first name) and sn (e.g., last name) attributes and you want the entry to have a cn (e.g., full name) attribute.

## Regulatory Governance Mapping

Oracle Virtual Directory helps meets regulatory compliance through the following mechanisms:

- Direct Data Access—avoiding copying data into a single repository
- Application Specific Views—can limit what attributes are available to applications on an application basis—even hiding the data from the LDAP schema
- Identity Data Firewall—can restrict specific queries; monitor, and send alerts on, out-of-policy behavior; and provide an audit trail

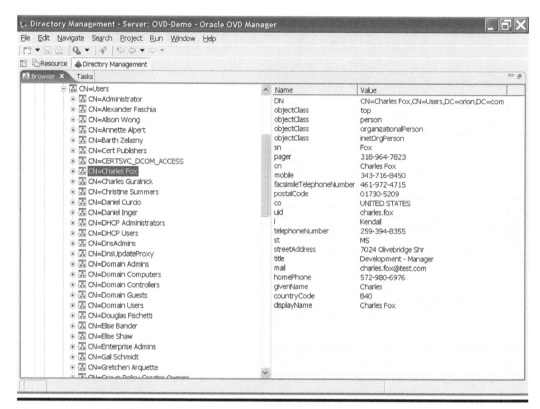

**Figure 8.12   Active directory data transformed in real-time to InetOrgPerson.**

- Data Transformation Support—can hide attribute names, attribute values, encrypt values, and even hide entries on a dynamic, policy-driven basis
- Provides a real-time complete view of identity data—when an auditor needs to see all of the person's identity information, OVD can provide a real-time view of this information in a much quicker and simpler fashion than a synchronization-based solution

## Summary

Organizations have identity information stored in multiple sources (the average number of sources is 100), and they are deploying applications that need to leverage a consolidated view of that identity information through standard protocols such as LDAP. These applications can be portals, single sign-on, J2EE, .Net, or even database-based applications such as Oracle Database Vault. Oracle Virtual Directory provides a fast, flexible, and easy-to-deploy solution that does not require any additional synchronization and leverages existing infrastructure investments, providing a greater ROI. Because it can connect to directories and databases while providing the capability to either view this data as a join or a union on an application-specific basis, it has become a secret weapon for many system integrators and architects. Finally, through the use of Direct Data Access, a strong security model, and data transformation capabilities, OVD allows organizations to more easily meet their regulatory requirements.

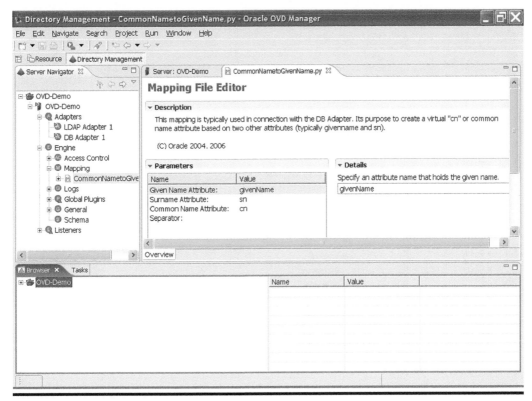

**Figure 8.13** CN mapping configuration screen.

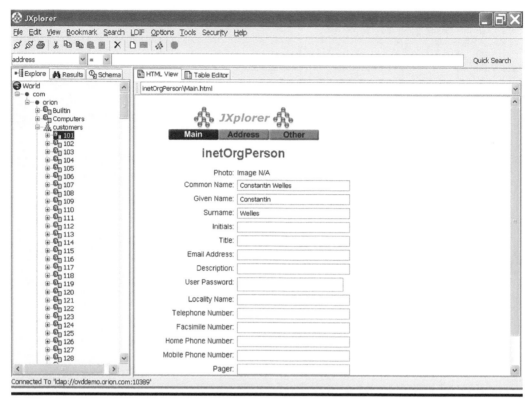

**Figure 8.14   Database entry prior to mapping.**

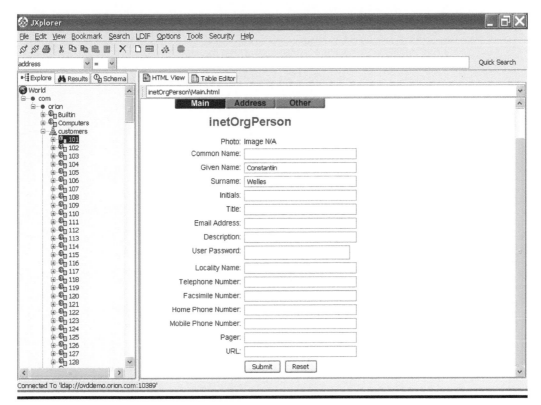

**Figure 8.15   Database entry post mapping.**

*Chapter 9*

---

# Oracle Security Developer Tools

---

Security Developer Tools include standards-based implementations of XML and Web services security protocols necessary to secure a Service Oriented Architecture (SOA)—a set of technologies and methodologies for accessing resources across a network. Security and interoperability are necessary requirements when resources are made accessible across heterogeneous networks. OracleAS Security Developer Tools programmatically allow a developer to extend the security of Oracle Application Server and Oracle Identity Management.

## Overview

Security tools are a critical component of any application development project. Each of these Java-based toolkits provides intuitive APIs. Oracle Security Developer Tools secures the application server with two Java libraries:

■ Oracle XML Security enables secure and interoperable exchange of data with an implementation of the World Wide Web Consortium (W3C) XML Signature and Encryption specifications, including Triple DES, AES-128, AES-256, AES-192, RSA-v1.5, RSA-OAEP, Diffie–Hellman, SHA1, SHA256, SHA512, RIPEMD-160, and Base64.
■ Oracle Web Services Security (WSS) provides a framework for authentication and authorization using existing security technologies as outlined by the Organization for the Advancement of Structured Information Standards (OASIS) specification for Web services security and supporting Username, X.509, and SAML Token Profiles.

### *Deployment of Cryptographic Architecture*

Cryptographic libraries are illustrated below in Figure 9.1. Cryptography is the basis of all modern data protection and is the foundation of modern non-repudiation and access control. The

155

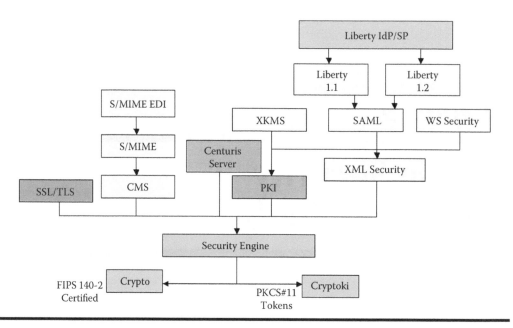

**Figure 9.1 Cryptographic libraries.**

cryptographic architecture serves as a preventative technical control when deployed within an infrastructure.

Oracle Crypto is a pure Java library that provides core cryptography algorithms. These APIs provide the developer with the tools necessary to build secure applications. A complete set of symmetric and asymmetric ciphers are included, along with signing, encryption, hashing, and pseudorandom number generator algorithms.

Oracle Crypto FIPS is a NIST-certified cryptographic module. The National Institute of Standards and Technology (NIST) maintains and coordinates validation programs for a number of cryptographic standards. FIPS PUB 140-2, Security Requirements for Cryptographic Modules (more commonly referred to as FIPS 140), specifies the security requirements that are to be satisfied by a cryptographic module utilized within a security system protecting unclassified information within computer and telecommunication systems. Oracle Crypto FIPS has been validated as meeting these requirements. FIPS 140-2 validation is a requirement for government licensing of cryptographic technology. More and more commercial organizations are also making FIPS 140-2 validation a licensing requirement as part of their risk management and best practices procedures. The same core cryptography algorithms that are available in Oracle Crypto are available in Oracle Crypto FIPS. Oracle Security Engine extends Oracle Crypto and Oracle Crypto FIPS by offering X.509-based certificate management functions. Security Engine is a superset of Oracle Crypto. The Oracle Cryptoki toolkit enables easy integration of Java applications with cryptographic hardware. Cryptoki allows implementers to utilize smart cards, USB tokens, cryptographic accelerator boards, and hardware security modules (HSMs) from their Java application. HSM & Smart Card Integration has the following functions:

■ Transparently integrates cryptographic hardware for performance or secure key storage
■ Works with any PKCS#11-compliant token

■ Used for building secure Java applets and applications that offer token-based authentication and digital signatures provided by smart cards

■ Supports Chrysalis, Eracom, nCipher, Rainbow, Sun, Thales—accelerators and HSMs, ACS, Aladdin, Arcot, Celocom, Datakey, Giesecke & Devrient, GemPlus, Rainbow iKey, Schlumberger, Spyrus—smart cards and authN tokens

Oracle XML Security implements XML Encryption and XML Signature standards in accordance with W3C specifications. Oracle XML Security ensures secure and interoperable exchange of data.

WSS implements both the preventative automated controls—the Trusted Access control domain and the Operational Control.

WSS is an OASIS specification that provides a framework for securing SOAP messages, using existing security technologies. Oracle WSS supports username Token, X.509 Certificate Token, SAML 1.x Token, Kerberos AP_REQ Token, and SOAP with Attachments Security.

SAML implements the preventative automated control, the Trusted Access control domain.

SAML (Security Assertions Mark-up Language) is a key framework for the exchange of security credentials among disparate systems and applications in an XML-based format. Managed by OASIS, SAML is an essential component of an interoperable Single Sign-On (SSO) environment. Oracle SAML implements both versions 1.0 and 1.1 of the specifications. SAML enables all SSO XML profiles and integrates with smart cards and hardware security modules for secure key storage. The SAML library is Java based and can be deployed in any JRE 1.2+ application environment.

Oracle S/MIME also implements the preventative automated control, the Trusted Access control domain.

Oracle S/MIME implements the IETF S/MIME (Secure Multipurpose Mail Extensions) specifications for secure e-mail. It secures e-mail using strong cryptography and is certified as interoperable with other S/MIME compliant products, such as Netscape/Mozilla Mail and Microsoft Outlook/Outlook Express.

Oracle S/MIME support includes the following:

■ S/MIME v2, v3, and v3.1 support as well as support for Enhanced Security Services (RFC 2634) such as digital receipts

■ EDI-INT AS1 and AS2, enabling the secure exchange of EDI over the Internet

■ JavaMail-compliant API portable to all Java platforms

■ PKCS #11 support for hardware accelerators and smart cards

■ Support for versions 2.0, 3.0, 3.1, and Enterprise Security Services (ESS). S/MIME is a requirement in other business-related protocols, such as EDI-INT AS1 and AS2.

The message syntax provides the basis of the non-repudiation preventative technical control.

Oracle CMS implements the IETF-defined Cryptographic Message Syntax (CMS) protocol. CMS defines data protection allowing for secure message envelopes. CMS supports signed, digested, authenticated, encrypted, enveloped, compressed data, signed receipts, and time stamps. CMS is compliant with RFC 2630 and PKCS #7, and also has stream I/O support for efficiently securing large data sizes. The CMS API supports unlimited levels of secure content wrapped in a Pure Java implementation. Support is also supplied for PKCS #11 support for hardware accelerators and smart cards.

Finally, we come to the Oracle Centuris PKI Component. Oracle Centuris PKI consists of sets of security protocols that enable the life-cycle management of a public key infrastructure. Centuris PKI integrates with PKCS#11 cryptographic hardware and supports the following:

- CMP/CRMF
- OCSP
- CRS
- TSP
- Key pair/certificate generation utilities

XKMS provides XML-based key and certificate management services and supports the W3C XKMS 2.0 XML format. Use of this library simplifies client access to PKI services and enables implementers to migrate off legacy PKI products without risk. XKMS includes XML signature and encryption for message security and includes support for HTTP, SOAP 1.1, and SOAP 1.2 bindings.

## Installation and Configuration

The following are included as sample programs for the Oracle Security Developer Tools Security Engine toolkit:

- der2pem.java—This program is a utility that converts DER-encoded ASN.1 structures to PEM (base 64) encoding.
- pem2der.java—This program is a utility that converts PEM-encoded (base 64) ASN.1 structures to DER encoding.
- GenCACert.java—Generates a key pair and self-signed CA certificate using either RSA or DSA keys.
- GenCert.java—Generates a certificate from a PKCS #10 certificate request.
- GenCertRequest.java—Generates a key pair and PKCS #10 certificate request, using either RSA or DSA keys.
- GenCRL.java—Generates a CA-signed certificate revocation list.
- GenSPKAC.java—Generates a key pair and signed-public-key-and-challenge certificate request of the type used by Netscape Web browsers.
- GenSPKACCert.java—Generates a certificate from a SPKAC request.
- KeyCertTest.java—Tests whether a given private key and certificate comprise a valid key pair.
- PKCS7Util.java—Utility for creating, extracting, and verifying PKCS #7 wrapped certificate (.p7c) and detached signature (.p7s) files.
- PKCS12Util.java—Utility for creating, extracting, and verifying PKCS #12 key/certificate (.p12) files.
- PrintASN1.java—Prints the structure and contents of an ASN1Object, with optional detail for certificates, CRLs, and private keys.
- VerifyCert.java—Checks the validity of a certificate based on its dates, signature, and (optionally) a CRL.
- VerifyCRL.java—Checks the validity of a CRL based on its dates and signature.

Oracle Security Developer Tools CMS toolkit includes a series of Java classes that implement the Trusted Access and Operational Control mechanisms which serve to mitigate the risks associated with normal business operations:

- CMSDataTest.java—This program generates a CMS 'id-data' Object, writes it to a file, reads the CMS 'id-data' Object from a file, and verifies it.
- CMSESSReceiptTest.java—This program generates a CMS 'id-ct-receipt' Object, writes it to a file, reads the CMS 'id-ct-receipt' Object from a file, and verifies it.
- CMSDigestedDataStreamsTest.java—This program generates a CMS 'id-digestedData' Object containing either a CMS 'id-data' or a CMS 'id-ct-receipt' Object, writes it to a file, reads the CMS 'id-digestedData' Object from a file, and verifies it.
- The CMSDigestedDataOutputStream class—This is used to generate the CMS 'id-digestedData' Object while it is verified by using the CMSDigestedDataContentInfo and the CMSDigestedDataInputStream classes.
- CMSDigestedDataCITest.java—This is the same as CMSDigestedDataStreamsTest.java except that the CMSDigestedDataContentInfo class is used to generate the CMS 'id-digestedData' Object.
- CMSEncryptedDataStreamsTest.java—This program generates a CMS 'id-encryptedData' Object containing either a CMS 'id-data' or a CMS 'id-ct-receipt' Object, writes it to a file, reads the CMS 'id-encryptedData' Object from a file, and verifies it.
- The CMSEncryptedDataOutputStream class is used to generate the CMS 'id-encryptedData' Object while it is verified by using the CMSEncryptedDataContentInfo and the CMSEncryptedDataInputStream classes.
- CMSEncryptedDataCITest.java—This is the same as CMSEncryptedDataStreamsTest.java except that the CMSEncryptedDataContentInfo class is used to generate the CMS 'id-encryptedData' Object.
- CMSSignedDataStreamsTest.java—This program generates a CMS 'id-signedData' Object containing either a CMS 'id-data' or a CMS 'id-ct-receipt' Object, writes it to a file, reads the CMS 'id-signedData' Object from a file, and verifies it.
- The CMSSignedDataOutputStream class—This is used to generate the CMS 'id-signedData' Object while it is verified by using the CMSSignedDataContentInfo and the CMSSignedDataInputStream classes.
- CMSSignedDataCITest.java—This is the same as CMSSignedDataStreamsTest.java except that the CMSSignedDataContentInfo class is used to generate the CMS 'id-signedData' Object.
- CMSEnvelopedDataStreamsTest.java—This program generates a CMS 'id-envelopedData' Object containing either a CMS 'id-data' or a CMS 'id-ct-receipt' Object, writes it to a file, reads the CMS 'id-envelopedData' Object from a file, and verifies it.
- The CMSEnvelopedDataOutputStream class—This is used to generate the CMS 'id-envelopedData' Object while it is verified by using the CMSEnvelopedDataContentInfo and the CMSEnvelopedDataInputStream classes.
- CMSEnvelopedDataCITest.java—This is the same as CMSEnvelopedDataStreamsTest.java except that the CMSEnvelopedDataContentInfo class is used to generate the CMS 'id-envelopedData' Object.

- CMSAuthenticatedDataStreamsTest.java—This program generates a CMS 'id-ct-authData' Object containing either a CMS 'id-data' or a CMS 'id-ct-receipt' Object, writes it to a file, reads the CMS 'id-ct-authData' Object from a file, and verifies it.
- The CMSAuthenticatedDataOutputStream class is used to generate the CMS 'id-ct-authData' Object while it is verified by using the CMSAuthenticatedDataContentInfo and the CMSAuthenticatedDataInputStream classes.
- CMSAuthenticatedDataCITest.java—This is the same as CMSAuthenticatedDataStreams-Test.java except that the CMSAuthenticatedDataContentInfo class is used to generate the CMS 'id-ct-authData' Object.
- CMSNestedDCITest.java—A program that generates and reads nested CMS objects using the CMSContentInfo classes.
- CMSNestedConnTest.java—A program that generates and reads nested CMS objects using the CMSOutputConnector and CMSInputConnector classes.
- Show.java—A program for displaying CMS objects.

## Deploying and Running the Application

The following are the executable commands for the sample programs for the Oracle Security Developer Tools CMS toolkit:

- CMSDataTest.java: java CMSDataTest -output filename.p7m -content DataContent—The required arguments are the filename to write the CMS 'id-data' object and the string, which forms the content.
  - output filename.p7m—Writes the CMS 'id-data' object to the specified file.
  - content DataContent—Specifies the content of the CMS object.
- CMSESSReceiptTest.java: java CMSESSReceiptTest -output file.p7m -contentType cType -signContentId contentId -origSignValue signatureValue—The required arguments are the filename to write the CMS 'id-ct-receipt' object; the fields of the Receipt, which are the content type of the message in response to which the receipt is being generated; the signed content identifier copied from the message in response to which the receipt is being generated; and the original signature value copied from the message in response to which the receipt is being generated.
  - output filename.p7m—Writes the CMS 'id-ct-receipt' object to the specified file.
  - contentType cType—The content type value. The possible values for cType are data|digestedData|signedData|encryptedData|envelopedData|authData.
  - signContentId contentId—The signed content identifier value.
  - origSignValue signatureValue—The original signature value.
- CMSDigestedDataStreamsTest.java: java CMSDigestedDataStreamsTest -output filename. p7m (-datacontent DataContent | -receiptContent ContentType signContentIdentifier origSignValue) -digest (MD5|SHA1) [-detached]—The required arguments are the filename to write the CMS 'id-digestedData' object, the digest algorithm, and either the CMS 'id-data' or 'id-ct-receipt' Object parameters.
  - output filename.p7m—Writes the CMS 'id-digestedData' Object to the specified filename.
  - content DataContent (if enclosed object is to be 'id-data')—Specifies the content of the CMS Object.

- contentType cType (if enclosed object is to be 'id-ct-receipt')—The content type value. The possible values for cType are data|digestedData|signedData|encryptedData|enveloped-Data|authData.
- signContentId contentId (if enclosed object is to be 'id-ct-receipt')—The signed content identifier value.
- origSignValue signatureValue (if enclosed object is to be 'id-ct-receipt')—The original signature value.
- digest (MD5|SHA1)—The digest algorithm to use: MD5 or SHA-1.
- detached—Specifies if the CMS 'id-digestedData' object is to be detached, i.e., the content over which the digest was calculated is not present.
■ CMSEncryptedDataStreamsTest.java: java CMSEncryptedDataStreamsTest -output filename.p7m (-datacontent DataContent | -receiptContent ContentType signContentIdentifier origSignValue) -encryptAlgorithm (3DES|RC2-40|RC2-64|RC2-128) [-useUnprotected-Attribute]—The required arguments are the filename to write the CMS 'id-encryptedData' object, the encryption algorithm, and either the CMS 'id-data' or 'id-ct-receipt' object parameters.
    - output filename.p7m—Writes the CMS 'id-encryptedData' object to the specified filename.
    - content DataContent (if enclosed object is to be 'id-data')—Specifies the content of the CMS object.
    - contentType cType (if enclosed object is to be 'id-ct-receipt')—The content type value. The possible values for cType are data|digestedData|signedData|encryptedData|envelopedData|authData.
    - signContentId contentId (if enclosed object is to be 'id-ct-receipt')—The signed content identifier value.
    - origSignValue signatureValue (if enclosed object is to be 'id-ct-receipt')—The original signature value.
    - encryptAlgorithm (3DES|RC2-40|RC2-64|RC2-128)—The digest algorithm to use: MD5 or SHA-1.
    - useUnprotectedAttribute—Specified if the set of unprotected attributes is to be used. The Content Identifier Attribute is used.
    - detached (Available only with CMSEncryptedDataCITest.java)—Specifies if the CMS 'id-encryptedData' object is to be detached, i.e., the content over which the digest was calculated is not present.
■ CMSSignedDataStreamsTest.java: java CMSSignedDataStreamsTest -output filename.p7m (-datacontent DataContent | -receiptContent ContentType signContentIdentifier origSignValue) -signers (signer-key.der signer-cert.der)+ [-certs cert.der+] [-crls crl.crl+] [-detached] [-useAttributes] [-useSPKI64|-useSPKI160] -verifyCert signer-cert.der -digest (MD5|SHA1)—The required arguments are the filename to write the CMS 'id-signedData' object, the signers, the signature verification certificate, the digest algorithm, and either the CMS 'id-data' or 'id-ct-receipt' object parameters.
    - output filename.p7m—Writes the CMS 'id-encryptedData' object to the specified filename.
    - content DataContent (if enclosed object is to be 'id-data')—Specifies the content of the CMS object.

- contentType cType (if enclosed object is to be 'id-ct-receipt')—The content type value. The possible values for cType are data|digestedData|signedData|encryptedData| envelopedData|authData.
- signContentId contentId (if enclosed object is to be 'id-ct-receipt')—The signed content identifier value.
- origSignValue signatureValue (if enclosed object is to be 'id-ct-receipt')—The original signature value.
- signers (signer-key.der signer-cert.der)—The list of one or more content signers. The private key signer-key.der and the certificate signer-cert.der must both be in the ASN.1 DER format. Selection of either RSA or DSS signatures is based on whether the signing key pair was generated using the DSA or RSA algorithm.
- certs cert.der—The list of one or more certificates that will be added to the CMS 'id-signedData' Object. The X509 certificate cert.der must be in the ASN1.DER format.
- crls crl.crl—The list of one or more CRLs that will be added to the CMS 'id-signedData' object. The CRL crl.crl must be in the ASN1.DER format.
- detached—Specifies if the CMS 'id-signedData' object is to be detached, i.e., the content over which the digest was calculated is not present. This is the same as creating external signatures.
- useAttributes—Specifies if the set of signed and unsigned attributes is to be used. The SigningTime signed attribute and the Content Identifier unsigned attribute are used.
- useSPKI64—Specifies that the 64-bit Subject Public Key Identifier is to be used as the signer identifier.
- useSPKI160—Specifies that the 160-bit Subject Public Key Identifier is to be used as the signer identifier.
- verifyCert signer-cert.der—Specifies the signer-cert.der should be used to verify the signature. The certificate must be in the ASN.1 DER format.

■ CMSEnvelopedDataStreamsTest.java: java CMSEnvelopedDataStreamsTest -output filename.p7m (-datacontent DataContent | -receiptContent ContentType signContentIdentifier origSignValue) [(-ktrecipient (recipient-cert.der (IASN|SPKI64|SPKI160))+ ) | (-kekrecipient -wrapAlg wrapAlgorithm (wrapping-key.der keyIdentifier)+)]+ [-certs cert.der+] [-crls crl. crl+] [-detached] [-useAttributes] ((-verifyRecipientKT recipient-key.der recipient-cert.der) | (-verifyRecipientKEK wrapping-key.der keyIdentifier))—The required arguments are the filename to write the CMS 'id-envelopedData' object, the recipient information, and either the CMS 'id-data' or 'id-ct-receipt' object parameters.

■ output filename.p7m—Writes the CMS 'id-encryptedData' Object to the specified filename.

■ content DataContent (if enclosed object is to be 'id-data')—Specifies the content of the CMS object.

■ contentType cType (if enclosed object is to be 'id-ct-receipt')—The content type value. The possible values for cType are data|digestedData|signedData|encryptedData|envelopedData| authData.

■ signContentId contentId (if enclosed object is to be 'id-ct-receipt')—The signed content identifier value.

■ origSignValue signatureValue (if enclosed object is to be 'id-ct-receipt')—The original signature value.

■ ktrecipient recipient-cert.der (IASN|SPKI64|SPKI160)—The list of one or more recipients. The Key Transport key management mechanism will be used to store the recipient information. The public key X.509 certificate of the recipient and the type of recipient identifier must be specified.

■ kekrecipient -wrapAlg wrapAlgorithm (wrapping-key.der keyIdentifier)—The list of one or more recipients. The Key Encryption (Wrapping) key management mechanism will be used to store the recipient information. Supported wrap algorithms are 3DES | RC2. The wrapping key and the key identifier must be specified.

■ certs cert.der—The list of one or more certificates that will be added to the CMS 'id-signed-Data' Object. The X.509 certificate cert.der must be in the ASN.1 DER format.

■ crls crl.crl—The list of one or more CRLs that will be added to the CMS 'id-signedData' object. The CRL crl.crl must be in the ASN1.DER format.

■ detached—Specifies if the CMS 'id-signedData' object is to be detached, i.e., the content over which the digest was calculated is not present. This is the same as creating external signatures.

■ useAttributes—Specifies if the set of signed and unsigned attributes is to be used. The Signing Time signed attribute and the Content Identifier unsigned attribute are used.

■ verifyRecipientKT recipient-key.der recipient-cert.der—Specifies the key pair that should be used to remove the envelope. The certificate must be in the ASN.1 DER format. Assumes recipient information is in the key transport key management mechanism format.

■ verifyRecipientKEK wrapping-key.der keyIdentifier—Specifies the information that should be used to remove the envelope. Assumes recipient information is in the key encryption (wrapping) key management mechanism format.

■ CMSAuthenticatedDataStreamsTest.java java: CMSAuthenticatedDataStreamsTest -output filename.p7m (-datacontent DataContent | -receiptContent ContentType signContentIdentifier origSignValue) ( (-ktrecipient (recipient-cert.der (IASN|SPKI64|SPKI160))+ ) | (-kekrecipient -wrapAlg wrapAlgorithm (wrapping-key.der keyIdentifier)+) ) [-certs cert.der+] [-crls crl.crl+] [-detached] [-digest (MD5|SHA1) -useAttributes] ((-verifyRecipientKT recipient-key.der recipient-cert.der)|(-verifyRecipientKEK wrapping-key.der keyIdentifier))—The required arguments are the filename to write the CMS 'id-ct-authData' object, the recipient information, and either the CMS 'id-data' or 'id-ct-receipt' object parameters.

■ output filename.p7m—Writes the CMS 'id-encryptedData' object to the specified filename.

■ content DataContent (if enclosed object is to be 'id-data')—Specifies the content of the CMS object.

■ contentType cType (if enclosed object is to be 'id-ct-receipt')—The content type value. The possible values for cType are data|digestedData|signedData|encryptedData|envelopedData|authData.

■ signContentId contentId (if enclosed object is to be 'id-ct-receipt')—The signed content identifier value.

■ origSignValue signatureValue (if enclosed object is to be 'id-ct-receipt')—The original signature value.

■ ktrecipient recipient-cert.der (IASN|SPKI64|SPKI160)—The list of one or more recipients. The Key Transport key management mechanism will be used to store the recipient information. The public key X.509 certificate of the recipient and the type of recipient identifier must be specified.

■ kekrecipient -wrapAlg wrapAlgorithm (wrapping-key.der keyIdentifier)—The list of one or more recipients. The Key Encryption (Wrapping) key management mechanism will be used to store the recipient information. Supported wrap algorithms are 3DES | RC2. The wrapping key and the key identifier must be specified.

- certs cert.der—The list of one or more certificates that will be added to the CMS 'id-signed-Data' object. The X.509 certificate cert.der must be in the ASN.1 DER format.
- crls crl.crl—The list of one or more CRLs that will be added to the CMS 'id-signedData' object. The CRL crl.crl must be in the ASN1.DER format.
- detached—Specifies if the CMS 'id-signedData' object is to be detached, i.e., the content over which the digest was calculated is not present. This is the same as creating external signatures.
- useAttributes—Specifies if the set of signed and unsigned attributes is to be used. The Signing Time signed attribute and the Content Identifier unsigned attribute are used.
- verifyRecipientKT recipient-key.der recipient-cert.der—Specifies the key pair that should be used to remove the envelope. The certificate must be in the ASN.1 DER format. Assumes recipient information is in the key transport key management mechanism format.
- verifyRecipientKEK wrapping-key.der keyIdentifier—Specifies the information that should be used to remove the envelope. Assumes recipient information is in the key encryption (wrapping) key management mechanism format.
- order recipient-key.der recipient-cert.der—If an enveloped (encrypted) message is to be viewed, the user may (optionally) specify a private-key/public-key (certificate) pair in the ASN.1 DER format to be used in decrypting the message text for display.

## Regulatory Governance Mapping

Data encryption can enhance security both inside and outside the database. A user may have a legitimate need for access to most columns of a table, but if one of the columns is encrypted and the user does not know the encryption key, the information is not usable as such within the control domains of

- Trusted Access
- Operational Control

These are covered as an automated control by use of the security developer toolkit. The security developer toolkit is vital for authorizing the operation of DoD information systems and for managing information assurance posture across DoD information systems consistent with Title III of the E-Government Act, FISMA, and DoD Directive 8500.1.

## Summary

OracleAS Security Developer Tools supports a comprehensive range of security standards and protocols, including the following:

- PKIX Standards
- X509v3 Certificates
- IETF S/MIME and CMS specifications
- Liberty Alliance Project federation standards
- OASIS SAML and Web Services Security specifications
- W3C XML Signature and Encryption specifications

# Chapter 10

# Oracle Access Manager

This chapter will describe in detail the role of the Oracle Access Manager (OAM) product as a member of the Oracle Identity Management Product Suite, which provides services related to business process and controls (automation, integration, and monitoring), security and identity management (mainly authentication/authorization, auditing, user account management, delegated administration, and data encryption), and data management (primarily storage and system management). The use of Access Manager for ITIL security, ISO 27001, and COBIT DS5 technical control is highlighted in the chapter.

## Overview

OAM has been designed based on a multitier distributed architecture comprising several components within one or more of the following categories.

### User Interface

The user interface components allow users to access the services provided by the Identity Management (IdM) Infrastructure, which includes actions such as creating new user accounts, updating user profile data, executing a business process related to IM, and self-management of their own user profile information.

### Enforcement Points

Components categorized as enforcement points provide mechanisms for controlling user access to the IdM system or to resources protected by established security policies. Although these components are not responsible for evaluating the policies and security rules, they ensure that every policy that protects access to a given resource will be enforced in all cases.

## Service Providers

The service provider components implement the actual IdM processes and services accessed by users and system administrators. Functionality provided by these components is made available through the user interface components already described.

# Extensions and Integration Points

Components categorized as extensions and integration points provide the necessary mechanisms to accommodate specialized business logic customized to fulfill business requirements. These components also allow OAM to interact and integrate with third-party software. Extensions and integration point components include packaged APIs (Event Plug-In API and Access Server SDK) and third-party interface implementations (e.g., WebLogic SSPI and WAS Connector). Table 10.1 outlines the functions of each component within the Access Manager.

## Example: Integration Access Manager with Oracle Portal

### Installing Oracle Portal

To install Oracle Portal against a preexisting Oracle Infrastructure, perform the following steps:

1. In Windows Explorer, navigate to E:\install_files\portal101202\disk1 and double-click the setup.exe file. This launches the Oracle Universal installer to install Oracle Portal 10.1.2.0.2.
2. Oracle Universal Installer should launch with the Welcome screen. Click Next.
3. Enter the Name as Portal and Path as E:\portal on the Specify File Locations screen, and click Next.
4. Select Oracle Application Server 10*g* on the Select a Product to Install screen, and then click Next.
5. Select Portal and Wireless on the Select Installation Type screen, and click Next.
6. You must have administrator privileges on the host for the installation to be successful. Check on the Administrator Privileges check box, and click Next.
7. Select Oracle Application Server 10*g* Portal on the Select Configuration Options screen.
8. Select Automatic Configure Ports on the Specify Port Configuration Options screen, and click Next.
9. Specify the host value ten.mydomain.com (or the host name in your environment where Oracle Internet Directory (OID) has been preinstalled) and port value 13060 (or the port for OID in your environment) for the OID instance that has been preinstalled on the Register with OID screen. Leave the Use Only SSL connections with this OID check box unchecked.
10. Specify cn=orcladmin and abcd1234 for username and password, respectively, on the Specify OID Log-in screen, and click Next.
11. On the Select Oracle Application Server 10*g* Metadata Repository screen, Database Connect string should be prepopulated with the hostname:port:Global Database name: Service name for the metadata repository. In our case, it is ten.mydomain.com:1521:infra.mydomain.com:infra.mydomain.com. Click Next.

**Table 10.1    Components**

| Component | Category | Description |
|---|---|---|
| WebPass | User interface | This component provides users with an entry point to gain access to identity management services provided by the identity server's applications (described later). |
| Policy Manager | User interface | The Policy Manager allows administrators to define security policies to protect applications. This component is not intended for external users. |
| WebGate | Enforcement points | This component is an extension of the Web server and is designed to function as an interceptor for all resource requests directed to the hosting Web server for policy enforcement purposes. |
| Identity server | Service provider | The Identity server exposes four applications designed to manage identity management infrastructure related data:<br>1. Management Console (administration and configuration data)<br>2. User Manager (user accounts)<br>3. Group Manager (groups)<br>4. Organization Manager (generic entities) |
| Access server | Service provider | The access server is responsible for evaluating access control policies against the user profile information of users signed into the system and determining if users are allowed to access the requested resources. |
| Access gates | Enforcement points/extensions | Access gates in general are used as custom-developed clients to perform protocol-level resource protection transactions against the access server. Access gates are created using the access server SDK; therefore, they are also considered extension components. |
| Access system console | User interface | This component allows administrators to manage the configuration settings of the access system, including, but not limited to, authentication schemes, resource types, Access Servers, and Access Gates\|WebGates configuration, among others. |

12. Specify the instance name as Portal and ias_admin password as abcd1234 (confirm the same password) on the Specify Instance Name and ias_admin Password screen, and click Next.
13. Click Install on the Summary screen.
14. Once the install completes, End of Installation screen will come up. Review the information, and click Exit.
15. To confirm that the installation of Oracle Portal was successful, open up Internet Explorer and type in the following URL: http://ten.mydomain.com:7778/pls/portal.
16. Click on the Log-in link, specify orcladmin as username with the password as abcd1234, and click OK. You should be logged in as orcladmin.

## Installing the OAM Identity Server

You use the identity server to manage identity information about users, groups, organizations, and other objects. Your installation may include one or more identity servers. Each instance of the identity server communicates with a Web server through a WebPass plug-in. The identity server performs four main functions:

- Reads from and writes to your LDAP directory server across a network connection
- Stores user information on a directory server and keeps the directory current
- Processes all requests related to user, group, and organization identification
- Directly retrieves and stores OAM configuration information stored in an LDAP repository (OID in this example)

To install the OAM Identity Server, perform the following steps:

1. In Windows Explorer, navigate to E:\install_files\oam101401, double-click the Oracle_ Access_Manager10_1_4_0_1_Win32_Identity_Server.exe file, and click Next. This command launches the OAM installer that will install the OAM Identity Server.
2. You need to have the administrative privileges to run the installation. If you are logged in as a different user, then you need to exit the installation, log in as the administrator, and then restart the installation. Then, click Next.
3. In the Destination Name text box, set the installation directory to E:\identity, and click Next.
4. Review the location to which the OAM Identity Server is getting installed and the total disk size it would take for the installation. Then, click Next.
5. Note that the installer begins copying the OAM Identity Server files. Next, select the Open Mode—No encryption option button for the identity client and identity server to communicate and, click Next.
6. You need to provide the identity server ID, host name, and port number for the identity server connection. For this installation, provide the following values, and then click Next.

   | *Parameter* | *Value* |
   | --- | --- |
   | Identity server ID | identity |
   | Host Name | ten.mydomain.com |
   | Port Number | 6022 |

   *Note*: You can use your own values for all these parameters on the basis of changes made to the environment setup.
7. If you are installing the first identity server instance on the host, then keep the default selected option button as Yes and click Next.
8. You can use SSL between the identity server and the directory server. By default, the "directory server hosting the user data is in SSL" and the "directory server hosting Oracle data is in SSL" check boxes are deselected. You will not be using SSL for this setup. Keeping the check boxes deselected, click Next.
9. The OID will be used as a user repository. This is used to host the user data for the identity server. In this case, you select OID from the Directory Server Type drop-down menu; click Next.
10. The directory server hosting user data and Oracle data could be in the same or different directories. In our case, the same OID instance will host both user and Oracle (Oblix) data. Select "Oracle data will be in the user data directory" and click Next.

11. The directory server schema needs to be extended to store the OAM schema. To configure the user repository with the OAM access manager schema, retain the Yes option button and click Next.
12. Provide the following information for the OID that hosts the user data and click Next.

    | *Parameter* | *Value* |
    |---|---|
    | Host machine or IP | ten.mydomain.com |
    | Port Number | 13060 |
    | Root DN | cn=orcladmin |
    | Root Password | abcd1234 |

13. Enter the Windows Service Name as identity, and click Next.
14. You can view the Readme file; then click Next.
15. You can review the server settings and click Finish.
16. Start the OAM Identity Server (identity) service.
    *Note*: In this environment, you start it from a batch file that runs a NET START command to start the identity service. You can also start it by navigating to Start > Control Panel > Administrative Tools > Services, right-clicking the OAM Identity Server (identity) service, and clicking Start.
17. You can verify the schema for the Oracle data (Oblix) in the OID by navigating to Oracle Directory Manager > Oracle Internet Directory Servers > orcladmin@ten.mydomain.com:13060 > Schema Management. You will find the Oracle (Oblix)-specific object classes (on Object Classes tab) and attributes (on Attributes tab) created when the OID schema was extended by the identity server installer.

## Installing the OAM WebPass

A WebPass is a Web server plug-in that passes information back and forth between a Web server and an identity server. A WebPass can communicate with multiple identity servers. Each Web server that communicates with the identity server must be configured with a WebPass. In an OAM (Oracle Access Manager) installation, at least one WebPass must be installed on a Web server and configured to communicate with at least one identity server. After installing an identity server and a WebPass, you must complete an initial identity system setup process to enable communication between the identity server and the WebPass. The WebPass performs the following functions:

■ Receives user requests and maps the URL to a message format
■ Forwards the request to an identity server
■ Receives information from the identity server and passes it to the Web server, which then communicates it to the user's browser

For this setup, the WebPass will be installed as a plug-in on OHS, which comes with the Oracle Infrastructure install. To install the OAM WebPass, perform the following steps:

1. In Windows Explorer, navigate to E:\install_files\oam101401, double-click the Oracle_Access_Manager10_1_4_0_1_Win32_OHS_WebPass.exe file, and click Next. This command launches the OAM installer that will install the OAM WebPass.
2. To install OAM WebPass, you need to have administrative privileges. If you are logged in as a different user, then you need to exit the installation, log in as the administrator, and then restart the installation. Then, click Next.

3. In the destination name text box, set the installation directory to E:\webpass, and click Next.
4. Review the location to which OAM WebPass is getting installed and the total disk size it would take for the installation. Then, click Next.
5. Note that the installer begins copying the OAM WebPass files. Next, select the Open Mode: No encryption option button for the WebPass and identity server to communicate—and click Next.
6. You need to provide the WebPass ID, host name, and port number for the identity server connection. For this installation, you can provide the following values and then click Next.

| Parameter | Value |
| --- | --- |
| WebPass ID | webpass |
| Host Name | ten.mydomain.com |
| Port Number | 6022 |

   *Note*: You can use your own values for all these parameters on the basis of changes made to the environment setup.
7. The Web server needs to be configured by modifying the configuration of the Web server directory. This change is reflected in the httpd.conf file for the OHS instance that is part of infrastructure installation. To automatically update this configuration, retain the automatic update selection and click Next.
8. You need to provide the absolute path for the httpd.conf file to the installer for WebPass. Click Browse and navigate to E:\infra\Apache\Apache\conf\httpd.conf, and then click Next. Again, click Next.
9. Note that the Web server configuration has been modified for the OHS. You need to restart the identity server and the Web server for the changes to take effect. To restart the identity server, click Start > Control Panel > Administrative Tools and double-click Services. Right-click the OAM Identity Server (identity) service, and click Restart.
   *Note*: Do not click Next before you start the identity server and restart the Web server.
10. To restart the Web server, execute the following commands in sequence from the <OHS_home>\opmn\bin:

```
E:\infra\opmn\bin>opmnctl stopproc process-type=HTTP_Server
E:\infra\opmn\bin>opmnctl startproc process-type=HTTP_Server
```

11. You can view the readme file; then click Next.
12. You can review the WebPass configuration settings; then click Finish.
13. To verify the WebPass installation, access the identity administration page from the following URL:

```
http://<hostname>.<domainname>/identity/oblix
```

   *Note*: For this environment, use the URL http://ten.mydomain.com:7777/identity/oblix, where 7777 is the port on which the OHS will route the access to the identity server.

Postinstallation configuration for OAM Identity Server—OAM requires the identity system console setup to complete the installation configuration. To complete the postinstallation configuration, perform the following steps:

1. Open the browser and enter the URL to access the Identity System Console in the following format, and then click Identity System Console.

```
http://<hostname>.<domainname>/identity/oblix
```

   *Note*: Before you begin, ensure that the OAM Identity Server (identity) service and the infrastructure OHS are started and running.

2. Note that the System Console Application is not set up. Then click Setup to perform the configuration.
3. For the directory server type for user data, select OID; then click Next.
4. You can view the note for the schema changes where the installer needs to update the OAM Identity schema into the directory. Scroll down, and click Next.
5. You need to specify the location of the LDAP server that will store user data. For this, provide the following parameters for the OID server; then click Next.

| Parameter | Value |
| --- | --- |
| Host | ten.mydomain.com |
| Port Number | 13060 |
| Root DN (Domain Name) | cn=orcladmin |
| Root Password | abcd1234 |
| Directory Server Security Mode | Open |

   Is the configuration data stored in this directory also? Yes.
6. The configuration DN is the directory tree where OAM stores the configuration data. The OAM Identity System and the OAM System need to use the same configuration data. The searchbase is the node in the directory tree where user data is stored. In our case, the searchbase will point to the parent of cn=Users container and ou=vendors container configured in OID. The configuration DN will point to the location where the o=oblix container will be created in OID. To set the searchbases and the configuration DN, provide the following values and click Next.

| Parameter | Value |
| --- | --- |
| Configuration DN | dc=mydopartners,dc=com |
| Searchbase | dc=mydopartners,dc=com |

7. The Person Object class defines the primary object class for people in the user directory. This will vary by the specific type of directory used for user information or if directory schema extensions are made to define a new type of "person" object. Provide the value for the person object class as inetOrgPerson, and click Next.
   *Note*: By default, retain the Auto configure object class check box as selected.
8. The Group Object class defines the primary object class for groups in the user directory. This will vary by the specific type of directory used for user information or if directory schema extensions are made to define a new type of default "group" object. Provide the values for the Group Object class as groupOfUniqueNames, and click Next.
   *Note*: By default, retain the Auto configure object class check box as selected.
9. The basic connection information for the directories is completed. You need to restart both the identity server and the OHS Web server for these changes to take effect and then perform the basic configuration schema mappings. After you restart (the next four steps), click Next.
   *Note*: You need to click Next only after you perform steps 10 through 13.
10. To stop the identity server, click Start > Control Panel > Administrative Tools, and double-click Services. Right-click the OAM Identity Server (identity) service, and click Stop.
11. To stop and start the OHS, browse to <Infra_home>\opmn\bin, and execute the following commands:

```
E:\infra\opmn\bin>opmnctl stopproc process-type=HTTP_Server
E:\infra\opmn\bin>opmnctl startproc process-type=HTTP_Server
```

12. To start the identity server, click Start > Control Panel > Administrative Tools and double-click Services. Right-click the OAM Identity Server (identity) service and click Start.

13. You can verify the configuration values set for the object class inetOrgPerson. After you review the complete schema mapping for this object class, click Yes.

14. You can verify the configuration values set for the group object class groupOfUniqueNames. After you review the complete schema mapping for this group class, click Yes.

15. OAM administrators have access to system configuration and system management functions. In this setup, one or more OAM master administrators need to be assigned. These users can configure the rest of the OAM installations. To identify these users, click Select User.

16. Search for Full Name as John Titor, for example, and click Go.

17. You can view the user John Titor. Click Add to select him as the master administrator.

18. Click Done to return to the Configure Administrators section. You can view that John Titor is now listed as master administrator. Click Next.

19. The default directories of the OAM identity server installation should be secured. Next, click Done.

20. Open the browser and enter the URL to access the Identity System Console in the following format, and then click Identity System Console.
http://<hostname>.<domainname>/identity/oblix

21. You can authenticate the master administrator you selected earlier. Enter the user name as john.titor and password as abcd1234 and click Login.

### Installing the OAM Policy Manager

The Policy Manager is installed on a Web server with a WebPass (under the same parent directory where WebPass is installed). The Policy Manager communicates with the Directory Server to write policy data and communicates with the access server over the Oracle Access Protocol to update the access server for policy modifications. When the Policy Manager receives requests from a WebGate instance, it queries the authentication, authorization, and auditing rules stored in the directory server. Based on the rules, the Policy Manager responds to the WebGate.

To install Oracle Access Manager Policy Manager, perform the following steps:

1. In Windows Explorer, navigate to E:\install_files\oam101401, double-click the Oracle_Access_Manager10_1_4_0_1_Win32_OHS_Policy_Manager.exe file, and click Next. This command launches the OAM installer that will install the OAM Policy Manager.

2. You need to have the administrative privileges to run the installation. If you are logged in as a different user, then you need to exit the installation, log in as the administrator, and then restart the installation. Then, click Next.

3. In the Destination Name text box, set the installation directory to E:\webpass, and click Next.
*Note*: The destination directory for WebPass installation further creates subdirectories for WebPass as E:\webpass\identity and for Policy Manager as E:\webpass\access.

4. Review the location to which OAM Policy Manager is getting installed and the total disk size it would take for the installation. Then, click Next.

5. The Policy Manager needs to connect to an LDAP server to store the policy data. Select the OID option from the drop-down option, and click Next.
*Note*: The policy data (similar to configuration data) is being accessed from OID (under o=oblix container).

6. Note that the installer prompts you to extend the LDAP schema to the Oracle schema. You have already extended the schema during the installation of the identity server. Select the No option button, and click Next.

   *Note*: Because you are storing both the configuration and policy data in the same instance of OID and you have already extended the schema for that instance of OID during the configuration data setup earlier, you choose not to extend the schema again. However, if you choose to store the policy data in a different instance of OID or in another LDAP directory, then you would need to extend the schema for that directory server instance in this step.

7. In this setup, you do not use SSL for any of the directory services. Leave the check box options deselected, and click Next.

8. Select the Open Mode: No encryption option button for the Policy Manager and access server to communicate, and click Next.

9. For installation of Policy Manager, the Web server (OHS) needs to be updated. In this case, the httpd.conf configuration file is updated. To confirm this update, retain the Yes option button, and then click Next.

   *Note*: You have already updated the httpd.conf file during the WebPass installation, and now you are again updating the same httpd.conf for Policy Manager installation.

10. Type E:\infra\Apache\Apache\conf\httpd.conf in the file location, and click Next.

11. You need to restart the Web server (OHS) so that changes done by the Policy Manager installer take effect. Execute the following commands in sequence from the <infra_home>\ opmn\bin, and then click Next.

    ```
    E:\infra\opmn\bin>opmnctl stopproc processs-type=HTTP_Server
    E:\infra\opmn\bin>opmnctl startproc process-type=HTTP_Server
    ```

12. You can view the readme file, and then click Next.

13. Note that Policy Manager has been successfully installed. Click Finish.

14. To verify the Policy Manager installation, access the Access Administration page from the following URL:

    ```
    http://<hostname>.<domainname>/identity/oblix
    ```

## Configuring the Access System Console

At this point, you can view the main OAM—The Access main page, but most of the links would be nonoperational. To configure the Access System Console, perform the following steps:

1. To configure the Access System Console, click Access System Console and then click Setup.

2. OID will be the user directory server where the access system can route the information for accessing user repositories. Select Oracle Internet Directory option from the drop-down menu, and click Next.

3. Provide the following information for the directory server hosting the user data, and click Next.

   | *Parameter* | *Value* |
   | --- | --- |
   | Host machine or IP | ten.mydomain.com |
   | Port Number | 13060 |
   | Root DN | cn=orcladmin |
   | Root Password | abcd1234 |
   | Directory Server Security Mode | Open |

4. You need to select the directory server hosting the configuration data. For this setup, select the OID option, and click Next.

5. You can store the configuration data and user data either in the same or in different LDAP servers. For this setup, you select the Store Configuration Data in the User directory server option, and click Next.

6. You can store the policy data and user data either in the same or in different LDAP servers. For this setup, you select the Store Policy Data in the user directory server option and click Next.

7. Provide the following information for the location for OAM configuration data, Searchbase, and Policybase. Then click Next.

    | Parameter | Value |
    |---|---|
    | Search Base | dc=mydopartners,dc=com |
    | Configuration DN | dc=mydopartners,dc=com |
    | Policy Base | dc=mydopartners,dc=com |

    *Note*: The o=oblix,dc=mydopartners,dc=com stores both the configuration and policy data.

8. Type the Person Object Class as inetOrgPerson, and click Next.

9. You need to restart the Web server (OHS). For this, perform the following steps, and then click Next.

    ```
    E:\infra\opmn\bin>opmnctl stopproc process-type=HTTP_Server
    E:\infra\opmn\bin>opmnctl startproc process-type=HTTP_Server
    ```

10. You need to specify the root directory for the policy domains. The subdirectories for policy domains will be created under the location that you specify. Type /, and click Next.

11. Select the Yes option button to configure the authentication schemas, and click Next.

12. To configure the authentication schema, select the Basic over LDAP check box and click Next.

13. Review the Basic Over LDAP authentication scheme configuration (retain all the default values), and click Next.

14. Select the Yes option button to configure policies that will protect the NetPoint Identity System and Access Manager, and click Next.

15. The installation for Policy Manager is complete. You need to restart the identity server and the Web server (the next three steps); then click Done.

16. To stop the identity server, click Start > Control Panel > Administrative Tools and double-click Services. Right-click the OAM Identity Server (identity) service, and click Stop.

17. You need to restart the Web server (OHS). For this, perform the following steps, and then click Next.

    ```
    E:\infra\opmn\bin>opmnctl stopproc process-type=HTTP_Server
    E:\infra\opmn\bin>opmnctl startproc process-type=HTTP_Server
    ```

18. To start the identity server, click Start > Control Panel > Administrative Tools and double-click Services. Right-click the OAM Identity Server (identity) service, and click Start.

19. To verify access system console setup, access the following URL and click Access System Console:

    ```
    http://<hostname>.<domainname>/access/oblix
    ```

20. Enter the user name as john.titor and password as abcd1234, and click Login.

21. You can view the Access System Console information.

## Installing the OAM Access Server

The access server plays a key role in authentication and authorization. Authentication involves determining the authentication method required for a resource and gathering credentials from the directory server, and then returning an HTTP response based on the results of credential validation to the access client (WebGate or AccessGate). Authorization involves gathering access information and granting access based on a policy domain stored in the directory and the identity established during authentication. To install the OAM Access Server, perform the following steps:

1. Before you can install an access server, you need to create an instance for it within the Access System Console. Failure to do so will cause your access server installation to fail. To create an instance for the access server, open the Access Administration page from the following URL, and click Access System console:
   `http://<hostname>.<domainname>/access/oblix`
2. Enter the user name as john.titor and password as abcd1234 and click Login.
3. Click on Access System Configuration tab. From the left pane, click Access Server Configuration, and then click Add.
4. In the Add a New Access Server section, provide the following values, and click Save.

   | Parameter | Value |
   | --- | --- |
   | Name | Access |
   | Hostname | ten.mydomain.com |
   | Port | 6035 |
   | Access Management Service | On |

   *Note*: Leave all the other values in the form in their default state.
5. Note that the AccessServer server instance is configured for the ten.mydomain.com server on port 6035. Click Logout and then OK to exit the Access Administration Console.
6. In Windows Explorer, navigate to E:\install_files\oam101401, and double-click the Oracle_Access_Manager10_1_4_0_1_Win32_Access_Server.exe file, and click Next. This command launches the OAM installer that will install the Access Manager.
7. To install Access Server, you need to have administrative privileges. If you are logged in as a different user, then you need to exit the installation, log in as the administrator, and then restart the installation. Then, click Next.
8. In the Destination Name text box, set the installation directory to E:\access, and click Next.
9. Review the location to which the access server is getting installed and the total disk size it would take for the installation. Then, click Next.
10. Notice that the installer begins copying the access server files. Next, select the Open Mode: No encryption option button for the access client (Web gates) and access server to communicate, and click Next.
11. You need to provide configuration information for the access server connection to the directory server containing Oracle configuration data that is running. For this installation, you can provide the following values, and then click Next.

    | Parameter | Value |
    | --- | --- |
    | Mode in which directory server containing Oracle configuration data is running | Open |

| | |
|---|---|
| Host Name | ten.mydomain.com |
| Port Number | 13060 |
| Root DN | cn=orcladmin |
| Root password | abcd1234 |
| Type of Directory Server | Oracle Internet Directory |

*Note*: You can use your own values for all these parameters on the basis of changes made to the environment setup.

12. The policy data is stored in OID. Select the Oracle Directory Option button, and click Next.
    *Note*: The policy data and configuration data are both stored in the same directory server instance of OID.

13. Provide the following values for the access server configuration details, and click Next.

| *Parameter* | *Value* |
|---|---|
| Access Server ID | Access |
| Configuration DN | dc=mydopartners,dc=com |
| Policy Base | dc=mydopartners,dc=com |

14. You can view the readme file, and then click Next.

15. You can review the access server configuration settings and click Finish. Next, you need to start the Access Server service.

16. Start the OAM Identity Server (Access) service.
    *Note*: You can start it by navigating to Start > Control Panel > Administrative Tools > Services, right-clicking the OAM Identity Server (Access) service, and clicking Start.

## Installing the OAM WebGate

Access Server uses a Web server plug-in to communicate with the Web server. Some plug-ins for standard Web servers are provided with OAM. These plug-ins are referred to as WebGates. In addition, using the APIs provided, additional plug-ins can be implemented. Such customized plug-ins are referred to as AccessGates. Because of their similarities of purpose, the terms Web-Gate and AccessGate are often used interchangeably. A WebGate performs these functions:

- Receives user requests and maps the URL to a message format that is understood by the access server
- Forwards the request to an access server for verifying credentials and authorization
- Receives authentication and authorization information from the access server
- Returns an appropriate reply to the user

To install the WebGate for OHS 1.x (that comes from the Oracle Application Server 10.1.4.0.1 Infrastructure installation), perform the following steps:

1. Similar to the access server installation, a WebGate must be defined in the configuration store before the WebGate can be installed. Open the browser and enter the URL in the following format to open the access system, and then click Access System Console:
   `http://<hostname>.<domainname>/access/oblix`

2. Enter the user name as john.titor and password as abcd1234, and click Login.

3. Click the Add New Access Gate section, provide the following values, and click Save.

| Parameter | Value |
|---|---|
| AccessGate Name | WebGate |
| Description | WebGate installed on OHS of Infrastructure |
| Hostname | ten.mydomain.com |
| Port | 7777 |
| Access Gate Password | abcd1234 |
| Retype Access Gate Password | abcd1234 |
| Access Management Service | On |
| Primary HTTP Cookie Domain | mydomain.com |
| Preferred HTTP Host | ten.mydomain.com:7777 |

*Note*: Leave all the other values in the form in their default state.

4. Note the warning regarding associating an access server with this AccessGate. Scroll down and click List Access Servers to associate the AccessGate with an Access Server.
5. Click Add to select a new access server for the AccessGate.
6. Select the ten.mydomain.com:6035 from the drop-down menu, and then click Add. Note that the AccessServer you installed previously is now associated with this AccessGate and will accept communication requests from the AccessGate.
7. In Windows Explorer, navigate to E:\install_files\oam101401, double-click the Oracle_ Access_Manager10_1_4_0_1_Win32_OHS_WebGate.exe file, and click Next. This command launches the OAM installer that will install the WebGate for OHS.
8. You need to have the administrative privileges to run the installation. If you are logged in as a different user, then you need to exit the installation, log in as the administrator, and then restart the installation. Then, click Next.
9. In the destination name text box, set the installation directory to E:\webgate, and click Next.
10. Review the location to which WebGate for OHS is getting installed and the total disk size it would take for the installation. Then, click Next.
11. Note that the installer begins copying the WebGate files for OHS. Next, select the Open Mode: No encryption option button for the transport security mode—and click Next.
12. Provide the following values for the WebGate configuration, and click Next.

| Parameter | Value |
|---|---|
| WebGate ID | WebGate |
| Password | abcd1234 |
| Access Server ID | Access |
| Host name | ten.mydomain.com |
| Port | 6035 |

13. The Web server needs to be configured by modifying the configuration of the Web server directory. This change is reflected in the httpd.conf file for the OHS. To automatically update this configuration, retain the automatic update selection and click Next.
14. You need to provide the absolute path for the httpd.conf file to the installer for WebPass. Click Browse and navigate to E:\infra\Apache\Apache\conf\httpd.conf, and then click Next.
15. Note that the Web server configuration has been modified. To restart the HTTP server, perform the following steps and click Next:
```
E:\infra\opmn\bin>opmnctl status
E:\infra\opmn\bin>opmnctl restartproc process-type=HTTP_Server
E:\infra\opmn\bin>opmnctl status
```

16. You can view the readme file, and then click Next.
17. You can review the WebGate for OHS configuration settings, and click Finish.
18. To verify the status of the installed WebGate, access the following URL:
    http://ten.mydomain.com:7777/access/oblix/apps/webgate/bin/webgate.cgi?progid=1

### Integrating the OAM with Oracle Single Sign-On and Oracle Portal

You will now integrate OAM with Oracle Single Sign-On (OSSO) in such a way that actual user authentication is handled by OAM and OSSO simply "trusts" the authentication performed by OAM. Oracle Portal will continue to perform user authorization after a successful user authentication. Oracle Portal still relies on OSSO for performing user authentication; the only difference is that OSSO is delegating the actual authentication to OAM, which it will "trust."

1. Define the list of host identifiers for the Oracle HTTP server that is serving OracleAS SSO. Use the Host Identifier's feature to enter the official name for the host and every other name by which the host can be addressed by the users. A request sent to any address on the list is mapped to the official host name, and applicable rules and policies are implemented. Log in to the Access System Console as john.titor.
2. To create a list of host identifiers for OHS serving OSSO, click Access System Configuration > Host Identifier > Add.
3. Enter all the possible variations of the host name using your host name and IP address combinations. Click + beside the host name variations to add more variations. Click Save when finished. Log out of the Access System Console.
4. Log in to the Policy Manager as john.titor.
5. Click Create Policy Domain in the left navigation pane. The Create Policy Domain page appears with the General tab highlighted. Enter OSSO as the Name and Oracle Single Sign-On Server as the Description. Then click Save.
6. Now configure the resources protected by this policy domain. Click the Resources tab of the OSSO policy domain. Click Add to add the first resource.
7. You will add two resources of the type http to protect using this policy domain—/sso/auth and /pls/orasso/orasso.wwsso_app_admin.ls_login.
   Using the values shown in the following table, create two resources. Click Save after configuring each resource and OK to confirm.

   | Parameter | Value | Value |
   | --- | --- | --- |
   | Resource Type | http | http |
   | Host Identifiers | ten.mydomain.com | ten.mydomain.com |
   | URL Prefix | /sso/auth | /pls/orasso/orasso.wwsso_app_admin.ls_login Description |

8. Now you will configure default rules. Click the Default Rules tab, and then click Add to create a new authentication rule with the following values. Click Save when done.

   | Parameter | Value |
   | --- | --- |
   | Name | OSSOAuth |
   | Description | OSSOAuth |
   | Authentication Scheme | Basic over LDAP |

9. Click the Actions subtab to configure authentication success or failure actions. Click Add and configure Return Attributes for Authentication Success with the following information. Click Save when done.

| Parameter | Value |
|---|---|
| Type | HeaderVar |
| Name | ossouser |
| Return Attribute | uid |

10. Configure policies for the OSSO policy domain. Click the Policies tab, and then click Add to create the policy with the following values. Click Save when done.

| Parameter | Value |
|---|---|
| Name | OSSOPolicy |
| Description | OSSOPolicy |
| Resource Type | http |
| Resource Operations | GET, POST |
| Resource | all |
| Host Identifiers | ten.mydomain.com |

11. Click the Authorization Rules tab. Click Add to create the authorization rule with the following values. Click Save when done.

| Parameter | Value |
|---|---|
| Name | OSSOAuthZ |
| Description | OSSO Authorization Rule |
| Enabled | Yes |
| Allow takes precedence | No |

12. Click Allow Access subtab within the Authorization Rules tab, and then click Add. Set the Role to Any one, then click Save.

13. Click the Default Rules tab and click the Authorization Expression subtab. Click Add to add an authorization expression. Select OSSOAuthZ from the list of authorization rules, and click Add. Scroll down, and click Save.

14. Click My Policy Domains in the left panel. Select the check box beside OSSO policy, and click Enable.

15. Now you will install and configure the OracleAS SSO Authentication plug-in. Compile the SSOOblixAuth.java file found here. Include e:\infra\sso\lib\ipastoolkit.jar and e:\infra\lib\ servlet.jar in the class path. Use the following command (all in one line). We are assuming that the location of SSOOblixAuth.java is the e:\input_files directory.

```
cd e:\input_files
e:\input_files>e:\infra\jdk\bin\javac -classpath e:\infra\sso\lib\
ipastoolkit.jar;e:\infra\lib\servlet.jar -d e:\infra\sso\plugin
SSOOblixAuth.java
```

16. The preceding command creates SSOOblixAuth.class and places it in the directory e:\infra\ sso\plugin\oblix\security\ssoplugin

17. You will now register the Java class with OracleAS SSO. Edit the policy.properties file in e:\infra\sso\conf, and replace the simple authentication plug-in with the plug-in that you created in the previous steps. Navigate to the line:

```
MediumSecurity_AuthPlugin=oracle.security.sso.server.auth.
SSOServerAuth.
```

Comment out the existing line, and add a new line to register your Java class. (When editing policy properties, take care not to insert a blank space at the end of a line.)

```
MediumSecurity_AuthPlugin=oblix.security.ssoplugin.SSOOblixAuth
```

18. Restart the single sign-on middle tier, and restart the OC4J instance OC4J for the changes to take effect:

```
E:\infra\opmn\bin>opmnctl restartproc process-type=HTTP_Server
E:\infra\opmn\bin>opmnctl restartproc process-type=OC4J_SECURITY
```

19. Lastly, you will verify the completion of integration. Using a separate browser window, access the Oracle Portal home URL http://ten.mydomain.com:7778/pls/portal. Click on Login link. The Basic over LDAP challenge should appear instead of the standard OSSO log-in page. Enter username as Marlin.Pohlman (for example) with the password of abcd1234, and click OK. You are now logged into Oracle Portal.

# Deployment Architecture

OAM provides extensive flexibility in the deployment of its components; however, careful planning and design is required to ensure the system performs optimally. Before installing and deploying any component, the following steps are recommended:

- Classify users: Determine how many different types of users will be using the system and the needs of each user type. User community definition and classification will allow for the optimization of the access points to keep the user experience consistent.
- Business process assessment: Much of the complexity involved in implementing an identity management (IdM) infrastructure is inherited from the business processes related to the operations and procedures of the user management life cycle for creating, maintaining, and deprovisioning user accounts. Reviewing and simplifying these procedures and practices within the organization lends itself to a higher level of corporate governance.
- Future growth planning: It is important to design the data structures and overall IdM infrastructure solution to support future requirements, which may or may not be known during the initial stages of deployment. Some examples of addressing unknown requirements may include planning for how new organization roles will develop and expected growth of the user population across existing and new user communities.

Oracle Access Manager is deployed primarily for providing access control to applications inside the corporation. This also includes user profile management functionality, such as allowing users to self-register for access to applications and resources of the organization, or modifying the specific data of their own profiles. To expose the user profile management functionality to users, the following deployment architecture is required:

DMZ Web tier: An instance of a Web server hosting the WebPass component protected by a WebGate resides within this tier. The WebPass and the WebGate components within the DMZ Web tier serve the following purposes:
- WebPass—exposes access to identity management functionality provided by the identity server hosted on the middle tier without allowing direct access to the corporate directory.
- WebGate—protects WebPass URLs and allows for user authentication and authorization to the IdM functionality.

Middle tier: An instance of the identity server and the access server resides in this tier for WebPass and WebGate connectivity, respectively.

Back-end tier: A directory server instance resides in this tier supporting connectivity for the identity and access servers.

The first tier (Web tier) contains the components responsible for exposing and protecting the user interface for IdM functionality and also the functionality that will enforce security policies for every resource request invoked within this tier. The aforementioned component functionality covers Web applications only, including protection of the Oracle Access Manager Web interfaces.

The second tier (middle tier) hosts the Oracle Access Manager Identity and Access Server components. The identity server provides services to the upper tier (Web tier), so users can access the IM functionality. The access server provides authentication/authorization and single sign-on services to applications hosted in the upper tier (Web tier) without placing additional security facilities in the applications themselves.

The third tier (back-end tier) hosts the data repositories containing user-identity-related information, which in this case are represented by directory servers. The identity and access servers store and extract their configuration metadata from the directory servers as well. A recommended best practice is to separate the directory server hosting OAM configuration metadata from those hosting user, group, and organization data.

## *Walkthrough*

Install OracleAS 10g.

Install the Oracle Infrastructure. The OracleAS Infrastructure 10g includes the Oracle Application Server Metadata Repository, OracleAS Single SSO server, and Oracle Internet Directory (OID). Ensure that servers where the Oracle Infrastructure and OAM are installed have fully qualified domain names, for example, hostname.domain.net. Install and set up OAM components.

Navigate to the Identity System Console and create an Oracle administrator (orcladmin) user to match the orcladmin user who already exists in the Oracle OID.

Next, protect the SSO log-in URL so that the WebGate challenges the user whenever the OracleAS Single SSO 10g is accessed:

```
/sso/auth/
```

The following activities are required to protect the SSO log-in URLs, or any other resources, using the access system.

1. Define an authentication scheme using the Access System Console.
   *Example:* Access System Console, Access System Configuration, Authentication Management, Add.
2. Create a policy domain using the Policy Manager.
   *Example:* Policy Manager, Create Policy Domain.
3. Add a resource to your policy domain using the Policy Manager.
   *Example:* Policy Manager, Create Policy Domain, Resources.
4. Define rules for your policy domain using the Policy Manager.
   *Example:* Policy Manager, Create Policy Domain, Default Rules.
5. Define an authorization action that sets a header variable with the ID of the user.
   *Example:* Policy Manager, Create Policy Domain, Default Rules, Authorization Expressions, Actions Authorization Success Return Type: HeaderVar Name: XXX_REMOTE_USER Return Attribute: loginAttribute, where XXX is any prefix (used because "REMOTE_USER" is often an internal header for HTTP servers) and loginAttribute is the attribute configured as the Login semantic type in the identity system. This name must map to the log-in name of the user stored in the OracleAS SSO repository. Some people have used the

"EMPLID" attribute, which will pass the Employee ID of the logged-in user. Upon successful authorization, the value of loginAttribute is passed on to the OracleAS 10g server.

6. In the authorization rule, allow access to Anyone.

*Example:* Policy Manager, Create Policy Domain, Authorization Rules, Name, Allow Access, Anyone Enable the Authorization rule.

*Example:* Policy Manager, Create Policy Domain, Authorization Rules, Name, Enable the Policy Domain.

*Example:* Policy Manager, My Policy Domains, Name, Modify, Enabled.

The configuration is now complete.

# Access Elements

In most cases, IdM implementations employ unique requirements within and across organizations. Complex requirements not addressed by deployment of out-of-the-box functionality are met by using the customization capabilities, classified as extension mechanisms, of OAM. As an introduction to the extension mechanisms of OAM, let us begin this discussion with a brief description of the most common types of customizations requested in organizational implementations.

## Business Logic

Business logic is usually embedded in IdM processes, especially user creation, user profile management, user activation/deactivation, and resource access provisioning. This business logic may require integration with other applications or repositories that are not supported out of the box by OAM. OAM provides interfaces that allow the invocation of custom code to communicate with external systems and applications according to the business logic being implemented.

Access control processes, especially authentication and authorization of users requesting access to protected resources, generally involve interactions with external systems or applications involved in the authentication or authorization transactions. To accommodate these needs, OAM provides APIs to extend the functionality provided out of the box for authentication and authorization. Developers may write custom code to perform authentication and authorization using external mechanisms, such as electronic token systems and smart cards.

Figure 10.1 describes the extension capabilities of OAM for IdM and access control. OAM has multiple APIs available for different purposes. There is a set of APIs for extending the functionality of the identity system (Identity Server) called Event Plug-In API and another set of APIs for the access system (Access Server), which is subdivided into three groups of APIs: Authentication/Authorization Plug-In APIs, Access Server API, and Access Manager API (Access Server API and Access Manager API together are known as the Access Server SDK).

### Oracle Access Manager—Event Plug-In API

OAM-IdM capabilities have two main components—previously described in the section on typical deployment architecture—the identity server and the WebPass. The identity server's functionality is divided in to three categories listed as follows:

- User management
- Group management
- Organization management

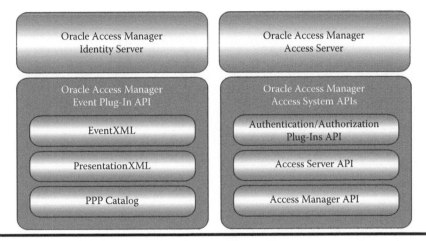

**Figure 10.1   Oracle Access Manager extension APIs.**

User management tasks are performed within the user manager application part of the Identity server. User Manager provides the mechanisms for users and administrators to manage identity data for system users, in other words, their user profiles.

Group Manager, which is another application of the identity server, performs group-management-related tasks. Group management operations include controlling user membership in groups, group creation, group profile management, and group removal. Group Manager also has the capability to manage dynamic groups even when the underlying directory server does not support dynamic groups natively.

The Organization Manager is also an application part of the identity system. This application is unique because it has some capabilities that the other two applications do not, for example, the capability to manage multiple structural object classes (structural object classes are data structures representing an entity, subject to having its own identity; e.g., a user, a group, a cell phone, an application, a printer, etc.). The organization management tasks are performed in this application, and these tasks include managing the life cycle of entities that are not users or groups but still have their own identity.

## Event Plug-In Execution Architecture

The architecture for extension plug-ins is described in Figure 10.2.

There are two different kinds of event plug-ins supported by the OAM identity system: library plug-ins and executables. Each kind of plug-in has advantages and disadvantages, which will be described in the following section.

### Library Plug-Ins

These can be written in C/C++ or any .NET-supported language for the case of managed library plug-ins (C#, VB.NET, J#, etc). They run within the OAM identity server's memory space and communicate back and forth with the server via direct API calls. Table 10.2 summarizes the advantages and disadvantages of library plug-ins.

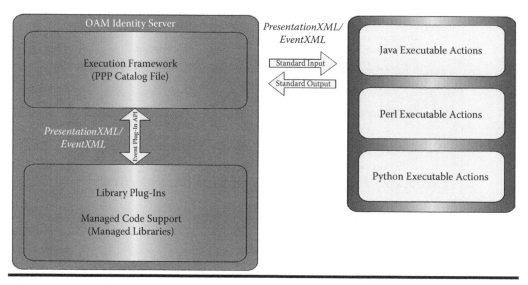

**Figure 10.2   Architecture for event plug-ins execution.**

**Table 10.2   Advantages and Disadvantages**

| Advantages | Disadvantages |
|---|---|
| Because the library plug-ins execute within the OAM Identity Server's memory space, they spawn threads and do not create processes; this is less expensive from the OS perspective and therefore allows for better scalability. | Faulty plug-ins can have very serious impacts on the OAM Identity Server's stability and may cause to crash if the plug-in is not thread-safe or it does not handle all exceptions properly. |
| Provide simple standards-based APIs to communicate with the OAM Identity Server. | A library plug-in can only utilize parameters exposed by the OAM Identity Server event management framework. |

# Executables

Executable plug-ins can be written in any compiled language that generates executables. For Java plug-ins, the JVM is the executable to be specified. All executable plug-ins generate processes communicating with OAM via their standard output stream in a single-threaded synchronized pipeline. For this reason, executable plug-ins are not scalable, and their use should be avoided for production implementations unless the load is not significant.

## Integration Access Manager with Oracle SSO (not eSSO)

Process overview—Integration of OAM with Oracle application server:

1. When a user attempts to access an OAM-protected application or Web resource, a WebGate intercepts the request.
2. WebGate requests the security policy from the access server to determine if the resource is protected.

3. When the resource is protected, WebGate prompts the user to authenticate.
4. The credentials entered by the user are validated against the directory for authentication.
5. When authentication is successful, an encrypted OAM SSO cookie is set on the user's browser.
6. After successful authentication, the access system determines if the user is authorized, by applying policies that have been configured for the resource.
7. Upon successful authorization, the access system executes the actions that have been defined in the security policy and sets an HTTP header variable that maps to the OracleAS 10*g* user ID.
8. The OracleAS SSO server recognizes the OAM HeaderVar, authenticates the user, and sets the OSSO cookie.

## Authentication and Authorization Plug-ins

The basic authentication and authorization services provided by OAM out of the box may not always meet the requirements of every implementation. As a result, extensive flexibility is provided within OAM that enables the accommodation of very sophisticated functionality for security management and access control.

Similar to the architecture of the event plug-ins, authentication and authorization plug-ins are libraries that are linked dynamically into the access server's memory space; however, the authentication/authorization plug-ins can only be written in C/C++.

The complexity involved in writing these plug-ins is significant; this is because authentication and authorization plug-ins have to be very reliable and robust, handle all exceptions properly, and be very thread-safe—otherwise, the consequences can be detrimental for the security framework, causing a loss of service and preventing all users from accessing applications/resources protected by the infrastructure.

Figure 10.3 shows the architecture for authentication/authorization plug-ins and other APIs for access management and access control.

Besides authentication/authorization plug-ins, it is possible to develop access server clients called Access Gates (described previously). These clients allow applications in general to leverage

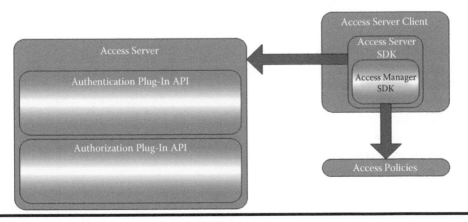

**Figure 10.3 Architecture for authentication/authorization plug-ins execution and access server APIs.**

authentication and authorization services from the access server. These clients can be written in C/C++, Java, and .NET languages such as C#, VB.NET, and other available languages. As described in Figure 10.3, access server clients can also create access policies programmatically using the Access Manager SDK, which is a separate API in the access server SDK.

# Installation and Configuration

This section does not intend to replace the documentation for installation and configuration of OAM; it provides very useful information about the parameters available in the configuration of every component that complements the installation process described in the available OAM documentation.

## *Identity System Installation Concepts*

The order in which components should be installed is shown as follows:

▪ Directory server
▪ Identity server
▪ WebPass

## *Directory Server Installation and Configuration*

OAM provides the functionality required to manage information stored in a directory server. This information is structured in a hierarchy designed to support the organization's IM process. To prepare OAM to manage this information, the directory schema needs to be extended to support the configuration metadata for OAM. The directory may already contain schema extensions to support organization-specific attributes and object classes; however, for OAM to manage this information, the system must be aware of such schema extensions and their associations so as to identify related objects.

The schema extensions required for OAM to represent configuration data include, but are not limited to the following:

▪ Password policies auxiliary object classes
▪ Location object classes
▪ Resources to be protected
▪ Policy domains
▪ Policy rules
▪ Attribute access control rules
▪ Attribute management configuration rules
▪ Object classes management

Other schema extensions are available to be leveraged based on organizational requirements and deployed functionality.

## Identity Server Installation and Configuration

The OAM Identity Server is the core component of the identity system and must access configuration metadata from the directory server. In this section, we present a detailed description of the most important configuration parameters for the OAM Identity Server.

## Transport Mode

The transport mode determines how information is exchanged between identity system components deployed in the infrastructure. There is one transport mode that exchanges data in cleartext and two transport modes that allow encryption of the data via SSL/TLS.

- Open mode: This transport mode allows data exchange in cleartext with no encryption on the data or via the communication channel. This mode is not recommended for production environments but is only for development or debugging.
- Simple mode: This transport mode provides a secure encrypted data exchange supported by the OAM Identity System. This mode uses SSL/TLS to encrypt the communication channel for data exchanged by the identity system components. In this case, a third-party PKI solution does not manage the certificates; rather, they are self-generated and self-signed by Oracle. This mode can be used for production environments; however, it is not a recommended implementation for Internet-facing infrastructures because of the inherent security risks associated with not using a recognized certificate provider.
- Certificate mode: This transport mode, like the simple mode, also exchanges data via a secure communication channel between system server components; the difference is that a recognized third-party certificate authority (CA), such as Verisign or RSA, generates the certificate used for SSL/TLS transactions.

## Auditing Configuration

One of the newest features of OAM is its capability to store auditing information in an RDBMS (currently supported at the time of this publication: MS Access and MS SQL Server). The aforementioned databases and the associated schema-generation scripts are supported out of the box. Other databases such as Oracle, DB2, and Informix are also supported as long as there are proper ODBC drivers available for the OS platform on which the system server components have been deployed. The databases must be prepared using the OAM DB Schema scripts (MS Access and MS SQL Server) or by creating the tables, indices, and other database artifacts manually within the database to be used for auditing (Oracle, MySQL, and others).

The parameters associated with the auditing capabilities are shown in Figure 10.4.

These parameters also include the ones for auditing a plaintext file.

Auditing a file requires administrators to specify the following parameters:

- Audit File: Administrators must specify an absolute path to the auditing file (e.g., c:\netpoint\identity\oblix\logs\audit.log).
- Audit File Maximum Size (bytes): This parameter is self-explanatory; it is the maximum size of the audit file whose path is specified in the Audit File Name parameter.

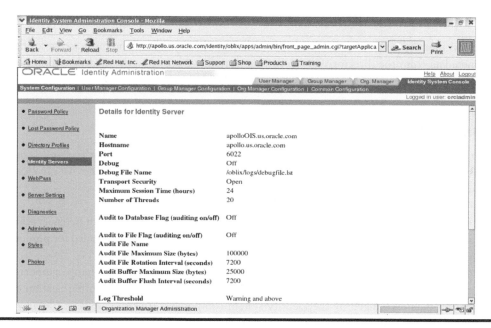

**Figure 10.4 Oracle Access Manager Identity Server auditing configuration parameters.**

■ Audit File Rotation Interval (seconds): This parameter specifies the number of seconds before the audit file is backed up and a new audit file is created to start logging again.
■ Audit Buffer Maximum Size (bytes): This parameter expresses the amount of bytes that the auditing buffer can hold before being flushed to the file. Auditing is a time-consuming operation and must be paid special attention because it can be configured to refresh the file immediately close to real-time, which may potentially impact system performance.
■ Audit Buffer Flush Interval (seconds): This parameter controls the periods when the contents of the auditing buffer will be written into the audit file. It is recommended to have a reasonable interval of time specified here, although this will depend on the requirements for auditing, which vary from implementation to implementation. A short interval will cause the buffer to flush very often, and this can cause a performance hit.

The format of each row of the file is controlled by the master auditing policy described next. This policy determines the amount of data to be written to the auditing file, which administrators should select carefully; do not log unnecessary data, because this could quickly consume the storage space on the server, thus affecting the stability of the system. Figure 10.5 describes the configuration of the master audit policy. As shown in the picture, the master audit policy comprises several elements, explained in detail as follows.

Date Type—This is the format of the date and time when the event occurred. The string yyyy-mm-ddThh:mm:ssTZD produces the following output: 2006\-05\-10T14:58:28 (May 10, 2006, 2:58 PM, 28 s).

Date Separator—This is the character used to separate the components of the date portion of the Date Type field. In this case, specifying – will produce \- because of "escaping"—the row fields are delimited by dashes.

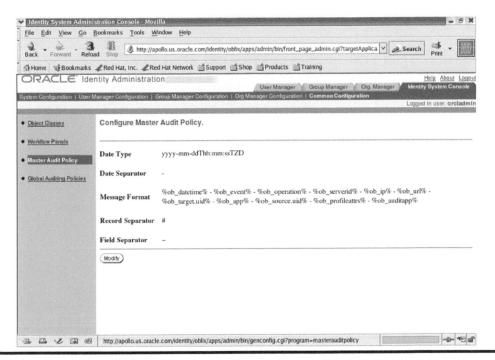

**Figure 10.5    Oracle Access Manager—master audit policy configuration.**

Message Format—This string contains OAM reserved field identifiers. The following extract from a sample audit file shows the values for each field given in Figure 10.5 previously.

05/10/2006 15:24:46 - ModifyProfile - SUCCESS - serv2003.oracle.com - 127.0.0.1 - /identity/oblix/apps/webpass/bin/webpass_iis.dll - cn=Abid Abasi,ou=APAC,cn=User s,dc=oracle,dc=com - User Manager - cn=orcladmin, cn=Users, dc=oracle,dc=com - -

Each row starts with the date and time expressed in the format defined by: mm/dd/yyyy. After the date, the first row element is 'ob_datetime', which displays the time when the event occurred. Following the time is the event type 'ob_event', which describes the task performed by the user. Then, the status of the task or operation 'ob_operation' is displayed after the event descriptor (this can take the value SUCCESS or FAILED). Then comes the identifier of the machine from where the event comes from, 'ob_serverid'; in other words, the HOST where the identity server that triggered the event is installed on and also the IP of that machine is available using 'ob_ip'. The 'ob_url' displays the relative path of installation of WebPass and the type of WebPass installed (namely, the kind of Web server where WebPass is installed—i.e., IIS). The element 'ob_target.uid' identifies the full DN of the recipient user. The element 'ob_app' is the name of the identity system application that generated the event; this can have the values of User Manager, Group Manager, or Organization Manager. Next comes the 'ob_source.id', which contains the DN of the user performing the operation causing the event to be triggered. After the DN of the action performer come the attributes associated with an event. Not all events have attributes associated; only the log-in, log-out, and password management events have user profile attributes associated to them. Auditing events can be enabled or disabled in the Global Auditing Policy screen, shown in Figure 10.6.

*Note*: 'ob_auditapp' is an undocumented parameter.

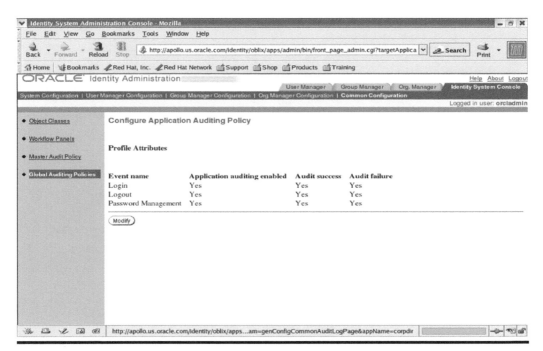

**Figure 10.6   Oracle Access Manager—global auditing policy configuration screen.**

## Execution Parameters

OAM is a multi-threaded process; therefore, there are some parameters important for administrators to understand so they can fine-tune the system.

Number of Threads: This parameter controls the number of worker threads created by the identity server to handle incoming calls. This parameter is rarely modified from the default, which is 20 threads. However, sometimes it is recommended to experiment. It is not advisable to increase this value higher than 40 threads per identity server process.

## WebPass Installation and Configuration

After installation of the identity server, it is the turn for WebPass, so that the identity system as a whole can be configured and administered.

WebPass is an extension of the Web server, and its purpose is to serve as an interface between users and the identity server functionality. WebPass uses proprietary APIs that each supported Web server exposes to application developers so that they can write extensions to the functionality of the Web server; having said this, there is a WebPass implementation for each supported Web server. Table 10.3 describes the different kinds of WebPass implementations and their corresponding supported Web servers.

WebPass communicates with the identity server using a proprietary protocol called NetPoint Identity Protocol (NIP) and uses the TCP/IP protocol to exchange data with the identity server. This data is exchanged in clear text and the transport mode configured for WebPass is set to Open, or encrypted using SSL for transport modes set to Simple or Certificate. (These two transport modes were already described in previous sections of this chapter.)

**Table 10.3   Web Servers and API**

| Web Server | API Implemented by WebPass |
|---|---|
| IIS and ISA | ISAPI (MS HTTP Server Extension API) |
| Apache | Apache SDK (this allows developers to write Web server modules which are compiled, loaded, and run within Apache Web server) |
| IPlanet (SUNOne HTTP Server) | NSAPI (API for extensions to IPlanet/SUNOne Web servers). |

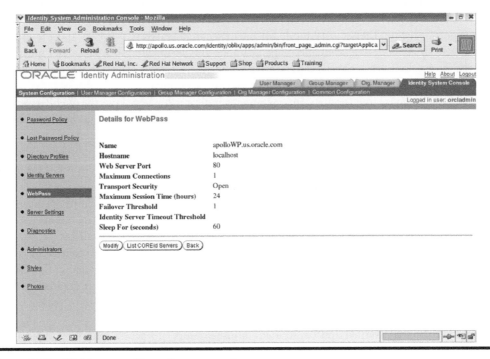

**Figure 10.7   WebPass configuration parameters.**

In the following section, the most important configuration parameters for WebPass will be described. As with the identity server, the information presented here does not intend to replace the installation documentation and the administration guides. It provides a more detailed explanation of each parameter, which will allow administrators to make better decisions when choosing values for these parameters. The configuration parameters for WebPass are shown in Figure 10.7. WebPass is installed on a Web server and not as a stand-alone component. The main parameters for WebPass are the following:

- Name
- Host name
- Web server port
- Maximum connections
- Transport security

- Maximum session time (hours)
- Failover threshold
- Identity server timeout threshold
- Sleep for (seconds)

Name: An arbitrary name for the WebPass component.

Host Name: The fully qualified name of the host having the Web server upon which the Web-Pass will be installed.

Web Server Port: The listening port of the Web server.

Maximum Connections: This parameter is used for load balancing and indicates the number of active connections to all available active servers. If more than one identity server is available as a primary, then this number determines how many primaries exist.

Transport Security: The security mode for data exchange between WebPass and the identity server. Three modes are available—open, simple, and certificate. This parameter must have the same value as the equivalent parameter or the identity server. These three transport security modes have been already explained in previous sections.

Maximum Session Time (hours): This parameter indicates for how long the WebPass session can be active without having to log in again. This parameter is in hours, as indicated by the user interface.

Failover Threshold: This parameter is used to control failover. It gives the number of identity servers that must go down before failover to the secondary identity servers. So, if the architecture deploys more than one primary server and this parameter is set to 1, as soon as one of the primary servers goes down, WebPass switches to the secondary identity servers.

Identity Server Timeout Threshold: This value is expressed in seconds and represents the time that has to elapse before considering the identity server as down or unavailable.

Sleep For (seconds): This parameter is used by the WebPass to determine how often WebPass will poll the primary identity servers to detect when they are up and running again. This parameter must be set to a reasonable value like 300 s, for instance, because there is some overhead in polling the identity server, especially when more primary servers need to be polled.

After WebPass is installed and configured, administrators can access four Web applications providing the interface to administer the configuration of the OAM Identity System. These four applications are the following:

- Identity System Console
- User Manager
- Group Manager
- Org. Manager

### Identity System Console

This application allows administrators to specify basic configuration information required by the underlying infrastructure to function properly. This basic configuration includes the following:

- System configuration
- System management

- Common configuration
- User Manager configuration
- Group Manager configuration
- Org. Manager configuration

## System Configuration

The menu items shown in Figure 10.8 comprise the system configuration section. To access the configuration parameters of WebPass, the user must select Configure WebPass from the left-hand side menu. All the configuration parameters for WebPass have been described previously. In this section, the discussion will be focused on directory options, password policies, and styles.

### Directory Profiles

OAM provides services to manage the information stored in the directory servers. This information can be organized and distributed across one or more directory servers. Some infrastructures keep the organization data separate from OAM configuration data, which is also stored in the directory server.

The way in which data is organized is defined by the creation of directory server profiles (DS profiles). DS profiles specify the location of specific information and the allowed operations that can be performed upon that data. Other parameters defined within a DS profile include the

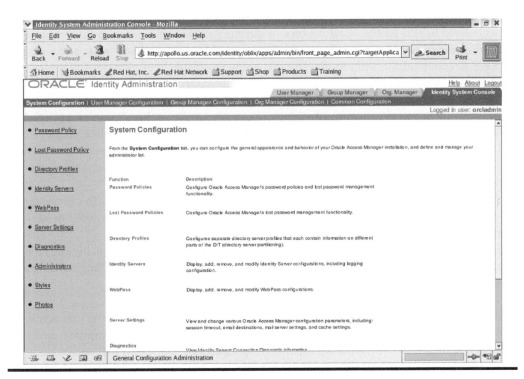

**Figure 10.8  System configuration for the Identity System.**

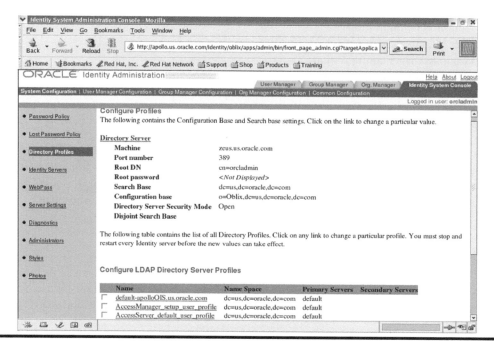

**Figure 10.9   Directory server profile configuration parameters.**

configuration settings for load balancing and failover. The picture in Figure 10.9 shows the structure of a directory profile.

A DS profile includes an identification name, a namespace—this being the DN suffix for the entries covered by this profile—and the type of directory server associated with this profile. Not all the directory servers have the same capabilities, so OAM needs to know what directory it is supposed to communicate with; so, features that are not available in every type of directory will not be used.

The section labeled Operations allows administrators to enable specific operations over the data covered by this profile. So, the administrator can potentially enable all operations or only a few depending on the characteristics of the profile. For example, a profile may be configured as a read-only profile because the data is received by replication from a writable master directory server, and this directory is only used to read information for authentication/authorization purposes or to display user profiles.

Also, different components within the installation can use different profiles. This is also specified in the profiles themselves. A more detailed description of each system is provided in sections to come.

Figure 10.10 details the load balancing and failover configuration. Load balancing and failover capabilities for directory servers are also available in OAM. The settings controlling the directory servers' load balancing and failover are the following:

Maximum Active Servers: This parameter indicates how many directory servers are active for the components using the profile to communicate with them. If four primary directory servers are defined, this parameter should be specified as 4, and OAM will load-balance the requests among the four directories. If only one directory server is available, this parameter is ignored.

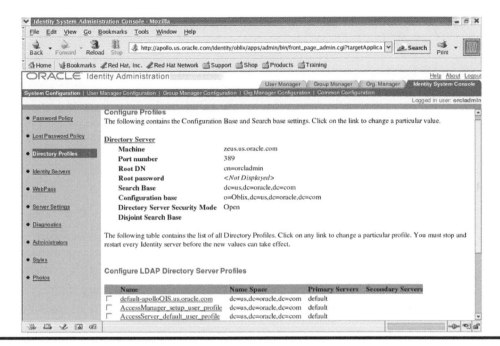

**Figure 10.10   Load balancing- and failover-related configuration settings.**

Failover Threshold: As for WebPass/identity server relationship, the failover threshold for directory servers indicates the number of directory servers to go down before initiating failover
to secondary directory servers. This parameter works in conjunction with the maximum
active servers.

Sleep For (Seconds): This parameter indicates how many seconds will elapse before the next
polling request to determine if a directory server previously down has come back to normal
activity.

## System Management

System management provides the functionality required to perform maintenance work on the
system. The only menu available in system management is Diagnostics, which displays a table with
diagnostics data, including connectivity information among all the components in the infrastructure. Figure 10.11 shows the diagnostics screen with all the information about all connections
opened among the components of the identity system. The figure also describes the diagnostics
screen for all the identity servers available in the infrastructure.

## Access Server Installation and Configuration

OAM Access Server is the core component of the access system. This component will access its
configuration from the directory server just like the identity server. In this section, we present a
detailed description of the most important configuration parameters for the OAM Access Server.

Some preliminary concepts to the access system installation and configuration are in order.
The access system cannot be installed alone; it has to be installed after the identity system. The

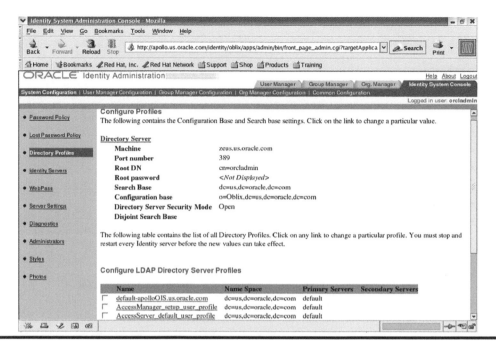

**Figure 10.11 Diagnostics screen for all identity servers available in this infrastructure.**

reason for this is mainly historical. Initially, COREid Products (Oblix band) only provided IM capabilities and no access control. After the access control functionality was added, the access system administration interface was integrated initially with WebPass, and now the Policy Manager application is provided independent of WebPass but still is associated with a Web server just like WebPass.

The first component of the access system that must be installed is the Administration User Interface. After installation, it must be configured through the Web-based setup process (described in the product's documentation). The Administration UI for the access system includes the Access System Console, which will be used to specify the configuration settings for the access server and WebGates to be installed afterwards, and the Policy Manager to create policy domains and security policies.

## System Configuration

This section allows administrators to delegate administrative privileges to other users. Figure 10.12 shows the administration screen to specify system administrators.

Master access administrators (MAAs) are those users allowed to modify the settings of the access system components such as access servers, WebGates, authentication schemes, policy domains, and access policies. They can also specify groups of delegated administrators and other MAAs.

MAAs can also create groups whose members will have privileges to manage one or more configuration elements of the access system. This is described in Figure 10.13.

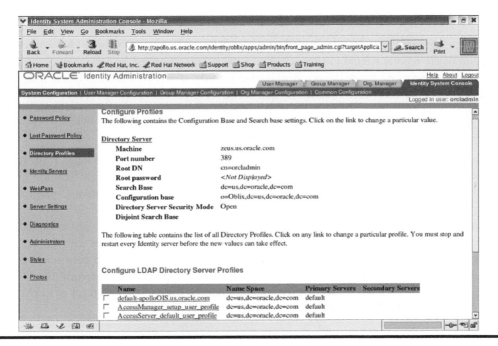

Figure 10.12   Configure administrators screen.

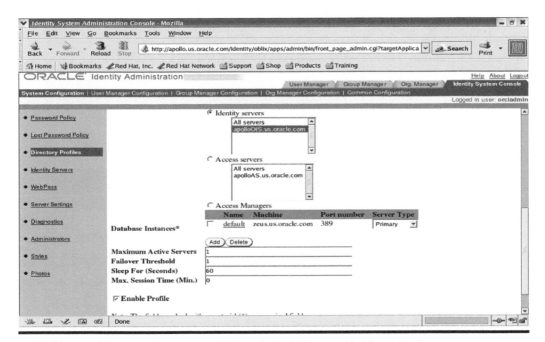

Figure 10.13   Create new group of delegated administrators for the access system.

## System Management

System management provides administrators with access to diagnostics screens; they can create, edit, and delete reports related to user access to applications protected by access policies defined in Access Manager; and purge the synchronization records, which are the result of the integrated automatic cache flush between the identity and access servers.

*Note*: Synchronization records are maintained by the access system and should not be managed by or deleted directly from the directory nor affected by any external interface.

The reports generated by OAM access system can be stored in a database or a file. If the report is stored in a database, an RDBMS profile needs to be created through the Create RDBMS Profile option at the bottom of the View Server Settings screen available in the System Configuration menu. Figure 10.14 describes this feature.

An RDBMS profile is created when OAM is required to interact with a database for auditing and reporting reasons. For compliance purposes, auditing and reporting to a database are very useful tools; they give a clear view of the system's operation and allow one to keep track of user accountability when accessing the enterprise resources and applications. Currently the ODBC (Open Database Connectivity) standard is supported for databases. Version 10.1.4 of OAM supports the following databases via ODBC:

- MySQL
- MS SQL Server
- Oracle database

In addition to ODBC, version 10.1.4 supports OCI to access Oracle's database.

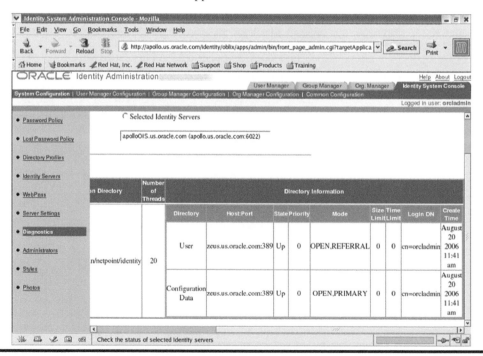

**Figure 10.14   Create RDBMS Profile configuration screen—Oracle Access Manager—system configuration.**

## *Access System Configuration*

The Access System Configuration menu allows administrators to specify the following elements:

- Access servers
- Access server clusters
- Access gates/WebGates
- Authentication schemes
- Authorization schemes
- Host identifiers sets

Access servers: Before installing an access server, the configuration entry describing that access server must be created first. The reason for this is that the access server being installed will connect to the directory server where the configuration data resides and will look for this configuration data to complete the installation. This concept also applies to access gates and WebGates.

Access server clusters: Access server clusters simplify the administration of the deployed components and provide automatic load-balancing capabilities. They must have two or more instances of access servers, which may not exist physically but the configuration data may have already been generated. When WebGates or access gates are associated with clusters, the installation will ignore the port number of the access server requested during installation; so when an access gate or a WebGate is installed, it will be connected to a cluster and will just accept the default port (6021) during installation.

Access gates/WebGates: These components are enforcement points for policies and credential collection. Similar to the access servers, the configuration data and any association with access servers or clusters must be specified before installing the component physically at its destination. There is a special type of access gate called WebGate, which is an extension of the Web server that insures that access policies are enforced properly on Web applications deployed on or accessed through (proxies) a Web server. Access gates are client components that also connect to an access server or a cluster of access servers, but they are not extensions of Web servers and can potentially stand on their own (depending on the implementation). There is an API that allows developers to write custom access gates called the access server SDK.

Authentication schemes: OAM's access system supports multiple mechanisms to collect and validate user credentials. These mechanisms are configured using authentication schemes, which have the following components:

- A challenge method: This determines how credentials are collected from users. The supported challenge methods are basic, form, none, and external.
- A set of plug-ins to process user credentials: After credentials are collected from the user, a set of authentication plug-ins (either out of the box or custom) will validate these credentials against LDAP or potentially an external system (i.e., RSA secure tokens or external non-LDAP repositories).

Authorization schemes: Sometimes, the decision regarding whether or not to allow an authenticated user to access a resource cannot be determined by simply evaluating attributes of the user profile as the standard authorization mechanisms would do. In some situations, authorization is contingent on the vote of a third-party application or system, or perhaps data stored on a different data repository. Authorization schemes rely on custom authorization plug-ins performing the custom authorization tasks against external authorization entities. The access system provides an API for developers to write custom authorization plug-ins, which can be associated with one or more authorization schemes.

Host identifers sets: To prevent security holes, the Host Identifiers feature of OAM allows administrators to specify all the possible names for a host or hosts to ensure proper policy enforcement on resources. The URLs referring to a Web application, for instance, can potentially be expressed using fully qualified host names, IP addresses, combinations of IP/host, name and ports, etc. This can present a security risk if not all the possible URL combinations are taken into account when enforcing policies, which rely on pattern matching to determine if a policy applies or not to a given application. Host Identifiers allow administrators to reduce the risk of a policy not being enforced because of a mismatch of the URL pattern owing to a host name or IP that has not been taken into account as part of a valid URL representing that resource. This can cause a protected resource to be accessed by unauthorized users because the policy protecting this resource will not be enforced. Host Identifiers and Preferred Host setting of WebGates ensure proper policy enforcement every time an application is accessed. Also, to prevent access to resources when a policy has not been identified for protecting an application, WebGate provides a parameter called DenyOn-NonProtected, which, once set to 'true' will automatically deny access to the application if there is no policy protecting it. In version 10.1.4, this configuration parameter is part of the WebGate parameters available in the user interface.

## Controlling Security with OAM

OAM allows organizations to define fine-grained security policies to protect their enterprise IT resources. OAM groups security policies in policy domains. A policy domain contains one or more resources/applications protected by a default set of policy rules or a special policy defined when a particular pattern is detected. It is important to understand that OAM relies on URL patterns to determine if a resource is protected or not. To be able to define policy domains and the policy rules within them, some elements need to be configured first. These elements have already been described in detail in previous sections, and they are listed here:

- Authentication/authorization schemes
- Resource types
- Host identifiers

During installation of OAM, an option is presented to the user to create a couple of default policy domains to protect OAM URLs for the OAM Identity System Console, User Manager, Group Manager, Org. Manager, Access System Console, and the Access Manager application (Web interface to create policy domains and security policies). Also, the installer creates a few authentication schemes automatically, and a couple of optional ones if the user chooses to, during Web-based setup of the access system.

## Creating Policy Domains and Security Policies

Policy Manager is the application that creates policy domains and security policies. Policy domains may protect a single application or a set of applications. It depends very much on the requirements of the organization and the number of applications to be protected. If the number is very large, applications should be logically grouped to keep the policies manageable. Enterprises having hundreds of applications integrated to the access system SSO framework may choose to define the policy domains in terms of the audience for each group of applications. An API to manage policy domains and security policies programmatically is also available for developers to build their own interfaces.

## Regulatory Governance Mapping

Security controls must be dealt with in a holistic context. Regardless of the source of the control criteria, be it internally or externally imposed, there is value in using a systematic approach to the overall design of the security controls. With the added emphasis on compliance with government regulatory agencies' requirements to first provide accurate data to the agencies and the public, and with the groundswell of cases of identity theft in the morning news, appropriate access control strategies become critical in every computer environment. In the area of regulatory compliance, no application is more critical to satisfying the requirements of ITIL Security, ISO 27001, and COBIT DS5 than Access Manager as a technical control. Breaking the issue of compliance into nine control domains, access control *maps* directly to the Trusted Access control domain. However, Operational Control and Segregation of Duties control domains are also areas in which the access control framework may be mapped.

- Trusted Access
- Operational Accountability and Transparency
- Segregation of Duties
- Operational Controls

Of primary interest to those implementing access control to satisfy a regulatory requirement is the audit policy configuration cited in Figure 10.5. As such, the Operational Accountability and Transparency control domain may also be satisfied by implementation of an access control system.

## Summary

OAM comprises two main subsystems—The Identity System and Access System.

The Identity System provides users the ability to control the life cycle of the user identities, groups and, organization assets subject to be identified. The identity system provides advanced workflow capabilities and extension mechanisms via Event Plug-In APIs. It also provides a Web services interface to allow developers to write IdM applications leveraging the Identity System's capabilities.

The Access System allows administrators to centralize the administration of access policies to control user access to resources and applications across the organization. It provides the capabilities to implement single sign-on across all applications and resources protected by policies in the Access System. It also provides the capability to extend the functionality of the access server to achieve authentication and authorization by communicating with external systems and identity data repositories. It provides an API to allow applications to incorporate security into their implementation without having to write all the capabilities of a full-blown security system as part of the application development.

The Identity System provides a customizable user interface, which is accomplished via modifying XSL stylesheets that are applied to in-memory XML streams to transform them into HTML with the desired look and feel for the user interface.

The Identity System has two main components—identity server and WebPass.

The Access System has four main components—Access System Console, Policy Manager, access servers, and WebGate/AccessGates.

The identity server has four applications used to administer identity data—Identity System Console, User Manager, Group Manager, and Org. Manager.

Identity System Console allows administrators to configure and customize the features of the other three applications. User Manager is an application that provides the capabilities to manage user accounts. Group Manager allows administrators to manage groups of users and create static, dynamic, or nested groups even when the underlying LDAP server does not support these natively. Org. Manager provides the ability to manage the life cycle of any organization asset represented as an entry in LDAP; very sophisticated implementations take advantage of the Org. Manager to represent user roles, resources, and applications.

APIs are provided for developers to leverage OAM functionality in their applications.

IdentityXML is an API exposed through Web services; it allows developers to access Identity System features such as workflow execution, user profile management, group profile management, password management, and many others.

Event Plug-In API is available to developers to extend the functionality of the Identity System with custom business logic.

Access Server SDK allows developers to integrate security services such as authentication and authorization in their custom-built applications that cannot be protected out of the box or have special integration requirements.

Authentication and Authorization Plug-In API allows developers to extend the authentication and authorization capabilities of the Access System by adding pluggable modules that accomplish authentication/authorization through external systems different from LDAP.

*Chapter 11*

# Oracle Web Services Manager

In today's business environment, agility and quick response to demanding markets is the key to the success of companies immersed in a tremendously competitive world, especially for global economies, where many countries compete to provide better products and services to their target global markets.

Enterprises face big challenges from the requirements imposed by regulations intended to standardize the procedures and practices necessary to maintain control of information security and guarantee data privacy within the organization and extending beyond its internal boundaries. Web services are important for providing a solid communications infrastructure between the operational and executive management. Specifically for Sarbanes–Oxley purposes, this system must supply information in real-time about material events. Further, the whistleblower requirements of Section 301 mandate an anonymous and secure communication system. The internal controls requirement of Section 404 and the financial accuracy requirements of Section 302 also require a secure communication system, because many important commands and controls are implemented through e-mail and messaging systems and important financial information travels through these communication channels.

This chapter will focus on the Business Process and Controls tier of the compliance architecture presented earlier. The main goal is to describe in detail the role of Oracle Web Services Manager (OWSM) as a member of the Oracle Identity Management Product Suite, which provides services related to Business Process and Controls (Automation, Integration, and Monitoring) applicable to Web services. Also, OWSM integrates with OAM to leverage the functionality related to Security and Identity Management (mainly Authentication/Authorization and Auditing) applied to Web services.

## Architecture

Oracle Web Services Manager provides enterprise IT administrators the ability to monitor, secure, and analyze the performance of Web services deployed on the IT infrastructure in a cost-effective fashion. The architecture of OWSM has the following components:

- PEP (policy enforcement points)
  - Client-side agents
  - Server-side agents
  - Gateways
- Administrative components
  - Monitor
  - Collector
  - Aggregator
- Policy Manager
- Administrator Console

## PEP (Policy Enforcement Points)

These components execute policy steps at various points during the Web service, called its *life cycle* (before the actual request, during the request, after the request, before the response, during the response and after the response). There are three types of PEPs in OWSM:

- Client-side agents: This kind of PEP is deployed within applications consuming Web services, in other words, applications performing as a Web services client. These agents are usually assigned the responsibility to collect data for capacity planning and perform logging for auditing purposes.
- Server-side agents: This kind of PEP is deployed within applications exposing Web services. These agents are usually employed in monitoring the performance and quality of service of the providers for capacity planning and scalability analysis.
- Gateways: This kind of PEP is deployed stand-alone. Gateways are especially powerful because they provide features not available in client- or server-side agents, like content routing, message modification, and protocol conversion.

All PEPs basically have the same purpose. The decision about deploying a client-side agent vs. server-side agents or gateways depends on the following factors:

- Functional requirements
- Ownership of Web services and applications
- Application development practices

If the service provider cannot accept SOAP messages over HTTP and must be transported through a message queue, then a gateway is required. If different Web services must be executed, depending on the contents of the initial request (content routing), this also requires a Gateway. Agents are used in situations where the functionality required is merely collecting and logging data.

Sometimes, applications are hosted externally and are not controlled by the organization using them. If this is the case, the recommended PEP type is an agent. The agent must be deployed into the application before making it available to the hosting party. Agents do not have any impact in the way managed Web services are invoked, as is the case for gateways.

Depending on how flexible applications are in terms of the way they were written, OWSM administrators may choose agents or gateways to manage Web services consumed or exposed by these applications.

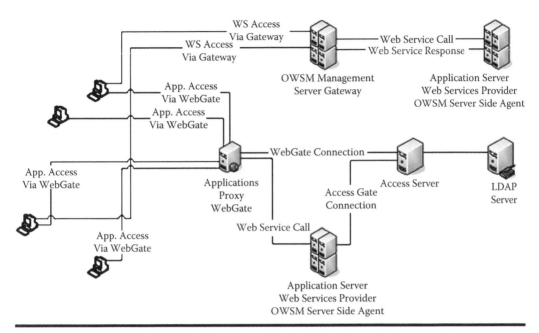

**Figure 11.1 Policy Enforcement Points distribution architecture.**

Figure 11.1 shows the location of agents and gateways and highlights each other's best applications:

As shown in the picture, agents are embedded into the applications themselves; they are actually deployed within the application's WAR file. The installation process of an agent generates a new WAR file, which is then deployed to the location of the original WAR file. Then the application server is restarted for the changes to apply. A good application for agents is logging and auditing. On the other hand, gateways are stand-alone PEPs, and they do not need to be placed on the host where applications are located. A good application for gateways is authentication/authorization of user access to Web services. Also, using gateways, it is possible to expose services that do not provide a SOAP-based interface to the client, which still has the ability to access it via SOAP over HTTP(S). This is due to the ability of the gateway to translate from one transport protocol to another without placing dependencies on the caller; in other words, a gateway makes the distinction between a client request and a service invocation, where client requests usually come over HTTP(S) and the service invocation may use a different transport protocol to invoke the service.

# Administrative Components

The following components provide the administration functionality for OWSM.

## Monitor

The monitor is responsible for collecting data and generating meaningful information to be displayed in the management console of OWSM. The monitor, in turn, has two subcomponents: the collector and the aggregator. Collectors are distributed as the agents and gateways. There is only one instance of the aggregator; it receives the data sent by the collectors, manipulates the data, and stores the results in the Metadata Repository database.

### Policy Manager

The Policy Manager allows administrators to define policies and configure policy steps, manage the life cycle of the policies, and facilitate registration of PEPs. The Policy Manager stores all the configuration information related to policies and registered PEPs in the Metadata Repository database.

### Administration Console

This is a Web application providing a central point of access to perform administrative tasks. The console displays information prepared by the aggregator component of the monitor. It also allows administrators to register agents, gateways, and services managed by them.

## Service-Oriented Architecture in OWSM

In order to understand the value of OWSM as a management tool, it is important to understand the concepts of Service-Oriented Architecture (SOA). Many SOA principles are applied in the design of OWSM's architecture, and that is what gives OWSM a unique and flexible design to provide a non-invasive approach to Web services management.

### The Power of SOA

SOA is arguably the most flexible and adaptable architecture model available for designing extensible, highly dynamic IT infrastructures prepared to rapidly evolve and adapt to changes in business requirements and technology trends.

OWSM is completely designed-based on the concept of services as self-contained functionality units performing their work without affecting the structure, behavior, or implementation of other business entities and other services that interact with them. This allows OWSM to provide a totally uninvasive approach to management of Web services infrastructures.

## Installation and Configuration

This section describes how OWSM is installed, deployed, and configured to suit the particular needs of an organization. The topics discussed here are not a mere repetition of the OWSM product documentation. The purpose of this section is to provide additional pieces of information that are not covered in too much detail in the product's documentation or describe best practices when installing and deploying OWSM components.

## Installation Packages and Configuration Files

OWSM installation is comprised by a series of ANT scripts (ANT is an open source scripting tool that allows us to build MAKE files to compile, deploy, and install software components and applications) that will perform the following main tasks:

- Create the installation files for all the components of OWSM.
- Create Web Application Archives for the Administration Console, the Policy Manager, the gateway, and the monitor.
- Create the Metadata Repository SQL scripts used to create and populate tables, views, and indices.
- Execute the SQL scripts to create and populate the Metadata Repository Database of OWSM.
- Before installing OWSM, it is recommended to carefully plan the deployment of each component in order to achieve the best performance as possible. Here are some suggestions of aspects to be considered for a good OWSM deployment:
  - Distribute the components in a multi-tier architecture. The diagram in Figure 11.2 shows a deployment architecture that serves as a reference for your design. In the picture there are five architecture tiers highlighted. These are the most typical, but there might be other tiers with additional components and services. Each tier in this architecture has a purpose, which is described below:
    - Web Proxies Tier: This tier front-ends clients who access enterprise applications over the Internet/intranet. This tier frequently hosts security checkpoint components (i.e., Oracle Access Manager's WebGates to enforce security policies protecting Web applications) used to secure user access to resources (Web applications, Web services, and other IT assets).
    - Application Middle Tier: This tier hosts the application containers. There are many ways in which applications are developed and deployed; for Web services in particular, in the context of OWSM, there are two ways in which Web services can be managed: via gateways and via agents. Gateways and agents are part of the OWSM Policy Enforcement point described later, but the decision on how to manage Web services via either agents or gateways determines how applications are deployed or even developed. In the picture in Figure 11.2, Applications deployed in this tier are configured to redirect calls to Web services through the Policy Enforcement Point Tier; this way, policies can be enforced by the Gateways on that tier.
    - OWSM Policy Enforcement Points Tier: This tier hosts components whose only purpose is to enforce policies, which are successions of steps, each of which performs a particular task at a given point in time during the life cycle of a Web service call. Notice in the diagram above, that there is an application container sitting on this tier. Doesn't that belong to the Middle Tier instead? Well, in this particular case the applications have PEP (Policy Enforcement Points) called Agents embedded into the applications themselves, therefore the container is placed on this tier and not on the Middle Tier.
    - Business Tier: The SOA architecture paradigm promotes the encapsulation of business functionality into atomic, loosely coupled, and reusable components known as

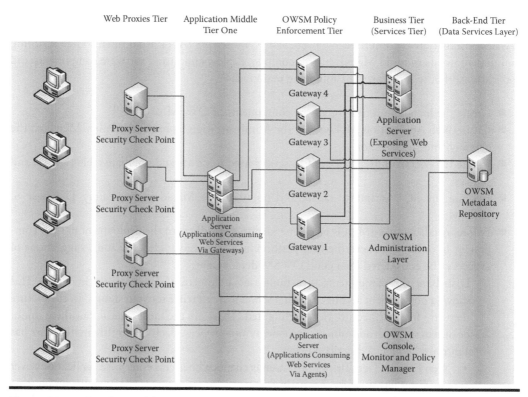

**Figure 11.2  Five-tier architecture.**

Services, which are the building blocks of complex business and enterprise applications, whose behavior is always consistent. This tier hosts the containers of actual Web services. Server-side agents can potentially be deployed as part of applications packaging together a set of Web services; in this case the diagram just shows the containers and no agents.

• Back-End Tier: This tier hosts the repositories where OWSM maintains its configuration for all the components. Notice in the diagram that all the components including the Administration Console, Policy Manager, agents, and gateways link to the Metadata Repository located on this tier.

## Preinstallation Recommendations

Before starting the installation it is recommended to modify the installation configuration files with some information related to the database connectivity. Table 11.1 describes what files these are and what you should do with them.

Once these configuration files have been prepared with the database connectivity information according to your existing database implementation, it is time to run the installer. The purpose of this installation is to generate the files necessary to deploy OWSM components onto their corresponding destinations. In a typical deployment scenario, the administration components are deployed in one machine and the enforcement points are deployed on different machines. So, the Administration Console, the monitor, and the Policy Manager are deployed together; the gateway

**Table 11.1   Pre-Install Configuration**

| File | Location | What to Do |
|---|---|---|
| Install.properties | <OWSM-Install-From Directory> | Configure the install.home.dir and the coresv.home.dir properties – for example: |
| | i.e.:/usr/local/owsm/ coresv | install.home.dir=/usr/local/owsm/ coresv_install_home |
| | | coresv.home.dir=/usr/local/owsm/ coresv_install_home |
| | | *Note: Both have to be the same.* |
| monitor_config_ installer.properties | | Configure the JDBC access parameters for the Monitor – i.e: |
| | | monitor.repository.url=jdbc:Oracle: thin: @localhost.localdomain:1521:PEDB2 |
| | | monitor.repository.driver=Oracle.jdbc. driver.OracleDriver |
| | | monitor.repository.userid=OWSM |
| | | monitor.repository.password=Oracle1 |
| gateway_config_ installer.properties | | gateway.repository.driver=Oracle.jdbc. driver.OracleDriver |
| | | gateway.repository.password=Oracle1 |
| | | gateway.repository.userid=OWSM |
| | | gateway.repository.url=jdbc:Oracle:thin: @ localhost.localdomain:1521:PEDB2 |
| ui_config_installer. properties | <OWSM-Install-From Directory>/config/ccore | |
| | i.e.:/usr/local/owsm/ coresv /config/ccore | Configure the authentication information for the Console Login – for example: |
| | | ui.authentication.provider=com.cfluent. accessprovider.sampledb. LocalDBAuthProvider |
| | | ui.authentication.provider.properties=\ |
| | | dbConnectionUrl=jdbc:Oracle:thin: @ localhost.localdomain:1521 :PEDB2|\ |
| | | dbDriver=Oracle.jdbc.driver.OracleDriver|\ |
| | | dbUser=OWSM|\ |
| | | dbPassword=Oracle1|\ |

*(continued on next page)*

**Table 11.1 (continued)   Pre-Install Configuration**

| File | Location | What to Do |
|------|----------|------------|
| | | maxConnections=10\|\ |
| | | idleTime=300\|\ |
| | | maxConnectionTime=120 |
| | | Also configure the jdbc connection string and authentication info – for instance: |
| | | ui.repository.url=jdbc:Oracle:thin: @ localhost.localdomain:1521:PEDB2 |
| | | ui.repository.driver=Oracle.jdbc.driver. OracleDriver |
| | | ui.repository.userid=OWSM |
| | | ui.repository.password=Oracle1 |
| | | ui.repository.maxConnections=10 |
| | | ui.repository.maxConnectionTime=120 |
| | | ui.repository.idleConnectionTime=1000 |
| | | ui.componentRepository. url=jdbc:Oracle:thin: @localhost. localdomain:1521:PEDB2 |
| | | ui.componentRepository.driver=Oracle. jdbc. driver.OracleDriver |
| | | ui.componentRepository.userid=OWSM |
| | | ui.componentRepository.password=Oracle1 |
| | | ui.componentRepository. maxConnections=10 |
| | | ui.componentRepository. maxConnectionTime=120 |
| | | ui.componentRepository. idleConnectionTime=1000 |

or gateways are deployed stand-alone or on the same machine as the other components; there is no restriction. For client- and server-side agents, they have to be deployed where the container applications reside. Remember that agents are embedded into the applications and constitute new Web Application Archives that are deployed in their corresponding application server containers.

It is also recommended to create a database user for OWSM and assign this user the DBA role at least until the OWSM dataload steps (described in the Installation process overview section) are complete.

## Installation Process Overview

This section only presents a brief overview of the installation process. This is well documented in the Installation and Configuration Guide, so please refer to this for the installation. Although this section does not delve too much into details of installation, it does intend to provide additional tips and recommendations to install components and deploy them according to recommended best practices.

The installation consists of the following steps:

- Execute the install.bat or install.sh (Windows and Unix, respectively).
- Create the SQL scripts via the dataloadconfigure option of coresv.bat|coresv.sh script.
- Initialize and load the metada into the database using the dataload option of the coresv. bat|coresv.sh script.
- Deploy the Administration Console Web Application (coresv deploy ccore).
- Deploy the Monitor (coresv deploy monitor).
- Deploy the Policy Manager (coresv deploy policymanager).
- Deploy the Default Gateway (coresv deploy Gateway).

### Components Distribution

Usually the components of a typical OWSM installation are organized as follows:

- Gateways are deployed to their own machines. It is possible to have multiple Gateways on the same machine; however, it is not recommended for performance and scalability reasons. It is also possible to have a load balancer in front of two or more machines hosting an OWSM Gateway. Gateways do not have built-in failover capabilities. Failover is implemented by configuring failover service URLs when registering services onto a gateway.
- The Admin Console, Policy Manager, and monitor are all kept together on the same machine. It is possible to have redundant instances of the administration components to keep as a failover infrastructure.
- The metadata database repository is also usually installed on its own machine. This is not usually part of the OWSM installation because most of the time there is a database already available before installation of OWSM.
- Agents are embedded in applications so the deployment and redundancy of agents depends on the physical deployment and redundancy of the applications hosting them.

# OWSM Administration

After all required OWSM components have been installed and configured, Administrators can then start registering services and configuring management policies. The first task to accomplish is the registration of the gateways in your installation.

## Registering a Gateway

To register a gateway, administrators log into the OWSM Administration Console and access the Policy Manager. The first time the Policy Manager is opened there are no components registered.

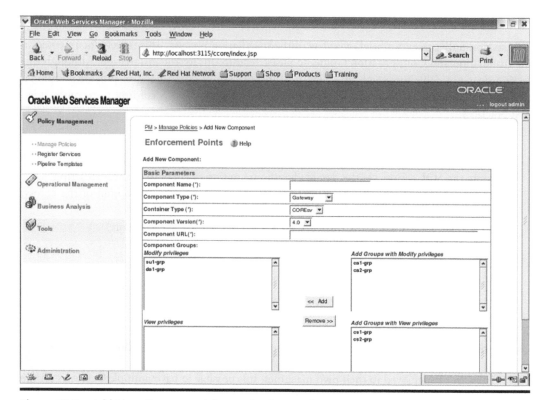

**Figure 11.3   Add New Component form—Register a Gateway.**

To register a Gateway, click on the Add New Component button. This will display the following form in the OWSM Administration Console in Figure 11.3:

To register the gateway it is required to provide a name for the component—which should be a descriptive name—and select the component type, which in this case is Gateway. Also select the Container Type and the Component Version. In the component URL enter the URL for the gateway (this is usually http://<host>:<port>/gateway). Once all the required information has been supplied proceed to click the Register button. A component ID is generated to uniquely identify the newly added component. This ID must be copied to the properties file in <OWSM Gateway Install Home>/config/gateway/gateway-config-installer.properties as the value of gateway. component.id property. Restart the Gateway's container by going to the host where the Gateway was deployed to and do a coresv.(sh|bat) start (startTomcat if you are using the bundled Tomcat container).

Before a gateway can process any service requests, the preceding steps must be completed successfully. Once the gateway is registered, it is time to add services to the gateway for it to manage. Return to the Manage Policies screen and select the Services link in the gateway's table entry. (There might be other components registered as well, like other gateways and client- or server-side agents; select the one you want to have the service registered onto.)

Gateways hide the actual End-Point URL of the services registered to them. There are some pieces of information needed to register services onto a gateway:

■ The URL of the WSDL descriptor for the service
■ The type of service this is (i.e., HTTP, JMS, other)

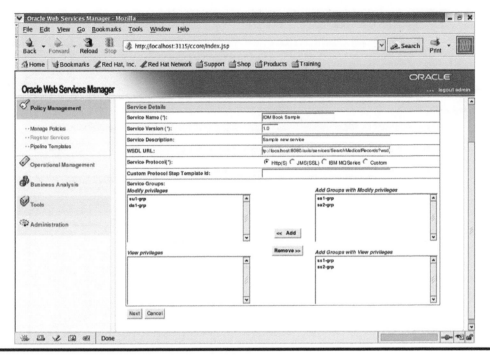

**Figure 11.4    Step 1—Add new service to a Gateway.**

The following screens illustrated in Figure 11.4 and 11.5 represent the steps to add a new service.

*Note:* It is important that you do not forget to Commit Policies after the service has been added, otherwise the gateway will not recognize the service as one registered to it.

In Step 1, administrators must provide a descriptive name for the service, a version, and a description. Then, the URL to the WSDL service descriptor is required. This URL must be valid and reachable in order to complete the registration process in Step 2. In the example shown above, the service protocol is HTTP(S); it might be different depending on the service being registered.

The preceding screen shows additional parameters for the service, such as timeouts and credential forwarding. Also, it is possible to configure failover URLs for this service to guarantee high availability.

## *Deploying Agents*

Agents are PEPs, just like gateways, although their capabilities and deployment procedure are different. Agents are not stand-alone components like the gateways, they are injected into the WAR file of applications hosting the agents. Only one agent can be installed per Web application. The steps to enable an agent are outlined as follows:

■ Register the agent just as described for the gateway (the procedures are very similar) and note the Component ID.
■ Modify the configuration files of the agent before installing the agent on the hosting machine to configure the Component ID and other properties of the agent.

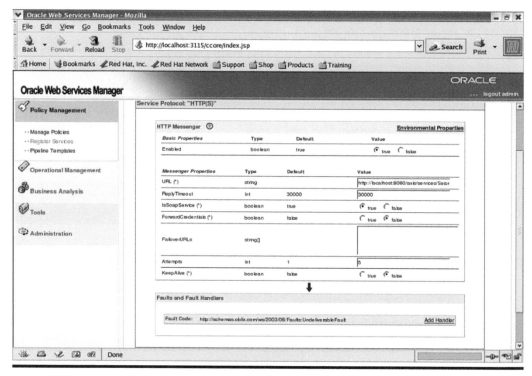

**Figure 11.5 Step 2—Add new service to a Gateway.**

- Run the coresv (sh|bat) command line tool to deploy the agent by injecting it in the target application's WAR.
- Deploy the new WAR file (with the injected agent) on the application server.

# Extensibility of OWSM

OWSM provides mechanisms to extend the functionality of the out-of-the-box components, making it possible to integrate with complex systems and fulfill special requirements within the organization. OWSM policies are active elements comprising steps, which in turn are functional units. These functional units can potentially interact with external systems to fulfill particular needs of a business process involving Web services. To accomplish the integration of custom logic within the policies, an API is available to developers allowing them to build custom pieces of functionality. These custom steps can be integrated into the policies enforced by agents and gateways.

## *Custom Step Development*

The process of developing custom steps is outlined in the Extensibility Guide of OWSM. A quote from the Extensibility Guide is shown below and will serve as a reference to start the discussion about this process:

"Developing a custom step that integrates with COREsv software involves completion of the following tasks:

- Define a Step Template and providing a unique ID, name and configurable parameters for the step.
- Extend the AbstractStep class by writing the implementation of the execute Method.
- Define fault codes (if needed) for the step.
- Deploy the custom step.
- If you have defined fault codes, assign appropriate fault handlers to the step.

By performing these tasks, you will also ensure that custom steps you develop are also compliant with Web services standards."

## Step: Templates

Step Templates are the equivalent of a deployment descriptor for a J2EE Web Application. Step Templates contain all the information about the custom steps, including the following:

- The name of the java class implementing the Custom Step
- A unique ID to identify the step within the system
- The name and type of Custom Step properties
- Descriptions of the purpose of the custom step and its properties

## Step: Interface

The Java API available to develop custom steps has an abstract class com.cfluent.policysteps. sdk. AbstractStep, which must be extended by the class implementing the custom step. Most of the methods have an implementation within the abstract class; however, the execute() method must be implemented by the developer of the custom step. This method contains the implementation of the step's functionality.

## Note: Exception Handling

It is very important to implement proper exception handling to guarantee the stability of the custom step as much as possible and avoid difficulties in diagnosing problems that may arise. The best practice is to catch as many specific exceptions and return the proper error codes. For run-time exceptions that may occur and are not evident at first hand, the execute method throws a Fault exception, which will generate a SOAPFault message propagated back to the message response, which can also be logged and audited.

## Step: Deployment

To deploy a custom step, the OWSM administrator needs to log into the OWSM console and navigate to the Policy Manager screen showing all registered components as illustrated in Figure 11.6:

Click on the Steps link in Figure 11.7. This will present the following screen to the user:

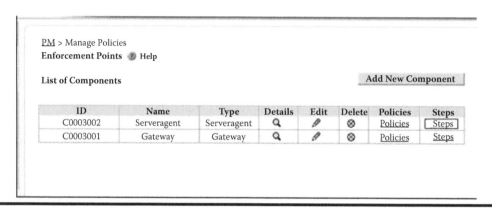

**Figure 11.6  Policy Manager—Registered components screen.**

Click on the Add New Step button on the upper right-hand corner of the screen shown in Figure 11.7. This will allow the administrator to upload the Custom Step Template created for the step as shown in Figure 11.8.

Once the template has been uploaded, the new step should appear in the list of steps for the component selected from the Policy Manager screen. Notice in Figure 11.8 that only Custom Steps can be deleted. Default Steps that come included with OWSM cannot be deleted.

The upload process causes OWSM to determine which custom properties to present in the configuration screen for the step and also allows it to instantiate the class implementing the step. In order to do this, the JAR file having all the classes used in the implementation of the Custom Step must be present in the CLASSPATH for the components to be able to find it.

## Security for Web Services

OWSM can also enforce access policies upon Web services calls leveraging the security services provided by Oracle Access Manager. OWSM provides a set of out of the box policy steps to enforce security policies upon a Web service call. This section provides some examples of how to configure these steps to achieve user authentication and authorization to a Web service call.

### Step 1: Extract Credentials

The Extract Credentials step, as its name implies, collects the credentials from a pre-defined source. The source—or location—of the credentials may be one of the following:

- HTTP: HTTP headers like the ones for Basic Authentication, which are placed in the transport protocol section of the SOAP message when submitted through HTTP.
- Xpath: When credentials are embedded into the SOAP message itself, an Xpath expression can be used to parse the credentials out of the SOAP envelope. This mechanism allows for any custom XML representation to be parsed to extract the credentials from the SOAP message.

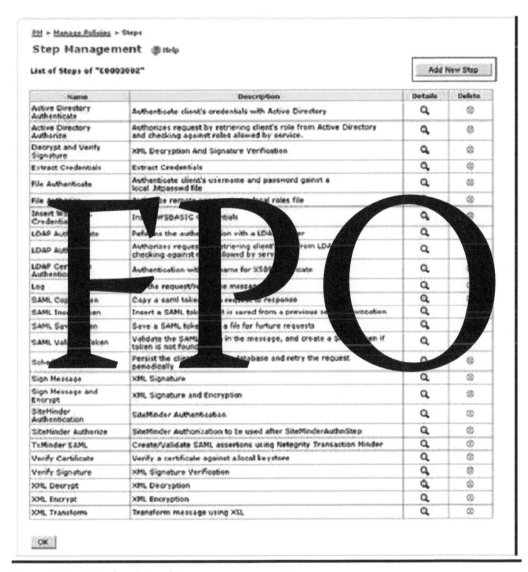

**Figure 11.7    List of registered steps per component.**

## *Step 2: OAM Authenticate/Authorized (COREid Authenticate/Authorize)*

Once credentials have been extracted, these are passed to the next step in the policy's pipeline, which usually is the Authenticate/Authorize step. This step uses an Access Gate defined in Oracle Access Manager, which connects to the Access Server of OAM to perform Authentication and apply access policies defined in Access Manager. This works as follows:

- OAM administrators create an Access Gate in OAM Access System Console.
- OAM administrators install the Access Gate in a directory accessible to the Policy Enforcement Point of OWSM; this is important because Access Gates are not remotely accessible to Gateways or Agents.

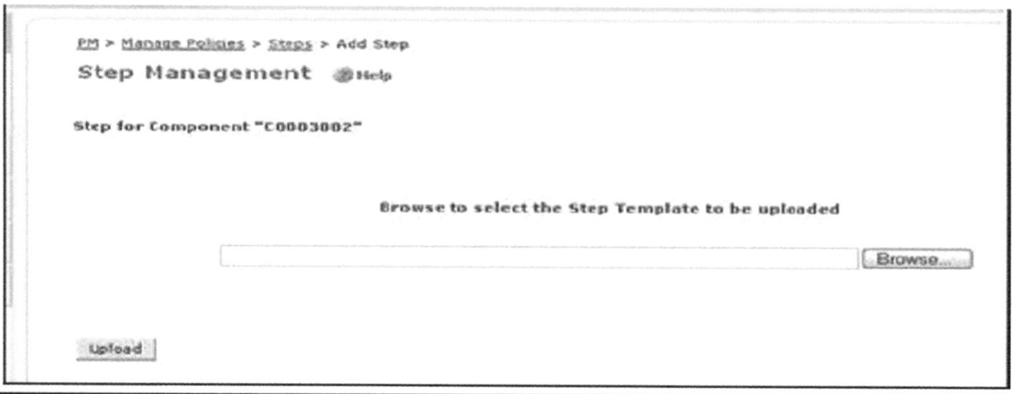

**Figure 11.8    Upload Template for the Custom Step.**

- OAM administrators create Policy Domains and Access Policies protecting the /gateway/ services/<Optional SID> (this is only required for services protected by a policy enforced by Gateways) and the URL of the Web service provider's end-point. It is recommended to create a Host Identifiers Set for applications and Gateways deployed in OWSM's installation.
- OWSM administrators register services to gateways or inject agents into Web services applications to enforce policies.
- OWSM administrators create a policy to protect a service request in OWSM Policy Manager.
- OWSM administrators add the Extract Credentials Step (already described) and the Authenticate/Authorize Step, which is configured to access the directory where the Access Gate was installed.

Figure 11.9 describes the Authentication Process in detail: Some clients access applications protected by WebGate (see Chapter 6 for details about WebGates); others call Web services deployed on the same application server as WebGate protected applications and yet others call Web services through an OWSM gateway. In all cases, Web services are protected by OWSM policies enforced by either an agent or a gateway. Policies enforced by agents or gateways use AccessGate type of connections to authenticate and perform authorization decisions. Application access through WebGates generates the ObSSOCookie, which can also be consumed by OWSM enforcement points using the Authenticate/Authorize step. This allows SSO between applications and Web services.

## Example: Authentication and Authorization Integrated with COREid

Designing an authentication and authorization strategy for distributed Web applications is a challenging task. The good news is that proper authentication and authorization design during the early phases of your application development helps to mitigate many top security risks.

When you consider authorization, you must also consider authentication. The two processes go hand in hand for two reasons: First, any meaningful authorization policy requires authenticated users. Second, the way in which you authenticate users (and specifically the way in which

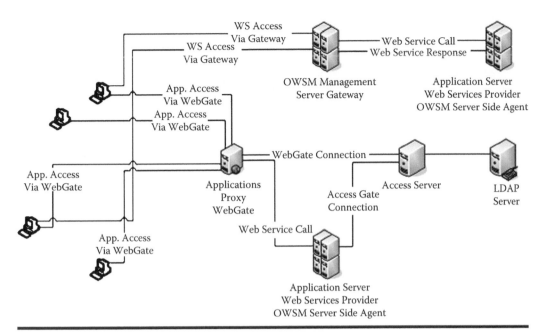

**Figure 11.9   Authentication process.**

the authenticated user identity is represented within your application) determines the available gatekeepers at your disposal.

In this example, we will walk through COREid's approach to policy enforcement of a Web service.

## *Policy Configuration*

In order to protect a Web service with a policy enforced through a gateway or an agent, the following procedure must be performed:

In OWSM Administration Console, click on Policy Management|Manage Policies.

A table with all registered Gateways and Agents is displayed. Select Policies link of the row corresponding to the registered Gateway or Agent supposed to enforce the policies for a given services. A list of all registered services and their associated policies is displayed.

From this screen select the Pencil Icon to edit the policy for the service in question. The edit policy screen is presented in Figure 11.10.

Click the Add Step Below link on the Log step in the Pipeline "Request". This will add a step to the policy's pipeline for the Request. Select Extract Credentials from the drop-down box as shown in Figure 11.11.

Click on the OK button and then select Configure link of the just added step. See screen in Figure 11.12.

Namespaces:

    soap=http://schemas.xmlsoap.org/soap/envelope

    wsse=http://docs.oasis-open.org/wss/2004/01/oasis-200401-wss-wssecurity-secext-
    1.0.xsd

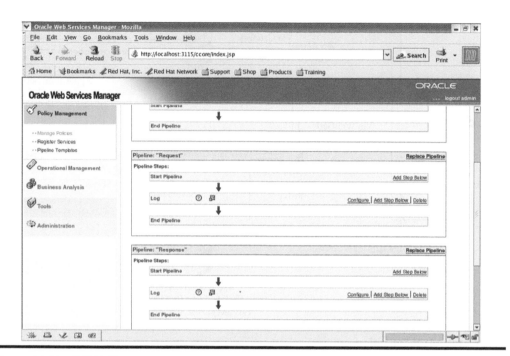

Figure 11.10    Edit Policy screen.

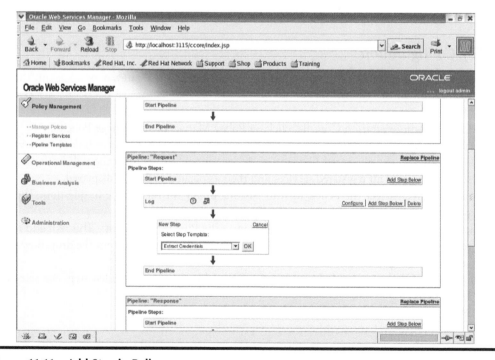

Figure 11.11    Add Step in Policy screen.

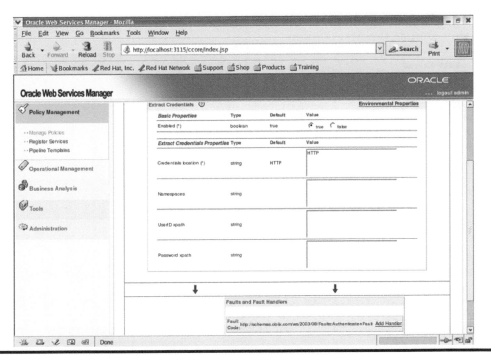

**Figure 11.12   Select the Configure link.**

UserID xpath: wsse:Username
Password: wsse:Password

Save the step.

Click on the Add Step Below link of the Extract Credentials step to add the next step, which
will be the COREid Authenticate/Authorize. Select the COREid Authenticate/Authorize
step from the dropdown list and click Ok.

*Note*: The next step in the process assumes that the Access Server SDK has already been installed
and configured. Please contact your OAM administrator if you are not sure of the above.

Part of the Authenticate/Authorize step configuration is specifying the Access Server SDK
installation directory where the Access Gate created by OAM administrator. Make sure you have
this information before configuring the Authenticate/Authorize Step in OWSM.

Figure 11.13 shows the details after the policy configuration has been completed.

## Create Policy Domain for OWSM services

OAM administrators must create policies to allow OAM to authenticate/authorize access to protected resources. In this case OWSM requires having the following URLs protected by a policy in
order to leverage the security management services of OAM:

/gateway/services/<ServiceID>
/OWSMProtectionTestApp/OWSMProtectionTestWSSoapHttpPort

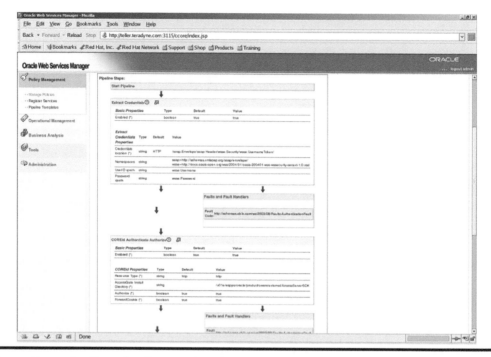

**Figure 11.13   Configured Policy—Authenticate/Authorize using COREid.**

In Access Manager console of OAM, click on New Policy Domain.

■ Provide a name—OWSM for instance.
■ Add two resources with the two URLs mentioned above.
■ Save the policy domain and enable it.

## Create Test Cases in OWSM Test Engine

OWSM has a test engine where all access to services can be tested and verified. In order to create a test case complete the following procedure:

In the OWSM Administration Console select Tools|Test Engine from the left-hand side menu bar.

Click on the Create New Test button.

Provide a name for the test and a brief description, then click Next button. The screen in Figure 11.14 should be presented.

Provide the following for each field.

## Provide the WSDL URL

Provide the WSDL URL of the Gateway for the ServiceID (SID) being protected. This can be obtained by going to the Gateway's Services Link, which displays the list of all registered services for the selected Gateway.

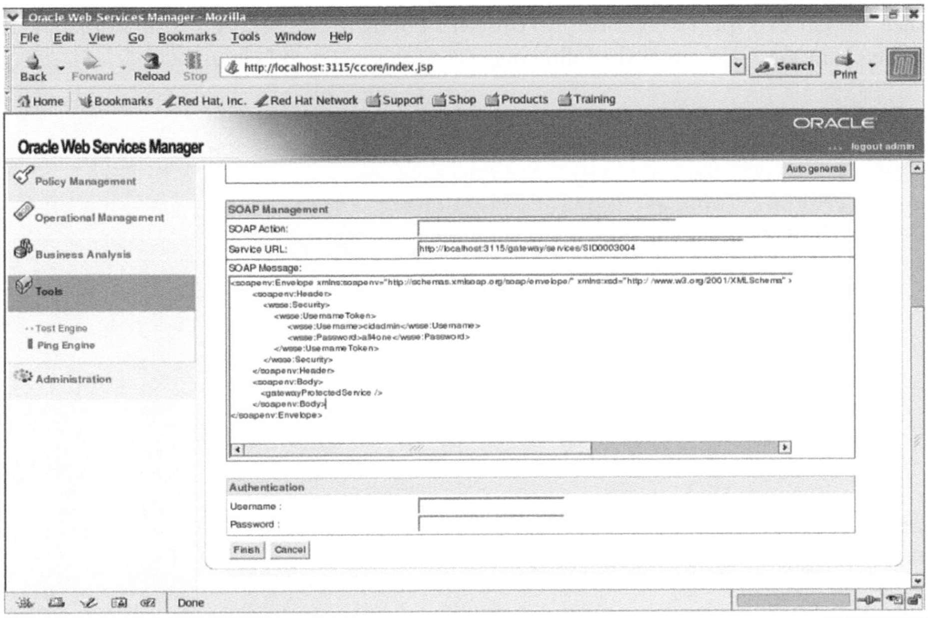

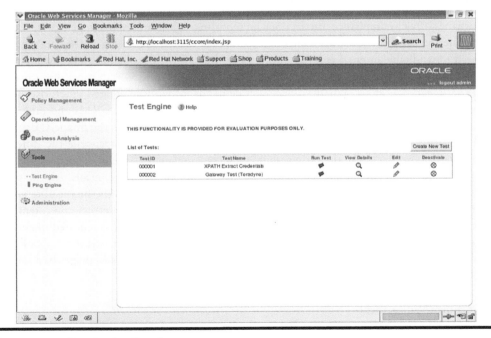

**Figure 11.14  Test Case Setup screen.**

**Figure 11.15  Test Engine Result screen.**

Click on Check Operations Button—this will populate the drop-down box for operations. Select the operation. Then enter the following text in the text area below:

```
<soapenv:Envelope
xmlns:soapenv="http://schemas.xmlsoap.org/soap/envelope/"
xmlns:xsd="http:/ /www.w3.org/2001/XMLSchema"
xmlns:xsi="http://www.w3.org/2001/XMLSchema-instance">
  <soapenv:Header>
    <wsse:Security>
      <wsse:UsernameToken>
        <wsse:Username>username</wsse:Username>
        <wsse:Password>password</wsse:Password>
      </wsse:UsernameToken>
    </wsse:Security>
  </soapenv:Header>
  <soapenv:Body>
    <!-- Web Service's Body -->
  </soapenv:Body>
</soapenv:Envelope>
```

Click the Finish button. The new test should be displayed on the list of test cases.

For the test case on the agent, the same procedure applies; the only difference is that the actual service URL for the WSDL and End Point should be provided as opposed to the gateway's URL as in the previous case.

## Regulatory Governance Mapping

For Sarbanes–Oxley compliance, the sections on reporting significant events, together with those on accurate and timely financial and other data, reveal a critical need to bring all the data together. The need for auditable internal controls also requires that all the data be integrated, work across various business processes, and be traceable. Sections 302, 404, and 409 thus call for a massive enterprise integration effort. Financial accuracy demands a highly integrated enterprise. If the information from the trio of core transactional systems (i.e., ERP, SCM, CRM) and other supporting functional automation systems is not integrated by a Web service, the financial data will remain inaccurate, and large amounts of resources will be required to reconcile the differing, though overlapping, data from the various sources. Such data remains open to distortion, loss, and corruption. Further, it becomes easy to prove the inadequacy of internal controls. All the places where data comes out of the transaction systems and is then entered into the financial reporting systems is a point of vulnerability, because of both unintentional human errors and intentional mischief. The possibility of providing real-time reports of material events, as required under Section 409, is extremely low. Of the nine control domains against which the existing body of compliance regulations and frameworks may be mapped, Oracle Web Services Manager best satisfies the following:

- Change Management
- Business Continuity and Availability
- Operational Monitor and Report
- Risk and Audit Management

- Operational Accountability and Transparency
- Operational Controls

When deploying a Web service for use by applications, it is not necessarily good enough to specify just the Web service interface and location. If the Web service takes longer to execute than the caller expects, the service will still fail. The specification for the amount of time it takes the service to return a result is part of the service's quality of service (QoS) specification. This aspect highlights the quality aspect of the Web service in conformance with the rules, the law, compliance with standards, and the established service level agreement. Oracle Web Services Manager serves to implement change control structures into functional service architecture, using the configuration cited in Figure 11.8. Operational reporting and audit management are achievable control objectives across all applications within the service bus. Fine-grained operational controls may be implemented within custom policy domains. The use of SOAP enables enforcement of secure operational controls within the domain governed but the auditing capabilities of the Collector and the Aggregator respectively enable automation of operational accountability and transparency.

## Summary

Oracle Web Services Manager is a comprehensive solution for managing and securing Web services infrastructures in a cost-effective fashion.

The architecture is based on the principles of SOA (Service-Oriented Architectures) and provides nonintrusive approaches to enforce policies upon execution of a Web service method.

OWSM provides two types of policy enforcement points (PEPs)—client/server agents and gateways.

Agents are injected into the applications themselves and are deployed in the same container. When an agent enforces policies, the Web service provider URL does not change and the policy is enforced upon all the Web services provided by the application within which the agent is embedded.

Gateways are a kind of Web Service Proxy. When gateways enforce policies, the service provider URL exposed is the one for the gateway supposed to enforce the policy. This gives Gateways the capability to transform from one transport protocol to another—like SOAP over HTTP to SOAP over JMS. Gateways can perform routing based on the content of the SOAP envelope (Agents do not have this capability). Gateways can enforce policies upon explicitly registered Web services, giving greater granularity when enforcing policies to Web services packaged within the same application.

Oracle Web Services Manager policies can be customized by developing custom steps that implement custom business logic and execute it when the policy containing the custom step is involved. The API for custom steps is described in OWSM Extensibility Guide.

# Chapter 12

# Oracle Identity Management

## Overview

Enterprise provisioning involves the management activities, business processes and technologies governing the creation, modification, and deletion of user access rights and privileges to an organization's IT systems, applications, and physical assets. Any system that attempts to resolve this business issue must address the challenge of tiered role management. From an IT perspective this involves mapping roles as user groups, where roles represent IT access privileges across multiple application domains. One accomplishes this by assigning role membership assignment modes, and allowing direct assignment by an administrator, based on business rule matching. To validate the implementation of business rules in an IT setting, any provisioning solution must include audit and compliance features. In a tiered role management environment where roles represent IT access privileges, this takes the form of resource-level segregation of duties (SoD) implemented as an attestation of access rights of a user and access to a resource. In this paradigm, roles become Oracle Identity Management resource objects and represent IT access privileges across multiple application within role membership assignment modes.

This approach facilitates the self-service assertion and approval workflow vital to attestation and audit and compliance. Role-level segregation of duties implemented as functional attestation of roles and role memberships provides business-role-to-IT-role mapping as well as a comprehensive role definition process. This may be leveraged to implement role mining and role engineering at a business process improvement level, establishing a functional identity-entity relationship, role polyarchy, and role provider management.

## Logical Architecture

Oracle Identity Manager (OIM) is an application that handles and selectively automates tasks that manage a user's access privileges.

These tasks include the following:

■ Creating access privileges to resources for users
■ Modifying privileges dynamically based on changes to user and business requirements
■ Removing access privileges from users

OIM has three logical tiers, as shown in Figure 12.1:

■ Presentation tier
■ Server tier
■ Data and enterprise integration tier

The presentation tier of OIM has two layers:

## *Presentation Layer*

This has two consoles for OIM: administrative console and design console.

The presentation layer consists of a Web browser running on a client machine, which handles the presentation using HTML, Java Applets, Java scripts, and applications that communicate with the business logic layer.

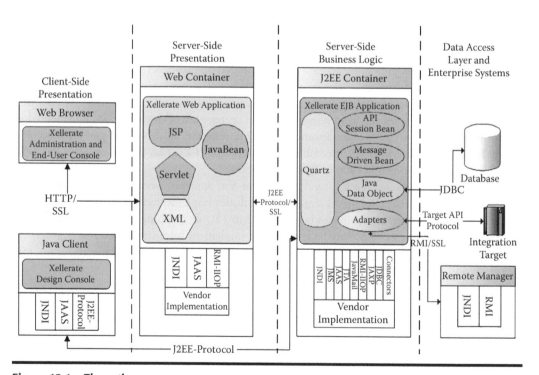

**Figure 12.1   Three tiers.**

## Dynamic Presentation Logic Layer

This is the logic for generating dynamic pages for the Administrative Console by using JSPs, Java servlets, XML, and JavaBeans.

The dynamic presentation layer (Figure 12.2) encompasses the logic for generating dynamic presentations and is done in the Web server using JSPs, servlets, XML, XSL, etc., to support the different kinds of browsers and presenting the content in its context of use.

## Business Logic Layer

The business logic of the enterprise application implemented in the middle tier has a J2EE application server that uses EJBs (Enterprise Java Beans) and other J2EE technologies to deploy the application as scalable and distributed (Figure 12.3).

(JDBC) connections and serves as an object-oriented wrapper around data sources.

The server tier of OIM is the interface between the presentation and data and enterprise integration tiers.

The application server for OIM:

■ Resides in the server tier
■ Provides the life-cycle management, security, deployment, and run-time services to the logical components that support OIM

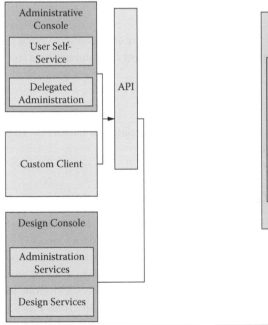

**Figure 12.2   Presentation layer.**

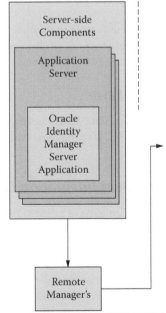

**Figure 12.3   Business logic layer.**

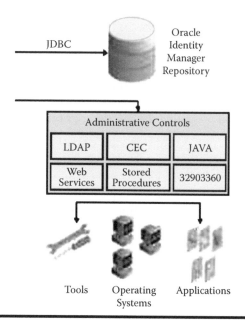

**Figure 12.4  Server tier.**

The server tier (see Figure 12.4) of OIM supports clustering, load balancing, security management, and scheduling.

The data and enterprise integration tier of OIM has two layers:

■ The data access layer, which has components enabling OIM to communicate with back-end data stores
■ A back-end data store that holds the relational substructure and leverages Oracle disaster and recovery features such as clustering, standby for redundant data storage, and replication

## Data Access Layer

This layer contains data access beans, which connect to the relational databases. This layer also manages the pool of Java database connectivity.

## Backend System Integration Layer

The back-end tier consists of a distributed set of relational databases and directories integrated to the middle tier using JDBC and JNDI, which are used to access multiple data sources (Figure 12.5).

However, in a compliance discussion, no component is more essential than the auditing, reconciliation, and attestation process. Reconciliation is the process by which OIM receives information from an external resource. Provisioning is the process by which OIM sends information to a target resource. By using reconciliation and provisioning, OIM can create a user record in a resource, then modify the privileges that the user has with the resource and, upon termination, remove the user record from the resource. OIM performs two types of reconciliation: trusted source and targeted resource reconciliation:

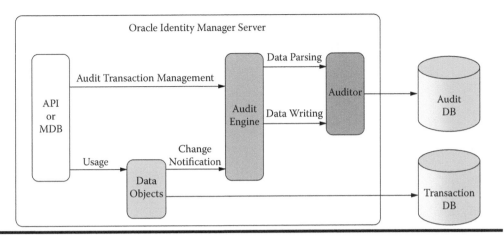

**Figure 12.5  Data tier.**

- *Targeted resource reconciliation* occurs when the audit criteria reconciles the resource request or change against the actual resource provisioned insuring access or the lack thereof in a ad hoc query bases.
- *Trusted source reconciliation* occurs when the audit criteria reconciles from a primary point of truth validating the resource access status against corporate policy.

Should reconciliation prove necessary, OIM can then perform three types of reconciliation events with an external resource: reconciliation insert, where the resource is provisioned and the status is updated; reconciliation update, where the status of the resource is changed in the database but the provisioning status remains unchanged; and reconciliation delete, where access is revoked and the status is reflected in the database.

OIM auditing consists of historical data, a reporting engine, and an interface. Archived data identifies users, the information that the users can access, the purpose for the access privileges, and the means for providing the information. You can capture, transport, store, retrieve, and remove historical data over its life cycle. Security is maintained at every part of the data life cycle.

Any action that a user takes in OIM translates into an application programming interface (API) call or into an MDB, picking up a message to process an action. To prevent the volume of audit records from affecting performance, the audit engine performs complex data extraction, processing, and recording (Figure 12.6). The audit engine works in parallel to the transaction processing within OIM. When a trigger for a defined event fires, the audit engine records the action and performs offline processing to generate and record the resource action.

There are two types of provisioning that OIM performs: day-one provisioning, which is the initial creation of access privileges to resources for users or the removal of these privileges from users; and day-two provisioning, the dynamic modification of user privileges with resources, based on changes to user and business requirements. Using these provisioning options, the manager can build an accurate picture of the user identities that it manages in both a trusted source and a targeted resource.

Remember there is a one-to-one relationship between the provisioning process and the workflow it represents. The final step is to attach the process task adapter to the process task.

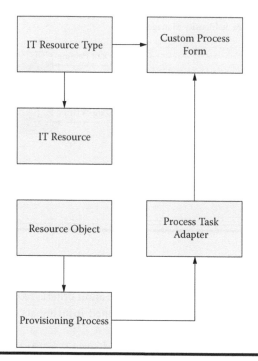

**Figure 12.6   Audit and attestation.**

# Administration

This section shows how to launch the server, reset passwords, grant resources, disable a resource, reset a locked administration screen, and create attestation reports from historical data.

## *How to Launch the Server*

Double-click the xlStartServer.bat command script, which resides in the E:\OIM902_server\ xellerate\bin directory on the server. Open the log-in page and enter the appropriate credentials in the User ID and Password fields and click Login. Open the log-in window launching the OIM design console and again enter the appropriate User ID and passwords, logging in. Developers then may use the design console to build OIM connectors (Figure 12.7). Administrators use the administrative console to manage OIM connectors. Using the My Account link, administrators can view and modify their account information, reset passwords, and designate a proxy administrator, as well as view, create, and modify information about requests and resources. Using the request link, administrators create and track requests of resources for users, as well as managing approval tasks. Using the To-Do list, link administrators can manage outstanding tasks and action items. The Users link enables management of records for OIM users. The user groups link in Figure 12.7 enables the same functionality for user groups. The Access Solicits link enables administrators to create and manage system policies as well, as shown in the following figure.

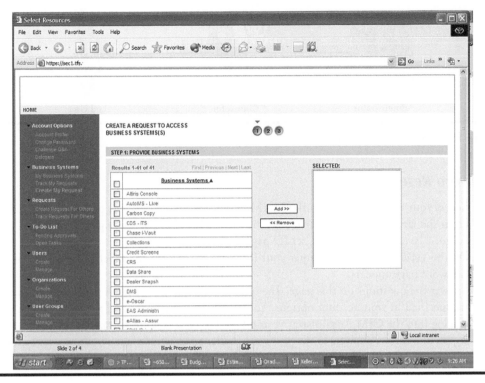

**Figure 12.7    OIM connector.**

## Self-Service Account Generation

To create an account for yourself:

1. Access your corporate portal link to OIM. The OIM landing page appears.
2. From the landing page for OIM, find the Self-Register label in the left navigation pane and click Create Request. The User Self-Registration page appears.
3. Enter your data.
    Required information is marked with an asterisk (*). Be sure to select and specify answers to password challenge questions if your system requires them. Depending on how your system administrator configured OIM, you may be required to specify answers to a number of challenge questions to reset your password when you forget it.
4. Click Submit Request.
    OIM informs you that the request has been submitted and displays the numeric ID of the request so that you can track it. Write down the Request ID after submitting your request. You need the request ID to track the status of your request.
    A link to the request appears.
5. If your request requires an approval, on the OIM landing page, click the Track Request option under Self-Register in the left navigation pane.
    The Track Self-Registration request page appears. You can check the status of your request on this page by entering the numeric ID of the request.

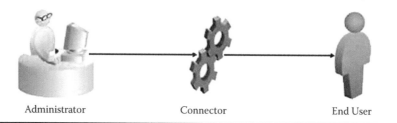

Administrator          Connector          End User

**Figure 12.8   Administrative console.**

## Password Reset

1. Access your corporate portal link to OIM. The OIM landing page appears.
2. From the landing page for OIM, find the Help label in the left navigation pane and click Forgot Password? The Verify User ID page appears.
3. On the Verify User ID page, enter your ID in the User ID field and click OK. The Change Password page appears.
4. Answer the questions on this page. The questions that appear on this page and the answers are specified in your account options. You select these questions and answers the first time you log into the OIM Administrative and User Console (Figure 12.8).
5. Supply the correct answers to the password challenge questions, enter your new password in both fields, and click Submit.

## Tracking Self-Registration Requests

To track the status of a self-registration request:

1. Access your corporate portal link to OIM. The OIM landing page appears.
2. In the left navigation pane, click Track Request under Self-Register. The Track Self-Registration page appears.
3. On the Track Self-Registration page, enter the ID of the request associated with your self-registration in the Request ID field.
4. Click Track Request. OIM displays the details regarding the self-registration request status.

# Administration of Users and User Entities

OIM supports three types of users:

■ System administrators are users who have both read access and write access to all forms and records.
■ Administrators of identity manager connectors are users who have read and write access rights to their own profiles, the records associated with them, as well as the profiles and records of any end users whom they supervise.
■ End users who are recipients of the resources that are provisioned to them by OIM. They have read access to their own user profile and the records associated with it.

These entities are associated with two functional entities:

Organizations, which take the form of records that represent a unit in a company's hierarchy, department, division, or cost center.

User groups are collections of one or more OIM users who share some functionality such as access rights, roles, or permissions for resources.

From the administrative console one can create organizations, users, and user groups; assign users to groups; set challenge questions; assign proxies; remove proxies; and reset passwords, as well as view and modify user profiles.

## *Assigning Connectors to Users*

Provisioning process is the process used to actually provision the resource to one or more users or organizations for which it was requested. Provisioning processes consist of a series of automated tasks that perform the steps necessary to grant access to a given resource. The provisioning process cannot be initiated until the approval process is complete, except in cases where an approval process has not been defined for the resource. OIM allows resources to be requested and provisioned to enterprise users. The resource can be an application, access to a database, rights to a directory structure on a network, or other entities to which access is vital. The manner in which access to the resource is granted and the permissions that you are given on that resource are governed by a provisioning process that an OIM Administrator defines. Access to a resource may be provisioned uniformly for all users, or Access may be provisioned in a unique fashion, based on variables such as the following:

■ Your role—for example, administrator, accountant
■ Your location
■ Your employment status—for example, full time, consultant
■ Your group or department designation
■ Other criteria that are deemed relevant

A resource is an external Web service, system, or application with which OIM communicates to perform provisioning, reconciliation, or compliance attestation. Some examples of resources with prepackaged connections include the following:

■ Operating systems such as Windows XP, 2000, Vista, Unix, Linux
■ Directory servers such as Oracle Internet Directory, Nestcape LDAP, MS Active Directory, Novell Directory in the Sun Java System Directory
■ Database servers such as Oracle 9*i*, 10*g*, My SQL, MS SQL
■ Security managers: ACF/2, IBM RACF, RSA Authentication Manager, CA Netegrity
■ Web access control applications: RSA ClearTrust, Tivoli Access manager
■ Collaboration and messaging such as Netscape Messaging Server, Microsoft Exchange, Novell Groupwise
■ Enterprise applications such as Oracle e-Business Suite, Siebel CRM, PeopleSoft Enterprise Application, and SAP applications

In this capacity OIM serves as a connector that holds all the information required to

Reconcile with an external source
Provision a user with a target resource

In addition to assigning a connector, the fields must be populated in the custom process form contained in the connector and that information must then be saved to the OIM database. There are three ways in which this assignment may occur:

Through direct provisioning
Provisioning using logical criteria such as membership rules and access policies
By form submitted requests

The direct provisioning route (Figure 12.9) directly connects connectors to end users via the following administrator action:

Using logical criteria, a connector can be assigned to a user using auto group membership rules and access policies. In this model the OIM provisioning manager evaluates criteria about the user making use of auto group memberships and access policies (Figure 12.10).

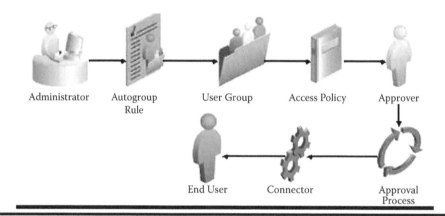

**Figure 12.9   Direct provisioning.**

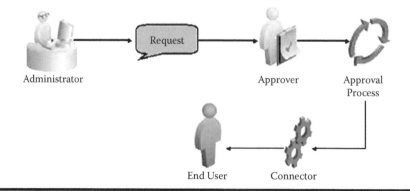

**Figure 12.10   Provisioning via logical criteria.**

For this to function correctly the administrator must

■ Assign an auto group membership rule to a user group
■ Build an access policy

Assigning the auto group membership rule to the user group enables OIM to add the end user to the access group. The addition of an access policy allocates the connector to the user as the user now belongs to the user group.

The final option is to leverage the built-in workflow system to assign user rights via association with a connector.

## Granting Resource Requests

To grant a resource request (Figure 12.11):

1. In the left navigation pane, click Requests, then click Resources. The Make a Request page appears. This page defaults to the Grant Resource option. Use this option to grant a resource to a specific user or organization.
2. Click Continue. The Create a Request To Provision Resource(s)—Step 1: Select Type page appears.
3. Click the Users option to assign a resource to one or many users. Select the Organization option to provision a resource to one or many organization(s).
   Click Continue.
   If you selected the Users option, the Create a Request To Provision Resource(s)—Step 2: Select User(s) page appears.
4. In the Results table, select the Users checkbox, then click Add to place the user name or names in the Selected list. Use the Remove button to delete any user or users in the Selected list:

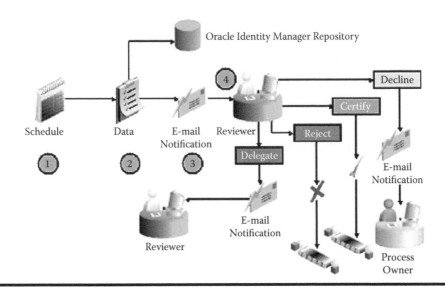

**Figure 12.11   Provisioning via request.**

To filter the list of users, select a key in the Filter By menu, enter selection criteria in the box next to this menu, and click Go.

If the request system form has any user-defined fields, these fields are displayed on the Step 2: Provide Additional Information page. These fields are created in the Design Console using the User Defined Field Definition form for Form Name=Requests. For more information, see the OIM Design Console Guide.

When you are done, click Continue.

The Create a Request To Provision Resource(s)—Step 3: Provide Resource page appears.

5. Select the resource name checkbox, then click Add to place the resource name in the Selected list. Use the Remove button to delete any user(s) in the Selected list.

To filter the list of users, select a key in the Filter By menu, enter selection criteria in the box next to this menu, and click Go.

When you are done, click Continue.

The Create a Request To Provision Resource(s)—Step 4: Provide Resource Data page appears. This page displays information about the resource and the user for this request.

6. If the information on this page is correct, click Continue, or click Back to make corrections. Any associated forms are displayed on the next page.

7. Enter the information requested in the Forms field and click Continue, or click Back to make corrections. If you click Continue, the Create a Request To Provision Resource—Step 5: Verify Information page appears.

8. To add a comment if desired, click the Add a comment link. The Add Request Comment page appears.

9. Enter your comment in the Comment field, and click Add Comment to insert your comment with your resource request. Or, click Clear to erase the text in the Comment field or Close to dismiss this page.

After adding a comment, this page displays the added comment.

10. After verifying the information, click Submit Now to make the request active.

11. To activate this request at a later time, then click Schedule for Later to define a date when the request becomes active. You can only specify a date that is later than today's date. The Schedule for Later page appears:

The Schedule for Later option is often used for new employees who are starting on a future date. After you define a date, the request is created, the approval process is initiated, approvers can approve the tasks, and the approval process can be completed. However, the provisioning process is not initiated until the scheduled date.

12. Use the calendar icon to define a date to activate your request, and then click Submit.

## Disabling a Resource Request

To disable a request:

1. In the left navigation pane, click Requests, then click Resources. The Make a Request page appears.

2. Select the Disable Resource radio button, and click Continue. The Create a Request To Disable Resource(s)—Step 1: Select Type page appears.

This page lets you select one of the following options:

Users: You can disable resources from one or many users.

Organizations: You can disable resources from one or many organizations. Select the appropriate option.

3. Click Continue. The Create a Request To Disable Resources—Step 2: Select User(s) page appears.

4. Select the user name checkboxes, then click Add to place the user names in the Selected list. Use the Remove button to delete any user or users in the Selected list.

To filter the list, select a key in the Filter By menu, enter selection criteria in the box next to this menu, and click Go.

When you are done, click Continue.

# Customizing the OIM Administrative Console

This section covers cosmetic enhancements to the administrative console such as functionality, branding, layout, and logos.

## *Branding the Console*

There are multiple ways built into the administrative console to brand the console as unique to your company. These include:

■ Customizing the overall layout of the Web pages of the console to match a corporate template. This is done from the administrative console as xelsysadmin by modifying the header banner

■ Modifying the descriptive text, links, and labels that appear on the Web page of the console. This is done from the administrative console as xelsysadmin by modifying the text in the footer banner of the console in the tjspLoginTiles.jsp file located in E:\jboss-4.0.2\server\default\deploy\XellerateFull.ear\xlWebApp.war\xlWebApp\tiles.

■ Replacing company and product logos within the style sheet with your own icons. This is done from the administrative console as xelsysadmin by modifying the logo at the left of the screen. In order to customize the log-in page of the administrative console.

1. Open the tjspLoginTiles.jsp file located in E:\jboss-4.0.2\server\default\deploy\XellerateFull.ear\xlWebApp.war\xlWebApp\tiles.

■ Changing the color, font, and txt alignment of the underlying XML to reflect a corporate standard. In order to change the background color for the header, do the following:

1. Stop the OIM server.

2. Use a text editor to open the Xellerate.css file located in E:\jboss-4.0.2\server\default\deploy\XellerateFull.ear\xlWebApp.was\css directory to reflect the new color scheme.

3. In this file create a new class called ExplorerMenu and add the new background color,

```
.ExplorerMenu
  {
  BACKGROUND-COLOR: <color>;
  }
```

where <color> represents the new color.

4. Use a text editor to open tjspClassicLayout.jsp file located in E:\jboss-4.0.2\server\ default\deploy\XellerateFull.ear\xlWebApp.war\layouts directory.
5. Replace the Sidebar element with the ExplorerMenu class.
6. Save changes and restart OIM Server.

## Functionality

There are five basic ways to change the functionality of the administrative console without modifying the underling code.

■ Customizing the self-registration process for creating user account—by making fields optional or mandatory.
■ Configuring how users can modify the profiles of their accounts.
■ Customizing the behavior of the fields within the Web pages of the administrative console.
■ Setting menu items that are available to users who belong to a specific group—by associating those to a specific group.
■ Customizing search pages. This is done from the Manage user form as xelsysadmin by modifying the Manage user buttons, predicate appends, and leading text. This may also include the number of search results returned.

### *How to Restore an Inadvertently Locked xelsysadmin User Account*

The xelsysadmin account is the super-user account for OIM; whenever this account is locked it can only be unlocked by accessing the associated Oracle database directly. This account cannot be unlocked using the Administrative Console or Design Console of OIM.

To unlock xelsysadmin user account, perform the following steps:

1. Stop the OIM server.
2. Open a DOS window.
3. From the DOS prompt enter sqlplus / nolog (a SQL prompt should appear).
4. Connect to the oracle database as an administrator (e.g., connect sys/sys@oracleserver as sysdba).
   Run the query.
5. SQL>UPDATE SYS.USR SET USR_LOCKED=0, USR_LOGON_ATTEMPTS_ CTR=0 WHERE USR_LOGON='XELSYSADMIN'
6. Restart the OIM server.

### *Creating Operational and Historical Reports*

In the attestation process no function is more critical than the generation of attestations to the reviewing party, which can, after inspection and testing, be used to certify that compliance criteria have been met. An administrator within OIM can create two types of reports for use in attestation, operational and historical:

Operational reports, which include information about resources that a user can access.
There are four types of operational reports that can be generated by OIM:
User resource matching: who has what.
User resource access list
Entitlement summary
Policy list
Historical reports, which contain information about resources that are associated with a user
throughout that user's employment with the company.
There are five types of historical reports that can be generated by OIM:
User Resource Access History
Resource Access List History
User Profile History
User Membership History
Group Membership History

In addition, OIM permits third-party applications to create eight additional reports:

Who Has What—a list of users and the resources with which they are provisioned
Direct Provisioned—resources that are directly provisioned to the target users, users who
directly provisioned by the resources for the target users, and the users who received the
resources
Requests Made—Displays requests that are created by users
Active Queue—Subset of the requests made that lists the resources approved by users
Requests Executed—Subset of the Active Queue report that shows the requests that are exe-
cuted by OIM
Reconciled Apps—lists the successful events associated with the reconciliation
Reconciled Users—displays the users who are added to OIM through reconciliation
Unreconciled Data—shows the reconciliation events that could not be matched to a specific
user, organization, or provisioning process

When using a third-party product one does not need to understand that data model or query
language to write queries for predefined reports. Information about data snapshot and lifetime
reports, as well as changes to those reports, are stored in XML formats in the UPA table of the
database. Any third party should be able generate reports from this table; however, if XML is not
the desired format, a SQL-compatible reporting tool can generate a report by retrieving data from
the UPA_USR, UPA_FIELDS, UPA_GRP_MEMBERSHIP and UPA_RESOURCE fields.

## *Attestation Processes*

Attestation processes make up the framework by which an attestation workflow is configured and
created (12.12). It contains

- Four types of users: The compliance manager, the system reviewer, the process owner, and
  the reviewer.
- Data
- An attestation schedule that may be periodic or executed on demand

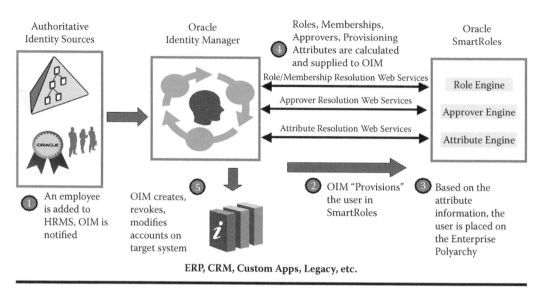

**Figure 12.12   Attestation workflow.**

The workflow moves through the process laid out as follows:

An approval process determines if a resource is to be approved or not for provisioning to one or more users or organizations for whom it was requested. Approval processes consist of a series of tasks that require responses from the users responsible for approving the provisioning of the resource. Because these responses are manually provided, they are assigned to an approver or a group of approvers.

Approvers can act upon all tasks in an approval process that are assigned to them. If an approver is assigned to a task in a request, he or she can view all tasks in the request. If you are an approver for a request, the request ID appears when you click the Pending Approvals link under To-Do. Within the approval process the system reviewer or process owners have four options when confronted with a resource request:

1. Decline the request and notify the process owner.
2. Certify the process as valid and approve.
3. Reject the process as invalid.
4. Delegate the request to an administrative proxy.

There are six steps in setting up the attestation process:

1. Configure OIM to enable attestation.
2. Configure the resource object of the connector so that its data can be reviewed during an attestation process.
3. Configure the process form of the connector so that its data is available for review during the attestation process.
4. Assign a manager to the user who is the recipient of the target resource. The manager must be responsible for reviewing the attestation process for the user.
5. Assign menu items to the two user groups responsible. One will be the user group responsible for creating and managing the attestation process. This group is designated the "process

owner"; the other group is the user group responsible for reviewing the attestation process itself. This group is designated the "reviewer group."

6. Assign administrative privileges and permissions to each of these groups.

When creating the attestation process, start with defining high-level information about the attestation process, the workflow, and the approval chain. Business process analysis at this stage will yield a high-level return for the organization. Next, define the scope and designate a reviewer for the attestation process. Remember to maintain a strict segregation of duties between the compliance manager, the system reviewer, the process owner, and the process reviewer. Define the administrative details of the attestation process. Specify how a user should have access rights to a resource and what the reviewer must consider when receiving the process. Verify the information gathered for the attestation workflow. Finally, assign groups of users to the attestation process who are responsible for review and management of the business process.

As a reviewer of an attestation process one has four actions, as outlined in Figure 12.11

■ Delegate it to another reviewer
■ Reject it
■ Certify it
■ Decline to act on it

An owner of an attestation process has more flexibility; they may view

■ High-level and detailed attestation information
■ The data and time the attestation process is submitted to a reviewer
■ The reviewer who received the attestation process
■ The status of the attestation process and whether the reviewer certified it, rejected it, declined it, or delegated it to another reviewer
■ The delegation path the attestation process has followed if delegated away

## Integration

The OIM Connector has a container that holds all of the information that OIM needs to reconcile with an external resource and provision a user with a target resource. A connector has seven components:

■ IT resource type
■ IT resource process
■ Form process
■ Task adapter
■ Resource object
■ Provisioning process
■ Process task

To create a connecter, one must create an IT resource type. This record represents the classification type, parameter fields, and encryption settings that are associated with a resource. Then define an IT resource. This record contains the values that OIM needs to communicate with a resource and access it as a system administrator for provisioning or reconciliation purposes, then create a custom process form. This record is a central storage mechanism that holds all OIM data needed to provision a user to a target resource or reconcile a user with an external resource. Once the custom process is defined, one must build a process task adapter. The process task adapter is a piece of Java code that is used to automate the completion of a provisioning process task. The process task adapter automates the creation of the user's account. This could be relational, LDAP, or XML based. There is a one-to-one relationship between the adapter and process task. Each process task is associated with a single adapter. The next step is to define a resource object. This record is a virtual representation of an OID resource and contains the details required to provision a user to the resource or reconcile the user and resource for audit attestation. The next step is to create a provisioning process flow. This process record contains steps that OIM must complete to perform provisioning or audit reconciliation with a resource.

## Transferring OIM Connectors

The benefits of reuse are self-evident to all but the most casual of users. The added efficiency and error reduction associated with the transfer of one OIM connector from one environment to another permits administrators to leverage and reuse many of the tedious and repetitive chores associated with system administration. With this in mind, OIM is designed to facilitate transfer of connectors or components of connectors from one environment to another. In fact, a system administrator may transport multiple OIM connectors between environments simultaneously. Before exporting OIM connectors, make sure to copy all associated external JAR files or the connector will fail. The JAR files that are used for provisioning can be found in:

E:\OIM902_server\xellerate\JavaTasks directory. The reconciliation focused JAR files are located in E:\OIM902_server\xellerate\ScheduleTask directory. To export an OIM connector so that it is operable in another environment:

1. Build an *.xlm file that contains the components of the connector.
2. Export this file into a designated location that can be accessed.
3. Paste any external JAR files into their designated locations.
4. Recompile the adaptors that are contained in the connector.
5. Define IT resources for the specific machines applications or services represented by the connector.
6. Assign the OIM connector to a user.
7. Populate the fields of the custom process form that is contained in the connector.
8. Save this information into the database.
9. Verify that the logon credentials used in the custom form can be used to access the external resource.

## Properly Exporting the File

Should the export of the file via the deployment form found in the OIM administrative console result in an invalid, corrupted, or 0KB XML file, check the following:

1. When exporting the file, verify no other users are also exporting files.
2. Verify that no reconciliation workflows or scheduled tasks are being run.

3. Reconfigure the minimum and maximum memory servers of the application server to 512MB and 1024MB, respectively, by stopping the OIM server, opening the run.bat file located in the application server, and locating the "set JAVA_OPTS=%JAVA_OPTS% -Xms256m -Xmx512m" to "set JAVA_OPTS=%JAVA_OPTS% -Xms512m -Xmx1024m".

Then, save and restart the OIM server.

# Installation and Configuration

This section outlines the steps for installing and configuring the components and service relating to the provisioning server.

## *Preparing a Database for OIM*

With the prepar_xl_db.bat script, administrators can prepare a database for OIM. This command takes the form of:

```
E:\OIM902_Installation\installServer\Xellerate\db\oracle>prepare_xl_db.bat
train92 E:\orant\ora92 sysadm sysadm
train92tbs E:\orant\ora92\oradata
train92tbs_01 TEMP sys
```

The OIM Diagnostic Dashboard is a Web application that can be used to verify the installation requirements for OIM. These requirements include:

- The proper preparation of the Oracle database
- The ability of OIM to connect with the database

To launch this tool, enter the URL in the address field. In the address field, the OIM administrator enters a URL that combines either the IP address of the application server or the name of the machine where the application server resides, as well as the application server's port number (e.g., 8067); the XIMDD thus takes the form:

```
http://<IP_address_or_machine_name>:<port_number>/XIMDD
```

Make sure the application server that hosts the OIM diagnostic dashboard is installed and configured properly and running during the operation.

Then run the prepare_xl_db.bat script in the form of
prepare_xl_db.bat tablespace E:\orant\ora92 sysadmin sysadmin databasename E:\orant\ora92\
    oradata tablespacename_01 TEMP sys
Where databasename is the name of the data store
tablespace is the name of the tablespace to be created
tablespacename_01 is the name of the datafile
E:\orant\ora92\oradata is the directory where the datafiles are to be placed
sys is the password for the sys user
If the script returns a message signifying successful execution, the database is prepared correctly.

## Installing the OIM Diagnostic Dashboard

The OIM dashboard is an application that runs on a JBoss application server and resides in the server tier of the OIM architecture. The diagnostic dashboard is available as a Web archive WAR file that can be found in E:\OIM902_Installation\DiagnosticDashboard.

Install and deploy the diagnostic dashboard before you install OIM. To install the OIM diagnostic dashboard:

> Copy the XIMDD.war file from the E:\OIM902_Installation\DiagnosticDashboard directory to the E:\jboss-4.0.2\server\default\deploy directory.
> Then, start the JBoss Application server.

## Installing the OIM Design Console

Enter the base directory where you install the design console. In this case E:\OIM902_client.

1. Double-click the setup_client.exe file located in the E:\OIM902_Installation\installServer directory. A welcome screen should occur.
2. Click Next. The target directory screen should appear.
3. In the Directory field, enter the base directory where OIM Design console is to be installed. In this case E:\OIM902_client. Do not include any spaces in the name of the base directory and verify that the base directory is identical to that specified in the OIM server.
4. Click Next. The base directory setting window should appear.
5. Click OK. The application server screen should appear.

## Installing Audit/Compliance Module

1. Double-click the setup_server.exe file, which is located in E:\OIM902_Installation\ installserver directory. A welcome message screen appears.
2. Click Next. The OIM Application Options screen appears.
3. Select the OIM with Audit and Compliance module option.
4. Click Next and select the oracle option to configure OID to work with the Oracle database.
5. Populate the database information screen with values that OIM uses to connect with the Oracle database.
6. Select the OIM Default Authentication option to use predefined settings to authenticate the administrative console.
7. Select the Oracle option to configure the OIM with the Oracle application server.

## Adding Audit/Compliance Module after a Default Installation

1. Delete the base directory for your OIM Server.
2. Run the setup_server.exe script and select the OIM with Audit and Compliance module option.
3. Complete the install, and you should be complete.

Caveat: Back up a copy of the base directory first (particularly the keystore files) before doing the reinstall.

As almost all of the OIM configuration information is in the database, your settings and configuration information will be maintained.

## Post Installation Tasks

Specifying OIM log level for the application server.

OIM supports five log levels:

- DEBUG
- INFO
- WARN
- ERROR
- FATAL

The levels are listed in descending order according to the amount of information logged. DEBUG logs the most information, and FATAL, the least.

The log4j.xml file, which is located in the E:\jboss-4.0.2\server\default\conf directory, is used for all logging functions in the application server. Within this XML file there is a general setting that uses an Xellerate tag. This setting is associated with all OIM components. The log level can be changed for all components associated with OIM by editing the priority value of this general setting.

The priority value tag one can set the log level for the application server to DEBUG, INFO, WARN, ERROR, or FATAL. Copy the jbossall-client.jar file and paste it into the E:\OIM902_client\xlclient\xlclient\ext directory.

The diagnostic dashboard can be used to check the preinstallation requirements for OIM as well as perform postinstallation checks and create reports to ensure that the OIM environment is installed and configured properly.

In a compliance attestation, such as a segregation of duties requirement or a PCI 1.1, Req 7 attestation diagnostic dashboard can be used to:

- Verify that an OIM user account is locked due to successive invalid logon attempts
- Create reports validating system properties associated with all Java Virtual Machines
- Verify information about the version numbers of the library and extension files
- Verify the scheduler is running
- Create detailed manifest about the library and extension files
- Verify the OIM can submit and process a Java Messaging Service message
- Verify Single Sign On is configured properly
- Verify that OIM can communicate with remote managers

The data encryption key in the OIM installation is identical to the one used to encrypt the data in the OIM database.

## Increasing the Size of the Java Pool

Should the database prerequisite check fail in the diagnostic dashboard, it may prove necessary to increase the size of the Java pool. The reason for this failure is that the current Java pool size of the Oracle database starts at 32 MB. As a result, it may not meet the 60 MB size requirement set by OIM. The solution is quite straightforward and simple:

1. Stop the OIM server.
2. Access the database by using the Oracle Enterprise Manager Console by selecting the Enterprise Manager Console command (in windows Start > Programs > Oracle - oracle_92home > Enterprise Manager Console).
3. In the Login window, select the Launch Standalone option, click OK, and wait for the enterprise manager console to appear.
4. On the main screen, select the Databases tree. The name of the database should appear.
5. Click on the database instance node. A Database Connect Information window appears
6. In this window enter "system" in the Username and Password fields; then select the Connect As drop-down list, select SYSDBA, and click OK.
7. Click the configuration form to make the window active.
8. Select the Memory tab. In the Java pool field enter 60, then click the Apply button that appears on the tab. A shutdown option should appear.
9. In the Shutdown Option window, select immediate shutdown and select OK to register the changes to the Java Pool.
10. Close the Oracle Enterprise manager console.
11. Restart the OIM server.

## Change the Authentication Mode from Default to Single Sign-On

Once OIM is installed, the administrator will, for compliance purposes, want to change the authentication mode from the application default setting to Single Sign-On. To do this, first stop the Oracle identity server. Then use a text editor to open the xlconfig.xml file, which is located in E:\OIM902_Server\xellerate\config directory. Then look for the code:

```
<Authentication>
Default
</Authentication>
```

Change that code unit to SSO.

## Verifying that the OIM Scheduler Is Running

A final service validation after the installation and configuration is the verification that the OIM scheduler is operational and program events are running as intended. Do the following in order to complete this final check:

1. Launch a Web browser.
2. In the address field enter:
   http://localhost:8087/xlScheduler/status

The status should appear as a response on the browser.

# Deployment Methodology

This section breaks deployment down into

- Requirements and architecture
- Planning and analysis
- Design
- Development
- Test
- Rollout and operations

It walks through a typical deployment as a benchmark for the implementer.

## *Requirements and Architecture*

When defining the requirements it is best to start with a broad approach to the vision. It is good, then, to focus on specific areas. Requirements should cover user base, usage patterns, organizational structure, roles, existing/future approval workflows, notification processes, target applications, password synch, and the required adapters. Database and applications and any third-party dependencies the provisioning effort might face should be included. Then, turning to existing data and data quality, calculate initial load requirements and define your approach, focusing on trusted sources for user data and passwords. Define physical locations and environments, taking into account hardware sizing on a transactional basis. Then, perform a gap analysis to identify areas of complex configuration and customization, and define acceptance test scenarios for those areas requiring configuration and customization.

In the requirement document detailed task definition, there should be a refinement of estimates to complete. Architectural and security reviews. It is good to practice the initial solution by starting with a small number of targets for one of the solutions (Password Management, Request Access Management, Audit/Compliance, Core Provisioning/Deprovisioning).

## *Planning and Analysis*

This phase takes the form of project structure. The planning phase focuses on timelines, team structure, and roles. The primary skill required for this phase is to understand the third-party software dependencies (app server/DB/OS) and hardware requirements for development, test, and production environments, prior to the beginning of the project. Figure 12.13 illustrates the OIM security model necessary for planning the security and compliance analysis.

## *Design*

This phase constitutes the detailed design, which consists of checkpoint and revalidation/refinement of estimates to complete the project. In this phase checkpoint and revalidations of the timeline are vital to the installation of the product in a development environment. It is within this phase that defined core provisioning operations take place and teams engage in internal development to

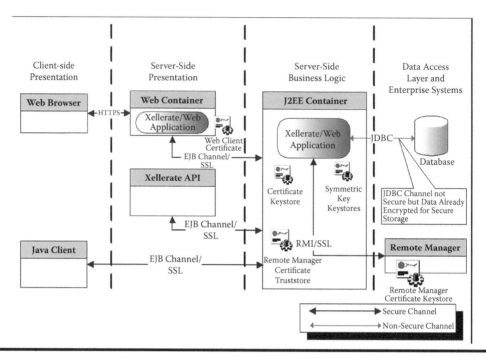

**Figure 12.13   OIM Security Model for Regulatory Compliance.**

build the connector/adapter interfaces. The completion of a proper design will significantly minimize the time it takes for the IDM team to bring applications under management.

Within system design, only three configurations exist that can be referred to as industry best practice. These are referred to as simple, clustered, and partitioned.

Figure 12.14 outlines the Simple deployment. Lacking the ability to scale, it does provide a secure architecture in which to provision users.

Figure 12.15 showcases a clustered deployment, which maintains the security model while providing the ability to scale.

Figure 12.16 showcases a partitioned deployment, which supplements the security model with network level security while providing the ability to scale. This design uses the most physical resources but provides maximum security.

## Development

This phase consists of unit and integration testing, the creation of a client deployment guide, and the installation of the product in a test environment. The diagram in Figure 12.17 denotes the security layers development should respect when implementing the deployment guide.

Figure 12.18 shows the relationship that should be maintained by OIM in relation to the LDAP directory and access server; no connector should be created that disintermediates this relationship.

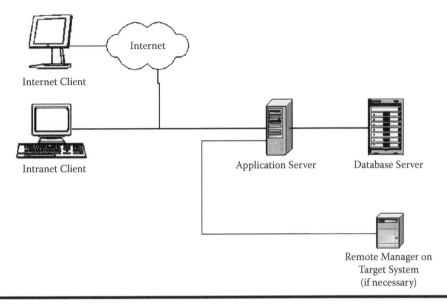

**Figure 12.14  Simple–Secure Deployment.**

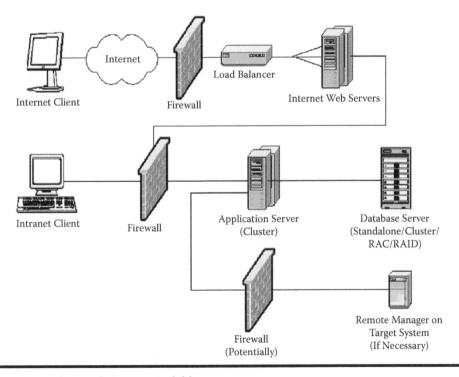

**Figure 12.15  Clustered–Secure–Scalable.**

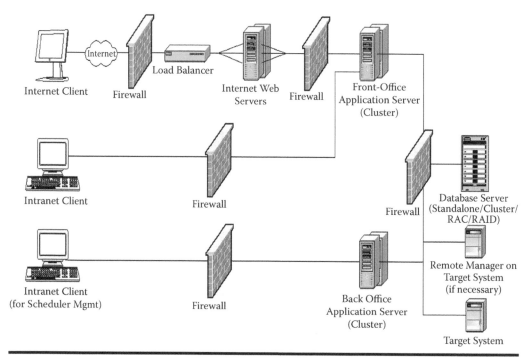

**Figure 12.16    Partitioned—Maximum protection through multitiered deployment.**

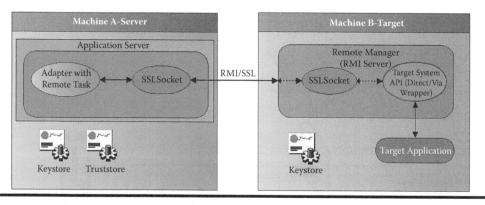

**Figure 12.17    Security layers in OIM.**

## Test

Within this phase, integration and system testing is the first task that must be completed. The second operation performance and stress testing takes place, with user acceptance testing being the final test.

## Rollout and Operations

Rollout and operation involves the installation of the product in a production environment. It is the rollout and operations and postproduction support of the provisioning system.

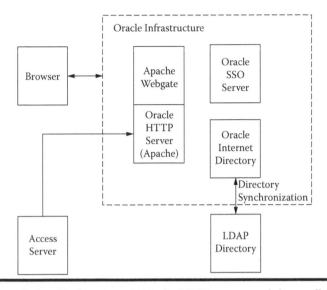

**Figure 12.18   The relationship between OIM, the LDAP server, and the application server.**

# Regulatory Governance Mapping

OIM provides audit and compliance reporting. You can use the audits and reports to capture and archive entity and transaction data for compliance monitoring and for IT-centric process and forensic auditing. OIM, with the audit and compliance modules, provides user profile audits, reports, and attestation.

The following out-of-the-box operational reports can be generated in OIM and can be used by administrators and auditors for operational and compliance purposes:

- Resource Access List: Queries all existing users provisioned to a resource
- Policy List: Displays a list of policies for a specified group
- Policy Detail: Displays complete details about specified policies
- OIM Password Expiration: Lists user password expiration settings
- User Resource Access: Queries access rights for users that match specified query parameters
- Summary: Lists the number of users for each status within each resource
- Attestation Requests by Process: Lists attestation requests by process
- Attestation Request Detail: Returns complete details of a specified attestation request
- Resource Password Expiration: Returns a list of users whose resource passwords are about to expire
- Group Membership: Lists the number of users in each group
- Attestation Process List: Lists all defined attestation processes
- Attestation Requests by Reviewer: Lists attestation requests by reviewer
- Group Membership Profile: Lists user group memberships

Revisiting Chapter 3 and examining the benefits of provisioning and workflow on the mapping results in a direct relationship between these eight of the nine control domains:

- Trusted Access
- Change Management
- Operational Awareness
- Records Management
- Audit and Risk Management
- Operational Accountability and Transparency
- Segregation of Duties
- Operational Controls

Of primary interest to those implementing Segregation of Duties and Operational Controls to satisfy a regulatory requirement is the event-logging capability.

## Oracle Smart Roles

Role-Based Access Control lends itself to enforcing the separation-of-duty (SoD) principle. The goal of SoD is to guard against internal fraud and errors by limiting the powers of individuals. As a result, accountability becomes automatically built into the governing policy of an enterprise. This fact is referred to henceforth as autonomous accountability. The classical example expressing assurance in accountability based on SoD is the rule that prohibits auditors from auditing themselves. An auditor must be designated to perform audits on actions of other individuals. Auditing oneself yields a conflict of interest in which the individual is confronted with two semantically exclusive interests. The first is the requirement for impartiality, whereas the second is the natural bias that one may exhibit toward oneself. One of the principal purposes of role-based access control is to provide a cost-effective and accurate approach to the management of access control data. However, the deployment of Role-Based Access Control when incorrectly implemented can result in the creation of a large number of user roles, which, in turn, need to be administered. In a large enterprise the number of roles can be in the hundreds or thousands; the number of users can be in the tens, hundreds of thousands, or in extreme circumstances, over a million; and the number of objects can easily exceed a million. In other words, the deployment of Role-Based Access Control replaces the very difficult and intractable problem of managing authorization data, scattered over numerous platforms and administrative domains, with a less difficult but significant problem of managing roles. SmartRoles simplifies this and completes IAM infrastructures by automatically tracking and managing what jobs people do, and integrating with provisioning systems to ensure the right access at the right times. It is an enterprise-class application for managing the life cycle of roles and membership data.

Features of this approach include

- Identity consolidation: where enterprise identities, IT resource definitions, and user accounts and entitlements are represented in an object-oriented, application-centric form
- Business role automation: In this process, business role definition is expressed through identity relationship in the context of an enterprise polyarchy where administrative processes define the relationship-based role providers
- IT role management: where policy-based role-control mechanisms such as approval workflows, rule-based membership, and attestation result in automated role-based provisioning

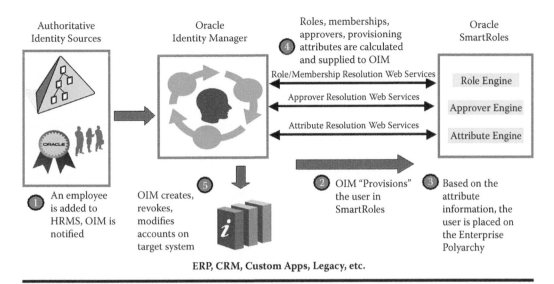

**Figure 12.19 Oracle Smart Role Integration.**

■ Attestation mechanism: that supports entitlement review and control mechanism review, user-centric and application-centric reviews, workflow, delegate and declines processes
■ Policy-based role synchronization: dynamic role and approver policy reconciliation

Using the policy enforcement engine within SmartRoles SoD is achieved by disseminating computing tasks along with associated permissions among multiple individuals (12.19). This is accomplished by first breaking a business process that presents a conflict of interest when viewed as a single set of transactions into its basic tasks that are free of conflict of interest. Once independent subtasks are identified, separate individuals are then authorized to perform each subtask, for instance, a role that evaluates a procurement process in an organization and one that authorizes payment represent a conflict of interest. SoD policies at the enterprise level mitigate the potential for fraud in the case of collusion attempts by automatically assigning different individuals to each of these two roles.

The access-matrix model directly manipulates access rights in that granting or revoking access to a resource explicitly refers to a particular permission. This approach yields a fine-grain level of control where each access type and its required permissions are related by a mapping that can be one-to-one at the finest level. For example, the read permission clearly means one can view the information contained in a resource but not modify it or add to it. To allow for updates, a new access right such as write or append is needed. Although this approach offers the advantage of fine-tuning an access control policy to accommodate any level of access needed, it can be costly to manage. The inherent cost factor becomes apparent with the increase in the number of managed users and resources. Furthermore, the effects from resources removed or added to the system as well as users leaving and joining an organization or simply changing job functions adds up to the complexity and overhead of maintaining such policy. For example, assigning an employee to a new function may require revoking his or her access rights to a large number of resources that are no longer needed for the tasks required by the new position. Similarly, functions of the new job may require access to various new resources. In this scenario, explicit revocation of access rights as well as the granting of new ones needs to span every old and new resource that is or used to be accessible to the user. Users sharing similar access to the same resources become members of a single group. The group as a single entity is then granted or denied access to the managed resources. Access decisions take into account the fact that a user is a member of one group or another. Grouping users is certainly one important aspect in addressing the scale of manageability in access-control systems but by itself is not sufficient. In addition to user groups, another important dimension in the manageability of access controls is the grouping of access rights. Following on the concept of managing users that share similar access capabilities as a unit, role-based access control evolves around the idea of grouping access rights pertinent to a particular functionality into a role abstraction. Access management as such is performed at a coarse-grain level as compared to individual privileges.

The appeal of SmartRoles is its inherent representation of real-world access control processes. In many situations, people perform day-to-day functions based on the role in the organizations to which they belong, within a community of people, or in society at large. A role is a higher-level concept that can be better understood as opposed to individual access rights or operations. In design, SmartRoles are compatible with the hierarchical organizations found in real life, such as those in an enterprise. SmartRoles can be easily mapped onto an already hierarchical structure of an organization.

The underlying SmartRoles foundations are:

■ Permissions are assigned to roles.
■ Users are assigned to roles.
■ Access decisions are based on users being members of applicable roles.

Key SmartRoles Features include:

■ Accurate and Authoritative Roles Repository: SmartRoles captures organizational information in terms of policies, approvals, and relationships into a comprehensive roles repository. It serves as the central source of information for roles and role membership.
■ Automated Context: Rich business roles information provides context to processes for user provisioning and access management.
■ Full Temporality: Temporal capabilities of SmartRoles enable users to track changes in organizational roles based on business events, plan and analyze roles based on future events, and retain an audit trail on who, what, when, and why people have access.

SmartRoles' top-down approach is to model and define business roles. Implementation begins by understanding the business framework and mapping the business relationships that exist within departments, across divisions, and throughout the extended enterprise of contractors, vendors, and partners. Role dependencies and conflicts are then computed, and the company receives governance recommendations for roles policy and practice, acting as an automated Trusted Access and Segregation of Duties control.

## Summary

We define provisioning as the process of providing IT resources to enable business functions to run. Provisioning makes the right resources available to the right processes and people at the right time. In review of the breadth and depth of the capabilities that OIM brings to bear on the organization it becomes evident that this becomes one of the major tools CxOs can leverage to bring an organization in line with regulators.

# Chapter 13

## Identity Management Audit and Attestation

### Enterprise Manager for Identity Management

The Oracle Enterprise Manager 10*g* Identity Management pack helps improve performance and availability and reduces the cost and complexity of managing the Oracle Identity and Access Management Suite. Most administrators react to these challenges after the fact, when they need to able to identify and resolve them prior to any adverse impact. They also would like to automate the custom and homegrown scripts they often use to manage the complex, distributed Identity and Access deployments, which can be error prone and increase management costs. Oracle Enterprise Manager 10*g* Release 3 helps address these challenges. Enterprise Manager Identity Management pack is integrated with the data center management solution. This enables administrators to perform key data center management operations such as service level management, and configuration management, in addition to monitoring the availability, performance, and load of the identity server components. Administrators will be able to monitor Identity services from end-user viewpoint and also allow, define, and monitor Service Levels of Identity Services. They will be able to capture and model the associations between the server components with single-step discovery. It also allows keeping track of key configuration parameters of Oracle Access Manager.

A centralized console combined with service and system dashboards provide IT managers and executives a top-down enterprise view with drill-down capabilities. This console reduces performance, availability, and configuration issues with your Identity and Access systems. It provides management capabilities for Oracle Access Manager, Oracle Identity Manager, and Oracle Identity Federation. It allows administrators to proactively monitor availability and performance of Identity deployments, cost-effectively and reliably.

### Enterprise Manager Elements

Elements of the Enterprise Manager include the following:

- The server tier
- The client tier
- The middle tier
- Communication components

### Server Tier

The server tier is a distributed, lightweight agent installed at each of the nodes, which are managed by OEM. A node can be any component of your database grid, such as a database server or an application server. Only one agent is installed at each node, irrespective of the number of database instances or application servers that the node comprises.

### Client Tier

With the Web-based architecture that is robust, reliable, and globally scalable, the OEM Console can be deployed and operated in a number of forms, thus giving one "manage from anywhere" flexibility. The client tier can take several forms:

### Web Browser

This thin client alleviates the necessity of installing any application to access the OEM Console.

The Console can be accessed via EM2Go using a PDA device capable of browsing the Internet.

Portal Oracle has designed a reporting framework, which can be used by portals to report on the health of the database to the end user.

### Middle Tier

The middle tier is Oracle Management Service (OMS), a powerful J2EE Web application. OMS works in conjunction with the Oracle database repository (called Management Repository) for its persistent data store.

### Communication Components

Communication between the Console and OMS, and between OMS and the agent(s), is via HTTP, thus making it easy to deploy OEM within firewall-protected environments. Secure Sockets Layer (SSL) can be enabled to allow secure communication between tiers.

### Consolidated Management

Each managed target has a "control page." The control page provides you with a view of the current state of the database by displaying a series of metrics that portray the overall health of the database. Summary metrics are displayed on the home page. If you find a metric of interest, you can bring up a comprehensive set of performance and health metrics via drill-down menus. Thus, the home page helps the DBA to quickly isolate and diagnose the root cause of problems facing the target. In addition, target home pages provide DBAs with direct access to configuration information as well as quick access to administrative functions. The target home page feature also promotes a consistent look and feel, irrespective of the type of target being monitored and managed.

Here is the basic information that you can view on the control page:

- General status information
- CPU information
- Availability
- Space usage
- Compliance information
- Job information
- Alerts

## Focusing on Enterprise Manager Identity Manager Pack Feature Function

Feature functions are:

- Proactive monitoring
- Improve quality of Identity and Access services Management for Oracle Access Manager, Oracle Identity Manager, and Oracle Identity Federation
- Single-step discovery and system modeling
- Complete system views include non-Oracle components like BEA WebLogic, IBM Websphere, Jboss, and Microsoft Active Directory
- Availability, performance, load, and security metrics
- Service-Level Management of Identity and Access Services
- End-user performance and availability perspective on authorization and authentication times
- Accelerate problem diagnosis and resolution time with minimal to no downtime.
- Policy-based configuration Management of Oracle Access Manager

## Electronic Discovery

Identity and Access deployments are complex and distributed over multiple hardware and software components. A single-step discovery process discovers all deployed Identity components and detects their associations with other managed entities such as hosts, application servers, directory servers, and databases. Discovery process will create Identity systems, which include Identity components along with associated managed entities that are running Identity components. For example, if Oracle Identity Manager is running on BEA WebLogic Application Server and using Oracle Internet Directory, discovery process will create an Identity Manager System that includes Oracle Identity Manager Server, BEA WebLogic Application Server, Oracle Internet Directory, the database backing the OID, and the hosts of all these components (Figure 13.1).

Monitoring Identity Systems along with dependent components will help in diagnosing any performance the problems. Oracle Enterprise Manager will also discover non-Oracle products and model them as part of Identity Systems.

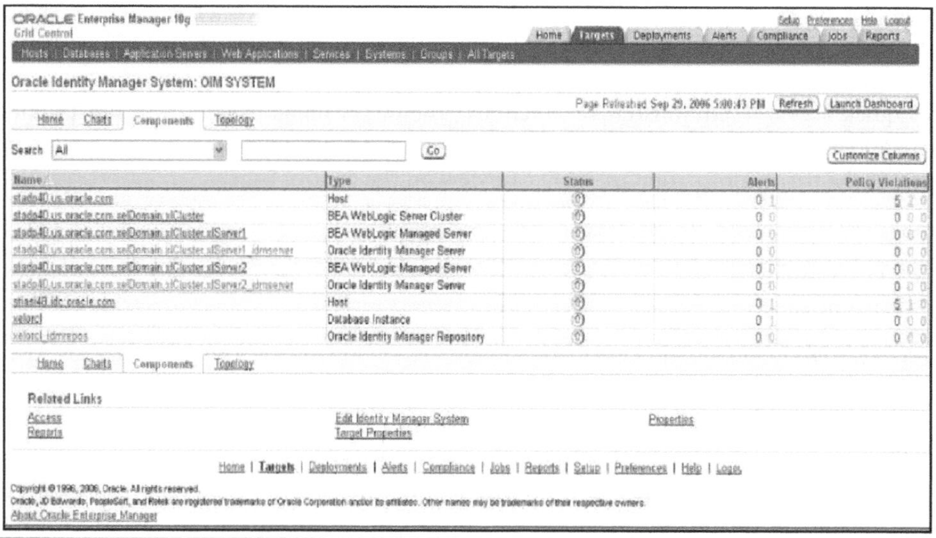

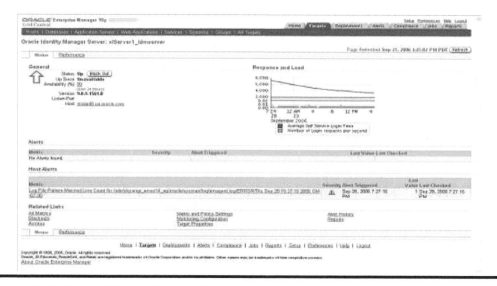

**Figure 13.1    Oracle Identity Manager System running on BEA WebLogic application server.**

## Monitoring and Diagnostics

Oracle Enterprise Manager monitors Identity components availability, performance metrics, load metrics, and security metrics such as successful authentications and failed authentications (Figure 13.2).

Administrators can set thresholds on these metrics and receive notifications when the thresholds are violated. All these metrics are available historically to compare with current performance. System performance views of all related components will help in correlating performance of Identity components with dependent components and diagnosing performance problems.

**Figure 13.2    Oracle Identity Manager Server homepage.**

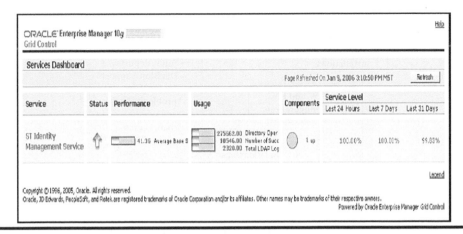

**Figure 13.3** Out-of-the-box service dashboards and reports can be used to report the availability, performance, and usage and service-level compliance dashboard.

## End-User Monitoring and Service-Level Management

Systems monitoring gives good insight into the health of Identity components, but it does not guarantee the accessibility of Identity services externally from an end-user perspective. Oracle Enterprise Manager enables monitoring Identity and Access services from an end-user point of view.

Using Oracle Enterprise Manager, identity or access services can be modeled and associated with identity or access systems that were created as part of discovery. Beacons deployed in remote locations can be used to monitor Identity service transactions externally from an end-user point of view. Metrics collected from the beacons can be used to determine availability and performance of identity or access services.

Service-level expectations can be defined in terms of service availability and performance. Defined service levels are monitored in real-time and service-level compliance is reported (Figure 13.3).

## Configuration Management for Oracle Access Manager

Performance problems are often caused by changes to the configuration parameters. Enterprise Manager 10*g* Release 3 supports Configuration Management for Oracle. Components include the following:

Access Manager. It allows tracking changes to configuration parameters. Administrators can take snapshots of the current configuration, compare configurations, and search configurations.

## Integration with Identity Suite 10g (10.1.4.0.1) Grid Control Plug-In

Grid Control plug-in released as part of Oracle Identity Management 10*g* Release enables management of Oracle Single Sign-On, Oracle Internet Directory, Directory Integration Platform and Delegated Administration Server. Identity Management capabilities in Enterprise Manager 10*g* Release 3 are compatible with the grid.

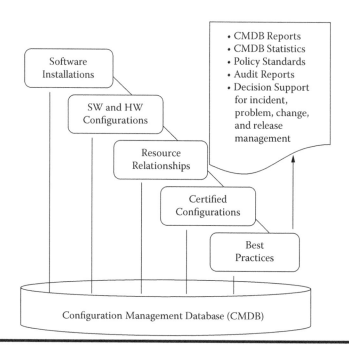

**Figure 13.4   Configuration Management Database.**

## Configuration Management Database

The configuration management database permits the discovery of hardware and software configurations as well as an inventory, including patch history and updates. This permits analysis of audit change and configuration comparisons against reference, saved, or live configurations (Figure 13.4). These components lead to model-based decision support wherein CMDB maintains inventory of all CIs and their relationship.

Dashboards display data regarding impact analysis, updates, baseline, and verification of change and serve as the foundation for compliance and change control. These dashboards map to ITIL and CoBIT frameworks and provide policy management and enforcement of security configuration policies.

## Identity Services Dashboard

Identity Services dashboard displays the availability, performance, usage, and service-level compliance of all critical Identity services. This is the most important screen for the IT operations managers and executives who commit to provide Identity services with certain level of service quality.

## Compliance System Dashboard

Compliance System dashboard provides an "at-a-glance" view of the overall health of all critical services. It shows their current availability, performance, and service-level compliance. Service dashboard allows smooth drill-downs to views that collaborate both end-user performance and

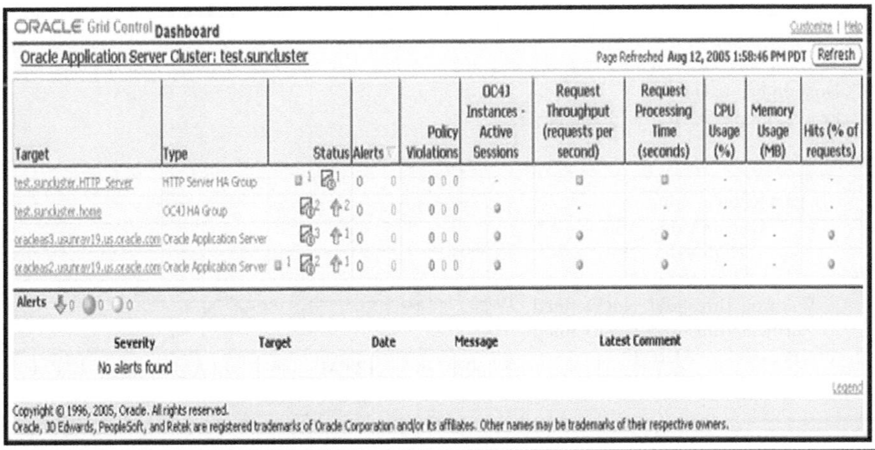

**Figure 13.5   Compliance System Dashboard.**

system infrastructure performance. It provides performance resolution diagnostic from a top-down approach (Figure 13.5).

The key to any Enterprise Service Bus (ESB)'s effectiveness as an SOA foundation is its ability to noninvasively enable the enterprise's existing systems and application to participate as equal citizens in the SOA. An ESB provides the implementation backbone for SOA in an IdM context. That is, it provides an IdM centric view of loosely coupled, event-driven SOA services with a highly distributed universe of named routing destinations across a multi-protocol message bus. When integrating IdM systems with other SOA systems, the Oracle SOA Process Manager provides the business process orchestration. These products put the power of business processes into the hands of the end users by means of various end-user reporting tools. Oracle Fusion allows users to quickly build a flexible, declarative, extendable environment to manage of all their business processes without building any orchestration or error-handling systems. The graphical SOA Process Manager (Figure 13.6) proves invaluable in creating and correcting identity-related business processes without coding.

## Oracle Identity Tracker

Tracker is a comprehensive antifraud software solution that works behind the scenes by verifying a host of factors used to confirm identity—from the computer/mobile device used to log in to a user's location and behavioral profiles. Based on these factors, Tracker scores risk and alerts the organization in real-time to potential fraud. Tracker can also trigger numerous follow-up actions, such as challenging the user.

Tracker conducts in-session risk analysis/scoring to verify users by their device, location, and behavior (see Figure 13.7). Tracker alerts the business in real-time, whenever a log-in or transaction is suspect. It does this by verifying the user's IP/geo-location, computer/device attributes, historical site usage, as well as a host of other factors, and comparing these with an existing profile (or predefined risk profile). Tracker may also be used to generate a dynamic alert or response to suspected fraud.

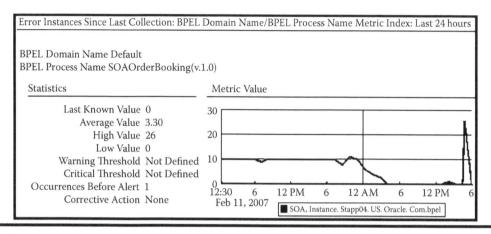

| Error Instances Since Last Collection: BPEL Domain Name/BPEL Process Name Metric Index: Last 24 hours |
| --- |

BPEL Domain Name Default
BPEL Process Name SOAOrderBooking(v.1.0)

| Statistics | | Metric Value |
| --- | --- | --- |
| Last Known Value | 0 | |
| Average Value | 3.30 | |
| High Value | 26 | |
| Low Value | 0 | |
| Warning Threshold | Not Defined | |
| Critical Threshold | Not Defined | |
| Occurrences Before Alert | 1 | |
| Corrective Action | None | |

**Figure 13.6   SOA and BPEL Compliance process.**

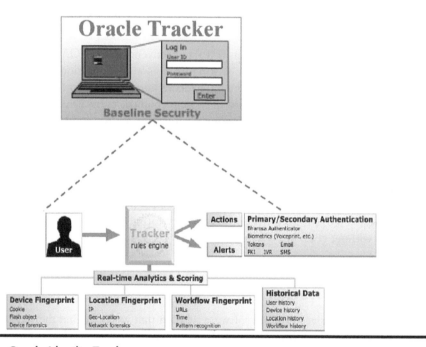

**Figure 13.7   Oracle Identity Tracker.**

## *"Gated" Security*

Risk scoring is done in real-time and sequentially during the course of a session. Scoring is repeated pre-, post-, and in-session for transactions and other online activities. No other method achieves higher accuracy and confidence.

## *Dynamic Rules-Based Authentication*

Based upon rules that may be customized by the business, Tracker can generate an alert and also govern a range of fluid responses, including secondary authentication out-of-band (via voice/SMS/e-mail) or through an online challenge (Oracle Authenticator).

## *Multifactor Online Security*

Device fingerprinting—Oracle uses proprietary methods to turn the end user's computer or mobile device into a strong second factor.

Location fingerprinting—Oracle Tracker checks the user's location at log-in and compares it with an account profile and other criteria (white/black list, etc.)

Workflow fingerprinting—Oracle Tracker uses proprietary methods to track online transactions and behavior against a historical profile in order to create a strong third factor.

Artificial intelligence—In addition to being rules-based, Tracker is also self-learning, in real-time. New fraud risks are detected, and rules are modified based upon past activity in the system.

As a stand-alone solution, Tracker offers strong, multifactor authentication security that can be implemented without requiring any change to the user experience.

Tracker, together with Authenticator, forms the organization's most powerful weapon in the fight against online identity theft.

## *Oracle Tracker Key Capabilities*

- Real-time monitoring of Web traffic builds profiles of normal user activity.
- Evaluates activities and context information against rules engine.
- Prompts for additional challenge questions or authentication.
- Blocks access or notifies administrators of potential fraudulent activity.
- Offline forensics analysis of audit data.

# Oracle Identity Authenticator

Authenticator includes a suite of highly secure Virtual Authentication Devices used to enter sensitive password and PIN data online. Oracle's data encryption technology combines the security strength of a device with the flexibility of the Web (Figure 13.8).

Authenticator includes a suite of highly secure Virtual Authentication Devices, which are used to enter sensitive password and PIN data online.

These devices are purely Web-based and server-driven. Virtual authentication devices are used at log-in or in session to protect against identity theft attacks, including trojans, phishing, screen scraping, and proxy-based fraud. Unlike traditional authentication methods, virtual authentication devices secure credentials, even on a compromised computer or Internet connection. Data is secured as it is entered on a user's machine and as it is transmitted over the wire.

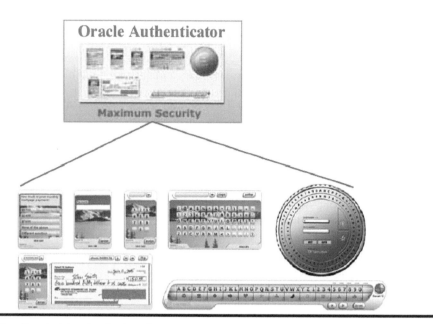

**Figure 13.8    Oracle Identity Authenticator.**

*Oracle Authenticator Key Capabilities:*

- Mutual authentication via personalized images.
- Virtual Authenticator devices protect passwords, PINs, and challenge questions against key loggers, man-in-the-middle attacks, OCR programs.
- Control and randomize placement of authenticators in the browser.

# Oracle Adaptive Access Manager

Adaptive Access manager creates stronger, step-up authentication based on access policies, and risk-based rules evaluation. It mutually authenticates users and Web sites with protection against identity theft Adapt policy-based authorizations to usage patterns, behavior, and anticipated risks (Figure 13.9).

VoicePad, an element of Adaptive Access manager, enables businesses to lower fraud risk and reduce operating costs through secure verification of consumer identities. VoicePad is a next-generation solution that offers improved and secure use of voice verification as a highly effective solution for out-of-band authentication. VoicePad allows for securing identities using biometric voiceprints and recognition of the user's phone, a combination known as a "voice token." The solution enables advanced protection of consumers without impacting their phone experience or a business's bottom line (Figure 13.10).

Together Authenticator, Web Gate, the Oracle Application Server, Oracle Access manager, and Oracle Tracker provide a secure conduit for sensitive personally identifiable information.

## Oracle Adaptive Authentication Key Capabilities

Risk-based authentication is superior when compared with "token"-based strong authentication alone:

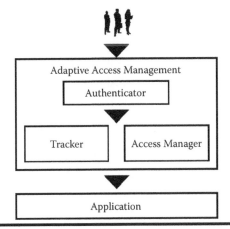

**Figure 13.9   Oracle Adaptive Access Manager.**

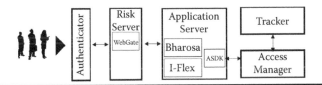

**Figure 13.10   Adaptive Access Process Flow.**

- Tokens imply higher cost/complexity and are not for large-scale consumer use.
- Passwords and PINs can still be compromised.
- Solution complements all token forms.

Nonintrusive and deep integration with applications:

- Proxy architecture or SOAP interfaces for quick and deep protection.
- Goes beyond detection to also BLOCK unauthorized access.
- Multi-tenant architecture works across multiple business units.

Rules never go out of date:

- Entire inventory of up-to-the-moment fraud rules available on demand.
- Tap into collective antifraud intelligence of entire global customer base.
- Ability to change rules in real-time.

# Oracle SSN Vault

SSN Vault, like Trusted Information Exchange, is an Oracle Consulting Solution that provides an additional method of securing personally identifiable information. SSN Vault, as shown in the following diagram (Figure 13.11), provides an electronic lockbox for Social Security numbers, providing the identity management system a token value in lieu of the actual user's Social Security

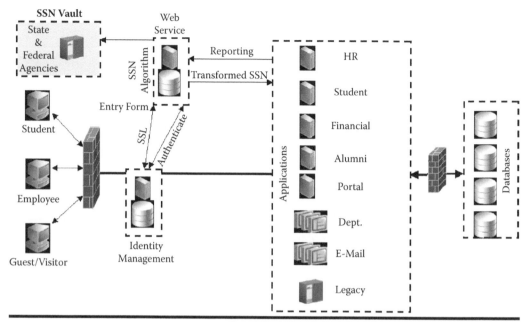

**Figure 13.11  SSN Vault.**

number. Another use of this solution is leveraging the electronic lockbox concept for credit cards, birthdates, or passport numbers.

## Oracle Identity Audit

Although log information does not provide control itself, it does provide evidence that controls are in place and working properly. Log information generally serves as the sample data used by auditors to perform tests of controls' operational effectiveness. Therefore, tamper resistance, correlation, and other auditing/logging features are quite important.

IdM components such as directory services, authentication mechanisms, access control capabilities, provisioning systems, and related tools all provide essential controls over identity information. Importantly, though, auditing requirements for most compliance situations need much more than what IdM alone can provide. In addition to the functions related to identity and access management, enterprises need data availability, physical security, policy adherence, and a variety of other technical necessities far outside the purview of identity management. Even the functions that an enterprise might choose to delegate to the IdM infrastructure often cannot fully accomplish the job.

Oracle Identity Audit tracks and analyzes user activity within enterprise applications to ensure conformity with business process best practices and standards. Oracle Identity Audit enables enterprises to confirm the integrity of their internal business processes by tracking user activity within enterprise applications and verifying it against established business process templates and best practices to detect insider fraud and further compliance initiatives. This solution enables administrators to detect and instantly alert the business to anomalous online user activity. A real-time engine compares user transactions against process templates and best practices. The engine then recognizes inconsistencies and generates real-time internal flags or alerts, which can allow

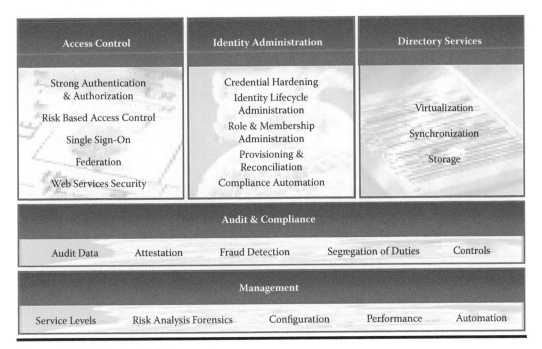

**Figure 13.12  Enhanced IdM ecosystem.**

the business to review and take corrective action; this results in an enhanced IdM ecosystem (Figure 13.12).

Oracle Identity Audit provides an important feedback mechanism that helps administrators determine whether policy objectives are being carried out. Enterprises require complete audit records to verify privilege settings, check whether users have accounts on approved systems, and generate other reports. Identity Audit trails also form a basis for accountability within the enterprise by tracking who requests access, why requests are granted or denied, and who approves requests. During investigations, audit records are required to conduct a thorough analysis of incidents. Because of their reliance on audit records for critical analysis, enterprises require that audit systems and the records they produce be protected from tampering. This implies using cryptographic technologies to sign or encrypt data such as the strategic use of Oracle Audit Vault in conjunction with Identity Audit. Enterprises may also require clear segregation of duties for administrators when the authority to modify audit settings and access audit records is restricted to a subset of administrators who do not perform user management functions; this feature leverages the Oracle Database Vault in tandem with the Identity Vault deployment.

# Chapter 14

# Oracle Integrating IdM and GRC Application Framework

In the past decade Oracle has evolved through acquisition and development from a database company into a comprehensive applications platform. In this context we view applications as a suite of modules that can provide an organization with robust transaction processing capability for accounting, distribution, manufacturing, and human resources business requirements. This chapter contains information about the high-level capabilities of the applications and how those applications exist within the compliance ecosystem.

## Oracle UMX User Management

Oracle User Management is a full-fledged role-based access control (RBAC) model that closely follows the RBAC ANSI standard (ANSI INCITS 359-2004) originally proposed by the National Institute of Standards and Technology (NIST). The RBAC Reference Model defines the following terms: objects, operations, permissions, roles, and users, as well as relations between the different components within the Oracle database.

Objects—"An object can be any system resource subject to access control, such as a file, printer, terminal, database record, etc."

In Oracle Applications this typically maps to records in relational tables/views, forms/HTML pages, and UI widgets.

Operations—"An operation is an executable image of a program, which upon invocation executes some function for the user."

Oracle Applications does not model operations separately; they are an implied part of our permission (function) definition. Examples of operations include Update, Escalate, Create, Invoke, Approve, Reject, etc.

Permissions—"Permission is an approval to perform an operation on one or more RBAC-protected objects."

In Oracle Applications this maps to what we have been referring to as functions, which are operations performed on objects. Examples are Invoke Service Request Form, Update Order, Approve Expense Report, Query Customers.

In Oracle Applications permissions are combined into Named Sets. Named Sets can be defined for two purposes, as Menus or Permission Sets. Each Named Set can also contain other Named Sets.

Menus are defined for navigation purposes and group UI pages into functional areas. Menus are granted to users through Responsibilities, which represent a special type of Role. Each menu item maps to a permission which optionally may be granted to the user as part of the menu/responsibility assignment. Menu items that are not granted as part of the menu/responsibility assignment will not be rendered unless the user is granted the permission separately.

Permission Sets are granted to users or roles independently of menus/responsibilities. Permission Sets are granted to users in order to enable menu items and other operations (functions) that should not be available to all users assigned a given menu/responsibility. Permission Sets are granted to users or roles through Permission Assignments.

Permission Assignments are granted with an optional Data Scope or Data Security Policy. Data Security Policies restrict operations so that they only can be performed on a subset of instances of the corresponding database object.

Approvals Management workflow is managed by the Oracle Approvals Management engine. The Oracle Approvals Management is a highly extensible approvals rules engine that allows organizations to simply and effectively define business rules determining who must approve a transaction originating within an Oracle Application. Implementers can devise simple or complex rules, as the organization requires, which then form part of the overall business flow.

Roles—"A role is a job function within the context of an organization with some associated semantics regarding the authority and responsibility conferred on the user assigned to the role."

Roles can also be included in Role Inheritance Hierarchies. This allows clients and product teams to set up hierarchies. Oracle Applications RBAC model supports what is referred to as General Role Hierarchies, which means any role can have multiple superior and sub-role relationships

Role Categories. Roles and Responsibilities can now be categorized into functional areas.

Oracle User Management supports Enterprise RBAC, which means that clients with corporate LDAP directories can synch groups and roles (including membership) between Oracle Applications and third-party systems.

Users—"A user is defined as a human being. Although the concept of a user can be extended to include machines, networks, or intelligent autonomous agents." Oracle Applications store user accounts in the FND_USER table; this is the preferred integration point with Oracle Identity manager.

## PeopleSoft Applications User Management

PeopleSoft User Management can use any LDAP-based data to autocreate the User Profile within itself upon the first "successful" authentication against LDAP (or Oracle Access Manager via LDAP) at runtime. The information needed to create this User Profile within itself would still need to be passed to PeopleSoft User Management, however, either via Oracle Access Manager or an LDAP lookup into Oracle Internet Directory.

Clients implementing PeopleSoft can utilize Oracle Access Management in the following ways:

1. PeopleSoft + Oracle Access Manager
   PeopleSoft delegates authentication tasks to Oracle Access Manager, which provides SSO capabilities. The user must be created in both PeopleSoft User Management and Oracle Access Manager. (Often, Oracle Access Manager relies on a Directory Server like AD, Oracle Internet Directory, and iPlanet, so the user entry will have to be created there as well.) Oracle Access Manager can be used in a larger context of providing SSO to other Web applications as well.
2. PeopleSoft + Oracle Identity Manager
   If user provisioning is one of the business drivers, then Oracle Identity Manager (Xellerate) can provision users and passwords to PeopleSoft.
3. PeopleSoft + Oracle Access Manager (OAM) + Oracle Identity Manager
   Oracle Identity Manager provisions users and passwords to the directory used by Oracle Access Manager, enabling SSO for PeopleSoft User Management. Oracle Identity Manager also provisions users and permissions to PeopleSoft User Management.
4. PeopleSoft + Oracle Internet Directory (also Oracle Virtual Directory)
   Here PeopleSoft User Management uses Oracle Internet Directory as the authentication store (and optionally roles). It also provisions users to the Directory. ESSO is not a part of this architecture here.
5. PeopleSoft + Oracle Access Manager + Oracle Internet Directory + Oracle Identity Manager (or if the architect wants to store different sets of users in different directories, they may combine PeopleSoft User Management + Oracle Access Manager + Oracle Internet Directory + Oracle Virtual Directory + Oracle Identity Manager + third-party directory)

## Deploying the PeopleSoft User Management Connector for Oracle Identity Manager

Deploying the connector involves the following steps:

- Step 1: Verify installation requirements
- Step 2: Copy the connector files
- Step 3: Configure the target system
- Step 4: Import the connector files
- Step 5: Configure the reconciliation module
- Step 6: Compile adapters

### Step 1: Verifying Installation Requirements

The installation requirements for the connector are the following:

Oracle Identity Manager Oracle Identity Manager release 8.5.3 or later
Target systems PSFT Base AR System 6.0
Target systems host platforms Microsoft Windows
Operating system Microsoft Windows 2003

## Step 2: Copying the Connector Files

The files to be copied and the destination directories to which they must be copied are the following:

PSFTBaseProvisioning.jar xellerate_installation\xellerate\JavaTasks

PSFTBaseReconciliation.jar xellerate_installation\xellerate\ScheduleTask

PSFT_Package_Package\PSFTAdapter\PeopleSoftBaseAdapter\XML\PSFTBaseConnector.xml xellerate_installation\xlclient\

## Step 3: Configuring the Target System

Configuring the target system involves performing the following procedures:

### 3.1 Create the APIs for the Component Interface

1. Open the Application Designer by clicking Start and then selecting Programs, Peoplesoft8.9hcm, and Application Designer. The Application Designer window is displayed.
2. In the Application Designer window, select Open from the File menu. The Open Definition dialog box is displayed.
3. In the Open Definition dialog box, select Component Interface from the Definition list.
4. Enter USER_PROFILE in the Name field, and then press Enter.
5. All the component interfaces with names that start with USER_PROFILE are displayed in the Open Definition dialog box.
6. Select the USER_PROFILE entry, and then click Open.
7. Click Yes in the message that is displayed. The Component Interface window for the USER_PROFILE definition is displayed.
8. In the Component Interface window for the USER_PROFILE definition, select PeopleSoft APIs from the Build menu. The Build PeopleSoft API Bindings dialog box is displayed.
9. In the Java Classes area of the Build PeopleSoft API Bindings dialog box, select the Build check box.
10. In the Target Directory field, specify the path of the directory in which you want the APIs to be created.
11. Click OK to close the message.

### 3.2 Create the Java Template for the Component Interface

1. On the right pane of the Component Interface window for the USER_PROFILE definition, right-click USER_PROFILE.
2. Select Generate Java Template from the shortcut menu. A message showing the name and path of the Java template is displayed.

### 3.3 Create the Application Engine Program

1. Open the Application Designer by clicking Start and then selecting Programs, Peoplesoft8.9hcm, and Application Designer. The Application Designer window is displayed.
2. In the Application Designer window, select New from the File menu. The New Definition dialog box is displayed.
3. In the New Definition dialog box, select Application Engine from the Definition list. The App Engine Program window is displayed.
4. In the App Engine Program window, select Action from the Insert menu.
5. From the list, select PeopleCode. Then, save the PeopleCode as EMPINF_AE by using the Save option from the File menu.
6. Double-click the PeopleCode action, and copy the following to the path statement:
   &File1 = GetFile("\\123.123.123.123\jdoe\txtfilename.txt, "w", %FilePath_Absolute);
   &LogFile = GetFile("\\123.123.123.123\temp\logfilename.log", "w", "a", %FilePath_Absolute);
7. Close the inner window, and save the PeopleCode.
8. Click Run to run the Application Engine program. The output is written to the path specified in the program.

## Step 4: Import the Connector Files

To import the connector files into Oracle Identity Manager:

1. Open the Oracle Identity Manager Administrative and User Console.
2. Click the Deployment Management link on the left navigation bar.
3. Click the Import link under Deployment Management. The Deployment Manager import window is displayed, along with a dialog box for locating files.
4. Locate and open the PSFTBaseConnector.xml file, which is in the xellerate_installation\xlclient directory. The Deployment Manager window is displayed.
5. In the Deployment Manager window, click Add File. The File Preview window showing the details of the selected file is displayed.
6. Click Next. The Substitution window is displayed.
7. Click Next. The Confirmation window is displayed.
8. Click View Selections. The contents of the XML file are displayed in the Deployment Manager import window. You may see a cross-shaped icon along with some nodes. You must remove these nodes. To do this, right-click each such node and then select Remove.
9. Click Import. The connector file is imported into Oracle Identity Manager.
10. Perform the same procedure to import the PSFTBaseXellerateUser.xml file.

## Step 5: Configure the Reconciliation Module

UserName Demo & Enter the Password Set up for Demo
Management server:Server Name IP address or computer name of the PeopleSoft User
Port: 0, Trusted Field: LoginName, Is Debug: Debug Feature YES, TimeStamp: Last Reconciliation time (none), DeleteUserFormName: SHR:DeletePeople, FormName SHR:People (Form name of the PeopleSoft User Management server to which the connection is to be made)

## Step 6: Compiling Adapters

The following adapters are imported into Oracle Identity Manager when the connector XML file is deployed. You must compile these adapters before you can use them to provision accounts on the target system.

```
adpPSFTCREATEUSER, adpPSFTUPDATEUSER, adpPSFTRESETPASSWORD,
adpPSFTUNLOCKUSER, adpPSFTLOCKUSER, adpPSFTUPDATEUSEREMPID,
adpPSFTADDORDELETEROLE, adpPSFTADDORDELETEEMAIL
```

To compile adapters by using the Adapter Manager form:

1. Open the Adapter Manager form.
2. To compile all the adapters that you have imported into the current database, select the Compile All option.
   To compile multiple (but not all) adapters, select the adapters you want to compile. Then, select the Compile Selected option.
3. Click Start. Oracle Identity Manager compiles the adapters.

## PeopleSoft Configuration for Use with Oracle Internet Directory

The Configure Directory component (PSDSSETUP) contains four pages that the administrator can use for specifying connection information and testing directory server connections. To enable the PeopleSoft system to successfully connect to Oracle Internet Directory, the implementer must enter the appropriate connection information. This includes the server name (DNS or IP address) and the listening port number. You also must enter the user-distinguished name (User DN) and associated password. The PeopleSoft application server uses the User DN and password to connect to the LDAP server to retrieve user profile information about the specific user signing in to the system. The User DN must reflect a user with the appropriate LDAP browse rights.

1. Access the Configure Directory–Directory Setup page.
2. Click to view graphic Configure Directory–Directory Setup page. Directory ID: Identifies the directory connection that you are creating. The directory ID that you enter can identify a specific LDAP server or a collection of LDAP servers depending on how many servers you add in the Server Name section. Description: Enter Oracle Internet Directory as the description.
3. Select Oracle Internet Directory from the list of options.
4. Default Connect DN (default connect distinguished name): Displays the default connect DN associated with the directory ID that you entered or selected on the initial search page. The connect DN is the ID that you can use to connect to Oracle Internet Directory. You can enter an alternative connect DN. Password: Enter the password associated with the directory-based account that appears in the Default Connect DN field. (*Note:* The password is stored in encrypted form in the database.) Server Name: Add LDAP directory servers to a connection list. You can add multiple servers for failover purposes using the plus button. All servers you add must participate in the same directory service. LDAP Server: Identify a specific LDAP server. You can use the DNS name or you can use IP address dotted notation. For example, either of the following formats is acceptable: ldap12.yourcompany.com or 192.201.185.90. Port: Enter the port number on which the LDAP server is configured

to receive search requests. The standard LDAP port is 389. If you do not specify the correct port, PeopleSoft Directory Interface cannot exchange data with Oracle Internet Directory server. SSL Port: If you are implementing SSL, enter the SSL port on Oracle Internet Directory.

5. Click to jump to top of pageClick to jump to parent topicSpecifying Additional Connect DNs.
6. Access the Configure Directory–Additional Connect DNs page.
7. Click to view graphic Configure Directory–Additional Connect DNs page.

The PeopleSoft application server uses the User DN and password specified on this page to connect to Oracle Internet Directory to retrieve user profile information about the specific user signing in to the system. The User DN must reflect a user with the appropriate LDAP browse rights.

User DN: Add any DNs that you need in addition to the default connect DN that you entered on the Directory Setup page. The default user ID is most likely an administrative ID. This enables you to set up a more secure user ID for the scope of the mapping.

## LDAP_Authentication Considerations

When using LDAP_Authentication, the default searching behavior can be overridden by entering attribute=%UserId% in the Search Attribute edit box on the In the Directory Setup page. When implementers insert this syntax, the system constructs the DN of the user by concatenating the search attribute plus the entered user name with the search base.

For example, given the setup depicted in the following example, if the user entered Pohlman in the User Name edit box of the sign-on page, the DN would be

```
uid=Pohlman,ou=TBU,o=tinyurl.com
```

This constructed DN would be used for the bind attempt rather than searching the directory with the search filter of

```
uid=Pohlman.
```

## SSO_Authentication Considerations

If implementers are using SSO_Authentication and LDAP_ProfileSynch to automatically generate profiles, then the value of the LDAP attribute mapped to User ID must be unique throughout the directory. The PeopleSoft User ID uniquely identifies a person within PeopleSoft, and a DN uniquely identifies a person within the directory. PeopleSoft maps the PeopleSoft User Profile to a directory entry by specifying the directory attribute that holds the value of the PeopleSoft User ID. Implementers may specify the appropriate mapping between the PeopleSoft system and primary directory using the User Profile Caching component. On the Mandatory User Properties page, implementers must equate the PeopleSoft User ID attribute with an LDAP attribute. For example, in many cases the PeopleSoft User ID is mapped to the LDAP attribute of uid. With a single sign-on token, the system can provide the Signon PeopleCode with only a user ID value to identify a person. Then the system must search the directory to find the corresponding DN. If multiple entries within the scope of the search have the same value on the User ID attribute, then PeopleSoft is unable to determine which entry corresponds to the user.

### LDAP_ProfileSynch Considerations

If implementers work with the NDS, Active Directory, or iPlanet directories and would like to assign roles dynamically at sign-on time, implementers can use the disabled example Signon PeopleCode that PeopleSoft has provided. Directory-specific information is included in the comments of the code.

## Siebel Universal Customer Master

Part of Oracle's Siebel Customer Data Integration (CDI) solutions, Universal Customer Master provides comprehensive functionality to manage customer data over the life cycle. Universal Customer Master (UCM) is a comprehensive customer data hub that unifies customer data across multiple business units and functionally disparate systems. What makes this product unique to corporate governance and identity management is its ability to control access to customer data and generate attestations on the use and custody of that data. It is also easily integrated with Oracle Identity Manager, Audit Vault, and Database Vault.

UCM provides a GUI for data stewards to manage customer data over the life-cycle activities include creating or importing customer information, to cleansing, matching, enhancing and distributing it. UCM has extensive capabilities to define and execute rules for matching and intelligently merging customer information coming from different sources. In order to create the single authoritative version of the customer profile, the customer master allows stewards to pick and choose attributes, or fields from different records.

UCM provides audit and capture of transactional data.

- Captures incoming source records from contributing systems and historical versions
- Provides data stewards the ability to restore customer profiles from any point in time
- Allows users to view all changes that have occurred to a record, including old and new values, and whoever made the change
- Audit records merge and unmerge events

The following tables are the primary integration points for Oracle Identity Manager and Oracle Audit Vault:

| | |
|---|---|
| S_UCM_ORG_EXT | Source and History table for accounts |
| S_UCM_CONTACT | Source and History table for contacts |
| S_UCM_ORG_CHLD | Source and History table for child objects of account |
| S_UCM_CON_CHLD | Source and History table for child objects of contact |
| EIM_UCM_ORG | EIM interface table for S_UCM_ORG_EXT |
| EIM_UCM_CON | EIM interface table for S_UCM_CONTACT |
| EIM_UCM_ORG_CHLD | EIM interface table for S_UCM_ORG_CHLD |
| EIM_UCM_CON_CHLD | EIM interface table for S_UCM_CON_CHLD |

Other integration points that can be used by Audit Vault and Oracle Identity Manager:

- Sending and receiving XML over HTTP
- MQ Series or MSMQ to exchange data in XML or any other format
- A provided ActiveX data control that can be embedded in a COM-based application

- J2EE or JSP within the provided Java framework
- A provided CORBA IDL

Integration with partners in a federated context:

- Data management processes invoke data quality service, which calls partner functions.
- Universal Connector provides uniform way for partners to integrate.
- Partners provide match scores and cleansing engine.
- UCM provides processes and UI to handle match results, and survivorship rules to merge and update correctly.
- Siebel UCM has pre-built Data Stewardship UI for manual review processes and ad hoc data correction.

The privacy management capabilities of UCM include

- Privacy attributes (part of the data mode)—do not call, do not e-mail, do not direct mail flags
- Rules engine to define privacy rules
- Rules repository

Sample Rules:
Set Privacy Status to "Pending" for a minimum of 45 days and is expressed in the following code segments:

```
IF ("Pending" period expires without the customer initiates privacy
activity)
THEN (update privacy fields)
IF (contact change for an account, e.g., co-borrowed deletion, primary
contact replacement)
THEN (apply more restrictive privacy policy to remaining contact)
IF (customer bought a vehicle in 48 contiguous states)
AND (subsequently moves to Puerto Rico)
THEN (send a new privacy notice in English and Spanish)
```

## *Audit and Attestation*

UCM captures incoming source records from contributing systems. Features, which may be leveraged for audit and attestation, include

- Data stewards roll back: the ability to restore customer profiles from any point in time
- Allows users to view all changes that have occurred to a record including old and new values, including a list of who made the change
- Audit records merge and unmerge events
- Data import management
- Primary method of getting data into UCM is through integration

Inserting data into UCM base tables is a four-step process:

- First, insert into Source Data and History (SDH) tables.
- Then, use UCM Batch Workflows to move data into base tables.

- Incoming records that match with an existing record in UCM are linked to the existing record and existing record is updated (Link and Update).
- Survivorship is invoked during Link and Update.

The advanced UCM features around dataimport include Intelligent Merge, Intelligent Update, Automerge, and Unmerge. All take advantage of the Survivorship infrastructure, which includes the following:

- Survivorship Rules, which determine the system allowed to contribute attributes to a customer record.
- System Confidence, which identifies the confidence level by which contribution to a given attribute or attribute group can be trusted.
- Attribute Group is a set of customer attributes that are usually processed together and treated as a single unit rather than individual attributes. For example, "Address" as an attribute group could consist of street address, city, province, country and postal code; administrators could base survivorship rules and confidence on the Address attribute group, instead of on individual attributes.
- Rule Evaluate Criteria that will be used to resolve conflicts in case of two equal weight/confidence rules.
- Rule Engine for executing of the survivorship rules during update and merge operations.
- Rule Administration UI for definition and activation of survivorship rules.
- Out-of-the-box Sample Rules for Account and Contact as a best-practice template for customer implementation.

## Siebel Branch Teller

Siebel Branch Teller is comprehensive transactional financial service operational control including a complete set of teller and supervisor transactions and a full set of support services. To support Check21 and customer authentication Siebel Branch Teller integrates two factor authentication mechanisms and supports U.S. regulatory compliance (CTR, BSA, Reg CC, and MIL) role-based transaction menus, entitlements, business rules, and workflows supporting account- and customer-centric processing.

## iFlex

Although technically a separate entity, at the time of this publication, with 83% ownership, the future merger of the product offerings is a certainty and is already reflected in the sales and support process. iFlex is one of the key components in satisfying the financial services governance requirements mandated by Basil II, GLBA, Sarbanes–Oxley, and GAAIP.

### *Reveleus*

Reveleus is a suite of analytical applications for the financial services industry focused in the areas of risk management, customer insight, and enterprisewide financial performance. Reveleus' Risk

Analytics product solves the most complex global challenges facing the financial industry with a focus on multijurisdictional Basel II compliance and operational risk management. Reveleus provides a stochastic modeling framework for estimation of business parameters. The Modeling Framework has been integrated with industry standard statistical packages like MATLAB for statistical analysis such as Optimizations, Regressions, etc. The modeling framework can also seamlessly work with any other statistical tools, such as SAS. Reveleus modeling framework can be used by banks for estimation of probability of default of a rating grade (PD) and loss-given-default for a facility (LGD). If, however, the PDs and LGDs have already been derived by the bank, the framework can still be utilized for running simulations and stress-testing their positions and decisions against various economic events. Moreover, we have found that many organizations plan to leverage the Reveleus Modeling Framework for certain lines of business where the processes are not fully implemented.

The framework provides base models to start with for PD, LGD Estimation but is also open for definition of newer business models for the purpose. Reveleus uses Logistic Regression and Naïve Bayes' method for PD estimation, whereas it uses Linear Regression for LGD Modeling.

- Business users can choose from a list of statistical methods for model development, viz.:
  - Logistic regression
  - Normalized logistic regression
  - Linear regression
  - Normalized linear regression
  - Stepwise linear regression
  - Bayesian analysis
- Business users can select independent and dependent variables from business definitions available in Reveleus Unified Meta Data Repository.
- Using the Reveleus modeling framework one can regress on one set of data and predict and/or back test on a completely different set of data.
- Business users can adopt a top-down approach in model development as Reveleus also offers the flexibility of portfoliowise regression.

## Mantas

Mantas is a Behavior Detection Platform that serves as a solution for detecting risk, enhancing customer relationships, and addressing regulatory requirements in the anti-money-laundering, trading, and broker-compliance areas.

Although regional and community banks are being held to the same regulations, risks, and exposures as multinational financial firms, they must balance that demand against significantly reduced resources. Mantas provides the regional banking market with a unique solution for compliance with anti-money-laundering (AML) regulation. By applying AI techniques along with statistical analysis, Mantas not only addresses current regulations, but also gives these institutions the flexibility and scale to adapt to rapidly changing business and regulatory requirements.

## Flexcube

Flexcube (cube—comprehensive universal banking experience) is a complete banking product suite for retail, consumer, corporate, investment and internet banking, and asset management and investor servicing with a focus on the entire gamut of banking operations namely cash, trade finance, treasury, securities, derivatives, and automated teller operations.

Flexcube allows the bank to choose an optimum set of modules that best suit its needs without being saddled with unnecessary components. The functional modules cover the broad categories of retail banking, treasury, trade finance, mutual funds, and delivery channels, and are based on the concept of universal banking. They include the areas of:

Retail banking: Provides browser-based access to all teller functions and all other retail banking operations, such as DDAs, savings and current accounts, term deposits, retail loans, mortgages, ACH, and clearing systems.

Corporate banking: Includes a graphical user interface (GUI) for commercial banking functions such as treasury, trade finance, investment banking, and cash management. The GUI also allows access to maintenance functions, including currency maintenance, and product definitions.

Internet banking: Flexcube@ provides HTML screens for performing retail and commercial banking over the Internet. The solution enables personalized screen layouts based on user profile, preferences, and user privileges.

Core modules form the foundation for operation of all the other functional modules. They provide a set of common services that are seamlessly accessed by all the other functional modules, such as accounting, customer information, risk management, and others.

General ledger: The user-definable, multicurrency General Ledger (GL) supports unlimited levels of account consolidation and reporting.

Customer information file: The Customer Information System captures and maintains relevant customer information to provide a detailed profile of a customer's relationship with the bank and between the customers.

Comprehensive MIS: MIS support, including profitability analysis, is provided at several levels such as customer, product, branch, business segment, bank, and any other user-defined MIS class.

Risk management: Flexcube provides online, centralized tracking of multicurrency customer limits across all branches. The lines can be defined for a single module or product across a combination of modules and products.

Standing instructions: The Standing Instructions module of Flexcube executes payment instructions for customers at periodic intervals. The module additionally handles sweeps based on projected value-dated balances between the Nostro accounts.

Clearing: The Clearing Module handles the back-office retail banking business such as inward clearing, outward clearing, check operations, and generation of related reports. It supports centralized, as well as decentralized, clearing operations.

Nostro reconciliation: This module helps in reconciling balances and transactions reported by correspondent banks in their statement of accounts.

Workflow management: This module handles the complete end-to-end processing of commercial contracts, right from the initiation of the contract or transaction, up to the point of closure. It also offers the option of document management system that helps retrieve the particular supporting document or contract that can be stored in various formats.

Fixed asset management: The Fixed Assets Module enables tracking of all the necessary information for events such as depreciation, revaluation, sales/transfer of assets, and disposal of assets.

Expense processing: The Expense Processing Module offers a comprehensive solution wherein banks can automate all the processes from preparing expense budgets to recording of all consequent expenses, including credit limits to vendors, contract settlements, advance payments, and final payments to vendors.

## *Daybreak*

Daybreak is a comprehensive consumer lending system that automates all aspects of financing from origination, to servicing and collections for installment loans, consumer leases, revolving products, and home equity lines of credit.

Daybreak installment loans: Closed-end, fixed-rate loans for multiple, user-defined collateral types

Daybreak lines of credit: A portfolio of revolving credit programs such as home equity lines of credit, in-store revolving credit programs, and overdraft credit lines

Daybreak leases: Consumer leases with sophisticated termination and remarketing programs

# Oracle Governance, Risk, and Compliance Manager

Oracle GRC Manager combined with Fusion Governance, Risk, and Compliance Intelligence (GRC Intelligence) provides advanced analytical and reporting capabilities. Dashboards and charts allow executives, business process owners, and auditors to promptly determine where the organization is in or out of compliance or where risks exist. GRC Manager automates the management and enforcement of internal controls and improves the efficiency of the compliance management process. GRC Manager includes a central repository. The central repository stores and manages content for all GRC initiatives, giving users a single view and access point to critical information including policies and procedures, process diagrams, control descriptions, test plans, control matrices, and remediation plans. The time and identity of users who access data is captured in an audit trail, preserving the chain of custody of compliance procedures and risk mitigation. GRC Manager is made up of the following:

- Stellent Financial Director
- Stellent Policy and Procedure Portal
- Internal Control Manager
- Internal Control Enforcer
- Stellent Universal Content Manager

## *Stellent Financial Director*

Stellent Financial Compliance Director: A Web-based software solution used to facilitate compliance with the Sarbanes–Oxley Act, as well as other global financial reporting mandates such as OMB A-123 in the U.S. federal space, Multilateral Instrument 52-109 in Canada, JSOX in Japan, KSOX in Korea, Loi de Securite Financiere in France, Turnbull Report in the U.K., Corporate Governance Code in Germany, or the Tabaksblat Code in the Netherlands.

## Stellent Policy and Procedure Portal

Stellent Policy and Procedure Portal uses hypertext Content Server Template (HCST) pages to render data while preserving content management. A developer can execute any Stellent UCM service with a properly constructed HCST. The most common use of HCSTs is to create check-in screens, search pages, and portal pages. Pages that execute custom services or database queries are also possible with proper coding. Hypertext Content Server Template is commonly used to customize searches, content info, and check-in pages. The hyperdata format, also known as HDA, is used to store tabular and unstructured data.

Most Content Server configuration files are in HDA format. The purpose behind the HDA format is to quickly serialize tabular data while retaining the flexibility of name-value pairs. It is similar in flexibility to XML. Unlike XML, however, the HDA format is more compact and focused on table-based data, so it is more quickly parsed.

HDA format contains four main sections:

1. A header describing the encoding used in the HDA
2. The LocalData section containing key-value pairs
3. All ResultSets containing tabular data
4. All OptionLists containing simple lists

HDA files are used throughout the content server for table-based configuration data. A developer uses them for the Component Definition File, which contains references for all resources in a custom component. Another commonly used HDA file is the Workflow Companion File, which contains state and history information about an item currently in workflow.

The HDA format is the default serialization of the primary data structure in the Content. Server. The Java object, which provides this function, is called a DataBinder and is located in intradoc.data.DataBinder. This Java object is used for service requests. The parameters in the request are stored in the LocalData for the DataBinder. The response data is attached as ResultSets, OptionLists, and new LocalData. This DataBinder is then used to render the response. Responses are HTML pages. In addition, the full DataBinder can be serialized back to the user in HDA format. This is an HDA-based Web service that occurs whenever the parameter IsJava=1 is sent in the request. The DataBinder is used for data structure Content Server features: user personalization, items in workflow, archives, and components. The data for these items is serialized out to HDA files on the file system. Many of these features are stored in the database.

## Internal Controls Manager (For E-Business Suite)

Oracle Internal Controls Manager is a comprehensive tool for executives, controllers, internal audit departments, and public accounting firms to document and test internal controls and monitor ongoing compliance. It is based on COSO (Committee of Sponsoring Organizations) standards.

Internal Control Manager permits companies to manage audit activities:

■ Define standard business processes.
■ Set up risks to which processes are exposed.
■ Set up controls that can mitigate process risk.
■ Set up the Organization Structure (Auditable Units), and map processes to this structure.

- Record your assessment of the organization's compliance with established controls and regulations.
- Create audit procedures to verify controls.
- Review the compliance of your business processes/systems and record audit results.

To set up Internal Controls Manager, more business process steps are required than technical:

1. Define standard business processes.
2. Set up a risk and controls library as well as the policies, procedures, and activities that allow an organization to address those risks.
3. Set up the organization structure (auditable units) and map processes to this structure.
4. Record the assessment of the organization's compliance with established controls and regulations.
5. Create audit procedures to verify controls.
6. Set up audit engagements to manage audit assignments.
7. Test for segregation of duties violations. Identify any combination of tasks in an enterprise as incompatible.
8. Set up business process certifications requiring process owners to provide assurance that their organization's processes are in compliance with the standards.
9. Set up financial statement certifications.
10. Record, track, and resolve findings. During the audit process, nonconformities to established standards are often discovered, and these anomalies are identified as "findings." They are typically items of material concern that violate sound accounting practice and accountability.
11. Setup roles and privileges security in the application is implemented through both function security and data security.
12. Implement Application Controls Monitoring (ACM) is an application built on top of Oracle Audit Trail within Internal Controls Manager. All change tracking is done via the capabilities offered by Audit Trail as follows: ACM seeds the setup data required to enable Audit Trail auditing on a particular set of E-Business Suite tables. Upon running the concurrent program "AuditTrail: Update Tables," a shadow table is created for each of these select tables. The shadow table will record the change history.

The two integration points in this process are the data security phase and the application controls, the monitoring of which can be configured to monitor and report on the configuration of Oracle Identity Manager and Oracle Access Manager.

## Internal Controls Enforcer (for PeopleSoft Enterprise)

Internal Controls Enforcer enables administrators to combat the cost of ongoing compliance by automating the management and enforcement of internal controls, ensuring that they remain in place with continuous monitoring, enabling better visibility and management of compliance projects, and driving accountability deeper throughout the organization.

Diagnostic tools delivered with the Internal Controls Enforcer detect changes in key controls within PeopleSoft and JD Edwards. Using ICE the audit administrator can monitor configurable controls such as accounting system settings, tolerances and limits, authorization and access, and business rules. Delivered diagnostics for monitoring key controls:

- PeopleSoft General Ledger: Journal edit rules
- PeopleSoft Expenses: Expense approval authority and limits
- PeopleSoft Accounts Payable: Segregation of duties; creation of one-time vendor; two-, three-, and four-way matching rules and tolerances; matching rules for incomplete source documents; duplicate invoice checks; and voucher limits
- PeopleSoft Accounts Receivable: Customer credit limits and write-off limits
- PeopleSoft Treasury: Bank reconciliation limits
- PeopleSoft Global Consolidations: Consolidation model settings, ownership percentages, locked periods, segregation of duties, row level security, and access to correction mode
- JD Edwards General Ledger: Journal options
- JD Edwards Accounts Payable: Segregation of duties; creation of matching rules and tolerances; and duplicate invoice rules (including voucher processing)
- JD Edwards Accounts Receivable: Customer credit limits, write-off limits, and receivables aging settings by company
- JD Edwards Expenses: Changes in expense management policies such as preferred suppliers, receipt required, daily allowance, and expense category

## Stellent UCM/FCD

However, it is important when integrating UCM/FCD to know the base Java classes and how they map to functional requirements of compliance.

- stellent/shared/classes/: Contains the Java class files for the Content Server and dependent libraries
- stellent/shared/config/resources/: Contains the core Web resources and configuration tables
- stellent/shared/config/resources/std_page.htm: Contains most of the HTML and IdocScript resources used on template pages
- stellent/shared/config/resources/std_services.htm: Contains the definition of most core services
- stellent/shared/config/resources/workflow.htm: Contains workflow-related services and data tables
- stellent/shared/config/resources/std_resources.htm: Commonly used configuration in data tables
- stellent/shared/config/resources/lang/: Localization strings for translating the interface into different languages
- stellent/shared/config/templates/: Contains the HTML templates returned after service requests

**Table 14.1    Regulatory Governance Mapping**

|  | Trusted Access | Change Management | Business Continuity and Availability | Operational Awareness | Records Management | Audit and Risk Management | Operational Accountability & Transparency | Segregation of Duties | Operational Controls |
|---|---|---|---|---|---|---|---|---|---|
| Oracle Enterprise Security Manager | X | X |  | X |  |  | X | X | X |
| Oracle UMX User Management | X | X |  | X |  |  | X | X | X |
| PeopleSoft Applications User Management | X |  |  | X |  |  |  | X | X |
| Siebel Universal Customer Master | X | X | X | X | X | X |  | X | X |
| Revelus | X |  |  | X | X | X | X | X | X |
| Mantas | X | X |  | X |  |  | X |  | X |
| Oracle Governance, Risk, and Compliance Manager |  | X | X | X | X | X | X | X | X |

# Summary

This chapter described identity and compliance applications common to a global enterprise and discussed the various Oracle applications that could be used to facilitate regulatory compliance. Although this book attempts to provide comprehensive coverage, the breadth and depth of the applications is too great for any one book or any one user to deal with completely. It would take an individual several years to understand both the technical platform and the applications they serve.

## Chapter 15

# Integrating IdM and GRC Technology Platform

Identity preservation is absolutely necessary for data security, as security cannot be based on anonymity. The first step occurs when the user authenticates himself or herself to the application server. The application server must then convey this identity in context to the database. The database can then apply the authorizations (privileges) and access control policies as well as auditing based on the user actually performing the actions. This chapter highlights products in the Oracle Data Technology Platform which may be coupled with Identity Management (IdM) to enable compliance. This section also highlights integration points against which OVD, OIM, OAM, and ESSO may be configured to audit, provision, and protect the data management layer.

## Database Vault

Oracle Database Vault (OVD) is one of a set of products that helps companies comply with the technical security requirements of various regulatory compliance regulations. In prior years, the database administrator (DBA) was required to be a trusted employee within an organization. The job/role gave the employee the authority to see any data within the system and control complete access to that system. This meant that they had the SELECT ANY TABLE system privilege. Database Vault prevents a DBA from accessing a table, even though the DBA continues to retain the SELECT ANY TABLE privilege. As the access the DBA has to data is typically at a lower level than that provided through an application, any auditing facilities designed into the application could be bypassed. With the advent of a number of regulatory compliance acts in a number of countries, this unique power of the DBA is now considered an unacceptable business risk. To mitigate this risk in an automated fashion, the Database Vault kernel still permits the user with the DBA role to select data from the table space but predicates the query in process, thus prohibiting the DBA user from viewing the data while permitting other job functions permitted by the domain owner. Database Vault is part of the database kernel, and thus is a more secure implementation than the one implemented in PL/SQL on top of the database.

The following components of Database Vault provide highly configurable access control:

Realms: A boundary set up around a set of objects in a schema. Specific conditions must exist to gain access.

Factors: Attributes of a user or the system at any given time. Factors contribute to the decision process of granting access, and combinations of several factors may be considered at once. This is multifactored authentication.

Identities: Specific values that factors may take on. Of the possible set of values for a given factor, some or all may have been assigned a name, which is an identity.

Rule sets: A collection of rules that are evaluated for purposes of granting access.

Command rules: Specific conditions that must be in effect for a given command to be executed on a given object or set of objects. This provides very granular control over what can be done to certain objects, and by whom.

Secure application roles: A role that can be activated by a session only under the condition of passing a rule set.

## Installation

### Clustered Installation

To install Database Vault in an RAC environment, perform the following steps:

1. Stop all RAC instances on all nodes.
2. Shut down all ASM instances on all nodes.
3. Stop all applications on all nodes.
4. Choose the RAC option in the Installation Method window.
5. Set Database Vault instance parameters on each node.

### Stand-Alone Installation

1. Stop all Oracle database processes:
   a. Shut down the database.
   b. Stop the listener.
   c. Stop the Oracle Enterprise Manager Database Control console.
   d. Stop the iSQL*Plus application server.
2. Run the installer: Database Vault has its own installer program, which is also called "runInstaller."
3. Restart Oracle database processes:
   a. Start up the database.
   b. Start the listener.
   c. Start the Oracle Enterprise Manager Database Control console.
   d. Start the iSQL*Plus application server.

### Installation Details

During the process of installing Database Vault in an existing database, you must specify the existing SYS password, the Destination path (defaults to Oracle home), User ID, and password for the Database Vault Owner account. The User ID and password for the Database Vault Account Manager account is optional. The last step of the automated installation process is to run the configuration assistants. When completed, the Details window displays the following message: "The "/u01/app/oracle/product/10.2.0/db_1/cfgtoollogs/configToolAllCommands" script contains all commands to be executed by the configuration assistants. This file may be used to run the configuration assistants outside of OUI." Update this script with passwords before executing. After Database Vault is installed, configure it by using Database Vault Administrator (DVA). DVA has a browser-based interface, and is the means by which implementers administer Database Vault. Using DVA, the administration can create, view, modify, and delete objects related to Database Vault. Log in using the Database Vault Owner account and password. The URL is the same as that for Oracle Enterprise Manager Database Control, except that it ends with "dva" instead of "em." An example of the URL for DVA is http://edrsr9p1.us.oracle.com:1158/dva.

## Realms

Realms contain objects such as tables, roles, and packages. The realm may also have users or roles defined as participants. The realm protects the objects it contains from users exercising system privileges such as SELECT ANY TABLE. So, any user privileged as such must be defined as a realm participant (or have a realm-participating role that has been granted to him or her) to access the protected objects.

## Roles

A number of database roles are created during the installation of Database Vault. These roles should be noted and recreated in OIM and enforced using ACM to satisfy the defense-in-depth requirement of ISO27001 and DCID 6/3.

DV_REALM_RESOURCE: This role should be granted to those database users who will own objects (such as tables or views). It provides the same privileges as the standard Oracle database.

RESOURCE role: A placeholder for the data to be protected.

DV_REALM_OWNER: The DV_REALM_OWNER role is used to enable users to manage objects in multiple schemas. This role should be granted to the database account owner who would manage several schema database accounts within a realm and the roles associated with the realm. A user granted this role can use powerful system privileges such as CREATE ANY, ALTER ANY, and DROP ANY within the realm.

DV_SEC_ANALYST: The DV_SECANALYST role has SELECT privileges on the DVSYS schema objects and portions of the SYS and SYSMAN schema objects needed for reporting on DVSYS-related and DVF-related entities. A user granted this role could check the DVSYS configuration by querying DVSYS views. Users granted this role also can read Oracle Database Vault reports and monitor Database Vault. Users with only this role are not able to create or maintain database users. The role is intended to provide reporting functionality on the Database Vault.

DV_PUBLIC: The DV_PUBLIC role is used to grant privileges on specific objects in the DVSYS schema. Oracle Database Vault does not allow you to directly grant object privileges in the DVSYS schema to PUBLIC. You must grant the object privilege on the DVSYS schema object to the DV_PUBLIC role, and then grant DV_PUBLIC to PUBLIC. The DV_PUBLIC role provides access to the PL/SQL procedures and functions used to enable access control to objects within the database and also to validate a DDL command for realm violations and command authorizations.

DV_ACCTMGR: The DV_ACCTMGR role is used for creating and maintaining database accounts and database profiles. A user granted this role can use the CREATE, ALTER, and DROP statements for users or profiles. However, a person with this role cannot use the DROP or ALTER statements for the DVSYS account, or change the DVSYS password.

DV_ADMIN: The DV_ADMIN role has the EXECUTE privilege on the DVSYS package, DBMS_MACADM, which is used for all access control configuration. DV_ADMIN has the reporting capabilities provided by the DV_SECANALYST role. A user granted this role has the EXECUTE privilege on all Oracle Database Vault administrative packages. Users granted this role also can run Oracle Database Vault reports and monitor Oracle Database Vault.

DV_OWNER: The most powerful of the Database Vault roles. The DV_OWNER role, which is created when Oracle Database Vault is first installed, has the most privileges on the DVSYS schema. It has the administration capabilities provided by the DV_ADMIN role and the reporting capabilities provided by the DV_SECANALYST role. Users granted this role also can run Oracle Database Vault reports and monitor Oracle Database Vault.

## Secure Application Roles

Secure application roles are created to require specific conditions to be true before taking advantage of permissions or privileges that are granted to the role. The conditions are represented as a single rule set. So, a secure application role consists entirely of a secure application role name and an associated rule set. Permissions granted to that role can only be exercised if the rule set evaluates to TRUE.

## Factors

A Database Vault factor is a building block for the configuration access control and overall database security. Each factor is named similar to a variable in an algebraic equation. Each factor has a value assigned to it. This value is called an *identity*. Factors are combined in logical ways with other factors in rules and rule sets to provide the basis for access control policies. A Database Vault factor is a building block for the configuration of security policies and overall database security. Each factor is a named piece of data, such as a user location, database IP address, or session user that Database Vault can recognize and secure. Each factor has a logical value assigned to it. This value is called an identity. Factors are combined in logical ways with other factors in rules and rule sets to provide the basis for security policies. Factors have several attributes: factor type, method, validation expression, and audit options.

The following predefined factors are automatically assigned values for each session:

Authentication_Method: Returns PASSWORD, KERBEROS, SSL, RADIUS, OS, or DCE, depending on the method of authentication. Proxy with certificate, distinguished name (DN), or username without using password returns NONE. You can use Identification_ type to distinguish between external and enterprise users when the authentication method is Password, Kerberos, or SSL.

Client_IP: Returns the IP address of a client session if the client connects through the listener, else the returned value is NULL.

Database_Domain: Domain of the database as specified in the DB_DOMAIN initialization parameter.

Database_Hostname: Returns the host name of the database as seen in the V$INSTANCE view.

Database_Instance: Returns the instance identifier as seen in the USERENV context.

Database_IP: Returns the IP address of the database server on the basis of the host name of the server.

Database_Name: Name of the database as specified in the DB_NAME initialization parameter.

Domain: Domain is a factor that does not have a predefined identity or method. It can be configured for your site. It is intended to be a named collection of physical factors, or configuration-specific or implementation-specific factors in the run-time environment.

Enterprise_Identity: The user's enterprisewide identity. For enterprise users, this returns the Oracle Internet Directory DN. For external users, this returns the external identity (Kerberos principal name, Radius and DCE schema names, OS username, and Certificate DN). For local users and SYSDBA and SYSOPER log-ins, this returns NULL. The value of the attribute differs by proxy method. For a proxy with DN, this returns the Oracle Internet Directory DN of the client. For a proxy with certificate, this returns the certificate DN of the client for external users. For global users, this returns the Oracle Internet Directory DN. For a proxy with username, this returns the Oracle Internet Directory DN if the client is an enterprise user, and NULL if the client is a local database user.

Identification_Type: Returns the way the user's schema is created in the database. Specifically, it reflects the IDENTIFIED clause in the CREATE/ALTER USER syntax.

Lang: The International Organization for Standardization (ISO) abbreviation for the language name, a shorter form than the existing LANGUAGE parameter.

Language: The language and territory currently used by your session, along with the database character set, in this form: language_territory.characterset.

Machine: Provides the client machine name for the current session.

Network_Protocol: Returns the network protocol being used for communication, as specified in the PROTOCOL=protocol portion of the connect string.

Proxy_Enterprise_Identity: Returns the Oracle Internet Directory DN when the proxy user is an enterprise user.

Proxy_User: Name of the database user who opened the current session on behalf of SESSION_USER.

Session_User: For enterprises users, returns the schema. This is the database user name by which the current user is authenticated. This value remains the same throughout the duration of the session.

Factors are evaluated at the session level.

## *Identities*

An identity is a value that is associated with a factor. The identity of a factor can vary according to the session, application, user, or even time of day. For example, when a user connects through a machine in the office, the DOMAIN factor identity is set to INTRANET with a TRUSTED trust level. When the same user connects from home, the DOMAIN factor identity is set to

INTERNET with an UNTRUSTED trust level. A factor can have an identity assigned by a combination of multiple factors. The identity of these factors can in turn be resolved by other factors. Using factors to resolve an identity is called an *identity mapping*. The DOMAIN factor is defined with three identities: SECURE, INTRANET, and INTERNET. If the assignment rule set is Null or Disabled, then these values are the only ones allowed that may be set with the SET_FACTORS function. Each identity defined must have a trust level assigned, even if it is the Trust Level Not Defined option. The trust level value can be used in rule sets and validation functions.

## Creating an Identity

1. Click the Create button in the Identities section on the Edit Factors page.
2. Enter the value of the identity; this is a VARCHAR2 data type.
3. Set the trust level. This may be set to Trust Level Not Defined if the trust level is not used in your instance.
4. Click OK to create the identity.

To integrate Database Vault with OIM focus on the identities API

```
DVSYS Schema Functions
```

Create identities and identity maps
CREATE_IDENTITY: Creates an identity
CREATE_IDENTITY_MAP: Defines a set of tests that are used to derive the identity of a factor from the value of linked child factors (subfactors)

## Modify Identities

CHANGE_IDENTITY_FACTOR: Associates an identity with a different factor
CHANGE_IDENTITY_VALUE: Updates the value of an identity
UPDATE_IDENTITY: Updates an identity
Delete identities and identity maps
DELETE_IDENTITY: Removes an identity
DELETE_IDENTITY_MAP: Removes an identity map for a factor

# Rule Sets and Command Rule

A rule set is a collection of rules that are evaluated together to produce a result. Each rule is defined as a WHERE clause expression. The rule set specifies whether the results of the rules are to be ANDed or ORed together. After each rule is evaluated, those results are ANDed or ORed together, and the result is a single value of TRUE or FALSE. A command rule defines the rules that must be followed to perform a command on an object. These commands include most data definition language (DDL) commands, and also SELECT, UPDATE, and DELETE. You can implement a command rule to restrict specific commands to specific objects or groups of objects.

# Data Vault Reports

Data Vault Audit Reports show Data Vault AUDIT_TRAIL$ records by Audit Event. This list is ordered by Timestamp DESCENDING.

- Command Authorization Audit Report
- Factor Audit Report
- Factor Evaluation and Factor Assignment audit events
- Realm Audit Report
- Realm Violation and Realm Authorization audit events
- Secure Application Role Audit Report
- MACSECURE Audit Report
- MACSECURE session initialization audits
- MACOLS Audit Report
- MACOLS session initialization audits and MAC OLS session label assignment audits

## *Alert on Data Vault Audit Events*

Upon installation an Audit alert is added for each type of custom Data Vault audit event using:

```
AUDSYS.SELAUD_ALERT_HANDLER.ADD_ALERT( PALERTNAME IN VARCHAR2, PALERTTYPE
IN VARCHAR2, PALERTRULE IN VARCHAR2, PAUDITDATASOURCE IN VARCHAR2,
PTABLEOWNER IN VARCHAR2, PTABLENAME IN VARCHAR2, PEMAILBODY IN VARCHAR2,
PEMAILPARAMS IN VARCHAR2, PRECIPIENTS IN VARCHAR_VARRAY);
```

To customize the message body, edit:

```
$DATA_VAULT_HOME/schema/selaud/sddvalr.sql
```

Associate recipients (e-mail or pager) with alert types:

```
AUDSYS.SELAUD_ALERT_HANDLER.ADD_ALERT_RECIPIENT
```

(*Note:* See $DATA_VAULT_HOME/schema/selaud/sddvrcp.sql for sample script.)

Data Vault implements Oracle standard auditing via a Selective Audit policy loaded during install. This is located in $DATA_VAULT_HOME/schema/selaud/dvselaud.xml.

- Audit Event Types
- Factor Evaluation Audit
- Based on factor audit options for the runtime retrieval status of a factor's identity
- Factor Assignment Audit
- Based on success/failure audit options of a factor's Assignment Rule Set
- Realm Authorization Audit
- Based on success/failure audit options of an assigned rule set
- Realm Violation Audit
- Based on success/failure audit options for the runtime determination of whether or not a user is authorized to use their system privileges within the realm
- Note that Realm Violations are not issued (or audited?) when DML system privileges are violated, as VPD is used to implement this feature.
- Command Authorization Audit
- Based on success/failure audit options of an assigned rule set
- Secure Role Audit

### Configuring Database Vault with Audit Vault

Register Data Vault as a custom audit source:

```
AUDSYS.SELAUD_TRAIL_HANDLER.REGISTER_TRAIL( PAUDITDATASOURCE => 'DV' ,
PTABLEOWNER => 'AUDSYS' ,PTABLENAME => 'AUDIT_TRAIL$' ,PDEFAULTTRAIL =>
'1' );
```

Store audit records in AUDSYS.AUDIT_TRAIL$.

Data Vault calls Audt Vault procedure at runtime to populate the AUDSYS.AUDIT_TRAIL$ table:

```
AUDSYS.SELAUD_TRAIL_HANDLER.ADD_AUDIT_EVENT(PAUDITDATASOURCE IN
VARCHAR2,PEVENT IN SELAUD_TRAIL_RECORD);
```

To add additional Data Vault custom events:

Call DVSYS.AUDIT_EVENT, which can be used to integrate external audit sources.

# Audit Vault

A key goal of enterprise auditing is that it should be easy to connect new audit sources. The audit collector association must also have minimal impact on the audit source. Implementers need an architecture that can work in many disparate environments. Audit Vault performs two functions essential to the enterprise:

■ Audit Consolidation: Audit Vault consolidates audit data (preferably on a separate machine) for secured centralized management, audit retention, and single database backup/recovery, query performance, and sophisticated analysis across various audit sources.

■ Behavior and Threat Analysis: Audit Vault is designed for high-performance reporting, analysis, and mining of read-only audit data stored in data warehousing structures. This information can be used for threat alerting and the creation of user profiles.

Audit Vault implements an architecture that implements a Collection process servicing a set of abstract components. Within any infrastructure there exists common processing that happens between any numbers of Collection use cases. By deconstructing the Collection process into components, Oracle's service-oriented approach promotes Component reuse, simplifying the job of writing new collectors.

Central to this discussion is the collector. The core activity of the collector is the reading/receiving of Native Audit Records and parsing them into a publicly accepted Common Audit Format.

### Collectors

Collector read/intercept Native Log Records and send them to Audit Vault through the AuditService; this results in greater security and less load on individual system components. On start or reset, the collector reads recovery information, configuration information, and policy information from Audit Vault. The AuditConfig provided by the AuditService contains this data. There are four types of collectors along with a collector shell. The taxonomy of collectors includes the following:

- Injected Collectors: These are part of the source system. They become part of the source system by injecting themselves through predefined hooks.
- Collectors for Web Applications: These can be injected into the Web Application as Java Loggers. They are injected by editing the logging configuration files (or an Admin GUI). They convert Java LogRecords to AuditVault Records.
- SysLog Daemon: We can implement a syslog daemon that sends log entries to Audit Vault. All components using syslog would then have their log records sent to Audit Vault.
- Polling Collectors: These collectors read native log data (in files or tables) and transform them into Audit Records. These collectors poll the native files/tables for new records.

Collector Shell (Agent)—A Collector can run in many environments. Injected Collectors run within the process space of the source, injecting only minimal overhead. However, regardless of where a Collector runs, it requires the following functionality from its environment:

- A Collector agent must be provided with an AuditService. Collectors use the Audit Service to communicate with Audit Vault to send audit data and receive configuration data.

Collectors are managed and monitored in that they are told in a system-oriented manner when to start and stop and provide metrics about their processes. A required metric is the Heartbeat metric. Examples of other metrics are CPU usage, IO usage, # of records sent, amount of audit sent, etc.

The collector can be in four states:

1. Error
2. Running
3. Unknown
4. Stopped

An agent is a component responsible for setting up the environment in which collectors run. The environment consists of the ChannelFactory, Proxy AuditService, and the ManagementAdaptor. The agent is also responsible for loading and creating the Collector Object.

Management and Monitoring Service manages all the collectors. It starts and stops collectors based on a schedule. It also exposes functions to manually start and stop collectors. It stores metrics about each collector. The only required metric is Heartbeat. It relies on a management repository to achieve its tasks.

A Management Service can also manage agents (collection shells). The Agent Management capability is not a requirement of the Management Service.

Audit Vault fulfills a number of HIPAA, SOX, and other regulatory compliance standards for auditing, including the following:

Enforcing Separation of Duties—Restricting even the DBA from accessing audit data.
Defining audit "policies" to capture the following—Unsuccessful log-ins, granting/revoking privileges, changing database object structures, accessing sensitive data (records/fields), etc.
Selective capturing of data changes by a user to see before and after data values. Capturing SQL statements
Retaining audit data

## Installation

The initial screen has Basic and Advanced options for installation type. The Basic installation type simplifies the installation process and prompts for a minimal set of inputs from the user to perform a full installation. The advanced installation is recommended in a high-security environment. Set up an Audit Vault Database. Then run $ AV AGENT HOME/ scripts/ sql/ setupav. sql as the Audit Vault user (avsys).

## Basic

In the basic install flow, the second screen allows for the user to enter the Audit Vault name—the name of the Audit Vault database—along with the path of the Audit Vault home, where the installation will occur.

1. The installer provides the account information for the users who will be created as part of the installation. Enter the Audit Vault Administrator. The password entered for the Administrator account will also be used for the standard database users (sys, system, sysman, dbsnmp).
2. For segregation of duties, a separate Auditor user should be created; then grant the Administrator user the AV_ADMIN role, and grant the Auditor user the AV_AUDIT role. In the basic installation the Administrator user name is used to derive the names of the two Database Vault users (DV Owner and DV Account Manager). The names of the DV Owner and Account Manager will be <av_admin_name>dvo and <av_admin_name>dva, respectively.

## Advanced

The advanced install flow for the Audit Vault server installation is similar to the advanced install flow for the normal database installation:

1. Enter the database users (sys, system, sysman, dbsnmp) to that of the Administrator, then enter the password details for the four standard database users.
2. The installer should then provide the names and passwords of the Database Vault Owner and Account Manager users. The Database Vault user names and passwords will not be derived from the AV Administrator, as in the case of the basic install flow.
3. The installer then enters the user name and password information for the Database Vault Owner and Account Manager. User input is required for the DV Owner, but optional for the DV Account Manager.

## Database Install

Database initialization parameters values as it pertains to Audit Vault.

```
REMOTE_LOGIN_PASSWORDFILE = default, EXCLUSIVE
PROCESSES = 200
OPEN_CURSORS = 300
JOB_QUEUE_PROCESSES = 10
UNDO_MANAGEMENT = AUTO
```

```
UNDO_TABLESPACE = <set>
DB_DOMAIN = <set>
DB_NAME = <set>
NLS_LANGUAGE = <set>
NLS_TERRITORY = <set>
```

Security-specific database initialization parameters and their recommended values should be always set as specified:

```
AUDIT_TRAIL = DB
AUDIT_SYS_OPERATIONS = TRUE
REMOTE_LISTENER = ''
REMOTE_OS_AUTHENT = FALSE
REMOTE_OS_ROLES = FALSE
OS_ROLES = FALSE
OS_AUTHENT_PREFIX = ''
RESOURCE_LIMIT = TRUE
SQL92_SECURITY = TRUE
O7_DICTIONARY_ACCESSIBILITY = FALSE
```

## Agent Configuration

1. Start Agent: To start the Audit Agent, the Management Service has to have the ability to execute commands at the agent machine.
2. Configure Agents: The Configuration Service will provide Creating/Updating Agent Configuration information. This information will be passed to the agent as part of the initialize call to the agent.

Stop Agent Collection: The service must provide a way to stop collection at an agent. This may be triggered based on a schedule or maybe explicitly requested by the Audit Admin.

## Web Applications

The Web Application collector is called AVAgent. Configure web.xml and orion-web.xml in $AV AGENT HOME/web-app/WEB-INF to the Web App name. The app name may also be configured in application.aml and orion-application.xml in $AV AGENT HOME/META-INF.

Then, Configure the DataSource and collector by editing the $AV AGENT HOME/web-app/WEB-INF/classes/oracle/av/audit/auditFactory.xml and changing the datasource setting. Add a new CollectorDefinition for the Collector and add an entry in collectorDefMap. Build and deploy EAR file to do this; run the following from $AV AGENT HOME:

```
jar cvf AVAgent.war web-app
jar cvf AVAgent.ear META-INF AVAgent.war
java -jar D:/oc4j/j2ee/home/admin.jar ormi://localhost
admin welcome -deploy -file AVAgen.ear
-deploymentName AVAgent
java -jar D:/oc4j/j2ee/home/admin.jar ormi://localhost
admin welcome -bindWebApp AVAgent AVAgent
http-web-site/AVAgent
```

# Enterprise User Security

An enterprise user is a user defined and managed in a directory. Each enterprise user has a unique identity across an enterprise. Enterprise users can be assigned enterprise roles, which determine their access privileges in databases. Enterprise roles are also stored and managed in a directory. An enterprise role consists of one or more global roles. A global role is a role administered in a directory, whose privileges are contained within a single database. You can thus think of an enterprise role as a container of global roles.

Installation and Configuration of Oracle Enterprise Manager for Enterprise User Security:

Task 1: Configure an Oracle Internet Directory.
Task 2: Install Oracle Enterprise manager.
Task 3: Configure Oracle Enterprise Manager for Enterprise User Security.
Task 4: Start Oracle Enterprise Security Manager.
Task 5: Log on to the directory.

Enterprise User Security is based on the Oracle Internet Directory. The Directory Server must be properly installed and configured before Enterprise Manager may be used to manage Enterprise User Security.

Oracle Enterprise Manager may be used to manage Enterprise User Security in two modes of operation.

1. Alternatively, Enterprise Security Manager may be launched from the same ORACLE_HOME as Enterprise Manager and used to connect directly to the Directory Server.
2. To launch Enterprise Security Manager from the Enterprise Manager ORACLE_HOME, enter the following at the command line:

```
oemapp esm
```

3. This will cause the Directory Log On box to appear.

Oracle Enterprise Manager enterprise users and their authorizations are managed in Oracle Internet Directory or other LDAP v3-compliant directory services. Enterprise users can be assigned enterprise roles that determine their access privileges in a database, and enterprise roles can be granted to one or more enterprise users.

## Schema-Independent Users

Oracle Advanced Security allows the separation of users from schemas so that multiple enterprise users can access a single, shared application schema. Administrators need to create a single enterprise user in the directory and point the user at a shared schema, which other enterprise users can also access. This allows administrators to create an enterprise user once in the directory. The enterprise user can then access multiple databases using only the privileges he or she needs, thus lowering the overhead of managing users in an enterprise.

Enterprise Security Manager manages one Directory Server, identified at the top of the main application tree. It has a series of menu operations that apply to this Directory Server. Users are managed in the Directory using Enterprise Security Manager. The application shows the directory to which it is connected and allows you to add, delete, and browse users in that directory. There are two ways to create enterprise users. The following section shows how you can use the Enterprise Manager Console Delegated Administration Services Web interface known as OiDDAS. Your second choice is to use the Enterprise Security Manager.

## Enterprise Manager Console

Enterprise Manager Console may be used to connect to the Oracle Management Server (OMS) and discover a Directory Server to manage.

Step 1. Open your browser to the DAS log-in page.
Example URL:
```
http://tynyurl.us.oracle.com:7777/oiddas
```
Step 2. Log into DAS as the "orcladmin" user.
Step 3. Select the "Configuration" tab.
Step 4. Select the "User Entry" subtab.
Step 5. Select "Add Object Class."
Step 6. From the list of object classes, select "orcladuser."
Step 7. After you add the "orcladuser" object class, click the "Next" button at the bottom of the form.
Step 8. Now we will add the attributes. The attributes we will add are
```
orclsamaccountname
krbprincipalname
orcluserprincipalname
```
To add the new attributes, click on the "Add New Attribute" button.
Step 9. Select the "orclsamaccountname" attribute from the "Directory Attribute Name" drop-down list.
Step 10. The UI Label will be the title of the attribute on the "DAS Create User" form.
Step 11. Check the "Viewable" check box so that you will be able to see the attribute on the DAS form.
Step 12. Perform steps 8 through 11 using the krbpricipalname and orcluserprincipalname attributes instead of the orclsamaccountname.
Step 13. Click the "Next" button to continue.
Step 14. On the next page click the "Create" button to create a new category for the "DAS Create User" form.
Step 15. Put the title of your new category in the "UI Label" field. In our example we will call our new category "DAS User Provisioning."
Step 16. Click the "Done" button.
Step 17. Click the "Order Category" button. Move the new category up the category list to where you want it. In our example we will put it under the "Basic Information" category.
Step 18. Now we will add our three attributes to the new category. Select your new category by clicking its radio button. Then click the "Edit" button.
Step 19. Move the "orclsamaccountname," "krbprincipalname," and "orcluserprincipalname" attributes from the list on the left to the list on the right.
Step 20. Click the "Done" button.
Step 21. Click the "Next" button.

Step 22. (Optional) If you want to include one of the new attributes in the Search Tables, select the attribute and click the "Move" button.

Step 23. Click the "Next" button.

Step 24. Click the "Finish" button.

When finished, navigate to the "DAS Create User" form by clicking on the "Directory" tab, and then click the "Create" button.

## Oracle Enterprise Security Manager

Enterprise Security Manager (ESM) program is a client/server program that allows you only to view users and add/revoke authorizations. To create users, log on to the directory as an administrator. By default, the directory administrator is the orcladmin user. Select the Users and Groups tab, then Select the User subtab and click the Create button to see the administration screen for creating a new user.

# Stellent Universal Content Manager

Content management is used to Capture, Manage, Store, Preserve, and Deliver content and documents related to organizational processes. Universal content manager stores all content in the same location; this includes Web content, compliance documents, records, business forms, video, and customer data stored in the same repository. Written in Java, Universal Content Manager supports the Service Oriented Architecture and Simple Object Access Protocol (SOAP). Universal content manager provides an extensible framework and a universal repository. This framework allows all items to be managed differently based on their type.

## Installation

1. The default administrator for the server is the user sysadmin, with the password idc.
2. Click Log into log in, which takes you to the dynamic home page.
3. Select the User Profile link, which returns the user profile page that contains information about the current user. You will see the fields User Name, Roles, Full Name, Password (w/Confirm), E-mail Address, User Type, and User Locale as well as User Personalization Settings.
4. Click the New Check In, which returns a content check-in form for adding new content items to the repository. Fill in the metadata for this item, such as the title and some comments, supply a Content ID, a unique identifier for all revisions of this item, then click Check In to add the content to the repository.
5. Other fields will include type, title author, and security group.
6. After a check-in, the Content Server extracts the text from the content item and enters it into the search engine's index, enabling users to quickly search for the item based on its content or its metadata.

The Content Server is an extensible Java framework. It uses data-driven resources to define services, which include the content management features in the server: check-in, checkout, workflow processing, subscriptions, conversion, and search.

## Integration Points

The Content Server has an internal architecture much like a middleware application. It stores data about content items on a file system and in a database. It stores user information in a database or an external Lightweight Directory Access Protocol (LDAP) repository. As such, this is the first integration point into Oracle Identity Management.

A service request initiates a series of events:

1. The user makes a Web request.
2. The Web server authenticates the user.
3. If the request is a service call, the Web server forwards it to the Content Server.
4. The Content Server parses request data and places this data in an HDA-based DataBinder object.
5. The server loads the definition for the service, including security information, a template page, and a list of actions to perform for this service.
6. The server validates that this user can run the service.
7. The server executes the service actions, which can be SQL queries or Java code. This action point may be leveraged as an access point for Oracle Identity Manager. Oracle Virtual Directory may also be inserted to extend service action into the Identity suite.
8. Each action pulls request parameters from the Data Binder and pushes the results back.
9. After all actions are complete, and no error occurred, the server loads the response template.
10. The server renders the template into HTML with the data in the DataBinder.
11. The server sends the response HTML to the Web server.
12. The Web server sends the HTML to the user.

# Records DB

Oracle Records DB provides a document audit trail and gives implementers the ability to enforce legal holds and quickly find vital information, lowering the risk and cost of legal discovery associated with FRCP Rule 33(d), which states that parties may reference "electronically stored information" as a type of business record from which answers to interrogatories may be derived. Records DB is used to establish the File Plan and the life-cycle management policies associated with the File Plan node. These properties/policies, including life-cycle instructions, can then be applied to a folder.

To Install Content DB:

1. Log on with administrator privilege.
2. Change directory to Disk1/Sources/CDB.
3. Execute run Installer the Oracle Universal Installer for 10*g*.
4. On the file Locations screen, enter /ora6/Sources/CDB/stage/products.xml for source and for Destination enter CDB_home with a Path of /ora6/CDB_area/ContentDB.

5. Let Oracle finish the Prerequisites checks and select your language.
6. Register with Oracle Internet Directory entering the Host and Port of your OID instance.
7. Specify your user log-in in the LDAP canonical form Username:cn=oracladmin Password *****.
8. Select the Records DB database entering the database ConnectionString: Example. orcl102 and the SYS password *****.
9. Create a Content Schema Password.
10. Specify SMTP Host and Port values.
11. Specify Instance name and the ias_admin Password.
12. This installer will execute the rest.
13. Enter the Oracle Enterprise Manager, Home Tab, and Select Enable/Disable Components.
14. Enable OC4J Content, HTTP_Server, OC4J_BPEL, Content, Web cache, home and OC4J_RM and start all system components.
16. Select Content, then select OC4J_RM.
17. Then select the OC4J_RM Node, and enter the Host Name/IP Address, Middle Tier, and select the Active check box.
18. Select OC4J_RM and start the process.
19. Click a name to edit the node configuration; click create non-HTTP Node to create a new non-HTTP node configuration. Click to create a new node configuration based on an existing one. Select a node configuration, and click "Delete" to remove an entry, then Activate the Service.
20. In Node configuration, click "Remove" on all Inactive Servers, activating FtpServer, FtpsServerExplicit, FtpsServerImplicit, and SecureEnterpriseSearchGroupAgent. Then enter the Node name in Display Name and fill in the Host Name/IP address. On Logging enter /ora6/CDB_area/ContentDB/content/log/Content/CDB_us_oracle_com_Node.log and select Text as the format.
21. Once OC4J_RM is started, Records DB should also be started.

Records DB is one of many automated controls that may be leveraged to satisfy U.S. Department of Defense (DoD) 5015.2 certification.

# Secure Enterprise Search

Secure Enterprise Search allows an enterprise to search all its enterprise data sources from a single interface. Oracle Secure Enterprise Search, a stand-alone product from Oracle, enables secure, high-quality, easy-to-use search across enterprise information assets.

## Deployment Guide

1. Set up an LDAP (Lightweight Directory Access Protocol) directory such as OID to authenticate users and provides the access control list (ACL) information that is stored in Secure Enterprise Search.
2. Decide what data to index, what method ("source type") to use to crawl those sources, and define the information needed to crawl them.

3. Define entry points. This is the point from which the crawler will start searching for links to follow.
4. Consider include and exclude rules. By default, if http://www.oracle.com is our start point, then a page called http://download.oracle.com would not be crawled, as it does not fit the default include rule (includes www.oracle.com). The best method is to create a page consisting of a long list of URLs to each page you want to be indexed.

Secure Enterprise Search features advanced security and data source connectivity, including pre-built connectors to diverse enterprise data sources such as Oracle Portal, Oracle Content DB, Oracle E-Business Suite, Siebel, Exchange, Sharepoint, Documentum, Filenet, Lotus Notes, OpenText Livelink, Hummingbird DM, as well as extensible XML.

# Oracle Data Integrator

Oracle Data Integrator is a key component of Oracle Fusion Middleware providing ETL (extract, transform, and load) services to Service-Oriented Architectures.

The ELT approach leverages the target database engines to perform the transformations, improving performance lower total cost. Data goes directly from sources to targets, and is transformed en route. The ELT architecture incorporates the best aspects of both manual coding and ETL approaches in the same solution. The ELT approach changes where and how data transformation takes place, and leverages the existing developer skills, RDBMS engines, and server hardware to the greatest extent possible. In operation, ELT relocates the data transformation step on the target RDBMS, changing the order of operations to: extract the data from the source tables, load the tables into the destination server, and then transform the data on the target RDBMS using native SQL operators. Two architecture elements should be considered when deciding whether to use Data Integrator:

SOA-Enabled: Oracle Data Integrator plugs into the Oracle SOA Suite through three key service access capabilities: data services, transformation services, and Web services access.

Web Services Access: Third-party Web services can be invoked as part of an Oracle Data Integrator workflow and used as part of the data integration processes. Requests are generated on the fly and responses processed through regular transformations.

## Integration Styles

Oracle Data Integrator supports three integration styles: data, events, and services. Integrator can move data directly from databases to different databases to or from applications to or from flat files. It also provides data or events to an Enterprise Service Bus or a message-oriented middleware transaction monitor, as such becoming part of a System-Oriented Architecture by providing data services and transformation services.

The Oracle Data Integrator approach allows a developer to accomplish integration in three steps:

1. Link the three sources together.
2. Declare the mappings between source and target fields.
3. Choose a built-in template to generate the data flow.

## User Interfaces

The four Oracle Data Integrator graphical modules are

- Designer: In this interface, users can define declarative rules for data transformation and data integrity. Database and application metadata can be imported or defined. Designer uses metadata and rules to generate scenarios for production. All project development is performed through this interface, and it is the main user interface for developers and metadata administrators at design time.
- Operator: In this interface, users can manage and monitor Oracle Data Integrator jobs in production. It is designed for production operators and shows the execution logs with error counts, the number of rows processed, execution statistics, the actual code that is executed, and so on. At design time, developers can also use Operator for debugging purposes. It is the main user interface at runtime.
- Topology Manager: In this interface, users can define the physical and logical architecture of the infrastructure. Servers, schemas, and agents are registered in the Oracle Data Integrator master repository through this interface, which is primarily used by the administrators of the infrastructure or project.
- Security Manager: In this interface, administrators can manage user accounts and privileges. It can be used to give profiles and users access rights.

## The Oracle Data Integrator Knowledge Modules

Oracle Data Integrator's KMs are the core of the product's integration architecture. Oracle Data Integrator's Knowledge Modules implement how the integration processes occur.

Each Knowledge Module type refers to a specific integration task:

- Reverse-engineering metadata from the heterogeneous systems for Oracle Data Integrator
- Handling Changed Data Capture (CDC)
- Loading data from one system to another, using system-optimized methods
- Integrating data in a target system, using specific strategies (insert/update, changing dimensions)
- Controlling data integrity on the data flow
- Exposing data in the form of services

These Knowledge Modules cover a wide range of technologies and techniques, from the messaging infrastructure to message-based integration compliant with the Java Message Services (JMS) standard. Within Data Integrator, a transformation job within Oracle Data Integrator can subscribe and source messages from any message queue or topic. Messages are captured and transformed in real-time and then written to the target systems. The JMS model supports transactions to ensure data integrity and message delivery from the source middleware to the target systems.

## Installation Instructions

1. Open the /setup/<system>/ directory on the CD, where <system> is the platform name. If the platform name is not present, select GenericUnix and open the Oracle Data Integrator setup program download directory.

2. On a Windows platform, run setup.exe; on a UNIX platform, run sh ./setup.bin.
3. Follow the instructions of the setup program.

# Compliance Designs

## *Data Integrity Firewall in the Integration Process*

The components involved in an integration process are the source applications, the processes that transform and integrate data, and the target applications. With Oracle Data Integrator, data integrity is managed in all these subsystems, creating a logical firewall that can be activated within the integration process separating sensitive relational substructures that may be required to be physically separated (e.g., EU data compliance).

## *Enforcing the Rules*

Oracle Data Integrator's Check Knowledge Modules help developers to automatically generate data integrity audits of their applications based on integrity rules that have been defined in the repository. Audits provide statistics on the quality of application data. They also isolate data that is detected as erroneous by applying the declarative rules. When erroneous records have been identified and isolated in error tables, they can be accessed directly from Oracle Data Integrator.

# Information Rights Management

Traditionally, information management policies are enforced through the security mechanisms provided by the IT infrastructure at the layer on which the document resides on a given server. For example, file access rights can be defined if the document resides on a disk, and objects rights can be defined at the DB layer if the document resides in a database. The problem with this approach is that server-side security is not "portable" and can be easily circumvented because in most instances these policies cannot be enforced when the document has been copied or moved into another location.

Oracle Information Rights Management (IRM) is a new form of information security technology that secures and tracks sensitive digital information everywhere it is stored and used. Conventional information management products only manage documents, e-mails, and Web pages while they remain stored within server-side repositories. Oracle Information Rights Management uses encryption to extend the management of information beyond the repository—to every copy of an organization's most sensitive information, everywhere it is stored and used—on end user desktops, laptops, and mobile wireless devices, in other repositories, inside and outside the firewall.

Oracle Information Rights Management is information-centric security, in that it secures information directly, rather than as a side-effect of placing copies of that information within access-controlled repositories. Oracle Information Rights Management is a Fusion Middleware service with profound and immediate synergies throughout the entire Oracle solution stack—particularly with Content Management, Records Management, and Identity and Access Management.

With IRM, information protection policies become portable and can be enforced regardless of the location of the document. By encrypting ("sealing") a document, IRM extends security, control, and tracking out to include information in use on remote end-user desktops, inside and outside the corporate firewalls. This solution enables documents or e-mails to be sealed at any stage in their life cycle, using sealing tools' integration into the Windows desktop, authoring applications, e-mail clients, content management, and collaborative repositories' environments.

## How Does Oracle Information Rights Management Work?

The author of a document (Word, Excel, etc.) or e-mail creates the document, and then seals it or classifies the document at a certain sensitivity level (internal only, confidential, attorney privileged, etc.). The document is then automatically encrypted. When a recipient receives the document and attempts to open it, a query is made to the centralized policy server, and access (i.e., decryption) is granted/denied based on the corporate policies governing this document (existence of a valid business reason for the recipient to use this document) or the preferences set by the original creator of the document. Policies can also be set to protect the document against altering, printing, copying, etc. Requests to the central policies server can be logged to enforce accountability across the organization, and maintain an audit trail for protected information. This provides the following:

1. Portable Security: With Oracle Information Rights Management, organizations can fully control how sensitive information is accessed and shared, and can maintain a detailed audit trail.
2. Centralized Enforcement: A centralized policy server, within Oracle Information Rights Management, enables customers to define information access control policies across the entire organization based on the sensitivity classification of the document and the identity of the user.
3. Simplicity and End-User Convenience: The free client software, Oracle Information Rights Management desktop, is integrated with the e-mail client, Windows, and various MS Office applications, providing end users with a convenient way to manage security around their documents.
4. Support for a wide range of file formats and applications: supports Exchange, Lotus Notes, Groupwise, MS Office applications. In addition, the following file formats are supported: PDF, CAD, TIFF, JPEG, PNG, GIF, etc.

Content Integration Suite (CIS) enables communication with Content Server and Image Server and is deployable on a number of J2EE application servers, in addition to working in non-J2EE environments.

This brief section provides information on installing and configuring CIS, and on integrating CIS with various servers and servlet engines. It also provides conceptual information on CIS and describes the UCPM API.

Content Integration Suite has a layered architecture that allows for its deployment in a number of different configurations. The architecture, at its core, is based on the standard J2EE "Command Design Pattern." The layers on top of the commands provide the APIs that are exposed to the end user.

This version of CIS uses the Universal Content and Process Management API (UCPM API) and consists of three main APIs, the SCS API for communication to Content Server, the SIS API for communication to the Image Server, and the CIS API for simultaneous communication to both servers (federated searching, generic contribution, etc.). The APIs wrap the communication from the Content Server or the Image Server into an object model that allows access to the individual object metadata.

The UCPM API allows application developers to focus on presentation issues rather than being concerned with how to access Content Server services (IdcCommand services). The UCPM API comprises a set of command objects that encapsulate distinct actions that are passed to the UCPM API and then "mapped" to the Content Server, the Image Server, or both. These commands include common functions such as search, checkout, and workflow approval. Each command is tied to one or more service calls. The UCPM API command objects have been developed in accordance with the J2EE Command Design Pattern.

This infrastructure is deployable in any J2EE-compliant application server or stand-alone JVM application. When deployed, the UCPM API will leverage the features in the environment, whether this is a J2EE application server or non-J2EE.

The UCPM API encapsulates Content Server business logic and validates the parameters of the incoming calls. The UCPM API handles communication to the Content Server or the Image Server, encapsulates socket communication logic (opening, validating, and streaming bits through the socket), and provides a strongly typed API to the available services.

CIS communicates with the Image Server through the use of Web services. Consequently, the protocol used is SOAP, and the application-level protocol definition is Web Services Description Language (WSDL).

The CIS Administration Application is the administration interface for Content Integration Suite (CIS). On an EAR installation (application servers), the CIS Administration Application is no longer deployed along with the Command EJBs. After deploying CIS to your application server, the CIS Administration Application must be deployed separately using the CIS Admin EAR file located in the /deployments/admin-ear directory of the unbundled CIS distribution file. Deploying the CIS Administration Application separately allows administrators to choose to not install it on a production server for security purposes. The default Web address of the CIS Administration Application after installation is

http://<hostname>:<port>/cis-admin.

On a WAR installation (Tomcat, etc.) the UCPM API and the CIS Administration Application are deployed using the CIS Server WAR file located in the /deployments/server-war directory of the unbundled CIS distribution file. We recommend using the WAR installation and Tomcat for your development environment. The default Web address of the CIS Administration Application after installation is

```
http://<hostname>:<port>/<.war file name>
```

You must enable the IP address of the application server. This allows the Content Server or Image Server to listen for connections from the application server. If you are connecting to both a Content Server and an Image Server, follow both sets of the following instructions:

Enabling the IP Address on Content Server:

1. On the Content Server instance, launch the System Properties editor. Select Content Server > "instance name" > Utilities > SystemProperties.
2. Select the Server tab.
3. Enter your application-server-specific information for the Hostname Filter and IP Address Filter.
   The wildcard (*) is accepted, but IP addresses must take the form x.x.x.x regardless of wildcards, and must be separated by a vertical bar.
   Example: 12.34.56.*|12.34.57.*|12.35.*.*
4. You must restart the Content Server for these changes to take effect.

Enabling the IP Address on Image Server:

1. On the Image Server instance, launch the IBPM Web Trust Config application (IBPM-WebTrustConfig.exe).

   The IBPM Web Trust Config application provides a listing of the IPs registered on this machine as "Trusted IPs" by the IBPM Web infrastructure. You can add and remove IPs from this list using this application.
2. Click ADD.
3. Enter the IP address of the WebSphere application server in the New IP field. Example: 10.20.1.2.
4. Click ADD.
5. Enable both Trusted by Web Services and Trusted by Web Content.
6. Close the IBPM Web Trust Config application.

You must install and enable the CIS_Helper component on your Content Server instance. The CIS_Helper.zip file is located in the /components directory of the unbundled CIS distribution file. You can install and enable the component by using either the Component Manager or the Component Wizard.

Installing the CIS Helper Component using the Component Manager:

1. Log on to the content server as an administrator and click Administration > Admin Server.
2. Click the button that corresponds to your server (for example, testserver7). The options and status page of the content server instance are displayed.
3. Click Component Manager in the menu on the left. The Component Manager page appears.
4. Click Browse opposite the Install New Component field. A file selection dialog box opens.
5. Select the CIS_Helper.zip file, and close the dialog box.
6. Click Install. A page appears, confirming what will be installed.
7. Click Continue.

   After this process is completed, a message appears stating that the component was uploaded and installed successfully.
8. Click Continue.
9. Enable the component and restart the content server.

Installing the CIS Helper Component using the Component Wizard:

1. Start Component Wizard: On Windows, select Start > Programs > Content Server > "instance name" > Utilities > Component Wizard.
2. The Component Wizard is started, with the Component List dialog box active.
3. Click Install. The Install dialog box appears.
4. Click Select. A file selection dialog box appears.
5. Select the CIS_Helper.zip file, and close the dialog box. The Install dialog box now displays all the files that will be installed.
6. Click OK. Once the required files are installed, a message will appear, asking whether the specified components should be enabled.
7. Click Yes. The CIS Helper component is loaded and enabled. The main Component Wizard window now shows a list of the component resources.
8. Close Component Wizard, and restart the content server.

## Modifying the Global Configuration

Once you have deployed the CIS Administration Application and restarted the application server, you can modify the global configuration as follows:

1. Launch the CIS Administration Application.
2. Click Adapter Configuration.
3. Click Modify Global Configuration.
4. Enter the SCS Command Web URL (the Web address clients use to communicate with the CIS servlets).
5. Optional—Enter the Server JNDI Properties (the JNDI properties used by the server to make JNDI connections).
6. Click Apply.

## Configuring an Adapter for Content Server

You must configure an adapter for each instance of Content Server and Image Server:

1. Launch the CIS Administration Application.
2. Click Adapter Configuration.
3. For new installations, click Create New SCS Adapter. To update an existing installation, click the adapter name (e.g., myadapter) on the Available Adapters to Configure list.
4. On the Adapter Properties page, specify these properties:
   Name: The name of the adapter (e.g., myadapter).
   Adapter Type: Type of communication transport.
    Socket—Open communication directly through Content Server.
    Web—Communicates via the Web server and requires individual authentication for each request.
   Host: The name or IP address of the Content Server instance (e.g., testserver7)
   Port: The Content Server port number (e.g., 4444).

Use Persistent Connections: Enable this check box if you want to keep the connection alive after a request is completed. If you enable persistent connections, the implementer must also configure them on the Content Server instance (via the providers interface).

Connection Timeout: When using persistent connections, this value is the maximum amount of time the connection will wait for response. Default is 20,000 ms.

## Running CIS Validation Tests for compliance

Two validation tests for installed adapters are available by clicking the Actions icon:

- Validate Mapped Directory Configuration: This will only pass if the properties for Content Mapping Location have been validly set.
- Validate Communication with Content Server: Returns configuration validation results. If communication is validated the message, "Communication to the content server is functioning correctly" will display.

# Trusted Information Sharing

Trusted Information Sharing is Oracle's military-grade IRM security application. This asset is so secure it is only sold as a consulting asset, meaning that no third-party implementer will ever participate in its deployment or configuration. It is not on the standard price list, and the majority of Oracle employees do not even know it exists. However, if you are a three-letter governmental organization, part of NATO, or a subcontractor of a three-letter agency, TIE is the protection asset to implement. We cannot disclose how the following features and functions are deployed or developed, so the author begs the indulgence of the curious reader in the interest of multinational security. We will tell you all we can and even show an example of how to code a policy.

Trusted Information Exchange (TIE) is built on established Oracle infrastructure technologies and provides applications and services to enable trusted information sharing across multiple organizations. Using an SOA network model/architecture and standardized security mechanisms including rights management, TIE implements a secure information "router" for the trusted information network. TIE provides a solution for secured horizontal sharing of sensitive/classified multimedia information from security watch lists to data sets and satellite imagery. TIE uniquely combines leading industry standards with innovation to provide the following:

- A scaleable, highly available Web-service-oriented architecture
- Information Rights Management using the ISO-REL standard
- Application and TIE ID Management through X.509 and PKI
- Push and pull data sharing between organizations
- High throughput (FTP or better) and high concurrency
- Virus, malicious code, file type, and "dirty" word checking
- Support for non-Oracle secure Web service interoperability
- TIE is designed to pass NSA CT&E evaluation for Guards.
- Cross-Domain Security Information Sharing—for sharing classified, multilevel security data across networks that are operating at different clearance levels (for DCID 6/3 PL4, PL5 systems)
  *Note*: Implementers must use Oracle's Cross Domain Security Solution (CDSS), another even more classified Consulting Offering. The required software licenses: Data Vault, OLS, ASO, RAC/GRID, Partitioning, TDE. CDSS falls under ITAR restrictions, so only U.S. citizens may participate in deployment.
- Cross-Organization Information Sharing—Interagency, sensitive, or classified data sharing across organizational domains
- Disconnected Information Sharing—Sharing of sensitive or classified data to disconnected devices
- Auditing and Verification—Centralized policy management and consolidation of audit records
- Adaptive Security—Adapt to changing security requirement and threats using configurable security policies that implement multifactored security, mandatory access control, separation of duties, auditing and alerting, and more.

TIE enables the following:

- Fully authenticated DB and Application access controls: TIEs that will do PKI authentication when exchanging content and content's metadata (contract/policy)

- Sender-side destination control: Originating organization TIE stipulates where content and content's metadata is disseminated and its policy for access
- Sender-controlled metadata handling: Originating organization TIE stipulates other conditions associated with the content as governed by the metadata, e.g., how long the content can be viewed, classification, release date, etc.
- Data and transport security: Content and content's metadata is encrypted and sent over SSL
- Access to content at an endpoint controlled by DB security
- Complete information flow audit trail: Entire information flow from originating organization to recipient organization can be audited
- Trusted Information Exchange Features
- Supports push or pull model for network transfers
- Provides high throughput (equal or better than FTP)
- Provides virus, malicious code, file type, and "dirty word" detection
- Supports streaming AES-256 encryption/decryption
- Supports low bandwidth or intermittent network connections
- Supports high concurrencies for push and pull models
- Scales both horizontally and vertically
- Built on proven 10gR2 RAC and AS10g cluster/grid configurations
- Supports non-Oracle Secure Web Services endpoints

Trusted Information Sharing was designed to satisfy the Homeland Security 9/11 Commission Report Recommendations, which included cultural shift from "need to know" to "need to share," restore a better balance between security and shared knowledge, and create a "trusted information network" using a decentralized network model—share data horizontally across agencies, coalition partners, etc. Grant and revoke access granted/denied based on rules set for the network. "Information rights management" data access controls.

Relevant Congressional acts TIE was designed to facilitate are the following:

- The Homeland Security Act, U.S. Patriot Act, Anti-Terrorism Act

Accreditations and Compliance:

- DCID 6/3 PL3, PL4, and PL5 and DITSCAP
- HIPAA, Sarbanes–Oxley, FISMA
- NSA Guard CT&E v3.1

Net-centric Operations:

- Share mission-critical information across domains and with coalition partners.
- Inform the warfighter "on the edge."
- Protect sources and methods. Maintain originator control of information.
- Secure justice and public safety: JPS Integration – TIS across jurisdictions and organizations. Combining crime fighting with counterterrorism analysis at all levels: local through national.
- Healthcare: HIPAA Compliance: Accountability, Auditing, Privacy security rules, Separation of Duties

Although we cannot show how TIE enforces policy, we can share some VPD code that enables the secure enforcement of policy.

### Example 1: Policy to expire data after certain date

```
BEGIN
  select expire_date into t_expire_date
  from policy_rules where recipient_id = 'FBI';
  if expire_date < SYSDATE then
    return ('1 = 1');
  else return ('1=2');
  end if;
  exception
  when others then
    NULL;
END;
```

### Example 2: Policy to anonymize data by hiding the names

```
BEGIN
  DBMS_RLS.ADD_POLICY(object_schema =>'HR', object_name=>'customer',
  policy_name=>'sp', function_schema=>'pol_admin',
policy_function=>'pf1',
  sec_relevant_cols=>'first, middle, last',
  sec_relevant_cols_opt=>dbms_rls.ALL_ROWS);
END;
```

### Example 3: Policy to ensure user is an employee

```
BEGIN
v_user := lower(sys_context('userenv',
  'session_user'));
  begin
  select manager_id into v_manager_id
  from hr.employees where lower(email) = v_user;
    is_employee:=1;
exception
  when no_data_found then is_employee:=2;
END;
```

### Example 4: Policy to restrict specific users within time interval

```
BEGIN
  select release_date, valid_period
 into t_release_date, t_valid_period
  from policy_rules where recipient_id = 'AGENT';
  if t_release_date+t_valid_period < SYSDATE then
    return ('1 = 1');
  else return ('1=2');
  end if;
  exception
  when others then NULL;
END;
```

Important concepts when deploying TIE:

- Principal: The entity being afforded the authorization with mechanism to prove identity
- Right: The action being afforded to the Principal
- Resource: The object that the Principal can perform the Right upon
- Condition: The conditions that must be satisfied to exercise the Right
- Issuer: The source of the authorization with mechanism to prove identity

TIE supports the following standards:

- Direct Internet Message Encapsulation (DIME)
- WSDL Extension for SOAP in DIME
- OASIS WS-S REL Token Profile 1.1
- OASIS Web Services Security 1.0 (WS-Security 2004)
- Web Services Security X.509 Certificate Token Profile
- SOAP Version 1.2
- XML-Signature Syntax and Processing
- XML Encryption Syntax and Processing
- WS-I Interop Basic Profile 1.1
- WS-I Attachments Profile 1.0
- WS-I Basic Security Profile
- WS-I, WS Security challenges, threats and countermeasures

Trusted Information Server is not for every enterprise. ITAR regulations severely restrict who can interact with the installation and maintenance of the product. However, for those interacting with the U.S. Defense Department and Homeland security, TIS is an important tool for meeting SAS70 compliance obligations.

# XML Publisher

Oracle Access Manager integrates with Oracle Database and Oracle XML Publisher to provide auditing and reporting capabilities for Web access management environment. XML Publisher reporting functionality allows one to

- Set up auditing data sources
- View and schedule reports
- Design report layouts
- Develop report queries and data models
- Perform administrative tasks, set up users, define runtime behaviors

By using XML publisher on OIM, the auditor can retrieve XML-formatted data from a data source and build reports that can be formatted in HTML, PDF, or Word. When integrated with OAM, the implementer can generate tailored reports about user access to applications to document which users are actually using their privileges and entitlements to do on a daily basis. Install a database to capture the XML logs. The next step is to set up OAM to log to that database. Follow the steps for setting up the database, importing the audit schema, and verifying the schema. Once that is done, log into the OAM console and enable OAM to connect to the audit database.

There are a number of reports the implementer can define that will provide information about users. Because OAM provides both identity administration (via OAM's Identity Server) and access management (via OAM's Access Server), administrators can generate reports that cover a history of a user's profile modifications as well as authentication and authorization events associated with that user profile. A list of attestation reports includes the following:

Identity

■ Group_History
■ Identity_History
■ Lockout_Users
■ Password_Changes_Interval
■ User_Profile_Modification
■ User
■ Users_Deactivated
■ Workflow_Time

Access

■ Authentication_Statistics
■ Authorization_Statistics
■ Failed_Authorization_By_Resource
■ Failed_Authorization_By_User
■ User_Access_Privilege

To complete the OAM setup, set the database auditing flag for the identity server and access server configuration. Log into the identity system console, navigate to the System Configuration tab, select Identity Servers in the left-hand navigation pane, click the link for the server you want to update, and click Modify. You will need to set the Audit to Database Flag (auditing on/off) to On. Once these configurations are set, the implementer must update the output format of the data to the auditing database. Once this task is complete, the implementer should select the profile attributes, such as Name, Department, Employee/Unique ID, Group Membership, Organization, or Group, that the auditor wants to include in the audit data. The next step is to log into XML Publisher and design the reports and publish the outcome. XML Publisher allows the developer to define a data mode, create or modify the query statements to the audit repository, and design the layout and present the data into a report formatted in HTML, PDF, or Word. Implementers can also schedule reports or run ad hoc queries. When beginning report design, the first task is enter the SQL query into the report builder interface. The result of the query is then returned to XML Publisher in the form of an XML template. The XML report will resemble the following:

```
<?xml version ="1.0" encoding="UTF-8"?>
<Rowset>
  <Row>
  <EVENTDATEANDTIME>2007-01-08T08:52:14.00+6:00</EVENTDATEANDTIME>
```

```
<SERVERID>identityserver_oracle01</SERVERID>
<WEBSERVERID</>
<EVENTNAME>AUTHN_FAIL</EVENTNAME>
<WORKFLOWINSTANCEID/>
<WORKFLOWTYPE/>
<WORKFLOWNAME/>
<WORKFLOWACTION/>
<ISPWDATTRMODIFIED>0</ISPWDATTRMODIFIED>
<ISGRMEMBERATTRMODIFIED>0</ISGRMEMBERATTRMODIFIED>
<LOCKOUTDURATION>0</LOCKOUTDURATION>
<URL>orcl2664:1880/ba/testba.html</URL>
<OPERATION>GET</OPERATION>
<TARGETUSERDN>cn=Marlin Pohlman,ou=OCS,ou=TBU,ou=NASA,ou=Oracle,o=coman
y,c=us</TARGETUSERDN>
<IPADDRESS>10.77.199.198</IPADDRESS>
<USERPROFILEATTRS>employeenumber=57933 employeetype=salary
loginid=pohlman</USERPROFILEATTRS>
<RESOURCESCHEME>HTTP</RESOURCESCHEME>
<WEBGATEID>wg204_orcl</WEBGATEID>
```

The auditor can then choose the information for the report, organize the fields, and start building out the template format. Formatting the report and defining how the information is laid out in the final report is accomplished using an RTF editor such as Microsoft Word and then saving the XML template as an RTF file. Using the general settings of the template layout, define the format to be displayed in the report. The formatting applied when the XML was converted to RTF is applied to the final output format, preserving layout, fonts, etc., then execute the report, and display it in the desire format.

## Hyperion Compliance Management Dashboard

The Compliance Management Dashboard combines internal control information with financial data to assist in providing an assessment of potential risk exposures, giving financial executives confidence in the appropriateness of financial statements and disclosures. The product provides easy-to-use screens, meters, and stoplights that quickly convey critical information. By bringing together account balances with assessments and tests of internal controls, the dashboard helps in delivering a risk assessment at the individual account and entity levels, taking into account the materiality of accounts and the risk levels of associated control activities. The dashboard can be leveraged to combine different sources of information, assisting in the delivery of an objective assessment of risk and generating greater confidence in financial statements.

The Compliance Management Dashboard performs the following functions:

- Assists in achieving transparency into potential risk exposures
- Easily helps identify remediation to gaps in internal control
- Helps companies gain confidence in the appropriateness of their financial statements and disclosures
- Assists in reducing the potential number of financial restatements

## The Hyperion Basel II Compliance Solution

The Hyperion Basel II Compliance solution combines analytical applications and reporting tools that help ensure compliance with Basel II Operational Risk Management. As stated earlier, to achieve compliance with Basel II, a banking institution must deliver appropriate reporting of operational risk exposures and loss data to its board of directors and senior management.

Credit risk analysis: Similarly, accurate monitoring and calculation of credit risk must be integrated into a bank's overall risk exposure. This analysis must include identification and measurement of weaknesses in a bank's portfolio for concentrations of risk by segment, geography, and counterparty, and calculate the appropriate capital to meet the risk exposure.

Data analysis challenge: A compliant institution must have a risk analysis framework that uses a combination of internal operational loss event data, relevant external operational loss event data, business environment and internal control factor assessments, and scenario analysis.

These reports must perform the following functions:

■ Address both companywide and line of business results.
■ Summarize operational risk exposure, loss experience, relevant business environment, and internal control assessments.
■ Identify and assess the operational risk inherent in all material products, activities, processes, and systems.

Hyperion Basel II compliance solution helps banks understand credit exposure by consolidating financial and operational data into a single version of the truth. Banks can thus assess credit exposures in multiple dimensions and automatically calculate and compare the effects of alternative risk-mitigation strategies.

## Hyperion XBRL Server

The XBRL server is an XLM-based transaction processor capable of enforcing financial business rules and policies in a service-oriented Architecture. XBRL tags enable automated software processing of financial data, thereby eliminating the need for tedious, costly manual data reentry and comparison. Once data has been tagged, software is used to select, analyze, store, and exchange information, thereby reducing the chances of error. Moreover, because it is a standardized language, XBRL enables efficient apples-to-apples comparison of financial data across multiple companies and industries. XBRL breaks down the language barriers of international financial reporting by converting data into a standardized format that is usable worldwide. Many regulators are introducing mandatory filing of financial statements in XBRL.

## Summary

Like Chapter 13, this section attempts to provide a list of tools and services that can be employed in conjunction with the Oracle Identity Management Suite to facilitate regulatory compliance. Although this book attempts to provide comprehensive coverage, the breadth and depth of the server technology is too great for any one book or any one user to deal with completely. It would take any single individual several years to understand both the technical platform and the applications they serve.

**Table 15.1   Regulatory Governance Mapping**

| | Trusted Access | Change Management | Business Continuity and Availability | Operational Awareness | Records Management | Audit and Risk Management | Operational Accountability and Transparency | Segregation of Duties | Operational Controls |
|---|---|---|---|---|---|---|---|---|---|
| Enterprise User Security | X | | | X | X | X | | X | X |
| Database Vault | X | X | | X | X | X | | X | X |
| Audit Vault | X | X | X | X | X | X | X | X | X |
| Stellent Universal Content Manager | X | X | | | X | X | | X | X |
| Records DB | X | X | X | X | X | | | | |
| Secure Enterprise Search | X | | | X | X | | | X | X |
| Oracle Data Integrator | X | X | | | X | X | | | X |
| Trusted Information Exchange | X | X | X | X | X | X | X | X | X |
| XML Publisher | | X | | X | X | X | X | | X |
| Hyperion: Business Compliance Dashboard | X | X | | X | X | X | X | X | X |
| Hyperion: Basel II Compliance | | X | | | X | X | X | | X |
| Hyperion: XBRL Server | | X | X | X | | | | | X |

# GOVERNANCE
# LANDSCAPE

# Chapter 16

## Asia Pacific and Oceana

What is Asia? Culturally, it is not a series of discrete parcels that match the borders of countries. For centuries Asian influences have paid scant regard to where one country ends and another begins. Attitudes and ideas have washed through the region unhindered by nationality. Centers of defined culture exist, but they blur at their margins, thanks to migration and population drift; and so Asia is both nuanced and interconnected. Oceana by contrast consists of discrete parcels of land separated until the 20th century by the tyranny of water. Oceana is defined as the South Pacific regions west of French Polynesia and east of Australia, which is included, and south of the Northern Marinas south to New Zealand, which is also included. This list includes Australia, Samoa, Tonga, New Caledonia, Vanuatu, Papua New Guinea, New Zealand, and the Solomon Islands, as well as numerous other smaller island territories. In this section we explore the existing legislative infrastructure in the context of our governance model. The mappings of the legislation to the nine control domains is outlined in Appendix A.

## Oceana

### Australia

Political System: The Commonwealth of Australia is a constitutional monarchy, a federation, and a parliamentary democracy.
Chief Privacy Officer/Minister Office of the Federal Privacy Commissioner http://www.privacy.gov.au

### Legislation

Victorian Electronic Records Strategy (VERS): Undertaken by Public Record Office Victoria (PROV) in conjunction with the Australian Commonwealth Scientific and Industrial Research Organisation (CSIRO). In 1999 the Victorian Department of Infrastructure implemented a Victorian Electronic Records Strategy (VERS)-compliant data capture system. Public Record Office Victoria has released an electronic record-keeping standard that applies to all Victorian government agencies.

DIRKS: The DIRKS methodology is a structured process for designing and implementing record-keeping systems. The DIRKS methodology is outlined in Australian Standard, AS ISO 15489-2002, Records Management. It was originally detailed in the precursor to this standard, Australian Standard, AS 4390-1996, Records Management.

DIRKS comprises eight steps:

1. Preliminary investigation
2. Analysis of business activity
3. Identification of record-keeping requirements
4. Assessment of existing systems
5. Identification of strategies for record keeping
6. Design of a record-keeping system
7. Implementation of a record-keeping system
8. Post implementation review

The DIRKS methodology is a clear and simple statement contained in the Australian Standard on Records Management, AS ISO 15489.

CLERP9: The Corporate Law Economic Reform Program (CLERP) is a vehicle for the ongoing review and reform of Australia's corporate and business regulation to ensure that it is modern, responsive ad promotes business activity. CLERP Paper No. 9 (Audit Reform and Corporate Disclosure) established a vision for promoting transparency, accountability, and shareholder rights. The law enhances auditor independence, achieves better disclosure outcomes, and improves enforcement.

AS/NZS:4360: Australian and New Zealand Risk Management Standard. AS/NZS:4360 was developed in response to a perceived need for practical assistance in applying risk management in public sector and private sector organizations. Related and dependent documents include the following:

SAA HB141-1999 Risk Financing Guidelines
SAA HB142-1999 A Basic Introduction to Managing Risk using the Australian and New Zealand Risk Management Standard
SAA/NZS HB143-1999 Guidelines for Managing Risk in the Australian and New Zealand Public Sector
SAA HB240-2000 Guidelines for Managing Risk in Outsourcing
SAA HB 231-2000 Information Security Risk Management Guidelines.
Emergency Risk Management—Applications Guide (Emergency Management Australia)

Privacy Act of 1988 (Amended 2001): This act creates a set of 11 Information Privacy Principles (IPPs), based on those in the OECD Guidelines that apply to the activities of most federal government agencies. The Privacy Amendment (Private Sector) Bill 2000 applies a set of National Privacy Principles developed by the Privacy Commissioner during 1997 and 1998, originally as a self-regulatory substitute for legislation. Privacy Principles, incorporated in the Privacy Act 1998 and Privacy Amendment (Private Sector) Act 2000

The Crimes Act: This act covers offenses relating to unauthorized access to computers, unauthorized interception of mail and telecommunications, and the unauthorized disclosure of Commonwealth government information.

The Federal Freedom of Information Act of 1982: This act provides for public access to government records.

Privacy Amendment (private sector) Bill (effective January 2002): This act extends privacy protections to the private sector.

## Miscellaneous Information

The Privacy Act of 1988: In contrast to the EU directive, organizations are required to obtain consent from customers for secondary use of their personal information for marketing purposes where it is "practicable"; "Wherever it is lawful and practicable, individuals must have the option of not identifying themselves when entering into transactions with an organisation."

## New Zealand

Political System: A parliamentary representative democratic monarchy (Implemented via First Nation Treaty)
Chief Privacy Officer/Minister: The Office of the Privacy Commissioner—Data Protection/Privacy Commission for New Zealand Parliamentary Democracy www.privacy.org.nz

## Legislation

As mentioned earlier, AS/NZS:4360 specifies the elements of the risk management process.

Article 21 of the Bill of Rights Act 1990: "Everyone has the right to be secure against unreasonable search or seizure, whether of the person, property, or correspondence or otherwise."

New Zealand's 1993 Privacy act: This act regulates the collection, use, and dissemination of personal information in both the public and private sectors. It also grants to individuals the right to have access to personal information held about them by any agency.

## Miscellaneous Information

New Zealand is a member of the Organization for Economic Cooperation and Development and has adopted the OECD Guidelines on the Protection of Privacy and Transborder Flows of Personal Data.

# Asia

## China

Political System: Communist state
   http://www.gov.cn/
Chief Privacy Officer/Minister: None

## Legislation

Article 37 of the Chinese constitution provides that the "freedom of the person of citizens of the People's Republic of China is inviolable," and Article 40 states that "freedom and privacy of correspondence of citizens of the People's Republic of China are protected by law."

Computer Information Network and Internet Security, Protection and Management Regulations: "The freedom and privacy of network users is protected by law. No unit or individual may, in violation of these regulations, use the Internet to violate the freedom and privacy of network users." Article 8 states that "units and individuals engaged in Internet business must accept the security supervision, inspection, and guidance of the public security organization."

Criminal Code: Sections 285 to 287 of the Criminal Code prohibit intrusions into computer systems and prescribe penalties for violations of the regulations.

Guidelines for Telecom Services: These stipulated that telecom operators should provide detailed lists of long distance calls, mobile phones, and information services for customers, and protect the rights and privacy of its customers.

## Hong Kong

Political System: Special Administrative Region of the People's Republic of China Communist State

www.gov.cn/

Chief Privacy Officer/Minister: Office of the Privacy Commissioner for Personal Data (PCO) Special Administrative Region of China www.pco.org.hk

## Legislation

Personal Data (Privacy) Ordinance 1996: The ordinance covers any data relating directly or indirectly to a living individual. Individuals have the right to confirm with data users whether their personal data are held, to obtain a copy of such data, and to have personal data corrected.

Basic Law of the Hong Kong Special Administrative Region Article 29 provides that "the homes and other premises of Hong Kong residents shall be inviolable. Arbitrary or unlawful search of, or intrusion into, a resident's home or other premises shall be prohibited." Article 30 provides that "the freedom and privacy of communications of Hong Kong residents shall be protected by law."

Personal Data (Privacy) Ordinance: The statutory provisions adopt features of a variety of existing data protection laws, and the draft version of the EU Directive is also reflected in several provisions. It lays down six principles to regulate the collection, accuracy, use, and security of personal data as well as requiring data users to be open about data processing and conferring on data subjects the right to be provided a copy of their personal data and to effect corrections.

Telecommunications Ordinance and the Post Office Ordinance: The Basic Law permits postal staff to examine, on the spot, the contents of nonletter postal materials.

## Miscellaneous Information

Data Protection Principle 1 states that personal data shall be collected by means that are lawful and fair under the circumstances of the case, and that the data subject be explicitly or implicitly informed, on or before collecting the data, regarding whether it is obligatory or voluntary for him to supply the data, and the data collected are adequate. Data Protection Principle 1 also requires that the data subject be explicitly informed, on or before collecting the data, of the purpose for which the data is to be used.

Data Protection Principle 2 requires that all practical steps be taken to ensure that personal data is accurate, and personal data shall not be kept longer than is necessary for the fulfillment of the purpose. "Inaccurate data" is defined in the law as data that is "incorrect, misleading, incomplete or obsolete."

Data Protection Principle 3 requires prescribed consent from the data subject before personal data can be used for a different purpose from the one specified at the time of collection.

Data Protection Principle 4 requires that all practical steps be taken to ensure that personal data held by a data user is protected against unauthorized access, processing, erasure, or other uses, with particular regard to physical location, data sensitivity, automatic systems security, data integrity, and people competence and data transmission.

Employee Privacy Information: Code of Practice on Human Resource Management

## Taiwan

Political System: Multiparty democratic regime encapsulated within a political de facto affiliation to People's Republic of China
Chief Privacy Officer/Minister: The Ministry of Justice Multiparty Democratic Regime http://www.gio.gov.tw

## Legislation

Article 12 of the 1994 Taiwanese Constitution states that "the people shall have freedom of privacy of correspondence."

The 1995 Computer-Processed Personal Data Protection Law: The act governs the collection and use of personally identifiable information by government agencies and many areas of the private sector. Individuals have a right of access and correction.

The 1995 Law Governing Protection of Personal Data Processed by Computers: This covers both the public and private sectors, but only computer processing systems with personal data.

The June 1999 Communication Protection and Surveillance Act: This act was to impose stricter guidelines on when and how wiretaps can be used.

Telecommunications Surveillance Act: Article 315 of Taiwan's Criminal Code states that a person who, without reason, opens or conceals a sealed letter or other sealed document efforts to collect information directly from the subject; provide for an appropriate security system; notify such person if information is collected about them from a third party; and provide rights of access, correction, and deletion.

The Official Information Act: This act allows for citizens to obtain government information 1934 Telegraph and Telephone Act: Phone tapping is a criminal offense under this act. Wiretaps can be conducted for security reasons.

## Japan

Political System: Constitutional monarchy
Chief Privacy Officer/Minister: Government Information Systems Planning Division of the Management and Coordination Agency & Prime Minister's Office Administrative Management Bureau

## Legislation

Article 21 of the 1946 Constitution: This states the following: "freedom of assembly and association as well as speech, press and all other forms of expression are guaranteed. 2) No censorship shall be maintained, nor shall the secrecy of any means of communication be violated."

Japan Personal Information Protection Act (2003): This was passed to control the spread of personal information. The law protects individuals' rights and welfare while preserving the usefulness of personal information

The 1988 Act for the Protection of Computer Processed Personal Data Held by Administrative Organs governs the use of personal information in computerized files held by government agencies.

Guidelines Concerning the Protection of Computer Processed Personal Data in the Private Sector: On March 4, 1997, the Ministry of International Trade and Industry (MITI) issued these guidelines.

The Law Concerning Access to Information Held by Administrative Organs: This law was approved by the Diet in May 1999 and allows any individual or company to request government information in electronic or printed form.

## Financial Instruments and Exchange Law (J-SOX)

Basic contents of the legislations:

1. Establishing cross-sectional framework of a wide range of financial instruments and services; establishing a comprehensive definition of collective investment scheme (funds) and wide-ranging definition of derivatives broadening the scope of "financial instruments firms"
2. Enhancing disclosure requirements; introduction of a statutory quarterly reporting system for listed companies; enhancing internal control over financial reporting; reviewing regulations on tender offers and large shareholding reports
3. Increasing the maximum criminal penalties against various market frauds and expanding the scope of penalties against *misegyoku*; increasing the maximum criminal penalties against such frauds as false annual reports and market manipulations, from 5 years in prison to 10 years
4. Providing organization structures for self-regulatory functions of exchanges in the form of stock corporations

## Miscellaneous Information

Japan is a member of the Organization for Economic Cooperation and Development and a signatory to the OECD Guidelines on Privacy and Transborder Dataflows.

## *Malaysia*

Constitutional monarchy:
http://www.smpke.jpm.my

## Description of Legislation

Communications and Multimedia Act: This act has several sections on telecommunications privacy. Section 234 prohibits unlawful interception of communications. Section 249 sets rules for searches of computers and includes access to encryption keys. Section 252 authorizes police to intercept communications without a warrant if a public prosecutor considers that a communication is likely to contain information that is relevant to an investigation.

The Digital Signature Act of 1997 and the Computer Crime Act of 1997: Section 8 of the Computer Crime Act allows police to inspect and seize computing equipment of suspects without a warrant or any notice. The suspect is also required to turn over all encryption keys for any encrypted data on his equipment. The act also outlaws eavesdropping, tampering with or falsifying data, sabotage through computer viruses or worms, among a host of cyber-crimes.

National Registration Department Voluntary Smart Cards for Infants: The issuance of voluntary chip-based ID cards to all newborn children. It includes number, name, parents' names, address, and citizenship status. It will later include the blood group of the child and other health information. The card would be used to identify children registering for school and for medical care.

## Miscellaneous Information

The Ministry of Energy, Communications, and Multimedia is drafting a Personal Data Protection act that creates legal protections for personal data as part of the "National Electronic Commerce Master Plan."

## Philippines

Political System: Republic
Chief Privacy Officer/Minister: http://www.gov.ph

## Legislation

The 1987 constitution: Article II of the 1987 constitution establishes the right of the people to be secure in their persons, houses, papers (interpreted to include digital files), and effects against unreasonable searches and seizures.

Article III of the constitution protects the right of privacy. Section 2 states, "The right of the people to be secure in their persons, houses, papers, and effects against unreasonable searches and seizures." Section 3 states, "(1) The privacy of communication and correspondence shall be inviolable. (2) Any evidence obtained in violation of this or the preceding section shall be inadmissible." Section 7 states, "The right of the people to information on matters of public concern shall be recognized. Access to official records, and to documents and papers pertaining to official acts, transactions, or decisions, as well as to government research data used as basis for policy development, shall be afforded the citizen, subject to such limitations as may be provided by law."

1998 Access Devices Regulation Act: This is a law intended to punish credit card fraud that outlaws the use of unauthorized access devices to obtain goods or services.

Republic Act 8972, the Electronic Commerce Act of 2000: Sections 8, 9, and 10 of the law give legal status to data messages, electronic writing, and digital signatures, making them admissible in court. Section 23 mandates a minimum fine and a prison term of 6 months to 3 years for unlawful and unauthorized access to computer systems, and extends the consumer act, RA7394, to transactions using data messages. Section 21 of the act requires the government to transact business with citizens through the Web.

The Anti-Wiretapping Law: This law requires a court order to obtain a telephone tap. The court order is to be awarded only if (1) the wiretap is used to pursue the commission of certain crimes including treason, espionage, or sedition; (2) there are reasonable grounds to believe that evidence gained will be essential to conviction; and (3) there are no other means of obtaining the evidence.

## Miscellaneous Information

There is no general data protection law, but there is a recognized right of privacy in civil law. The Civil Code also states that "every person shall respect the dignity, personality, privacy, and peace of mind of his neighbors and other persons," and punishes acts that violate privacy of private citizens, public officers, or employees of private companies.

## Singapore

Political System: Parliamentary republic
Chief Privacy Officer/Minister: The National Trust Council http://www.ida.gov.sg

## Legislation

E-Commerce Code for the Protection of Personal Information and Communications of Consumers of Internet Commerce: The code encourages providers to ensure the confidentiality of business records and personal information of users, including details of usage or transactions, and prohibits the disclosure of personal information.

Computer Misuse Act, the Electronic Transactions Act, and the Nation Computer Board (Amendment) Act: The CMA prohibits the unauthorized interception of computer communications.

Guidelines Regulating Scanning of Computers by Internet Services Providers (ISPs): The infocomm Development Authority of Singapore issued guidelines regulating the scanning of computers by ISPs.

The Model Data Protection Code for the Private Sector: When data is to be transferred to someone (other than the individual or the organization or its employees), the organization shall take reasonable steps to ensure that the data that is to be transferred will not be processed inconsistently with this Model Code. Accountability for the organization's compliance with the principles rests with the designated persons, even though other persons within the organization may be responsible for the day-to-day collection and processing of personal data. In addition, other persons within the organization may be delegated to act on behalf of the designated persons. The identity of the persons designated by the organization to oversee the organization's compliance with the principles shall be made known upon request.

## Miscellaneous Information

The Singapore constitution is based on the British system and does not contain any explicit right to privacy. There is no general data protection or privacy law in Singapore.

All of the ISPs are operated by government-owned or governed-controlled companies.

## South Korea

Political System: Republic
Chief Privacy Officer/Minister: Minster of Government Administrate www.korea.net

## Legislation

The Constitution Article 16, 17, and 18: The constitution provides for protection of privacy and secrecy of communications. Article 16 states, "All citizens are free from intrusion into their place of resides. In case of search or seizure in a residence, a warrant issued by a judge upon request of a prosecutor has to be presented." Article 17 states, "The privacy of no citizen may be infringed." Article 18 states, "The privacy of correspondence of no citizen shall be infringed."

The Act on the Protection of Personal Information Managed by Public Agencies 1994: This act sets rules for the management of computer-based personal information by government agencies.

The Basic Act on Electronic Commerce: Chapter III of the act requires that "electronic traders shall not use, nor provide to any third party, the personal information collected through electronic commerce beyond the alleged purpose for collection: Individuals also have rights of access, correction, and deletion."

Law on Protection of Communications Secrecy Act: This act regulates wiretapping. A court order is required to place a tap. Intelligence agencies are required to obtain permission from the chief judge of the High Court or approval from the president for national security cases.

Article 54 of the Telecommunication Business Act: This act prohibits persons who are (or have been) engaged in telecommunication services from releasing private correspondence.

Act Relating to Use and Protection of Credit Information of 1995: Credit reports are protected by the Act Relating to Use and Protection of Credit Information of 1995.

Postal Services Act: Postal privacy is protected by the Postal Services Act.

The Act on Disclosure of Information by Public Agencies: This act is a freedom of information act that allows Koreans to demand access to government records. It enforces a constitutional right to information.

## Miscellaneous Information

The Ministry of Information and Communication (MIC) guidelines requires consent before collecting "sensitive information" such as political orientation, birthplace, and sexual orientation, and ISPs wishing to collect information about users under 14 must obtain parental consent.

South Korea is a member of the Organization for Economic Cooperation and Development and has adopted the OECD Guidelines on the Protection of Privacy and Transborder Flows of Personal Data.

## Thailand

Political System: Constitutional monarchy
Chief Privacy Officer/Minister: Commissioner, Official Information Commission—National Information Technology Committee (NITC)

### Description of Legislation

### Constitution

Article 34: The rights, honor, and privacy of family members are recognized and must be protected. Public statements and publicity of a statement or picture, no matter by what means, are not allowed if they adversely affect the rights, honor, or privacy of a person unless the publicity is in the public interest.

Article 37: Individuals have the right to lawful communication. Search, seizure, or exposure of lawful communications or any attempt to eavesdrop on such communications is prohibited unless through laws on national security or peace and order.

Article 58: People are entitled to access to information concerning the records of government agencies except when disclosure of such information will jeopardize national security, public safety, or interests protected by the law of any individual.

Thailand Data Protection Law: The Data Protection law prohibits misuse of information and affords rights to data owners. It is unique in that it is the first Asian standard that covers technology that can track a Web surfer's behavior and also covers location technology.

Electronic Transactions Act: Electronic Transaction Act B.E. 2544 (2001)—To promote consumer protection and allocate the liability incurred from the technological risks.

Electronic Data Interchange Law: Establishes the legal framework in concluding of electronic contracts.

Bylaw of Section 78 of the Thai Constitution (Universal Access Law): To create an equitable information society by promoting universal access to information in the National Information Infrastructure (NII).

Electronic Signature Law: The law allows electronic documents to be used as evidence in court and makes digital signatures legally binding.

The Official Information Act: The act guarantees access to public information for all citizens and establishes a code of information practices for the processing of personal information by state agencies. Section 4 of the act defines personal information as information relating to "the particular private matters" of a person that can identify that person.

## India

Political System: Republic
Chief Privacy Officer/Minister: Controller of Certifying Authorities

### Legislation

India's Information Technology Act, 2000: The Information Technology Act is a set of laws intended to provide a comprehensive regulatory environment for electronic commerce and also addresses computer crime, hacking, damage to computer source code, breach of confidentiality, and viewing of pornography.

Clause 49: The companies which are required to comply with the requirements of the revised Clause 49 shall submit a quarterly compliance report to the stock exchanges as per sub Clause VI (ii), of the revised Clause 49, within 15 days from the end of every quarter. The report shall be signed either by the compliance officer or the chief executive officer of the company. The company shall obtain a certificate from either the auditors or practicing company secretaries regarding compliance of conditions of corporate governance.

## Miscellaneous Information

National Association of Software and Service Companies (NASSCOM): The Indian chamber of commerce that serves as an interface to the Indian software industry. The consortium was set up to facilitate business and trade in software and services and to encourage advancement of research in software technology.

## Summary

With China's entry into the WTO, international firms are becoming excited about the lifting of the barriers to potentially the largest consumer market in the world. Since China's current economic reform was launched in 1978, foreign firms have shown tremendous enthusiasm about the emerging China market. Since China's "open door" policy began in 1978, Chinese consumers have experienced an unprecedented consumer revolution. However, because of historical, economic, and other related reasons, regional differences exist in the development of consumerism in Asia. Regulatory compliance impacted three key dimensions of growing consumerism in Asia: health consciousness, environmental consciousness, and confidence in business ethics.

By contrast, progress in improving corporate governance in much of the Western world has not come by a considered program of reform, but rather as a spasmodic reaction to scandal or incompetence. These reforms suggest a change in effective accountability (the second criterion of sound governance in any country). The important part the banks played in the Asia/Pacific rim has greatly diminished, and in its place there are now better-structured boards, more effective company auditors, and, occasionally, more active shareholders. An increase of interest, and, where appropriate, action on their part, is serving restore the balance that the banks' withdrawal from the scene has impaired.

# Chapter 17

# Europe and Africa

It is a commonplace of political commentary on the European Union to claim that European integration lacks a cultural dimension similar to that of the individual nation states that make up the Union. A trading community not a centralized state system; rather, the nation state can be viewed as having collectively outsourced legislative and financial authority through multiple levels of aggregation through mutually binding ratified treaties. In examination there are three sets of forces that will continue to bring about change in the field of corporate governance within Europe and the trading communities and nation states which exist within her borders. The first are market forces, primarily driven by investors and the providers of corporate funds; the second forces are the ever-rising expectations of society; and finally, there are regulatory forces of one kind or another pursued by national and international authorities. The following regulations are those that to date support investor protection and individual privacy.

## European Union

EC 8th Directive on Company Law and Corporate Governance: The directive establishes an audit regulatory committee to govern entities of public interest. The objective of the 8th directive is twofold:

- Enhance global efficiency and competitiveness of businesses in the EU
- Strengthen shareholders' rights and third parties' protection

This governance covers many of the major areas the Turnbull guidance outlines and is in effect a more comprehensive version of the American Sarbanes–Oxley statute. Areas of coverage include Directive on Statutory Audit outlining the following:

- Auditor Independence & Audit Committee
- Group Audit consolidated
- Quality & Transparency in Auditing
- Regulatory Framework (in-country)
- Article 39: monitor effectiveness of IC, Internal Audit, & Risk

Also included is management of companies of public interest enforcing the following:

- 3.1.3 Collective Board responsibility
- 3.1.1 Governance Statement
- Existence & nature of risk management
- Adoption of a Code of Corporate Governance

EU codes, Action Plan, and Directive help coordinate oversight of public auditors by national regulatory bodies and enforce the independence of auditors by vesting authority to decide their appointment and remuneration in a board of directors audit committee rather than regular management. The directive specifies a clear chain of authority in the audit of group companies, and adopts international auditing standards as a baseline for all audits.

The Action Plan associated with the directive requires that the board of management collectively certify a Governance Report in the Annual Report so that the management team is held responsible for the accuracy of the reporting. It also requires that management consciously articulate and review the existence and nature of the worldwide financial internal control system, and specifies the Governance Code with which it complies or in relation to which it explains deviations.

Union Data Protection Directive standardizes the protection of data privacy for European Union citizens, while allowing for the free flow of information between member states. As a result, companies based outside the European Union now find themselves scrambling to understand the implications of the directive for their business operation. The impact will vary depending on a company's involvement and presence in a member state. The ease with which electronic data flows across borders has led to a concern that data protection laws could be circumvented by simply transferring personal information to a third country where the law did not apply. The data could then be processed in that country, frequently called *data haven*, without any limitations. For this reason, most data protection laws include restrictions on the transfer of information to third countries, unless the information is protected in the destination country. A European Directive imposes an obligation on member states to ensure that any personal information relating to European citizens is protected by law when it is exported to, and processed in, countries outside Europe. It states that

> The Member States shall provide that the transfer to a third country of personal data which are undergoing processing or are intended for processing after transfer may take place only if the third country in question ensures an adequate level of protection.

EU Directive 95/46 Article 286 of the EC Treaty provides that community acts on the protection of individuals with regard to the processing of personal data and the free movement of such data also apply to institutions and bodies. This article also provides for an independent supervisory body responsible for monitoring the application of such community acts.

EU Directive 95/46 on the right to privacy: The EU Directive 95/46/EC on the protection of individuals with regard to the processing of personal data and on the free movement of such data limits and regulates the collection of personal information.

EU Directive 97/66: Concerning the processing of personal data and the protection of privacy in the telecommunications sector passed 15 December 1997. EU Directive 97/66 addresses the processing of personal data and the protection of privacy in the telecommunications sector.

EU Directive 2002/58/EC: This directive seeks to protect the fundamental rights and observes the principles embodied in the charter of fundamental rights of the European Union. In particular, this directive seeks to ensure full respect for the rights of individuals with regard to personally identifiable information.

Electronic surveillance in the workplace: Article 8 of the ECHR also provides a right to respect for one's "private and family life, his home and his correspondence," subject to certain restrictions.

Article 29 Working Party Document 5401/01: Workers do not abandon their right to privacy and data protection in the workplace. They are provided an expectation of a certain degree of privacy in the workplace as they develop a significant part of their relationships within the workplace.

Markets in Financial Instruments Directive (MiFID) establishes a single market and regulatory regime for investment services across the 25 member states of the European Union. The key objectives of this directive are the following:

1. To complete the EU single market for investment services
2. To respond to changes/innovations in the securities markets
2. To protect investors as a supplement to the Investment Services Directive (Directive 93/22/EEC)

MiFID is one of the cornerstones of the European Commission's Financial Services Action Plan introduced in 1999, whose 42 measures are bringing substantial changes to the regulation of the EU financial services markets. MiFID was introduced under the "Lamfalussy" procedure designed to speed up the introduction of legislation based on a four-level approach recommended by a committee. MIFID serves to supplement the Prospectus Directive, the Market Abuse Directive, and the Transparency Directive.

The MiFID Level 1 Directive: Directive 2004/39/EC sets out a detailed "framework" for the legislation. Twenty articles of this directive stipulate the introduction of technical implementation measures, which are to be adopted via a directive and a regulation. The European Commission, following the receipt of technical advice from the Committee of European Securities Regulators and negotiations in the European Securities Committee with oversight by the European Parliament, adopted these technical implementation measures. The implementation measures were officially published on September 2, 2006.

## Key Aspects of MiFID

Authorization, regulation, and pass porting: Firms covered by MiFID will be authorized and regulated in their "home state." Once a firm has been authorized, it will be able to use the MiFID passport to provide services to customers in other EU member states. These services will be regulated by the member state in their home state.

Client classification: MiFID requires firms to classify clients as eligible counterparties, professional clients, and retail clients. Clear procedures must be in place to classify clients and assess their suitability for each type of investment product. The appropriateness of any investment advice or suggested financial transaction must be verified before being given.

Client order handling: MiFID has requirements relating to the information that needs to be captured when accepting client orders, ensuring that a firm is acting in a client's best interests and as to how orders from different clients may be aggregated.

Pretrade transparency: MiFID requires that operators of continuous order-matching systems must make aggregated order information available at the five best price levels on the buy and sell side; for quote-driven markets, the best bids and offers of market makers must be made available.

Posttrade transparency: MiFID requires firms to publish the price and volume of all trades, even if executed outside of a regulated market.

Best execution: MiFID requires that firms take all reasonable steps to obtain the best possible result in the execution of an order for a client. The best possible result is not limited to execution price but also includes cost, speed, and likelihood of execution and settlement.

Systematic internalizer: A systematic internalizer is a firm that executes orders from its clients against its own book or against orders from other clients. MiFID will treat systematic internalizers as miniexchanges; hence, for example, they will be subject to pre- and posttrade transparency requirements.

## Austria

Chief Privacy Officer/Minister: Data Protection Commission
Political System: Federal republic
Web URL: http://www.austria.gv.at/e/

## Description of Legislation

Datenschutzgesetz (DSG) 2000: Data protection law that incorporates the EU Directive into Austrian law. Some sections of the data protection law (Datenschutzgesetz–DSG) have constitutional status.

Code of Criminal Procedure: Wiretapping, electronic eavesdropping, and computer searches are regulated by the code of criminal procedure.

The Auskunftspflichtgesetz: A freedom of information law that obliges federal authorities to answer questions regarding their areas of responsibility. It does not permit citizens to access documents, just to receive answers from the government on the content of information.

## Miscellaneous Information

Austria is a member of the Council of Europe, has ratified the Convention for the Protection of Individuals with Regard to Automatic Processing of Personal Data (ETS No. 38), and ratified the European Convention for the Protection of Human Rights and Fundamental Freedoms.

## Belgium

Chief Privacy Officer/Minister: Belgian Privacy Office
Political System: Federal Parliamentary Democracy under Constitutional Monarchy
National Data Protection Authority: President—Consultative Commission for Protection of Privacy
Web URL: http://www.fgov.be

## Description of Legislation

The Belgian constitution recognizes the right of privacy and private communications. Article 12 states that "everyone has the right to the respect of his private and family life."

Article 29 states that "the confidentiality of letters is inviolable ... The law establishes confidentiality of letters entrusted to the postal service."

Law on privacy protection in relation to the processing of personal data: The Belgian law applies to automatic processing of personal data and to manual files compiled and stored in a logical manner enabling systematic consultation. Processing of personal data, according to the Belgian law, covers any operation with automatic procedures relating to the recording or storing of personal data.

Data Protection Act of 1992: This law governs the processing and use of personal information. Amending pre-existing legislation to update this act and make it consistent with the EU.

Criminal Procedure Code: The code gives the judge authority to request the cooperation of experts or network managers to help decrypt telecommunications messages that have been intercepted. The experts or network managers may not refuse.

## Miscellaneous Information

Belgium is a member of the Council of Europe, has ratified the Convention for the Protection of Individuals with Regard to Automatic Processing of Personal Data (ETS No. 108), and ratified the European Convention for the Protection of Human Rights and Fundamental Freedoms.

# Bulgaria

Chief Privacy Officer/Minister: State Commission for the Protection of Personal Data
Political System: Parliamentary democracy
Web URL: http://www.government.bg

## Description of Legislation

Bulgarian Constitution of 1991: The constitution recognizes rights of privacy, secrecy of communications, and access to information.

Article 32: The privacy of citizens shall be inviolable; the home shall be inviolable.

Article 34: This pertains to the freedom and confidentiality of correspondence.

Article 41: Everyone shall be entitled to seek, obtain, and disseminate information. Citizens shall be entitled to obtain information from state bodies.

Personal Data Protection Act of 1997: This was established under the Treaty for Association Personal Data Protection Act of 1997. Entities collecting personal information must inform people why their personal information is being collected and allow them reasonable access.

The Law for Access to Information: This allows for access to government records except in cases of state security or personal privacy.

## Miscellaneous Information

Bulgaria is a member of the Council of Europe and has signed the Protection of Individuals with Regard to Automatic Processing of Personal Data (ETS No. 108).

## Czech Republic

Chief Privacy Officer/Minister: Office for Personal Data Protection
National Data Protection Authority: The Office for Personal Data Protection
Political System: Parliamentary democracy
Web URL: http://www.vlada.cz/1250/eng/

### Description of Legislation

The 1993 Charter of Fundamental Rights and Freedoms: This provides for extensive privacy rights.

Article 7: This states that Inviolability of the person and of privacy is guaranteed. It may be limited only in cases specified by law.

Article 10: Individuals are entitled to protection of dignity, personal integrity, reputation, protection against unauthorized interference in his or her personal and family life, protection against unauthorized gathering, and publication or other misuse of his or her personal data.

Article 13: This insures secrecy of letters and records. Similar protection is extended to messages communicated by telephone, telegraph, or other such facilities.

101 ACT of April 4, 2000, on the Protection of Personal Data: It implements the basic requirements of the EU Directive, but the police and intelligence services are exempted.

Czech Penal Code: This covers the infringement of the right to privacy in the definitions of criminal acts of infringement of the confidentiality of communications. Unauthorized use of personal data systems is considered a crime.

Freedom of Information Law: The law is based on the U.S. Freedom of Information Act and provides for citizens' access to all government records held by state bodies.

### Miscellaneous Information

The Czech Republic is a member of the Council of Europe, but has not signed the Convention for the Protection of Individuals with Regard to Automatic Processing of Personal Data.

## Denmark

Chief Privacy Officer/Minister Registerilsynet
National Data Protection Authority: Danish Data Protection Agency
Political System: Constitutional monarchy
Web URL: http://www.datatilsynet.dk

### Description of Legislation

Act on Processing of Personal Data: The act incorporates the European Union Data Protection Directive into Danish law. It replaces the Private Registers Act of 1978.

The Danish Constitution of 1953: This contains two provisions relating to privacy and data protection. Section 71 provides for the inviolability of personal liberty. Section 72 states that "the dwelling shall be inviolable." This includes telegraph and telephone communications.

The Administrative Procedures Act of 1985 the Payment Cards Act of 1994: The focus of the proposal is on rules, which are important for consumers and provide protection of consumers using payment instruments.

Access to Health Information Act of 1993: All citizen of Denmark are provided with a Danish Central Personal Registration (CPR). The misuse of this information is strictly prohibited.

The Access to Information Act and the Access to Public Administration Files Act: This freedom of information act governs access to government records.

## Miscellaneous Information

Denmark is a member of the Council of Europe and has signed the Convention for the Protection of Individuals with Regard to Automatic Processing of Personal Data (ETS No. 108).

## Greenland

The original unamended Danish Public and Private Registers Acts of 1979 continues to apply within Greenland, as a self-governing territory. The 1988 amendments that brought Denmark into compliance with the Council of Europe's Convention 108 do not apply to Greenland. Greenland is not part of the European Union and therefore has not adopted the EU Privacy Directive. Greenland's data protection requirements are much less stringent than those of Denmark and the other nations of the EU.

## *Estonia*

Chief Privacy Officer/Minister: Data Protection Inspectorate
Political System: Parliamentary democracy
Web URL: http://www.dp.gov.ee/eng/

## Description of Legislation

The 1992 Estonia constitution: The constitution recognizes the right of privacy, secrecy of communications, and data protection.

Article 42: This states that "no state or local government authority or their officials may collect or store information on the persuasions of any Estonian citizen against his or her free will."

Article 43: This states that "everyone shall be entitled to secrecy of messages transmitted by him or to him by post, telegram, telephone or other generally used means."

Article 44: This states that "Estonian citizens shall have the right to become acquainted with information about themselves held by state and local government authorities."

Personal Data Protection Act: The act protects the fundamental rights and freedoms of persons with respect to the processing of personal data.

Databases Act: This act is a procedural law for the establishment of national databases. The law sets out the general principles for the maintenance of databases and prescribes requirements and protection measures for data processing.

The Digital Signatures Act: This act provides the necessary conditions for using digital signatures and lays down the procedure for exercising supervision over the provision of certification services and time-stamping services.

1994 Surveillance Act: It regulates the interception of communications.

Telecommunications Act: Surveillance agencies can obtain information on the sender and receiver of messages by written or oral request. Telecommunications providers are also required to delete data within one year and prevent unauthorized disclosure of users' information.

## Miscellaneous Information

Estonia is a member of the Council of Europe and has signed the Convention for the Protection of Individuals with Regard to Automatic Processing of Personal Data (ETS No. 108).

# Finland

Chief Privacy Officer/Minister: Data Protection Ombudsman–Data Protection Commission for Finland
Political System: Republic
Web URL: http://www.tietosuoja.fi

## Description of Legislation

The Constitution Act of Finland: The secrecy of correspondence and of telephone and other confidential communications shall be inviolable.

The Personal Data Protection Act: The law replaced the 1987 Personal Data File Act to make Finnish law consistent with the EU Data Protection Directive.

Personal Data Act (523/1999): The objectives of this act are to guarantee, in the processing of personal data, the protection of private life and the other basic rights that safeguard the right to privacy, as well as to promote the development of, and compliance with, good processing practice.

Act on the amendment of the Personal Data Act (986/2000): The Personal Data Act accommodates the constitutional reform and the EU Data Protection Directive.

Coercive Criminal Investigations Means Act: Electronic surveillance and telephone tapping are governed by the criminal law.

The Publicity (of Public Actions) Act: Provides for a general right to access any document created by a government agency, or sent or received by a government agency, including electronic records.

Workplace Data Protection Legislation: Workers need to know what data the employer is collecting about them. The personal data must be adequate, relevant, and not excessive. The employer must implement appropriate technical and organizational measures at the workplace.

## Miscellaneous Information

Finland is a country that has traditionally adhered to the Nordic tradition of open access to government files.

Finland is a member of the Council of Europe and has signed and ratified the Convention for the Protection of Individuals with Regard to Automatic Processing of Personal Data (ETS No. 108).

## *France*

Chief Privacy Officer/Minister: President National Commission for Freedom of Information (The Commission Nationale de L'informatique et des Libertes (CNIL))
Political System: Republic
Web URL: http://www.cnil.fr
National Data Protection Authority: La Commission Nationale de l' Informatique et des Libertés

### Description of Legislation

Law 78-17 of January 6, 1978, on Data Processing, Data Files, and Individual Liberties: This act has provisions regarding the use, storage, and availability of personally identifiable information.

Act of August 6, 2004 relating to the protection of individuals with regard to the processing of personal data: This act supplements the 78 Data processing law adding the aggregation and analysis of personally identifiable information as a function open to operational transparency.

The Data Protection Act (Loi relative à la sécurité quotidienne): Anyone wishing to process personal data must register and obtain permission in many cases relating to processing by public bodies. Individuals must be informed of the reasons for collection of information and may object to it. Individuals have rights to access information being kept about them and to demand the correction and deletion of this data.

The French Liberty of Communication Act: The act requires all persons wishing to post content on the Internet to identify themselves, by publishing their name and address or to their host provider. The law requires ISPs to keep logs of all data.

### Miscellaneous Information

France is a member of the Council of Europe and has signed and ratified the Convention for the Protection of Individuals with Regard to Automatic Processing of Personal Data (ETS No. 108).

## *Germany*

Chief Privacy Officer/Minister: German Federal Privacy Commissioner (Bundesbeauftragte fur den Datenschutz)
National Data Protection Authority: Office of the Federal Data Protection Commissioner
Political System: Federal republic
Web URL: http://www.bfd.bund.de

### Description of Legislation

The TransPuG (2002): By correlating accounting standards and company management/control standards to state-of-the-art international criteria, the TransPuG tightens accounting standards, risk management responsibility, and auditor accountability.

The 4th Financial-Market Support Law (2002): With a focus on shielding shareholders while developing better market opportunities of capital market participants, the 4th Law seeks to regulate the adjustment of share prices and financial analyst liability while making transparent a company's directors' dealings.

The Cromme Commission Report (2003): A government-originated commission that was appointed by Germany's justice minister, the Cromme Report summarizes how increased transparency and liability can improve company performance, competitiveness, and access to capital.

The Datenschutz (1994): This German data protection act protects employee and consumer information. This should be examined together with the EU privacy directive because implementing security that deals with data becomes extremely complex when the two intersect.

Bundsebar Germany's eGovernment initiative: bundonline2005.de houses more than 100 authorities and offices that deliver 450+ services to the populace. This is one in a series of European governments that is going virtual and sparking an extensive local security debate. When considering German regulations, note that the country's federalist framework is made up of 16 states. National law is intertwined with state-based laws and ministries.

Governing Legislation: Federal Data Protection Act (amended 2001) Teleservices Data Protection Act: Under the act, German citizens have the right to withdraw consent to have user data collected, processed, and used without stating reasons as well as inspect any user data saved.

Article 10 of the Basic Law: Privacy of letters, posts, and telecommunications shall be inviolable.

Federal Data Protection Law: The purpose of this law is "to protect the individual against violations of his personal right (Personlichkeitsrecht) by handling person-related data." The law covers collection, processing, and use of personal data.

The Telecommunications Carriers Data Protection Ordinance of 1996: This ordinance protects privacy of telecommunications information.

The Information and Communication Services (Multimedia) Act of 1997L: The act details protection for information used in computer networks. The Act also sets out the legal requirements for digital signatures.

German Stock Corporation Act ("AktG"): Boards of listed companies must declare annually the compliance with the recommendations of the Government Commission German Corporate Governance Code published by the Federal Ministry of Justice.

Document Management and Electronic Archiving (DOMEA): This guideline focuses on records management and transparency of standard operations.

Germany's 2nd and 3rd Laws for the Promotion of the Financial Markets: This act allows management to take defensive actions against unsolicited takeover bids on the condition that these actions are in the corporation's best interest. The law explicitly states that management may solicit competing bids. These laws increase transparency and level the playing field in the market for corporate control.

KonTraG (Gesetz zur Kontrolle und Transparenz im Unternehmensbereich [1998]): A goal of the KonTraG is to improve corporate governance in German enterprises. As a result, regulations from the Handels and corporate law were changed. The KonTraG specifies and extends regulations of the HGB (commercial code) and the AktG (law on limited companies). Dealing with the responsibility of the business owner for his or her business, the KonTraG mandates that owners must do everything in their power to manage the business in a risk-averse way.

The German Safe Custody Act (Depotgesetz): Governs the safekeeping and management of securities on behalf of third parties.

BDSG the German Federal Data Protection Act (BDSG): Governs use of Personally Identifiable Information in both public and private functions.

## Miscellaneous Information

Germany is a member of the Council of Europe and has signed and ratified the Convention for the Protection of Individuals with Regard to Automatic Processing of Personal Data (ETS No. 108).

# Greece

Chief Privacy Officer/Minister: Hellenic Data Protection Authority
Political System: Parliamentary democracy
Web URL: http://www.dpa.gr/

## Description of Legislation

The Constitution of Greece: The constitution recognizes the rights of privacy and secrecy of communications. Article 19 states that "the privacy of correspondence and any other form of communication is absolutely inviolable."

Law on the Protection of Individuals with regard to the Processing of Personal Data

Article 5 of the Greek Code of Administrative Procedure: The article is a new Freedom of Information Act that provides citizens the right to access administrative documents.

## Miscellaneous Information

Greece is a member of the Council of Europe and has signed and ratified the Convention for the Protection of Individuals with Regard to Automatic Processing of Personal Data (ETS No. 108).

Greece was the last member of the European Union to adopt a data protection law, and its law was written to directly apply the EU Directive into Greek law.

# Hungary

Chief Privacy Officer/Minister: The Parliamentary Commissioner for Data Protection and Freedom of Information
Political System: Parliamentary democracy
Web URL: http://www.obh.hu/

## Description of Legislation

Constitution of the Republic of Hungary: "Everyone in the Republic of Hungary shall have the right to good reputation, the inviolability of the privacy of his home and correspondence, and the protection of his personal data."

Protection of Personal Data and Disclosure of Data of Public Interest: This legislation covers the collection and use of personal information.

## Miscellaneous Information

Hungary is a member of the Council of Europe and has signed and ratified the Convention for the Protection of Individuals with Regard to Automatic Processing of Personal Data (ETS No. 108).

## *Ireland*

Chief Privacy Officer/Minister: Data Protection Commissioner
Political System: Republic
Web URL: http://www.irlgov.Ie

### Description of Legislation

Irish constitution: Although not an express right to privacy in the Irish constitution, the Supreme Court has ruled that an individual may invoke the personal rights provision in Article 40.3.1 to establish an implied right to privacy.

Data Protection Act (effective 1988) and (Amendment) Bill, 2002: The Data Protection Act was passed to implement the 1981 Council of Europe Convention for the Protection of Individuals with Regard to Automatic Processing of Personal Data.

The Freedom of Information Act: This became effective April 1988. The act grants the public access to documents created by government agencies and requires that government agencies make internal information available.

Data Protection Order for Registration of January 9, 2001: The Data Protection Commission issued an order requiring telecommunications companies and Internet service providers to register their databases of customer information under the Data Protection Act of 1988.

European Communities (Data Protection) Regulations, 2001: Directive 95/46/EC protection of individuals with regard to the processing of personal data and on the free movement of data.

### Miscellaneous Information

Ireland is a member of the Council of Europe and, as mentioned, it introduced the 1988 Data Protection Act to give effect to Convention for the Protection of Individuals with Regard to Automatic Processing of Personal Data.

## *Isle of Man, Territory of United Kingdom*

Chief Privacy Officer/Minister: Data Protection Registrar
Political System: Parliamentary democracy (British Columbia, Dependent)
Web URL: http://www.odpr.org

### Legislation

The Isle of Man Data Protection Act of 1986: This act is based on the 1984 U.K. Data Protection Act. The Office of the Data Protection Registrar enforces the act.

## *Italy*

Chief Privacy Officer/Minister: Supervisory Authority ("Garante") for Personal Data Protection—Italian Data Protection Commission
Political System: Republic
Web URL: http://www.governo.it, http://www.privacy.it/dll998171.html

## Description of Legislation

Employee Data Protection Provisions: Authorisation No. 1/2002 Concerning Processing of Sensitive Data in the Employment Context: This legal act affords employees greater autonomy over personal data gathered in the workplace.

The 1948 Constitution: The constitution has limited provisions relating to privacy.

Article 15 states that "the liberty and secrecy of correspondence and of every form of communication are inviolable."

The Italian Data Protection Act: The Data Protection Act of 1996 implements the EU Data Protection Directive. It covers both electronic and manual files, and their use within government information, journalism, scientific and research.

EU Telecommunications Privacy Directive: In March 1998, the parliament issued a legislative decree adopting the provisions of the EU Telecommunications Privacy Directive.

## Miscellaneous Information

Italy is a member of the Council of Europe and has signed and ratified the Convention for the Protection of Individuals with Regard to Automatic Processing of Personal Data (ETS No. 108).

## Latvia

Chief Privacy Officer/Minister: Data Protection Inspectorate Parliamentary
Political System: Democracy
Web URL: http://www.mk.gov.lv/eng/

## Legislation

Constitutional Law on Rights and Obligations of a Citizen and a Person: The state guarantees the confidentiality of correspondence, telephone conversations, telegraph, and other communications.

The Law on Personal Data Protection of March 23, 2000: The law is based on the EU Data Directive and the Council of Europe Convention No. 108. The bill creates a Data Protection Inspectorate.

The Law on Freedom of Information act of November 1998: Guarantees public access to all information in "any technically feasible form." Individuals may use it to obtain their own records.

## Miscellaneous Information

Latvia is a member of the Council of Europe and has signed the Convention for the Protection of Individuals with Regard to Automatic Processing of Personal Data (ETS No. 108).

## Lithuania

Chief Privacy Officer/Minister: The State Data Protection Inspectorate Parliamentary
Political System: Democracy
Web URL: http://www.Irak.It

## Description of Legislation

Article 22 of the Constitution: "The private life of an individual shall be inviolable. Personal correspondences, telephone conversations, telegraph messages, and other intercommunications shall be inviolable."

Law on Legal Protection of Personal Data: The law regulates the processing of all types of personal data. It lays down rules regarding the collection, processing, transfer, and usage of data, including general means of protecting personal data and rights of access and correction.

The Penal Code of the Republic of Lithuania: There are specific privacy protections in laws relating to telecommunications, radio communications, statistics, the population register, and health information.

The 1996 Law on the Provision of Information to the Public: This law provides for a limited right of access to official documents and to documents held by political parties, political and public organizations, trade unions, and other entities.

## Luxembourg

Chief Privacy Officer/Minister: The Commission a la Protection des Donnees Nominatives
Political System: Constitutional monarchy
Web URL: http://www.gouvernement.lu/gouv/fr/gouv/
Legislation
Article 28 of the constitution: The secrecy of correspondence is inviolable.
Act Concerning the Use of Nominal Data in Computer Processing effective 1979: The law pertains to individually identifiable data in both public and private computer files. It also requires licensing of systems used for the processing of personal data.

### Miscellaneous Information

There is no general freedom of information law in Luxembourg. Luxembourg is a member of the Council of Europe and has signed and ratified the Convention for the Protection of Individuals with Regard to Automatic Processing of Personal Data (ETS No. 108).

## Netherlands

Chief Privacy Officer/Minister: Registratiekamer; The Registration Chamber Dutch Data Protection Authorities
Political System: Constitutional monarchy
Web URL: http://www.registratiekamer.nl

### Legislation

The constitution: The constitution grants citizens an explicit right to privacy. Article 10 states that everyone shall have the right to respect for his privacy, without prejudice to restrictions. Rules to protect privacy shall be laid down by act of parliament in connection with the recording and dissemination of personal data. The constitution also establishes rules concerning the rights of persons to be informed of data recorded concerning them and of the use that is made.

The Personal Data Protection Act of 2000: This bill is a expanded version of the 1988 Data Registration Act and brings Dutch law in line with the European Data Protection Directive and regulates the disclosure of personal data to countries outside of the European Union.

Telecommunications Act effective December 1998: This act requires that Internet service providers have the capability by August 2000 to intercept all traffic with a court order and maintain users logs for 3 months.

The Government Information Public Access Act of 1991: This act is based on the constitutional right of access to information. It creates a presumption that documents created by a public agency should be available to everyone.

## Miscellaneous Information

The Netherlands is a member of the Council of Europe and has signed and ratified the Convention for the Protection of Individuals with Regard to Automatic Processing of Personal Data ETS No. 108).

# Poland

Chief Privacy Officer/Minister Bureau of Inspector General for the Protection of Personal Data
Political System: Republic
Web URL: http://www.giodo.gov.pl

## Description of Legislation

### The Polish Constitution

Article 47: "Everyone shall have the right to legal protection of his private and family life, of his honor and good reputation and to make decisions about his personal life."

Article 51: "No one may be obliged, except on the basis of statute, to disclose information concerning his person. Public authorities shall not acquire, collect nor make accessible information on citizens other than that which is necessary in a democratic state ruled by law. Everyone shall have a right of access to official documents and data collections concerning himself. Limitations upon such rights may be established by statute. Everyone shall have the right to demand the correction or deletion of untrue or incomplete information, or information acquired by means contrary to statute. (5) Principles and procedures for collection of and access to information shall be specified by statute."

The Law on the Protection of Personal Data Protection: The law is based on the European Union Data Protection Directive. Under the law, personal information may only be processed with the consent of the individual. Everyone has the right to verify his or her personal records.

Access to Information Act: Provides for access to records held by government agency and private actors performing public duties.

Classified Information Protection Act: This act was adopted as a condition to entering NATO and provides the government a national security clause to the Access to Information Act.

## Miscellaneous Information

There is no general freedom of information act in Poland.

Poland is a member of the Council of Europe and has signed the Convention for the Protection of Individuals with Regard to Automatic Processing of Personal Data (ETS No. 108).

# Portugal

Chief Privacy Officer/Minister: National Data Protection Commission (Comissao Nacional de Proteccao de Dados—CNPD)
Political System: Parliamentary democracy
Web URL: http://www.cnpd.pt

## Legislation

### Portuguese Constitution

"Article 35: All citizens have the right of access to any computerized data relating to them and the right to be informed of the use for which the data is intended, under the law; they are entitled to require that the contents of the files and records be corrected and brought up to date. The law shall determine what is personal data as well as the conditions applicable to automatic processing, connection, transmission and use thereof, and shall guarantee its protection by means of an independent administrative body. Computerized storage shall not be used for information concerning a person's ideological or political convictions. Access to personal data of third parties is prohibited, except in exceptional cases as prescribed by law. Citizens shall not be given an all-purpose national identity number. Everyone shall be guaranteed free access to public information networks and the law shall define the regulations applicable to the transnational data flows and the adequate norms of protection for personal data and for data that should be safeguarded in the national interest."

Portuguese Data Protection Act (The 1998 Act on the Protection of Personal Data): This incorporates act adopts the EU Data Protection requirements into Portuguese law.

Freedom of Information Law 65/93, of 26 August 1993: This law provides for access to government records in any form by any person. It contains a personal privacy provision.

## Miscellaneous Information

Portugal is a member of the Council of Europe and has signed and ratified the Convention for the Protection of Individuals with Regard to Automatic Processing of Personal Data (ETS No. 108) and the OECD Guidelines on the Protection of Privacy and Transborder Flows of Personal Data.

# Slovakia

Chief Privacy Officer/Minister: Commissioner for the Protection of Personal Data in Information Systems
Political System: Parliamentary democracy
Web URL: http://www.Government.gov.sk

## Description of Legislation

The 1992 Constitution: The constitution provides protection for privacy, data protection, and secrecy of communications.

Article 16: Everyone has the right to protection against the unwarranted collection, publication, or other illicit use of his personal data.

Article 22: The privacy of correspondence and secrecy of mailed messages and other written documents and the protection of personal data are guaranteed.

The Act on Protection of Personal Data in Information Systems: The act closely tracks the EU Data Protection Directive and limits the collection, disclosure, and use of personal information; also, transfers to other countries are limited unless the country has "adequate" protection.

Article 11 of the Civil Code: Per this article "everyone shall have the right to be free from unjustified interference in his or her privacy and family life." This includes unjustified treatment of personal data.

The Act on Free Access to Information: It sets broad rules on disclosure of information held by the government.

## Miscellaneous Information

Slovakia is a member of the Council of Europe.

## Slovenia

Chief Privacy Officer/Minister: Inspectorate
Political System: Parliamentary democratic republic
Web URL: http://www.sigov.si

## Description of Legislation

The 1991 Constitution: Article 35 deals with the Protection of the Right to Privacy and of Personal Integrity.

Article 38 on the Protection of Personal Data states, "The protection of personal data relating to an individual shall be guaranteed. Any use of personal data shall be forbidden where that use conflicts with the original purpose for which it was collected. Each person has the right to be informed of the personal data relating to him, which has been collected."

Law on Personal Data Protection: The new law is based on the EU Data Protection Directive and the COE Convention No. 108.

The Law on Telecommunications: This law requires telecommunications service providers to "guarantee the confidentiality of transmitted messages and of personal and non-personal data known only to them."

The Electronic Commerce and Electronic Signature Act: This act regulates electronic commerce, which includes commerce in the electronic form on distance.

## Miscellaneous Information

Slovenia is a member of the Council of Europe.

## Spain

Chief Privacy Officer/Minister: Agencia de Proteccion de Datos (Data protection commission for Spain)
Political System: Parliamentary monarchy
Web URL: http://www.ag-protecciondatos.es

### Legislation

The Constitution: The constitution recognizes the right to privacy, secrecy of communications, and data protection.

Organic Law 5/1992 on the Regulation of the Automatic Processing of Personal Data: The Spanish Data Protection Agency was formally created by Royal Decree 428/1993 of 26 March.

Law of Information Society Services and Electronic Commerce (LSSI): This law applies to any business that engages in commerce, stating that those Web sites now have to register with the government.

The Spanish Data Protection Act (LORTAD): This act was amended in December 1999 to implement the EU Data Protection Directive. The act covers files held by the public and private sector and establishes the right of citizens to know what personal data is contained in computer files and the right to correct or delete incorrect or false data. Personal information may only be used for the purpose for which it was collected.

### Miscellaneous Information

There are also additional laws in the penal code, and relating to credit information, video surveillance, and automatic tellers. The government issued a decree on digital signatures in September 1999.

Spain is a member of the Council of Europe and European Union and has signed the Convention for the Protection of Individuals with Regard to Automatic Processing of Personal Data (ETS No. 108).

## Sweden

Chief Privacy Officer/Minister: Datainspektionen—Data Protection Commission for Sweden & Swedish Data Inspection Board
Political System: Constitutional monarchy
Web URL: http://www.din.se

### Legislation

Sweden's constitution: The constitution, which consists of several different legal documents, contains several provisions that are relevant to data protection. Section 2 of the Instrument of Government Act of 1974 provides, inter alia, for the protection of individual privacy. It is also important to note that the European Convention on Human Rights has been incorporated into Swedish law as of 1994. The ECHR is not formally part of the Swedish Constitution but has, in effect, similar status.

Personal Data Act of 1998 (amended in January 2000): Sweden enacted the Personal Data Act of 1998 to bring Swedish law into conformity with the requirements of the EC Directive on data protection.

Freedom of the Press Act of 1766: Sweden is a country that has traditionally adhered to the Nordic tradition of open access to government files. The world's first freedom of information act was the Riksdag's (Swedish Parliament) "Freedom of the Press Act of 1766." The act required that official documents should "upon request immediately be made available to anyone making a request" at no charge. The Freedom of the Press Act is now part of the constitution and decrees that "every Swedish citizen shall have free access to official documents."

## Miscellaneous Information

Sweden is a member of the Council of Europe and has signed and ratified the Convention for the Protection of Individuals with Regard to Automatic Processing of Personal Data (ETS No. 108).

## Turkey

Chief Privacy Officer/Minister: N/A
Political System: Republican parliamentary democracy
Web URL: http://www.mfa.gov.tr

## Description of Legislation

Article 20 of the Turkish Constitution regulates the right to respect for private life as follows: "Everyone has the right to demand respect for his private and family life. Privacy of individual and family life cannot be violated." Article 20 also prohibits the search or seizure of any individual, his private papers, or his belongings unless there exists a decision duly passed by a judge on the grounds such as national security or public order, and unless there exists an order of an agency authorized by law in cases where delay is deemed prejudicial.

Article 22 of the Constitution, as amended in October 2001, preserves the secrecy of communication and provides that "Communication shall not be impeded nor its secrecy be violated, unless there exists a decision duly passed by a judge in cases explicitly defined by law, and unless there exists an order of an agency authorized by law in cases where delay is deemed prejudicial."

Civil Code Article 24 states "an individual whose personal rights are unjustly violated may bring a civil action against such violation to prevent such violation and/or the compensation of damages arising from such violation."

Banking Law No. 5411, which entered into force on 1 November 2005, also provides a number of provisions dealing with the protection of personal data concerning the customers of banks.

Article 73 requires the directors, managers and other personnel of banks to keep personal information about their customers confidential. Under Article 159 of the Banking Law, violation of such requirement is subject to an imprisonment from 1 to 3 years as well as an administrative fine. In the case that such violation is made for the purposes of obtaining a benefit, the penalty shall be increased by one sixth.

The new Turkish Employment Law, which entered into force on 10 July 2003 and replaced the old Employment Law No. 1475, provides that the employer is obliged to use the personal data of its employees in accordance with the laws and the principle of good faith, and not to disclose any such personal data if the relevant employee has a reasonable benefit in the confidential treatment of such data.

Bank Cards and Credit Cards Law No. 5464, which entered into force on 1 March 2006, also includes certain provision aimed to protect the personal data of the bank cards and credits cards holders.

Pursuant to Article 23 of the Bank Cards and Credit Cards Law, member merchants/shops cannot use, store or copy the personal data regarding their customers, which they obtain during the utilization of credit cards or bank cards in their shop/work place, without written consent of the relevant customer. Card issuing institutions are also required to keep such information confidential other than the purposes of marketing their services. Article 39 of the Bank Cards and Credit Cards Law provides that violation of such requirements is subject to imprisonment from 1 to 3 years as well as an administrative fine.

The BDDK adopted the Information Technology Control Objectives for Basel II in October 2007 (ITGI, 2007b) which refers to the Control Objectives for Information and related Technology (CobiT) framework at the sub-domain level for controlling the operational risks, and to integrate and harmonize them in order to project an aggregated IT checklist for ORM. In the article, the control objectives in Information Control Models (ICMs) have been evaluated and mapped to the operational risk categories in Basel II which are defined as loss event types, rather than bridging the Basel II principles and CobiT principles, so that the ICMs can be compared against the Basel II requirements' fulfillment.

Turkey is a member of the Council of Europe and has signed the Council's Convention for the Protection of Individuals with Regard to Automatic Processing of Personal Data (ETS No. 108) in 1981.3 Turkey has not, however, ratified that Convention yet.

Under the National Program for the Harmonization of Turkish Legislation with European Union Law, the Turkish Government has committed to harmonize its legislation.

Accordingly, the Draft Law to mainly follow the Draft Law mainly follows the European Union Data Protection Directive No. 95/46/EC and the Commission Decision 2001/497/EC of 15 June 2001 on standard contractual clauses for the transfer of personal data to third party countries.

Alignment with the EU acquis on personal data protection was one of the short term priorities of the Turkish Government under the 2003 Accession Partnership Document published by the European Commission. The Draft Law was aimed to be enacted by December 2004 under the National Program of 2003, and the Personal Data Protection Authority was aimed to be established in 2005. However, neither the Draft Law has been enacted, nor the Personal Data Protection Authority has been established.

"Banking Regulation and Supervision Agency (BDDK) establishes COBIT as BIS II standard."

## Miscellaneous Information

Turkey is a member of the Council of Europe and has accepted the Council's monitoring mechanism.

## *United Kingdom*

Chief Privacy Officer/Minister: Information Commissioner, Data Protection Registrar—United Kingdom's Data Protection Registry
Political System: Constitutional monarchy
Web URL: http://www.open.gov.uk

## Legislation

Human Rights Act of October 2, 2000: In 1998, the Parliament approved the Human Rights Act that will incorporate the European Convention on Human Rights into domestic law, a process which will establish an enforceable right of privacy.

Data Protection Act of 1998: The legislation implements the requirements of the European Union's Data Protection Directive. It provides for limitations on the use of personal information, access to records, and requires that entities that maintain records register with the Data Protection Commissioner. It covers all manual and electronic records.

Employee Privacy Legislation: This outlines privacy-centric employment practices. It focuses on records management and limits employer monitoring at work.

Health and Social Care Bill (see Section 59 on the disclosure of Health Care information): Focuses on the privacy of patient data and doctor patient confidentiality.

Freedom of Information Act 2000: This act provides citizen access to public records not deemed threatening to national security or interests.

## Miscellaneous Information

The United Kingdom is a member of the Council of Europe and has signed and ratified the Convention for the Protection of Individuals with Regard to Automatic Processing of Personal Data (ETS No. 108) along with the European Convention for the Protection of Human Rights and Fundamental Freedoms. In addition to these commitments, the United Kingdom is a member of the Organization for Economic Cooperation and Development and has adopted the OECD Guidelines on the Protection of Privacy and Transborder Flows of Personal Data.

# Non-EU European Countries and Africa

The remainder of this chapter covers those countries that are not signatories to the Treaty of Maastricht but which by proximity or in the case of South Africa by membership in the Commonwealth of Nations in the Balfour Declaration at the Imperial Conference in 1926 and the Lomé Convention which provides economic advantage to 71 African nations including South Africa enjoy EU affiliate status.

## Iceland

Chief Privacy Officer/Minister: Icelandic Data Protection Commission (Datatilsynet)
Political System: Republic
Web URL: http://www.iceland.org

### Description of Legislation

Constitution: "Searching, seizure, and examination of letters and other papers as well as any breach of the secrecy to be observed in postal, telegraph, and telephone matters shall take place only under a judicial order."

The Act on Protection of Individuals with regard to the Processing of Personal Data: This act governs the processing of personal information and serves to ensure compliance with the EU Directive.

Law on Criminal Procedure: This law on wiretapping, tape recording, or photographing without consent requires a court order and must be limited to a short period of time. After the recording is complete, the target must be informed and the recordings must be destroyed after they are no longer needed.

The Freedom of Information Act of 1996 (Upplysingalog): This act governs the release of records. Under the act, individuals (including nonresidents) and legal entities have a legal right to documents.

### Miscellaneous Information

Iceland is not an EU member state, but has been granted associate status as a member of the Council of Europe and has signed and ratified the Convention for the Protection of Individuals with Regard to Automatic Processing of Personal Data (ETS No. 108) and has adopted the OECD Guidelines on the Protection of Privacy and Transborder Flows of Personal Data.

## Norway

Chief Privacy Officer/Minister: Datatilsynet—The Data Inspectorate
Political System: Constitutional monarchy
Web URL: http://www.datatilsynet.no

### Legislation

General Legal Protection of "Personality": The Norwegian Supreme Court has held that there exists in Norwegian law a general legal protection of "personality" that embraces a right to privacy.

The Personal Data Registers Act of 2000: It is designed to update Norwegian law and closely follows the EU Directive, even though Norway is not a member of the EU.

The Telecommunications Act: This act imposes a duty of confidentiality on telecommunications providers. However, Internet service providers must keep extensive logs of usage for 6 months to 1 year.

The Public Access to Documents in the (Public) Administration: This act provides for public access to government records.

Rules for the protection of personal data (Personal Data Protection Act): Aligned closely with the EU data protection act, this goes beyond the Directive, offering an even greater level of protection.

### Miscellaneous Information

Norway is a member of the Council of Europe. Norway is a party to the 1992 Agreement on the European Economic Area (EEA).

## Russia

Chief Privacy Officer/Minister
Political System: Republic
Web URL: http://www.government.gov.ru/english

## Description of Legislation

The Constitution of the Russian Federation: The constitution recognizes rights of privacy, data protection, and secrecy of communications.

Article 23: Everyone shall have the right to privacy of correspondence, telephone communications, mail, cables, and other communications.

Article 24: It shall be forbidden to gather, store, use and disseminate information on the private life of any person without his or her consent.

Russian Federation on Information, Informatization, and Information Protection of January 1995: The law covers the processing of personal information by the private and civil sector. Citizens and organizations have the right of access to the documented information about them, to correct it, and supplement it.

Law of the Russian Federation on Information, Informatization, and Information Protection also serves as a freedom of information law.

1995 Communications Act: The 1995 Communications Act protects secrecy of communications.

System for Operational Research Actions on the Documentary Telecommunication Networks (SORM-2): This requires Internet service providers to install surveillance devices and high-speed links to the FSB (Federal Security Service), which would allow the FSB direct access to the communications of Internet.

## Miscellaneous Information

The Russian law does not establish a central regulatory body for data protection. Responsibility for data protection rests with the data controllers.

## Switzerland

Chief Privacy Officer/Minister: Data Protection Commission—Data protection/privacy commission for Switzerland
Political System: Federal republic
Web URL: http://www.edsb.ch

## Description of Legislation

Article 36: "All persons have the right to receive respect for their private and family life, home, mail, and telecommunications. All persons have the right to be protected against abuse of their personal data."

The Federal Act of Data Protection of 1992: This act regulates personal information held by government and private bodies. The act requires that information be legally and fairly collected and places limits on its use and disclosure to third parties. Private companies must register if they regularly process sensitive data or transfer the data to third parties. Transfers to other nations must be registered, and the recipient nation must have equivalent laws. Individuals have a right of access to correct inaccurate information. Federal agencies must register their databases.

## Miscellaneous Information

In addition to the Data Protection Act, there are also legal protections for privacy in the Civil Code and Penal Code, and special rules relating to workers' privacy from surveillance, telecommunications information, health care statistics, and professional confidentiality, including medical and legal information, medical research, police files, and identity cards.

Switzerland is not an EU member state, but has been granted associate status and has adopted the OECD Guidelines on the Protection of Privacy and Transborder Flows of Personal Data.

## Ukraine

Chief Privacy Officer/Minister: State Committee of Communications and Computerization
Political System: Republic
Web URL: http://www.kmw.gov.ua

## Description of Legislation

The Constitution of Ukraine: The constitution guarantees the right of privacy and data protection.

Article 32 states, "No one shall be subject to interference in his or her personal and family life, except in cases envisaged by the Constitution of Ukraine. The collection, storage, use and dissemination of confidential information about a person without his or her consent shall not be permitted."

April 2000 Presidential Order: Adopts regulations on the protection of information in data-transmitting networks.

The 1992 Act on Information: This act provides a right of access to government records.

## South Africa

Chief Privacy Officer/Minister: Human Rights Commission
Political System: Republic
Web URL: http://www.gov.za

## Description of Legislation

Section 14 of the South African Constitution of 1996: Everyone has the right to privacy, which includes the right not to have their privacy of communications infringed upon.

Section 32: Everyone has the right of access to any information held by the state, and any information that is held by another person and that is required for the exercise or protection of any rights.

The Access to Information Act of February 2000: The bill covers both public and private sector entities and allows for access, rights of correction, and limitations on disclosure of information.

The Interception and Monitoring Act of 1992: This act regulates the interception of communications.

King II (South Africa Corporate Governance for South Africa): King II focuses on good corporate governance and operational transparency. Whereas King I advocated an integrated approach to the good governance in the interests of a wide range of stakeholders, King II addresses issues such as financial risk and audit.

Electronic Communications and Transactions Bill and Promotion of Access to Information Act No. 2 of 2000: The main purpose of the act is to facilitate E-commerce by creating legal certainty and promoting trust and confidence in electronic transactions. It provides for functional equivalence of electronic documents, recognition of contracts, digital signatures, electronic filing, and evidence.

International privacy issues: South Africa does not have a privacy commission, but has a Human Rights Commission that was established under Chapter 9 of the constitution.

## Summary

The European Economic Community came into being following the signing of the Treaty of Rome in 1957. These members were France, West Germany, Italy, Belgium, the Netherlands, and Luxembourg. The United Kingdom joined in 1972 with the passing of the European Communities Act, together with Denmark and the Irish Republic. In 1981, Greece joined; in 1986, Spain and Portugal, and in 1995, Sweden, Austria, and Finland, to make a current European Union of 15 members. An important development came in 1986 with the signing by the then 12 of the Single European Act (SEA). The aim of the SEA was to eliminate the remaining barriers to the single internal market within the deadline of December 31, 1992. The establishment of the "Four Freedoms," i.e., a free movement of goods, persons, services, and capital, was achieved.

With regard to regulatory compliance, EU accession countries have to comply with a wide range of EU legislation. The need to change their business models, contracts, and systems to comply with competition law, employment law, and laws covering consumer protection, intellectual property, and data protection has largely been dealt with by the individual governments' adoption of the acquis communautaire, the body of EU law contained in EC directives. Adoption of the acquis was a necessary precondition of qualification for entry. This insures the impacts of Markets in Financial Instruments Directive (MiFID) and EC 8th Directive on Company Law and Corporate Governance are certain not to be the last legislation passed in the financial service sector.

# Chapter 18

## Latin America

This chapter examines international business activity in Latin America, from Mexico in the north to Argentina and Chile in the south. The structure of this chapter follows a fairly standard format of examining first the legal business drivers in which international business takes place in Latin America, followed by legal analysis by country and, to a limited extent, by industry sector, and by issue. The overarching goal is to identify and clarify the legal drivers that are central to international business in Latin America at the start of the twenty-first century. Today, Latin America is the fourth largest region in the world in measures of international business, trailing the United States and Canada, the European Union (EU), and East Asia. International trade of Latin American countries amounted to over $300 billion in 1998, and incoming foreign direct investment was over $70 billion in 1998, trailing the United States and Canada, the European Union, and East Asia. Latin America with its oil wealth, population, and ecology is emerging as a growing international player, and proper regulatory governance is the key to capitalizing on those assets.

### Argentina

Chief Privacy Officer/Minister: National Directorate for the Protection of Personal Data
Political system: Federal republic
Web URL: http://www.argentina.gov.ar

#### *Legislation*

Articles 18 and 19 of the Argentine constitution provide (in part), "The home is inviolable as is personal correspondence and private papers; the law will determine what cases and what justifications may be relevant to their search or confiscation. The private actions of men that in no way offend order nor public morals, or prejudice a third party, are reserved only to God's judgment, and are free from judicial authority. No inhabitant of the nation will be obligated to do that which is not required by law, nor be deprived of what is not prohibited." Article 43, enacted in 1994, provides a right of "habeas data" [537]: "Every person may file an action to obtain knowledge of the content and purpose of all the data pertaining to him or her contained in public records or databanks, or in private ones whose purpose is to provide reports; and in the case of falsehood of information or its use for discriminatory purposes, a person will be able to demand the deletion, correction, confidentiality or update of the data contained in the above records. The secrecy of journalistic information sources may not be affected."

The Personal Data Protection Law (PDLP) No. 25,326 went into effect in April 2001. It is the strongest privacy law in South America, covering all private and publicly held personal data, mandating that all data collectors register with the government, and prohibiting the transfer of personal data to countries that lack adequate levels of data protection. In general, the law, adopted on the EU model, distinguishes between "personal data" and "sensitive data" and provides different treatment, depending upon the classification of the data. *Sensitive data* is defined as data that reveals ethnic and racial origin, political opinions, religion, moral or philosophical opinions, and health and sexual preference information. All other information is defined by implication as *personal data*. Argentine data protection rules cover personal data recorded in datafiles, registers, databanks, or other technical means that are public, as well as those that are private whose purpose is to provide reports. This includes those the purpose of which is more than exclusively personal, and those that are intended for the assignment or transfer of personal data. Collection of sensitive data is given additional protections and is prohibited unless authorized by law. With respect to personal data, the transfer of such information is only permitted when the assignment is necessary to further a legitimate interest of the assignor or the assignee and with the express prior consent of the assignee. The Data Privacy Decree also prohibits the transfer of personal data to countries that do not provide adequate levels of privacy protection.

Decree 1570-2001 (the Exchange Control Decree) limits the amount of money that may be withdrawn from an Argentine bank or sent abroad. The Exchange Control Decree was prompted by a run on Argentine banks, which had caused nearly 20 percent of the total bank deposits to leave the country. The Exchange Control Decree restricts individuals or legal entities from withdrawing more than $1000 per month from their bank accounts. In addition, checks in excess of $250 may not be cashed, but may only be deposited in Argentine bank accounts. In addition, individuals are not allowed to leave the country with more than $1000 in cash, and the transfer of money abroad is prohibited with the exception of import or export sales.

The Argentina Civil Code prohibits the transfer of data "which arbitrarily interferes in another person's life: publishing photos, divulging correspondence, mortifying another's customs or sentiments or disturbing his privacy by whatever means." This article has been applied to protect the privacy of the home, private letters, and several situations involving intrusive telephone calls and neighbor's intrusions into one's private life.

The Credit Card Act regulates credit card contracts between consumers and financial institutions, specifically the interest rates that banks charge to consumer credit cards. Article 53 restricts the possibility of transferring information from banks or credit card companies to credit reporting agencies. There is a specific right of access to personal data of a financial character. Under Article 8.1 of the regulation, the data subject (a client of a bank) has a right of access to the information and to know the reason why he or she was included in its databases.

City of Buenos Aires Privacy Law gives all persons the right to ask for and receive information held by the local authorities and creates a right of judicial review. Individuals have the right under habeas data to update, rectify, maintain the confidentiality of, or suppress information about themselves.

## *Miscellaneous Information*

The EU decided that Argentina could be considered as providing an adequate level of protection for personal data, meeting the requirements of the EU data protection directive. The adequacy finding implies that all transborder data flows between Argentina and the EU are presumptively considered in compliance with the EU directive. Argentina is the first country in Latin America to obtain such adequacy approval.

On May 2003, government documents obtained by the Electronic Privacy Information Center revealed that ChoicePoint, a U.S. company, had entered into a contract with the U.S. Government to provide international data from public registries obtained from Argentina, Brazil, Colombia, Costa Rica, and Mexico. The transfer of personal information abroad is a matter of much concern to the governments of those countries, as these countries have strict data protection laws (e.g., Argentina) or are about to enact data protection bills (e.g., Colombia, Costa Rica, and Mexico).

# Brazil

Chief Privacy Officer/Minister: N/A
Political System: Federal republic
Web URL: http:// www.brazilsf.org/gov.htm

## *Description of Legislation*

Brazil was the first country in Latin America to introduce habeas data into its constitution of 1988. Article 5, section LXXII states that habeas data will be granted: (1) to assure the knowledge of information related to the person of the plaintiff that consist in registrations or databases of government entities or of public character and (2) for the rectification of data, when it is not preferred to make it for secret, judicial, or administrative procedure.

Article 5 of the 1988 constitution of Brazil provides, in part, the following:

"The privacy, private life, honor and image of persons are inviolable, and the right to compensation for property or moral damages resulting from the violation thereof is ensured."

"The home is the inviolable asylum of the individual, and no one may enter it without the dweller's consent, save in the case of 'in flagrante delicto' or disaster, or to give help, or, during the day, by court order."

"The secrecy of correspondence and of telegraphic, data and telephone communications is inviolable, except, in the latter case, by court order, in the events and in the manner established by the law for purposes of criminal investigation or criminal procedural discovery."

"Access to information is ensured to everyone and confidentiality of the source is protected whenever necessary for the professional activity."

The 1990 Code of Consumer Protection and Defense: Allows all consumers to access information derived from personal and consumer data stores in files, archives, registries, and databases, as well as their respective sources. Consumer files and data shall be objective, clear, true, and written in a manner easily understood, and shall not contain derogatory information for a period over five years.

Senate Bill No. 61: Implements EU-style rules on consent, notification, access, registration, and security. As currently written, however, its rules on cross-border transmission of personal data appear to be significantly weaker than the EU directive's.

Informatics Law of 1984: Protects the confidentiality of stored, processed, and disclosed data, and the privacy and security of physical, legal, public, and private entities. Citizens are entitled to access and correct their personal information in private or public databases.

Wiretapping Law: In 1996, a law regulating wiretapping was enacted. Official wiretaps are permitted for 15 days, renewable on a judge's order for another 15 days, and can only be resorted to when police suspect serious crimes punishable by imprisonment, such as drug smuggling, corruption, contraband smuggling, murder, and kidnapping.

Computer Crimes Act of July 2000: This act amends a 1940 law to update it to include computer crimes descriptions and penalties for such crimes.

Bill 3494/2000: Bill for the structuring and use of databases regarding third parties and regulating the procedural right of habeas data.

Projeto de Lei da Camara no. 6981/2002: Establishes rules for the protection of personal data.

Projeto de Lei da Camara no. 6541/2002: Includes a new crime in the Criminal Code—the publication and commercialization of addresses and personal data without due consent.

Projeto de Lei do Senado 2000, Article 1, §1, 2 (on cyber-crimes): It states that undue use or publication of one's personal data without consent may lead to imprisonment, from one to six months, and fine.

Projeto de Lei da Camara no. 3356/2000: Focuses on data protection and the relation between Internet users and providers.

Projeto de Lei da Camara no. 3360/2000: It also deals with data protection and the relation between Internet users and providers.

Projeto de Lei da Camara no. 3494/2000: It establishes the structure and use of personal databases and regulates habeas data.

Projeto de Lei da Camara no. 1682/99: It defines the violation of electronic communication as crime.

Projeto de Lei da Camara no. 84/99: It determines computer crimes and sanctions (privacy violation liable to imprisonment, from one to six months).

Federal Senate Bill no. 61, 1996: It promotes the privacy of personal data in conformance to the Organization for Economic Cooperation and Development (OECD) guidelines to affect both public and private sector databases.

Projeto de Lei da Camara no. 4102/93: It regulates the constitutional right to data protection and defines computer crimes.

## Miscellaneous Information

Brazil signed the American Convention on Human Rights on September 25, 1992.

Individuals have a constitutional right of habeas data, which has been adopted into law to access information about them held by public agencies.

# Chile

Chief Privacy Officer/Minister: N/A
Political System: Republic
Web URL: http://www.gobiernodechile.cl/

## *Legislation*

Article 19 of Chile's constitution: Secures for all persons "Respect and protection for public and private life, the honor of a person and his family. The inviolability of the home and of all forms of private communication. The home may be invaded and private communications and documents intercepted, opened, or inspected only in cases and manners determined by law."

Act No. 19628, Law for the Protection of Private Life of October 28, 1999: This law has 24 articles covering processing and use of personal data in the public and private sector, and the rights of individuals to access, correction, and judicial control. The law contains a chapter dedicated to the use of financial, commercial, and banking data, and specific rules addressing the use of information by government agencies.

Spam and unsolicited commercial communications Consumer Protection Law (No. 19.955): This law is the first regulation that addresses some of the problems related to spam and unsolicited commercial communications. The law establishes an opt-out system and provides that any electronic commercial e-mail must indicate the name of the sender, the precise description of what is advertised, and a valid address where the consumer can send a message to avoid any future e-mail (Article 28B). The same provisions are applicable to advertisements coming via regular mail, fax, or telephone. These communications must indicate an easy mechanism to avoid similar distribution in future.

Chile–EU Trade Agreement Article 30: This agreement establishes a political and economic association between Chile and the EU. The parties agree to cooperate on the protection of personal data to improve the level of protection and avoid obstacles to trade that requires transfers of personal data. Cooperation on personal data protection may include technical assistance in the form of exchange of information and experts, and the establishment of joint programs.

## *Miscellaneous Information*

Chile signed the American Convention on Human Rights on August 20, 1990. There is no data protection authority, and each affected person does enforcement of the law individually.

# Colombia

Chief Privacy Officer/Minister: NA
Political system: Federal republic
Web URL: http://www.presidencia.gov.co

## *Legislation*

Medical records: Medical Records Law No. 23 addresses the privacy of patient data; no enforcement mechanism exists.

Statutory Law No. 139/2004 (August 31, 2004) This statute addresses the constitutional right of habeas data; no enforcement exists.

# Ecuador

Chief Privacy Officer/Minister: President
Political system: Federal republic
Web URL: http://www.presidencia.gov.ec/

## *Legislation*

Data Protection Bill (2006): The present law intends to guarantee and protect the personal data based in archives, registries, data banks, or other usual techniques of data processing, as much public as prevailed, to "guarantee the right to the honor and the privacy of the people, as well as the access to the information that on the same ones is registered, of conformity to the established thing in the political Constitution of the Republic of Ecuador Personal data that affect the personal or familiar right to privacy quality of the data."

Article 4—Quality of data: The data of a personal character gathered must be adapted to, as well as pertinent and nonexcessive in relation to the scope and intended purposes, and should not be used for aims incompatible with those for which the data had been gathered. The quality of data must conform to the following:

Those parties requesting information about their personal data will have the right of notification in an express, precise, and unequivocal way.

Article 7—Consent of the holder: The treatment of data of a personal character will require the free, express, and unequivocal consent of the holder of the personal data, unless forbidden by law.

Transparency and Access to Information Law of 2004 declares that the right of access to information is guaranteed by the state.

## *Miscellaneous Information*

The Government of Ecuador has formulated consumer protection legislation in anticipation of transborder E-commerce. In addition, the government has established special departments and offices for consumer protection, consumer education, information, and complaints handling. An informal communications network exists among the organizations of the region dedicated to consumer protection and encourages the creation, development, and use of national and international data banks. Electronic trade is in its infancy in Ecuador, and it is yet unclear what transborder data flow problems and concerns will emerge as connectivity and access spread across the country.

# Mexico

Chief Privacy Officer/Minister: N/A
Political system: Federal republic
Web URL: http://www.presidencia.gob.mx

## Description of Legislation

Article 16 of the 1917 Mexican Constitution: "One's person, family, home, papers or possessions may not be molested, except by virtue of a written order by a proper authority, based on and motivated by legal proceedings. The administrative authority may make home visits only to certify compliance with sanitary and police rules; the presentation of books and papers indispensable to verify compliance with the fiscal laws may be required in compliance with the respective laws and the formalities prescribed for their inspection. Correspondence, under the protective circle of the mail, will be free from all inspection, and its violation will be punishable by law."

Mexican E-Commerce Act of June 7, 2000: The law amends the Civil Code, the Commercial Code, the Rules of Civil Procedure, and the Consumer Protection Act. It covers consumer protection, privacy, and digital signatures and electronic documents. It includes a new article in the Federal Consumer Protection Act giving authority to the government "to provide for the effective protection of the consumer in electronic transactions or concluded by any other means, and the adequate use of the data provided by the consumer." The E-Commerce Act of 2000 includes some provisions related to privacy, including a provision that prohibits the processing of personal data without consumer consent. In September 2001, however, an EU-style privacy law was proposed in the Mexican Congress, which outlines a national privacy regime modeled largely on the EU data protection directive.

Article 6 (data protection): The law mandates the establishment of a national data protection authority as well as rules on sensitive data, notification, access, third-party and international data transfer, data verification, and minimum-security levels for personal data records. Additionally, under Article 6 of the proposed law, the treatment of data of a personal nature (which covers any personally identifiable data, including photographic and acoustical information) requires express consent from the affected party. The proposed law encompasses both electronic and manual data treatment, and applies equally to public and private bodies.

Article 1 chapter VIII: To coordinate the use of code of ethics by providers, including the principles of this law. The statute also creates a new chapter on consumer law titled: "Rights of Consumers in Electronic Transactions and Transactions by Any Other Means."

Article 76: This article applies to the dealings between providers and consumers in transactions effected by electronic means. The following principles must be observed:

a. Providers shall use information provided by consumers in a confidential manner, and shall not be able to transfer it to third parties, unless there is express consent from the consumer or a requirement from a public authority.
b. Providers must use technical measures to provide security and confidentiality to the information submitted by the consumer, and notify the consumer, before the transaction, of the characteristics of the system.
c. Providers must respect consumer decisions not to receive commercial solicitations.

Chapter 6 of Mexico's Postal Code: The postal code recognizes the inviolability of correspondence and guarantees the privacy of correspondence.

The 1939 General Communicator Law: Provides penalties for interrupting communications and divulging secrets.

The Law against Organized Crime effective from November 1996: This law allows for electronic surveillance with a judicial order. The law prohibits electronic surveillance in cases of electoral, civil, commercial, labor, or administrative matters and expands protection against unauthorized surveillance to cover all private means of communications, not merely telephone calls.

## Miscellaneous Information

Mexico is a member of the Organization for Economic Cooperation and Development, but does not appear to have adopted the OECD Guidelines on the Protection of Privacy and Transborder Flows of Personal Data. Mexico has also signed the American Convention on Human Rights.

# Paraguay

Chief Privacy Officer/Minister: N/A
Political system: Republic
Web URL: http://www.paraguaygobierno.gov.py

## Description of Legislation

Data Protection Act of December 28, 2000: Processing of sensitive information is not permitted, and information about economic status requires prior written approval of the individual. The courts can apply fines and sanctions.

# Peru

Chief Privacy Officer/Minister: N/A
Political system: Republic
Web URL: http://www.rcp.net.pe

## Legislation

The 1993 Constitution sets out extensive privacy, data protection, and freedom of information rights.

Article 2 states, "Every person has the right: To solicit information that one needs without disclosing the reason, and to receive that information from any public entity within the period specified by law, at a reasonable cost. Information that affects personal intimacy and that is expressly excluded by law or for reasons of national security is not subject to disclosure. Secret bank information or tax information can be accessed by judicial order, the National Prosecutor, or a Congressional investigative commission, in accordance with law and only insofar as it relates to a case under investigation.

V. To be assured that information services, whether computerized or not, public or private, do not provide information that affects personal and family intimacy.

VI. To honor and good reputation, to personal and family intimacy, both as to voice and image. Every person affected by untrue or inexact statements or aggrieved by any medium of social communication has the right to free, immediate and proportional rectification, without prejudice to responsibilities imposed by law.

IX. To secrecy and the inviolability of communications and private documents. Communications, telecommunications or instruments of communication may be opened, seized, intercepted or inspected only under judicial authorization and with the protections specified by law. All matters unconnected with the fact that motivates the examination are to be guarded from disclosure. Private documents obtained in violation of this precept have no legal effect. Books, ledgers, and accounting and administrative documents are subject to inspection or investigation by the competent authority in conformity with law. Actions taken in this respect may not include withdrawal or seizure, except by judicial order."

Freedom of information is constitutionally protected under the right of habeas data.

Penal Code: Article 154 of the Penal Code states that "a person who violates personal or family privacy, whether by watching, listening to or recording an act, a word, a piece of writing or an image using technical instruments or processes and other means, shall be punished with imprisonment for not more than two years."

Penal Code: Article 151 of the Penal Code states "that a person who unlawfully opens a letter, document, telegram, radio telegram, telephone message or other document of a similar nature that is not addressed to him, or unlawfully takes possession of any such document even if it is open, shall be liable to imprisonment of not more than 2 years and less than 60 to 90 days."

Telecommunications and Wiretapping Law of July 12, 2001: Gives government sweeping powers to monitor private telephone calls. The State through Osiptel (Peru's largest telephone provider) can identify both parties on the call and the location of both parties.

Law against Spam, law 24,893 passed 2004: The antispam law of 2004 makes the unauthorized distribution of commercial e-mail a civil crime subject to financial and criminal sanctions.

## Miscellaneous Information

Peru signed the American Convention on Human Rights on July 28, 1978, but withdrew from the jurisdiction of the American Court of Human Rights in July 1999.

# Uruguay

Chief Privacy Officer/Minister: NA
Political system: Federal republic
Web URL: http://www.parlamento.gub.uy

## Legislation

Transparency and Access to Information Law of 2004 declares that the right of access to information is guaranteed by the State.

Article 72 of the Constitution, which provides: "The enumeration of rights, duties, and protections established in the Constitution, does not exclude other rights which are inherent to the human personality or are derived from the republican form of government."

Article 28 protects individuals' documents and correspondence of any nature (letters, telegraphic, or telephone communications) from all sorts of interception, unless those procedures are performed in compliance with applicable laws. When referring to telephone communications, some scholars have interpreted that such a rule does not only guarantee the inviolability of the content of the conversation but also of the records containing the list of calls made and received by a particular person.

Article 296 of the Penal Code guarantees the privacy of correspondence, establishing that whoever opens an envelope containing a letter (that is not directed to that person) with the intent of learning about its content is guilty of a felony. Article 298 of the Code also punishes the disclosure of information obtained by any means similar to those referred to in Article 296. Article 297 punishes the interception of telephone or telegraphic communications.

The Uruguayan Tax Code (Decree Law No. 14.306) and Banking Law No. 15.322 also regulate privacy and confidentiality in their respective areas. Acts 16.790 and 16.713 that protect the confidentiality of job history and other labor records replaced Act 14.306.

Law No. 16.616, enacted on October 20, 1994, regulates the national statistical system. It establishes that the individual information obtained must be treated with the utmost confidentiality, and that a link should exist between the data requested and the objectives of the statistics or census.

Law No. 16.011, which regulates the writ of relief, offers a procedural base to articulate the habeas data.

Decree No. 396/003 regulates processing of personal data in public and private healthcare sectors.

Article 694 of Law No. 16.736 establishes freedom of information at the governmental level and establishes the petitioner's right to amend or rectify erroneous or inaccurate information.

Processing of personal data in public and private healthcare sectors—Decree No. 396/003.

Law no. 17.838 of 2004 (September 24, 2004)—Regulation of commercial personal information and habeas data action.

Law 17,984—Database of the central bank with information about debtors (2006).

## Venezuela

Chief Privacy Officer/Minister: NA
Political system: Federal republic
Web URL: http://www.venezuela.gov.ve/

### Legislation

Data Protection and Habeas Data Law for Venezuela passed in 2004: The privacy, private life, honor, and image of persons are inviolable. There is a specific right of access to personal data as well as rules on sensitive data, notification, access, third-party and international data transfer, and data verification.

## Summary

Periods of crisis are fertile ground for the development of reform proposals, both at the national and international level. In the midst of economic disruption and social pain, it is only natural that policymakers, members of multilateral organizations, academics, and representatives from the private sector reexamine what went wrong and what could be done to prevent the emergence of future crises.

Latin America exemplifies this process. The region has spawned numerous reforms, some that have worked well and others that have not. However, in most cases of success, the solution involved actions from both national authorities and the international community. The debt crisis of the early 1980s, perhaps the deepest and most costly for the region in recent times, took a number of attempts at resolution until, finally, the implementation of the Brady Plan laid the groundwork for recovery. At the domestic level, exchange-rate-based stabilization programs proved to be the effective remedy for containing hyperinflation.

However, when the next crisis, the so-called tequila crisis, erupted at the end of 1994, the sustainability of fixed exchange rate regimes began to be questioned, and Mexico opted for a flexible exchange rate. Because the connection between banking and exchange rate crises was identified, an overhaul of the regulatory and supervisory framework of domestic financial institutions was commonly agreed on as a needed reform. Five factors affect the long-term governance and compliance efforts of all companies within Latin America:

1. The government/business relationship and its great significance in Latin America relative to that in the United States. The reform of the government sector and the institutionalization of democracy have greatly affected the governance environment in Latin America. Likewise, the relationship of these countries to the United States is the key to international business in the region.
2. The impact of subregional integration schemes on competition in the region, including that between local and multinational firms. The future of Latin America will depend on what kind of regional economic integration can best support economic development.
3. Financial flows into the region and policies to avoid financial crises. Financial flows have been dominated by foreign direct investment in the 1990s, but this has not precluded recurring episodes of financial crisis in the region.
4. The entry and operation of foreign multinationals, and the reaction of local firms to the onslaught of multinational corporations from the United States, Europe, and elsewhere. At the same time, local firms are expanding internationally, demonstrating new capabilities that enable these firms to compete.
5. The relation of the informal economy to international business in the region. This part of the economy, constituting easily more than 1/3 of the total economy in many countries, poses the greatest challenge to corporate governance to the international business conducted there.

## Chapter 19

# North America

## North American Payment Card Industry—Visa, Mastercard, American Express, Discover, and JCL

Visa USA instituted the CISP, first mandated in June 2001. The program is intended to protect Visa cardholder data, no matter where it resides. The idea is to ensure that cardholders, merchants, and service providers maintain the highest information security standards. CISP compliance is required of all merchants and service providers that store, process, or transmit Visa cardholder data. The program applies to all payment channels, including retail (brick-and-mortar), mail/telephone order, and E-commerce.

The MasterCard SDP Program is a proactive, global solution offered by MasterCard through its acquiring members. The program provides acquiring members the ability to deploy security compliance programs, assisting online merchants and member service providers to better protect against hacker intrusions and account data compromises. The program takes a proactive approach to security by identifying common possible vulnerabilities in a merchant Web site and makes recommendations for short- and long-term security improvements. The solution addresses the security issues that online merchants and their acquiring banks face in the virtual world and concerns arising from these issues, such as Internet fraud, chargebacks, brand image damage, consumer information safety and privacy, and the cost of replacing stolen account numbers.

To achieve compliance, merchants and service providers must adhere to the Payment Card Industry (PCI) Data Security Standard, which offers a single approach to safeguarding sensitive data for all card brands. This standard is a result of the collaboration between Visa and MasterCard and is designed to create common industry security requirements. Using the PCI Data Security Standard as the framework, the Visa and MasterCard security programs provide the tools and measurements needed to protect against cardholder data exposure and compromise.

MasterCard's Site Data Protection Plan and Visa's Cardholder Information Security Program are parallel in design. Both stipulate separate compliance validation requirements for merchants and service providers, which vary depending on the size of the company. Compliance levels are defined based on annual transaction volume and corresponding risk exposure.

The requirements are the following:

Build and maintain a secure network
> Requirement 1: Install and maintain a firewall configuration to protect cardholder data.
> Requirement 2: Do not use vendor-supplied defaults for system passwords and other security parameters.

Protect cardholder data
> Requirement 3: Protect stored cardholder data.
> Requirement 4: Encrypt transmission of cardholder data across open, public networks.

Maintain a vulnerability management program
> Requirement 5: Use and regularly update anti-virus software.
> Requirement 6: Develop and maintain secure systems and applications.

Implement strong access control measures
> Requirement 7: Restrict access to cardholder data by business need-to-know.
> Requirement 8: Assign a unique ID to each person with computer access.
> Requirement 9: Restrict physical access to cardholder data.

Regularly monitor and test networks
> Requirement 10: Track and monitor all access to network resources and cardholder data.
> Requirement 11: Regularly test security systems and processes.

Maintain an information security policy
> Requirement 12: Maintain a policy that addresses information security.

Participating companies can be barred from processing credit card transactions and higher processing fees can be applied; and in the event of a serious security breach, fines of up to $500,000 can be levied for each instance of noncompliance.

Acquirers are responsible for ensuring that all of their merchants comply with the PCI Data Security Standard requirements; however, merchant compliance validation has been prioritized based on the volume of transactions, the potential risk, and exposure introduced into the payment system.

All merchants fall into one of the four merchant levels based on transaction volume over a 12-month period. Transaction volume is based on the aggregate number of card transactions. Of note is a safe harbor rule version 1.1 of the PCI compliance standard, which states that MasterCard and Visa will fully exempt acquirers from data security-related noncompliance assessments, investigative costs, and issuer reimbursement costs if the compromised entity is found to have been compliant with the Payment Card Industry (PCI) Data Security Standard at the time of the compromise, and was registered as compliant at the time of the compromise. Oracle Direct currently holds the status of PCI 1.1 compliant.

# United States

In the wake of 9/11, national security has been at the top of everyone's list. North Americans have seen the U.S. government take actions in the hope of preventing such an event from occurring again. These actions include the implementation of new security measures at airports, new legislation to allow easier investigation and identification of terrorist activities, and the call for the use of new technologies to aid in this fight against those who would harm the United States and its way of life. The sweeping, and hopefully not rash, legislation and technologies that have been proposed and in some instances implemented are The Patriot Act, the use of Echelon and Carnivore (government surveillance systems), biometric technology such as face recognition systems, and the use of national ID cards for all citizens. Each of these items has a set of issues and concerns that may affect personal privacy in the name of national security. In this chapter we will discuss each of these items, what it is, how it works, and its implications for privacy in the short and long term.

## United States: Government and Public Sector

ITAR—The ITAR regulation specifically refers to military and military-related information. It states that military information systems and data may only be serviced by U.S. citizens; this applies to all DoD agencies as well as contractors, who have two choices: hire only U.S. citizens for the positions in question or prevent non-U.S. citizens from seeing the data. The latter can be accomplished with Oracle technology (e.g., Database Vault), though the possibility of system administrators (root) reading database files directly, and network admins viewing data transmitted in cleartext, still exist. These vulnerabilities can be eliminated with the Advanced Security Option to encrypt data on the network, and Transparent Data Encryption (included in ASO) to encrypt sensitive data on disk. Often, firms with these kind of requirements are handling some form of classified data, and require that the users can only read/write specific rows. This requirement is met by Oracle Label Security.

Title 21 Code of Federal Regulations (21 CFR Part 11) Electronic Records; Electronic Signatures (also known as A Risk-Based Approach to Pharmaceutical Current Good Manufacturing Practices (cGMP) for the 21st century)—The Food and Drug Administration (FDA) has issued regulations that provide criteria for acceptance by FDA, under certain circumstances, of electronic records, electronic signatures, and handwritten signatures executed to electronic records as equivalent to paper records and handwritten signatures executed on paper. These regulations, which apply to all FDA program areas, are intended to permit the widest possible use of electronic technology, compatible with FDA's responsibility to promote and protect public health.

12 CFR Part 30—Requirement for a written safety and soundness compliance plan pursuant to Appendix B, titled "Interagency Guidelines Establishing Standards For Safeguarding Customer Information." This federal regulation mandates secure access control, financial transparency, and secure record retention for all financial services insured by or doing business with the U.S. federal government.

Accessibility of DoD Web sites to people with disabilities—All federal public Web sites comply with the requirements of Section 508 of the Rehabilitation Act (29 U.S.C. 794d), designed to make online information and services fully available to individuals with disabilities. Organizations should review Section 508 and accompanying guidance to ensure that their public Web sites meet the requirements.

Audit Report D-2001-130—Governs activity on collecting, creating, sharing, and reviewing personally identifiable information about individuals and their viewing habits at Government Web sites. This report implements Section 646 of the Treasury and General Government Appropriations Act 2001. As contained in Public Law 106-554, the Consolidated Appropriations Act requires the Inspector General of each government department to submit a report to Congress that discloses the agency's activity on collecting or reviewing singular data, or the creation of aggregate lists that include personally identifying information, about individuals who access the

Department's Internet Web sites. This report also implements Management and Budget (OMB) Memorandum M99-18. The memorandum governs privacy policies on federal Web sites and directs agencies to post clear privacy policies on Web sites and on any Web page where substantial personal information is collected from the public. The policy states that if an agency collects information, it must disclose the information collected and why and how it will be used.

CJCSI 6212.01C: Interoperability and Supportability of Information Technology and National Security Systems—This mandate issued by the chairman of the joint chiefs of staff establishes policies and procedures for the J-6 interoperability requirements and supportability certification and validation of Joint Capabilities Integration and Development Systems. This mandate implements the Clinger–Cohen Act covering Net-Centric Operations and Warfare (NCOW), Global Information Grid (GIG), and Key Interface Profiles.

CJCSI 6510.01—This mandate issued by the chairman of the joint chiefs of staff provides joint policy and guidance for information assurance (IA) and computer network defense (CND) operations in accordance with (IAW) references and assesses those measures that protect and defend information and information systems by ensuring availability integrity, authentication, confidentiality, and non-repudiation. This includes providing for restoration of information systems by incorporating protection, detection, and reaction.

CJCSM 3150.07A—This defines the Global Information Grid and provides the Joint Staff, military services, combatant commands, and other addressees pertinent summary information on the global communications events that have occurred. It also provides the Joint Staff, combatant commands, services, and other designated addressees pertinent information concerning conditions that impose serious degradation of communications operations within the transport layer of the grid.

CJCSM 6510.0: Defense-in-Depth: IA and Computer Network Defense (CND)—Integrates an organized, manned, equipped, and trained workforce to guard and secure information and information systems by providing the security services/attributes of availability, authentication, confidentiality, integrity, and non-repudiation. IA processes function to protect and defend against unauthorized activity. IA incorporates protection, detection, response, restoration and reaction capabilities, and processes to shield and preserve information and information systems.

Computer Security Enhancement Act of 2001 (HR1259)—This act amends the National Institute of Standards and Technology Act and requires the institute to develop uniform standards for the cost-effective security and privacy of sensitive information in federal systems.

Government Network Security Act 2003—This act (H.R. 3159) requires that federal agencies protect their computers and networks from the security risks posed by peer-to-peer file sharing.

Computer Fraud and Abuse Act (CFAA)—The act established two new felony offenses for the unauthorized access of "federal interest" computers and a misdemeanor for unauthorized trafficking in computer passwords. The act enhanced and strengthened an intermediate Fraud and Abuse Act established in 1984. It also complemented the Electronic Communications Privacy Act of 1986, which outlawed the unauthorized interception of digital communications.

One of the felony offenses established addresses the unauthorized access of a federal-interest computer with the intention to commit fraudulent theft. The other felony was established to address "malicious damage," which involves altering information in, or preventing the use of, a federal-interest computer. A malicious damage violation would have to result in a loss to the victim of $1000 or more, except in cases involving the alteration of medical records.

The legislation was designed to address only federal and interstate computer crimes because of concern that the act could infringe on individual states' rights and computer crime laws. A federal-interest computer is defined as "one exclusively for the use of a financial institution or the U.S. government, or, in the case of a computer not exclusively for such use, used by or for a financial institution or the U.S. government, and the conduct constituting the offense affects such use, or which is one of two or more computers used in committing the offense, not all of which are located in the same State." Financial institutions covered by the act specifically include federally insured banks, thrifts, and credit unions; registered securities brokers; and members of the Federal Home Loan Bank System, the Farm Credit Administration, and the Federal Reserve System. A felony conviction under the Computer Fraud and Abuse Act could result in a prison term of 5 years for a first offense and 10 years for a second offense.

The act established as a federal misdemeanor trafficking in computer passwords with the intent to commit fraud that affects interstate commerce.

The Computer Security Act of 1987 was enacted to mandate that federal agencies such as the Federal Reserve and the Treasury Department take extra measures to prevent unauthorized access to computers holding sensitive information. The Computer Abuse Amendments Act of 1994 expanded the 1986 act to address the transmission of viruses and other harmful code. The Patriot Act of 2001 also amended the CFAA.

DCID 6/3—In 1999, the DoD established new guidance for information systems with the Director of Central Intelligence Directive (DCID) 6/3 [DCID 6/3]. DCID 6/3 specified requirements for ensuring adequate protection of certain categories of intelligence information that is stored or processed on an information system. The DCID 6/3 focused on the same core objectives stated in NISPOM and BS 7799: protecting the confidentiality of information, protecting data integrity, and protecting data availability.

DISA Instruction 630-225-7: Web Policies and Products, Internet, Intranet, and World Wide Web Policy—This provides the technical security policies and requirements for providing a secure remote access environment to users in Department of Defense (DOD) components.

DoD Directive 8320.2: Data sharing in a Net-Centric Department of Defense—This establishes policies and responsibilities to implement data sharing. It directs the use of resources to implement data sharing among information capabilities, services, processes, and personnel interconnected within the Global Information Grid (GIG), as defined in DoD Directive 8100.1.

DoD Directive 8500.1: Information Assurance—This establishes policy and assigns responsibilities under reference to achieve Department of Defense (DoD) IA through a defense-in-depth approach that integrates the capabilities of personnel, operations, and technology, and supports the evolution to network-centric warfare.

DoD Global Information Grid Architecture (V 2.0) Management Plan: Global Information Grid Architecture (V 2.0) Management Plan—This plan establishes DoD computing policy and responsibilities under reference to enable the secure storage, processing, exchange, and use of information necessary for the execution of the DoD mission. The plan ensures effective, efficient, and economical acquisition, life-cycle management, and use of GIG personal, local, regional, and global computing environments.

DOD Instruction 5200.40: DoD Information Technology Security Certification and Accreditation Process (DITSCAP)—The DITSCAP establishes a standard process, set of activities, general task descriptions, and a management structure to certify and accredit IT systems that will maintain the security posture of the defense information infrastructure. The DITSCAP presents a four-phase infrastructure-centric approach and establishes a standard process, set of activities, general task descriptions, and a management structure to certify and accredit. Of particular interest to identity management professionals are E2.1.51–1.56; these include the following:

E2.1.51. Security Test and Evaluation (ST&E)—Examination and analysis of the safeguards and security posture.

E2.1.52. Sensitive Information—Information concerning the loss, misuse, or unauthorized access to or modification of which could adversely affect the national interest or the conduct of federal programs, or the privacy to which individuals are entitled less than 5 U.S.C. Section 552a.

DoD Instruction 5215.2: Computer Security Technical Vulnerability Reporting—This instruction focuses on the issue of secure (trusted) access and the ability to monitor and report violations.

DoD Instruction 5230.29: Security and Policy Review of DoD Information for Public Release—This instruction has specific focus on the release of personally identifiable information in the policy. Trusted access, records management are focus areas

DoD Instruction 8500.2: Information Assurance Implementation—This instruction implements policy, assigns responsibilities, and prescribes procedures for applying integrated, layered protection of the DoD information systems and networks under DoD Directive 8500.1

DoD Mobile Code Guidance—This directive establishes policy and assigns responsibilities for the use of commercial wireless devices, services, and technologies in the DoD Global Information Grid. It applies to all commercial wireless devices, services, and technologies, including voice and data capabilities. For data, strong authentication, non-repudiation, and personal identification are required. This guide has a specific requirement for change management on mobile code.

DoD X.509 Certificate Policy Version 9.0 & DoD Key Recovery Policy Version 3.0—The United States Department of Defense (DoD) has developed a key management infrastructure (KMI) to provide engineered solutions (consisting of products and services) for security of networked computer-based systems. Part of this KMI is a public key infrastructure (PKI), consisting of products and services that provide and manage X.509 certificates for public key cryptography.

Security management services provided by the PKI include the following:

- Key generation/storage/recovery
- Certificate generation, update, renewal, rekey, and distribution
- Certificate revocation list (CRL) generation and distribution
- Directory management of certificate-related items
- Certificate token initialization/programming/management
- Privilege and authorization management
- System management functions (e.g., security audit, configuration management, archive, etc.)

DoDD 3020.26: COOP Policy and Planning: 4.1—The DoD shall have a comprehensive and effective Defense Continuity Program that ensures DoD Component Mission Essential Functions. This document mandates the identification, assessment, and security of physical and cyber systems and assets so vital to the nation that their incapacitation or destruction would have a debilitating impact on national security, national economic security, or national public health and safety.

DoDD 3020.40: A DoD risk management program that seeks to ensure the availability of networked assets critical to Dod missions. v

DoDD 8000.1: Defense Information Management Program—Protection of the department's critical infrastructures requires participation by all hands to identify potential vulnerabilities, defend against exploitation, and, if exploited, minimize the impact to overall mission. CIP embraces traditional aspects of security (antiterrorism/force protection, operational security, and infrastructure assurance).

DoDD O 8530.1: Military Health Service Information System (IS)—This encompasses all automated IS applications, enclaves, outsourced IT-based processes, and platform information technology. This document covers availability, trusted access, record management, and audit and risk management.

Executive Order 12356—In 1982 this order was issued to provide a uniform method of classifying, declassifying, and safeguarding national security information.

Executive Order 12829—Introduced in 1993, this order established a National Security Program to safeguard federal government classified information that is released to contractors, licensees, and grantees of the U.S. government.

FIPS 200: Minimum Security Requirements for Federal Information and Information Systems—The use of FIPS 200 is compulsory and binding on federal agencies for all information within the federal government other than that information that has been determined pursuant to Executive Order 12958. The security-related areas include (i) access control; (ii) awareness and training; (iii) audit and accountability; (iv) certification, accreditation, and security assessments; (v) configuration management; (vi) contingency planning; (vii) identification and authentication; (viii) incident response; (ix) maintenance; (x) media protection; (xi) physical and environmental protection; (xii) planning; (xiii) personnel security; (xiv) risk assessment; (xv) systems and services acquisition; (xvi) system and communications protection; and (xvii) system and information integrity.

H.R. 6, The Energy Policy Act of 2005, Title XII-Electricity (the network reliability provision)—This authorizes the creation of a self-regulatory electric reliability organization (ERO) that spans North America, with FERC oversight in the United States. The legislation respects the international character of the North American electric transmission system by ensuring that Canadian and Mexican interests in the reliability of the interconnected North American electric grid are fully considered. The reliability legislation amends Part II of the Federal Power Act to add new section 215, making reliability standards for the bulk-power system mandatory and enforceable.

FISMA Act of 2002—Federal Information Management Act (FISMA) Public Law 107-347 implemented as NIST 800-37 provides a comprehensive framework for ensuring the effectiveness of information security controls over information resources that support federal operations and assets. It recognizes the highly networked nature of the current federal computing environment and provides effective governmentwide management and oversight of the related information security risks, including coordination of information security efforts throughout the civilian, national security, and law enforcement communities. Under FISMA, the National Institute of Standards and Technology (NIST) is chartered to develop the standards and guidelines for agency IT security requirements. Its December 2006 publication (Special Publication 800-53 (SP 800-53): Recommended Security Controls for Federal Information Systems) details the specific elements required in an overall security plan (national security systems are covered by other standards). The controls detailed in SP 800-53 cover all aspects of security from high-level business processes to detailed hardware and software functions. These security controls fall into three classes: technical controls, operational controls, and management controls.

## Technical Controls

Technical controls are those security mechanisms used by an information system's hardware, software, or firmware to secure the system and its information. There are four families of security controls in this class: Identification and Authentication, Logical Access Control, Accountability and Audit, and System and Communication Protection.

More on FISMA and how Oracle products implement Technical Controls is covered in Appendix B.

Freedom of Information Act/Privacy Act—The goal of the NSA/CSS Freedom of Information Act/Privacy Act Office is to release as much information as possible, consistent with the need to protect information under the exemption provisions of these laws.

GISRA—The Defense Authorization Act of 2001 contained the Government Information Security Reform Act (GISRA). GISRA required agencies to implement efforts to secure electronic information and systems; to thoroughly assess their security management practices; and to report on their security programs, processes, technology, and personnel to the Office of Management and Budget (OMB).

Memorandum 00-13: Privacy Policies and Data Collection of Federal Web Sites & Memorandum 99-18: Privacy Policies on Federal Web Sites—Each agency is required by law and policy to establish clear privacy policies for its Web activities and to comply with those policies. Agencies are to post clear privacy policies on agency principal Web sites. This memo extends to contractors, who are also required to comply with those policies when operating Web sites on behalf of federal agencies.

NISPOM: DoD 5220.22-M National Industrial Security Program Operating Manual (NISPOM)—NISPOM represents an industrial security process that is based on sound threat analysis and risk management practices. This DoD directive covers Information System Security, Classification, and Records Management.

NIST 800-53: Security Controls for Federal Information Systems—NIST 800-53 drafts an Ontology of Identity Credentials—This document establishes the foundation for federal identity management with a focus on authorization and access control. It provides the broadest possible range of identity credentials and supporting documents insofar as they pertain to identity credential issuance. Priority is given to examples of primary and secondary identity credentials issued within the United States.

NIST 800-53: Techniques and Procedures for Verifying the Effectiveness of Security Controls in Federal Information Systems—This provides techniques and procedures for implementing FIPS 199 Homeland Security Presidential Directive #7, #12, and Public Law 107-347 Section III Federal Information Security Management Act of 2002. This document focuses on the selection and employment of appropriate security controls for an information system. Chapter Two describes the fundamental concepts associated with security control, including the structural components of security controls and taxonomy, the minimum security (baseline) controls, and assurance in the effectiveness of security controls. Chapter Three describes the process of selecting and specifying security controls for an information system, including the organization's approach to managing risk, the security categorization of the system, and the selection of minimum (baseline) security.

NIST 800-59: Guideline for identifying an Information System as a National Security System—The document provides guidance on how to determine whether an information system meets the new legislative definition for "national security systems" (FISMA, Title III, Public Law 107-347).

NIST 800-60: Guide for Mapping Types of Information and Information Systems to Security Objectives and Risk Levels—This series of seven documents provides a structured, flexible framework for selecting, specifying, employing, and evaluating the security controls in federal information systems. It contains the basic guidelines for mapping types of information and information systems to security categories. This guideline is less prescriptive for mission-based information than for administrative and support information because there is significantly less commonality of mission information types among agencies.

NIST SP 800-30: Risk Assessment Guide for Information Technology Systems: Risk Management Guide for Information Technology Systems—This guide provides a common foundation for system users to evaluate and mitigate operational risk. Section 2 provides an overview of risk management, how it fits into the system development life cycle (SDLC), and the roles of individuals who support and use this process. Section 3 describes the risk assessment methodology and the nine primary steps in conducting a risk assessment of an IT system. Section 4 describes the risk mitigation process, including risk mitigation options and strategy, approach for control implementation, control categories, cost–benefit analysis, and residual risk. Section 5 discusses the good practice and need for an ongoing risk evaluation and assessment.

NSA/CSS-NISCAP—In 2001, NSA/CSS developed the NISCAP in support of DCID 6/3 [NISCAP]. The NISCAP defines a standard C&A process for systems designed to process information under the purview of the director, National Security Agency (DIRNSA). Additionally, NISCAP describes the security documentation required to support the process. The guide discusses the roles and responsibilities of the organizations involved in the system security certification process, the security requirements associated with systems to which this guide applies (Director of Central Intelligence Directive 6/3), the process to be followed in achieving security certification and accreditation of a system, and the security documentation used to support the certification process and subsequent accreditation of the system.

NSTISSAM COMPUSEC 1-99: Advisory Memorandum on the Transition from the Trusted Computer System Evaluation Criteria to the International Common Criteria for Information Technology Security Evaluation—This focuses on the insider threat and the potential damage that such an individual could cause when targeting today's information systems (IS). It points out the various weaknesses (vulnerabilities) in today's IS an insider might exploit and highlights approaches to solving these problems. The commission highlighted two areas for particular attention. First, personnel security lies at the very heart of our security system, and the trustworthiness of those who deal with sensitive and classified information must be ensured. Second, IS security requires increased attention. The commission acknowledged that an insider threat can take the form of employees, contractors, service providers, or anyone with legitimate access to a system. All insiders have some degree of physical or administrative access to ISs. The greater the individual's knowledge of and access to the system, the greater the potential threat from that person, with individuals having privileged access posing the greatest potential threat.

NSTISSI 1000: National Security Telecommunications and Information Systems Security Instruction—This describes the National Information Assurance Certification and Accreditation Process (NIACAP), which establishes the minimum national standards for certifying and accrediting national security systems. This process provides a standard set of activities, general tasks, and a management structure to certify and accredit systems that will maintain the IA and security posture of a system or site. The NIACAP agreements are documented in the System Security Authorization Agreement, or SSAA. The SSAA documents the conditions of the C&A for an IS. The SSAA is a formal agreement among the DAAs, certifier, user representative, and program manager. The SSAA is used throughout the entire NIACAP process to guide actions, document decisions, specify IA requirements, document certification tailoring and level of effort, identify possible solutions, and maintain operational systems security. The SSAA has the following functions:

- Describes the operating environment and threat
- Describes the system security architecture
- Establishes the C&A boundary of the system to be accredited
- Documents the formal agreement among the DAAs, certifier, program manager, and user representative
- Documents all requirements necessary for accreditation
- Minimizes documentation requirements by consolidating applicable information into the SSAA (security policy, concept of operations, architecture description, test procedures, etc.)
- Documents the NIACAP plan
- Documents test plans and procedures, certification results, and residual risk
- Forms the baseline security configuration document

NSTISSP—National Security Telecommunications and Information Systems Security Policy NSTISSP #11 is a national security community policy governing the acquisition of IA and IA-enabled information technology products. The policy was issued by the Chairman of the National Security Telecommunications and Information Systems Security Committee (NSTISSC), now known as the Committee on National Security Systems (CNSS), in January 2000 and was revised in June 2003. The policy mandates that departments and agencies within the executive branch shall acquire, for use on national security systems, only those COTS products or cryptographic modules that have been validated with the International Common Criteria for Information Technology Security Evaluation, the National Information Assurance Partnership (NIAP) Common Criteria Evaluation and Validation Scheme (CCEVS), or by the National Institute of Standards and Technology (NIST) Federal Information Processing Standards (FIPS). Cryptographic Information Assurance (IA) shall be considered a requirement for all systems used to enter, process, store, display, or transmit national security information.

OMB Circular A-130: Management of Federal Information Systems: "Federal Agency Responsibilities for Maintaining Records About Individuals." OMB A130 Transmittal Number 4: Management of Federal Information Resources "Security of Federal Automated Information Systems." This Transmittal 4 is intended to guide agencies in securing government information resources as they increasingly rely on an open and interconnected National Information Infrastructure. It stresses management controls, such as individual responsibility, awareness and training, and accountability, and explains how they can be supported by technical controls. Among other things, it requires agencies to ensure that risk-based rules of behavior are established. The issuance dealt primarily with how the federal government manages its information holdings, particularly information exchange with the public. Systematic attention to the management of government records is an essential component of sound public resources management, which ensures public accountability. Together with records preservation, it protects the government's historical record and guards the legal and financial rights of the government and the public.

PDD-63 Critical Infrastructure Protection—Addresses the cyber and physical infrastructure vulnerabilities of the federal government by requiring each department and agency to work to reduce its exposure to new threats. The directive authorized NSA to develop means to protect "unclassified sensitive" information. For the first time in its 32-year history, the NSA was assigned responsibilities outside its traditional foreign eavesdropping and military and diplomatic communications security roles.

Public Law 100-235: Computer Security Act of 1987—This law instructs public agencies to perform research and to conduct studies, as needed, to determine the nature and extent of the vulnerabilities of, and to devise techniques for the cost-effective security and privacy of, sensitive information in federal computer systems. Agencies must establish a plan for the security and privacy of each federal computer system identified by that agency, pursuant to subsection (a), that is commensurate with the risk and magnitude of the harm resulting from the loss, misuse, or unauthorized access to or modification of the information contained in such system.

Public Law 93-579 (Privacy Act of 1974)—The purpose of this act is to provide certain safeguards for an individual against an invasion of personal privacy by requiring federal agencies to:

- Permit an individual to determine what records pertaining to him are collected, maintained, used, or disseminated by such agencies; permit an individual to prevent records pertaining to him obtained by such agencies for a particular purpose from being used or made available for another purpose without his consent
- Permit an individual to gain access to information pertaining to him in federal agency records, to have a copy made of all or any portion thereof, and to correct or amend such records; collect, maintain, use, or disseminate any record of identifiable personal information in a manner that ensures that such action is for a necessary and lawful purpose, that the information is current and accurate for its intended use, and that adequate safeguards are provided to prevent misuse of such information
- Permit exemptions from such requirements with respect to records provided in this act only when an important public policy need for such exemption as has been determined by specific statutory authority
- Be subject to civil suit for any damages that occur as a result of willful or intentional action which violates any individual's rights under this act

Removal of Personally Identifying Information: OASD Memorandum, "Removal of Personally Identifying Information under the Information of Freedom Act (FOIA)"—All public records shall be open to inspection and copying by any citizen of the state during regular business hours by the custodian of the records for the appropriate public body. However, any record the disclosure of which would constitute an invasion of personal privacy is closed to public scrutiny. Agencies holding such criminal records may delete any information, before release, which would disclose the names of witnesses, intelligence personnel, and aids or any other information of a privileged and confidential nature.

System Security Engineering Capability Maturity Model—The SSE-CMM describes the essential characteristics of an organization's security engineering process necessary to ensure good security engineering. The model for the SSE-CMM is made up of a number of process areas (PAs). These PAs are considered to be the basic fundamental parts of the majority, if not all, activities. The PAs that go to make up the SSE-CMM model are themselves divided into a number of parts called base practices (BPs). It is not the how of the BP that is important but the fact that the BP is performed. Each of the identified BPs is considered to contribute toward the effective performance of the PA, and therefore, all BPs within a particular PA must be performed. However, it is considered that some organizations will not need to perform some PAs, because of the nature of their activities, and thus, PAs are not mandatory for compliance with the model. The PAs themselves are divided into three categories: the engineering PAs, the project PAs, and the organizational PAs.

The project and organizational PAs are essentially the same as those of the SE-CMM. In some a change of focus has taken place; they are dealing with security engineering specifically rather than systems engineering as a whole. It should also be pointed out at this juncture that a fundamental tenant of the SSE-CMM is that security engineering should be integrated with systems engineering rather than remaining a separate entity. The engineering PAs have been specifically developed for the SSE-CMM.

The National Strategy to Secure Cyberspace: Strategy to secure Cyberspace signed by the President. The National Strategy for Homeland Security and is complemented by a National Strategy for the Physical Protection of Critical Infrastructures and Key Assets—The purpose of this document is to engage and empower Americans to secure the portions of cyberspace that they own, operate, control, or with which they interact. These responsibilities include the following:

■ Developing a comprehensive national plan for securing the key resources and critical infrastructure of the United States
■ Providing crisis management in response to attacks on critical information systems
■ Providing technical assistance to the private sector and other government entities with respect to emergency recovery plans for failures of critical information systems

Rainbow Series Library—The Rainbow Series (sometimes known as the Rainbow Books) is a series of computer security standards published by the United States government in the 1980s and 1990s. These standards describe a process of evaluation for trusted systems. In some cases, U.S. government entities (as well as defense contractors) require formal validation of computer technology using this process as part of their procurement criteria. Many of these standards have influenced, and have been superseded by, the Common Criteria. The series was originally published by the U.S. Department of Defense Computer Security Center, and then by the National Computer Security Center. The rainbow series is a library of 37 documents that address specific areas of computer security. Each of the documents is a different color; as a result books have nicknames based on the color of its cover. For example, the Trusted Computer System Evaluation Criteria was referred to as "The Orange Book." Books applicable to Identity Management include the following:

■ CSC-STD-001-83 [Orange Book]
■ DOD Trusted Computer System Evaluation Criteria [DOD 5200.28]
■ CSC-STD-002-85 [Green Book]
■ DoD Password Management Guidelines
■ CSC-STD-003-85 [Light Yellow Book]
■ Guidance for Applying the DoD Trusted Computer System Evaluation Criteria in Specific Environments
■ CSC-STD-004-85 [Yellow Book II]
■ Technical Rationale Behind CSC-STD-003-85: Computer Security Requirements
■ CSC-STD-005-85
■ DoD Magnetic Remanence Security Guideline

CAC-BWG (PKI 4 PIV -D1172.2)—This is based on the Defense Management Council (DMC) decision of Sep 1999 to adopt a universal DoD Smart Card. The DoD Common Access Card (CAC) is designed to provide physical and logical access and act as a class 4 PKI hardware token. It includes multiple media (mag stripe, chip, and bar code).

RFID (DFARS-RFID Req) MIL-STD-129P 70 FR 53955 Defense Federal Acquisition Regulation Supplement (DFARS) Department of Defense Practice Military Marking for Shipping and Storage—This standard provides the minimum requirements for uniform military marking for shipment and storage. Passive RFID tags shall be applied to case shipments and palletized unit load shipments. The item packaging (unit pack) for items requires a unique identification (UID) mark under this supplement.

Federal Reserve Act, 12 U.S.C. 248(i),(j), and (o)—This act requires the board to publish once each week a statement showing the condition of each Federal Reserve Bank and a consolidated statement for all Federal Reserve Banks. Such statements shall show in detail the assets and liabilities of the Federal Reserve Banks, single and combined, and shall furnish full information regarding the character of the money held as reserve and the amount, nature, and maturities of the paper and other investments owned or held by Federal Reserve Banks.

Federal Reserve Act, 12 U.S.C. 342—Enacts the International Banking Act of 1978 regarding the acceptance of electronic deposits. This act has a change management and records management requirement.

Federal Reserve Act, 12 U.S.C. 360—This act has a reporting requirement and a security requirement. The Federal Reserve agent shall each day notify the Board of Governors of the Federal Reserve System of all issues and withdrawals of Federal Reserve notes to and by the Federal Reserve Bank to which he or she is accredited. The said Board of Governors of the Federal Reserve System may at any time call upon a Federal Reserve Bank for additional security to protect the Federal Reserve notes issued to it.

Federal Reserve Act, 12 U.S.C. 4001-4010—This grants the reserve the ability to regulate nonbank banks, impose a moratorium on certain securities and insurance activities by banks, recapitalize the Federal Savings and Loan Insurance Corporation, allow emergency interstate bank acquisitions, streamline credit union operations, regulate consumer check holds, and for other purposes. Within the act these powers are interpreted as electronic regulation and automation of operations for nonbank banks.

Federal Reserve Act, 12 U.S.C. 464—This act defines reserve requirements. Each depository institution is required to maintain reserves against its transaction accounts as the Board may prescribe by regulation solely for the purpose of implementing monetary policy.

IGES for Safeguarding Customer Information, 12 CFR § Part 364, Appendix B—Section 39(a) requires the agencies to establish operational and managerial standards relating to the following: (1) internal controls, information systems, and internal audit systems, in accordance with section 36 of the FDI Act (12 U.S.C. 1831m); (2) loan documentation; (3) credit underwriting; (4) interest rate exposure; (5) asset growth; and (6) compensation, fees, and benefits.

IGES for Safety and Soundness, 12 CFR § Part 364, Appendix A—Section 39 of the Federal Deposit Insurance Act requires the Federal Deposit Insurance Corporation to establish safety and soundness standards. Pursuant to section 39, this part establishes safety and soundness standards by guideline. An institution should have internal controls and information systems that are appropriate to the size of the institution and the nature, scope, and risk of its activities.

IGES for Safeguarding Customer Information (bank holding companies and their nonbank subsidiaries or affiliates (except brokers, dealers, persons providing insurance, investment companies, and investment advisors), 12 CFR Part 225, Appendix F—These Interagency Guidelines Establishing Information Security Standards (Guidelines) set forth standards pursuant to sections 501 and 505 of the Gramm–Leach–Bliley Act (15 U.S.C. 6801 and 6805). These guidelines address standards for developing and implementing administrative, technical, and physical safeguards to protect the security, confidentiality, and integrity of customer information.

IGES for Safeguarding Customer Information (Edge or agreement corporation), 12 CFR 211.5: Subchapter II of chapter 53 of Title 31, United States Code, commonly known as the "Bank Secrecy Act"—This generally requires financial institutions to, among other things, keep records and make reports that have a high degree of usefulness in criminal, tax, or regulatory proceedings. The supervisory agencies' implementing regulations incorporate the minimum components of a compliance program as generally set forth in the Bank Secrecy Act at 31 U.S.C. 5318(h). These components are: (1) a system of internal controls to ensure ongoing compliance; (2) independent testing of compliance by the institution's personnel; (3) the designation of an individual or individuals responsible for coordinating and monitoring day-to-day compliance; and (4) training for appropriate personnel.

The International Lending Supervision Act of 1983 (ILSA), 12 U.S.C. 3901, et seq., requires each federal banking agency to evaluate the foreign country.

IGES for Safeguarding Customer Information, Appendix D-2 (State Member Banks), 12 CFR Part 208, Appendix D-1: Section 39 of the Federal Deposit Insurance Act 1 (FDI Act)—This requires each federal banking agency (collectively, the agencies) to establish certain safety and soundness standards by regulation or by guideline for all insured depository institutions. Under section 39, the agencies must establish three types of standards: (1) operational and managerial standards; (2) compensation standards; and (3) such standards relating to asset quality, earnings, and stock valuation as they determine to be appropriate.

United States: Listed Companies and Private Corporations

Sarbanes–Oxley—No single piece of legislation has impacted the public sector more than the Public Company Accounting Reform and Investor Protection Act of 2002 drafted by Paul Sarbanes and Michael Oxley. In the wake of corporate accounting scandals, Congress passed the Sarbanes–Oxley Act in July 2002. Its purpose is to prevent such a crisis from occurring again and restore the public's faith in corporate America's financial reporting. Every company whose stock trades on a U.S.-based stock exchange must conform to this legislation. Given the pervasiveness of this mandate and its impact, it is worth devoting a section-by-section inspection to determine where automated compensating controls may be leveraged.

Title I: Public Company Accounting Oversight Board

Section 103. Auditing, quality control, and independence standards and rules: In all assurance engagements related to both disclosure and internal control evaluations and attestations, company management and auditors should obtain an understanding of disclosure and internal controls sufficient to plan the assurance engagement by performing procedures to:

Understand the design of the controls relevant to the attestation

Determine whether those controls have been placed in operation

Section 104. Inspections of registered public accounting firms: COSO defines internal control as a process. This internal control process can be affected by an entity's operating environment, including directors, officers, managers, and other personnel. It is designed to provide reasonable assurance about achieving objectives in three primary categories and consists of five interrelated components. These objectives and components are summarized as follows:

Control Objectives

1. Operations, asset protection, and security
2. Financial reporting
3. Compliance

Control Components

1. Control environment
2. Risk assessment
3. Control activities
4. Information and communications
5. Monitoring

Section 108. Accounting standards:

Prioritize requirements—To perform an overall risk assessment, specific assets or processes should be prioritized in terms of their criticality to the enterprise.

Identify risks—After ranking and prioritizing important assets that need to be protected and safeguarded, specific threats to those assets can be identified.

Determine likelihood—After identifying the major risks that represent the greatest threats to the most valuable assets of the enterprise, the entity should estimate the likelihood of these risks occurring.

### Title II: Auditor Independence

Section 204. Auditor reports to audit committees: To support an assessed disclosure/internal control risk below the maximum level, the assuror should obtain sufficient competent evidential matter. To be competent, evidence must be both relevant and valid. Relevance is related to the type of evidence available, whereas validity is dependent on the source and circumstances under which the evidence is obtained. In this section detective controls such as those within Internal Controls Manager, PeopleSoft Internal Controls Enforcer, and Audit Vault may be leveraged.

Section 205. Conforming amendments: SAS-80 discusses evidential matter in the context of an electronic data processing environment. It addresses the point that even though the internal/external auditor's assurance objectives do not change whether information is processed manually or electronically, the methods of applying assurance procedures may be influenced by the method of processing. SAS-80 notes that it may be difficult or impossible for auditors to access certain information for inquiry, inspection, or reperformance without using information technology itself in the form of computer-assisted auditing techniques (CAATs).

### Title III: Corporate Responsibility

Section 301. Public company audit committees: This deals with process and procedures involving standards governing internal/external auditors providing financial reporting and compliance assurance services. This in turn focuses the practitioner toward COSO, and by association, COBIT.

Section 302. Corporate responsibility for financial reports: As discussed in Section 202, risk assessment is the process of identifying and analyzing both internal and external risks and threats to achieving an entity's goals and objectives. Risk assessment can be performed on the level of either the whole enterprise or entity, or a specific application or transaction. Risk assessment processes on both the entity level and application level form the basis of determining how to manage risk through control activities.

### Title IV: Enhanced Financial Disclosures

Section 401. Disclosures in periodic reports: This chapter includes risk/control evaluations for both entitywide and application levels, and includes specific control activities for operational and general ledger account groupings common to typical commercial businesses. The overall framework and design for each of the risk/control matrices are based on the basic principles and control criteria established in Internal Control-Integrated Framework (the COSO Report).

Section 404. Management assessment of internal controls: Sections 302 and 404 of the Sarbanes–Oxley Act of 2002 (SOX) specifically require public companies to establish, implement, and evaluate their internal controls for purposes of financial statement reporting (i.e., "disclosure controls") and operational integrity. In establishing rules to implement both sections 302 and 404, the Securities and Exchange Commission (SEC) makes reference to existing auditing standards issued by the American Institute of Certified Public Accountants (AICPA) regarding auditing and internal controls.

Section 408. Enhanced review of periodic disclosures by issuers: This chapter includes risk/control evaluations for both entitywide and application levels, and includes specific control activities for operational and general ledger account groupings common to typical commercial businesses. The overall framework and design for each of the risk/control matrices are based on the basic principles and control criteria established in Internal Control-Integrated Framework (the COSO Report).

Title VIII: Corporate and Criminal Fraud Accountability
  Section 802. Criminal penalties for altering documents

Title XI: Corporate Fraud and Accountability
  Section 1102. Tampering with a record or otherwise impeding an official proceeding: The Sarbanes–Oxley Act is a far-reaching piece of legislation. Although the act has many facets, including criminal penalties for corporate officers, those relevant to this discussion are the following:

- Corporate officers must certify, and will be held responsible for, financial statements.
- All financial processes must be documented and appropriate controls identified.
- Auditors must attest that this has been done on an annual basis.

In examination, 12 IT Control Objectives, which align with the PCAOB Auditing Standard No. 2 and Control Objectives for information and related technology, can be mapped to Sarbanes–Oxley:

- Acquire and maintain application software AI2
- Acquire and maintain technology infrastructure AI3
- Enable Operations AI4
- Install and accredit solutions and changes AI7
- Manage changes AI6
- Define and manage service levels DS1
- Manage third party services DS2
- Ensure system security DS5
- Manage the configuration DS9
- Manage problems and incidents DS8, DS10
- Manage data DS11
- Manage the physical environment and operations DS12, D13

Fair Credit Reporting Act—Congress enacted the Fair Credit Reporting Act (FCRA) to protect consumers from the disclosure of inaccurate and arbitrary personal information held by consumer reporting agencies. It enables individuals to have access to their own data profile. Individuals have a right to learn who has accessed their files. Although the FCRA regulates the disclosure of personal information, it does not restrict the amount or type of information that can be collected. Under the FCRA, consumer-reporting agencies may only disclose personal information to third parties under specified conditions. Additionally, information may be released to a third party with the written consent of the subject of the report or when the reporting agency has reason to believe the requesting party intends to use the information:

■ For a credit, employment, or insurance evaluation
■ In connection with the grant of a license or other government benefit
■ For another "legitimate business need" involving the consumer

Privacy Act of 1974—This act was designed to protect individuals from a powerful and potentially intrusive federal government. It incorporates the Code or Fair Information Practices recommended by the Department of Health, Education, and Welfare and empowers individuals to control the federal government's collection, use, and dissemination of sensitive personal information. The act prohibits agencies from disclosing records to third parties or other agencies without the consent of the individual to whom the record pertains.

The code emphasized five principles:

1. There should be no records whose very existence is private.
2. An individual must be able to discover what information is contained in his or her record and how it is used.
3. An individual must be able to prevent information collected for one purpose from being used for another purpose without consent.
4. An individual must be able to correct or amend erroneous information.
5. Any organization creating, maintaining, using, or disseminating records of identifiable personal data must ensure the reliability of the data for its intended purpose and must take precautions to prevent misuse.

Family Education Rights and Privacy Act—Congress passed the Family Educational Rights and Privacy Act (also known as the Buckle Amendment) to protect the accuracy and confidentiality of student records; it applies to all schools receiving federal funding. The act prevents educational institutions from disclosing student records or personally identifiable information to third parties without consent, but does not restrict the collection or use of information by schools. The statute also requires educational institutions to give students and their parents access to school records and an opportunity to challenge the content of records they believe to be inaccurate or misleading.

Right to Financial Privacy Act—This act was designed to protect the confidentiality of personal financial records by creating a statutory Fourth Amendment protection for bank records. The Right to Financial Privacy Act states that "no Government authority may have access to or obtain copies of, or the information contained in the financial records of any customer from a financial institution unless the financial records are reasonably described" and at least one of the following applies:

■ The customer authorizes access.
■ There is an appropriate administrative subpoena or summons.
■ There is a qualified search warrant.

- There is an appropriate judicial subpoena.
- There is an appropriate written request from an authorized government authority.

The statute prevents banks from requiring customers to authorize the release of financial records as a condition of doing business and states that customers have a right to access a record of all disclosures.

Privacy Protection Act of 1980 (PPA)—Congress enacted this act ("PPA") to reduce the effect of law enforcement searches and seizures on publishers. The PPA prohibits government officials searching or seizing any work, product, or documentary materials held by a "person believed to have a purpose to disseminate to the public a newspaper, book, broadcast, or similar form of public communication," unless there is probable cause to believe the publisher has committed or is committing a criminal offense to which the materials relate. The PPA effectively forces law enforcement to use subpoenas or voluntary cooperation to obtain evidence from those engaged in First Amendment activities.

Cable Communications Policy Act of 1984—Congress passed the Cable Communications Policy Act ("1984 Cable Act" or "Cable Act") to amend the Communications Act of 1934. The Cable Act establishes a comprehensive legislation for cable regulation and sets forth strong protections for subscriber privacy by restricting the collection, maintenance, and dissemination of subscriber data. The act prohibits cable providers from using the cable system to collect "personally identifiable information" concerning any subscriber without prior consent, unless the information is necessary to render service or detect reception. The act also prohibits operators from disclosing personally identifiable data to third parties without consent, unless the disclosure is either necessary to render a service provided by the cable operator to the subscriber or if it is made to a government entity pursuant to a court order.

The Patriot Act of 2001, in section 211, addressed the question of whether this act covers data collection by cable companies that offer cable modems and Internet service provider services. The Patriot Act allows cable operators to disclose any personal information, including that transmitted through cable modems, to law enforcement agents without the consent of the subscriber.

The Patriot Act of 2001, in section 312, requires certain U.S. financial institutions to apply due diligence to correspondent accounts maintained for certain foreign financial institutions. U.S. financial institutions covered by the final rule must establish a due diligence program that includes appropriate, specific, risk-based, and, where necessary, enhanced policies, procedures, and controls that are reasonably designed to detect and report known or suspected money-laundering activity conducted through or involving any correspondent account established, maintained, administered, or managed in the United States.

At a minimum, the due diligence program must accomplish the following: (1) determine whether the account is subject to enhanced due diligence under section 312 (see later discussion of the notice of proposed rule making); (2) assess the money-laundering risk posed, based on a consideration of relevant risk factors; and (3) apply risk-based policies, procedures, and controls to each such correspondent account reasonably designed to detect and report known or suspected money-laundering activity.

The Electronic Communications Privacy Act—Congress passed the Electronic Communications Privacy Act (ECPA) to expand the scope of existing federal wiretap laws, such as the Wiretap Act, to include protection for electronic communications. ECPA expands the privacy protections of the Wiretap Act in five significant ways:

1. ECPA broadens the scope of privileged communications to include all forms of electronic transmissions, including video, text, audio, and data.
2. ECPA eliminates the requirement that communications be transmitted via common carrier to receive legal protection.
3. ECPA maintains restrictions on the interception of messages in transmission and adds prohibition on access to stored electronic communications.
4. ECPA responds to the Supreme Court's ruling in *Smith v. Maryland* that telephone records are not private and restricts law enforcement access to transactional information pertaining to users of electronic communication services.
5. ECPA broadens the reach of the Wiretap Act by restricting both government and private access to communications.

Virtually all online services offer some sort of "private" activity, which allows subscribers to send personal e-mail messages to others. The federal Electronic Communications Privacy Act (ECPA) makes it unlawful for anyone to read or disclose the contents of an electronic communication. This law applies to e-mail messages.

However, there are three important exceptions to the ECPA:

1. The online service may view private e-mail if it suspects that the sender is attempting to damage the system or harm another user. However, random monitoring of e-mail is prohibited.
2. The service may legally view and disclose private e-mail if either the sender or the recipient of the message consents to the inspection or disclosure. Many commercial services require a consent agreement from new members when signing up for the service.
3. If an employer owns the e-mail system, the employer may inspect the contents of employee e-mail on the system. Therefore, any e-mail sent from a business location is probably not private. Several court cases have determined that employers have a right to monitor e-mail messages of their employees.

Law enforcement officials may access or disclose electronic communications only after receiving a court-ordered search warrant. The Patriot Act of 2001 amended the ECPA. See sections 209, 211, 212, and 815 of the Patriot Act for those amendments.

Computer Security Act—This act assigns the National Bureau of Standards responsibility for developing standards and guidelines for the security of federal computer systems, drawing upon technical guidelines developed by the National Security Agency, when such guidelines are consistent with the requirements for protecting sensitive information. H.R. 145 also provides for a Computer Systems Advisory Board to identify emerging federal computer security and privacy issues, advise the NSA on these issues and report its findings to the Office of Management and Budget (OMB), NSA, and Congress. The law amends the Brooks Act of 1965 by updating the term *computer* and requires the establishment of security plans by all operators of federal computer systems that contain sensitive information; and requires mandatory periodic training for all persons involved in management, use, or operation of federal computer systems that contain sensitive information. The purpose of H.R. 145, the Computer Security Act of 1987, as amended, is to improve the security and privacy of sensitive information in federal computer systems. It achieves this purpose through improved training, aimed at raising the awareness of federal workers about computer system security, by establishing a focal point within the government for developing computer system security standards and guidelines to protect sensitive information, and by requiring agencies to establish computer system security plans.

Video Privacy Protection Act of 1988—The act prohibits videotape service providers from disclosing customer rental records without the informed, written consent of the consumer. Furthermore, the act requires video service providers to destroy personally identifiable customer information within a year of the date it is no longer necessary for the purpose for which it was collected.

Telephone Consumer Protection Act of 1991 (TCPA)—This was enacted in response to consumer complaints about the proliferation of intrusive telemarketing practices and concerns about such practices on consumer privacy. The act amends Title II of the Communications Act of 1934 and requires that the Federal Communications Commission (FCC or Commission) promulgate rules "to protect residential telephone subscribers' privacy rights." In response to TCPA, the FCC issued a report and order requiring any person or entity engaged in telemarketing to maintain a list of consumers who request not to be called.

Driver's Privacy Protection Act of 1994—Congress passed the Driver's Privacy Protection Act as an amendment to the Omnibus Crime Act of 1994; it restricts the public disclosure of personal information contained in state department motor vehicle (DMV) records. Although the Driver's Privacy Protection Act generally prohibits DMV officials from knowingly disclosing personally identifiable information contained in records, it delineates several broad exceptions. One of them is the classification of information from drivers' licenses and motor vehicle registrations as a "thing in interstate commerce" that can be regulated by Congress similar to any other commodity.

Communications Assistance for Law Enforcement Act of 1994 (CALEA)—Congress passed the CALEA (also commonly known as the Digital Telephony Act) to preserve the government's ability to intercept communications over digital networks. The act requires phone companies to modify their networks to ensure government access to all wire and electronic communications as well as to call-identifying information. The law also includes several provisions enhancing privacy, including a section that increased the standard for government access to transactional data.

Telecommunications Act of 1996—In this act, Congress included a provision addressing widespread concern over telephone companies' misuse of personal records, requiring telephone companies to obtain the approval of customers before using information about users' calling patterns (or CPNI [customer proprietary network information]) to market new services. The statute requires telephone companies to obtain approval before using customers' information. Under the FCC's rule, telephone companies must give customers explicit notice of their right to control the use of their CPNI and obtain express written, oral, or electronic approval for its use.

Health Insurance Portability and Accountability Act of 1996 (HIPAA)—The Kennedy–Kassebaum Health Insurance Portability and Accountability Act contains a section known as "Administrative Simplification," which mandates the development and adoption of standards for electronic exchanges of health information. It also requires the development of privacy rules to govern such electronic exchanges. The proposal requires consumer consent before companies share medical data or detailed information about consumer spending habits. The act also requires companies to disclose their privacy policies prior to engaging in data transactions with users. The rules mandate the following:

- Patients must get a clear, written explanation of how information is used, kept, and disclosed.
- Patients must be able to get copies of their records and request amendments.
- Patients must give authorization before information is disclosed and can request restrictions on disclosure.

- Providers and health plans cannot demand a patient's blanket approval to disclosure before giving treatment.
- Health information can be used for health purposes only, with few exceptions.
- Providers and health plans must adopt written privacy procedures, train employees, and designate a privacy officer.

The standards also specify civil penalties of up to $25,000 per person and criminal penalties of up to $250,000 and 10 years in prison for improper use or disclosure of health information.

Children's Online Privacy Protection Act of 1998 (COPPA)—This was passed to protect children's personal information from its collection and misuse by commercial Web sites. On October 20, 1999, the Federal Trade Commission issued a Final Rule implementing the act, which went into effect on April 21, 2000. COPPA requires commercial Web sites and other online services directed at children 12 and under, or which collect information regarding users' age, to provide parents with notice of their information practices and obtain parental consent prior to the collection of personal information from children. The act further requires such sites to provide parents the ability to review and correct information about their children collected by such services. COPPA was designed to ensure that children's ability to speak, seek out information, and publish would not be adversely affected. As a result operators have to:

- Post their privacy policy.
- Get parental consent.
- Get fresh consent when information practices change in a material way.
- Allow parents to review personal information collected from their children.
- Allow parents to revoke their consent, and delete information collected from their children at the parents' request.

Gramm–Leach–Bliley Act (GLBA) of 1999—Signed law in November 1999, the GLBA is a comprehensive piece of legislation affecting financial institutions. The "Obligations with respect to disclosures of personal information" provision prompts notices from banks, brokerage firms, and insurance companies explaining their position on privacy as it relates to your personal information. The law provides that financial institutions allow for an "opt-out" provision for consumer privacy. The section, entitled "Protection of nonpublic personal information," mandates that financial institutions implement "administrative, technical and physical safeguards" for customer records and information. Specifically, these safeguards are designed to:

- Insure the security and confidentiality of customer records and information
- Protect against any anticipated threats or hazards to the security and integrity of such records
- Protect against unauthorized access to or use of such records or information that would result in substantial harm or inconvenience to any customer

The GLBA states that any financial institution that provides financial products or services to consumers must comply with the privacy provisions of Subtitle A of Title V of the GLBA and the Privacy Rule. A company has consumers if they provide financial products or services to individuals, not businesses, to be used primarily for their personal, family, or household purposes. A side effect of this act is that all U.S. educational institutions that participate in the self-funded Perkins loan program are now classified as financial services institutions.

Patriot Act of 2001—The Patriot Act was the first direct change to a law as a result of the terrorist attacks on 9/11. This act is also referred to as the "Anti-terrorism Surveillance Legislation." The Patriot Act is 342 pages long and makes changes to over 15 different statutes. Items changed include the following: electronic surveillance, search warrants, funding of investigative taskforces, money laundering, financial records, seizure of funds, counterfeiting, protecting the borders, immigrant status and detentions, benefits for immigrants, authority to pay rewards for information, providing for victims of terrorism, information sharing between agencies, strengthening criminal laws against terrorism, and improving intelligence.

Section 202, Authority to Intercept Voice Communictions in Computer Hacking Investigations

Domestic Security Enhancement Act of 2003 (Patriot II)—Some of the key provisions of the Domestic Security Enhancement Act of 2003 include the following:

Section 201, "Prohibition of Disclosure of Terrorism Investigation Detainee Information"—
  Safeguarding the dissemination of information related to national security
Section 202, "Distribution of 'Worst Case Scenario' Information"—This introduces new FOIA
  restrictions with regard to the Environmental Protection Agency. Section 202 of this act
  restricts FOIA requests to reports, which may serve as "a roadmap for terrorists." Reducing
  public access to "read-only" methods for only those persons "who live and work in the geo-
  graphical area likely to be affected by a worst-case scenario"
Section 301-306, "Terrorist Identification Database"—These sections authorize creation of
  a DNA database on "suspected terrorists," including association with suspected terrorist
  groups, and noncitizens suspected of certain crimes or of having supported any group designated as terrorist.
Section 312, "Appropriate Remedies with Respect to Law Enforcement Surveillance Activities"—This section terminates all state law enforcement consent decrees before September
  11, 2001, not related to racial profiling or other civil rights violations, that limit such agencies from gathering information about individuals and organizations. It also places substantial restrictions on court injunctions.

Bank Protection Act, 12 U.S.C. 1882—This requires each savings association to adopt appropriate security procedures to discourage robberies, burglaries, and larcenies and to assist in the identification and prosecution of persons who commit such acts.

Fraud and Related Activity in Connection with Computers 18 U.S.C. 1030—Require protection against unauthorized disclosure for reasons of national defense or foreign relations, or any restricted data, as defined in paragraph y of section 11 of the Atomic Energy Act of 1954.

Electronic Signatures in Global and National Commerce Act (E-Sign) Pub.L.No. 106-229—The ESIGN Act facilitates the use of electronic records and signatures in interstate and foreign commerce and removes uncertainty about the validity of contracts entered into electronically.

Bank Secrecy Act, 31 U.S.C. 5311—Under 12 CFR 21.21, all national banks must develop, administer, and maintain a program that ensures and monitors compliance with the BSA and its implementing regulations, including record keeping and reporting requirements. Senior management is responsible for ensuring an effective system of internal controls for the BSA.

Check Clearing for the 21st Century Act, 12 U.S.C. 5001—The Check 21 Act authorizes a new negotiable instrument called a *substitute check*, which is a paper reproduction of an original check, and provides that a properly prepared substitute check is the legal equivalent of an original check. The act facilitates electronic check exchange by enabling banks to sort and deliver checks electronically and, where necessary, to create legally equivalent substitute checks for presentment to banks that have not agreed to accept checks electronically.

Home Owner's Loan Act 12 U.S.C. 1464(d)—This act contains a provision to ensure and monitor the security of home owners' personally identifiable information.

Supervisory Committee 12 U.S.C. 1761 & 1761d—The supervisory committee shall make, or cause to be made, an annual audit and shall submit a report of that audit to the board of directors and a summary of the report to the members at the next annual meeting of the credit union; shall make, or cause to be made, such supplementary audits as it deems necessary or as may be ordered by the Board.

Risks Involving Client/Server Computer Systems, FIL-82-96—The statement addresses the risks and fundamental controls associated with a client/server environment. Management should ensure that appropriate risk management practices are in place for all information systems. Standard development methodologies that ensure appropriate controls need to be followed for all information systems, regardless of the methodology, platform, or technology used.

Electronic Banking Examination Procedures, FIL-14-97—This deals with the examination procedures that address the safety and soundness of electronic banking and audit of records.

Security Risks Associated with the Internet, FIL-131-97—Unless otherwise protected, all data transfers, including electronic mail, travel openly over the Internet and can be monitored or read by others. Appendix A discusses applicable security measures.

Suspicious Activity Reporting, FIL-124-97—This section ensures that a member bank files a Suspicious Activity Report when it detects a known or suspected violation of federal law, or a suspicious transaction related to a money-laundering activity or a violation of the Bank Secrecy Act.

Electronic Financial Services and Consumer Compliance, FIL-79-98—The guidance contains two sections: "Compliance Regulatory Environment," which summarizes relevant sections of the federal consumer protection laws and regulations that address electronic financial services, and includes interim compliance policy guidance with practical examples for applying existing consumer laws and regulations; and "The Role of Consumer Compliance in Developing and Implementing Electronic Services," which discusses the importance of compliance officer involvement in the design, development, implementation, and monitoring of electronic banking operations.

Electronic Commerce and Consumer Privacy, FIL-86-98—The privacy of consumer personal information has become an increasing concern with the rapid growth in electronic commerce conducted over the Internet, emerging electronic payment systems, and collection of personal information—this act addresses all these issues. How the information is used by the entity collecting the information, particularly for purposes other than the original transaction, and whether personal information is transferred to third parties, and how they will use it also come under the purview of this act.

Pretext Phone Calling, FIL-98-98—Although this advisory primarily concerns the unauthorized access to customer account information through pretext phone calling, unauthorized access to sensitive account information may occur through other means as well, including burglary, illegal or unauthorized access to the institution's computer systems, and bribing employees with access to personal account information. Institutions should have effective procedures and controls in place to limit access to confidential information on a need-to-know basis, and to prevent unauthorized access to customer information through these and other means.

Offshore Outsourcing FIL-49-99: Bank Service Company Act—Few legal restrictions apply to financial service companies sending customer data to foreign countries. Financial institution customers may not opt out of these information transfers to nonaffiliated service providers if the transfer is for a purpose described in section 502(e) of the GLBA. For example, the opportunity to opt out does not apply when the information transfer is to: (1) service or process a financial product or service that the customer requested or authorized or (2) maintain or service the customer's account.

Annual Independent Audits and Reporting Requirements, 12 CFR Part 363—(a) Audited financial statements: Each insured depository institution shall prepare annual financial statements in accordance with generally accepted accounting principles: which shall be audited by an independent public accountant. (b) Management report: Each insured depository institution annually shall prepare, as of the end of the institution's most recent fiscal year, a management report signed by its chief executive officer and chief accounting or chief financial officer

Minimum Security Procedures, 12 CFR 326, Subpart A—This subpart is issued to ensure that all insured nonmember banks as defined in 12 CFR 326.1 establish and maintain procedures reasonably designed to ensure and monitor compliance. They should also provide for a system of internal controls to ensure ongoing compliance; provide for independent testing for compliance to be conducted by bank personnel or by an outside party; designate an individual or individuals responsible for coordinating and monitoring day-to-day compliance; and provide training for appropriate personnel.

Privacy of Consumer Financial Information, 12 CFR 332—This act governs the treatment of nonpublic personal information about consumers by the financial institutions. If an institution holds ownership or servicing rights to an individual's loan that is used primarily for personal, family, or household purposes, the individual is to be considered a consumer and possesses a right to privacy of that information

Procedures for Monitoring Bank Secrecy Act Compliance, 12 CFR 326, Subpart B—This sets forth requirements for state nonmember banks to establish and maintain procedures to ensure and monitor their compliance with the BSA.

Suspicious Activity Reports, 12 CFR 353—The purpose of this part is to ensure that an insured state nonmember bank files a Suspicious Activity Report when it detects a known or suspected criminal violation of federal law or a suspicious transaction related to a money-laundering activity or a violation of the Bank Secrecy Act. This part applies to all insured state nonmember banks as well as any insured, state-licensed branches of foreign banks.

e-CFR 12 CFR 208.61—Authority, purpose, and scope. Pursuant to section 3 of the Bank Protection Act of 1968 (12 U.S.C. 1882), member banks are required to adopt appropriate security procedures to discourage robberies, burglaries, and larcenies, and to assist in the identification and prosecution of persons who commit such acts.

## United States: Nonprofit

New York and California have passed legislation on SOX "clones," targeting nonprofit accountability. In a similar vein, the U.S. Senate Finance Committee conducted hearings in June 2004 and published some proposed actions to raise the bar for nonprofit accountability. The legislation mandates the following:

■ A requirement for nonprofits to have their Internal Revenue Service (IRS) tax-exempt status reviewed every 5 years, with extra documents and a new processing fee
■ Increased information disclosures on IRS Form 990, including annual performance goals and measurements for meeting those goals

- Require Form 990 to be signed by an organization's chief executive officer (CEO) or equivalent under penalties or perjury
- Penalties for failure to file a complete and accurate 990
- Appropriate $10 million for various forms of nonprofit accreditation
- Establishment of an Exempt Organization Hotline for reporting abuses by charities and complaints by donors and beneficiaries
- Limit board size to 15 members

There is public pressure for a higher level of scrutiny and regulation of U.S. nonprofits. Although only two provisions of SOX apply to both nonprofit and publicly traded companies (whistleblower protection and document preservation), best practices that emerge from SOX compliance and have been implemented by state legislation include the following:

- Requirements for a more effective board whose members understand and adhere to their fiduciary obligations and recognize their responsibility in governing the nonprofit
- Higher level of management and staff accountability
- Effective protocols to ensure that the nonprofit remains in compliance with SOX and nonprofit "industry standards" and addresses future standards
- Better competitive positioning by making known that the nonprofit adheres to the SOX platinum standard in its operating practices
- Greater credibility and ability to recruit high-quality board members and to attract the favorable attention of major donors, foundations, and other funding sources

Internal Revenue Service Commissioner's Testimony—As part of the Senate Finance Committee's June 2004 hearings on nonprofit accountability, by Mark W. Everson, the commissioner of the IRS, the administration's FY 2005 budget contains a number of legislative incentives for nonprofit accountability that were originally announced by the Treasury Department in March 2002 to combat abusive transactions. These proposals include statutory changes that create better, coordinated disclosure of abusive transactions; although the administration is committed to encouraging gifts to charity, it also wants to ensure that taxpayers are accurately valuing property they donate to charity.

Section 501(c)(3)—This provides that the assets of an organization cannot inure to the benefit of private shareholders or individuals. If an organization pays or distributes assets to insiders in excess of the fair market value of the services rendered, the organization can lose its tax-exempt status. Organizations also will be asked for details concerning the independence of the governing body that approved the compensation and details of the duties and responsibilities of these managers with respect to the organization. Other stages will follow, and will include looking at various kinds of insider transactions, such as loans or sales to executives and officers. Five-year review of tax-exempt status by the IR. The staff discussion recommended that:

On every fifth anniversary of the IRS' determination of the tax-exempt status of an organization that is required to apply for such status, the organization is required to file with the IRS such information as would enable the IRS to determine whether the organization continues to be organized and operated exclusively for exempt purposes (i.e., whether the original determination letter should remain in effect). Information filed would include current articles of incorporation and by-laws, conflicts of interest policies, evidence of accreditation, management policies regarding best practices, a detailed narrative about the organization's practices, and financial statements.

This recommendation requires nonprofits to submit documentation every 5 years that proves to the IRS that the organization continues to comply with its 501(c)(3) designation.

Form 990 requirements—Form 990 requires that the CEO (or equivalent officer) of a tax-exempt organization sign a declaration under penalties of perjury that the CEO has put in place processes and procedures to ensure that the organization's federal information return and tax return (including Form 990T) complies with the Internal Revenue Code and that the CEO was provided reasonable assurance of the accuracy and completeness of all material aspects of the return. These declarations are part of the information or tax return.

What does this mean for federally registered nonprofits? This ruling requires a nonprofit CEO to sign an affidavit under penalties of perjury that the organization's Form 990 complies with the Internal Revenue Code and that the CEO is providing assurance of the accuracy and completeness of all material aspects of the return. (The financials accurately reflect the financial position of the nonprofit.) This affidavit should be part of the information or tax return.

In accordance with legislation, the recommendation is that nonprofit executives and board members should be held to the same criminal liability standards as those of their private sector counterparts.

Penalties for failure to file a complete and accurate Form 990—The present law penalty for failure to file or to include required information is $20/day up to the lesser of $10,000 or 5 percent of gross receipts per return (increased to $100/day up to $50,000 per return for organizations with gross receipts over $1 million in a year). Under the proposal, the penalty for failure to file is doubled, and for organizations with gross receipts over $2 million per year, the present law penalty is tripled. Failure to file a required Form 990 for 2 consecutive years (or for 3 of 4 years) could result in loss of tax exemption, or other penalties such as loss of status as an organization to which deductible contributions may be made.

What does this mean for nonprofits? There will be severe penalties for failing to file a Form 990. The proposals recommend loss of tax exemption or loss of status as an organization to which deductible contributions may be made. For a nonprofit, this means the organization can no longer tell donors that their contributions are tax exempt. In other words, the "nonprofit" is out of business.

Required disclosure of performance goals, activities, and expenses in Form 990 and in financial statements—Charitable organizations with over $250,000 in gross receipts are required to include in Form 990 a detailed description of the organization's annual performance goals and measurements for meeting those goals (to be established by the board of directors) for the past year and goals for the coming year. The purposes of this requirement are to assist donors to better determine an organization's accomplishments and goals in deciding whether to donate, and not as a point of review by the IRS. Charitable organizations are required to disclose material changes in activities, operations, or structure. Charitable organizations are required to accurately report the charity's expenses, including any joint cost allocations, in its financial statements and Form 990. Exempt organizations are required to report how often the board of directors met, and how often the board met without the CEO (or equivalent) present.

What does this mean for nonprofits? Transparency is the predominant theme of these recommendations. The Congressional staff may have been spurred on by the volume of public complaints about nonprofit organizations that, for every donor dollar, contribute very little to programs. In recent years, the media has conducted many investigations of bogus charities, and certainly, some charities that are "household names" have abused donor trust by misdirecting donations to exorbitant salaries, expenses, and other abuses. Note that these disclosures are required to be presented on Form 990. The accuracy of these disclosures could carry criminal liability if the other proposal on CEO signatures is enacted into law.

Nonprofits are required to make documents publicly available. Public oversight is critical to ensuring that an exempt organization continues to operate in accordance with its tax-exempt status. For charitable organizations, public oversight provides donors with vital information for determining which organizations have the programs and practices that will ensure that contributions will be spent as intended. Oversight is facilitated under present law by mandated public disclosure of information returns and applications for tax-exempt status.

Disclosure of financial statements—Exempt organizations are required to disclose to the public the organization's financial statements.

Web site disclosure—Exempt organizations with a Web site are required to post on such site any return that is required to be made public by present law, the organization's application for tax exemption, the organization's determination letter from the IRS, and the organization's financial statements for the five most recent years.

What does this mean for federally registered nonprofits? The recommendations are aimed at ensuring that the public has access to information that is vital to decide whether to make a donation or not. Of particular note is the recommendation that the nonprofit's Web site be employed to present those documents currently required (Form 990).

California's "Nonprofit Integrity Act" (SB1262): Provisions that Apply to Nonprofits with Budgets in Excess of $2 Million—The state of California passed a "Nonprofit Integrity Act" that imposes many of the features of SOX on nonprofits with budgets in excess of $2 million operating in that state.

Key provisions of this law include the following:

Nonprofits will be required to have an annual audit performed by a CPA who is "independent" as defined by U.S. government auditing standards.
The results of the audit will need to be made available to the public and the attorney general.
Nonprofits will be required to have an audit committee whose membership cannot include staff and must not overlap more than 50 percent with the finance committee; the audit committee can include members who are not on the organization's board of directors.

New York Nonprofit Integrity Act (S4836-A) requires that not-for-profits, other than private foundations, with annual gross revenues less than $1 million and total assets less than $3 million verify that the annual report "fairly presents" the financial condition of the corporation. A more comprehensive verification requirement affects nonprofits with annual gross revenues of at least $1 million or at least $3 million in assets. For nonprofit entities (excluding private foundations and Type A corporations that do not register with the attorney general) that meet this second threshold, raised from an original proposal of $250,000 or more in gross revenues, S4836-A applies strict financial reporting standards. Among other provisions, this standard requires the president or CEO and the treasurer or CFO to certify the accuracy and validity of the annual report as well as the adequacy of the internal controls. The legislation also tightens the reins on interested-party contracts and board compensation. The establishment of an executive committee with 3 or more board members is required of entities with boards of more than 25 directors. For nonprofits that meet the second threshold, or whose financial statements are to be audited by a public accountant, the legislation mandates the establishment of an audit committee of three or more board members who lack any business ties to the organization. (State law currently requires that nonprofit organizations with revenues over $250,000 must file audited financial statements.)

What does this mean for nonprofits in California and New York? To ensure greater account-ability in executive compensation, the law requires that the board approve the compensation, including benefits, of the corporation's president or CEO, and its treasurer or CFO, for the purposes of ensuring that these executives' compensation packages are reasonable.

The laws also require disclosure of written contracts between commercial fundraisers and non-profits and available for review on demand from the attorney general's office. Fundraisers must be registered with the attorney general's office.

## United States: State and Local Government

Real ID Act Bill Number H.R. 418 for the 109th Congress—To establish and rapidly implement regulations for state driver's license and identification document security standards, to prevent terrorists from abusing the asylum laws of the United States, to unify terrorism-related grounds for inadmissibility and removal, and to ensure expeditious construction of the San Diego border fence. Pursuant to H. Res. 151, the text of H.R. 418, as passed House, was appended as Division B to the end of H.R. 1268. Division B was further modified in conference. H.R. 1268 became P.L. 109-13 on 5/11/2005.

Title I: Amendments to Federal Laws to Protect Against Terrorist Entry - (Section 101)—Amends Immigration and Nationality Act (INA).

Title II: Improved Security for Driver's Licenses and Personal Identification Cards - (Section 202)—This prohibits federal agencies from accepting state-issued driver's licenses or identification cards unless such documents are determined by the secretary to meet minimum security requirements, including the incorporation of specified data, a common machine-readable technology, and certain antifraud security features.

Title III: Border Infrastructure and Technology Integration - (Section 301)—This increases the utilization of ground surveillance technologies to enhance U.S. border security. Requires technologies to include video camera, sensor, and motion detection technologies.

Breach Notification Laws—These include Arizona SB 1338, Arkansas SB 1167, California SB 1386, Colorado HB 1119, Connecticut SB 650, Delaware HB 116, Florida HB 481, Georgia SB 230, Hawaii SB 2290, Idaho SB 1374, Illinois HB 1633, Indiana HB 1101, Kansas SB 196, Louisiana SB 205, Maine LD 1671, Minnesota HF 2121, Montana HB 732, Nebraska LB 876, Nevada SB 347, New Hampshire HB 1660, New Jersey A4001, New York S 3492 & S 5827, North Carolina SB 1048, North Dakota SB 2251, Ohio HB 104, Oklahoma HB 2357, Pennsylvania SB 712, Rhode Island HB 6191, Tennessee HB 2170, Texas SB 122, Utah SB 69, Washington SB 6043, and Wisconsin SB 164.

Typical state breach disclosure state laws require direct notification between the third party organization with th compromise and each affected individual. Private information is defined in the legislation to be any of the following: Social Security numbers, driver's license number, bank account numbers, credit/debit card numbers, as well as any other personal identifying information. State disclosure laws are a significant improvement because affected parties are unaware of their increased risk of identity theft and the public would not know of the magnitude of the problem through mass media reports. Typical requirements include the following:

Trigger Requirement - Information Materially Compromised or Likelihood of Harm Before Notification—Some states require the organization whose security was breached to themselves determine if the compromised private information is "likely" to result in identity theft. Not surprisingly, this has resulted in some organizations not reporting breaches that most objective observers would consider likely to result in identity theft. Other states have a trigger depending on the number of people affected (for instance, greater than 1000 people). Other states exempt certain organizations from having to report.

Timing Requirements—Many states require notification following a trigger event over varying periods of time. Individuals should be warned in enough time to protect themselves from increased identity theft risk.

Monitoring and Enforcement Requirement—Some states require organizations to monitor their systems to be able to better determine breach events but, as stated previously, the type of monitoring required is vague and changes dynamically. A national breach disclosure law should eliminate the requirement for monitoring but levy a significant civil/criminal penalty if a breach is exposed that was not first reported by the organization.

Type of Notification Requirement—Notification can be written using 2-day postal delivery, electronic, or telephonic, depending on the state in question.

Notification Information Requirement—In many states elements of the following information need to be reported for breach events to both the affected individuals and a public clearinghouse. This includes number of records breached, type of private information compromised, breach mechanism, number of people affected, estimated cost of breach damage, steps taken to prevent breach from recurring, and steps for the affected individual to protect themselves from increased identity theft risk specific to this event.

Prebreach Measures Requirement—In advance of any breach many states (including California Civil Code Section 1798.81.5) require a business to implement and maintain reasonable security procedures and practices and to contractually require the same of any nonaffiliated third parties to whom personal information is transferred. Some states also require businesses to utilize appropriate data destruction methods when disposing of records containing personal information.

The proposed federal legislation encompasses the following:

- Consumer Data Security and Notification Act of 2005 - HR 3140
- Personal Data Privacy and Security Act - S 1789
- Data Accountability and Trust Act - HR 4127
- Information Protection and Security Act - S 500
- Consumer Access Rights Defense Act (CARD) of 2005 - HR 3501
- Consumer Notification and Financial Data Protection Act of 2005 - HR 3374
- Financial Data Protection Act of 2005 - HR 3997
- Comprehensive Identity Theft Prevention Act - S 768
- Identity Theft Protection Act - S 1408
- Notification of Risk to Personal Data Act - S 751
- Notification of Risk to Personal Data Act - HR 1069
- Identity Theft Notification and Credit Restoration Act of 2003 - HR 3233
- Identity Theft and Credit Restoration Act of 2003 - S 1633
- Identity Theft Consumer Notification Act - HR 5474

Credit Freeze Laws—A security freeze lets consumers stop predators from getting credit in their names. A security freeze locks, or freezes, access to the consumer credit report and credit score. Without this information, a business will not issue new credit. When the consumer wants to get new credit, he or she uses a PIN to unlock access to the credit file. These states give consumers this important weapon to prevent identity theft. Two types are available:

Acquisition-based trigger—Strong consumer-oriented notification requirement based on loss of information.

Risk-based trigger—Loss of information does not trigger notice automatically.

Notice is subject to some analysis by breached entity of the degree of risk to consumers before notice is required. Some risk triggers are more consumer-friendly than others. (For example, S 1789 and HR 4127 as proposed in the 2006 Congress require a presumption of notice unless "no risk" exists. Weaker laws require some risk before notice.)

- California CIS-10 California Civil Code sections 1785.11.2-1785.11.6
- Colorado SB 05-137
- Connecticut SB 650
- Delaware SB109 'Clean Credit and Identity Theft Prevention Act'
- Florida Statute Section 501.005 et seq. (2006 HB 37)
- Hawaii Title 26 Revised Statutes Section 1 et seq. (HB 1871)
- Illinois 815 ILCS 505/2MM
- Kansas S.B. 196
- Kentucky Ch367 Revised Statutes Sections 1-3 (HB 54)
- Louisiana Statutes Annotated § 9.3571(H) to (Y)
- Maine 10 MRSA §1313-C
- Minnesota Senate Bill 2002
- Nevada NRS 598C
- New Hampshire Revised Statutes Annotated 359B:23 (SB334)
- New Jersey Statute 56:11-44 et seq.
- New York CLS Gen. Bus. §380-a (k)-(n), §380-t bill version AB 7349
- North Carolina General Statutes §75-63
- Oklahoma Title 24 Statutes Sections 149 and 150 (SB 1748)
- Rhode Island Statutes 6-48-1 et seq. (H7148)
- South Dakota SB180
- Texas Business & Commerce Code Ann. § 20.031 to 20.039
- Utah Code Ann. §13-45-102, 13-45-201 et seq. bill version SB 71
- Vermont Statutes Annotated, Title 9, Sections 2480a to 2480j
- Washington Sec. 19.182 RCW
- Wisconsin Statutes (AB 912) Section 138.25

FRCP e-Discovery—On April 12, 2006, the United States Supreme Court approved, without comment or dissent, proposed amendments to the Federal Rules of Civil Procedure that will significantly alter the way in which litigants must handle discovery of "electronically stored information." The new rules and amendments have been sent to Congress and will take effect on December 1, 2006, unless Congress enacts legislation to modify, reject, or defer the amendments. Among other changes, the proposed amendments will modify Rules 16, 26, 33, 34, 37, and 45, as follows:

Rule 16(b): The court's pretrial scheduling order can include provisions concerning electronically stored information.

Rule 26(b)(2): There is no duty to produce data reasonably identified as inaccessible, though the court may still order production upon good cause, with conditions.

Rule 26(b)(5): Creates a "claw back" procedure whereby a party can request the return of inadvertently produced privileged documents.

Rule 26(f): Parties must meet and confer on E-discovery issues before the pretrial scheduling conference.

Rule 33(d): Parties may reference "electronically stored information" as a type of business record from which answers to interrogatories may be derived.

Rule 34: Production request may specify desired E-data format and response must state any objection to requested format; "ordinary" (aka "native") file format or "reasonably useable" form is production default.

Rule 37: Provides "safe harbor" (i.e., no discovery sanctions) for inadvertent E-data loss if based on "routine, good faith operation" of an IT system.

Rule 45: Applicable new E-discovery rules extend to subpoenas.

# Canada

Political System: Parliamentary democracy

Web URL: www.privecom.gc.ca

Chief Privacy Officer/Minister: Federal Privacy Commissioner—Bureau for Data Protection/Privacy Commissioner of Canada

Description of Legislation

Personal Information Protection and Electronic Documents Act—The act adopts the CSA International Privacy Code (a national standard: CAN/CSA-Q830-96) into law for enterprises that process personal information "in the course of a commercial activity," and for federally regulated employers with respect to their employees. It does not apply to information collected for personal, journalistic, artistic, literary, or noncommercial purposes.

The Canadian Securities Administrators (CSA) issued Notice 52-313, which proposed some significant changes with regards to the CEO/CFO certification process, especially the requirements dealing with reporting on internal control over financial reporting (ICFR). This decision, which effectively shifts the responsibility for evaluating ICFR from an external auditor to the board of directors, impacts a number of stakeholders, including corporate directors, senior management, auditors and Canadian capital markets.

Multilateral Instrument 52-110, Audit Committees, states that "an audit committee must review the issuer's financial statements, MD&A, and annual and interim earnings press releases before the issuer publicly discloses this information."

This measure enhances investor protection as follows:

1. Public companies design and maintain effective ICFR to ensure reliable financial reporting in annual filings, quarterly filings, and in continuous disclosure releases.
2. Material weaknesses, if any, are disclosed properly to inform investors of their existence.

The Federal Privacy Act—Provides individuals with a right of access to personal information held by the federal public sector. In addition, the act contains provisions regulating the confidentiality, collection, correction, disclosure, retention, and use of personal information. Individuals may request records directly from the institution that has the custody of the information. The act establishes a code of fair information practices that applies to government handling of personal records.

Personal Information in the Private Sector—This provides individuals with a right of control regarding personal information held by private sector entities doing business within the province of Quebec. The Quebec's Private Sector Act has four principles:

1. A person or a corporation must have a serious and legitimate reason for establishing a file on someone.
2. Every individual has the right to access his or her file, unless the rights of third parties must be protected or there is a serious reason for refusing access.
3. Every individual has the right to rectify an incorrect, incomplete, or obsolete file.
4. Every person or corporation that opens a file on an individual has an obligation of confidentiality.

The right to professional secrecy actually takes precedence over privacy legislation, which is expressly set out in the Québec Private Sector Act. Within the act, only public interest can be raised as an exception to the protection and access obligations. Religions are not subject to the legislation when ruling on religious matters concerning relations between individuals and religious authorities.

The Canadian Security Intelligence Service Act—This authorizes the interception of communications for national security reasons and includes a policy for encryption that allows for broad development, use, and dissemination of encryption products.

The Telecommunications Act—This provides protection for the privacy of individuals, including the regulation of unsolicited communications.

The Federal Access to Information Act (R.S. 1985, c. A-1)—This act provides individuals with a right of access to information held by the federal public sector. The act gives Canadians and other individuals and corporations present in Canada the right to apply for and obtain copies of federal government records. "Records" include letters, memos, reports, photographs, films, microforms, plans, drawings, diagrams, maps, sound and video recordings, and machine-readable or computer files.

C-36 The Anti-Terrorism Act—This act deals with measures to deter, disable, identify, prosecute, convict, and punish terrorist groups. The law mandates investigative tools to law enforcement and national security agencies, and enacts controls ensuring individual identity safeguards. C-36 enacts stronger laws against hate crimes and propaganda with a records management provision.

The Suppression of Terrorist Financing Convention relates to the freezing of terrorist property by prohibiting dealing in any property of a person engaged in terrorist activities and prohibiting making available funds and financial or other related services to terrorists. C-36 allows a Federal Court judge to order the seizure and forfeiture of property used in or related to terrorist activity.

Under Bill C-36, the Criminal Code will also be amended to establish provisions aimed at disabling and dismantling the activities of terrorist groups and those who support them.

## Summary

Unfortunately, the trend is clearly heading toward more regulation, not less. Always consult experienced legal counsel (or your organization's audit or compliance department) for legal advice with regulatory issues that could materially affect your organization. Although this chapter highlights the most common regulatory concerns surrounding identity management and information technology regulatory compliance, it cannot provide complete guidance for every situation or jurisdiction. Many of the experts I have met with over the years prefer to apply known regulations narrowly and do not want to open the door to unanticipated compliance costs (a common concern for internal experts) or expand the scope of compliance work without having the billable expertise to address it (typical for external experts). If that happens during your implementation, ensure that you complete your due diligence by advising your organization's responsible executive (corporate counsel or chief compliance office) of your concerns in writing and leaving the matter in his or her hands. Remember, no piece of technology or application can make a company compliant. Regulatory compliance is a result of people, process, and procedure. No technology can take the place of proper due diligence.

# APPENDICES

# Appendix A

# Regulatory to Technical Control Mapping

**Table A.1    Multinational Regulatory Compliance Mapping**

| | Trusted Access | Change Management | Business Continuity and Availability | Operational Monitor and Report | Records Management | Audit and Risk Management | Operational Transparency | Segregation of Duties | Operational Control |
|---|---|---|---|---|---|---|---|---|---|
| **Asia/Pacific and Oceana** | | | | | | | | | |
| *Australia* | | | | | | | | | |
| Victorian Electronic Records Strategy (VERS) | X | X | * | X | * | X | X | X | X |
| DIRKS | X | X | * | X | * | X | X | X | X |
| CLERP9 | X | * | * | * | * | X | X | X | X |
| AS/NZS:4360 | X | X | * | X | * | * | X | X | X |
| Privacy Act of 1988 (Amended 2001) | X | * | * | * | * | X | X | X | X |
| The Crimes Act | X | X | X | X | * | X | X | X | X |
| The Federal Freedom of Information Act of 1982 | X | X | * | * | * | X | * | X | X |

**Table A.1 (continued)  Multinational Regulatory Compliance Mapping**

| | Trusted Access | Change Management | Business Continuity and Availability | Operational Monitor and Report | Records Management | Audit and Risk Management | Operational Transparency | Segregation of Duties | Operational Control |
|---|---|---|---|---|---|---|---|---|---|
| Privacy Amendment (private sector) Bill | X | X | X | X | X | X | X | X | X |
| The Privacy Act of 1988 | X | X | * | * | * | * | X | X | * |
| **New Zealand** | | | | | | | | | |
| AS/NZS:4360 | X | X | X | X | X | * | X | X | X |
| Article 21 of the Bill of Rights Act 1990 | X | X | X | X | X | X | X | X | X |
| **China** | | | | | | | | | |
| Chinese Constitution: Article 37 | X | X | X | X | X | X | X | X | X |
| Computer Information Network and Internet Security Protection and Management Regulations | X | X | X | * | * | * | X | X | X |
| Criminal Code: Sections 285 to 287 | X | X | X | X | * | X | X | X | X |
| Guidelines for Telecom Services | X | X | X | X | * | X | X | X | X |
| **Hong Kong** | | | | | | | | | |
| Personal Data (Privacy) Ordinance 1996 | X | * | * | * | * | * | X | X | X |
| Basic Law of the Hong Kong Special Administrative Region: Article 29 | X | X | X | X | * | X | X | X | X |
| Personal Data (Privacy) Ordinance | X | * | X | X | * | * | X | X | X |
| Telecommunications Ordinance and the Post Office Ordinance | X | X | X | X | * | X | X | X | X |
| Data Protection Principle 1 | X | * | X | X | * | * | X | X | X |
| Data Protection Principle 3 | X | X | * | * | * | X | X | X | X |
| Data Protection Principle 4 | X | X | X | * | * | * | X | X | X |

**Table A.1 (continued) Multinational Regulatory Compliance Mapping**

| | Trusted Access | Change Management | Business Continuity and Availability | Operational Monitor and Report | Records Management | Audit and Risk Management | Operational Transparency | Segregation of Duties | Operational Control |
|---|---|---|---|---|---|---|---|---|---|
| Employee Privacy Information: Code of Practice | X | X | X | X | * | X | X | X | X |
| Draft Code of Practice on Monitoring and Personal Data Privacy at Work | X | X | X | * | X | X | X | X | X |
| **Taiwan** | | | | | | | | | |
| Article 12 of the 1994 Taiwanese Constitution | X | X | X | X | X | X | X | X | X |
| The 1995 Computer-Processed Personal Data Protection Law | X | * | X | * | * | X | X | X | X |
| The 1995 Law Governing Protection of Personal Data Processed by Computers | X | X | X | X | X | X | X | X | X |
| The June 1999 Communication Protection and Surveillance Act | X | X | X | * | * | X | X | X | X |
| Telecommunications Surveillance Act: Article 315 | X | * | * | * | * | * | X | X | X |
| The Official Information Act | X | * | * | X | * | X | X | X | X |
| 1934 Telegraph and Telephone Act | X | X | * | * | X | X | X | X | X |
| **Japan** | | | | | | | | | |
| Article 21 of the 1946 Constitution | X | X | X | * | * | * | X | X | X |
| Japan Personal Information Protection Act (2003) | X | X | X | X | * | X | X | X | X |
| The 1988 Act for the Protection of Computer Processed Personal Data Held by Administrative Organs | X | X | X | X | * | * | X | X | X |

**Table A.1 (continued)   Multinational Regulatory Compliance Mapping**

| | Trusted Access | Change Management | Business Continuity and Availability | Operational Monitor and Report | Records Management | Audit and Risk Management | Operational Transparency | Segregation of Duties | Operational Control |
|---|---|---|---|---|---|---|---|---|---|
| Guidelines Concerning the Protection of Computer-Processed Personal Data in the Private Sector | X | X | * | X | * | X | X | X | X |
| The Law Concerning Access to Information Held by Administrative Organs | X | X | * | X | * | X | X | X | X |
| ***Malaysia*** | | | | | | | | | |
| Communications and Multimedia Act | X | X | X | X | X | X | X | X | X |
| The Digital Signature Act of 1997 and the Computer Crime Act of 1997 | X | X | X | X | * | X | X | X | X |
| National Registration Department Voluntary Smart Cards for Infants | X | X | X | * | * | * | X | X | X |
| The Ministry of Energy Communications and Multimedia Personal Data Protection | X | X | * | * | * | * | X | X | X |
| ***Philippines*** | | | | | | | | | |
| Article II of the 1987 Constitution | X | X | * | * | * | X | X | X | X |
| Article III of the 1987 Constitution | X | X | * | * | * | X | X | X | X |
| 1998 Access Devices Regulation Act | X | X | X | X | * | X | X | X | X |
| Republic Act 8972 the Electronic Commerce Act of 2000: Sections 89 and 10 | X | * | * | * | * | X | X | X | X |
| The Anti-Wiretapping Law | X | X | X | * | * | X | X | X | X |

**Table A.1 (continued)   Multinational Regulatory Compliance Mapping**

| | Trusted Access | Change Management | Business Continuity and Availability | Operational Monitor and Report | Records Management | Audit and Risk Management | Operational Transparency | Segregation of Duties | Operational Control |
|---|---|---|---|---|---|---|---|---|---|
| **Singapore** | | | | | | | | | |
| E-Commerce Code for the Protection of Personal Information and Communications of Consumers of Internet Commerce | X | X | X | X | * | X | X | X | X |
| Computer Misuse Act the Electronic Transactions Act and Nation Computer Board (Amendment) Act | X | X | X | X | X | X | X | X | X |
| Guidelines Regulating Scanning of Computers by ISPs | X | X | X | X | X | X | X | X | X |
| The Model Data Protection Code for the Private Sector | X | X | X | X | * | X | X | X | X |
| **South Korea** | | | | | | | | | |
| The Constitution: Articles 16 to 18 | X | X | X | X | X | X | X | X | X |
| The Act on the Protection of Personal Information Managed by Public Agencies 1994 | X | * | * | * | * | X | X | X | X |
| The Basic Act on Electronic Commerce: Chapter III | X | * | * | * | * | X | X | X | X |
| Law on Protection of Communications Secrecy Act | X | X | X | * | * | X | X | X | X |
| Article 54 of the Telecommunication Business Act | X | X | X | X | X | X | X | X | X |
| Act Relating to Use and Protection of Credit Information (1995) | X | X | * | * | * | X | X | X | X |
| Postal Services Act | X | X | X | X | X | X | X | X | X |

**Table A.1 (continued)  Multinational Regulatory Compliance Mapping**

| | Trusted Access | Change Management | Business Continuity and Availability | Operational Monitor and Report | Records Management | Audit and Risk Management | Operational Transparency | Segregation of Duties | Operational Control |
|---|---|---|---|---|---|---|---|---|---|
| The Act on Disclosure of Information by Public Agencies | X | X | * | X | * | X | X | X | X |
| The Ministry of Information and Communication (MIC) | X | X | X | * | * | X | X | X | X |
| **Thailand** | | | | | | | | | |
| Constitution Article 34 | X | X | X | X | X | X | X | X | X |
| Constitution Article 37 | X | X | X | X | X | X | X | X | X |
| Constitution Article 58 | X | X | X | X | * | X | X | X | X |
| Thailand Data Protection Law | X | X | X | * | * | X | X | X | X |
| Electronic Transactions Act | X | X | X | * | * | * | X | X | X |
| Electronic Data Interchange Law | X | X | X | X | * | X | X | X | X |
| Bylaw under Section 78 of the Thai Constitution (Universal Access Law) | X | X | * | X | X | X | X | X | X |
| Electronic Signature Law | X | X | X | X | * | X | X | X | X |
| The Official Information Act | X | X | X | * | * | * | X | X | X |
| **India** | | | | | | | | | |
| Information Technology Act 2000 | X | X | X | * | * | X | X | X | X |
| Security and Exchange Board StIndia Clause 49 | X | * | * | * | X | X | X | * | * |
| **European Union and Africa** | | | | | | | | | |
| **European Union** | | | | | | | | | |
| EU 8th Directive / FDICIA—EU Corporate Governance | X | * | * | * | X | X | X | * | * |
| EU Directive on the Transfer of PII Data | X | * | * | * | * | * | X | X | X |

**Table A.1 (continued)   Multinational Regulatory Compliance Mapping**

| | *Trusted Access* | *Change Management* | *Business Continuity and Availability* | *Operational Monitor and Report* | *Records Management* | *Audit and Risk Management* | *Operational Transparency* | *Segregation of Duties* | *Operational Control* |
|---|---|---|---|---|---|---|---|---|---|
| EU Directive 95/46 Article 286 | X | X | X | * | * | * | X | X | X |
| EU Directive 95/46/EC | X | X | X | X | * | X | X | X | X |
| EU Directive 97/66 | X | * | X | * | * | X | X | X | X |
| EU Directive 2002/58/EC | X | X | X | * | * | X | X | X | X |
| Electronic Surveillance in the Workplace: Article 8 | X | X | X | * | X | X | X | X | X |
| Article 29 Working Party Document 5401/01 | X | X | X | X | X | X | X | X | X |
| Markets in Financial Instruments Directive (MiFID) | X | * | X | * | * | * | * | * | * |
| **Austria** | | | | | | | | | |
| Datenschutzgesetz (DSG) 2000 | X | * | * | * | * | * | X | X | X |
| Code of Criminal Procedure | X | X | X | X | * | X | * | X | X |
| The Auskunftspflichtgesetz | X | X | X | X | * | X | * | X | X |
| **Belgium** | | | | | | | | | |
| Belgian Constitution. Recognizes the right of privacy and private communications | X | X | X | X | * | X | * | X | X |
| Article 29 | X | X | X | X | * | X | X | X | X |
| Law on Privacy Protection in Relation to the Processing of Personal Data | X | X | X | * | * | X | X | X | X |
| Data Protection Act of 1992 | X | X | X | X | * | X | X | X | X |
| Criminal Procedure Code | X | X | * | X | * | X | * | X | X |
| **Bulgaria** | | | | | | | | | |
| Bulgarian Constitution of 1991 | X | X | X | X | X | X | X | X | X |
| Article 32 | X | X | X | * | * | X | X | X | X |

**Table A.1 (continued)   Multinational Regulatory Compliance Mapping**

| | Trusted Access | Change Management | Business Continuity and Availability | Operational Monitor and Report | Records Management | Audit and Risk Management | Operational Transparency | Segregation of Duties | Operational Control |
|---|---|---|---|---|---|---|---|---|---|
| Article 34 | X | X | X | X | X | X | X | X | X |
| Article 41 | X | X | X | X | * | X | * | X | X |
| Personal Data Protection Act of 1997 | X | * | X | * | * | X | * | X | X |
| The Law for Access to Information | X | X | X | X | * | X | * | X | X |
| **Czech Republic** | | | | | | | | | |
| The 1993 Charter of Fundamental Rights and Freedoms | X | X | X | X | * | X | X | X | X |
| Article 7 | X | X | X | X | * | X | X | X | X |
| Article 10 | X | X | X | * | * | X | X | X | X |
| Article 13 | X | X | X | X | * | X | X | X | X |
| 101 Act of 4 April 2000 | X | X | X | X | * | X | X | X | X |
| Czech Penal Code | X | X | X | X | * | X | X | X | X |
| Freedom of Information Law | X | X | X | X | * | X | * | X | X |
| **Denmark** | | | | | | | | | |
| Act on Processing of Personal Data | X | X | X | X | * | X | X | X | X |
| The Danish Constitution of 1953 | X | X | X | * | * | X | * | X | X |
| The Administrative Procedures Act of 1985 the Payment Cards Act of 1994 | X | X | * | * | * | * | * | X | X |
| Access to Health Information Act of 1993 | X | X | X | X | * | X | X | X | X |
| The Access to Information Act and the Access to Public Administration Files Act | X | X | X | X | * | X | X | X | X |

**Table A.1 (continued)    Multinational Regulatory Compliance Mapping**

| | Trusted Access | Change Management | Business Continuity and Availability | Operational Monitor and Report | Records Management | Audit and Risk Management | Operational Transparency | Segregation of Duties | Operational Control |
|---|---|---|---|---|---|---|---|---|---|
| **Estonia** | | | | | | | | | |
| The 1992 Estonia Constitution | X | X | X | X | * | X | X | X | X |
| Article 42 | X | X | X | * | * | X | X | X | X |
| Article 43 | X | X | X | X | * | * | * | X | X |
| Article 44 | X | X | X | X | * | X | * | X | X |
| Personal Data Protection Act | X | X | X | * | * | X | * | X | X |
| Databases Act | X | X | * | X | * | X | * | X | X |
| The Digital Signatures Act | X | X | X | X | X | * | X | X | X |
| 1994 Surveillance Act | X | X | X | X | * | X | X | X | X |
| Telecommunications Act | X | X | * | * | * | X | * | X | X |
| **Finland** | | | | | | | | | |
| The Constitution Act of Finland | X | X | X | * | * | X | X | X | X |
| The Personal Data Protection Act | X | * | X | * | * | X | * | X | X |
| Personal Data Act (523/1999) | X | X | * | * | * | X | * | X | X |
| Amendment to Personal Data Act (986/2000) | X | X | * | * | * | X | * | X | X |
| Coercive Criminal Investigations Means Act | X | X | X | X | * | X | X | X | X |
| The Publicity (of Public Actions) Act | X | X | X | X | * | X | X | X | X |
| Workplace Data Protection Legislation | X | * | X | * | * | * | * | X | X |
| **France** | | | | | | | | | |
| Law 78-17 of 6 January 1978 on Data Processing Data Files and Individual Liberties | X | X | * | * | * | X | X | X | X |

**Table A.1 (continued)    Multinational Regulatory Compliance Mapping**

| | Trusted Access | Change Management | Business Continuity and Availability | Operational Monitor and Report | Records Management | Audit and Risk Management | Operational Transparency | Segregation of Duties | Operational Control |
|---|---|---|---|---|---|---|---|---|---|
| Act of 6 August 2004 | X | X | * | * | * | X | * | X | X |
| The Data Protection Act | X | X | * | * | * | X | * | X | X |
| The French Liberty of Communication Act | X | X | * | * | * | * | * | X | X |
| **Germany** | | | | | | | | | |
| The TransPuG Law (2002) | X | * | X | * | X | * | * | X | * |
| The 4th Financial Market Support Law (2002) | X | * | * | * | * | * | * | X | * |
| The Cromme Commission Report | X | X | * | X | X | * | X | X | * |
| The Datenschutz Law (1994) | X | X | * | X | X | * | * | * | * |
| Bundsebar Germany's eGovernment initiative | X | * | X | * | * | * | * | X | * |
| Governing Legislation: Federal Data Protection Act | X | * | * | * | * | X | * | X | X |
| Article 10 of the Basic Law | X | X | * | * | * | X | * | X | X |
| Federal Data Protection Law | X | X | * | * | * | X | * | X | X |
| The Telecommunications Carriers Data Protection Ordinance of 1996 | X | X | * | * | * | X | * | X | X |
| The Information and Communication Services (Multimedia) Act of 1997 | X | X | X | X | * | * | X | X | X |
| German Stock Corporation Act (AktG) | X | X | * | * | * | * | * | X | X |
| Document management and electronic archiving (DOMEA) | X | X | * | * | * | X | * | X | X |
| Germany's 2nd and 3rd Laws for the Promotion of the Financial Markets | X | * | * | * | * | * | * | X | X |

**Table A.1 (continued)  Multinational Regulatory Compliance Mapping**

| | Trusted Access | Change Management | Business Continuity and Availability | Operational Monitor and Report | Records Management | Audit and Risk Management | Operational Transparency | Segregation of Duties | Operational Control |
|---|---|---|---|---|---|---|---|---|---|
| KonTraG - Gesetz zur Kontrolle und Transparenz im Unternehmensbereich (1998) | X | * | * | * | * | * | * | X | X |
| The German Safe Custody Act (Depotgesetz) | X | X | * | * | * | * | * | X | X |
| BDSG the German Federal Data Protection Act (BDSG) | X | * | * | * | * | * | * | X | X |
| **Greece** | | | | | | | | | |
| The Constitution of Greece | X | X | X | X | * | * | X | X | X |
| Article 19 of the constitution | X | X | * | X | * | X | X | X | X |
| Law on the Protection of Individuals with regard to the Processing of Personal Data | X | X | * | * | * | X | * | X | X |
| Article 5 of the Greek Code of Administrative Procedure | X | X | * | * | * | X | * | X | X |
| **Hungary** | | | | | | | | | |
| Constitution of the Republic of Hungary | X | X | X | X | * | X | X | X | X |
| Protection of Personal Data and Disclosure of Data of Public Interest | X | X | X | * | * | X | * | X | X |
| **Iceland** | | | | | | | | | |
| Constitution research and seizure | X | X | X | X | * | X | X | X | X |
| The Act on Protection of Individuals with regard to the Processing of Personal Data | X | X | X | * | * | * | X | X | X |
| Law on Criminal Procedure | X | X | * | * | * | * | * | X | X |
| The Freedom of Information Act of 1996 (Upplysingalog) | X | X | * | * | * | X | * | X | X |

**Table A.1 (continued)    Multinational Regulatory Compliance Mapping**

| | Trusted Access | Change Management | Business Continuity and Availability | Operational Monitor and Report | Records Management | Audit and Risk Management | Operational Transparency | Segregation of Duties | Operational Control |
|---|---|---|---|---|---|---|---|---|---|
| **Ireland** | | | | | | | | | |
| Data Protection Act (effective 1988) and (Amendment) Bill 2002 | X | X | * | * | * | X | * | X | X |
| The Freedom of Information Act | X | X | X | * | X | X | * | X | X |
| Data Protection Order for Registration of 9 January 2001 | X | X | * | * | * | X | * | X | X |
| European Communities (Data Protection) Regulations 2001 | X | X | X | * | * | * | * | X | X |
| Isle of Man Territory of United Kingdom The Isle of Man Data Protection Act of 1986 | X | X | * | * | * | * | * | X | X |
| **Italy** | | | | | | | | | |
| Employee Data Protection Provisions | X | X | X | * | * | X | * | X | X |
| The 1948 Constitution | X | X | X | X | * | X | X | X | X |
| The Italian Data Protection Act | X | * | * | * | * | * | * | X | X |
| EU Telecommunications Privacy Directive | X | X | * | * | * | * | * | X | X |
| **Latvia** | | | | | | | | | |
| Constitutional Law on Rights and Obligations of a Citizen and a Person | X | X | X | * | * | * | X | X | X |
| The Law on Personal Data Protection of 23 March 2000 | X | * | * | * | * | * | * | X | X |
| **Lithuania** | | | | | | | | | |
| Article 22 of the Constitution | X | X | X | X | * | X | X | X | X |
| Law on Legal Protection of Personal Data | X | * | * | * | * | * | * | X | X |

**Table A.1 (continued) Multinational Regulatory Compliance Mapping**

|  | Trusted Access | Change Management | Business Continuity and Availability | Operational Monitor and Report | Records Management | Audit and Risk Management | Operational Transparency | Segregation of Duties | Operational Control |
|---|---|---|---|---|---|---|---|---|---|
| The Penal Code of the Republic of Lithuania: | X | X | * | * | * | X | X | X | X |
| The 1996 Law on the Provision of Information to the Public | X | X | * | X | * | X | * | X | X |
| *Luxemburg* | | | | | | | | | |
| Article 28 of the Constitution | X | X | X | X | * | X | X | X | X |
| Act Concerning the Use of Nominal Data in Computer Processing effective 1979 | X | X | X | * | * | * | X | X | X |
| *Netherlands* | | | | | | | | | |
| The Constitution | X | X | X | * | * | * | * | X | X |
| The Personal Data Protection Act of 2000 | X | X | * | * | * | * | * | X | X |
| Telecommunications Act effective December 1998 | X | X | * | * | * | * | X | X | X |
| The Government Information Public Access Act of 1991 | X | X | * | * | * | X | * | X | X |
| *Norway* | | | | | | | | | |
| General Legal Protection of "Personality" | X | * | X | X | * | X | X | X | X |
| The Personal Data Registers Act of 2000 | X | * | * | * | * | * | * | X | X |
| The Telecommunications Act | X | X | X | * | * | X | X | X | X |
| The Public Access to Documents in the (Public) Administration | X | X | * | X | * | X | * | X | X |
| Rules for the protection of personal data (Personal Data Protection Act) | X | * | * | * | * | * | * | X | X |

**Table A.1 (continued)   Multinational Regulatory Compliance Mapping**

| | Trusted Access | Change Management | Business Continuity and Availability | Operational Monitor and Report | Records Management | Audit and Risk Management | Operational Transparency | Segregation of Duties | Operational Control |
|---|---|---|---|---|---|---|---|---|---|
| **Poland** | | | | | | | | | |
| The Polish Constitution: Article 47 | X | * | X | * | * | * | * | X | X |
| The Polish Constitution: Article 51 | X | * | X | * | * | * | * | X | X |
| The Law on the Protection of Personal Data Protection | X | * | * | * | * | * | * | X | X |
| Access to Information Act | X | X | X | X | X | * | * | X | X |
| Classified Information Protection Act | X | X | X | X | X | * | X | X | X |
| **Portugal** | | | | | | | | | |
| Portuguese Constitution: Article 35 | X | * | X | * | * | * | * | X | X |
| Portuguese Data Protection Act | X | * | * | * | * | * | * | X | X |
| Freedom of information Law 65/93 of 26 August 1993 | X | X | * | * | * | X | * | X | X |
| **Russia** | | | | | | | | | |
| The Constitution of the Russian Federation 23 and 24 | X | X | X | * | * | * | * | X | X |
| Russian Federation on Information Informatization and Information Protection of January 1995 | X | * | X | * | * | X | * | X | X |
| Freedom of Information | X | X | X | X | * | X | * | X | X |
| 1995 Communications Act | X | X | X | * | * | * | * | X | X |
| System for Operational Research Actions on the Documentary Telecommunication Networks | X | X | X | * | * | * | X | X | X |

**Table A.1 (continued)   Multinational Regulatory Compliance Mapping**

| | Trusted Access | Change Management | Business Continuity and Availability | Operational Monitor and Report | Records Management | Audit and Risk Management | Operational Transparency | Segregation of Duties | Operational Control |
|---|---|---|---|---|---|---|---|---|---|
| **Slovakia** | | | | | | | | | |
| The 1992 Constitution: Article 16 and 22 | X | X | * | * | * | X | * | X | X |
| The Act on Protection of Personal Data in Information Systems | X | X | * | * | * | X | * | X | X |
| Article 11 of the Civil Code | X | X | X | * | * | * | * | X | X |
| The Act on Free Access to Information | X | * | * | * | * | * | * | X | X |
| **Slovenia** | | | | | | | | | |
| The 1991 Constitution: Article 35 on the Protection of the Right to Privacy and of Personal Integrity | X | X | X | X | * | X | * | X | X |
| Article 38 on the Protection of Personal Data | X | X | * | * | * | * | * | X | X |
| Law on Personal Data Protection | X | * | * | * | * | * | * | X | X |
| The Law on Telecommunications | X | X | X | * | * | * | * | X | X |
| The Electronic Commerce and Electronic Signature Act | X | X | X | X | * | * | X | X | X |
| **Spain** | | | | | | | | | |
| The Constitution | X | X | X | X | * | * | X | X | X |
| Organic Law 5/1992 on the Regulation of the Automatic Processing of Personal Data | X | X | X | X | X | * | * | X | X |
| Law of Information Society Services and Electronic Commerce (LSSI) | X | X | X | X | * | X | * | X | X |
| The Spanish Data Protection Act (LORTAD) | X | * | * | * | * | * | * | X | X |

**Table A.1 (continued)   Multinational Regulatory Compliance Mapping**

| | Trusted Access | Change Management | Business Continuity and Availability | Operational Monitor and Report | Records Management | Audit and Risk Management | Operational Transparency | Segregation of Duties | Operational Control |
|---|---|---|---|---|---|---|---|---|---|
| **Sweden** | | | | | | | | | |
| Sweden's Constitution | X | * | * | * | * | * | * | X | X |
| Personal Data Act of 1998 (amended in January 2000) | X | * | * | * | * | * | * | X | X |
| Freedom of the Press Act of 1766 | X | X | * | * | * | X | * | X | X |
| **Switzerland** | | | | | | | | | |
| Article 36 of the Constitution | X | X | * | * | * | * | * | X | X |
| The Federal Act of Data Protection of 1992 | X | X | * | * | * | * | * | X | X |
| **Turkey** | | | | | | | | | |
| Article 22 of the Constitution states secrecy of communication is fundamental | X | X | X | * | * | * | * | X | X |
| **Ukraine** | | | | | | | | | |
| The Constitution of Ukraine | X | X | X | * | * | * | * | X | X |
| Article 32 of the Constitution | X | * | X | * | * | * | * | X | X |
| April 2000 Presidential Order | X | X | X | X | X | * | * | X | X |
| The 1992 Act on Information | X | X | X | X | * | X | * | X | X |
| **United Kingdom** | | | | | | | | | |
| Human Rights Act of 2 October 2000 | X | X | X | X | X | X | X | X | X |
| Data Protection Act of 1998 | X | * | * | * | * | * | * | X | X |
| Employee Privacy Legislation | X | X | * | * | * | * | X | X | X |
| Health and Social Care Bill (see Section 59) | X | X | * | * | * | * | X | X | X |
| Freedom of Information Act 2000 | X | X | * | * | X | X | * | X | X |

**Table A.1 (continued)   Multinational Regulatory Compliance Mapping**

| | Trusted Access | Change Management | Business Continuity and Availability | Operational Monitor and Report | Records Management | Audit and Risk Management | Operational Transparency | Segregation of Duties | Operational Control |
|---|---|---|---|---|---|---|---|---|---|
| **South Africa** | | | | | | | | | |
| Section 14 and 32 of the South African Constitution of 1996 | X | X | X | * | * | * | * | X | X |
| The Access to Information Act of February 2000 | X | X | X | * | * | * | * | X | X |
| The Interception and Monitoring Act of 1992 | X | X | X | * | * | X | X | X | X |
| King II (Corporate Governance for South Africa) | X | * | * | * | * | * | * | X | X |
| Electronic Communications and Transactions Bill and Promotion of Access to Information Act | X | * | * | X | * | * | X | X | X |
| **Latin America** | | | | | | | | | |
| **Argentina** | | | | | | | | | |
| Articles 18 and 19 of the Argentine Constitution | X | X | X | X | * | X | X | X | X |
| The Personal Data Protection Law(PDLP) No. 25326 | X | * | * | X | * | X | * | X | * |
| Decree 1570-2001 (the Exchange Control Decree) | X | X | X | * | X | X | X | X | * |
| The Argentina Civil Code | X | X | X | X | * | X | X | X | X |
| The Credit Card Act | X | * | * | X | * | * | * | X | * |
| City of Buenos Aires Privacy Law | X | * | * | X | * | X | X | X | * |
| **Brazil** | | | | | | | | | |
| Constitution, Article 5 Section LXXII, dictates Habeas Data | X | * | * | X | X | X | * | X | X |
| Article 5 of the 1988 Constitution of Brazil | X | X | X | X | * | X | X | X | X |

**Table A.1 (continued)   Multinational Regulatory Compliance Mapping**

| | Trusted Access | Change Management | Business Continuity and Availability | Operational Monitor and Report | Records Management | Audit and Risk Management | Operational Transparency | Segregation of Duties | Operational Control |
|---|---|---|---|---|---|---|---|---|---|
| 1990 Code of Consumer Protection and Defense | X | * | * | * | * | X | * | X | * |
| Senate Bill No. 61 | X | * | X | X | * | X | X | X | X |
| Informatics Law of 1984 | X | * | X | X | * | X | X | X | X |
| Wiretapping Law of 1996 | X | X | X | X | * | * | X | X | X |
| Computer Crimes Act of July 2000 | X | X | X | X | X | X | X | X | X |
| Bill 3494/2000 | X | X | X | X | * | X | X | X | X |
| Projeto de Lei da Camara no. 6981/2002 | X | X | X | X | * | X | X | X | X |
| Projeto de Lei da Camara no. 6541/2002 | X | X | X | X | * | X | X | X | X |
| Projeto de Lei do Senado 2000 art 1 §1, 2 (on cybercrimes) | X | X | X | X | * | X | X | X | X |
| Projeto de Lei da Camara no. 3356/2000 | X | X | X | * | * | X | X | * | X |
| Projeto de Lei da Camara no. 3360/2000 | X | X | X | X | * | X | X | * | X |
| Projeto de Lei da Camara no. 3494/2000 | X | X | X | X | * | X | X | X | * |
| Projeto de Lei da Camara no. 1682/99 | X | X | X | X | * | X | X | X | X |
| Projeto de Lei da Camara no. 84/99 | X | X | X | X | * | X | X | X | X |
| Federal Senate Bill no. 61 1996 | X | X | X | X | * | X | X | * | * |
| Projeto de Lei da Camara no. 4102/93 | X | X | X | X | * | X | X | X | X |
| *Chile* | | | | | | | | | |
| Article 19 of Chile's Constitution | X | X | X | X | * | X | X | X | X |

**Table A.1 (continued)  Multinational Regulatory Compliance Mapping**

| | Trusted Access | Change Management | Business Continuity and Availability | Operational Monitor and Report | Records Management | Audit and Risk Management | Operational Transparency | Segregation of Duties | Operational Control |
|---|---|---|---|---|---|---|---|---|---|
| Act No. 19628 Law for the Protection of Private Life of 28 October 1999 | X | X | X | X | * | X | X | X | X |
| Spam and unsolicited commercial communications Consumer Protection Law (No.19.955) | X | * | X | X | * | X | X | * | * |
| Chile–EU Trade Agreement Article 30 | X | X | X | X | * | * | X | X | * |
| **Columbia** | | | | | | | | | |
| Medical Records Law No. 23 | X | X | X | X | * | X | X | X | X |
| Statutory Law No. 139/2004 (31 August 2004) | X | X | X | X | * | X | X | X | X |
| **Ecuador** | | | | | | | | | |
| Data Protection Bill (2006) | X | * | X | X | * | X | X | * | * |
| Ecuador Habeas Data Law Article 4—Quality of the data | X | * | X | X | * | X | X | X | * |
| Ecuador Habeas Data Law Article 7—Consent of the holder | X | * | X | X | * | X | X | X | * |
| Transparency and Access to Information Law of 2004 | X | X | * | * | * | X | X | X | X |
| **Mexico** | | | | | | | | | |
| Article 16 of the 1917 Mexican Constitution | X | X | * | * | * | X | X | X | X |
| Mexican E-Commerce Act of 7 June 2000 | X | X | X | * | * | X | * | X | * |
| Mexico Federal Personal Data Protection Law Article 6 (Data Protection) | X | X | X | X | * | X | X | X | * |

**Table A.1 (continued)   Multinational Regulatory Compliance Mapping**

| | Trusted Access | Change Management | Business Continuity and Availability | Operational Monitor and Report | Records Management | Audit and Risk Management | Operational Transparency | Segregation of Duties | Operational Control |
|---|---|---|---|---|---|---|---|---|---|
| Mexico Federal Personal Data Protection Law Article I Chapter VIII | X | X | X | X | * | X | X | X | X |
| Mexico Federal Personal Data Protection Law Article 76 Sec I, II, and III | X | X | X | X | * | X | X | X | X |
| Chapter 6 of Mexico's Postal Code | X | X | X | X | * | X | X | X | X |
| The 1939 General Communicator | X | X | X | X | * | X | X | X | * |
| The Law Against Organized Crime effective November 1996 | X | X | * | * | * | X | X | X | X |
| **Paraguay** | | | | | | | | | |
| Data Protection Act of December 28 2000 | X | X | * | * | * | X | X | X | * |
| **Peru** | | | | | | | | | |
| The 1993 Constitution Article 2 Sec VIx | X | X | * | X | * | X | X | X | X |
| Penal Code, Article 154 | X | X | X | X | * | X | X | X | * |
| Penal Code, Article 151 | X | X | X | X | * | X | X | X | * |
| Telecommunications and Wiretapping Law of 12 July 2001 | X | X | * | * | * | X | * | X | X |
| **Paraguay** | | | | | | | | | |
| Data Protection Act of December 28 2000 | X | X | X | * | * | X | X | X | X |
| **Uruguay** | | | | | | | | | |
| Transparency and Access to Information Law of 2004 | X | X | * | X | X | X | * | X | X |
| Article 72 of the Constitution | X | X | X | X | X | X | X | X | X |
| Article 28 protects individuals' documents and correspondence | X | X | X | X | * | X | * | X | X |

**Table A.1 (continued)   Multinational Regulatory Compliance Mapping**

|  | Trusted Access | Change Management | Business Continuity and Availability | Operational Monitor and Report | Records Management | Audit and Risk Management | Operational Transparency | Segregation of Duties | Operational Control |
|---|---|---|---|---|---|---|---|---|---|
| Article 296 of the Penal Code | X | X | X | X | * | X | X | X | X |
| The Uruguayan Tax Code (Decree Law No. 14.306) and Banking Law No. 15.322 | X | X | X | X | * | X | X | * | * |
| Law No. 16.616 enacted on 20 October 1994 | X | X | X | X | * | X | X | X | * |
| Law No. 16.011 | X | X | X | X | * | X | X | X | X |
| Decree No. 396/003 | X | X | X | X | * | X | X | X | * |
| Article 694 of Law No. 16.736 | X | * | X | X | * | X | * | X | X |
| Decree No. 396/003 | X | * | X | X | * | X | * | X | X |
| Law 17984—Database of the Central Bank with information about debtors (2006) | X | * | * | X | * | X | * | * | * |
| **Venezuela** | | | | | | | | | |
| Data Protection and Habeas Data Law for Venezuela passed in 2004 | X | * | * | X | * | X | * | * | * |
| **North America** | | | | | | | | | |
| **United States of America** | | | | | | | | | |
| *United States: Government and Public Sector* | | | | | | | | | |
| ITAR | X | X | X | X | * | * | X | X | * |
| Title 21 Code of Federal Regulations (21 CFR Part 11) Electronic | X | * | * | X | * | X | * | X | * |
| 12 CFR Part 30 | X | * | * | X | * | X | * | X | * |
| Section 508 of the Rehabilitation Act (29 U.S.C. 794d) | X | X | * | X | * | X | X | X | X |

**Table A.1 (continued)  Multinational Regulatory Compliance Mapping**

| | Trusted Access | Change Management | Business Continuity and Availability | Operational Monitor and Report | Records Management | Audit and Risk Management | Operational Transparency | Segregation of Duties | Operational Control |
|---|---|---|---|---|---|---|---|---|---|
| Audit Report D-2001-130 | X | * | * | * | * | X | * | * | * |
| CJCSI 6212.01C | X | * | * | * | * | * | X | * | X |
| CJCSI 6510.01 | X | * | * | * | * | * | * | * | X |
| CJCSM 3150.07A | X | * | * | * | * | * | X | * | X |
| CJCSM 6510.0 | X | X | * | * | * | * | X | * | X |
| Computer Security Enhancement Act of 2001 (HR1259) | X | X | X | * | * | * | * | * | X |
| Government Network Security Act 2003 | X | X | X | * | * | * | * | * | X |
| Computer Fraud and Abuse Act (CFAA) | X | X | X | X | * | X | X | X | * |
| The Computer Security Act of 1987 | X | X | X | X | * | X | X | X | * |
| DCID 6/3 | X | * | * | * | * | X | * | X | X |
| DISA Instruction 630-225-7 | X | X | * | X | * | * | * | X | X |
| DoD Directive 8320.2 | X | X | * | * | * | X | X | * | * |
| DoD Directive 8500.1 | X | * | * | * | X | * | X | * | X |
| DoD Global Information Grid Architecture (V 2.0) Management Plan | X | * | * | X | * | * | * | * | X |
| DOD Instruction 5200.40: DoD Information Technology Security Certification and Accreditation DITSCAP E2.1.51-52 | X | * | * | * | * | * | * | * | X |
| DoD Instruction 5215.2 | X | X | X | * | * | * | X | X | X |
| DoD Instruction 5230.29 | X | X | X | X | * | X | X | X | * |
| DoD Instruction 8500.2 | X | X | X | * | * | * | X | * | * |

**Table A.1 (continued)** **Multinational Regulatory Compliance Mapping**

| | Trusted Access | Change Management | Business Continuity and Availability | Operational Monitor and Report | Records Management | Audit and Risk Management | Operational Transparency | Segregation of Duties | Operational Control |
|---|---|---|---|---|---|---|---|---|---|
| DoD Mobile Code Guidance | X | * | X | X | * | * | X | X | X |
| DoD X.509 Certificate Policy Version 9.0 and DoD Key Recovery Policy Version 3.0 | X | X | X | X | X | * | X | * | X |
| DoDD 3020.26: COOP Policy and Planning: 4.1 | X | X | * | X | * | * | X | X | X |
| DoDD 3020.40: Defense Critical Infrastructure Program (DCIP) | X | X | * | * | * | * | X | * | X |
| DoDD 8000.1: Defense Information Management Program | X | X | * | * | * | * | * | * | X |
| DoDD O 8530.1 | X | X | * | * | * | * | X | * | X |
| Executive Order 12356 | X | X | X | * | * | * | * | * | * |
| Executive Order 12829 | X | X | X | * | * | * | * | * | * |
| FIPS 200 | X | * | * | * | * | * | * | X | * |
| H.R. 6 The Energy Policy Act of 2005 Title II | X | * | * | * | * | * | X | X | X |
| FISMA Act of 2002 | X | X | X | * | * | * | * | * | * |
| Freedom Of Information Act/ Privacy Act | X | X | X | X | * | X | * | X | * |
| GISRA: The Defense Authorization Act of 2001 | X | X | * | X | * | * | * | * | X |
| Memorandum 00-13 and 99-18: Privacy Policies | X | X | X | X | * | * | * | X | X |
| NISPOM: DoD 5220.22-M | X | X | X | * | * | * | * | * | X |
| NIST 800-53: Security Controls for Federal Information Systems | X | X | X | * | * | X | * | X | * |
| NIST 800-53: Techniques and Procedures for Verifying the Effectiveness of Security Controls | X | * | X | * | * | * | * | * | X |

**Table A.1 (continued)   Multinational Regulatory Compliance Mapping**

| | Trusted Access | Change Management | Business Continuity and Availability | Operational Monitor and Report | Records Management | Audit and Risk Management | Operational Transparency | Segregation of Duties | Operational Control |
|---|---|---|---|---|---|---|---|---|---|
| NIST 800-59 | X | X | X | * | * | * | * | X | X |
| NIST 800-60 | X | * | * | * | * | * | * | * | X |
| NIST SP 800-30 | X | * | * | * | * | * | * | X | * |
| NSA/CSS-NISCAP | X | * | X | X | * | X | * | * | X |
| NSTISSAM COMPUSEC 1-99 | X | X | X | * | * | * | * | * | X |
| NSTISSI 1000 | X | * | X | X | * | * | * | * | * |
| NSTISSP | X | * | * | * | * | * | X | X | X |
| OMB A130 Transmittal Number 4 | X | X | X | * | * | * | * | X | * |
| OMB Circular A-130 | X | X | X | X | X | X | X | * | * |
| PDD-63 Critical Infrastructure Protection | X | X | * | * | * | * | X | * | * |
| Public Law 100-235 | X | X | X | * | * | * | X | X | * |
| Public Law 93-579 (Privacy Act of 1974) | X | X | X | * | * | * | X | X | * |
| Removal of Personally Identifying Information | X | X | * | X | * | X | X | X | * |
| System Security Engineering Capability Maturity Model | X | * | * | X | X | * | * | X | X |
| The National Strategy to Secure Cyberspace | X | X | * | * | * | * | * | X | X |
| Rainbow Series Library | X | * | * | * | * | * | * | * | X |
| CAC-BWG (PKI 4 PIV -D1172.2) | X | X | X | * | * | X | X | X | X |
| RFID (DFARS-RFID Req) MIL-STD-129P 70 FR 53955 | X | X | X | * | * | X | X | X | X |
| Federal Reserve Act 12 USC 248(I), (j), and (o) | X | X | X | X | * | * | X | X | X |
| Federal Reserve Act 12 U.S.C. 342 | X | X | * | * | * | * | X | X | X |
| Federal Reserve Act 12 U.S.C. 360 | X | X | * | * | * | X | X | X | X |

**Table A.1 (continued)   Multinational Regulatory Compliance Mapping**

| | Trusted Access | Change Management | Business Continuity and Availability | Operational Monitor and Report | Records Management | Audit and Risk Management | Operational Transparency | Segregation of Duties | Operational Control |
|---|---|---|---|---|---|---|---|---|---|
| Federal Reserve Act 12 USC 4001-4010 | X | X | * | * | * | * | X | X | X |
| Federal Reserve Act 12 U.S.C.Gramm 464 | X | X | X | * | * | * | * | X | X |
| IGES for Safeguarding Customer Information 12 CFR § Part 364 Appendix B | X | X | * | * | * | X | X | X | * |
| IGES for Safety and Soundness 12 CFR § Part 364 Appendix A | X | * | * | X | * | * | * | X | * |
| IGES for Safeguarding Customer Information Bank holding companies and their non-bank subsidiaries or affiliates (except brokers, dealers or persons providing insurance, investment companies, and investment advisors) 12 CFR Part 225 Appendix F | X | X | * | * | * | * | * | X | X |
| IGES for Safeguarding Customer Information (Edge or agreement corporation) 12 CFR 211.5 | X | X | X | X | * | X | * | * | * |
| IGES for Safeguarding Customer Information (Edge or agreement corporation) 12 CFR 211.9 | X | X | X | X | * | X | * | * | * |
| IGES for Safeguarding Customer Information (uninsured state-licensed branch or agency of a foreign bank) 12 CFR 211.24 | X | X | X | * | X | * | * | * | |
| IGES for Safeguarding Customer Information Appendix D-2 (State Member Banks) 12 CFR Part 208 Appendix D-1 and D-2 | X | X | X | X | * | X | * | * | * |

**Table A.1 (continued)   Multinational Regulatory Compliance Mapping**

| | Trusted Access | Change Management | Business Continuity and Availability | Operational Monitor and Report | Records Management | Audit and Risk Management | Operational Transparency | Segregation of Duties | Operational Control |
|---|---|---|---|---|---|---|---|---|---|
| United States: Listed Companies and Private Corporations SOX Public Company Accounting Reform and Investor Protection Act of 2002 | X | * | * | * | * | * | * | * | * |
| Fair Credit Reporting Act | X | * | * | * | * | * | X | * | X |
| Privacy Act of 1974 | X | * | * | * | * | * | * | X | * |
| Family Education Rights and Privacy Act | X | X | * | * | * | * | * | X | * |
| Right to Financial Privacy Act | X | X | X | * | * | * | * | X | * |
| Privacy Protection Act of 1980 (PPA) | X | X | X | X | X | * | X | * | X |
| Cable Communications Policy Act of 1984 | X | X | X | * | * | * | * | X | * |
| The Electronic Communications Privacy Act | X | X | * | * | * | X | X | * | * |
| Computer Security Act | X | X | X | * | * | * | X | * | * |
| Video Privacy Protection Act of 1988 | X | X | X | X | * | X | X | * | * |
| Telephone Consumer Protection Act of 1991 (TCPA) | X | X | X | X | * | X | X | * | X |
| Driver's Privacy Protection Act of 1994 | X | X | * | X | * | * | X | X | * |
| Communications Assistance for Law Enforcement Act of 1994 (CALEA) | X | X | * | * | * | X | X | X | X |
| Telecommunications Act of 1996 | X | X | X | * | * | * | * | * | X |
| Health Insurance Portability and Accountability Act of 1996 (HIPAA) | X | X | * | * | * | X | * | * | * |

**Table A.1 (continued)  Multinational Regulatory Compliance Mapping**

| | Trusted Access | Change Management | Business Continuity and Availability | Operational Monitor and Report | Records Management | Audit and Risk Management | Operational Transparency | Segregation of Duties | Operational Control |
|---|---|---|---|---|---|---|---|---|---|
| Children's Online Privacy Protection Act of 1998 (COPPA) | X | * | * | * | * | * | * | * | * |
| Gramm–Leach–Bliley Act of 1999 | X | * | * | * | * | * | * | * | X |
| Patriot Act of 2001 | X | * | * | * | * | X | * | X | * |
| USA Patriot Act Section 312 | X | * | * | * | * | * | * | X | * |
| Special Due Diligence for Correspondent Accounts and Private Banking Accounts Domestic Security Enhancement Act of 2003 (Patriot II) | X | X | X | * | * | * | * | X | X |
| Bank Protection Act 12 U.S.C. 1882 | X | X | X | X | X | X | X | X | X |
| Fraud and Related Activity in Connection with Computers 18 USC 1030 | X | X | X | X | X | X | X | X | X |
| Electronic Signatures in Global and National Commerce Act (E-Sign) Pub.L.No. 106-229 | X | X | X | X | X | X | X | X | * |
| Bank Secrecy Act 31 U.S.C. 5311 | X | X | X | X | X | * | X | X | X |
| Check Clearing for the 21st Century Act 12 U.S.C. 5001 | X | X | X | X | * | X | X | X | X |
| Home Owner's Loan Act 12 U.S.C. 1464(d) | X | X | X | X | * | X | X | X | X |
| Supervisory Committee 12 U.S.C. 1761 and 1761d | X | X | X | * | * | * | X | X | X |
| Risks Involving Client/Server Computer Systems FIL-82-96 | X | X | X | X | X | * | X | X | * |
| Electronic Banking Examination Procedures FIL-14-97 | X | X | X | * | X | * | X | X | X |
| Security Risks Associated with the Internet FIL-131-97 | X | X | X | * | X | X | X | X | * |

**Table A.1 (continued)   Multinational Regulatory Compliance Mapping**

| | Trusted Access | Change Management | Business Continuity and Availability | Operational Monitor and Report | Records Management | Audit and Risk Management | Operational Transparency | Segregation of Duties | Operational Control |
|---|---|---|---|---|---|---|---|---|---|
| Suspicious Activity Reporting FIL-124-97 | X | X | X | X | X | * | X | X | X |
| Electronic Financial Services and Consumer Compliance FIL 79-98 | X | X | X | * | * | * | X | X | X |
| Electronic Commerce and Consumer Privacy FIL-86-98 | X | X | X | X | * | X | X | X | X |
| Offshore Outsourcing FIL-49-99: Bank Service Company Act | X | X | X | X | * | * | X | * | * |
| Annual Independent Audits and Reporting Requirements 12 CFR Part 363 | X | X | X | * | * | * | X | X | X |
| Minimum Security Procedures 12 CFR 326 Subpart A | X | X | X | * | X | * | * | X | X |
| Privacy of Consumer Financial Information 12 CFR 332 | X | X | X | X | * | X | X | X | X |
| Procedures for Monitoring Bank Secrecy Act Compliance 12 CFR 326 Subpart B | X | X | X | * | * | * | X | X | X |
| Suspicious Activity Reports 12 CFR 353 | X | X | X | * | X | * | X | X | X |
| Minimum Security Devices and Procedures 12 CFR 208.61 | X | X | X | X | X | * | X | X | X |
| Payment Card Industry CISP/DSS | X | * | * | X | * | * | * | X | * |
| *United States: Nonprofit Organizations* | | | | | | | | | |
| IRS Form 990 | X | * | * | * | * | * | * | X | X |
| Secton 501( c )(3) | X | X | X | X | * | X | * | * | * |
| California's Nonprofit Integrity Act SB1262 | X | X | * | * | * | * | X | * | X |
| New York Nonprofit Integrity Act S4836-A | X | X | * | X | * | * | X | * | * |

**Table A.1 (continued)    Multinational Regulatory Compliance Mapping**

| | Trusted Access | Change Management | Business Continuity and Availability | Operational Monitor and Report | Records Management | Audit and Risk Management | Operational Transparency | Segregation of Duties | Operational Control |
|---|---|---|---|---|---|---|---|---|---|
| **United States: State and Local Government** | | | | | | | | | |
| Real ID Act Bill Number H.R.418 for the 109th Congress | X | X | X | * | * | * | * | X | X |
| State Breach Notification Laws | X | * | X | * | * | * | * | X | X |
| Credit Freeze Laws | X | * | * | * | * | * | * | * | X |
| FRCP e-Discovery | X | * | * | * | * | * | X | * | X |
| **Canada** | | | | | | | | | |
| CSA 52-313 | X | * | * | * | X | X | X | * | * |
| PIPEDA CAN/CSA-Q830-96 | X | * | X | * | * | * | * | X | * |
| The Federal Privacy Act | X | * | X | * | * | * | X | * | X |
| Personal Information in the Private Sector | X | * | * | * | * | * | * | X | * |
| The Canadian Security Intelligence Service Act | X | X | X | X | * | * | * | * | X |
| The Telecommunications Act | X | X | X | * | * | * | X | X | X |
| The Federal Access to Information Act (R.S. 1985c. A-1) | X | * | X | * | * | * | X | * | X |
| C-36 The Anti-Terrorism Act | X | X | X | * | * | * | * | X | X |

*Notes:*

X Denotes the control requirement required by the legislative mandate; the controls from left to right are

- Trusted Access
- Change Management
- Business Continuity and Availability
- Operational Monitor and Report
- Records Management
- Audit and Risk Management
- Operational Transparency
- Segregation of Duties
- Operational Control

* Denotes the control requirement is not explicitly required by the legislative mandate.

**Table A.2    Primary Frameworks Mapped to Control Domains**

|  | Trusted Access | Change Management | Business Continuity and Availability | Operational Monitor and Report | Records Management | Audit and Risk Management | Operational Transparency | Segregation of Duties | Operational Control |
|---|---|---|---|---|---|---|---|---|---|
| Joint EU Framework (ISO/IEC 27001:2005, ITIL, and CobiT ) | X | X | X | X | X | X | X | * | * |
| COBIT | X | X | X | X | X | X | * | X | * |
| ISO/IEC 27001:2005 | X | * | X | X | X | X | X | X | * |
| ITIL | * | X | X | X | X | X | * | * | * |
| BSI IT-Grundschutz Methodology | X | X | X | X | X | X | X | * | X |
| Capability Maturity Model Integration (CMMI) | X | X | X | X | X | * | * | * | * |
| ISF Standard of Good Practice (SoGP) | X | X | X | X | * | * | X | * | * |
| GAIT and GAISP | X | * | * | * | * | X | X | * | * |
| NIST | * | * | * | * | X | X | * | X | * |
| COSO and Turnbull Guidance | X | * | * | X | X | X | X | X | X |
| SAS70 | * | X | X | X | * | X | * | X | X |

*Notes:*

X Denotes the framework may be used to measure the control requirement

- Trusted Access
- Change Management
- Business Continuity and Availability
- Operational Monitor and Report
- Records Management
- Audit and Risk Management
- Operational Transparency
- Segregation of Duties
- Operational Control

* Denotes the framework does not express a metric used to measure the control requirement.

**Table A.3    Oracle Technical Control Mapping versus Control Domains**

| | Trusted Access | Change Management | Business Continuity and Availability | Operational Monitor and Report | Records Management | Audit and Risk Management | Operational Transparency | Segregation of Duties | Operational Control |
|---|---|---|---|---|---|---|---|---|---|
| **GRC Intelligence** | | | | | | | | | |
| Balanced Scorecard | * | X | * | X | X | X | X | * | X |
| Business Intelligence | * | * | * | X | X | X | X | * | * |
| Fusion GRC Intelligence | X | X | * | X | * | X | X | X | X |
| Enterprise Planning and Budgeting | * | X | * | X | X | X | * | * | * |
| **Organizational Policy Management** | | | | | | | | | |
| Oracle Learning Management | * | X | * | * | X | * | * | * | * |
| Universal Content Manager (Policy and Procedure Portal) | X | X | * | * | X | X | * | * | * |
| Enterprise Learning Management | * | X | * | * | X | * | * | * | * |
| **Organizational Risk and Compliance Management** | | | | | | | | | |
| Financial Consolidation Hub | * | * | * | X | X | X | * | * | * |
| GRC Manager | X | X | * | X | X | X | X | X | X |
| Application Access Controls | X | X | * | * | * | * | * | * | * |
| Application Configuration Controls | * | X | * | * | * | * | * | * | * |
| Project Portfolio Management | * | * | * | X | X | X | * | * | * |
| Enterprise Manager: IT Governance Pack | X | X | X | X | X | X | X | X | X |
| **Industry-Specific Risk and Compliance Management** | | | | | | | | | |
| Discreet Manufacturing | * | X | * | X | X | * | X | * | * |
| Process Manufacturing | * | X | * | X | X | * | X | X | * |
| G-Log Global Trade | * | * | * | X | X | * | * | * | * |

**Table A.3 (continued)   Oracle Technical Control Mapping versus Control Domains**

| | Trusted Access | Change Management | Business Continuity and Availability | Operational Monitor and Report | Records Management | Audit and Risk Management | Operational Transparency | Segregation of Duties | Operational Control |
|---|---|---|---|---|---|---|---|---|---|
| IFlex Reveleus | X | X | * | X | X | X | X | * | * |
| iFlex Mantas | X | * | * | X | * | * | * | * | * |
| Adverse Event Reporting (FDA) | X | X | * | X | X | X | * | X | X |
| Clinical Trial Management | X | X | * | X | X | * | * | X | X |
| **Business Process Management** | | | | | | | | | |
| BPEL Process Manager | * | X | * | X | X | X | X | X | X |
| Tutor (Business Process Documentation) | X | X | * | * | X | * | * | * | * |
| Business Activity Monitoring | * | X | X | X | * | X | * | * | X |
| **Content and Records Management** | | | | | | | | | |
| Siebel Universal Customer Master | X | X | X | X | X | * | * | X | X |
| Trusted Information Sharing | X | X | * | X | X | * | * | X | X |
| Universal Records Manager | X | X | X | * | X | * | * | * | * |
| Universal Content Manager | X | X | * | * | X | * | * | * | * |
| Information Rights Management | X | X | * | X | X | * | * | X | X |
| Content Database | X | X | * | * | X | * | * | * | * |
| Records Database | X | X | X | * | X | * | * | * | * |
| **Configuration and Change Management** | | | | | | | | | |
| Enterprise Manager: Change Management Pack | * | X | X | X | * | * | * | * | X |
| Enterprise Manager: Provisioning Pack | * | X | * | X | * | * | X | X | X |
| Enterprise Manager: Configuration Management Pack | * | X | X | * | * | * | * | * | X |

**Table A.3 (continued)    Oracle Technical Control Mapping versus Control Domains**

| | Trusted Access | Change Management | Business Continuity and Availability | Operational Monitor and Report | Records Management | Audit and Risk Management | Operational Transparency | Segregation of Duties | Operational Control |
|---|---|---|---|---|---|---|---|---|---|
| **Identity and Access Management** | | | | | | | | | |
| Internet Directory | X | X | * | X | X | * | * | * | * |
| Virtual Directory | X | * | X | X | * | X | * | X | X |
| IdM Suite: Access Manager | X | X | * | X | * | * | * | X | * |
| IdM Suite: Identity Federation | X | * | * | * | * | * | * | * | * |
| IdM Suite: Identity Manager | X | X | * | X | * | * | X | X | * |
| Enterprise Single Sign-On | X | * | * | X | * | * | * | * | * |
| Web Services Manager | X | * | * | X | * | * | * | X | X |
| Enterprise Manager: Identity Management Pack | X | X | X | X | X | X | X | X | X |
| **Data Protection and Accountability** | | | | | | | | | |
| Advanced Security Option | X | * | * | * | * | * | * | * | * |
| Oracle Label Security | X | * | * | * | X | * | * | X | * |
| Audit Vault | X | X | X | X | X | X | * | X | X |
| Oracle Database | X | * | X | X | X | * | * | * | * |
| Database Vault | X | X | X | X | X | X | * | X | * |
| Secure Enterprise Search | X | * | X | X | X | * | * | * | * |
| **Information Lifecycle Management** | | | | | | | | | |
| Automatic Storage Management | * | X | X | X | X | * | * | * | X |
| Oracle Recovery Manager (RMAN) | * | X | X | X | X | * | * | * | * |
| Oracle Data Guard | X | X | X | X | X | * | * | X | X |
| Oracle Secure Backup | X | X | X | X | X | * | * | X | * |
| Oracle CDP (Flaskback) | * | X | X | X | X | * | * | * | * |

**Table A.3 (continued)   Oracle Technical Control Mapping versus Control Domains**

*Notes:*

- ◼ Trusted Access
- ◼ Change Management
- ◼ Business Continuity and Availability
- ◼ Operational Monitor and Report
- ◼ Records Management
- ◼ Audit and Risk Management
- ◼ Operational Transparency
- ◼ Segregation of Duties
- ◼ Operational Control

\* Denotes the technical control represented by the properly configured Oracle product does not address control.

**Table A.4  Oracle Technical Control COBIT v4 Control Mapping (Part I: PO and AI)**

| | PO1 Define a Strategic IT Plan | PO2 Define the Information Architecture | PO3 Determine Technological Direction | PO4 Define the IT Processes, Organization, and Relationships | PO5 Manage the IT Investment | PO6 Communicate Management Aims and Direction | PO7 Manage IT Human Resources | PO8 Manage Quality | PO9 Assess and Manage IT Risks | PO10 Manage Projects | AI1 Identify Automated Solutions | AI2 Acquire and Maintain Application Software | AI3 Acquire and Maintain Technology Infrastructure | AI4 Enable Operation and Use | AI5 Procure IT Resources | AI6 Manage Changes | AI7 Install and Accredit Solutions and Changes |
|---|---|---|---|---|---|---|---|---|---|---|---|---|---|---|---|---|---|
| GRC Intelligence | * | × | * | × | × | × | * | * | × | × | × | × | * | × | × | * | × |
| Balanced Scorecard | * | * | * | * | * | × | * | * | × | × | × | * | * | * | * | * | * |
| Business Intelligence | * | * | * | * | * | * | * | * | * | * | * | * | * | * | * | * | * |
| Fusion GRC Intelligence | * | * | * | * | * | * | × | * | * | × | * | * | × | × | * | * | × |
| Enterprise Planning and Budgeting | * | × | * | × | × | × | * | * | * | × | * | × | * | * | × | * | * |
| Organizational Policy Management | * | * | * | × | * | × | * | * | * | × | * | * | * | × | * | * | |
| Oracle Learning Management | * | * | * | × | * | × | * | * | * | × | * | * | * | × | * | * | * |
| Universal Content Manager (Policy and Procedure Portal) | * | * | * | × | * | × | * | × | * | * | * | * | × | × | * | * | * |
| Enterprise Learning Management | * | * | * | × | * | × | * | * | * | * | * | * | * | × | * | * | * |
| Organizational Risk and Compliance Management | × | × | * | × | × | * | × | × | × | × | * | × | × | × | * | * | × |
| Financial Consolidation Hub | * | * | * | * | * | * | * | * | * | * | * | * | * | * | * | * | * |

**Table A.4 (continued)   Oracle Technical Control COBIT v4 Control Mapping (Part I: PO and AI)**

| | PO1 Define a Strategic IT Plan | PO2 Define the Information Architecture | PO3 Determine Technological Direction | PO4 Define the IT Processes, Organization, and Relationships | PO5 Manage the IT Investment | PO6 Communicate Management Aims and Direction | PO7 Manage IT Human Resources | PO8 Manage Quality | PO9 Assess and Manage IT Risks | PO10 Manage Projects | AI1 Identify Automated Solutions | AI2 Acquire and Maintain Application Software | AI3 Acquire and Maintain Technology Infrastructure | AI4 Enable Operation and Use | AI5 Procure IT Resources | AI6 Manage Changes | AI7 Install and Accredit Solutions and Changes |
|---|---|---|---|---|---|---|---|---|---|---|---|---|---|---|---|---|---|
| GRC Manager | * | X | * | * | X | * | X | X | X | * | X | * | * | * | * | * | X |
| Application Access Controls | * | * | * | * | * | * | * | * | X | * | X | X | X | X | * | X | * |
| Application Configuration Controls | * | * | * | * | * | * | * | * | X | * | X | X | X | X | * | X | * |
| Project Portfolio Management | X | * | * | X | X | X | * | * | * | X | * | * | X | * | * | * | * |
| Enterprise Manager: IT Governance Pack | X | X | * | X | X | * | X | X | X | X | * | X | X | * | * | X | X |
| Industry-Specific Risk and Compliance Management | * | X | * | X | * | X | * | X | X | X | * | X | X | * | * | * | * |
| Discreet Manufacturing | * | X | * | X | * | X | * | X | X | X | * | X | X | * | * | * | * |
| Process Manufacturing | * | X | * | X | * | X | * | X | X | X | * | X | X | * | * | * | * |
| G-Log Global Trade | * | X | * | X | * | X | * | X | X | X | * | X | * | * | * | * | * |
| IFlex Reveleus | * | * | * | X | * | * | * | X | X | * | * | * | * | * | * | * | * |

| | 1 | 2 | 3 | 4 | 5 | 6 | 7 | 8 | 9 | 10 | 11 | 12 | 13 | 14 | 15 | 16 | 17 | 18 | 19 | 20 |
|---|---|---|---|---|---|---|---|---|---|---|---|---|---|---|---|---|---|---|---|---|
| iFlex Mantas | * | * | * | X | * | * | * | * | * | * | * | * | * | * | * | * | * | * | * | * |
| Adverse Event Reporting (FDA) | * | * | * | X | * | X | * | * | X | X | X | * | * | * | * | * | * | * | * | * |
| Clinical Trial Management | * | * | * | X | * | X | X | * | X | X | * | * | * | * | * | * | * | * | * | * |
| Business Process Management | * | * | * | X | * | * | * | * | X | X | X | * | X | * | * | * | * | * | * | * |
| BPEL Process Manager | * | * | * | X | * | X | * | X | X | X | X | * | X | * | * | * | * | * | * | * |
| Tutor (Business Process Documentation) | X | X | * | X | * | X | * | * | * | * | * | * | X | * | * | * | * | * | * | * |
| Business Activity Monitoring | * | * | * | X | * | * | * | * | * | * | * | * | * | * | * | * | * | * | * | * |
| Content and Records Management | * | * | * | * | * | * | * | X | X | * | * | * | * | * | * | * | * | * | * | * |
| Siebel Universal Customer Master | * | * | * | * | * | * | * | X | X | * | * | * | * | * | * | * | * | * | * | * |
| Trusted Information Sharing | * | * | * | * | * | * | * | * | X | * | * | * | * | * | * | * | * | * | * | * |
| Universal Records Manager | * | * | * | * | * | * | * | X | * | * | * | * | * | * | * | * | * | * | * | * |
| Universal Content Manager | * | * | * | * | * | * | * | * | * | * | * | * | * | * | * | * | * | * | * | * |
| Information Rights Management | * | * | * | * | * | X | * | * | X | * | * | * | * | * | * | * | * | * | * | * |
| Content Database | * | * | * | * | * | * | * | * | * | * | * | * | * | * | * | * | * | * | * | * |
| Records Database | * | * | * | * | * | * | * | * | * | * | * | * | * | * | * | * | * | * | * | * |
| Configuration and Change Management | * | * | * | * | * | * | * | * | * | * | * | * | X | X | X | X | X | X | X | X |
| Enterprise Manager: Change Management Pack | * | * | * | * | * | * | * | * | * | * | * | * | X | X | X | X | X | X | X | X |
| Enterprise Manager: Provisioning Pack | * | * | * | * | * | * | * | * | * | * | * | * | X | X | X | X | X | X | X | X |

**Table A.4 (continued)   Oracle Technical Control COBIT v4 Control Mapping (Part I: PO and AI)**

| | PO1 Define a Strategic IT Plan | PO2 Define the Information Architecture | PO3 Determine Technological Direction | PO4 Define the IT Processes, Organization, and Relationships | PO5 Manage the IT Investment | PO6 Communicate Management Aims and Direction | PO7 Manage IT Human Resources | PO8 Manage Quality | PO9 Assess and Manage IT Risks | PO10 Manage Projects | AI1 Identify Automated Solutions | AI2 Acquire and Maintain Application Software | AI3 Acquire and Maintain Technology Infrastructure | AI4 Enable Operation and Use | AI5 Procure IT Resources | AI6 Manage Changes | AI7 Install and Accredit Solutions and Changes |
|---|---|---|---|---|---|---|---|---|---|---|---|---|---|---|---|---|---|
| Enterprise Manager: Configuration Management Pack | * | * | * | * | * | * | * | * | * | * | * | X | X | * | * | X | X |
| Identity and Access Management | * | * | * | X | * | * | * | * | * | X | * | * | * | * | * | * | * |
| Internet Directory | * | * | * | * | * | * | * | * | * | * | * | * | * | * | X | X | * |
| Virtual Directory | * | * | * | * | * | * | * | * | * | * | * | * | * | * | * | X | * |
| IdM Suite: Access Manager | * | * | * | X | * | * | * | * | * | * | * | * | * | * | X | * | * |
| IdM Suite: Identity Federation | * | * | * | * | * | * | * | * | * | * | * | * | * | * | * | * | * |
| IdM Suite: Identity Manager | * | * | * | X | * | * | X | * | * | X | X | * | * | * | X | X | * |
| Enterprise Single Sign-On | * | * | * | * | * | * | * | * | * | * | * | * | * | * | * | * | * |
| Web Services Manager | * | * | * | * | * | * | * | * | * | * | X | * | * | * | * | * | * |
| Enterprise Manager: Identity Management Pack | * | * | * | X | * | * | X | * | * | X | X | * | * | * | * | * | * |
| Data Protection and Accountability | * | * | * | * | * | * | * | * | * | * | * | * | * | * | * | * | * |

| | | | | | | | | | | | | | | | | | | |
|---|---|---|---|---|---|---|---|---|---|---|---|---|---|---|---|---|---|---|
| Advanced Security Option | * | * | * | * | * | * | * | * | * | * | * | * | * | * | * | * | * | * |
| Oracle Label Security | * | * | * | * | * | * | * | * | * | * | * | * | * | * | * | * | * | * |
| Audit Vault | * | * | * | * | * | * | * | * | * | X | * | * | * | * | * | * | * | * |
| Oracle Database | * | * | * | * | * | * | * | * | * | X | * | * | * | * | * | * | * | * |
| Database Vault | * | * | * | * | * | * | * | * | * | * | * | * | * | * | * | * | * | * |
| Secure Enterprise Search | * | * | * | * | * | * | * | * | * | * | * | * | * | * | * | * | * | * |
| Information Lifecycle Management | * | * | X | * | * | * | * | * | * | * | * | * | * | * | * | * | * | * |
| Automatic Storage Management | * | * | X | * | * | * | * | * | * | * | * | * | * | * | * | * | * | * |
| Oracle Recovery Manager (RMAN) | * | * | X | * | * | * | * | * | * | * | * | * | * | * | * | | | * |
| Oracle Data Guard | * | * | X | * | * | * | * | * | * | * | * | * | * | * | * | * | * | * |
| Oracle Secure Backup | * | * | X | * | * | * | * | * | * | * | * | * | * | * | * | * | * | * |
| Oracle CDP (Flaskback) | * | * | X | * | * | * | * | * | * | * | * | * | * | * | * | * | * | * |

*Notes:*

X  Denotes the technical control represented by the properly configured Oracle product satisfies the control.

*  Denotes the technical control represented by the properly configured Oracle product does not address control.

**Table A.5 Oracle Technical Control COBIT v4 Control Mapping (Part II: DS and ME)v**

| | DS1 Define and Manage Service Levels | DS2 Manage Third-Party Services | DS3 Manage Performance and Capacity | DS4 Ensure Continuous Service | DS5 Ensure Systems Security | DS6 Identify and Allocate Costs | DS7 Educate and Train Users | DS8 Manage Service Desk and Incidents | DS9 Manage the Configuration | DS10 Manage Problems | DS11 Manage Data | DS12 Manage the Physical Environment | DS13 Manage Operations | ME1 Monitor and Evaluate IT Performance | ME2 Monitor and Evaluate Internal Control | ME3 Ensure Regulatory Compliance | ME4 Provide IT Governance |
|---|---|---|---|---|---|---|---|---|---|---|---|---|---|---|---|---|---|
| GRC Intelligence | X | * | X | * | * | X | * | * | * | * | * | * | X | X | X | X | X |
| Balanced Scorecard | * | * | X | * | * | * | * | * | * | * | * | * | X | X | X | * | * |
| Business Intelligence | * | * | * | * | * | * | * | * | * | * | * | * | * | * | X | X | * |
| Fusion GRC Intelligence | * | * | X | * | * | * | * | * | * | * | * | * | X | * | X | X | X |
| Enterprise Planning and Budgeting | * | * | * | * | * | X | * | * | * | * | * | * | * | X | * | * | * |
| Organizational Policy Management | X | * | * | * | * | * | X | * | * | * | * | * | * | * | * | * | X |
| Oracle Learning Management | * | * | * | * | * | * | X | * | * | * | * | * | * | * | * | * | * |
| Universal Content Manager (Policy and Procedure Portal) | X | * | * | * | * | * | X | * | * | * | * | * | * | * | * | * | X |
| Enterprise Learning Management | * | * | * | * | * | * | X | * | * | * | * | * | * | * | * | * | * |

| Control | | | | | | | | | | | | | | | | | |
|---|---|---|---|---|---|---|---|---|---|---|---|---|---|---|---|---|---|
| Organizational Risk and Compliance Management | X | * | * | X | X | * | X | * | * | * | X | * | X | X | X | X | X |
| Financial Consolidation Hub | * | * | * | * | * | * | * | * | * | * | * | * | * | * | * | * | * |
| GRC Manager | X | * | * | X | X | * | X | * | * | * | X | * | X | X | X | X | X |
| Application Access Controls | X | * | * | X | * | * | * | * | * | * | X | * | X | * | X | X | * |
| Application Configuration Controls | X | * | * | X | X | * | X | * | * | * | X | * | X | X | X | * | * |
| Project Portfolio Management | X | * | * | * | * | * | * | * | * | * | * | * | * | * | * | * | * |
| Enterprise Manager: IT Governance Pack | X | * | X | X | X | X | X | * | X | X | X | X | X | X | X | X | X |
| Industry-Specific Risk and Compliance Management | * | * | * | * | * | * | * | * | * | * | X | X | X | X | X | X | * |
| Discreet Manufacturing | * | * | * | * | * | * | * | * | * | * | X | * | * | * | * | * | * |
| Process Manufacturing | * | * | * | * | * | * | * | * | * | * | X | * | * | * | * | * | * |
| G-Log Global Trade | * | * | * | * | * | * | * | * | * | * | X | * | X | * | X | * | * |
| IFlex Reveleus | * | * | * | * | * | * | * | * | * | * | X | * | * | * | * | X | * |
| iFlex Mantas | * | * | * | * | * | * | * | * | * | * | * | X | X | X | X | X | * |

**Table A.5 (continued)  Oracle Technical Control COBIT v4 Control Mapping (Part II: DS and ME)v**

| | DS1 Define and Manage Service Levels | DS2 Manage Third-Party Services | DS3 Manage Performance and Capacity | DS4 Ensure Continuous Service | DS5 Ensure Systems Security | DS6 Identify and Allocate Costs | DS7 Educate and Train Users | DS8 Manage Service Desk and Incidents | DS9 Manage the Configuration | DS10 Manage Problems | DS11 Manage Data | DS12 Manage the Physical Environment | DS13 Manage Operations | ME1 Monitor and Evaluate IT Performance | ME2 Monitor and Evaluate Internal Control | ME3 Ensure Regulatory Compliance | ME4 Provide IT Governance |
|---|---|---|---|---|---|---|---|---|---|---|---|---|---|---|---|---|---|
| Adverse Event Reporting (FDA) | * | * | * | * | * | * | * | * | * | * | * | * | X | X | X | X | * |
| Clinical Trial Management | * | * | * | * | * | * | * | * | * | * | * | * | X | X | X | X | * |
| Business Process Management | X | * | * | * | * | * | * | * | * | * | * | * | X | X | * | * | * |
| BPEL Process Manager | X | * | * | * | * | * | * | * | * | * | * | * | X | * | * | * | * |
| Tutor (Business Process Documentation) | X | * | * | * | * | * | * | * | * | * | * | * | * | * | * | * | * |
| Business Activity Monitoring | X | * | * | * | * | * | * | * | * | * | * | * | * | X | * | * | * |
| Content and Records Management | * | X | * | * | X | * | * | * | * | * | X | * | * | * | * | X | * |
| Siebel Universal Customer Master | * | * | * | * | X | * | * | * | * | * | X | * | * | * | * | X | * |

| | Trusted Information Sharing | Universal Records Manager | Universal Content Manager | Information Rights Management | Content Database | Records Database | Configuration and Change Management | Enterprise Manager: Change Management Pack | Enterprise Manager: Provisioning Pack | Enterprise Manager: Configuration Management Pack | Identity and Access Management | Internet Directory | Virtual Directory |
|---|---|---|---|---|---|---|---|---|---|---|---|---|---|
| | * | * | * | * | * | * | * | * | * | * | * | * | * |
| | X | X | X | X | X | X | X | X | * | X | * | * | * |
| | * | * | * | * | * | * | X | X | X | X | X | * | * |
| | * | * | * | * | * | * | X | X | X | X | * | * | * |
| | * | * | * | * | * | * | X | X | * | X | * | * | * |
| | * | * | * | * | * | * | * | * | * | * | * | * | * |
| | X | X | X | X | X | X | * | * | * | * | * | * | * |
| | * | * | * | * | * | * | * | * | * | * | * | * | * |
| | * | * | * | * | * | * | X | X | X | X | * | * | * |
| | * | * | * | * | * | * | * | * | * | * | * | * | * |
| | * | * | * | * | * | * | * | * | * | * | * | * | * |
| | * | * | * | * | * | * | * | * | * | * | * | * | * |
| | X | X | X | X | X | X | * | * | * | * | X | X | X |
| | * | * | * | * | * | * | * | * | * | * | X | * | * |
| | * | * | * | * | * | * | * | * | * | * | * | * | * |
| | X | * | * | X | * | * | * | * | * | * | * | * | * |
| | * | * | * | * | * | * | * | * | * | * | * | * | * |

**Table A.5 (continued)  Oracle Technical Control COBIT v4 Control Mapping (Part II: DS and ME)v**

| | DS1 Define and Manage Service Levels | DS2 Manage Third-Party Services | DS3 Manage Performance and Capacity | DS4 Ensure Continuous Service | DS5 Ensure Systems Security | DS6 Identify and Allocate Costs | DS7 Educate and Train Users | DS8 Manage Service Desk and Incidents | DS9 Manage the Configuration | DS10 Manage Problems | DS11 Manage Data | DS12 Manage the Physical Environment | DS13 Manage Operations | ME1 Monitor and Evaluate IT Performance | ME2 Monitor and Evaluate Internal Control | ME3 Ensure Regulatory Compliance | ME4 Provide IT Governance |
|---|---|---|---|---|---|---|---|---|---|---|---|---|---|---|---|---|---|
| IdM Suite: Access Manager | * | * | * | * | X | * | * | * | * | * | * | * | * | * | * | * | * |
| IdM Suite: Identity Federation | * | X | * | * | X | * | * | * | * | * | * | * | * | * | * | * | * |
| IdM Suite: Identity Manager | * | X | * | * | X | * | * | * | * | * | * | * | * | * | * | * | * |
| Enterprise Single Sign-On | * | * | * | * | X | * | * | * | * | * | * | * | * | * | * | * | * |
| Web Services Manager | X | * | * | X | X | * | * | * | * | * | * | * | * | * | X | * | * |
| Enterprise Manager: Identity Management Pack | X | * | * | X | X | * | * | * | * | * | * | * | * | * | X | * | * |
| Data Protection and Accountability | * | * | * | * | X | * | * | * | * | * | X | * | * | * | * | * | * |
| Advanced Security Option | * | * | * | * | X | * | * | * | * | * | X | * | * | * | * | * | * |

| Product | | | | | | | | | | | | | | | | |
|---|---|---|---|---|---|---|---|---|---|---|---|---|---|---|---|---|
| Oracle Label Security | * | * | * | * | X | * | * | * | * | X | * | * | * | * | * | * |
| Audit Vault | * | * | * | * | X | * | * | * | * | X | * | * | * | * | * | * |
| Oracle Database | * | * | * | * | X | * | * | * | * | X | * | * | * | * | * | * |
| Database Vault | * | * | * | * | X | * | * | * | * | X | * | * | * | * | * | * |
| Secure Enterprise Search | * | * | * | * | X | * | * | * | * | X | * | * | * | * | * | * |
| Information Lifecycle Management | * | * | * | X | X | * | * | * | * | X | * | * | * | * | * | * |
| Automatic Storage Management | * | * | * | X | X | * | * | * | * | X | * | * | * | * | * | * |
| Oracle Recovery Manager (RMAN) | * | * | * | X | * | * | * | * | * | X | * | * | * | * | * | * |
| Oracle Data Guard | * | * | * | X | X | * | * | * | * | X | * | * | * | * | * | * |
| Oracle Secure Backup | * | * | * | X | X | * | * | * | * | X | * | * | * | * | * | * |
| Oracle CDP (Flashback) | * | * | * | X | * | * | * | * | * | X | * | * | * | * | * | * |

Notes:

X  Denotes the technical control represented by the properly configured Oracle product satisfies the control.

*  Denotes the technical control represented by the properly configured Oracle product does not address control.

**Table A.6 Oracle Technical Control COBIT v4 DS5 Ensure System Security Control Mapping**

| | DS5.1 Management of IT Security | DS5.2 IT Security Plan | DS5.3 Identity Management | DS5.4 User Account Management | DS5.5 Security Testing, Surveillance, and Monitoring | DS5.6 Security Incident Definition | DS5.7 Protection of Security Technology | DS5.8 Cryptographic Key Management | DS5.9 Malicious Software Prevention, Detection, and Correction | DS5.10 Network Security | DS5.11 Exchange of Sensitive Data |
|---|---|---|---|---|---|---|---|---|---|---|---|
| GRC Intelligence | X | X | * | * | X | X | * | * | * | * | * |
| Balanced Scorecard | X | * | * | * | * | * | * | * | * | * | * |
| Business Intelligence | * | * | * | * | * | * | * | * | * | * | * |
| Fusion GRC Intelligence | * | X | * | * | X | X | * | * | * | * | * |
| Enterprise Planning and Budgeting | * | * | * | * | * | * | * | * | * | * | * |
| Organizational Policy Management | * | * | * | * | * | * | * | * | * | * | * |
| Oracle Learning Management | * | * | * | * | * | * | * | * | * | * | * |
| Universal Content Manager (Policy and Procedure Portal) | * | * | * | * | * | * | * | * | * | * | * |
| Enterprise Learning Management | * | * | * | * | * | * | * | * | * | * | * |
| Organizational Risk and Compliance Management | * | * | * | X | X | * | X | * | X | * | * |
| Financial Consolidation Hub | * | * | * | * | * | * | * | * | * | * | * |
| GRC Manager | * | * | * | * | * | * | * | * | * | * | * |
| Application Access Controls | * | * | * | X | X | * | X | * | X | * | * |
| Application Configuration Controls | * | * | * | * | X | * | X | * | X | * | * |
| Project Portfolio Management | * | * | * | * | * | * | * | * | * | * | * |
| Enterprise Manager: IT Governance Pack | X | X | X | X | X | X | X | X | * | X | X |

**Table A.6 (continued)  Oracle Technical Control COBIT v4 DS5 Ensure System Security Control Mapping**

| | DS5.1 Management of IT Security | DS5.2 IT Security Plan | DS5.3 Identity Management | DS5.4 User Account Management | DS5.5 Security Testing, Surveillance, and Monitoring | DS5.6 Security Incident Definition | DS5.7 Protection of Security Technology | DS5.8 Cryptographic Key Management | DS5.9 Malicious Software Prevention, Detection, and Correction | DS5.10 Network Security | DS5.11 Exchange of Sensitive Data |
|---|---|---|---|---|---|---|---|---|---|---|---|
| Industry-Specific Risk and Compliance Management | * | * | * | * | X | * | * | * | * | * | * |
| Discreet Manufacturing | * | * | * | * | * | * | * | * | * | * | * |
| Process Manufacturing | * | * | * | * | * | * | * | * | * | * | * |
| G-Log Global Trade | * | * | * | * | * | * | * | * | * | * | * |
| IFlex Reveleus | * | * | * | * | * | * | * | * | * | * | * |
| iFlex Mantas | * | * | * | * | X | * | * | * | * | * | * |
| Adverse Event Reporting (FDA) | * | * | * | * | * | * | * | * | * | * | * |
| Clinical Trial Management | * | * | * | * | * | * | * | * | * | * | * |
| Business Process Management | * | * | * | * | X | * | * | * | * | * | * |
| BPEL Process Manager | * | * | * | * | X | * | * | * | * | * | * |
| Tutor (Business Process Documentation) | * | * | * | * | * | * | * | * | * | * | * |
| Business Activity Monitoring | * | * | * | * | * | * | * | * | * | * | * |
| Content and Records Management | * | X | * | X | X | * | * | * | * | * | X |
| Siebel Universal Customer Master | * | X | * | X | * | * | * | * | * | * | X |
| Trusted Information Sharing | * | X | * | X | * | * | * | * | * | * | X |
| Universal Records Manager | * | X | * | * | * | * | * | * | * | * | X |
| Universal Content Manager | * | X | * | * | * | * | * | * | * | * | X |

**Table A.6 (continued)    Oracle Technical Control COBIT v4 DS5 Ensure System Security Control Mapping**

| | DS5.1 Management of IT Security | DS5.2 IT Security Plan | DS5.3 Identity Management | DS5.4 User Account Management | DS5.5 Security Testing, Surveillance, and Monitoring | DS5.6 Security Incident Definition | DS5.7 Protection of Security Technology | DS5.8 Cryptographic Key Management | DS5.9 Malicious Software Prevention, Detection, and Correction | DS5.10 Network Security | DS5.11 Exchange of Sensitive Data |
|---|---|---|---|---|---|---|---|---|---|---|---|
| Information Rights Management | * | X | * | X | X | * | * | * | * | * | X |
| Content Database | * | X | * | * | * | * | * | * | * | * | X |
| Records Database | * | X | * | * | * | * | * | * | * | * | X |
| Configuration and Change Management | * | * | * | * | * | * | * | * | X | X | * |
| Enterprise Manager: Change Management Pack | * | * | * | * | * | * | * | * | X | * | * |
| Enterprise Manager: Provisioning Pack | * | * | * | * | * | * | * | * | * | * | * |
| Enterprise Manager: Configuration Management Pack | * | * | * | * | * | * | * | * | * | X | * |
| Identity and Access Management | X | X | X | X | X | * | X | X | * | * | X |
| Internet Directory | X | X | X | X | X | * | X | X | * | * | * |
| Virtual Directory | X | X | X | X | * | * | X | * | * | * | X |
| IdM Suite: Access Manager | X | X | X | X | * | * | X | * | * | * | X |
| IdM Suite: Identity Federation | X | X | X | X | * | * | X | * | * | * | X |
| IdM Suite: Identity Manager | X | X | X | X | * | X | X | * | * | X | * |
| Enterprise Single Sign-On | X | X | X | X | * | * | X | * | * | * | * |
| Web Services Manager | X | X | X | X | * | * | X | * | * | * | X |
| Enterprise Manager: Identity Management Pack | X | X | X | X | X | X | X | X | * | X | X |

**Table A.6 (continued) Oracle Technical Control COBIT v4 DS5 Ensure System Security Control Mapping**

| | DS5.1 Management of IT Security | DS5.2 IT Security Plan | DS5.3 Identity Management | DS5.4 User Account Management | DS5.5 Security Testing, Surveillance, and Monitoring | DS5.6 Security Incident Definition | DS5.7 Protection of Security Technology | DS5.8 Cryptographic Key Management | DS5.9 Malicious Software Prevention, Detection, and Correction | DS5.10 Network Security | DS5.11 Exchange of Sensitive Data |
|---|---|---|---|---|---|---|---|---|---|---|---|
| Data Protection and Accountability | X | X | X | X | X | * | X | X | * | X | * |
|   Advanced Security Option | X | X | * | X | * | * | X | X | * | X | * |
|   Oracle Label Security | X | X | * | * | * | * | X | * | * | * | * |
|   Audit Vault | X | X | X | X | X | * | X | * | * | * | * |
|   Oracle Database | X | X | * | * | * | * | X | * | * | * | * |
|   Database Vault | X | X | X | X | * | * | X | * | * | * | * |
|   Secure Enterprise Search | X | X | * | * | * | * | X | * | * | * | * |
| Information Lifecycle Management | X | X | * | * | * | * | X | X | * | * | * |
|   Automatic Storage Management | X | X | * | * | * | * | * | * | * | * | * |
|   Oracle Recovery Manager (RMAN) | X | * | * | * | * | * | * | * | * | * | * |
|   Oracle Data Guard | X | X | * | * | * | * | X | * | * | * | * |
|   Oracle Secure Backup | X | X | * | * | * | * | X | X | * | * | * |
|   Oracle CDP (Flaskback) | X | * | * | * | * | * | * | * | * | * | * |

*Notes:*

X Denotes the technical control represented by the properly configured Oracle product satisfies the control.

* Denotes the technical control represented by the properly configured Oracle product does not address control.

**Table A.7  Risk versus Maturity of COBIT**

*Risk versus Compliance State*

| RISK | | | | | | | | |
|---|---|---|---|---|---|---|---|---|
| High | | | | | AI.6 | | | |
| | | | | | DS.5 | | | |
| | | DS.9 | AI.5 | | DS.10 | | | |
| | | | | | AI.4 | | | |
| | | | | | DS.2 | | | |
| | DS.13 | | | | | | | |
| | | DS.7 | | | | M.1 | | |
| | | AI.3 | | | | DS.12 | DS.4 | |
| | | | DS.11 | PO.10 | | | | |
| | | AI.2 | | | | | | |
| | | DS.3 | | | DS.1 | | | |
| | | M.2 | | | | | | |
| Low | Low | | | | | | | High |

→ COMPLIANCE STATE →

**Table A.8  Oracle Technical Control ITIL Control Mapping**

| | Final 6 Books | | | | | | Service Delivery | | | | | | | Service Support | | | | | | | | |
|---|---|---|---|---|---|---|---|---|---|---|---|---|---|---|---|---|---|---|---|---|---|---|
| | Software Asset Management | Project Management | Planning for Service Management | Application Management | Security Management | ICT Infrastructure Management | SD-Implement (Planning for the Implementation of Service Management) | SD-SCM (IT Service Continuity Management) | SD-FinMgmt (Financial Management for IT Services) | SD-CapMgmt (Capacity Management) | SD-AvaMgmt (Availability Management) | SD-SerMgmt (Service-level Management) | SD-Relation (Relationship between Processes) | SS-Implement (Planning for the Implementation of Service Management) | SS-Tools (Service Management Software Tools) | SS-ConMgmt (Configuration Management) | SS-RelMgmt (Release Management) | SS-ChgMgmt (Change Management) | SS-ProMgmt (Problem Management) | SS-IncMgmt (Incident Management) | SS-SerDesk (The Service Desk) | SS-Relation (Relationship between Processes) |
|---|---|---|---|---|---|---|---|---|---|---|---|---|---|---|---|---|---|---|---|---|---|---|
| GRC Intelligence | X | X | X | * | * | * | X | * | X | * | * | X | * | X | X | * | X | X | * | * | * | * |
| Balanced Scorecard | * | * | * | * | * | * | * | * | * | * | * | X | * | * | X | * | * | * | * | * | * | * |
| Business Intelligence | * | * | * | * | * | * | * | * | * | * | * | X | * | * | X | * | * | * | * | * | * | * |
| Fusion GRC Intelligence | * | * | * | * | * | * | * | * | * | * | * | X | * | * | X | * | X | * | * | * | * | X |
| Enterprise Planning and Budgeting | X | X | X | * | * | * | X | * | X | * | * | * | * | X | X | * | * | X | * | * | * | * |
| Organizational Policy Management | * | * | * | * | * | * | * | * | * | * | * | * | * | X | X | * | * | X | * | X | * | X |
| Oracle Learning Management | * | * | * | * | * | * | * | * | * | * | * | * | * | X | X | * | * | * | * | X | * | * |

**Table A.8 (continued)   Oracle Technical Control ITIL Control Mapping**

| | Service Support | | | | | | | | | Service Delivery | | | | | | | Final 6 Books | | | | | |
|---|---|---|---|---|---|---|---|---|---|---|---|---|---|---|---|---|---|---|---|---|---|---|
| | SS-Relation (Relationship between Processes) | SS-SerDesk (The Service Desk) | SS-IncMgmt (Incident Management) | SS-ProMgmt (Problem Management) | SS-ChgMgmt (Change Management) | SS-RelMgmt (Release Management) | SS-ConMgmt (Configuration Management) | SS-Tools (Service Management Software Tools) | SS-Implement (Planning for the Implementation of Service Management) | SD-Relation (Relationship between Processes) | SD-SerMgmt (Service-level Management) | SD-AvaMgmt (Availability Management) | SD-CapMgmt (Capacity Management) | SD-FinMgmt (Financial Management for IT Services) | SD-SCM (IT Service Continuity Management) | SD-Implement (Planning for the Implementation of Service Management) | ICT Infrastructure Management | Security Management | Application Management | Planning for Service Management | Project Management | Software Asset Management |
| Universal Content Manager (Policy and Procedure Portal) | X | * | * | * | X | * | * | X | X | * | * | * | * | * | * | * | * | * | * | * | * | * |
| Enterprise Learning Management | * | * | * | * | * | * | * | X | X | * | * | * | * | * | * | * | * | * | * | * | * | * |
| Organizational Risk and Compliance Management | * | * | * | X | X | * | X | X | X | X | X | X | X | X | * | X | X | X | X | * | X | X |
| Financial Consolidation Hub | * | * | * | * | * | * | * | * | * | * | * | * | * | X | * | * | * | * | * | * | * | * |
| GRC Manager | * | * | * | X | X | * | X | X | X | X | X | X | X | X | * | * | X | X | X | * | X | X |
| Application Access Controls | * | * | * | * | X | * | X | * | * | * | * | * | * | * | * | * | X | X | X | * | * | X |

| | 1 | 2 | 3 | 4 | 5 | 6 | 7 | 8 | 9 | 10 | 11 | 12 | 13 | 14 | 15 | 16 | 17 | 18 | 19 | 20 | 21 | 22 |
|---|---|---|---|---|---|---|---|---|---|---|---|---|---|---|---|---|---|---|---|---|---|---|
| Application Configuration Controls | X | * | * | * | * | X | * | * | * | * | * | * | * | * | * | X | * | * | * | * | * | * |
| Project Portfolio Management | * | X | * | * | * | X | X | * | * | * | * | X | X | * | * | * | * | * | * | * | X | * |
| Enterprise Manager: IT Governance Pack | X | X | * | X | X | X | X | * | X | X | X | X | X | X | X | X | X | X | * | X | X | X |
| Industry-Specific Risk and Compliance Management | * | * | * | * | X | X | * | * | X | * | * | * | * | * | * | X | X | * | * | * | X | * |
| Discreet Manufacturing | * | * | * | * | * | X | * | * | * | * | * | * | * | * | * | * | * | X | * | * | X | * |
| Process Manufacturing | * | * | * | * | * | X | * | * | * | * | * | * | * | * | * | X | * | X | * | * | X | * |
| G-Log Global Trade | * | * | * | * | * | * | * | * | X | * | * | * | * | * | * | * | * | * | * | * | * | * |
| IFlex Reveleus | * | * | * | * | * | * | * | * | X | * | * | * | * | * | * | * | * | * | * | * | * | * |
| iFlex Mantas | * | * | * | * | * | * | * | * | X | * | X | X | * | * | * | X | * | * | * | * | X | * |
| Adverse Event Reporting (FDA) | * | * | * | * | * | X | * | * | * | * | * | * | * | * | * | X | * | * | * | * | * | * |
| Clinical Trial Management | * | * | * | * | * | * | * | * | * | * | * | * | * | * | * | * | * | * | * | * | * | * |
| Business Process Management | X | * | X | * | * | * | * | * | * | * | X | X | X | * | * | * | * | * | X | * | * | X |
| BPEL Process Manager | X | * | X | * | * | * | * | * | * | * | X | X | X | * | * | * | * | * | X | * | * | * |
| Tutor (Business Process Documentation) | X | * | X | * | * | * | * | * | * | * | X | X | X | * | * | * | * | * | X | * | * | * |
| Business Activity Monitoring | X | * | X | * | * | * | * | * | * | * | X | X | X | * | * | * | * | * | X | * | * | * |

**Table A.8 (continued)  Oracle Technical Control ITIL Control Mapping**

| | SS-Relation (Relationship between Processes) | SS-SerDesk (The Service Desk) | SS-IncMgmt (Incident Management) | SS-ProMgmt (Problem Management) | SS-ChgMgmt (Change Management) | SS-RelMgmt (Release Management) | SS-ConMgmt (Configuration Management) | SS-Tools (Service Management Software Tools) | SS-Implement (Planning for the Implementation of Service Management) | SD-Relation (Relationship between Processes) | SD-SerMgmt (Service-level Management) | SD-AvaMgmt (Availability Management) | SD-CapMgmt (Capacity Management) | SD-FinMgmt (Financial Management for IT Services) | SD-SCM (IT Service Continuity Management) | SD-Implement (Planning for the Implementation of Service Management) | ICT Infrastructure Management | Security Management | Application Management | Planning for Service Management | Project Management | Software Asset Management |
|---|---|---|---|---|---|---|---|---|---|---|---|---|---|---|---|---|---|---|---|---|---|---|
| | *Service Support* | | | | | | | | *Service Delivery* | | | | | | | | *Final 6 Books* | | | | | |
| Content and Records Management | * | * | * | * | * | * | * | * | * | * | * | * | X | * | * | * | * | X | * | * | * | * |
| Siebel Universal Customer Master | * | * | * | * | * | * | * | * | * | * | * | * | * | * | * | * | * | * | * | * | * | * |
| Trusted Information Sharing | * | * | * | * | * | * | * | * | * | * | * | * | * | * | * | * | * | * | * | * | * | * |
| Universal Records Manager | * | * | * | * | * | * | * | * | * | * | * | * | * | * | * | * | * | * | * | * | * | * |
| Universal Content Manager | * | * | * | * | * | * | * | * | * | * | * | * | * | * | * | * | * | * | * | * | * | * |
| Information Rights Management | * | * | * | * | * | * | * | * | * | * | * | * | * | * | * | * | * | * | * | * | * | * |
| Content Database | * | * | * | * | * | * | * | * | * | * | * | * | X | * | * | * | * | * | * | * | * | * |

| | Records Database | Configuration and Change Management | Enterprise Manager: Change Management Pack | Enterprise Manager: Provisioning Pack | Enterprise Manager: Configuration Management Pack | Identity and Access Management | Internet Directory | Virtual Directory | IdM Suite: Access Manager | IdM Suite: Identity Federation | IdM Suite: Identity Manager | Enterprise Single Sign-On | Web Services Manager | Enterprise Manager: Identity Management Pack |
|---|---|---|---|---|---|---|---|---|---|---|---|---|---|---|
|  | * | X | X | X | X | * | * | * | * | * | * | * | * | * |
|  | * | * | * | * | * | * | * | * | * | * | * | * | * | * |
|  | * | X | X | X | X | * | * | X | X | * | * | * | X | X |
|  | * | X | X | X | X | X | X | X | X | X | X | X | X | X |
|  | * | * | * | * | * | X | X | X | X | X | X | X | X | X |
|  | * | * | * | * | * | * | * | * | * | * | * | * | * | X |
|  | * | * | * | * | * | * | * | * | * | * | * | * | * | * |
|  | X | * | * | * | * | * | * | * | * | * | * | * | * | X |
|  | * | * | * | * | * | * | * | * | * | * | * | * | * | * |
|  | * | X | X | X | X | X | * | * | * | * | * | X | X | X |
|  | * | * | * | * | * | * | * | * | * | * | * | * | * | * |
|  | * | * | * | * | * | * | * | * | * | * | * | * | * | * |
|  | * | X | X | X | X | * | * | * | * | * | * | * | X | * |
|  | * | * | * | * | * | * | * | * | * | * | * | * | * | * |
|  | * | * | * | * | * | * | * | * | * | * | * | * | * | * |
|  | * | * | * | * | * | * | * | * | * | * | * | * | * | * |
|  | * | * | * | * | * | * | * | * | * | * | * | * | * | * |
|  | * | * | * | * | * | * | * | * | * | * | * | * | * | * |

**Table A.8 (continued)   Oracle Technical Control ITIL Control Mapping**

| | Service Support | | | | | | | | Service Delivery | | | | | | | | Final 6 Books | | | | | |
|---|---|---|---|---|---|---|---|---|---|---|---|---|---|---|---|---|---|---|---|---|---|---|
| | SS-Relation (Relationship between Processes) | SS-SerDesk (The Service Desk) | SS-IncMgmt (Incident Management) | SS-ProMgmt (Problem Management) | SS-ChgMgmt (Change Management) | SS-RelMgmt (Release Management) | SS-ConMgmt (Configuration Management) | SS-Tools (Service Management Software Tools) | SS-Implement (Planning for the Implementation of Service Management) | SD-Relation (Relationship between Processes) | SD-SerMgmt (Service-level Management) | SD-AvaMgmt (Availability Management) | SD-CapMgmt (Capacity Management) | SD-FinMgmt (Financial Management for IT Services) | SD-SCM (IT Service Continuity Management) | SD-Implement (Planning for the Implementation of Service Management) | ICT Infrastructure Management | Security Management | Application Management | Planning for Service Management | Project Management | Software Asset Management |
| Data Protection and Accountability | * | * | * | X | X | * | * | * | * | * | * | * | X | * | X | * | * | X | * | * | * | * |
| Advanced Security Option | * | * | * | * | * | * | * | * | * | * | * | * | * | * | * | * | * | X | * | * | * | * |
| Oracle Label Security | * | * | * | * | * | * | * | * | * | * | * | * | * | * | X | * | * | X | * | * | * | * |
| Audit Vault | * | * | * | X | X | * | * | * | * | * | * | * | * | * | * | * | * | X | * | * | * | * |
| Oracle Database | * | * | * | * | X | * | * | * | * | * | * | * | X | * | X | * | * | X | X | * | * | * |
| Database Vault | * | * | * | X | X | * | * | * | * | * | * | * | * | * | X | * | * | X | * | * | * | * |
| Secure Enterprise Search | * | * | * | * | * | * | X | X | * | * | X | X | * | * | * | * | * | X | * | * | * | * |
| Information Lifecycle Management | * | * | * | * | X | * | * | * | * | * | * | * | X | * | X | * | * | X | * | * | * | * |

| | | | | | | | | | | | | | | | | | | | | | | |
|---|---|---|---|---|---|---|---|---|---|---|---|---|---|---|---|---|---|---|---|---|---|---|
| Automatic Storage Management | * | * | * | * | * | * | * | * | X | * | X | X | * | * | X | * | * | * | * | * | * | * |
| Oracle Recovery Manager (RMAN) | * | * | * | * | * | X | * | X | * | X | * | X | X | * | * | X | * | * | * | * | * | * |
| Oracle Data Guard | * | * | * | * | * | * | * | X | * | X | * | X | X | * | * | X | X | * | * | * | * | * |
| Oracle Secure Backup | * | * | * | * | X | * | * | X | * | X | * | X | X | * | * | X | X | * | * | * | * | * |
| Oracle CDP (Flaskback) | * | * | X | * | * | * | * | X | * | X | * | X | X | * | * | X | * | * | * | * | * | * |

*Notes:*

X  Denotes the technical control represented by the properly configured Oracle product satisfies the control.

*  Denotes the technical control represented by the properly configured Oracle product does not address control.

# Appendix B

# FISMA Technical Control Mapping

The Federal Information Security Management Act (FISMA) was passed in late 2002 as Title III of the 2002 E-Gov Act. The Government Information Security Reform Act (GISRA), which expired in 2002, had many of the same provisions as FISMA. The basic purpose of FISMA is to strengthen information security programs at federal agencies by providing a framework for information security. FISMA requires agencies to evaluate their information system's security requirements and to develop and execute plans for securing them. In support of this and other related legislation, the Office of Management and Budget (OMB) requires each federal agency to:

- Develop security plans
- Ensure that overall responsibility for security is assigned to an appropriate official
- Periodically review the security mechanisms in place for their information systems
- Officially accept the security risks associated with information systems prior to initial operation and again periodically once the systems are in place
- Define the following technical controls and position solutions to mitigate risks:
  - Logical access control tools (Table B.1)
  - Accountability and audit tools (Table B.2)
  - Identification and authentication tools (Table B.3)
  - System and communication protection tools (Table B.4)
  - Operational controls (Table B.5)

Operational controls are largely procedural in nature and, in general, deal with the business processes used to support management and technical controls. The Operational Controls class includes nine families of security controls: Personnel Security, Physical and Environmental Protection, Contingency Planning and Operations, Configuration Management, Hardware and Software Maintenance, System and Information Integrity, Media Protection, Incident Response, and Security Awareness and Training. Oracle has tools that can help satisfy requirements in both the Contingency Planning and the Incident Response families.

**Table B.1    Logical Access Control Tools**

| Control Name | Oracle Features/Components Used |
|---|---|
| AC-1 Access control policy and procedures | Oracle Consulting Services and Oracle partners can help review your access control policies and procedures. |
| AC-2 Account management | When a user leaves the organization or access is no longer required or valid due to a job change, Oracle Identity Manager revokes access on demand or automatically, as dictated by role- or attribute-based access policies.<br><br>Oracle Identity Manager can also provide continuous monitoring of rogue and orphan accounts. By combining denial access policies, workflows, and reconciliation, an enterprise can execute the requisite corrective actions when such accounts are discovered, in accordance with security and governance policies.<br><br>To maintain better control over and provide improved visibility into all provisioning processes, Oracle Identity Manager enables end users and administrators to track request status in real-time, at any point during a provisioning transaction. Account managers can also be notified when account status is changed due to changes such as termination or alteration.<br><br>Oracle Identity Manager reports on both the history and the current state of the provisioning environment. The system captures all necessary data to answer the question "Who has access to What, When, How, and Why?" Oracle Identity Manager's reporting and auditing capabilities enable an enterprise to cost effectively cope with ever increasingly stringent regulatory requirements.<br><br>Enterprise User Security, an Oracle Database Enterprise Edition feature, gives you the ability to centrally manage database users and authorizations in one central place. Enterprise User Security increases security in many ways:<br><br>Centralized provisioning and deprovisioning of database users.<br><br>Centralized password management and self-service password reset capability.<br><br>Centralized management of authorizations using global database roles.<br><br>Oracle Directory Synchronization Service, part of Oracle Internet Directory, permits synchronization between Oracle Internet Directory and other directories and user repositories such as Microsoft Active Directory and SunONE. |
| AC-3 Access enforcement | Oracle Access Manager is a state-of-the-art solution for both centralized identity management and access control, providing an integrated standards-based solution that delivers authentication, Web single sign-on, access policy creation and enforcement, user self-registration and self-service, delegated administration, reporting, and auditing. |

**Table B.1 (continued)   Logical Access Control Tools**

| *Control Name* | *Oracle Features/Components Used* |
|---|---|
| AC-3 Access enforcement (continued) | Oracle Database Vault, an option for the Oracle database, enforces access based on multiple requirements to provide greater certainty that users are who they state themselves to be. Oracle Database Vault can prevent highly privileged users, including powerful application DBAs and others, from accessing sensitive applications and data in Oracle databases outside their authorized responsibilities. |
| | Oracle Label Security, also an option for the Oracle database, provides fine-grained access control and implements and maintains row-level security for sensitive data that is subject to privacy and compliance regulations. |
| AC-4 Information flow enforcement | Based on SAML and SOAP, the Oracle Identity Governance Framework provides CARML and XACML assertions to enforce information flow controls and provide fit-for-use and fit-for-purpose attestations. |
| AC-5 Separation of duties | The access enforcement technologies mentioned in section AC-3, when configured based on "least privileged" model, can also provide and control the minimum authorization users require to accomplish their job. |
| | Oracle Database Vault enforces separation of duty, a critical requirement when applications and databases are consolidated, by ensuring that the privileged DBAs are limited to managing the database but not allowed to access the application data. This separation-of-duty architecture establishes the strong internal controls necessary to meet various regulatory requirements. |
| | Oracle Audit Vault, a solution that provides the ability to consolidate, monitor, and analyze audit information from multiple Oracle databases, provides separation of duties to prevent unauthorized access and modification of audit information. |
| AC-6 Least privilege | Oracle has robust support for roles, allowing application developers to break down access privileges into a least-privilege model. Application users can have many roles active depending on their job responsibility. |
| | The access enforcement technologies mentioned in section AC-3 will allow organizations to provide the minimum access a user requires to do his or her job. Technology, however, is only a facilitator when it comes to least privilege. Policies and procedures must first be established so that the supporting technologies can be configured properly. |
| AC-7 Unsuccessful log-in attempts | Oracle Enterprise Single Sign-On, part of the Oracle Identity Management Suite, enables centralized management of password policy enforcement. Oracle GRC Manager takes this capability and leverages information gathered by the Virtual Directory and Audit Vault to enforce and track log-in attempts. |

**Table B.1 (continued)   Logical Access Control Tools**

| Control Name | Oracle Features/Components Used |
|---|---|
| AC-8 System use notification | Oracle GRC Manager in conjunction with Virtual Directory and Audit Vault is able to aggregate and consolidate statistics on system use and initiate notification of parties leveraging the BPEL workflow system. |
| AC-9 Previous log-on notification | When used in conjunction Oracle GRC Manager and Audit Vault may be leveraged to provide a history of data and application log-on. |
| AC-10 Concurrent session control | |
| AC-11 Session lock | |
| AC-12 Session termination | |
| AC-13 Supervision and review—access control | Attestation, Oracle Audit functionality, fine-grained auditing, OAM reports, and Audit Vault enable non-reputable review of access controls and user activity. |
| AC-14 Permitted actions without identification and authentication | The Oracle Identity Governance framework permits capability-based action based on inherited XACML and CARML assertions. |
| AC-15 Automated marking | The Oracle Identity Governance framework permits information marking via XACML and CARML assertions to determine special handling. |
| AC-16 Automated labeling | Oracle Label Security is a security option for the Oracle database which provides the ability to assign classification labels to sensitive data inside the Oracle database and manage user access to the sensitive data through a process called access mediation. Oracle Label Security addresses a variety of data classification requirements ranging from the simple assignment of a classification label to an employee record to the enforcement of multilevel security for the protection of national security information. |
| AC-17 Remote access | Through its use of Rules and Factors, Oracle Database Vault can restrict or deny access to the Oracle database based on the IP address the user is connecting from, such as an untrusted remote location. It can also require encryption to be implemented on that connection as well. Oracle Advanced Security Option is necessary to provide encryption of network traffic. |
| AC-18 Wireless access restrictions | Oracle Application Server supports wireless security. |
| AC-19 Access control for portable and mobile devices | IdM support mobile devices. |

**Table B.1 (continued)  Logical Access Control Tools**

| Control Name | Oracle Features/Components Used |
|---|---|
| AC-20 Use of external information systems | Oracle Identity Governance framework when used in conjunction with Oracle Federation and Information Rights Management permits granular policy definition when to untrusted systems. |

**Table B.2  Accountability and Audit Tools**

| Control Name | Oracle Features/Components Used |
|---|---|
| AU-1 Audit and accountability policy and procedures | Oracle Consulting Services and Oracle Partners can help review your auditing and accountability policy and procedures. |
| AU-2 Auditable events | Discuss control of audited events. How many events we audit. Alerts. Audit Vault centralization and securing of audits. |
| AU-3 Content of audit records | Mentions centralization again (Audit Vault) … what do audit records include? |
| AU-4 Audit storage capacity | Selective auditing to minimize storage capacity. |
| AU-5 Response to auditing processing failures | Oracle Grid Control provides warnings and alerts when storage reaches capacity. |
| AU-6 Audit monitoring, analysis, and reporting | Audit Vault provides for audit monitoring, analysis, and reporting; fine-grained auditing provides for alerts. |
| AU-7 Audit reduction and report generation | Oracle Fusion GRC Intelligence provides selective viewing or reporting of certain audit events. |
| AU-8 Time stamps | Time stamps on audits are provided in all Oracle products. |
| AU-9 Protection of audit information | Audit Vault affords cryptographically nonreputable data storage, creating a write-once read-many data repository. |
| AU-10 Non-repudiation | Oracle Audit Vault provides cryptographically nonreputable recorded proof of individual action—dig signatures, time stamps, etc. |
| AU-11 Audit record retention | Content DV/Records DB and Audit Vault provide for cryptographically secure, nonreputable audit record retention. |

**Table B.3    Identification and Authentication Tools**

| Control Name | Oracle Features/Components Used |
|---|---|
| IA-1 Identification and authentication policies and procedures | Oracle Consulting Services and Oracle Partners can help agencies review their identification and authentication policies and procedures. |
| IA-2 User identification and authentication | Oracle database natively supports password authentication or via Oracle Advanced Security Option provides support for strong authentication methods such as tokens, PKI, smart cards and biometrics.<br><br>These same authentication form factors are supported in Oracle's Identity and Access Management solutions. Oracle Identity and Access Management solutions provide a shared service that can employ consistent identification and authentication at the application level as stated in the IA-2 of SP 800-53.<br><br>Oracle Identity Federation, one of Oracle's Identity and Access Management solutions, provides the infrastructure that enables identities and their relevant entitlements to be propagated across security domains—this applies to domains existing within an organization as well as between organizations.<br><br>It is important to uniquely identify the user throughout the identity life cycle. Proxy Authentication and Client Identifier, features in the Oracle database, enable identity preservation to the database level so user can be uniquely identified in the Oracle database.<br><br>Oracle Identity Manager is a best-in-class user provisioning and administration solution that automates the process of adding, updating, and deleting users accounts from applications and directories. Oracle Identity Manager can synchronize or map passwords across managed resources and enforce differences in password policies among these resources. This addresses the personal identity verification requirement in FISMA. |
| IA-3 Device identification and authentication | Oracle Sensor-Based Service Offering supports FIPS 1999 device identification and authentication requirement. |
| IA-4 Identifier management | Oracle Identity Manager automates the process of provisioning IT resources across heterogeneous business processes and managed platforms. It instantly connects users to the resources they need to be productive, and revokes unauthorized access to protect proprietary information, enhance security and automate regulatory compliance.<br><br>Oracle Identity Manager supports separation of approval and provisioning workflows. Approval workflow enables an enterprise to model its preferred or best-practice approval processes for managing resource access requests. This addresses the personal identity verification requirement in FISMA. |

**Table B.3 (continued)   Identification and Authentication Tools**

| Control Name | Oracle Features/Components Used |
|---|---|
| IA-5 Authenticator management | Oracle Identity Manager's self-service capabilities allow users to manage their own passwords across managed resources. In case a user forgets his password, Oracle Identity Manager can present customizable challenge questions to enable self-service identity verification and password retrieval. |
| | Oracle Identity Manager features very rich password policy management capabilities. Most best-practice password policies are supported out of the box and are configurable via an intuitive user interface. Supported password complexity requirements include password length, alphanumeric and special characters usage, upper and lower case usage, full or partial exclusion of username, and historical passwords. |
| | Oracle Identity Manager can synchronize or map passwords across managed resources and enforce differences in password policies among these resources. |
| | Oracle Identity Manager can manage deployment and termination of strong authentication solutions such as the RSA SecurID solution. |
| | In the Oracle database: |
| | ■ Passwords are always hashed when transmitted for authentication purposes. |
| | ■ Password complexity routines and password profiles are supported. |
| | ■ Personal Identity Verification requirement is supported. |
| IA-6 Authentication feedback | Oracle ESSO, Oracle Wallet, and Oracle Access Manager enforce the Authentication feedback mandate of FIPS 140-2. |
| IA-7 Cryptographic module authentication | Oracle Advanced Security Option satisfies FIPS 140-2 certification when authenticating to cryptographic modules. |

**Table B.4    System and Communication Protection Tools**

| Control Name | Oracle Features/Components Used |
| --- | --- |
| SP-1 Application partitioning | Oracle applications and system management tools are separate products that have no interdependencies. |
| SP-2 Information system partitioning | Oracle supports logical and physical partitioning of information in the same database but does not enforce its use. |
| SP-4 Denial of service protection | Session usage information combined with the ability to block IP addresses and network domains/ resource monitoring and session control provide support for preventing successful denial-of-service (DoS) attacks. |
| SP-5 Resource priority | Resource Consumer Groups in the database ensure that server resources are not intentionally or inadvertently monopolized. Users and applications are also allocated disk quotas. |
| SP-6 Boundary protection | Oracle supports the use of firewalls in secure network architectures. |
| SP-8 Transmission integrity | Oracle Advanced Security checksumming detects modifications of packets, replays of packets, and missing packets. Checksumming provides data integrity (to check to see that data has not been tampered with during transmission). Oracle Advanced Security provides support for the Secure Socket Layer (SSL) protocol. SSL support in Oracle secures Net8 and networks. It provides encryption of network traffic and authentication of clients and servers using public-key technology. With SSL, Oracle servers can authenticate clients by using industry-standard X.509 version 3 certificates. |
| SP-9 Network disconnect | TCP timeouts are supported for the database, and http session timeouts are supported for the Oracle Single Sign-On Server. |
| SP-10 Information transmission | Oracle Advanced Security checksumming detects modifications of packets, replays of packets, and missing packets. Checksumming provides data integrity (to check to see that data has not been tampered with during transmission). Oracle Advanced Security provides support for the Secure Socket Layer (SSL) protocol. SSL support in Oracle secures Net8 and networks. It provides encryption of network traffic and authentication of clients and servers using public-key technology. With SSL, Oracle servers can authenticate clients by using industry-standard X.509 version 3 certificates. |
| SP-11 Trusted path | Encrypted network communication and strong I&A are supported. |
| SP-12 Duress alarm | Assisted by fine-grained auditing or selective audit. |
| SP-13 Cryptographic key management | Oracle supports PKI and PKCS#11 for key management. |
| SP-15 Public key infrastructure certificates | Oracle10g Certificate Authority. An Oracle10g Application Server component that generates and publishes X.509 V3 PKI certificates to support strong authentication methods. |

**Table B.4 (continued)  System and Communication Protection Tools**

| Control Name | Oracle Features/Components Used |
|---|---|
| SP-16 Use of encryption | Oracle Advanced Security provides support for the Secure Socket Layer (SSL) protocol. SSL support in Oracle provides encryption of network traffic and authentication of clients and servers using public-key technology. With SSL, Oracle servers can authenticate clients by using industry-standard X.509 version 3 certificates. In addition, the database supports the encryption of stored data. |

**Table B.5  Operational Control Tools**

| Control Name | Oracle Features/Components Used |
|---|---|
| CP-5 Off-site backup storage sites | Data Guard maintains one or more synchronized copies of a customer's production data. An Oracle9i Data Guard configuration consists of a collection of loosely connected systems that combine the primary database and physical standby databases into a single, easily managed disaster recovery solution. |
| CP-6 Information backup and restore | |
| CP-7 Backup mechanisms | |
| CP-10 Information system recovery | |
| IR-5 Intrusion detection systems and tools | Fine-grained auditing or selective audit or mantas can be an integral part of an intrusion detection and response control strategy. They can be used as tripwires for malicious and dubious activity. |
| CM-1 Off-site backup storage sites | Not Applicable |
| CM-2 Baseline configuration | Oracle Grid Control: The goal of baseline configuration is realized within Oracle's grid core technologies, Oracle Application Server, and Oracle Real Application Clusters, permanently logically controlled from a special monitoring component, Oracle Grid Control (GC). In the event of abnormal situations (high load, insufficient response time, service not available, etc.) the GC acts like an agent and sends respective traps to the ASCC. If an error condition is reported, the ASCC initiates a check in the corresponding inventory list for the failed server. Depending on the policies and actions that are defined for the failed system, it automatically triggers a corrective action. This action could result in a reboot of the same server or the provisioning and boot of a spare server with an identical image. |
| CM-3 Configuration change control | Oracle Application Configuration Controls monitor more than 500 internal controls for the Oracle E-Business Suite, provides continuous monitoring for changes in application configuration controls, and includes the ability to set up auditing parameters to enforce organizational tolerances across multiple instances. |

**Table B.5 (continued)** **Operational Control Tools**

| Control Name | Oracle Features/Components Used |
|---|---|
| CM-4 Monitoring configuration changes | Oracle Application Configuration Controls monitor more than 500 internal controls for the Oracle E-Business Suite, provides continuous monitoring for changes in application configuration controls, and includes the ability to set up auditing parameters to enforce organizational tolerances across multiple instances. |
| CM-5 Access restrictions for change | Oracle Application Access Controls deliver a library of segregation-of-duties (SOD) controls, including more than 200 rules for the Oracle E-Business Suite and provide the ability to detect and prevent access control violations. |

Management controls are largely procedural in nature and, in general, deal with the business processes used by an organization to manage the security of the information systems. The Management Control class includes five families of security controls: Risk Assessment, Security Planning, Acquisition of Information Systems and Services, Review of Security Controls, and Security Accreditation.

# FISMA Background and Related Standards

FISMA utilizes NIST Special Publication (SP) 800–37, Guide for the Security Certification and Accreditation of Federal Information Systems, as its compliance standard. NIST SP 800–37 provides guidelines for certifying and accrediting information systems supporting the executive agencies of the federal government. NIST SP 800–37 applies to all federal information systems other than those systems designated as national security systems, as defined in FISMA.

Some of the key responsibilities of the agencies under FISMA are summarized as follows and include (these items are from the FISMA documentation on the Department of Homeland Security's Web site—http://www.fedcirc.gov/library/legislation/FISMA.html):

■ Providing information security commensurate with the associated risk
■ Performing a risk assessment
■ Implementing policies and procedures that reduce information security risks in a cost-effective manner
■ Conducting periodic testing of information security measures
■ Having a qualified Chief Information Security Officer whose primary responsibility is information security
■ Conducting ongoing evaluation and adjustment of the information security program

These requirements are, for the most part, very similar to those of GISRA. The main difference with FISMA is the integration with National Institute of Standards and Technology (NIST). Under FISMA, federal agencies are to use the standards proposed by NIST to determine information security measures for their operations. According to the legislation, "the secretary shall make standards [NIST standards] … compulsory and binding to the extent determined necessary by the secretary to improve the efficiency of operation or security of federal information systems." Essentially, federal agencies must achieve compliance with NIST standards under FISMA.

In addition to modifying GISRA, FISMA had a number of other effects including:

- Repealing the Computer Security Act of 1987
- Documenting inventory of information systems

Similar to legislation such as HIPAA and GLBA, FISMA is mandating federal agencies to have an information security program that includes the full life cycle of information security, including risk assessments, security policies and procedures, use of technology, and ongoing compliance efforts. FISMA also provides some room for agencies to determine what information security measures are best for them. From a security assessment perspective, FISMA should be reviewed in detail if working with a federal agency.

The certification and accreditation package consists of the following documents:

- System security plan (SSP)
- Security assessment report
- Plan of action and milestones (POAM)

The key document for the certification and accreditation process is the system security plan (SSP), detailed in NIST Special Publication 800–18, Guide for Developing Security Plans for Information Technology Systems. The purpose of the SSP is to:

- Provide an overview of the system's security requirements and describe the controls in place or planned for meeting those requirements
- Delineate responsibilities and expected behavior of all individuals who access the system

## DoD Information Technology Security Certification and Accreditation Process

DoDI 5200.40 (DITSCAP) establishes a standard DoD-wide process, set of activities, general tasks, and a management structure to certify and accredit information systems (IS). Certification and accreditation (C&A) uses a single-document approach for all classified and unclassified systems in the DoD. All the information relevant to the C&A is collected into one document, the systems security authorization agreement (SSAA), which is then submitted to the Designated Approval Authority for approval.

## National Information Assurance Certification and Accreditation Process

The National Security Telecommunications and Information System Security Instruction (NSTISSI) 1000 defines the National Information Assurance Certification and Accreditation Process (NIACAP). The NIACAP establishes a standard national process, set of activities, general tasks, and a management structure to certify and accredit systems that will maintain the information assurance (IA) and security posture of a system or site. NSTISSI 1000 provides an overview of the NIACAP process, roles of the people involved, and the documentation produced during the process. More detailed procedures will be included in the NIACAP implementation manual when it is released.

## Defense Information Assurance Certification and Accreditation Process

The Defense Information Assurance Certification and Accreditation Process (DIACAP) (now in draft form) will supersede the DITSCAP (DoDI 5200.40). The DIACAP will establish the standard DoD process for identifying, implementing, and validating IA controls, for authorizing the operation of DoD information systems, and for managing IA posture across DoD information systems consistent with Title III of the E-Government Act, FISMA, and DoD Directive 8500.1. All DoD systems will be required to transition to DIACAP in the future.

The DIACAP is independent of the system life cycle, and its activities may be initiated at any system life-cycle stage—during acquisition, during operation, or at the inception of a major system modification. Generally, the earlier in the system life cycle the DIACAP is initiated, the less expensive and problematic is the implementation of IA capabilities and services.

## Response to Suspected Threats or Intrusions

All of these concerns and possibly many others could be drawn from the organizational assessment. This is far from an extensive list of possible management concerns. You will have to understand customers and their motivations to identify the real management concerns. These could be the same reasons for requesting the evaluation, but there are usually more. Technical concerns should be addressed equally with the organizational concerns. Technical concerns usually come from senior technicians and are not normally expressed by management. Some of these could be:

- Blame for findings
- Impact to normal operations
- System downtime
- Loss of data

# Appendix C

# Oracle Governance Risk and Compliance Ecosystem

Image C1: Oracle Governance, Risk & Compliance Products (END-C01.TIF)
Image C2: Oracle IT Governance Solution Set (END-C02.TIF)
Image C3: Oracle GRC - Financial Integrity Solution Set (END-C03.TIF)
Image C4: Oracle GRC - Legal Risk Solution Set (END-C04.TIF)
Image C5: Oracle GRC - Enterprise Risk Solution Set (END-C05.TIF)
Image C6: Oracle GRC - Oracle GRC Ecosystem (END-C06.TIF)

## Credits

Co-Authors & Contributors:
  Alex Lopez - Oracle Product Development
  Mark Wilcox - Oracle Product Development
  David Saslav - Oracle Product Development
  Phil Hunt - Oracle Product Development
  Viresh Garg - Oracle Product Development
  Bob Wells - Oracle Consulting
  Anshu Sharma - Oracle Product Development
  Vishal Parashar - Oracle Product Development
  Lane Leskela - Oracle Marketing
  Ted Sherill IV - Oracle Sales
  Pateek Misshra - Oracle Product Development

Editor:
  Amy L. Van Antwerp

Special Thanks:

Heather Wellard - Austrlian Bankers Association

Steve Detrick - Oracle Security Architect

Mary Ann Davidson - Oracle Chief Security Officer

Dick Heart - SXIP

**Image C1   Oracle Governance, Risk, and Compliance Products**

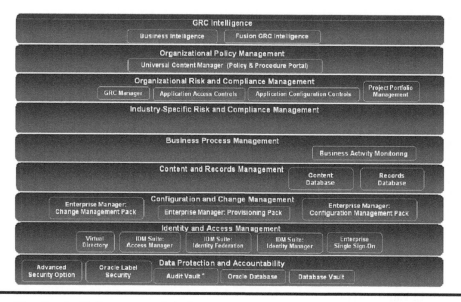

**Image C2   Oracle IT Governance Solution Set**

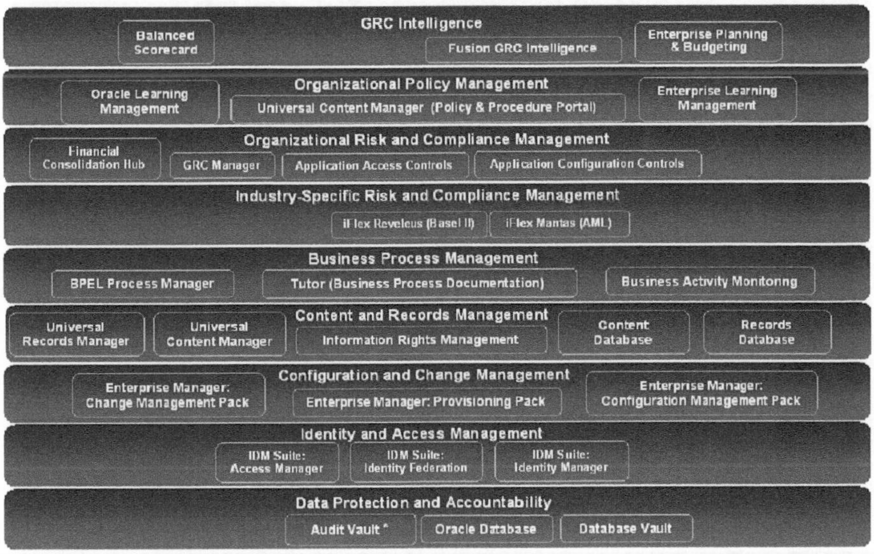

**Image C3 Oracle GRC: Financial Integrity Solution Set**

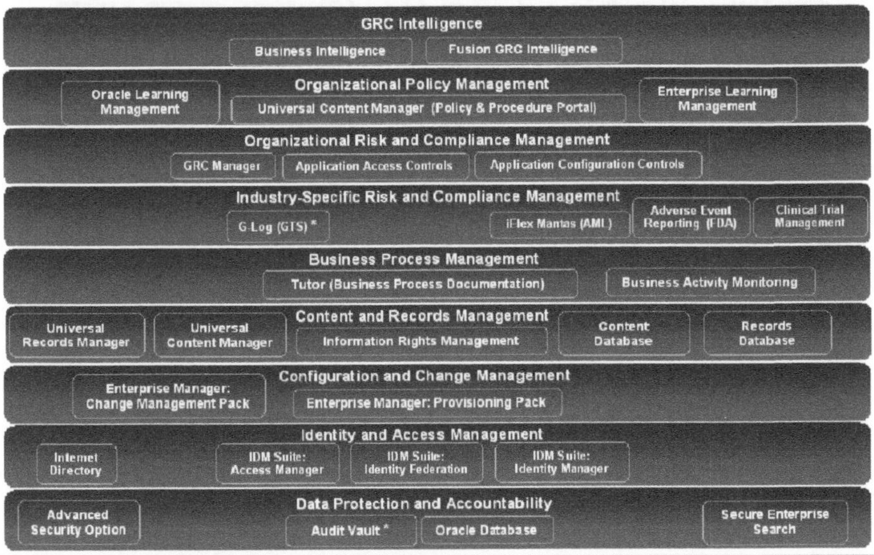

**Image C4 Oracle GRC: Legal Risk Solution Set**

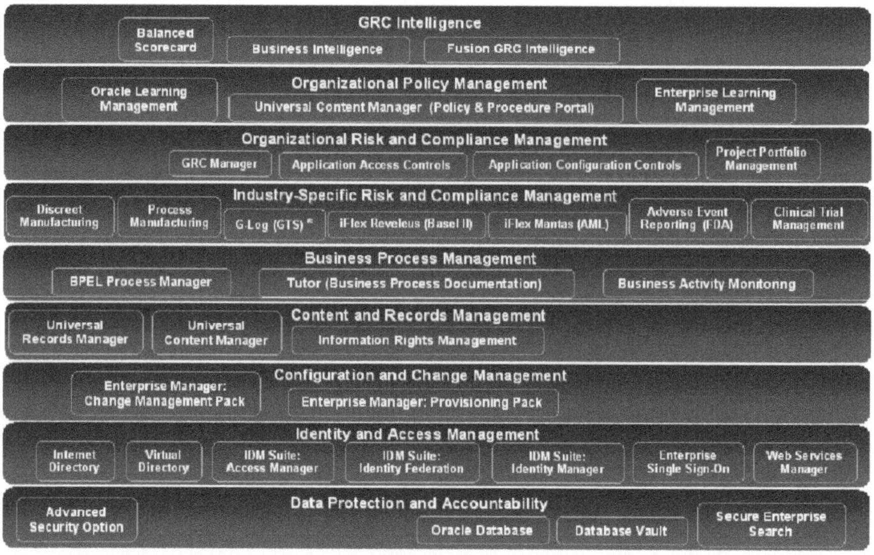

| GRC Intelligence | | |
|---|---|---|
| Balanced Scorecard | Business Intelligence | Fusion GRC Intelligence |

| Organizational Policy Management | | |
|---|---|---|
| Oracle Learning Management | Universal Content Manager (Policy & Procedure Portal) | Enterprise Learning Management |

| Organizational Risk and Compliance Management | | | |
|---|---|---|---|
| GRC Manager | Application Access Controls | Application Configuration Controls | Project Portfolio Management |

| Industry-Specific Risk and Compliance Management | | | | | |
|---|---|---|---|---|---|
| Discreet Manufacturing | Process Manufacturing | G-Log (GTS) ® | i-Flex Reveleus (Basel II) | i-Flex Mantas (AML) | Adverse Event Reporting (FDA) | Clinical Trial Management |

| Business Process Management | | |
|---|---|---|
| BPEL Process Manager | Tutor (Business Process Documentation) | Business Activity Monitoring |

| Content and Records Management | | |
|---|---|---|
| Universal Records Manager | Universal Content Manager | Information Rights Management |

| Configuration and Change Management | |
|---|---|
| Enterprise Manager: Change Management Pack | Enterprise Manager: Provisioning Pack |

| Identity and Access Management | | | | | | |
|---|---|---|---|---|---|---|
| Internet Directory | Virtual Directory | IDM Suite: Access Manager | IDM Suite: Identity Federation | IDM Suite: Identity Manager | Enterprise Single Sign-On | Web Services Manager |

| Data Protection and Accountability | | | |
|---|---|---|---|
| Advanced Security Option | Oracle Database | Database Vault | Secure Enterprise Search |

**Image C5    Oracle GRC: Enterprise Risk Solution Set**

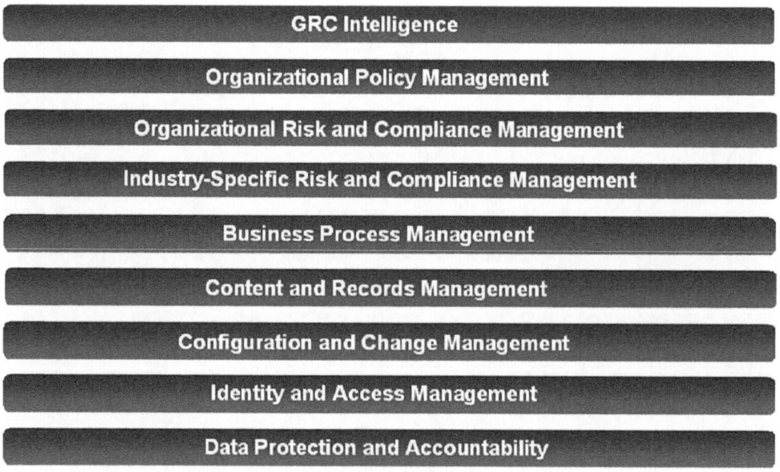

| GRC Intelligence |
|---|
| Organizational Policy Management |
| Organizational Risk and Compliance Management |
| Industry-Specific Risk and Compliance Management |
| Business Process Management |
| Content and Records Management |
| Configuration and Change Management |
| Identity and Access Management |
| Data Protection and Accountability |

**Image C6    Oracle GRC: Oracle GRC Ecosystem**

# INDEX

# Index